Lecture Notes in Computer Science

Lecture Notes in Artificial Intelligence   14136

Founding Editor

Jörg Siekmann

Series Editors

Randy Goebel, *University of Alberta, Edmonton, Canada*
Wolfgang Wahlster, *DFKI, Berlin, Germany*
Zhi-Hua Zhou, *Nanjing University, Nanjing, China*

The series Lecture Notes in Artificial Intelligence (LNAI) was established in 1988 as a topical subseries of LNCS devoted to artificial intelligence.

The series publishes state-of-the-art research results at a high level. As with the LNCS mother series, the mission of the series is to serve the international R & D community by providing an invaluable service, mainly focused on the publication of conference and workshop proceedings and postproceedings.

Fumiya Iida · Perla Maiolino · Arsen Abdulali ·
Mingfeng Wang

Editors

Towards Autonomous Robotic Systems

24th Annual Conference, TAROS 2023
Cambridge, UK, September 13–15, 2023
Proceedings

 Springer

Editors
Fumiya Iida 🆔
University of Cambridge
Cambridge, UK

Perla Maiolino 🆔
University of Oxford
Oxford, UK

Arsen Abdulali 🆔
University of Cambridge
Cambridge, UK

Mingfeng Wang 🆔
Brunel University London
Uxbridge, UK

ISSN 0302-9743   ISSN 1611-3349 (electronic)
Lecture Notes in Artificial Intelligence
ISBN 978-3-031-43359-7   ISBN 978-3-031-43360-3 (eBook)
https://doi.org/10.1007/978-3-031-43360-3

LNCS Sublibrary: SL7 – Artificial Intelligence

This Springer imprint is published by the registered company Springer Nature Switzerland AG
The registered company address is: Gewerbestrasse 11, 6330 Cham, Switzerland

Paper in this product is recyclable.

Preface

This volume contains the papers presented at TAROS 2023, the 24th Towards Autonomous Robotic Systems (TAROS) Conference, held at the Department of Engineering, University of Cambridge, Cambridge, UK, during September 13–15, 2023 (https://taros-conference.org/).

TAROS is the longest-running UK-hosted international conference on robotics and autonomous systems (RAS), and is aimed at the presentation and discussion of the latest results and methods in autonomous robotics research and applications. The conference offers a friendly environment for robotics researchers and industry to take stock and plan future progress. It welcomes senior researchers and research students alike, and specifically provides opportunities for research students and young research scientists to present their work to the scientific community.

The papers in this volume were 40 full papers selected from 70 submissions under single-blind peer review process in which submissions received an average of two reviews each. The conference program included an academic conference, industry exhibitions, robot demonstrations, and other social events. TAROS 2023 covered topics of robotic systems, human–robot interaction, soft robotics, robot navigation and planning, robot control, and industrial robots, and highlights included – 4 Keynote lectures by world-leading experts in robotics, including Sethu Vijayakumar from University of Edinburgh, UK; Jamie Shotton from Wayve Technologies Ltd., UK; Amanda Prorok from University of Cambridge, UK; and Gert Kootstra from Wageningen University, The Netherlands – 20 Oral paper presentations and Poster presentations, covering various topics in robotics – a forum including people from industry, government and UK-RAS – and a Women in Robotics session. This year the conference also included sessions and contributions from the following EPSRC Centres for Doctoral Training (CDT): RAS, FARSCOPE, AIMS, and AgriForwards.

The TAROS 2023 Organizing Committee would like to thank all the authors, the reviewers, and the conference sponsors, including Mathworks, Jacobs, Queen Mary University of London, and Springer for their support of the conference.

September 2023

Fumiya Iida
Perla Maiolino
Arsen Abdulali
Mingfeng Wang

The original version of the frontmatter was revised. The frontmatter inadvertently contained an Invited Talk "Human Evaluation of Robotic Grippers for Berry Picking" which is not part of this volume. Therefore this Invited Talk has been removed from the frontmatter.

Organization

Organizing Committee

General Chair

Fumiya Iida   University of Cambridge, UK

Program Chairs

Perla Maiolino   University of Oxford, UK
Arsen Abdulali   University of Cambridge, UK
Mingfeng Wang   Brunel University London, UK

Publicity Chair

Veronica Egorova   University of Cambridge, UK

Program Committee

Invited Speakers

Amanda Prorok   University of Cambridge, UK
Sethu Vijayakumar   University of Edinburgh, UK
Gert Kootstra   Wageningen University, The Netherlands
Jamie Shotton   Wayve Technologies Ltd., UK

External Reviewers

Su Lu   Case Western Reserve University, USA
Chapa Sirithunge   University of Cambridge, UK
Huijiang Wang   University of Cambridge, UK
Fan Ye   University of Cambridge, UK
Wenxing Liu   UK Atomic Energy Authority, UK
Kai-Fung Chu   Hong Kong Polytechnic University, China
Xiaoping Zhang   University of Cambridge, UK
Hui Ben   University of Newcastle, UK

N'Zebo Richard Anvo	Costain, UK
Elijah Almanzor	University of Cambridge, UK
Mingfeng Wang	Brunel University London, UK
Mark Post	University of York, UK
Christopher Peers	University of Leeds, UK
Yuhui Wan	University of Leeds, UK
Ibragim Atadjanov	Universidad Rey Juan Carlos, Spain
Taku Sugiyama	University of Cambridge, UK
Sundara Tejaswi Digumarti	University of Oxford, UK
Nived Chebrolu	University of Oxford, UK
Michael Ishida	University of Cambridge, UK
Abu Bakar Dawood	Queen Mary University of London, UK
Roderich Gross	University of Sheffield, UK
Nicolas Herzig	University of Sussex, UK
Hui Fang	Loughborough University, UK
Antonia Tzemanaki	University of Bristol, UK
Marc Hanheide	University of Lincoln, UK
Wenxing Liu	University of Manchester, UK
Simon Watson	University of Manchester, UK
Chenguang Yang	South China University of Technology, China
Joe Louca	University of Bristol, UK
Lorenzo Jamone	Queen Mary University of London, UK
Guowu Wei	University of Salford, UK
Russell Buchanan	University of Oxford, UK
Luigi Campanaro	University of Oxford, UK
Stefan Poslad	Queen Mary University of London, UK
Matteo Russo	University of Nottingham, UK
Oliver Shorthose	University of Oxford, UK
Alessandro Albini	University of Oxford, UK
David Marquez-Gamez	University of Oxford, UK
Jingcheng Sun	University of Leeds, UK
Oliver Hardy	University of Lincoln, UK
Ketao Zhang	Queen Mary University of London, UK
Shan Luo	King's College London, UK

Contents

Machine Vision

Multi-robot Systems

Agri-Food Robotics

Plant Phenotyping Using DLT Method: Towards Retrieving the Delicate Features in a Dynamic Environment

Srikishan Vayakkattil$^{(\boxtimes)}$, Grzegorz Cielniak , and Marcello Calisti

Lincoln Institute for Agri-Food Technology, College of Science, University of Lincoln, Lincoln LN2 2LG, UK
LAR@lincoln.ac.uk
https://lar.lincoln.ac.uk/

Abstract. Passive phenotyping methodologies use various techniques for calibration, which include a variety of sensory information like vision. Contrary to the state-of-the-art, this paper presents the use of a Direct Linear Transformation (DLT) algorithm to find the shape and position of fine and delicate features in plants. The proposed method not only finds a solution to the motion problem but also provides additional information related to the displacement of the traits of the subject plant. This study uses DLTdv digitalisation toolbox to implement the DLT modelling tool which reduces the complications in data processing. The calibration feature of the toolbox also enables the prior assumption of calibrated space in using DLT.

Keywords: Plant phenotyping · Direct Linear Transformation · 3D reconstruction · shape estimation

1 Introduction

Due to the increase in population, there is a high necessity of an increase in food production [18]. To increase food production, an in-depth study of a crop's lifecycle is vital. To support this growing demand, Coppens et al. present a comprehensive study of different traits of plants along with their living conditions. Vision is a primary asset to observe the lifecycle of a plant and with the advancements in sensor technology, vision-based plant phenotyping is the conventional state-of-the-art method to meet the cause [4,7]. In this method, the images of individuals or groups of plants are collected and studied. The use of images both 2D and 3D for the study of structural, physiological and performance-related plant characteristics has also made it possible to understand plants even if the actual plant is not available [7].

The use of 3D point clouds is one of the common practices in no destructive phenotyping [5]. In recent years, the use of both minimal equipment and specialised knowledge has led to an increase in the use of the structure from motion

F. Iida et al. (Eds.): TAROS 2023, LNAI 14136, pp. 3–14, 2023.
https://doi.org/10.1007/978-3-031-43360-3_1

technique [14,17]. One of the major problems faced while using this technique for plant phenotyping is the necessity of continuous motion of the equipment [12].

Plants are complex structures, which include fine and delicate parts such as stalks (or sometimes pedicels), leaves and roots. Retrieving images from these structures is one of the challenges faced [12]. Apart from this in an actual field, there are different factors such as wind that causes the delicate features of the plant to move. The structure from motion (sfm) does not have the ability to tackle such a problem of motion since they rely on triangulation [3,6]. The article [16] also underlines that in dynamic environments standard approaches of sfm, as well as SLAM, fail to provide robust localization.

Compared to the sfm approach, which provides dimensionless 3D points with colour, texture, and shape information but lacks scale information can be used for quantitative analysis of plant features such as the number of fruits and stalks. The close-range photogrammetry DLT method provides the scale information that is crucial in plant phenotyping [19].

In this paper the feasibility of using the Direct Linear transformation (DLT) method to reconstruct the 3D shape of the delicate feature of the plant, the stalk in a dynamic environment is verified. Thus in this article, we plan to:

– defining a methodology using the DLT method of 3D reconstruction to aid the phenotyping of fine and delicate features of plants such as stalks.
– test the method in both static and dynamic environments.
– Also, check and report the repeatability of the proposed method.

2   Proposed Method

We plan to create the shape of delicate objects such as stalks of strawberries using cameras. The basic idea is to have two or more cameras capturing images of space from different orientations. If the space is calibrated, it is possible to generate the 3D position of any point in the calibrated space. This concept is used to reconstruct the shape of the stalk of strawberries. Different coloured markers are used to identify the exact position of points in different frames and orientations. Since the method uses images from different orientations at the same time, it is not affected by motion. Videos can be used to tackle the problem of motion.

A prevalent method in computer vision and photogrammetry to generate three-dimensional (3D) point models is called Direct Linear Transformation (DLT). The technique is based on the mathematical principle of projective geometry, which explains the connection between a 3D point and its projection onto a 2D picture [13].

The DLT algorithm involves a two-step process to determine the camera parameters and the reconstruction of the 3D point coordinates. The initial step is to identify the camera matrix, which describes the position as well as the orientation of the camera in reference to the 3D point [9]. This is accomplished through the use of a series of correspondences between the 3D point coordinates and the image coordinates of the point's projection.

In the second phase, the 3D point coordinates are reconstructed from the camera matrix and the image coordinates [9]. This is accomplished by solving a series of linear equations obtained from the correspondences. The solution of these equations yields the 3D coordinates of the point in the camera's reference frame.

Fig. 1. The Calibration box.

The DLT algorithm provides significant benefits over existing approaches for 3D point modelling [8]. It is relatively simple to implement and does not require any prior knowledge of the camera parameters. It is also robust to errors in correspondence and can manage a large number of points.

However, the DLT algorithm has some limitations as well [9]. It assumes that the camera is calibrated, and that the correspondences are exact. It also assumes that the camera is in a fixed position and does not take into account any motion of the camera.

In conclusion, DLT is a powerful and widely used method for 3D point modelling in computer vision and photogrammetry [9]. It is relatively simple to implement and can handle a large number of points. However, it does have some limitations, and it is important to consider these when using the method for real-world applications [8]. These include the size of the calibration, number of cameras, the view of the camera.

3 Experimental Procedure

There are several software tools available for implementing the DLT algorithm, including DLTdv, which is a commonly used software package for digitizing 3D points from images. The DLTdv digitizing tool is user-friendly and easy to use, and it provides a variety of options for data processing and visualization. The technique uses post-processing rather than real-time shape reconstructions, this enables manual interpretation of the points even when the automatic interpretation fails.

DLTdv operates by importing image files and control point data, and then using the DLT algorithm to calculate the 3D coordinates for each point in the image. The software also includes tools for data visualization, such as the ability to create 3D point clouds and to export data to other software packages [10].

Fig. 2. The experimental setup with two cameras.

In order to calibrate the space and to visualise the space, a cube-shaped box was constructed with wooden sticks of a length of 15 cm and a diameter of 4mm (Fig. 1). Markers were placed at 20 predetermined points, at 8 vertices and at the midpoint of every 12 edges. The 3D printed joints of PCP are used to connect the wooden sticks to create the calibration box of dimensions $16 \times 16 \times 16$ (in cm). By adjusting the size and the number of points and the size of the calibration box, it is possible to vary the efficiency of the model. Two cameras DSC-RX100M4 from Sony are selected for vision-based measurement. The camera setup (Fig. 2)

is used to record both the static and dynamic (external force applied) state of
the stalk.

Here we used videos of 15 Hz for frame rate for dynamic modelling and a single frame for static modelling anything less than this rate proved to be missing
significant information about the models (here, strawberry stalk). The calibration box is kept such that the stalk of the strawberry is inside the box (ideally
in the middle). This frame of image is captured using both cameras at the same
time, after which the box is removed. The statics state of the strawberry is
excited by applying an unknown force to the strawberry. The video of the strawberry stalk in motion is captured in both cameras until it comes to rest (static
state) to study the dynamic state of the stalk (Fig. 3).

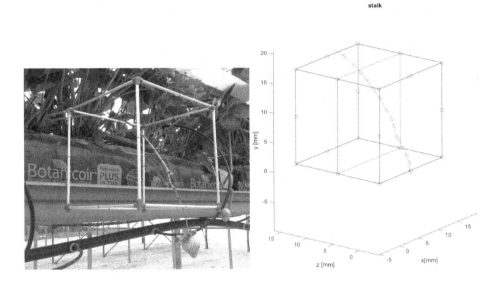

Fig. 3. The original stalk and reconstructed stalk.

The proposed estimation algorithm is implemented in Matlab using the
DLTdv digitizing tool. A set of 20 predetermined points were used to create the
calibration coefficients. In DLTdv, the calibration coefficients are used to correct
distortion and perspective effects in the images and to convert the image coordinates to the true coordinates of the scene. These coefficients are determined
by performing a calibration process on the camera, which involves capturing
images of a known pattern or object, and then using these images to calculate
the calibration coefficients.

Markers were placed on the stalk of the strawberry to point and track it in
the 3D space. Manually, from a single frame each marker was converted into
the 3D-points. Kalman filter along with an average DLT residual threshold of 5
(approx.). The DLT residual threshold is a parameter used in the DLTdv (Direct

Linear Transformation Digitizing Tool) software to determine the accuracy of the reconstructed 3D coordinates. The residual is the difference between the predicted image coordinates and the actual image coordinates of the points, and the threshold is the maximum residual value that is allowed before a point is considered to be an outlier. The length of the stalk is also measured from the first and last marker on the stalk and noted.

The DLT residual threshold is used to filter out points that have a large residual, indicating that there may be an error in the correspondence between the 3D object point and the 2D image point. These points are considered outliers and are not included in the calculations to determine the camera matrix and the 3D coordinates of the points.

All the experiments were conducted in a strawberry-growing polytunnel facility in natural conditions. Two sets of experiments were used for the validation of the proposed passive phenotyping method. These are:

- static: reconstruction of the stalks when it is not moving.
- dynamic: reconstruction of the stalks while it is moving.

Static testing helps to understand the error in reconstruction while dynamic testing showcases the ability to tackle the motion problem. By applying a small torque on the strawberry and exciting the stalk a reasonable testing condition is created. A total of 5 tests were carried out for statics while a single test was carried out for dynamic testing.

4   Observations and Results

Table 1. Table showing the actual value and measured value of the stalk

Actual length (in cm)	reconstructed length (in cm)	Error (in %)
25.6	25.2331	1.43
16.5	16.417	0.503
7.9	7.5119	4.91
10	10.6309	6.306
11.5	11.3174	0.158
32	31.599	1.253
18.9	17.23	8.8359

Using the DLTdv digitizing tool the positions of the markers on the stalks in 3D space are generated. The obtained 3D points were then plotted along with the calibration box and the characteristics were observed. Since the reconstructed shape is the shape produced by connecting the shape of the maker points, the number of points does affect the final reconstructed shape of the stalk. However, if the shape of the stalk to be are simple, the number of the maker can be reduced. This help to reduce the computational cost of reconstruction (Table 1).

The total length of the reconstructed stalk is calculated as the sum of Euclidean distances from each marker simultaneously from the first to the last. This length called reconstructed length is then compared to the actual length of the stalk, measured manually. The error of reconstruction is calculated as

$$Error = \frac{actual\ length - reconstructed\ length}{actual\ length} \times 100 \qquad (1)$$

Fig. 4. The dynamic test results. (a) Strawberry stalk with 15 marker points. (b, c, d) Displacement along X, Y and Z axis, respectively

The dynamic model in which the stalk of the strawberry is excited by an unknown torque by poking the strawberry follows the same step of the reconstruction as that of static. While in the static reconstruction, only a single frame of the video is considered the dynamic method a continuous frame of the whole video is considered. It was found that since the reconstruction utilises the position of markers, additional information such as the damping in different axis can be retrieved.

Figure 4 show the displacement in X, Y and Z axis when from the time of excitement until it comes to rest. It can be noted that there are few disturbances

10 S. Vayakkattil et al.

in the respective graphs. They are two reasons for these errors. First, the disturbance was caused due to small wind in the facility and second, errors were produced while choosing the exact pixels of markers. This can be reduced by increasing the size and point of the calibration box. And also by using a camera of higher resolution. The accuracy of DLT-based methods, including DLTdv, can be influenced by factors such as camera calibration errors and the quality of control point measurements [11,15].

The time required for the reconstruction depends on a number of parameters such as whether the reconstruction is dynamic or static, and the number of markers number of points on the calibration box, and the number of views of the camera. On average, the calibration of 20 points box takes around 5 min to calculate the calibration coefficients. And static reconstruction of a single frame (with 10 to 15 points) takes 3 min on average to reconstruct with a two-camera setup. While the dynamic reconstruction of the setup requires an addition of 4 s per frame per point. The automated tracking feature in the toolbox can help to reduce the time while using dynamic reconstruction.

5 Additional Testing

Additional tests were conducted to validate the method and compare it with the existing technologies commonly used in phenotyping.

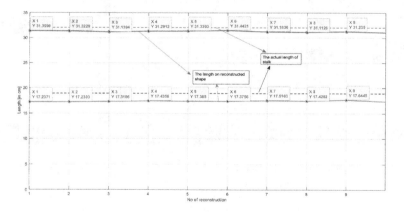

Fig. 5. The graph shows the variation in length with repeated reconstruction of the same stalk of length 32 cm (top) and 18.9 cm (bottom).

In order to test the repeatability of the experiment, the shape reconstruction of a single stalk needs to be repeated. The reconstruction of a single stalk is repeated 10 times. This is carried out by keeping the calibration coefficients constant. The repeatability test helps to better understand the adaptability of using DLT of close-range photogrammetry in plant phenotyping. The variation

Fig. 6. The actual triangle flag.

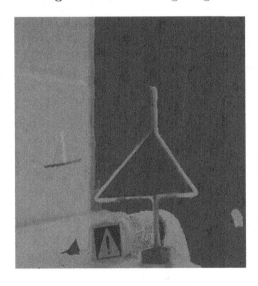

Fig. 7. The reconstructed triangle flag using sfm (Agisoft Metashape).

in length with respect to the reconstruction of the stalk can be analyzed from the graph Fig. 5.

A comparison test with structure from motion was carried out using the Agisoft Metashape software. A triangle-shaped flag with a predefined dimension was used to perform the comparison test Fig. 6. The test was performed

Fig. 8. The reconstructed triangle flag using DLT (DLTdv).

following the procedure similar to [2], with the same camera used for above mention test. After the acquisition of the videos. With the help of the software Agisoft MetaShape, these videos were transformed into dense coloured 3d point clouds, which were subsequently imported in Matlab for further processing using [1] Fig. 7. Once the same flag was reconstructed using the DLTdv toolbox the predefined measurements were analysed and compared using both techniques, Fig. 8.

Table 2. Table showing the actual value and measured value of the triangle flag using the DLT(DLTdv) and SFM (Agisoft) methods of reconstruction

	true length (in cm)	length using DLT (in cm)	Error in DLT (in %)	length using SFM (in cm)	Error in SFM (in %)
a	8.707	8.923	−2.4808	10.133	−16.377
b	5.581	5.7701	−3.88	7.6002	−36.183
c	7.003	7.0802	−1.10	7.1372	−1.91
L1	2.853	3.0169	−5.7819	3.5796	−25.511
L2	8.5	8.034	5.4823	9.6503	−13.5330
L3	9.594	9.8474	−2.64123	11.1309	−16.01

Since the SFM does not provide any information on the scale, here the axis was standardised to that of the yellow marker in the image. Even then from Table 2 it can be analysed how effective the DLTdv is to provide qualitative analysis of plants.

6   Conclusion

The proposed phenotyping method, based on the DLT model, could calculate the shape of the delicate features of plants, even if they are in motion. Experimental investigations verified that the method can generate the 3D point cloud of relevant features of plants with reasonable errors. The method can be used for different applications involving any kind of shape or position estimation. The ability to counter motion problems with minimal economical cost and specific knowledge enables the technique to be used in complex environments.

It should be also noted that, unlike other methods like SFM or SLAM, the proposed methods will provide additional information on changes in positions over time, which has immense application, especially in plant phenotyping. Hence we suggest an alternate solution that can be used in outdoor and indoor conditions to study the individual characteristics of the plant in close-range analysis.

Acknowledgements. The authors would like to people the strawberry growing facility at the University of Lincoln for providing help towards collecting the data. This research is fully funded by the Lincoln Agri-Robotics (LAR), University of Lincoln as part of the PhD process of Srikishan Vayakkattil. The research had added support from Research England.

References

1. Agisoft: Agisoft metashape user manual: Standard edition, Agisoft website vol. 1.6, 28 (2021)
2. Al Khalil, O.: Structure from motion (SFM) photogrammetry as alternative to laser scanning for 3D modelling of historical monuments. Open Sci. J. **5** (2020)
3. Avidan, S., Shashua, A.: Trajectory triangulation: 3D reconstruction of moving points from a monocular image sequence. IEEE Trans. Pattern Anal. Mach. Intell. **22**, 348–357 (2000)
4. Coppens, F., Wuyts, N., Inzé, D., Dhondt, S.: Unlocking the potential of plant phenotyping data through integration and data-driven approaches. Current Opin. Syst. Biol. **4**, 58–63 (2017)
5. Dandois, J.P., Ellis, E.C.: High spatial resolution three-dimensional mapping of vegetation spectral dynamics using computer vision. Remote Sens. Environ. **136**, 259–276 (2013)
6. Dani, A.P., Kan, Z., Fischer, N.R., Dixon, W.E.: Structure and motion estimation of a moving object using a moving camera. In: Proceedings of the 2010 American Control Conference, pp. 6962–6967. IEEE (2010)
7. Dhondt, S., Wuyts, N., Inzé, D.: Cell to whole-plant phenotyping: the best is yet to come. Trends Plant Sci. **18**, 428–439 (2013)
8. Faugeras, O., Faugeras, O.A.: Three-Dimensional Computer Vision: A Geometric Viewpoint. MIT Press, Cambridge (1993)
9. Faugeras, O.D.: What can be seen in three dimensions with an uncalibrated stereo rig? In: Sandini, G. (ed.) ECCV 1992. LNCS, vol. 588, pp. 563–578. Springer, Heidelberg (1992). https://doi.org/10.1007/3-540-55426-2_61
10. Hedrick, T.L.: Software techniques for two-and three-dimensional kinematic measurements of biological and biomimetic systems. Bioinspiration Biomimetics **3** (2008)

11. Huang, J., Wang, Z., Xue, Q., Gao, J.: Calibration of a camera-projector measurement system and error impact analysis. Measur. Sci. Technol. **23** (2012)
12. Li, Z., Guo, R., Li, M., Chen, Y., Li, G.: A review of computer vision technologies for plant phenotyping. Comput. Electron. Agric. **176** (2020)
13. Longuet-Higgins, H.C., Prazdny, K.: The interpretation of a moving retinal image. Proc. Roy. Soc. London Ser. B Biolog. Sci. **208**, 385–397 (1980)
14. Paulus, S.: Measuring crops in 3D: using geometry for plant phenotyping. Plant Methods **15** (2019)
15. Remondino, F.: Heritage recording and 3D modeling with photogrammetry and 3D scanning. Remote Sens. **3**, 1104–1138 (2011)
16. Saputra, M.R.U., Markham, A., Trigoni, N.: Visual slam and structure from motion in dynamic environments: a survey. ACM Comput. Surv. (CSUR) **51**, 1–36 (2018)
17. Smith, M.W., Carrivick, J.L., Quincey, D.J.: Structure from motion photogrammetry in physical geography. Prog. Phys. Geogr. **40**, 247–275 (2016)
18. Tomlinson, I.: Doubling food production to feed the 9 billion: a critical perspective on a key discourse of food security in the UK. J. Rural. Stud. **29**, 81–90 (2013)
19. Xue, Y., Zhang, S., Zhou, M., Zhu, H.: Novel SfM-DLT method for metro tunnel 3D reconstruction and visualization. Undergr. Space **6**, 134–141 (2021)

Rapid Development and Performance Evaluation of a Potato Planting Robot

Elijah Almanzor$^{(\boxtimes)}$, Simon Birell, and Fumiya Iida

Department of Engineering, University of Cambridge, Cambridge CB2 1PZ, UK
{eda26,sab233,fi224}@cam.ac.uk

Abstract. Agriculture is characterised by noisy semi-structured conditions, and production uncertainty which present obstacles to automation. This paper introduces PotatoBot, a specialised robot designed for planting potatoes in a small niche market with limited resources. By adopting an agile-like approach and integrating off-the-shelf modular components, the agri-robotics prototype was developed rapidly and cost-effectively. The system combines Mask R-CNN and PCA for potato pose localisation and utilises a custom end-effector for efficient grasping within standard box crates. Extensive metrics, farmer engagement, and laboratory simulations were used to evaluate performance. Our approach enables the rapid development of an affordable robotic system, particularly suited for niche farming markets with tight profit margins.

Keywords: Agriculture · Jersey Royal Potatoes · Robotic Planting · Computer Vision · Robotics

1 Introduction

Agricultural mechanisation has brought numerous benefits to crops like wheat, corn, cotton, and potatoes, improving yields, efficiency, and sustainability. However, certain crops, such as strawberries [1], peppers [2], and others [3–5], still rely on manual harvesting due to the challenges posed by noisy, uncertain, and semi-structured field environments, along with the significant variations in geometry, appearance, and market standards of the produce. This problem is further exacerbated by the global issue of labour shortages [6], particularly in the UK and its Channel Islands [7,8]. Robotics and autonomous systems have emerged as potential solutions to address these challenges [9]. However, the adoption of these technologies comes with risks and uncertainties [10], as well as higher capital costs, which create barriers to entry into agriculture, known for its smaller profit margins. To overcome these barriers, agri-robots must operate efficiently in challenging agricultural conditions, adapt to environmental variability, and demonstrate affordability and reliability to attract farmers.

Supported by organization Jersey Farmers Union.

F. Iida et al. (Eds.): TAROS 2023, LNAI 14136, pp. 15–25, 2023.
https://doi.org/10.1007/978-3-031-43360-3_2

In the case of Jersey Royals potatoes, which account for a substantial portion of Jersey's agricultural turnover, manual seed planting is currently the norm (see Fig. 1). Existing mechanical planters have inefficiencies, such as planting multiple seed potatoes in the same location and damaging the shoots responsible for producing marketable potatoes. These planters are also heavy, leading to soil compaction, and pose hazards in wet conditions and on steep inclines.

Fig. 1. a) Jersey Royals with shoots in a standard Jersey box. b) Labourer planting potatoes in a straight line.

Robotic planting of Jersey Royals potatoes faces two primary challenges. Firstly, visually identifying the potatoes within crate boxes is difficult due to their random and tightly packed configurations, varying shapes and sizes, and the muddy and dusty environment. Secondly, the robot needs to pick potatoes in different poses, including underneath the box crate handlebar, and plant them in a straight line with proper spacing and orientation. Currently, there are no robots capable of performing this planting process. Unlike transplanting other tuber vegetables like sweet potatoes using detached shoots [11], the pick and planting process for Jersey Royals resembles fruit harvesting but in the opposite direction. The standard Jersey boxes are an important asset in the Jersey potato planting infrastructure. Hence, the robot must be designed in a way that it can be seamlessly integrated into the farmers' operations. However, developing a specialised robot for this niche market with limited economic resources incurs high costs and logistical challenges. To mitigate these challenges, testing in simulated farm conditions as a physical twin is necessary to reduce on-site iterations and developmental costs, especially in the early stages of robot development [12].

Despite advances in big-data machine learning (ML), some agri-robotic systems still rely on classical hand-crafted vision techniques [1–3] due to the lack of suitable datasets, which are expensive to acquire and label. However, these are not suitable for localising the Jersey Royals. ML-based computer vision approaches include YOLO [5], and Mask R-CNN [13]. YOLO struggles with distinguishing closely packed objects, while Mask R-CNN excels in accurately localizing contiguous produce. Control approaches can be open or closed-loop. Open-loop approaches estimate the pose of the target object and execute commands without positional corrections [2,3], while closed-loop approaches use sensor information for position or velocity correction, leading to higher success rates [1,5]. The choice of end-effector for grasping produce is also crucial. Different crops like strawberries, peppers, and lettuces have specific market criteria for harvesting [1,2,5], while Jersey Royal seed potatoes have fewer commercial requirements as they are not the directly sold produce. However, the gripper still needs to be robust enough to handle potatoes of varying geometry and pose within the box.

This paper introduces the PotatoBot, a robotic solution for planting potato tuber seeds resembling manual human planting. It addresses the challenges faced by Jersey farmers and emphasises the use and customisation of off-the-shelf technologies to rapidly develop an effective agricultural system within commercial constraints. Through farmer consultation and laboratory simulations, the research demonstrates the potential of robotic automation in addressing labour shortages. An Agile-like approach was employed to minimise iterations and anticipate technological challenges. Performance evaluation was conducted using intensive metrics to guide future iterations and provide performance indicators for farmers.

2 Methodology

2.1 PotatoBot Robotic System

The PotatoBot consists of a Universal Robot UR10 robotic manipulator, mounted on a wheeled platform (Fig. 2a). A rapid development approach based on the 'Agile' project management [14] was implemented. The system was broken down into small separate tasks which were solved in an iterative manner to allow the development of the system to continue. Jersey farmers were kept in the loop during the development to ensure the progress of the system was kept grounded. The use of off-the-shelf hardware and software allowed the PotatoBot system to be built and analysed in the space of 10 weeks.

The platform is designed to be attachable as a trailer to a vehicle for a stop-and-plant approach similar to human planting. The end-effector is a pneumatic spear gripper equipped with a RealSense D415 RGB-D camera (Fig. 2b). The system utilizes the open-source Robotics Operating System (ROS) with Python3 for compartmentalizing different functionalities into separate scripts (Fig. 2c). Commercial viability set by the Jersey Farmers Union requires the robot to be under £75k with a 90% success rate and a cycle time of 3.5 s. The current cost of the PotatoBot system is approximately £32k. The whole system is powered using standard UK 230 V mains with compressed air also coming from a mains supply.

The gripper is fabricated using aluminium extrusions (Fig. 2b.1 and 2b.2). The slender design aims to prevent collisions when picking near the crate walls and minimise visual occlusion in the camera view (see Fig. 4b), which can affect stereo depth estimations. A pneumatic double-acting actuator with needles was employed for quick picking and release. Two needles are used to prevent the rotation of the picked potatoes around the piercing axis. Thin and slender needles minimize the probability of contact or damage to the shoots compared to other

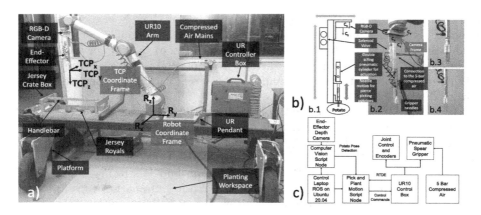

Fig. 2. a) PotatoBot system with its components. b) Spear Gripper: *1.* Side profile diagram of the gripper. *2.* Image of the gripper. *3.* Solenoid valve in the off position. *4.* Solenoid valve in the on position. c) High-level schematic of the PotatoBot's software and hardware.

end-effector mechanisms with fingers. It was found that 5 bar gives sufficient piercing force for consistent grasp and release of potatoes. The overall cost of the gripper is approximately £250, making it more cost-effective than off-the-shelf grippers which can cost up to thousands of pounds[1].

For computer vision, we implemented Mask R-CNN using Detectron2 and Python PyTorch libraries, due to its high performance [13], and the availability of libraries and pre-trained network weights. Due to the unavailability of pre-existing datasets for potatoes, a dataset of Jersey Royal potatoes was created. A preliminary field study was conducted to assess the lighting conditions in Jersey's fields and warehouses. Figure 3a shows that the lighting in the field remains relatively consistent during the day. The most significant change in image quality occurs in the evening. A total of 157 laboratory images were captured at different heights for this study. At the time of the investigation, the test potatoes did not possess shoots as they were unavailable outside of the planting seasons. To simulate the well-lit field conditions, all training images were captured in a brightly illuminated room. A small number of training data were used to expedite the integration process and reduce time and labour costs. The VGG Image Annotator tool was used to label two classes: Jersey Royal and Handlebar to determine if potatoes were occluded by the handlebar using the control methods (see Fig. 4). The training images included potatoes in various orientations and box densities (see Fig. 3b.1, 3b.2, and 3b.3 for examples), with some containing additional vegetables as negative samples (Fig. 3b.4). The network was trained on Google Colab for 500 epochs. Transfer learning was employed due to the limited training data, using the COCO dataset. Using 15% of the training data as

---

[1] https://robotiq.com/products/2f85-140-adaptive-robot-gripper.

validation, no overfitting was observed. Inference and evaluation were conducted on the laptop's GPU (RTX2060m) at an average speed of 7 FPS.

a) Images in the field and in the warehouse

b) Training images

Fig. 3. a) Variations of the lighting conditions in the field and in the storage warehouse. b) Examples of the training images. 1. A crate with a low density of potatoes. 2. A crate with medium density. 3. A fully crowded crate. 4. A crate with the distractors.

The largest predicted mask is picked as the current target potato. The position of the target's bounding box centre within the depth camera frame is transformed into the robot's base frame using transformation matrices. Principal component analysis (PCA) was then applied to the detected 2D mask of the target to find the principal axes which correspond to the long-ways orientation.

Figure 4a shows the flowchart for both control methods. Control Method 1 (CM1) does not consider the handlebar; it only performs vertical picking and moves the robot's end-effector to View Position 1 before picking individual potatoes (Fig. 4b.1 to 4b.3). After picking, the planting sequence is initiated. Since there were no simulated soil rows in the laboratory, arbitrary positions with potato-sized spacing (10 cm) on the solid ground was used as planting locations. In Control Method 2 (CM2), an augmentation of CM1, the robot has the option to perform picking at a 45-degree angle if the centre of the target potato is close to the handlebar. To address the occlusion of smaller potatoes by the handlebar, a second viewing position, View Position 2 (Fig. 4b.4), was introduced for final verification. Once no more targets are present, the pick and plant experiment is considered complete. Due to the open-loop approach, all the individual positions, such as the plant locations in Fig. 4a, the view positions or pre-pick and pick poses uses heuristical values found empirically to avoid self or environmental collisions.

2.2   Setup and Experiments

The box crates were placed on the right-hand side of the robot (see Fig. 2a). There were six types of experiments conducted to analyse the vision and pick-and-plant performance. Tests A, B, C, and D had the handlebar removed for simplicity. Random changes were made to the test potatoes and their positions

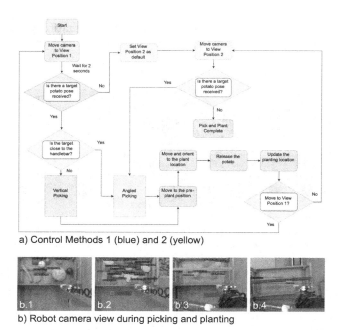

a) Control Methods 1 (blue) and 2 (yellow)

b) Robot camera view during picking and planting

Fig. 4. a) Control method for the Pick-and-Plant (PnP) process. Control Method 1 (CM1, blue) does not consider the handlebar. Control Method 2 (CM2, yellow), an augmentation of CM1, accommodates the box handlebar through angled picking and by having a second viewing position in case of visual occlusions. b) Example camera views of the different experiments with label predictions. *1.* Five potatoes with the distractors and without the handlebar at View Position 1. *2.* Twenty potatoes without the handlebar (medium density) at View Position 1. *3.* Five potatoes with the handlebar at View Position 1. *4.* Example of View Position 2. (Color figure online)

to test robot generalizability. Test A involved five Jersey potatoes in the box, and 10 pick-and-plant experiments were conducted to evaluate performance on a low density of potatoes. Initial robot view images were captured for vision test data. Test B was a vision-only test with distractors, evaluating the performance of the vision system when non-potato objects were present in the crate. Ten images were collected. Test C was another vision-only experiment. Using the *Pillow* library, the brightness and contrast of validation images were adjusted to simulate varying weather and lighting conditions in field settings. Different enhancement factors (ranging from 0.5 to 1.5) were used to represent different lighting conditions. Test D was similar to Test A, but with 20 potatoes in the crate to assess the effects of higher density on performance under simplified conditions. Tests E and F were conducted with the box handlebar and a low density of potatoes to compare the performance of the two control methods, with Test F also including a vision test.

2.3   Metrics

For computer vision, the standard metric for the COCO dataset [15] is the *Average Precision* (AP). AP uses the area of the precision-recall curve, where the *Precision* is a function of *Recall* at interpolated values.

Metrics were created for the pick and plant operations. The *Picking Attempts Rate*, $PAR = \frac{Total\ Successful\ Pick\ and\ Plant}{Number\ of\ Attempts}$, is a measure of the systems picking efficiency. If the robot misses, crashes or drops the potato after three attempts, it was considered a failure. Any more than three failed attempts are unacceptable for a commercial application as repeats greatly lengthen the robot's cycle time. *Picking Success Rate*, $PSR = \frac{Total\ Successful\ Pick\ and\ Plant}{Total\ Number\ of\ Potatoes}$, is a measure of the overall success of the system for a given experiment. The *Miss, Crash* and *Drop* rates are measured by their proportions to the total unsuccessful pick and plant attempts. The *Cycle Time* is the duration of the robot to move to the view positions, detect, pick and plant the target and return to the pre-plant position.

An additional three metrics are introduced for comparing the planted seeds by human labourers (baseline) against the robot's performance. The first is the *Normalised Averaged Potato Gap*, $NAPG = \frac{\sum_i^{P_n} G_i}{(P_n-1)\bar{L}}$, a measure of the average gap between the planted potatoes. Normalisation allows for comparison between different pictures taken at different heights and angles. G_i is the pixel distance between each consecutive potato, P_n is the number of potatoes, and $\bar{L}$ is the mean length of all the potatoes within a given image. The second is the *Normalised Averaged Potato Distance to Line*, $NAPDL = \frac{\sum_i^{P_n} D_i}{P_n \bar{W}}$ which measures the straightness of a planted line using linear regression. D_i is the pixel distance of each potato to the regression line, and $\bar{W}$ is the average width of the potatoes in a given image. The third metric is the *Average Angle*, which uses the PCA method.

3   Experimental Results

Results for Vision Test C are shown in Fig. 5. The performance remained high at higher brightness and contrast levels. However, performance declined when the images were darkened which shows that more training data is required.

Table 1 demonstrates that the Precision and Recall metrics were consistently close to 1, indicating accurate and correct predictions by the network for the majority of potato instances. However, in Test B with distractors, there was a single misclassification of a non-potato object. The inclusion of more negative samples in the dataset is expected to address this issue. Test F had the lowest Recall value at 0.88, caused by the occlusion of the potatoes from the handlebar.

Table 2 presents the results of the Pick-and-Plant experiments. The simplest experiment (Test A) achieved a high success rate of 96% for pick and plant tasks. However, as the density increased to 20 potatoes (Test D), the success rate dropped to 91% due to increased crash and miss failures. Despite this, dropping potatoes was not a factor in any of the failures, indicating the robustness of vertical picking. Unsuccessful potato planting resulting from crashing, miss, and

22   E. Almanzor et al.

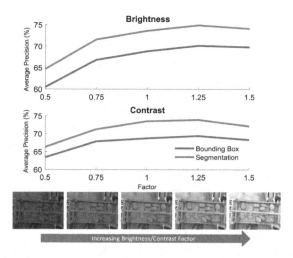

Fig. 5. Effects of brightness and contrast (*Test C*) on Average Precision (AP). At higher brightness and contrast, the network retains high AP values. Performance suffers at lower brightness and contrast.

Table 1. Detectron 2 vision metrics on the different image test experiments.

Metrics	No Handlebar			With Handlebar
	Vision Test A	Vision Test B	Vision Test D	Vision Test F
Experiment Type	Low Density	Distractors	Medium Density	Control Method 2
Precision	1	0.98	1	1
Recall	1	1	0.99	0.88
Average Precision (Bounding Box %)	79.68	74.05	76.87	68.83
Average Precision (Mask Segmentation %)	81.50	82.33	82.37	71.3

drop failures were attributed to the open-loop approach as localisation errors are not corrected during the trajectory. The performance was the poorest in the experiment involving the handlebar (Test E) using CM1, with a 60% pick and plant success rate. The main cause of failure in Test E was crashing into the handlebar. By incorporating the CM2 extension for angled picking, the success rate improved to 87%, significantly reducing the occurrence of crashes. The picking attempts efficiency also increased from 60% to 83%. This highlights the value of being able to pick potatoes under the handlebar. However, the drop and miss rates doubled, indicating that angled picking leads to less robust grasping and exacerbates the localization error. The robot's cycle time in general is slower than the human baseline of 3.5 s. It was found that the distance between picking and planting positions is the primary factor contributing to the cycle time bottleneck. Table 2 and Fig. 6 reveals that the robotic planted lines performed poorer than the human baseline in terms of the planted line metrics, with angled picking (Test F) being the worst. These differences are attributed to the bouncing and rotation of potatoes after release. The less robust angled picking in Test F was also due to the segmented mask detection which leads to the larger area becoming the target mask, resulting in less accurate orientation detection by the PCA algorithm and spear needles' grasp point no longer being at the centroid of the potato.

Table 2. Pick and plant performances of the robotic system in the various test experiments.

Metrics	No Handlebar		With Handlebar	
	PnP Test A	PnP Test D	PnP Test E	PnP Test F
Pick and Plant Performance				
Experiment Type	Low Density	Medium Density	Control Method 1	Control Method 2
Picking Attempts Rate (%)	92	86	56	83
Planting Success Rate (%)	96	91	60	87
Crash Rate (%)	50	66	75	8
Drop Rate (%)	0	0	5	31
Miss Rate (%)	50	34	20	61
Average Cycle Times				
Vertical Picking Time (s)	$9.17, \sigma = 0.32$	$9.21, \sigma = 0.43$	$9.35, \sigma = 0.49$	$9.73, \sigma = 0.42$
Vertical Picking Average (s): $9.34, \sigma = 0.84$				
Angled Picking Time (s)	N/A	N/A	N/A	$10.38, \sigma = 0.65$
Plant Line Performances				
	Human Baseline		PnP Test A	PnP Test F
NAPG	$1.10, \sigma = 0.20$		$1.28, \sigma = 0.40$	$1.50, \sigma = 0.76$
NAPDL	$0.12, \sigma = 0.09$		$0.26, \sigma = 0.16$	$0.34, \sigma = 0.38$
Average Angle	$-3.94, \sigma = 10.31$		$5.77, \sigma = 15.48$	$-4.45, \sigma = 39.99$

PnP, pick-and-plant; N/A, Not Available; σ, Standard Deviation.

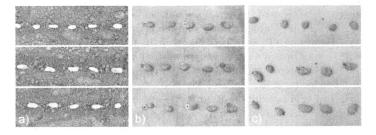

Fig. 6. Example planted lines for the a) Human baseline. The human baseline performance was derived from field images captured in Jersey (Fig. 6a), b) Test A, 5 potatoes without the crate handlebar using Control Method 1, and c) Test F, 5 potatoes with the crate handlebar using Control Method 2.

4   Discussion

PotatoBot achieved an 87% success rate with an average cycle time of 10.38 s, falling slightly short of the goal of a 90% success rate within 3.5 s to be commercially viable. However, our agile-like approach allowed for rapid development within a 10-week time frame through the integration of customised off-the-shelf modular components and minimisation of costs by avoiding field tests at this stage. Observing real farm operations and consulting experienced farmers helped recreate important farm conditions in the laboratory as a physical twin, reducing on-site system iterations. Intensive metrics were utilized to compare future iterations, providing performance indicators for farmers and reducing barriers to entry and uncertainties associated with new farming technology. The developmental approach used in this project can be applied to other crops that require rapid and cost-effective development.

The custom pneumatic spear gripper was chosen for rapid potato picking, simplicity of control, and cost efficiency. Future work will consider methods of automatic sanitation for disease prevention. For potato pose detection, PCA integrated with Mask R-CNN was used to achieve rudimentary grasping based on position and yaw orientation. Mask R-CNN performed well in laboratory-simulated conditions, but more representative training data is needed to enhance performance in real-world conditions. A heuristical approach was taken to define waypoints and achieve a working robotic planter without additional sensors in the open-loop control methodology. However, this approach suffered from inaccurate potato pose estimations, leading to inefficient picking attempts, misses, dropped potatoes, and collisions. To reduce these as well as tolerate faster dynamic movements of the potatoes, future work will consider visual-servoing methods. Future versions of PotatoBot will have a smaller design to minimize traversal distances to meet commercial viability. Automated crop row detection and field testing with full crates are also necessary for the robot to be field-ready.

References

1. Xiong, Y., Ge, Y., Grimstad, L., From, P.J.: An autonomous strawberry-harvesting robot: design, development, integration, and field evaluation. J. Field Rob. **37**(2), 202–224 (2020). https://onlinelibrary.wiley.com/doi/abs/10.1002/rob.21889
2. Bac, C.W., Hemming, J., van Tuijl, B., Barth, R., Wais, E., van Henten, E.J.: Performance evaluation of a harvesting robot for sweet pepper. J. Field Rob. **34**(6), 1123–1139 (2017). https://onlinelibrary.wiley.com/doi/abs/10.1002/rob.21709
3. Silwal, A., Davidson, J.R., Karkee, M., Mo, C., Zhang, Q., Lewis, K.: Design, integration, and field evaluation of a robotic apple harvester. J. Field Rob. **34**(6), 1140–1159 (2017). https://onlinelibrary.wiley.com/doi/abs/10.1002/rob.21715
4. SepúLveda, D., Fernández, R., Navas, E., Armada, M., González-De-Santos, P.: Robotic aubergine harvesting using dual-arm manipulation. IEEE Access **8**, 121889–121904 (2020)
5. Birrell, S., Hughes, J., Cai, J.Y., Iida, F.: A field-tested robotic harvesting system for iceberg lettuce. J. Field Rob. **37**(2), 225–245 (2020). https://onlinelibrary.wiley.com/doi/abs/10.1002/rob.21888

6. Roser, M.: Employment in Agriculture. Oxford, United Kingdom (2022). https://ourworldindata.org/employment-in-agriculture
7. NFU Online, Establishing the labour availability issues of the UK Food and Drink Sector (2021)
8. British Summer Fruits, The Impact of Brexit on the Soft Fruit Industry (2017)
9. Duckett, T., et al.: Agricultural robotics: the future of robotic agriculture (2018)
10. NFU Mutual, Agri-tech Report (2022)
11. Liu, Z., Wang, X., Zheng, W., Lv, Z., Zhang, W.: Design of a sweet potato transplanter based on a robot arm. Appl. Sci. **11**(19) (2021). https://www.mdpi.com/2076-3417/11/19/9349
12. Junge, K., Pires, C., Hughes, J.: Soft sensorized physical twin enabling lab2field transfer and learning from demonstration for raspberry harvesting (2023). https://doi.org/10.21203/rs.3.rs-2511021/v1
13. Ge, Y., Xiong, Y., From, P.J.: Instance segmentation and localization of strawberries in farm conditions for automatic fruit harvesting. IFAC-PapersOnLine **52**(30), 294–299 (2019). 6th IFAC Conference on Sensing, Control and Automation Technologies for Agriculture AGRICONTROL 2019. https://www.sciencedirect.com/science/article/pii/S2405896319324565
14. Sharma, S., Sarkar, D., Gupta, D.: Agile processes and methodologies: a conceptual study. Int. J. Comput. Sci. Eng. **4**, 05 (2012)
15. Lin, T.-Y., et al.: Microsoft COCO: common objects in context. In: Fleet, D., Pajdla, T., Schiele, B., Tuytelaars, T. (eds.) ECCV 2014. LNCS, vol. 8693, pp. 740–755. Springer, Cham (2014). https://doi.org/10.1007/978-3-319-10602-1_48

An Automated Precision Spraying Evaluation System

Harry Rogers[1]([✉])(iD), Beatriz De La Iglesia[1](iD), Tahmina Zebin[2](iD),
Grzegorz Cielniak[3](iD), and Ben Magri[4]

[1] School of Computing Sciences, University of East Anglia, Norwich NR4 7TJ, UK
{Harry.Rogers,B.Iglesia}@uea.ac.uk
[2] School of Computer Science, Brunel University London, Uxbridge UB8 3PH, UK
tahmina.zebin@brunel.ac.uk
[3] School of Computer Science, University of Lincoln, Lincoln LN6 7TS, UK
gcielniak@lincoln.ac.uk
[4] Syngenta Ltd., Bracknell RG42 6EY, UK
ben.magri@syngenta.com

Abstract. Data-driven robotic systems are imperative in precision agriculture. Currently, Agri-Robot precision sprayers lack automated methods to assess the efficacy of their spraying. In this paper, images were collected from an RGB camera mounted to an Agri-robot system to locate spray deposits on target weeds or non-target lettuces. We propose an explainable deep learning pipeline to classify and localise spray deposits without using existing manual agricultural methods. We implement a novel stratification and sampling methodology to improve classification results. Spray deposits are identified with over 90% Area Under the Receiver Operating Characteristic and over 50% Intersection over Union for a Weakly Supervised Object Localisation task. This approach utilises near real-time architectures and methods to achieve inference for both classification and localisation in 0.062 s on average.

Keywords: Agri-Robotics · Computer Vision · XAI

1 Introduction

Precise chemical usage is an essential objective in sustainable precision spraying applications and a number of Agri-robot systems are being developed to provide data-driven solutions. According to the 2019 European Union (EU) Green Deal [3], modern Agri-robot precision sprayers will have to undergo further regulatory assessment to ensure systems can minimize the usage of chemicals. Hence, formulating an evaluation methodology to assess the spraying effect in terms of whether the applied chemical has landed correctly on desired targets or has misfired is of crucial importance in assessing these systems.

This work is supported by the UK Engineering and Physical Sciences Research Council [EP/S023917/1]. This work is also supported by Syngenta as the Industrial partner.

F. Iida et al. (Eds.): TAROS 2023, LNAI 14136, pp. 26–37, 2023.
https://doi.org/10.1007/978-3-031-43360-3_3

Despite the large amounts of research and development within Agri-robotics, traditional manual methods of evaluating precision spraying systems are still used. Therefore, our goal is to develop a vision system for Agri-robot precision sprayers that identifies spray deposits on target weeds and non-target crops.

Our own dataset has been generated, with our industrial partner Syngenta, as there are no publicly available datasets for this task. Precision spraying was completed with an Agri-robot system called the XY Sprayer and a human controller. Added to the system was a Canon 500D camera which took images before and after spraying. This generated a binary classification scenario. We have labelled half of the test data in our dataset with bounding boxes for a Weakly Supervised Object Localisation (WSOL) task to localise around spray deposits.

We propose an eXplainable Artificial Intelligence (XAI) pipeline using Convolutional Neural Networks (CNNs). After classification, a Class Activation Map (CAM) is generated by visualising the final layers of CNNs, which allow for the computation of an importance map of the final feature extraction layer. Using these CAMs we can localise around spray deposits to complete weakly supervised object localisation by only labelling half of the test data. Within the pipeline classification performance is improved from a traditional random data split with a novel stratification method and additional novel sampling method.

To evaluate our pipeline we use classification metrics, F1-Score and Area Under the Receiver Operating Characteristic (AUROC) using the classification labels. To evaluate CAMs, XAI metrics Deletion, Insertion, and WSOL are used. We test CNN and CAM inference speed on GPU and CPU devices to identify near real-time methods. From the results, we find that real time classification and localisation is possible for spray deposits on lettuces and weeds.

The core contributions of this paper are:

1. Formulation for a stratification and sampling methodology for binary classification for image specific feature selection.
2. A near real-time methodology for binary weakly supervised object localisation that only requires half of the test data split to be labelled with bounding boxes.

The remainder of this paper is organised as follows. Section 2 introduces related work on Agri-robot precision spraying system evaluations and XAI methods for generating and evaluating CAMs. Section 3 introduces the experimental setup for the XY sprayer, and the associated data collection and pre-processing stages. Section 4 provides details of the XAI pipeline, network architectures, and other implementation details. The performance of the developed CNNs and CAM explanations are reported and evaluated in Sect. 5. Finally, the paper's conclusions and future work are presented in Sect. 6.

2   Related Work

2.1   Agri-Robot Precision Sprayer System Evaluations

There are many types of precision spraying systems that have been developed within the Agri-robotics domain. One of the current commercial state-of-the-art systems developed by John Deere [1], uses computer vision and machine learning to target weeds. This system says it can reduce herbicide usage but does not identify if a target is sprayed or where the spray deposit has actually landed.

Within literature, ground based systems have been developed with examples of ATVs [17], and Agri-robot platforms [13] using CNNs to first identify target weeds and then spray them. Both systems evaluate the spraying of targets and do not use traditional agricultural methods of water sensitive papers or tracers. However, both use vague definitions of classes for spraying and require human intervention for the classification.

Other ground based systems have also been developed but use traditional agricultural methods. For example, Kim et al. [12] presents a novel platform for spraying fruit trees, Farooque et al. [7] proposes a disease detection methodology for potatoes, Wang et al. [22] put forward a real-time detection system for weed spraying in corn fields, Fu et al. [8] presents a detection system for weed spraying in cabbage fields. However, all evaluate their methods with water sensitive papers. Water sensitive papers do show a good estimate of spray deposits that create deposition values. However, it is an estimate that requires placement and retrieval of the papers for analysis after spraying, so requires human intervention. Alongside this, water sensitive papers do not have the same texture as the targets and systems we are aiming for. This can create differences between actual (in the field) and estimated deposits.

Developments in precision spraying Agri-robotics have also been completed with tracer based methodologies. Some systems include pesticide spraying in early-stage Maize [24] using Rhodamine dye, weed control in lettuce fields [19] with UV dyes, and pesticide application in orchards [14] applying Tartrazine dye. Tracers are very effective at identifying quantities of applied chemicals but each method mentioned uses a specific dye that is not generalisable to other chemical applications. Tracers also require further analysis from either additional expensive equipment or other means depending on the tracer used.

Despite agricultural methods being effective for the evaluation of spray deposits, a visual aid for the detection of spray deposits is also easier to explain and validate.

2.2 eXplainable Artificial Intelligence

XAI within this paper is used for feature extraction from CNNs to localise around spray deposits. CAMs are computed and visualised to create a heatmap that is overlaid on an image to show regions of interest. CAMs can also be evaluated with several metrics to show how effective each method is for the CNN it is applied to.

When looking at CAM methods as we do not know the number of spray deposits within an image, localising around multiple deposits would be realistic, GradCAM++ [2] therefore should be considered. GradCAM++ is a direct development from GradCAM [20], one of the first CAM methods. Both methods use a target class that is passed into the last convolutional layer in the CNN posed.

GradCAM takes the average of the gradients calculated whereas GradCAM++ uses a weighted combination of positive partial derivatives of the gradients. Comparing GradCAM++ to other gradient based methods such as LayerCAM [11], HiResCAM [6], and FullGrad [21], GradCAM++ is lightest computationally when being used in conjunction with CNNs for near real-time inference, whilst also being effective with multiple object instances. More recently, CAM methods have moved towards using gradient free solutions. EigenCAM [16] returns the Singular Value Decomposition (SVD) of the activations in the CNN, therefore the CAM will correspond with the dominant object in the image. There are other gradient free methods like Abalation-CAM [5] and ScoreCAM [23], but these methods are computationally expensive and could not be considered for a near real-time Agri-robot precision spraying system. Gradients have also been combined with EigenCAM to create EigenGradCAM, where gradients are multiplied by activations and then SVD is applied. We will compare GradCAM++, EigenCAM, and EigenGradCAM to identify an accurate method that will work in real-time.

CAM performance can be evaluated using multiple metrics; for our scenario we will use Deletion, Insertion, and WSOL [18]. To evaluate the effectiveness of an explanation, two complementary metrics are commonly used: Deletion and Insertion. Deletion gauges the change in classification confidence that occurs when various regions of an image are removed. In contrast, Insertion measures the change in confidence resulting from the addition of regions, either with surrounding noise or without any surrounding context. WSOL is much simpler, this measures the Intersection over Union (IoU) of regions of high interest with labelled objects.

From literature, CAMs have been tested for their effectiveness of explanations. However, they have not been used for real time inference of a WSOL task within Agri-robotics. Therefore, we will use evaluation metrics in conjunction with real-time testing to evaluate deployable methods.

3   Experimental Setup and Dataset Description

The XY Sprayer depicted in Fig. 1 was developed as an experimental Agri-robot precision spraying system by Syngenta. The system is used to evaluate spraying effectiveness of spray plates, it uses an XY gantry system with an adjustable floor. Mounted to the system is a Canon 500D camera to capture images. Syngenta recommended a spraying height of 30 cm from the tray bed with a spray time of 8 ms and a pressure of 3 bar as these are similar measurements into deployed systems. The camera was 45 cm away from the tray bed.

3.1   Data Collection Procedure

Lettuces were cultivated and transplanted into trays of commonly found, randomly sown weeds. This was to generate synthetic data similar to what could be

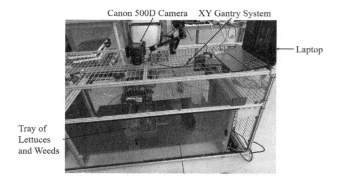

Fig. 1. XY Sprayer with tray of lettuces and weeds.

found on lettuce farms. Trays were placed into the XY sprayer system to be captured by the Canon 500D camera before spraying. Once images were collected, spraying was completed with a human controller. The dataset collected contains 178 images, with 89 images for both non sprayed and sprayed classes. In Fig. 2 is an example tray before and after spraying. Identifying spray by human eye is difficult in the overall image, therefore a zoomed-in target that has been sprayed is also shown to illustrate the difficulty of the identification task.

Fig. 2. Tray image comparison of sprayed (Top Left), and non sprayed (Top Right). Zoomed in comparison of the same target between sprayed (Bottom Left), and non sprayed (Bottom Right).

3.2   Data Pre-processing: Augmentation

After data collection, images were labelled and randomly split using a 70%, 20%, and 10% ratio for training, validation, and test, respectively. For CNNs to become generalisable and robust vast amounts of data is required. However, to our knowledge this is the only dataset containing non sprayed and sprayed lettuces and weeds. Therefore, multiple augmentations are applied to our dataset to increase the data available for training CNNs. Augmentations include flips, rotations, blurring, brightness, and contrast alterations. Thus, our training split has increased from 122 images to 854, creating an overall dataset of 910 images.

4   XAI Pipeline

In the proposed XAI pipeline we select the dataset type of random, stratified, or stratified sampling. CNNs based on the dataset type selected are trained and then evaluated with multiple classification metrics. Following the best performing CNNs we compute CAMs using a variety of methodologies. We then evaluate the explanation of the CAM using XAI metrics. Average inference time of CNNs and CAM computation is then completed.

4.1   Network Architectures

Experiments with two pre-trained CNNs, DenseNet121 [10] and ShuffleNetV2 [15] have been completed. Networks are pre-trained on the ImageNet [4] dataset. Table 1 shows a comparison of the Top-1 ImageNet scores, parameters, file size in MegaBytes (MB), and Giga Floating Point Operations per Second (GFLOPs). These networks are selected on their ability to complete classification tasks to a similar level whilst being designed for different goals. DenseNet121 is designed to be a larger heavier, potentially more accurate network. Whereas ShuffleNetV2 is designed to be lightweight but also accurate.

Table 1. Network comparisons

Network	ImageNet Top-1	Parameters (Million)	File Size (MB)	GFLOPs
DenseNet121	74.4%	7.9	30.4	2.83
ShuffleNetV2 2x	76.2%	7.3	28.4	0.58

All networks are given the same learning parameters during the training phase. A batch size of 4 with each image being resized down to 864×1296 pixels is used. Due to spray deposits being incredibly small, resizing the images to any smaller can lead to information loss and therefore makes it much more difficult to locate spray deposits. In the pipeline, a Stochastic Gradient Descent optimiser with a learning rate of 0.001, momentum of 0.9, and weight decay of 0.1 has been used. Additionally, a learning rate scheduler that decays the learning rate, with a step size of 5, and a gamma constant of 0.3 was used.

4.2 Stratification and Sampling

Stratification of a dataset is the process of dividing data into subgroups based on a specific criterion. For our dataset we split our data into two strata using the classification labels sprayed or non sprayed.

Let $x_1, x_2, .., x_n$ be our data, where y_i is a binary variable indicating spray deposits or not. Let $g(y_i)$ be a function that assigns data to its stratum:

$$g(y_i) = \begin{cases} 1 & \text{if } y_i = 1 \\ 2 & \text{if } y_i = 0 \end{cases} \tag{1}$$

After using $g(y_i)$ we numerically sort each strata based on filenames. Strata then has $image_x$ sprayed have the same index as $image_x$ non sprayed. Sampling can then be completed by taking the same random index from both strata. Stata data (Stratification in Sect. 5) is used to compare against sampling. Sampling is only used in the training split of the data (Train sampling in Sect. 5).

4.3 Classification Metrics

F1-score and AUROC are used to assess our networks, both of which are defined and calculated in literature [9].

4.4 CAM Metrics

CAMs are heatmaps of spatial locations that are regions of interest from CNNs used to classify an image. To evaluate the CAMs generated and features identified within the CAMs, Deletion, Insertion, and WSOL are used [18]. Spray deposits are the only objects localisation can occur with in this dataset. Therefore, only the sprayed test images will be used for evaluation of CAMs with the average score for each metric being reported in Sect. 5.

For Deletion and Insertion, the confidence of the CNNs prediction will be recorded with Deletion and Insertion increasing by 1% until the entire image is deleted or inserted. After plotting the confidence values against the amount of image deleted or inserted, the Area Under the Curve (AUC) is calculated using the Trapezoidal Rule:

$$AUC = \frac{h}{2} \left[y_0 + 2 \left(y_1 + y_2 + y_3 + \cdots + y_{n-1} \right) + y_n \right] \tag{2}$$

where y is the prediction confidence, n is equal to the number of plotted points, and h is equal to the increase in Deletion or Insertion change. Therefore, Deletion scores that are lower are better and Insertion scores that are higher are better.

The metric commonly used within WSOL is IoU and can be calculated as the area of overlap divided by the area of union. Mathematically it is defined:

$$IoU(A, B) = \frac{A \cap B}{A \cup B} \tag{3}$$

where A and B are the prediction and ground truth bounding boxes, respectively. IoU will show how effective the CAM method is at localising around spray deposits.

4.5   Speed Test

Inference times of CNNs on the test set are recorded using an NVIDIA GeForce RTX 3070 Ti GPU and Intel Core i7-1800H CPU. The average CAM computation time is also recorded, to identify which method could be deployed.

5   Results and Performance Evaluation

The best scoring metrics are in bold for all tables in this section. Table 2 displays classification metrics using different data split methods. For both tested CNN architectures, F1-score of 94.1% is achieved for Non Sprayed, F1-score of 93.3% for Sprayed, and AUROC of 93.7% with stratification and train sampling. The DenseNet121 architecture performs similarly with the stratification data split. CAMs from these CNNs will be evaluated, considering stratification and train sampling as the best data split method.

The data split method has a massive increase on the metric scores. The DenseNet121 and ShuffleNetV2 increase by 16.4% F1-Score for Non Sprayed, 21.9% F1-Score for Sprayed, and 18.7% AUROC when using stratification and train sampling when compared to the random data split. The addition of train sampling has a positive effect for ShuffleNetV2 with increases of 5.3% F1-Score for Non Sprayed, 7.6% F1-Score for Sprayed, and 6.2% AUROC.

Table 2. Classification Results

Model	Data Split Method	F1-Score Non Sprayed (%)	F1-Score Sprayed (%)	AUROC (%)
DenseNet121	Random	77.7	71.4	75.0
	Stratification	**94.1**	**93.3**	**93.7**
	Train Sampling	**93.3**	**94.1**	**93.7**
ShuffleNetV2 2x	Random	77.7	71.4	75.0
	Stratification	88.8	85.7	87.50
	Train Sampling	**94.1**	**93.3**	**93.7**

Table 3 displays the average inference speed using a GPU and CPU. ShuffleNetV2 achieves 0.012 s on GPU and 0.014 s on CPU. DenseNet121 achieves 0.036 s on GPU and 0.056 s on GPU. Considering identical classification scores and faster inference, ShuffleNetV2 is more effective.

Table 3. Model Inference Speed Test

Network	Average Inference GPU (s)	Average Inference CPU (s)
DenseNet121	**0.036**	0.056
ShuffleNetV2 2x	**0.012**	0.014

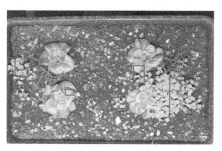

(a) Bounding boxes for spray deposits in test image.

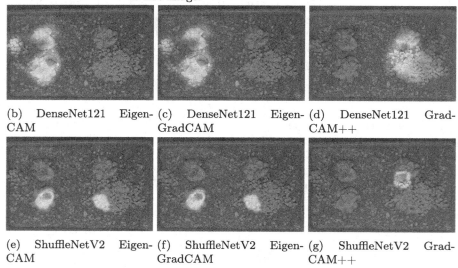

(b) DenseNet121 Eigen-CAM

(c) DenseNet121 Eigen-GradCAM

(d) DenseNet121 Grad-CAM++

(e) ShuffleNetV2 Eigen-CAM

(f) ShuffleNetV2 Eigen-GradCAM

(g) ShuffleNetV2 Grad-CAM++

Fig. 3. Class Activation Maps for all methods and models for sprayed test image.

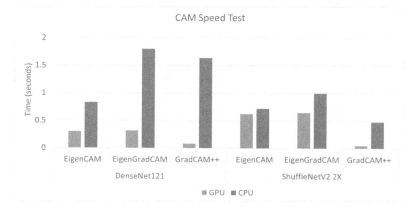

Fig. 4. CAM average inference speed on CPU and GPU for both architectures.

Using the best data split methodology of stratification and sampling, CAMs are generated and then evaluated with Deletion, Insertion, and WSOL and are reported in Table 4. With DenseNet121, GradCAM++ performs the best in all metrics with 49.85% Deletion, 84.63% Insertion, and 56.6% WSOL. Similarly, GradCAM++ achieves the best Deletion score 36.02%, and Insertion score 24.76% with ShuffleNetV2. EigenGradCAM achieves a 54.5% score for WSOL with ShuffleNetv2. These results indicate GradCAM++ consistently outperforms other CAM methods across the architectures tested, with a slight exception where EigenGradCAM has a marginally higher WSOL score with ShuffleNetV2.

Table 4. CAM Results

Model	CAM Method	Deletion (%)	Insertion (%)	WSOL (%)
DenseNet121	*EigenCAM*	56.10	78.22	45.0
	EigenGradCAM	50.98	56.07	23.0
	GradCAM++	**49.85**	**84.63**	**56.6**
ShuffleNetV2 2x	*EigenCAM*	37.10	20.70	53.7
	EigenGradCAM	37.41	22.80	**54.5**
	GradCAM++	**36.02**	**24.76**	53.7

Figure 3 displays the CAMs for a test image, including a bounding box ground truth of spray deposits. While EigenCAM and EigenGradCAM generate similar CAMs with activations across both architectures, GradCAM++ shows different CAMs using gradients only. This discrepancy between CAM results in Table 4 is shown visually in Fig. 3 when using activations or gradients.

Table 5. CAM Speed Test

Model	CAM Method	Average Inference GPU (s)	Average Inference CPU (s)
DenseNet121	*EigenCAM*	0.305	**0.832**
	EigenGradCAM	0.319	1.804
	GradCAM++	**0.083**	1.638
ShuffleNetV2 2x	*EigenCAM*	0.621	0.719
	EigenGradCAM	0.645	0.996
	GradCAM++	**0.050**	**0.483**

In Table 5 inference speed test results of the CAM methods are reported. GradCAM++ for both models is the fastest on the GPU with an average 0.083 s inference time for the DenseNet121, and an average 0.050 s inference time for the ShuffleNetV2. However, EigenCAM is faster on the CPU with DenseNet121 with an average inference time of 0.832 s. For the ShuffleNetV2, on the CPU Grad-CAM++ is still the fastest with an average inference time of 0.483 s. Figure 4 illustrates a chart to show the variance in speed.

6 Conclusion

Our results indicate that this system could be deployed onto Agri-robot precision spraying systems to evaluate spraying effectiveness. Adding a camera can cheaply and effectively meet EU Green Deal requirements with a generalisable approach.

CNNs are able to distinguish sprayed from non sprayed weeds and lettuces with over 90% AUROC, localise around spray deposits in a WSOL task with an average IoU of over 50%, and complete inference for both within real-time. Using the ShuffleNetV2 architecture and GradCAM++ CAM method we can achieve a total classification and localisation time of 0.062 s on average.

This evaluation system could be improved by quantifying spray deposition values to compare to water sensitive papers and tracers. Therefore, we are going to segment spray deposits and create deposition values for our future work.

References

1. John Deere. https://www.deere.com/en/sprayers/see-spray-ultimate/
2. Chattopadhay, A., Sarkar, A., Howlader, P., Balasubramanian, V.N.: Grad-CAM++: generalized gradient-based visual explanations for deep convolutional networks. In: 2018 IEEE Winter Conference on Applications of Computer Vision (WACV), pp. 839–847. IEEE (2018)
3. Commission, E.: The European green deal. In: European Commission (2019). https://bit.ly/3fje1au
4. Deng, J., Dong, W., Socher, R., Li, L.J., Li, K., Fei-Fei, L.: ImageNet: a large-scale hierarchical image database. In: 2009 IEEE Conference on Computer Vision and Pattern Recognition, pp. 248–255 (2009). https://doi.org/10.1109/CVPR.2009.5206848
5. Desai, S., Ramaswamy, H.G.: Ablation-CAM: visual explanations for deep convolutional network via gradient-free localization. In: 2020 IEEE Winter Conference on Applications of Computer Vision (WACV), pp. 972–980 (2020). https://doi.org/10.1109/WACV45572.2020.9093360
6. Draelos, R.L., Carin, L.: Use HiResCAM instead of grad-cam for faithful explanations of convolutional neural networks (2020). https://doi.org/10.48550/ARXIV.2011.08891. https://arxiv.org/abs/2011.08891
7. Farooque, A.A., et al.: Field evaluation of a deep learning-based smart variable-rate sprayer for targeted application of agrochemicals. Smart Agric. Technol. **3**, 100073 (2023). https://www.sciencedirect.com/science/article/pii/S2772375522000387
8. Fu, H., Zhao, X., Wu, H., Zheng, S., Zheng, K., Zhai, C.: Design and experimental verification of the YOLOv5 model implanted with a transformer module for target-oriented spraying in cabbage farming. Agronomy **12**(10) (2022). https://www.mdpi.com/2073-4395/12/10/2551
9. Hossin, M., Sulaiman, M.N.: A review on evaluation metrics for data classification evaluations. Int. J. Data Min. Knowl. Manag. Process **5**(2), 1 (2015)
10. Huang, G., Liu, Z., van der Maaten, L., Weinberger, K.Q.: Densely connected convolutional networks (2018)
11. Jiang, P.T., Zhang, C.B., Hou, Q., Cheng, M.M., Wei, Y.: LayerCAM: exploring hierarchical class activation maps for localization. IEEE Trans. Image Process. **30**, 5875–5888 (2021)

12. Kim, J., Seol, J., Lee, S., Hong, S.W., Son, H.I.: An intelligent spraying system with deep learning-based semantic segmentation of fruit trees in orchards. In: 2020 IEEE International Conference on Robotics and Automation (ICRA), pp. 3923–3929 (2020). https://doi.org/10.1109/ICRA40945.2020.9197556
13. Liu, J., Abbas, I., Noor, R.S.: Development of deep learning-based variable rate agrochemical spraying system for targeted weeds control in strawberry crop. Agronomy **11**(8), 1480 (2021)
14. Liu, L., Liu, Y., He, X., Liu, W.: Precision variable-rate spraying robot by using single 3D lidar in orchards. Agronomy **12**(10) (2022). https://www.mdpi.com/2073-4395/12/10/2509
15. Ma, N., Zhang, X., Zheng, H.-T., Sun, J.: ShuffleNet V2: practical guidelines for efficient CNN architecture design. In: Ferrari, V., Hebert, M., Sminchisescu, C., Weiss, Y. (eds.) Computer Vision – ECCV 2018. LNCS, vol. 11218, pp. 122–138. Springer, Cham (2018). https://doi.org/10.1007/978-3-030-01264-9_8
16. Muhammad, M.B., Yeasin, M.: Eigen-CAM: class activation map using principal components. In: 2020 International Joint Conference on Neural Networks (IJCNN). IEEE, July 2020. https://doi.org/10.1109/IJCNN48605.2020.9206626
17. Partel, V., Charan Kakarla, S., Ampatzidis, Y.: Development and evaluation of a low-cost and smart technology for precision weed management utilizing artificial intelligence. Comput. Electron. Agric. **157**, 339–350 (2019)
18. Petsiuk, V., Das, A., Saenko, K.: RISE: randomized input sampling for explanation of black-box models (2018). https://arxiv.org/abs/1806.07421
19. Raja, R., Nguyen, T.T., Slaughter, D.C., Fennimore, S.A.: Real-time weed-crop classification and localisation technique for robotic weed control in lettuce. Biosys. Eng. **192**, 257–274 (2020)
20. Selvaraju, R.R., Cogswell, M., Das, A., Vedantam, R., Parikh, D., Batra, D.: Grad-CAM: visual explanations from deep networks via gradient-based localization. Int. J. Comput. Vis. **128**(2), 336–359 (2019). https://doi.org/10.1007/s11263-019-01228-7
21. Srinivas, S., Fleuret, F.: Full-gradient representation for neural network visualization (2019). https://arxiv.org/abs/1905.00780
22. Wang, B., Yan, Y., Lan, Y., Wang, M., Bian, Z.: Accurate detection and precision spraying of corn and weeds using the improved YOLOv5 model. IEEE Access **11**, 29868–29882 (2023). https://doi.org/10.1109/ACCESS.2023.3258439
23. Wang, H., et al.: Score-CAM: score-weighted visual explanations for convolutional neural networks (2020)
24. Zheng, K., Zhao, X., Han, C., He, Y., Zhai, C., Zhao, C.: Design and experiment of an automatic row-oriented spraying system based on machine vision for early-stage maize corps. Agriculture **13**(3) (2023). https://www.mdpi.com/2077-0472/13/3/691

Smart Parking System Using Heuristic Optimization for Autonomous Transportation Robots in Agriculture

Roopika Ravikanna[✉], James Heselden, Muhammad Arshad Khan,
Andrew Perrett, Zuyuan Zhu, Gautham Das, and Marc Hanheide

School of Computer Science, University of Lincoln, Lincoln, UK
18724409@students.lincoln.ac.uk

Abstract. A typical commercial berry farm is spread across quite a few hectares and has over hundreds of rows and tens of pickers operating on a daily basis. The berries in these farms are grown in a poly-tunnel parallel row based environment. This work develops a heuristic assignment technique called Smart Parking. Smart Parking is used for allocating parking spaces to autonomous transportation robots that assist fruit pickers working in such farms. The Smart Parking algorithm developed is put to test in a simulation software. It is also integrated with a robot controller called RASberry, which is a cutting-edge research project for running an entirely automated strawberry farm. The robots utilised for autonomous transportation in the RASberry project and the real-world trials in this study are Thorvald by Saga Robotics. To monitor and evaluate the effectiveness of Smart Parking, a number of real-world tests are carried out using the RASberry-Thorvald system. Smart Parking performs better than Standard Parking in terms of mechanical conservation and task completion time, as shown by graphical trend lines and statistical tests.

Keywords: Autonomous Robots · Multi-Robot Systems · Agricultural Robots · Multi-Agent Distribution · Human-Robot Interaction · Multi-Robot Planning · Swarm Robotics

1 Introduction

With 8.8 billion tonnes of strawberries produced worldwide, soft fruit output has increased by 600% in the UK during the past 25 years [3]. Their time is more precious, especially during this labour scarcity in agriculture, where labour expenses often account for 50% of crop production [7]. Since most soft fruits are high-value crops, their growers make good candidates for agricultural technology investors. One of the main industrial uses for autonomous agricultural robots is transportation, particularly in the horticulture and fruit production industries. Due to their utility in minimising downtime of fruit pickers, which they may put into their primary work of picking, transportation robots are appreciated by both fruit pickers and agri-industries in the production of soft fruit. The use

F. Iida et al. (Eds.): TAROS 2023, LNAI 14136, pp. 38–50, 2023.
https://doi.org/10.1007/978-3-031-43360-3_4

of autonomous transportation robots in the production of soft fruit benefits the fruit pickers by enhancing their daily crop production and optimising their profits while they are on the job. According to UK-RAS's predictions for the future of agri-robotics: as the technology develops, different levels of shared autonomy in which a human operator directs high-level execution will be visible [10].

The number of robots a human can control at once, along with the robotic system's performance of the necessary sensory-motor coordination on the ground, will help motivate the coexistence of human supervisors and robot agents in such a paradigm [10]. This paper aims to facilitate and optimise the use of autonomous transportation robots that operate in a parallel aisle or poly-tunnel environment. A typical commercial berry farm is spread across quite a few hectares and has over hundreds of rows and tens of pickers operating on a daily basis [1]. The importance of this contribution is due to the huge scale of area at which commercial horticulture and berry farms operate.

2   Context and Problem Statement

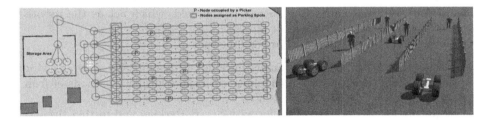

Fig. 1. (left) Graphical representation of the field's Topological map, (right) Illustrative image of the picker(s)-robot(s) system

This problem statement is fundamentally a dynamic assignment problem where a number of robots must be instantly assigned to a variety of jobs. In this instance, the workers are strawberry pickers dispersed across the poly-tunnel farm environment who require a transportation robot to move their full trays of strawberries to the storage section. Here, minimising robot travel is the main goal in task assignment for robots followed by shortening the time it takes to complete the activity. The previous work on intelligent parking for autonomous agricultural robots [2] is followed up in this paper. In that earlier work, various heuristic assignment algorithms for autonomous transportation robots were thoroughly analysed, compared, and evaluated using simulation software. The main conclusions and presumptions from that research have been cited often in this work. This piece, like [2], is a component of the RASberry project, which is supported by UKRI for a partnership between Saga Robotics and the University of Lincoln. The RASberry system can be characterised as a coordinated fleet of specialised mobile platforms that safely navigate through the strawberry environment and communicate with human workers to complete a task (such as transporting a tray of picked fruit) [8]. The mobile platform's control software is tailored to the jobs so it is essential there won't be any changes to the environment. The RASberry coordinator works on a topological level. Work is done by the RASberry coordinator at the topological level. Figure 1 displays a topological map of the test farm, where all of the experiments for this study are conducted and it also shows an illustrative example image of the system. Nodes, which are independent spatial points connected to one another, define it. The task points to be assigned to the robots are represented by the nodes within the rows. The individual robots are capable of supporting and interacting with human workers in a natural fashion [8]. Thorvald, a modular, all-purpose, lightweight outdoor mobile platform designed for autonomous operation in the agricultural domain, is the robotic platform used in this research [8]. The Riseholme test farm has a fully operational RASberry system. The majority of the experiments for this publication were conducted on the University of Lincoln campus [8].

Finding the best parking spots for autonomous transportation robots based on the spatial distribution of fruit pickers throughout the field can be summed up as the problem at hand. It falls under the category of an unbalanced assignment problem since n robots must be assigned to m task points. The task points in this case are the head nodes of each row in the field, which act as the robots' parking or waiting areas.

The highlights of this research are as follows:

– Creating a heuristic algorithm (Smart Parking) to dynamically assign parking places to a multi-robot system changing with the transient locations of fruit pickers.
– Integrating the RASberry controller with Smart Parking and testing the system in a real-world setting.
– Comparing the performance of Smart Parking versus Standard Parking, which involves employing fixed, unchanging parking places using a simulation software.

3   Related Work and Methodology

The Hungarian technique [14], often referred to as Hungarian planning, is a combinatorial optimisation technique used to solve the assignment problem. It can be used to determine the best solution for any balanced assignment problem. A collection of augmenting paths are found iteratively by the Hungarian algorithm in a weighted bipartite graph. An augmenting path is a graph path that alternates between matched and mismatched vertex locations starting with an unmatched vertex on one side of the bi-partition and ending at an unmatched vertex on the other uneven edges. The bipartite graph's n vertices determine the Hungarian algorithm's time complexity, which is $O(n3)$.

It may be fairly assumed that the number of robots will always be lower than the number of tasks in this unbalanced assignment situation. Since the job locations are not known in advance, they cannot be precisely predicted in real time.

In this study, simulation software was used to test out robot parking locations that were calculated using the Hungarian Algorithm. In a nutshell, the heuristic approach (Smart Parking) surpassed the Hungarian Algorithm outcomes.

This might be because Hungarian technique does not have a temporal aspect to it and gives an optimal solution for a given scenario of resources and tasks at a single instance of time. There is no allowance for unpredictability with the appearance of tasks. In case of Fruit farms, the exact node and time at which the picker calls for the robot cannot be anticipated with the current system. Therefore, a simple yet reasonable judgement of optimal parking spots depending on the pickers' transient positions works better, as this makes room for uncertainties. Also, the computational complexity of the Hungarian Technique becomes exponentially greater with the increase in number of tasks and resources, rendering it unsuitable to make quick decisions in real time. Most other assignment techniques like Linear bottleneck assignment [4], Monge-Kantorovich transportation [5] are also NP-hard and computationally complex. The heuristic method was chosen for further implementation in the real-time robot system due to this.

It can be observed that while the results form the simulation show that the Smart Parking heuristic performs better throughout, it can also be observed that the performance of Hungarian Technique worsens as the ratio of robots to pickers (resources to tasks) decreases and also gets increasingly complex.

Finding solid approximations to difficult optimisation issues is the goal of the problem-solving strategy known as heuristic optimisation. In heuristic optimisation, a set of straightforward guidelines or tactics is used to direct the search for the ideal answer without ensuring that the answer discovered is universally optimal.

In the earlier work of this project, various heuristic strategies to assign parking places to a group of robots were devised and tested for effectiveness on simulated software [2]. According to the findings of the previous study [2], the Cumulative Ranking Technique, a newly developed heuristic optimisation technique, outperforms the other ranking techniques when it comes to reducing robot travel distance and overall task completion time. Cumulative ranking technique is loosely based on rank-maximal matching or greedy matching [6]. Therefore, the design of a Smart Parking System for autonomous agricultural robots in a poly-tunnel environment incorporates the Cumulative Ranking Technique. When using the picker locations in the field to combine the parking place priority for each picker, the Cumulative Ranking System evaluates the best parking positions.

The system's implicit decision to assign parking spots in ascending order of proximity to the picker's location as the priority in this case seems intuitive. Figure 2 shows a visual representation of this. Action flow of the robot(s) is shown in Fig. 3. The controller assigns parking spaces to the robots in real time based on the pickers' current positions as obtained from a smart trolley device (SMTD). SMTD is a portable gadget with GPS connectivity that is connected to the trolley, which is used to summon a robot to the trolley's current location. For each picker present, a cycle within the system repeats. A typical cycle starts by

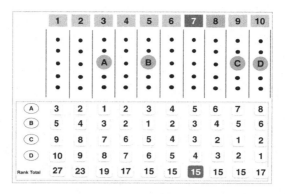

Fig. 2. Cumulative Ranking Method

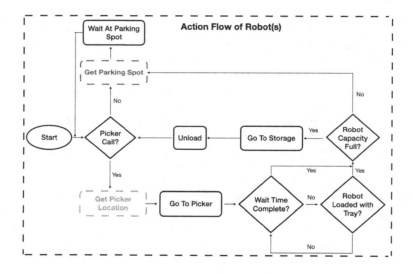

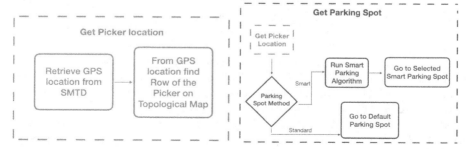

Fig. 3. Action Flow Diagram of the Robot(s)

giving the robot the parking space chosen according to the selected algorithm, after finishing its navigation, it will sit still there. If a picker requests a tray collection, the system identifies the closest idle robot to the picker and entrusts it with the task. Next, the robot will find the picker and wait till the picker has acknowledged that the loading is finished or the wait time has lapsed, then if the robot is filled up to its capacity, it will navigate to the storage area, else it goes to the recommended parking spot and the cycle repeats.

4 Experiments Using Software Simulator

This system's simulation programme was created in Python using the Simpy module. This software is created as a discrete event simulation system, just like in [11]. The test environment is a branched rectangular field with several parallel rows that feature evenly spaced nodes or way points that the pickers pass through during their journey. Based on information from [2], each row is considered to be 120 m long, with a field node to node distance of 5 m. This results in 24 nodes per row. Picker time is a variable that represents the amount of time it takes a picker to move from one node to another, or the amount of time they spend picking at each node. This is estimated to be approximately 1240 s based on actual data collected from fruit pickers, with some variation, being mindful of people's uncertainties.

As with real robots, the robot is instructed to move at a speed of 0.5 m/s. The number of rows in the field, the number of pickers, and the number of robots can all be altered in the simulation software as necessary for the experiment. Two methods are available for determining the parking spaces: Standard Parking, which uses a heuristic technique to designate the row headers at the centre or mid-field as Smart Parking. While the robots wait in the conventional or smart parking spots depending on the type of experiment, the system outputs a random selection of picker sites for each experiment. Depending on when they load their virtual tray of strawberries, the pickers each cry out for a robot at various points from the beginning. The robot(s) then departs from its parking space to serve them. The main metric provided by the simulation software is the robot distance and time to finish these tasks. The two sets of experiments run in the simulation programme use three robots in a setting of 50 rows with variable numbers of pickers (ranging from 3 to 15). Another involves three robots and five pickers in situations where the number of rows varies from 10 to 50. The experimental outcomes of each situation under consideration were averaged across 100 picker location trials.

5   Experiments in the Real World

Smart Parking Algorithm is integrated with the RASberry-Throvald controller and the performance is tested out at a strawberry farm with actual human pickers for some scenarios.

5.1   The Robot Controller, RASberry

A collection of ROS systems called RASberry is created to handle everything necessary for automating a robot deployment in an agriculture/food production setting. Component systems include many different things like robot control, methods for fruit counting, yield projections, and analyses of human behaviour architectures for communications and environment representations. It is a built in collaboration with Saga Robotics and the University of Lincoln. A centralised coordination system called the RASberry Coordinator was created to react to requests for on-demand jobs, like a picker asking for a robot. It is responsible for both the work distribution, which follows the straightforward first-come, first-served using topological-filtering in each robot's approach and route planning to break routing impasses. The parking-spot allocation method currently in use, Standard Parking chooses the closest vacant occupied node from a predetermined list that is closest to the robot's current location. When using the Smart Parking algorithm, the Standard Parking technique is substituted.

5.2   Experimental Configuration

Real-world polytunnels have extensive rows of strawberry plants with a mixture of diseased/unripe fruits and ripe fruits hanging from them. For the purpose of this experiment, this is imitated wooden pegs strung along a thread liner that represent strawberry fruits hanging from the plants in the rows of poly-tunnels. This synthetic recreation of the environment is done to avoid wastage of crop and build a controlled setting that could be replicate similar settings across experiments. The frequency of the pegs distributed is in relation to the yield density of strawberries during the peak harvest season (based on data from the Riseholme yield poly-tunnel for strawberry growing in June/July 2022). Indicative pegs on this line will also include a scaled illustration fruits that are unripe or sick using pegs of a different colour to that representing ripe ones. This is to simulate a realistic plucking challenge for the research. Each strawberry picker has a cart with an SMTD, which they push as they move through the poly-tunnel rows, filling it with the strawberries they have just picked. During real harvest, the robot is summoned at the conclusion of each tray of strawberries by pressing a button on the SMTD. Here in the experiments, every time someone fills a tray with pegs, a robot is called in the same way (Note: the tray size has been appropriately changed to account for the volume difference between strawberries and pegs) (Fig. 4).

Fig. 4. Real World Experimental Setup: (top-left) Poly-tunnel environment; (top-right) SMTD; (bottom-left) A Thorvald robot in the poly-tunnel environment; (bottom-right) Red pegs placed along the plant rows. (Color figure online)

5.3   Human Fruit Pickers in Experimental Trials

A total of 8 studies were carried out with the Throvald Robot and RASberry controller in a realistic setting. These trials tested the Smart Parking module's performance in terms of Robot Travel Distance in contrast to Standard Parking after it had been integrated with the controller. The eight trials are really divided into four pairs, each pair with the same set of conditions.

6   Results and Discussions

The results from simulated experiments are shown in Fig. 5. It can be observed that the Robot Travel distance is notably lesser during all of the experiments with Smart Parking as opposed to Standard Parking. It has been reflected in the Plots. Also, the percentage change in Robot Travel Distance increases linearly as the Robot to Picker ratio decreases and also when the Robot to Rows ratio decreases. This means that the positive effect of using Smart Parking versus Standard Parking increases in more stringent cases of Robot Resources. There is approximately 12% decrease of robot travel distance while using Smart Parking thereby causing conservation of mechanical and power consumption of Robot Resources. This also means a lesser wait time for the pickers as they would be attended to more quickly due to lesser robot travel time.

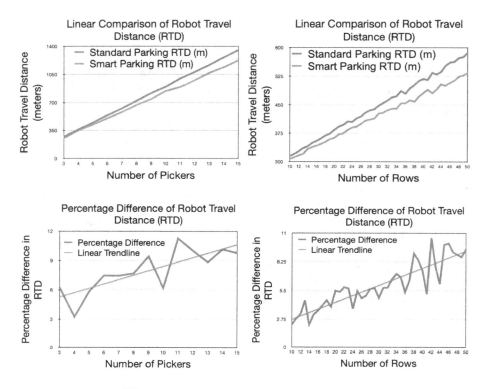

Fig. 5. Results from Simulated Experiments

The real world experiments for each scenario were run twice, once with Standard Parking and once with Smart Parking turned on in the controller. The four different experimental settings are as follows: one picker and one robot with a capacity of two trays, two pickers and one robot with a capacity of two trays, two pickers and one robot with a capacity of four trays, and two pickers and one robot with a capacity of six trays. Participants for each of the 4 sets of tests were different human fruit pickers with comparable degrees of ability. Each experiment's robot trajectory was recorded for performance evaluation. Robot travel trajectories are plotted for each of the four sets of the real-world experiments in Fig. 6. When employing Smart Parking instead of Standard Parking, up to 22% of the space is saved.

Table 1. Key findings from Paired T-Test to validate results from simulated and real world experiments.

Parameters	Row Variation Test	Picker Variation Test	Real World Test
Null Hypothesis H0	$\mu = 0$	$\mu = 0$	$\mu = 0$
Alternate Hypothesis H1	$\mu < 0$	$\mu < 0$	$\mu < 0$
Alpha α	0.05	0.05	0.05
P-value	$p < 0.001$	$p < 0.001$	$p = 0.043$
Test Statistic T	-12.6312	-6.0358	-2.4974
Sample Size	41	13	4
Skewness	-0.5364	-0.1314	-1.6453
Kurtosis	-0.782	-1.4907	2.8782
Effect Size	1.97	1.67	1.25
Result	H0 rejected	H0 rejected	H0 rejected

A statistical technique known as the Paired T-technique was used to verify the significance of the results. Results and analysis of this are provided in Table 1 for both real world and simulated experiments. In all of the studies, it can be seen that the Robot Travel distance is significantly lower with Smart Parking than with Standard Parking. The null hypothesis for each of the cases stated that there would be no change in Robot Travel Distance when switching from Standard Parking to Smart Parking and the alternative hypothesis stating a decrease in mean distance travelled by robots when employing Smart Parking. Both in simulated and actual experiments, with a confidence interval of 0.05, the null hypothesis is disproved, proving the performance betterment in using Smart Parking.

48   R. Ravikanna et al.

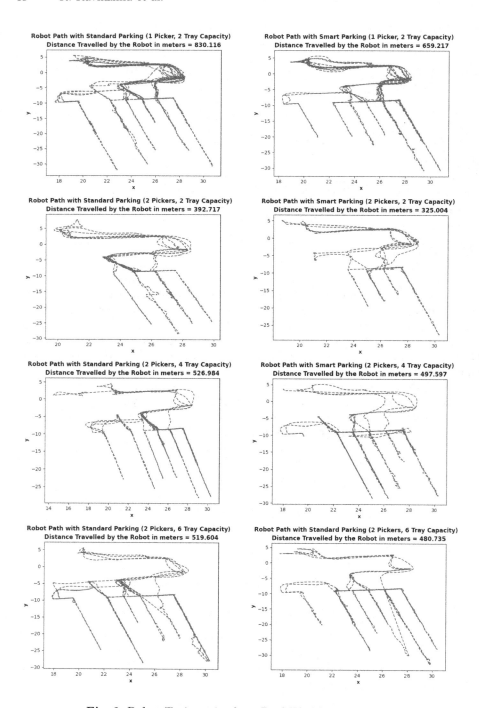

Fig. 6. Robot Trajectories from Real World Experiments

7 Future Work and Conclusion

After implementing and validating Smart Parking in agricultural autonomous transportation robots, the next step in this research is to predict in advance the robot needs of fruit pickers while picking in the field. To do this, a probabilistic model of pickers' behaviour across yield spectrum would need to be developed. This project's basic work is currently underway, and it seeks to deliver a comprehensive automation of the transportation robot system in the agricultural area along with Smart Parking [9].

Acknowledgements. The Engineering and Physical Sciences Research Council [EP/S023917/1] and Saga Robotics provided funding for this work.

References

1. Cheshire, L.: Dyson Farming extends UK strawberry season. Fruitnet (2021). https://www.fruitnet.com/fresh-produce-journal/dyson-farming-extends-uk-strawberry-season/184759.article
2. Ravikanna, R., Hanheide, M., Das, G., Zhu, Z.: Maximising availability of transportation robots through intelligent allocation of parking spaces. In: Towards Autonomous Robotic Systems: 22nd Annual Conference, TAROS 2021, Lincoln, UK, 8–10 September 2021, Proceedings 22, pp. 337–348 (2021)
3. Horticulture Statistics 2020. assets.publishing.service.gov.uk. https://assets.publishing.service.gov.uk/government/uploads/system/uploads/attachment_data/file/1003935/hort-report-20jul21.pdf. Accessed 10 Apr 2023
4. Villani, C.: Topics in Optimal Transportation, p. 66 (2003)
5. Burkard, R., Mauro, D., Martello, S.: Assignment Problems. Chapter 6.2 Linear Bottleneck Assignment Problem, p. 172 (2008)
6. Irving, R.: Greedy matchings. Technical report Tr-2003-136, University of Glasgow (2003)
7. Agriculture in the UK Evidence Pack assets.publishing.service.gov.uk. https://assets.publishing.service.gov.uk/government/uploads/system/uploads/attachment_data/file/1106562/AUK_Evidence_Pack_2021_Sept22.pdf. Accessed 12 Apr 2023
8. Johan From, P., Grimstad, L., Hanheide, M., Pearson, S., Cielniak, G.: Rasberry-robotic and autonomous systems for berry production. Mech. Eng. **140**, S14–S18 (2018)
9. Pal, A., Das, G., Hanheide, M., Candea Leite, A., From, P.: An agricultural event prediction framework towards anticipatory scheduling of robot fleets: general concepts and case studies. Agronomy **12**, 1299 (2022)
10. Duckett, T., et al.: Agricultural robotics: the future of robotic agriculture. arXiv Preprint arXiv:1806.06762 (2018)
11. Das, G., Cielniak, G., From, P., Hanheide, M., et al.: Discrete event simulations for scalability analysis of robotic in-field logistics in agriculture-a case study (2018)
12. Baxter, P., Cielniak, G., Hanheide, M., From, P.: Safe human-robot interaction in agriculture. In: Companion of the 2018 ACM/IEEE International Conference on Human-Robot Interaction, pp. 59–60 (2018)

13. Fox, C., Gao, J., Ghalamzan Esfahani, A., Saaj, M., Hanheide, M., Parsons, S. (eds.): TAROS 2021. LNCS (LNAI), vol. 13054. Springer, Cham (2021). https:// doi.org/10.1007/978-3-030-89177-0
14. Kuhn, H.: The Hungarian method for the assignment problem. Nav. Res. Logist. Q. **2**, 83–97 (1955)

Closed-Loop Robotic Cooking of Soups with Multi-modal Taste Feedback

Jierui Shi, Arsen Abdulali, Grzegorz Sochacki[✉], and Fumiya Iida

University of Cambridge, Cambridge CB2 1TN, UK
gks33@cam.ac.uk

Abstract. Cooking soup is a complex dynamic process, where the properties and taste of ingredients change during long temperature exposure. Furthermore, the simmering process of a soup also causes evaporation of the water, which increases the salt density in a bouillon. To mitigate this problem, we developed a closed-loop robotic system that allows cooking soups based on salinity and pH sensing. By taking into account that both salinity and pH are subject to change during the cooking, we recorded the salinity and pH over a complete course of cooking by an expert human and employed a proportional controller that adds salt and water into the soup. For the evaluation, we employed the proposed approach to cook a tomato soup with three different initial conditions. The results suggest that the system reaches the target pH and salinity reasonably close, even for significantly different soup bases.

Keywords: Robotic Cooking · Taste Feedback · Closed-loop Control

1 Introduction

Culinary arts play an essential role in human evolution. Apart from the balanced nutrition content, each dish evolved by capturing the taste preferences and traditions of a particular cuisine. Even experienced chefs, sometimes, have difficulties to reproduce a meal with a certain taste. In the case of robotic cooking, with a limited taste perception, cooking the food becomes significantly more challenging.

The research on robotic cooking remains in its infancy. There are multiple levels of integration of robots into cooking process. One of the basic robotic cooking approaches is teleoperated robots, e.g., Bolano et al. developed a CookieBot system that enables remotely decorate cakes [1]. Another level of autonomy is the robotic system assisting humans in tedious and repetitive tasks. For instance, in [2], the authors proposed an autonomous robotic solution to load dishes into dishwashers. Other examples of robotic assistants are robots performing an open-loop stir-fry [3] and selecting ingredients according to a recipe [4]. More advanced robo-chef are involved in the actual cooking process. In their early work, Beetz et al. developed a cooking platform that enabled the robot to make pancakes from the recipes [5]. Later on, this approach was extended in [6],

F. Iida et al. (Eds.): TAROS 2023, LNAI 14136, pp. 51–62, 2023.
https://doi.org/10.1007/978-3-031-43360-3_5

where the robot learned to cook pancakes from video demonstrations. Similarly, Zhang and Nikolaidis proposed using videos from the internet to teach robots to cook [7]. Recently, the researchers in [8] have employed the Batch Bayesian Optimization that optimizes the contact of ingredients in an omelette based on human feedback. Having no taste feedback, this approach rather optimizes the target recipe, whereas the cooking is performed in an open-loop fashion. To cook dishes comparable to the ones made by a human, however, sensing the taste during the cooking process is inevitable.

Sensing taste and interpreting the taste signal for robotic applications are challenging. There are several sensing methods presented in the literature [9] and commercial products [10,11] that were generally used for accessing the quality or content of the food, e.g., cheese [12], fruits [13], meats [14], honey [15], wine [13], etc. These methods, however, are inapplicable for the robotics control as they require homogenization process [14] or additional chemicals [16]. Practical robotic systems with taste feedback, on the other hand, utilize simple low dimensional feedback. For instance, in [17], the closed-loop control with salinity feedback was proposed to cook scramble eggs. Only salinity feedback is generally limited to measurement of the salt content. By replacing the chewing process of a human, the researchers in [18] were able to track salinity changes while mechanically processing the food. The additional time dimension, in this case, helped to measure the content of both salt and tomatoes in tomato scrambled eggs. This approach, however, is inapplicable for cooking soups, where the mechanical processing does not introduce significant changes of conductance. Additionally, long exposure to the heat required for cooking a soup, evaporates water from the soup. The water and salt content should be optimized with respect to other ingredients, which makes one-dimensional taste feedback rather impractical.

In this paper, we proposed the first practical approach to robotic cooking of soups. To adjust the salt and water content in a closed-loop setting, we employed an additional sensing channel of the pH. The combination of salinity and pH signals helps the robot to maintain the ratio of the ingredients to the total volume of the bouillon, and prevent the excessive amount of salt and water. To adjust the salinity and pH levels, we developed a closed-loop controller that adds salt and water during the cooking. To prove the concept the proposed system was employed for cooking tomato soup. The performance of the proposed controller is evaluated for three different initial conditions. The results show that the system is able to reach the target levels of salinity and pH reasonably close for various soup bases.

2   Control Model

2.1   Problem Definition

Cooking soup is a dynamic process, where the properties of ingredients change from raw to cooked, and the water content also changes due to evaporation. Experienced chefs usually address this issue either by adding extra water before or during cooking. Furthermore, the ratio of the ingredients to the total volume of the bouillon is also essential. While sensing the salt density in a water solution is a relatively simple task, measuring the content of other ingredients is nontrivial. In this work, we employ pH sensing as an additional taste dimension to help the robot infer the ratio of the bouillon to other ingredients. The pH measurements are invariant to the amount of salt in solution, which makes them convenient to use for our task. pH closely mimics one of the basic human tastes - sourness [19]. The innate human response to low pH is negative [20], but it is strongly affected by acquired taste, and is considered positive in the context of many dishes. The central idea of our approach is that the ingredients in a bouillon change the pH level to higher or lower values than the pH of the water. Thus, the closer the pH readings of the soup to the pH of the water, the smaller the ratio of ingredients to water. This assumption generally holds for soups where the total pH of ingredients deviates from the level of water. Therefore, the main requirement of using our approach is to take the pH measurement after making a soup base and before adding the water, ensuring that it differs from the water pH, which is 7 for pure water at 25 °C, and a very similar value for tap water [21]. pH varies between foods, even among foods of very similar origin. For example, the breasts and thighs of broilers and spent hens were homogenized with water in a 1:4 proportion, and their pH was recorded. Significant differences in pH were found in these meats. The spent hen breast had a pH of 5.64, and the thigh was 6.37, while the corresponding values for broiler were 6.43 and 6.83 [22]. Perception of sourness is largely dependent on age and dish [23]. Older people report lower intensity when exposed to the same stimuli. Water solutions of ascorbic acid always cause negative pleasantness, the sensation becoming stronger with concentration. The sensation is different when studied in apple drink. In this case, people report peak pleasantness at a non-zero concentration of the acid [23].

To cook the soup, our system requires target values for both salinity and pH levels. The target values can generally be measured from the dishes cooked by an experienced chef. The proportional controller can then be utilized to reach target values towards the end of cooking.

2.2   Closed-Loop Control Model

We implement the feedback system using a proportional controller detailed in Fig. 1. At each moment, the controller uses the values of salinity and pH of the human chefs' soup at that specific time as setpoints. While cooking autonomously, the robot continuously compares the current pH and conductance voltages to the setpoints discussed earlier. We denote these setpoints as pH_{target} and G_{target}, where G stands for conductance.

The controller is described by Eqs. (1) and (2). As we see the mass of the salt added m_{salt} and the mass of the water added m_{water} are proportional to the error for the corresponding measurements(pH and G), but only when the error is positive. This is a necessity caused by the fact that both the water and salt can be added, but cannot be removed.

$$m_{salt} \propto G_{target} - G \text{ (when } G_{target} > G)$$
(1)

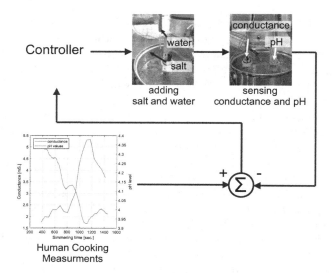

Fig. 1. Proportional controller enabling real-time closed-loop control of soup's salinity and pH.

$$m_{water} \propto pH_{target} - pH \ (\text{when } pH_{target} > pH) \tag{2}$$

The controller interacts with the soup by adding either water or salt. The addition of the water will lower the conductance, by lowering ion concentration in the soup, and increase pH by diluting low pH tomatoes. Adding the salt on the other hand increases conductance, by introducing extra Na+ and Cl- ions. The feedback is applied every 60 s. Multiple updates during the cooking allow close replication of the human cooking and mitigate the obvious issue that adding water not only increases the pH but also decreases the conductance.

3 Experimental Setup

3.1 Robotic System

The robotic system, depicted in Fig. 2a, is developed based on an admittance-type robotic arm (UR5) hanging down from a metal frame stretching alongside the kitchen worktop. The robot has access to a salt mill filled with crystal salt and a hob, where the tomato soup simmers. Moreover, the water tank is placed above the kitchen and connected through an electric valve to the end effector. The controller is implemented on a laptop, which interfaces with all parts of the system as shown in Fig. 3. The laptop also records measurements from the probes via a data acquisition device (DAQ) and interfaces to the water valve, salt dispenser, and proximity sensor via Arduino.

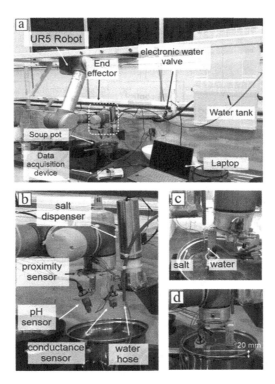

Fig. 2. Experimental setup. a) Robotic kitchen used for the experiment. UR5 arm hanging down from a metal frame is used for manipulation. The water tank is placed above the cooking area and an electronic valve is used to control the water flow. b) Closeup of the robot's end effector, showing the position of the water hose, pH and conductance sensors, and proximity sensor. c) The robot adds both salt and water to the soup. d) Closeup the robot probing pH.

The end-effector of the arm is depicted in Fig. 2b. It is a 3D print holding proximity sensors, a conductance probe, and a pH electrode. The conductance probe is in the form of an open circuit with two electrodes. To prevent electrolyzing (due to the current flow between anode and cathode) and build-ups of oxide films on the electrodes, the conductance probe is inserted into a soup only during the sensing, i.e., one-second interval per each measurement. The average value of each interval is used for control. The conductance measurements are collected with a frequency of approximately 2 samples per minute. The conductance probe is practically a voltage divider circuit in series with a $220\,\Omega$ resistor. The equation to convert conductance voltage V_g to conductance G[mS] as follows,

$$G = \left(\frac{5}{V_g} - 1\right) \times \frac{1000}{220}. \tag{3}$$

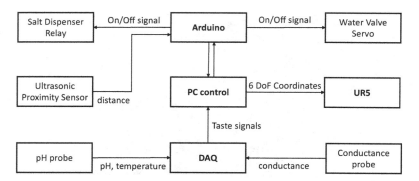

Fig. 3. Diagram showing dataflow in the cooking robot. PC is the center of the system that controls the robotic arm, and valves and records the measurements.

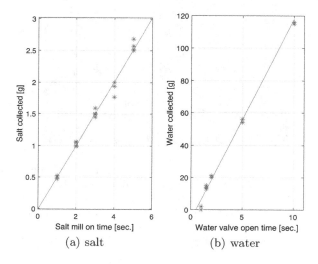

(a) salt   (b) water

Fig. 4. Figures showing a linear correlation between control inputs and the amount of ingredients added by the robot. a) Relation between the time of pressing salt mill and weight of the salt collected. b) Relation between water valve opening and weight of water added.

The pH probe measures the voltage difference between two electrodes at the end of the probe. However, due to the small voltage change during the experiment and susceptibility to significant noise, it is desirable to take as many measurements as possible to ensure accuracy. To achieve this, the pH probe is continuously immersed in the soup.

Therefore, the two sensors are mounted at different altitudes. Specifically, the conductance sensor is positioned 20 mm higher than the pH sensor (as shown in Fig. 2d). When adjusted to an initial height where the pH probe is approximately 5 mm below the soup level, the pH probe will be constantly taking measurements.

During the conductance measurement, the UR5 arm briefly lowers by 20 mm and returns to the previous position. However, during this one-second measurement interval, the measurements from the pH probe are discarded, as the movement cause variations in the voltage measured. Due to its high output resistance, the pH electrode needs to be buffered before reading with an operational amplifier. RENESAS 7611 was used for this task, in such a way that neutral pH resulted in the output of 1.65 V. Moreover, applying the Nernst Equation for water boiling temperature (373K) we get a slope of 0.074 V per 1 pH. Therefore, the final formula to convert electrode voltage into pH is:

$$\text{pH} = 7.0 - \frac{V_{pH} - 1.65}{0.074}. \tag{4}$$

Soup surface level varies during cooking as well, either due to evaporation or water being added. To ensure consistent and accurate measurements, it is essential to keep the probes at a constant height relative to the soup surface. The ultrasonic distance sensor mounted on the end actuator constantly monitors the distance from the soup, and communicates with the PC, which then sends a signal to UR5 to adjust the height, maintaining roughly the same distance from the soup to the probes.

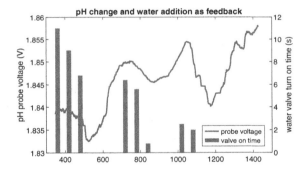

Fig. 5. Figure showing changes of pH during simmering of the soup (blue) and amount of water added as feedback (red). (Color figure online)

Adding salt and water is controlled through time modulation, by switching on the corresponding supply, i.e., salt mill and water valve (see Fig. 2c), for a specific duration. The relation between the time the salt mill/water valve remains on and the resulting addition of salt and water are depicted in Fig. 4. Both graphs show that there is a linear relationship. The constant is approximately 0.5 g/sec for salt and 11 g/sec for water. This result is combined with Eqs. (3), and (4), meaning that the time for keeping the salt mill/water valve on is proportional to the difference in conductance/pH voltages. The remaining problem is finding that proportional constant. If the constant is too small, the pH and conductance of the cooking soup will not converge to the ground truth soup. If the proportional constant is too large, the amount of salt and water added to the soup may overshoot. These overshoots cannot be easily corrected as removing water/salt from the soup is not feasible, and they should be avoided. The example of closed-loop control with the amount of water added is depicted in Fig. 5.

Fig. 6. Figure showing the cooking procedure for the soup. 1) Soup base is prepared by frying onions and adding canned tomatoes. Then the soup simmers for an extended amount of time (2), while being probed periodically (3).

3.2   Experimental Procedure

In this section, we explain the cooking procedure employed to obtain the measurements from *Human chef* cooking, as well as during *Closed-loop* cooking of the soup by a robot. The cooking algorithm is depicted in Fig. 6 with a following description:

1. In a saucepan, melt unsalted lard and cook diced onions for 2 min, then add canned chopped tomatoes and cook for a further 3 min. The hob temperature is high for this step. The mass of ingredients for onions, lard, and tomatoes are 70 g, 20 g, and 400 g respectively. No measurement is taken.
2. The contents (soup base) from the previous step is transferred to a cooking pot, and around 200 ml of water is then added to the pot. The hob temperature is medium for this step, and the soup is usually brought to a boiling temperature within 3 min. The whole cooking process lasts for around 25 min. *Human chef*: In addition to the 200 ml of water added at the start, a further 300 ml of water is added. Water added is accurate to the nearest 10 ml. 15 min into the step, 5g of salt is added, accurate to the nearest 0.1 g. The cooking process ends after another 10 min.
   Closed-loop: add salt and water according to probe measurement feedback. The feedback mechanism is elaborated in the following sections.
3. The measurements are interactively recorded while cooking for *Human chef* case. In the case of *closed-loop* control, the measurements are used in a proportional controller.

3.3   Experimental Conditions

To test the effectiveness of the proposed closed-loop control, we prepared three experimental conditions, i.e., *standard, flavored*, and *tomato only*. First, the base of the soup is cooked the same way from similar ingredients as during cooking by a human chef. Having a similar initial condition, a robot controller can simply follow the procedure of the ground truth data. Second, the soup base is additionally flavored with vinegar and salt. This helps to shift the initial condition and let the robot reach the level of desired pH and salinity. Last, the soup base is cooked using tomato only. This setting helps to assess the initial condition with low pH and salinity.

3.4   Data Processing

The conductance and pH signals measured by respective sensors are generally noisy. There are several reasons for the noise to appear. For instance, the additional salt and water supplied in a closed-loop requires some time to reach a homogeneous distribution of salt density and temperature. Bigger chunks of the ingredients can appear between electrodes causing the deviation of conductance from the average of the soup. The range of measurements is small for pH probe readings, ranging between 1.75 V to 1.90 V, which will be affected by white noises due to the electronics in the probe itself. To obtain reliable values when sampling real-time, the data were filtered by the following steps.

Removing Outliers. Both pH data and conductance data were cropped between 300–1500 s, as the first few minutes of data obtained are unstable due to adding water, temperature change (bringing to boiling temperature), robotic arm movement, etc. Then, we detect and remove outliers in conductance and pH signals individually. The voltage signal obtained by the pH sensor is linearly related to the actual pH value according to Nernst Equation. The reasonable range in this case of pH readings is 3.5–5.0 (e.g., pH signals measured during expert cooking varied in a range from 3.9 to 4.4). Therefore, any sample outside the aforementioned range is considered to be an outlier and removed from the data stream.

Signal Filtering. After the previous steps, a moving average window is applied to both the pH and conductance data to obtain smooth curves. The moving window size used is 500 and 3 for pH and conductance data respectively, corresponding to around a minute of data. The data processed during run-time follow the same manner, but as the filter requires a window size of approximately a minute of data, the processed data obtained is always half a minute behind the current running time.

4   Results and Discussion

Figure 7 shows the comparison of changes in pH and conductance levels for closed-loop cooked soups for three different starting soup bases. Their terminal

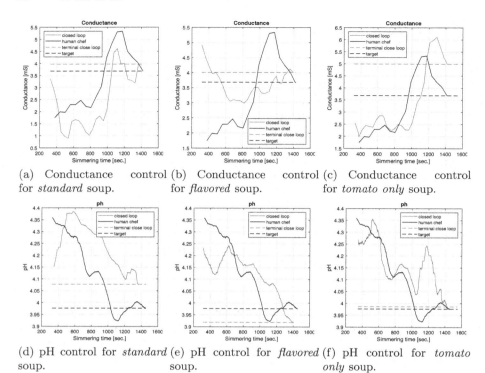

(a) Conductance control for *standard* soup.

(b) Conductance control for *flavored* soup.

(c) Conductance control for *tomato only* soup.

(d) pH control for *standard* soup.

(e) pH control for *flavored* soup.

(f) pH control for *tomato only* soup.

Fig. 7. Figure showing the performance of the robot in reproducing human cooked soup in terms of pH and conductivity.

values for both robot-cooked and ground truth soups are marked with dashed lines. Figure 7a and Fig. 7d show the case when the starting soup base is the same as the ground truth soup base. The closed-loop plots look like a delayed version of the ground truth plots. The terminal pH obtained by the closed-loop control are slightly higher because the closed-loop control caused the amount of water added to overshoot. The difference for the terminal value of conductance is small, yet higher than the ground truth value, possibly due to ground truth curving downwards towards the end. The salt control performed better in comparison.

Figure 7b and Fig. 7e show the case when the starting soup base is additionally flavoured with salt and vinegar. The pH plot showed that the pH value dropped more over the course of the time because the soup consists mostly of sour ingredient. Additionally, as the pH value only dropped below the reference value curve in the last few minutes, there was not enough time for the system to react, causing the terminal closed-loop pH value to fall below the terminal ground truth pH value. The closed-loop control end conductance is slightly higher than terminal ground truth value for the same reason as described in standard soup base.

Figure 7c and Fig. 7f show the case when the starting soup base is made only from tomatoes. The conductance overshoot after the time when the human chef added the salt, and it did not get enough time to fall down again. This is probably due to time delays in the system coming from time needed for the salt to dissolve. The pH followed the ground truth very closely until the system has started reacting to the salt addition by the human. At this moment the pH error grew, but was corrected fast enough to result in a soup very similar to the ground truth.

5   Conclusion

In this paper, we developed the robotic system that is able to cook soups based on conductance and pH data observed in human expert's cooking. The proposed closed-loop controller helps to maintain the ratio of ingredients to water, which helps to solve the problem with evaporation. To show that the proposed controller is able to reach the target starting from arbitrary initial condition, we performed evaluation for three use-cases, i.e., standard recipe, flavored with vinegar, and soup with unflavored tomato base. The experimental results suggest that the proposed system is able to approach the target salinity and pH level with reasonable accuracy.

In our future work, we plan to explore additional dimensions of the taste. Furthermore, we plan to develop a system distinguishing proportion of different ingredients in the base of the soup.

References

1. Bolano, G., Becker, P., Kaiser, J., Roennau, A., Dillmann, R.: Advanced usability through constrained multi modal interactive strategies: the cookiebot. In: 2019 19th International Conference on Advanced Robotics (ICAR), pp. 213–219 (2019)
2. Voysey, I., George Thuruthel, T., Iida, F.: Autonomous dishwasher loading from cluttered trays using pre-trained deep neural networks. Eng. Rep. 3(5), e12321 (2021)
3. Liu, J., et al.: Robot cooking with stir-fry: bimanual non-prehensile manipulation of semi-fluid objects. IEEE Robot. Autom. Lett. 7(2), 5159–5166 (2022)
4. Inagawa, M., Takei, T., Imanishi, E.: Development of a tower-type cooking robot. In: 2021 IEEE/SICE International Symposium on System Integration (SII), pp. 455–460 (2021)
5. Beetz, M., et al.: Robotic roommates making pancakes. In: 2011 11th IEEE-RAS International Conference on Humanoid Robots, pp. 529–536 (2011)
6. Danno, D., Hauser, S., Iida, F.: Robotic cooking through pose extraction from human natural cooking using OpenPose. In: Ang Jr, M.H., Asama, H., Lin, W., Foong, S. (eds.) IAS 2021. LNNS, vol. 412, pp. 288–298. Springer, Cham (2022). https://doi.org/10.1007/978-3-030-95892-3_22
7. Zhang, H., Nikolaidis, S.: Robot learning and execution of collaborative manipulation plans from youtube cooking videos. arXiv preprint arXiv:1911.10686 (2019)
8. Junge, K., Hughes, J., Thuruthel, T.G., Iida, F.: Improving robotic cooking using batch Bayesian optimization. IEEE Robot. Autom. Lett. 5(2), 760–765 (2020)

9. Di Rosa, A.R., Leone, F., Chiofalo, V.: 7 - electronic noses and tongues. In: Pico, Y. (ed.) Chemical Analysis of Food, 2nd edn, pp. 353–389. Academic Press (2020)

10. Astree electronic tongue - taste analysis. https://www.alpha-mos.com/astree-electronic-tongue-taste-analysis#electronic-tongue. Accessed 30 Jan 2022

11. "ts-5000z" intelligent sensor technology. http://www.insent.co.jp/en/products/ts5000z_index.html. Accessed 20 Jan 2022

12. Valente, N.I.P., Rudnitskaya, A., Oliveira, J.A.B.P., Gaspar, E.M.M., Gomes, M.T.S.R.: Cheeses made from raw and pasteurized cow's milk analysed by an electronic nose and an electronic tongue. Sensors **18**(8), 2415 (2018)

13. Rodriguez-Méndez, M.L., et al.: Analysis of grapes and wines using a voltammetric bioelectronic tongue: correlation with the phenolic and sugar content. In: 2014 IEEE SENSORS, pp. 2139–2142 (2014)

14. Liu, D., et al.: Evolution of taste compounds of dezhou-braised chicken during cooking evaluated by chemical analysis and an electronic tongue system. J. Food Sci. **82**(5), 1076–1082 (2017)

15. Oroian, M., Paduret, S., Ropciuc, S.: Honey adulteration detection: voltammetric e-tongue versus official methods for physicochemical parameter determination. J. Sci. Food Agric. **98**, 02 (2018)

16. Lipkowitz, J., Ross, C., Diako, C., Smith, D.: Discriminating aging and protein-to-fat ratio in cheddar cheese using sensory analysis and a potentiometric electronic tongue. J. Dairy Sci. **101**, 01 (2018)

17. Sochacki, G., Hughes, J., Hauser, S., Iida, F.: Closed-loop robotic cooking of scrambled eggs with a salinity-based 'taste' sensor. In: 2021 IEEE/RSJ International Conference on Intelligent Robots and Systems (IROS), pp. 594–600 (2021)

18. Sochacki, G., Abdulali, A., Iida, F.: Mastication-enhanced taste-based classification of multi-ingredient dishes for robotic cooking. Front. Robot. AI **9**, 108 (2022)

19. Gravina, S.A., Yep, G.L., Khan, M.: Human biology of taste. Ann. Saudi Med. **33**(3), 217–222 (2013)

20. Mela, D.J.: Why do we like what we like? J. Sci. Food Agric. **81**(1), 10–16 (2001)

21. Banks, D., Birke, M., Flem, B., Reimann, C.: Inorganic chemical quality of European tap-water: 1. distribution of parameters and regulatory compliance. Appl. Geochem. **59**, 200–210 (2015)

22. Lee, S.-H., Kim, H.-Y.: Comparison of quality and sensory characteristics of spent hen and broiler in South Korea. Animals **11**(9), 2565 (2021)

23. Chauhan, J., Hawrysh, Z.J.: Suprathreshold sour taste intensity and pleasantness perception with age. Physiol. Behav. **43**(5), 601–607 (1988)

A Folding Morphing-Wheg Duct-Entry Robot for Nuclear Characterisation

Dominic Murphy[✉], Manuel Giuliani, and Paul Bremner

Bristol Robotics Laboratory, University of the West of England, Bristol, UK
{dominic3.murphy,manuel.giuliani,paul2.bremner}@uwe.ac.uk

Abstract. This paper explores the design and development of a folding robot required to survey and characterize nuclear facilities only accessible via 125 mm diameter entry ducts. The enclosed legacy facilities at old nuclear sites like Sellafield in the UK have limited access. The condition, radioactive characteristics and accessibility of the enclosed environments is unknown and for decommissioning to take place, these environments must be mapped and characterised. For a robot to carry out this task, one of the key requirements is the ability of the robot to traverse rough terrain and obstacles that could be found inside the facility. To accommodate this, while fitting through the entry duct, the chosen design utilizes morphing whegs (wheel-legs), for locomotion. These are shape-changing wheels that can open out into a set of legs that rotate around an axle, allowing greater traction, diameter, and object traversal ability than wheels alone. The design and morphology of a folding morphing-wheg robot for nuclear characterisation, as well as the manufacture and testing of a prototype is discussed in this paper. A preliminary evaluation of the robot has shown it is capable of climbing up a maximum step height of 150 mm, while having a wheel diameter of 100 mm and being able to fit through a 125 mm duct.

Keywords: Folding Robot · Morphing Wheg · Nuclear Decommissioning

1 Introduction

With use, nuclear facilities are exposed to radiation and inevitably the buildings and equipment used in the nuclear processes become radioactive. This radioactive material poses a hazard to human and animal life and effectively renders a large area of land unusable if the radioactive material is not successfully removed or rendered safe. These environments are complex and due to degradation of the facilities, unstructured and unclean. Nuclear decommissioning is the process whereby a nuclear facility is dismantled so that it no longer requires measures for radiation protection. The term encompasses the immediate decommissioning of power plants, the dismantling and demolishing of buildings, the management

© The Author(s), under exclusive license to Springer Nature Switzerland AG 2023
F. Iida et al. (Eds.): TAROS 2023, LNAI 14136, pp. 63–74, 2023.
https://doi.org/10.1007/978-3-031-43360-3_6

and disposal of nuclear waste, and the remediation of the land. Nuclear decommissioning is a global problem of enormous societal importance and is set to become increasingly important in the future as Nuclear power becomes more widespread [8].

The Sellafield site in Cumbria, United Kingdom, is one of the oldest nuclear sites in the world. Many major developments in the 20th century nuclear industry were pioneered at this site, including the world's first commercial nuclear power station - Calder Hall - and many other world firsts. [1]. Due to the age of the facilities and the lack of precedent, documentation is very poor and decommissioning was not a consideration when building and operating the site. This makes the current task of decommissioning all the more difficult. There are approximately 170 nuclear facilities at Sellafield which require decommissioning over the next 100 years, at an estimated cost of £100 billion. While the decommissioning of the site has begun, many of these facilities are in unknown states and have been deemed too radioactive for humans to enter. For decommissioning operations to be conducted safely and efficiently it is important that the state, layout and radioactivity of the facility is known. [11] "Characterisation is extremely important because it allows the most appropriate and effective methods of decontamination, dismantling/demolition, and waste management to be subsequently applied and therefore affects decommissioning safety and cost."

Decommissioning and characterisation operations at Sellafield are currently carried out manually and with some bespoke mechanical systems. These bespoke solutions are both time consuming and expensive to deploy, and manual handling is costly, slow and potentially dangerous. There is the potential to develop less expensive, modular robotic systems which can be used effectively in many nuclear environments. These environments are complex and due to degradation of the facilities, unstructured and unclean. Objects such as pipes, cables and other nuclear detritus may lay across open spaces and impede the movement of any robot inside.

The nuclear decommissioning industry is a highly regulated and relatively conservative industry, and so far this has prevented the use of many robotic tools, though many are currently in development in academia and industry (e.g., [2,4,12,13]). A high degree of importance is put on reliability and robustness of processes, as the consequences of a failure can be so high. For this reason simple tools are preferred and thus far high levels of automation have been rejected to continue the use of traditional demolition machinery. Any robotic tool must be designed carefully to be suitable for the industry and task.

This paper presents the design and development of a folding robot for access into nuclear facilities through 125 mm diameter entry ducts (Fig. 1). The robot uses a morphing-wheg design to move over both flat surfaces and obstacles up to 150 mm height. We present the robot's design and software (Sect. 3). We also show a first prototype and discuss results from a preliminary evaluation (Sect. 4).

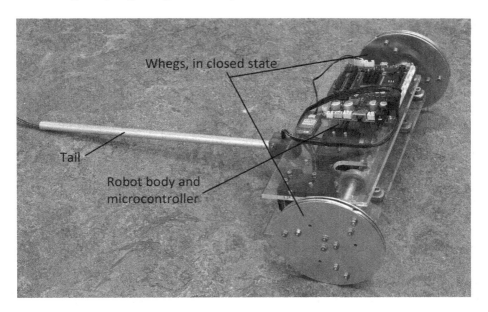

Fig. 1. The robot

2   Related Work

A robot that has previously been designed for entry through the 125 mm diameter ducts at Sellafield is the MIRRAX (Miniature Inspection Robot for Restricted Access eXploration) robot [6]. This robot is a 3 segment folding robot with the shape inspired by the Hitachi-GE Nuclear Energy Robot, which is also designed for duct entry. With the robot 'opened up' and the three segments parallel to each other, the robot can move though a duct driven by its four omni-wheels. Once inside the facility the robot can then close to a 'U' shape providing a stable platform. The robot carries two LIDARs, a camera and a G-M tube. This robot has been designed to be low cost and is deemed sacrificial. Through discussion with the creators, it had been found that this robot is limited by its lack of ability to move over rough terrain, with omni-wheels only being suitable for movement on flat, smooth surfaces, with even carpet being difficult. The design of the MIRRAX robot was inspired by the PMORPH2 and PMORPH2 robots made by Hitachi Corp for use in decommissioning the Fukushima Daiichi Nuclear plant following the 2011 nuclear accident. These are also folding robots designed to move through pipes, as well as move on flat ground. They are tracked robots that perform similar tasks to that required at Sellafield and have been deployed successfully at Fukushima.

2.1   Whegs

In light of the primary limiting factor of previous duct-entry robots outlined above we have selected wheel-legs or 'whegs' to be used as the method of loco-motion. Whegs are a system in which legged locomotion is implemented by a number of legs rotating around an axis. The advantage of whegs over conventional wheels centres around the ability of the design to traverse rough terrain and obstacles [5, 9, 10]. Whegs are implemented in two main forms, the first with fast-spinning, flexible legs which cause the vehicle to 'bounce' over objects, and the second with slower moving, stiffer legs that hook onto objects, allowing the vehicle to crawl over them. For this design, whegs designed to crawl over objects have been chosen. These provide good ability to traverse obstacles while doing so in a relatively safe manner. The slower, more gradual movement allows for more careful route planning by the operator, and reduces the risk of the robot tipping over or damaging itself. The slower movement also reduces vibration, aiding the use of sensing equipment and potentially leading to better quality sensing.

2.2   Morphing Whegs

For wheeled and wheged robots, the object traversal ability has a direct cor-relation with the size of the wheels or whegs. Without significant lateral force to provide friction, wheeled vehicles are not able to traverse obstacles larger in size than the wheel's radius. In practice this ratio is even smaller for smooth wheels. If whegs are shaped to hook onto objects they can traverse objects of greater size, [3, 14] potentially nearing the diameter of the wheg, though again, we see that the ability to traverse objects is limited by the diameter of the whegs. For this task the size of the duct limits the diameter of the wheels or whegs that can be entered into it. To work around this problem, and to maximize the obstacles traversal ability of the robot, 'morphing whegs' have been chosen. These are mechanisms that transform between wheels and whegs, with the effect of increasing the diameter of the system, as well as the traction properties on rough surfaces [7]. It is envisaged that the robot will be entered into the duct while in the 'wheel state', as the diameter of the wheels will be smaller that of the whegs, which would be too large to fit through. Once beyond the duct, wheels and whegs each have use cases depending on the terrain being traversed. Whegs are most useful in crossing uneven terrain, climbing over obstacles that wheels cannot and generally in situations where wheels lack traction. Wheels are useful where speed is required, as they can turn more rapidly without trans-ferring vibration and jarring forces to the robot, and in situations where more accurate sensor data and odometry is needed, as the jarring movement of the whegs may degrade these capabilities.

3   Robot Hardware and Software Design

This section describes the design and implementation of the presented folding morphing-wheg duct-entry robot. We first present the design process of the mech-anisms required to actuate the morphing whegs in Sect. 3.1. We then describe the

hardware design for the overall robot in Sect. 3.2. Finally, we give an overview
of the robot's ROS-based software in Sect. 3.3.

3.1 Morphing Wheg Design

For the state of the whegs to be actively controlled, a force is required to deploy
and retract them. This presents a challenge as either a control signal and electric
power must be transmitted to the rotating wheg, or a mechanical force must
be transmitted. In the case of the whegs being powered via an electric signal
and current, a motor and mechanical system would need to be mounted on
the rotating wheg. This presents a problem as wiring cannot easily be passed
through continuously rotating junctions. A potential way to work around this
is passing a signal and current to the wheg via a slip ring, an electromechanical
device that utilises rotary sliding contacts to pass power over a rotating linkage.
Mechanically there are multiple ways power transmission can be achieved. These
methods can essentially be simplified to either a linkage moving axially along the
rotating axis of the wheg shaft that transmits a force to the wheg mechanism,
or coaxial shaft mechanism in which the relative angle of two moving shafts is
controlled to actuate a mechanism.

Fig. 2. A diagram showing whegs actuated via a co-axial shaft mechanism

Figure 2 shows a wheg mechanism that is controlled via a co-axial shaft mechanism. Here the whegs are actuated by the relative motion of the inner gear,
connected to an inner shaft, and the wheg hub, connected to an outer shaft. The
relative angle of the two shafts sets the opening angle of the whegs. In normal
operation, the two shafts will rotate at the same speed, allowing the wheg to
rotate continuously. To deploy or retract the whegs the relative velocity of the
whegs is changed until the desired relative angle is achieved. A test rig for this
system was built (Fig. 3). This uses two Dynamixel motors with rotary encoders
which allow the exact rotational positions of the two shafts to be tracked. A PID
controller is implemented in code, and used to set the relative angle of the two
shafts, with the inputs being the shaft positions and a desired angular offset,

and the output being the speeds of the two shafts. This controller is shown in Fig. 4.

Fig. 3. A test rig of a coaxial mechanism designed to actuate morphing whegs

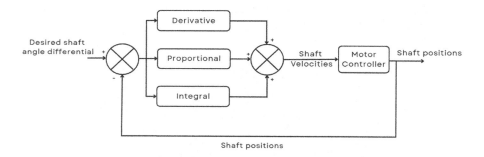

Fig. 4. A PID controller used to control the wheg actuation

The test rig functioned well with full control over the degree to which the whegs were open during continuous forward and reverse motion of the wheg system as a whole. If this system were to be implemented on a robot it would need to be made more robust. The current gear mechanism is unsuitable for practical use as the large forces generated during wheged movement would be transferred directly through the teeth of the gears, likely leading to them sheering off. A future version, as well as being made smaller and constructed in steel rather than plastic, would either utilise a mechanical linkage for wheg actuation or much thicker herringbone gears, which can be loaded more heavily than the thin spur gears currently used.

Another, simple way of implementing morphing whegs is to use a wire pull mechanism. This consists of a wire passed through a hollow axle that can be tensioned to actuate the legs. A 'swivel' or rotary coupling must be included in the wire to allow for continuous rotation of the whegs without the wire becoming twisted or tangled.

While the coaxial actuation method is generally more robust, as it does not rely on cables that can become tangled, stretch or break and provides a higher degree of control over the actuation, it requires more development before it can be implemented on a robot. For this reason, to produce a working prototype quickly the wire-pull mechanism was chosen.

3.2 Robot Hardware

With the aforementioned design features, a robotic tool for duct-entry nuclear decommissioning has been developed. The robot is connected via a tether to its 'tail' and is able to move around inside to the nuclear environment to gather sensory data for characterisation. The robot is a two wheged differential-drive design with a folding tail, allowing it to enter into a duct, as shown in Fig. 5a. The shape has been optimised to minimise the projected side on area when in the folded configuration, allowing the robot to fit into and be pushed through a 125 mm duct. Once through the duct, the robot is lowered to the ground by its tether and can unfold the tail to move about. The robot is able to move on smooth ground while in the wheel configuration, and opening up the whegs to traverse rougher terrain when required. Sensing and imaging equipment can be deployed via a hinged arm that swings out above the robot and provides an overhead vantage point, as shown in Fig. 5b. This allows unobstructed sensing and imaging for characterisation and operator feedback. The ducts Conceptual drawings of the robot in its folded and unfolded states are shown in Figs. 5a and 5b respectively.

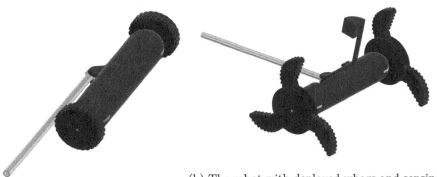

(b) The robot with deployed whegs and sensing
(a) The robot in its folded state   equipment

Fig. 5. Concept of the completed robot

The robot moves about by rotating the wheels or whegs and dragging the tail behind it. The tail is required to oppose the forward rotary motion of the whegs, without which the main body of the robot would rotate rather than the wheels.

Steering is conducted through varying the speeds of the two wheels relative to each other.

3.3   Robot Software

The software for the folding morphing-wheg robot is based upon the Turtle-bot3 ROS2 stack. This framework allows for control from either a base PC or a bluetooth controller. ROS integration allows for future inclusion of navigation, mapping and vision packages. An OpenCR board is used to read and write signals to the motors and onboard computing is performed using a Raspberry Pi single board computer. More complex computation, such as for image processing and SLAM can take place on the base PC. A high level system diagram can be seen in Fig. 6. This is the architecture used in testing for basic operation with a bluetooth controller and without ROS.

4   Prototype and Preliminary Evaluation

An initial prototype has been manufactured to test the morphing wheg design and folding concept (Fig. 9a). A wire pull mechanism is used to actuate the whegs. This consists of a central capstan rotated by a Dynamixel servo that tensions a wire. This wire is attached via rotary couplings to two wires that run through the centre of the two hollow axles and into the wheg mechanisms. Inside the body of the wheg mechanism this wire splits into 3 and when tensioned, actuates the wheg mechanism to open the legs. To close the legs, the tension from the wire is released and springs, which were tensioned during opening, pull the mechanism closed. The wire mechanism is shown in Figs. 7 and 8.

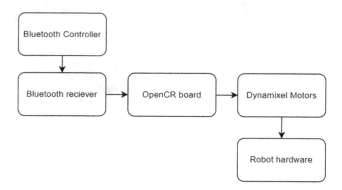

Fig. 6. A diagram showing the system architecture

4.1 Evaluation

The prototype has been tested in a range of scenarios and in both wheel and wheg configurations. Generally it has been found that the robot operates well and as intended, though with limitations. Some of these limitations are due to constraints during the build of the prototype and are not inherent to the overall concept. It is likely a further prototype designed taking into account the evaluation of this prototype can address these. It has been found that while having a wheel diameter of 100 mm and fitting through a 125 mm duct, the robot could climb a step of 150 mm height. In the wheeled configuration the robot can move about a smooth surface quickly and effectively. Figures 9a and 9b show the robot climbing over a breeze block.

Fig. 7. Motor and capstan used to tension wheg wire

4.2 Limitations and Future Work

One of the problems that became apparent during testing is the potential for the whegs to become stuck during the forward movement of the robot. Certain types of terrain or objects such as those made from pliable materials that can become caught in the wheg, or those containing high aspect ratio pockets in which whegs can become stuck present the highest risk. In most scenarios the robot can simply be steered or reversed to free itself, and with knowledge of the types of terrain that present a risk to the robot an operator can avoid becoming stuck in the first place. The shape of the whegs used in the prototype is likely one that is more prone than necessary to becoming stuck, as this was not a major consideration during design. Future required testing would need to look at different shapes of wheg and how this influences the likelihood of them becoming stuck in a variety of different terrain types. Another problem arises due to the relative rotation of the two whegs. If the angular orientation of the whegs is the same, or in 120° increments, the robot chassis remains level to the ground during forward movement, with the whegs creating a vertical bouncing movement. If the whegs are out of sync, the robot rolls side to side, and yaws back and forth during forward movement. This can create problems with controlling the robot and traversing obstacles if the user is not mindful of this problem.

Fig. 8. The wire mechanism splitting into three to actuate the whegs

Further work will focus on both the physical hardware of the robot and the software, with the potential of adding autonomy as well as video teleoperation. To make the whegs less prone to becoming stuck, the shape can be altered and the degree to which they open can be made variable rather than an open-closed toggle. The wire-pull mechanism used to actuate the whegs is likely not robust enough or reliable enough for use beyond prototype testing. In a future version of the robot this would be changed to either a coaxial shaft actuation mechanism or a system using motors on board the whegs. The traction of the whegs must be improved and a rubber tread can be added to achieve this, as well as increasing the width of the whegs. Research will need to be conducted on the implementation of sensors on the robot. Due to the uneven nature of the robot movement when using whegs, any sensors implemented on the robot would be subject to vibration and unpredictable rapid movements. This is likely to impact the quality of captured data and steps may need to be taken to reduce the impact of the uneven movement.

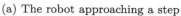

(a) The robot approaching a step   (b) The robot climbing onto the step

Fig. 9. The robot moving with whegs applied

5 Conclusion

This paper proposes the design and control mechanism of a novel wheged robot for use in restricted access nuclear decommissioning as well as the design of mechanical systems for morphing wheel-leg robots. The robot proposed is a folding ground based mobile robot for use in restricted access nuclear environments accessible only via 125 mm ducts. The robot uses morphing-whegs to achieve this. Whegs are systems in which multiple 'legs' rotate around an axis, giving a resemblance of legged motion via a simple control mechanism. Morphing whegs are whegs that can transform between wheels and whegs, depending on which state is desirable for a given terrain. The paper proposes mechanisms for the actuation of morphing whegs. Three mechanisms are proposed, a 'wire-pull' mechanism, in which a wire with a rotary coupling passes through a hollow axle into the hub of the wheg, and can be pulled to actuate the whegs. A coaxial shaft mechanism, where one shaft passes through another hollow shaft, and the relative angle of the two shafts can be controlled to actuate a mechanism, and a third mechanism in which a slip ring is used to control a motor mounted inside the wheg hub. A preliminary evaluation of the robot has been carried out. The robot was found to function well in both wheeled and wheged states. In the wheeled configuration the robot can move quickly on smooth ground, in the wheg state it was found that the robot can climb a step of 150 mm height. Further work will focus on improving the mechanical design of the robot to bring it to a state more suitable for commercial use, as well as the improving the software for teleoperation and potential autonomy.

Acknowledgment. This work was supported by UK Engineering and Physical Sciences Research Council (EPSRC) for the Centre for Doctoral Training in Future Autonomous Robotic Systems (grant no. EP/S021795/1).

References

1. Nuclear provision: the cost of cleaning up Britain's historic nuclear sites 2019. https://www.gov.uk/government/publications/nuclear-provision-explaining-the-cost-of-cleaning-up-britains-nuclear-legacy/nuclear-provision-explaining-the-cost-of-cleaning-up-britains-nuclear-legacy. Accessed 15 Sept 2022
2. Bird, B., et al.: A robot to monitor nuclear facilities: using autonomous radiation-monitoring assistance to reduce risk and cost. IEEE Robot. Autom. Mag. **26**(1), 35–43 (2018)
3. Chen, S.C., Huang, K.J., Chen, W.H., Shen, S.Y., Li, C.H., Lin, P.C.: Quattroped: a leg-wheel transformable robot. IEEE/ASME Trans. Mechatron. **19**, 730–742 (2014)
4. Groves, K., West, A., Gornicki, K., Watson, S., Carrasco, J., Lennox, B.: Mallard: an autonomous aquatic surface vehicle for inspection and monitoring of wet nuclear storage facilities. Robotics **8**(2), 47 (2019)
5. Kim, Y.S., Jung, G.P., Kim, H., Cho, K.J., Chu, C.N.: Wheel transformer: a wheel-leg hybrid robot with passive transformable wheels. IEEE Trans. Rob. **30**, 1487–1498 (2014)

44

6. Martin, H., Watson, S., Lennox, B., Poteau, X.: Miniature inspection robot for restricted access exploration (MIRRAX). In: WM Symposia, vol. 2018 (2018)
7. İrem Mertyüz, Tanyıldızı, A.K., Taşar, B., Tatar, A.B., Yakut, O.: FUHAR: a transformable wheel-legged hybrid mobile robot. Robot. Auton. Syst. **133**, 103627 (2020)
8. Sell, R., Aryassov, G., Petritshenko, A., Kaeeli, M.: Kinematics and dynamics of configurable wheel-leg. In: Proceedings of the 8th International DAAAM Baltic Conference Industrial Engineering, pp. 19–21 (2012)
9. Smith, L.M., Quinn, R.D., Johnson, K.A., Tuck, W.R.: The tri-wheel: a novel wheel-leg mobility concept, pp. 4146–4152 (2015)
10. Sun, T., Xiang, X., Su, W., Wu, H., Song, Y.: A transformable wheel-legged mobile robot: design, analysis and experiment. Robot. Auton. Syst. **98**, 30–41 (2017)
11. Tsitsimpelis, I., Taylor, C.J., Lennox, B., Joyce, M.J.: A review of ground-based robotic systems for the characterization of nuclear environments. Prog. Nucl. Energy **111**, 109–124 (2019)
12. Wei, Z., Song, G., Zhang, Y., Sun, H., Qiao, G.: Transleg: a wire-driven leg-wheel robot with a compliant spine. In: 2016 IEEE International Conference on Information and Automation (ICIA), pp. 7–12. IEEE (2016)
13. West, C., et al.: A debris clearance robot for extreme environments, pp. 148–159 (2019)
14. Zheng, C., Lee, K.: Wheeler: wheel-leg reconfigurable mechanism with passive gears for mobile robot applications. In: 2019 International Conference on Robotics and Automation (ICRA), pp. 9292–9298. IEEE (2019)

Autonomy

Occupancy Map Abstraction for Higher Level Mission Planning of Autonomous Robotic Exploration in Hazardous Nuclear Environments

David Batty[1]([✉]), Lupo Manes[1], Andrew West[2], Maulik Patel[1], Ipek Caliskanelli[1], and Paolo Paoletti[3]

[1] School of Engineering, University of Liverpool, L3 5RF Liverpool, UK
d.w.batty@liverpool.ac.uk
[2] Department of Electrical and Electronic Engineering, University of Manchester, Manchester M13 9PL, UK
[3] RACE, Culham Science Centre, Abingdon OX14 3DB, UK

Abstract. In the nuclear industry, the need for improved reliability in current and future technology hinders the deployment of autonomous robotic systems. The following research aims to develop a method of reliably mapping a large environment and abstracting the map into a sparse node graph to create a more efficient data form. The proposed data form allows for efficient storage whilst maintaining important map features and coverage. The method utilises an expanding node algorithm to convert standard occupancy maps to a sparse node graph representation. The algorithm's effectiveness has been tested on simulated maps and real-world maps to test the compression factor for a wide range of scenarios. The algorithm is expanded to function on a semi-unknown map abstracting during exploration.

Keywords: Occupancy Map · Map Abstraction · Mobile Robot · Autonomous Navigation · Radiation Hazard Avoidance

1 Introduction

As the nuclear industry in the United Kingdom moves forward, increasing focus is being placed on decommissioning legacy and recently decommissioned nuclear facilities and assets. The Nuclear Decommissioning Authority (NDA) are at the forefront of leading the implementation of protocols and policies in the clean-up effort. Recently the NDA released a set of "Grand Challenges" [8] to accelerate the technical innovation in nuclear decommissioning. One of these challenges involves creating and developing technologies and methods to move humans away from harm. This challenge is critical for reducing the risks posed to the workforce by many factors involved in hands-on tasks. Whilst the challenge of removing humans from harm can be achieved through various technological advances such as the use of VR or augmented reality allowing for remote operation, the key area of focus for this research is the utilisation of robotic systems to reduce the

F. Iida et al. (Eds.): TAROS 2023, LNAI 14136, pp. 77–88, 2023.
https://doi.org/10.1007/978-3-031-43360-3_7

need for humans to enter hazardous locations to perform routine tasks. These tasks range from routine inspection of operational facilities to the exploration and survey of legacy decommissioned facilities [12]. Currently, these types of inspections are carried out by highly trained operators wearing radiological protective suits and breathing apparatus that, due to contamination, are typically deemed single-use and treated as contaminated waste after each operation. This method of working for routine tasks is costly and exposes the operators to physical and radiological danger. However, with technological advances, these tasks are becoming suitable for a robotic system. This would allow the operators to teleoperate and, ideally, supervise missions from the safety of a remote location. Additionally, this change in work methods would increase operator safety and efficiency while reducing the costs of these tasks [11].

One of the main problems facing the deployment of robotic systems is the safety concerns with deploying a device into an active environment and ensuring the system's reliable operation when exposed to harsh environments. Three main factors pose a problem to a robotic system. The first two, temperature and humidity, are standard for various environments, and off-the-shelf components are typically relatively resilient to high temperature and humidity levels. Nuclear industry environments are unique, except for aerospace applications, as they feature the potential for increased radiation levels that a robotic system would be exposed to during regular operation [1]. Typical off-the-shelf components are susceptible to damage and failure from relatively low radiation dosage levels [7]. This damage can cause various effects, from memory corruption to system failures [13]. This potential for system failure has led the nuclear industry to prefer systems to be deployed in a tethered configuration when deployed. Whilst guaranteed high-speed network communications between the user and the robot is an advantage, the tether dramatically restricts the range of exploration into complex facilities with a risk of snagging and tangling during missions. The logical solution would be to operate the robotic system wirelessly. However, this poses a significant challenge the following research aims to solve. This challenge is that an untethered system would be significantly more challenging to recover in case of a system failure or loss of signal with the user. In this event, the robot would be unable to return to the base. It could become an obstacle to future robotic missions and pose issues to other operations. The disabled robot would likely need to be recovered by deploying human operators into the environment. At that point, the purpose of utilising robots is negated because human operators are still required to enter the environment [5,10].

The following research focuses on furthering the capabilities of semi-autonomous ground vehicles. Currently, the industry's concern about the reliability of the technologies is holding back potential deployments of robotic systems into real-world scenarios. One of the main methods of improving the trust of the systems is to develop a method of allowing complex path planning and mapping to be carried out onboard the robot without relying on a centralised server. Existing literature solutions require a high-power computer to achieve the computation needed to process occupancy maps with multiple layers of information, for example, the work by A West et al. Additionally, the current literature explored in the next section, only carried out the higher-level path and mission planning on relatively small and straightforward environments. This research aims to design a method of abstracting the current practice of storing mapping data into a sparse node graph representation. This method of modelling the environment will allow for significantly larger areas with even more data layers to be efficiently stored and computed using relatively low-power computing units. With robots looking to be deployed into mainstream facilities, the ability for the robot to achieve autonomy using low-power computers will significantly reduce the costs involved, further improving the argument for deploying systems into nuclear environments. This paper investigates the current state of research in this field (Sect. 2), outlines how the algorithm functions (Sect. 3), tests the effectiveness of the algorithm in simulation and real-world testing (Sect. 4), explores application when the environment is unknown (Sect. 5) and concludes with potential applications of the work (Sect. 6).

2   Related Work

This research is primarily inspired to be a precursor step, to research carried out into developing a state-based risk framework for navigation in a hazardous environment, featuring radiation and temperature levels that may cause harm to the robot exploring them [4]. This concept utilises an assessment of the current health of the robot, combined with an estimation of the environmental exposure expected along a selection of potential paths, to determine which path will either cause the lowest harm to the robot or, if the damage is inevitable, which path will cause the least cumulative damage to the robot. The path planning for this method is standard occupancy map-based path planning. Additionally, research was conducted into mapping radiation in a similar environment, and exploring how to locate possible radiation sources and subsequently avoid them during navigation, to reduce the system's exposure [6,14]. Both methods are at the forefront of developing autonomy using ground rover navigation in a hazardous environment. However, they both feature the drawback of utilising occupancy maps for path planning. Given that multiple additional layers are added to the cost maps, both implementations' computation requirements are significant and require a high-power computer. These methods are also shown to work on relatively small single-room maps; however, for these systems to reach maturity, they must be capable of handling maps significantly beyond the reach of a tethered system.

The above systems represent state of the art for avoiding radiation based on a mapped radiation environment. Several projects have been developed to achieve the radiation mapping and localisation of the radiation source. CARMA, now succeeded by CARMA II, developed at the University of Manchester, is designed to be capable of autonomously searching for radiation sources. The system is based on the Clearpath Husky platform and is designed to patrol around a known area taking periodic readings to detect radiological leaks or contamination [9]. The system could avoid these radiation sources once detected.

Finally, several systems have successfully reached a high technological readiness level to be tested in active environments. The most notable ground-based systems are, firstly, Mirrax [3]. This system has been designed to be deployed through port holes at Sellafield and reconfigured inside a more traditional ground-based rover. Mirrax features a sensor set capable of mapping the environment to which it is deployed. However, this robot is currently limited by regulations to be teleoperated and tethered, significantly reducing the range of exploration. Another similar system is project Lyra, formally Vega [2]. Like Mirrax, this system is currently deployed in both active and non-active testing areas. However, it is also limited by requiring teleoperation and tethering. Both systems, whilst having the potential to be deployed with semi-autonomous capabilities, require more proven reliability of these technologies to be approved for active testing of the systems.

3   Methodology

From the related work, the main limiting factor of the methods proposed is the significant amount of computational power required to work with even relatively small maps. Typically, from literature, this would be solved by utilising either a high power computer onboard the robot, which is heavy and expensive, or a network link to a server to achieve the computation. In a hazardous environment in a nuclear plant however, it is not practical to deploy expensive systems due to contamination concerns, meaning the robot is usually unable to be removed and suitably decontaminated to be used elsewhere. The following procedure aims to abstract the occupancy map into a sparse nodal representation of the environment. This primarily aims to compress the data form that the map represents. The key features of the map must be maintained to allow any path planning carried out on the compressed version to have access to all the necessary features. The method creates a series of nodes by converting open spaces into nodes. The more open the area, the more spread out the nodes are placed. More complex areas feature a denser placing of nodes to preserve features.

When abstracting the map there are two main parts of the method, the first is to create a node and define the free space radius around the node. This currently is the key heuristic used in determining the most suitable candidate nodes to be selected. The algorithm operates on an iterative basis and the cycle of finding nodes based on the eligible neighbours continues until there are not suitable nodes remaining. Suitable nodes are filtered based on having a free space radius above a certain threshold, mainly the radius of the robot plus a turning tolerance. Another area of note is that if all possible neighbours are calculated, this leads to higher then acceptable computation times. It was found during experimentation that considering every fifth cell when selecting neighbours, allows for the best reduction in computation whilst still functioning in the intended manner across a range of testing worlds. Figure 1 shows the outline of the algorithm, followed by a graphical example of the algorithm, Fig. 2.

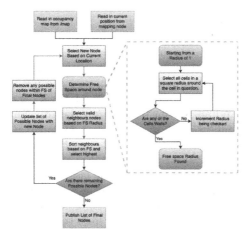

Fig. 1. Flowchart outlining algorithm for Occupancy Map Abstraction

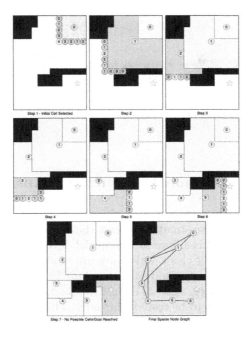

Fig. 2. Visual Example of Abstraction Applied to a Simple Occupancy Map

4   Implementation

Following the trend of robotics research, the system was developed using the ROS framework. The robotics community is progressively adopting the ROS framework for the speed at which it can be used to implement complex systems and the vast libraries allowing for hardware integration without needing to rewrite code [12]. For both methods, the primary computation was conducted on a setup ROS Noetic running on Ubuntu 20.04, on a computer with an Intel Core i7 10-core CPU and an Nvidia RTX 3070Ti laptop. Further testing is also carried out with the same setup running on an Aaeon Core Up Squared Pro, single-board computer for operation onboard the physical rover. The simulation and real-world testing will utilise Hector Mapping as the mapping node for these experiments. Gmapping is a node that uses the laser depth point cloud produced from LiDAR, either simulation or real-world sensor, to compute a 2D occupancy map of the environment [13]. For this testing, the cell size of the mapping was left at the default of 5 cm to allow for a relatively high resolution to be mapped. Hector mapping can also determine the pose of the sensor in the environment using the additional Gmapping SLAM (simultaneous location and mapping) package included in the library. Both sources of information are published as ROS topics which can be received by the abstraction node to be computed and run onboard the computer. An example of how the abstraction fits into the data flow is shown in Fig. 3.

Fig. 3. High-level Data flow from raw point cloud data to sparse node abstraction

5   Simulated Environment Testing and Analysis

The effectiveness of the algorithm proposed in this paper was assessed through a series of simulations. These simulations test the algorithm in a controlled and repeatable environment. This allows for the initial development of the algorithm due to the input data being clean and easily obtainable. The simulation environment of choice is Gazebo, an industry-standard Physics simulation package that allows the seamless integration of digital robots to be simulated, allowing a wide range of environments to be tested efficiently. This range allows for specific behaviours of the algorithm to be tested in isolation and combination to ensure that the system responds as expected. To test the algorithm effectively, generation of a series of maps of varying sizes and complexities is required to analyse the effectiveness of the algorithm's compression. Set-up shown in Fig. 4 and 5.

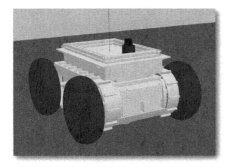

Fig. 4. Miti Rover Digital Twin

Fig. 5. RViz Output of Simulated World

Using Gazebo, it is simple to construct a series of maps to emulate typical scenarios that the system would find during operation. For this testing, three simulation maps were created. Firstly, a simple hexagonal arena ensured the algorithm was functioning correctly. Secondly, a maze-type structure was built. This maze featured diverging and converging paths and dead ends to ensure the algorithm could handle these features. Finally, a multi-room building was constructed to compare real-world testing later in the report. To simulate a real-world environment, further hazards such as tables, chairs and barrels were added to the world to allow the map to feature some nonstandard shapes.

Each of the tests was carried out in a standard manner. The robot was loaded into the world and teleoperated by the user around the map, as shown in Fig. 4, until a complete map was captured using the Gmapping package. Teleoperation was achieved using the Turtlebot3 teleop node. This stage was completed by simply running the abstraction node, which runs once when it sees a suitable map published into the map topic. Figure 5 shows an example of world abstraction; each sphere in the RViz window represents an assigned node. For each test, the initial node was set to be the starting spawn location of the robot. Due to the complete nature of the map, the algorithm should only be run once to abstract the whole environment.

Following the successful abstraction of the map, it is possible to determine how compressed the abstraction of the occupancy map has become whilst ensuring that the map's features have been maintained. Initially, this is done by comparing the total number of unoccupied cells in the occupancy map against the total number of nodes in the abstracted map. These values are absolute and were run post-computation. Additionally, testing was conducted to determine the proportion of occupancy map cells considered when an A* path-planning algorithm [14] is performed on the occupancy map. If a cell is checked for its heuristic value, it has been considered. This value is the average taken from several pairs of points positioned randomly around the map. This value indicates the performance increase achieved through the abstraction, as when considering path planning, not all cells of an occupancy map will be considered. This comparison is more indicative than measuring compute time of the algorithms, as factors such as language and library inefficiencies and data source loading delays cannot be ruled out and tested comparably. The following figure, Fig. 6 shows this analysis applied to four artificially created maps like a real-world environment. The worlds range from TB Arena (approx. 4 m × 4 m) to Large Office (approx. 20 m × 20 m).

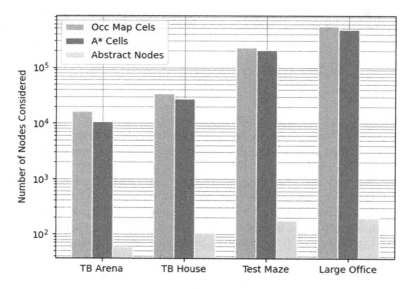

Fig. 6. Simulated Environment Free space cells vs considered cells vs nodes in abstraction comparison

It can easily be seen that the nodal abstraction provides a data form that is consistently several orders of magnitude more compressed than the raw occupancy map data, whilst visually maintaining the essential features of the map. This whilst maintaining coverage of the map, with 99.9 percent of the unoccupied cells falling withing the free space radius of one of the nodes, meaning that every cell is still reachable by the new abstract network. Simulation testing has shown that the proposed algorithm functions in the intended manner under various conditions. For example, when looking at the house model, the occupancy map created consisted of 72300 unoccupied cells. A* running at the extremities of the map required the evaluation of 53103 cells. Following abstraction, this map is reduced to 102 nodes that have 100 percent coverage of cells within the building. Simulation has also been done to ensure that, given a random list of nodes, the robot can traverse between all the nodes.

6   Real-World Testing and Analysis

Following the successful simulation, the next logical progression is to test the effectiveness of the algorithm compression on real-world maps. These maps differ from the simulations due to the level of noise and unpredictability compared to the pure nature of the maps produced in the simulation. The exact mapping and abstraction nodes from the simulation testing were used, with the main difference being that the data was collected using a real LiDAR, RPLiDAR LiDAR S2 from SLAMtec. The rover was teleoperated around an environment to test the mapping and abstraction in real time (Fig. 7).

Fig. 7. Miti Rover by Rover Robotics with SLAMTEC LiDAR

Testing proved successful with a few key points to consider to achieve good results. The robot's speed was limited to 0.5 ms-1 to avoid issues with Hector mapping losing synchronisation. The abstraction was carried out after mapping was conducted on the Intel/NVidia-based laptop, and successfully onboard the robot on the Aaeon Core Squared Pro board, to show that the abstraction can be handled on the system without impacting the performance of the robot's operation. Figure 8 shows the testing setup and the successful abstraction in a sizeable looping environment.

Due to the real-world nature of the data collected, some minor clean-up was conducted to remove some minor particulate noise caused by reflections from the environment. This clean-up was later solved by using a higher-quality sensor. The next section features a similar numerical analysis comparing the raw number of cells against the number of nodes the abstracted map required to represent them. During the simulation testing, utilising maps generated from the teleoperation based mapping of a real-world environment around the lab. Three separate maps were generated to test the abstraction, the first was a single room (approx. 15 m × 20 m), the second was of two connected rooms and a corridor (approx. 30 m × 25 m) and the third was a large loop connecting both labs (approx. 50 m × 40 m). The resulting data from these tests are showing in Fig. 9.

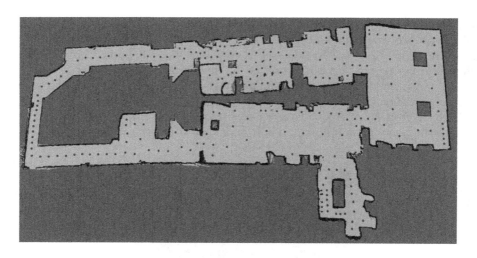

Fig. 8. Real-World Mapping and Abstraction Result

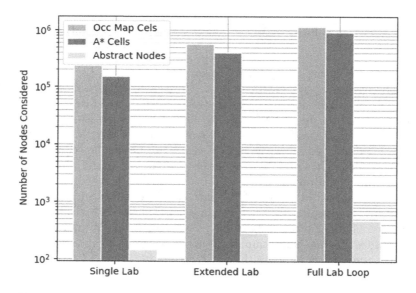

Fig. 9. Real- World Testing Free space cells vs considered cells vs nodes in abstraction comparison

As with the simulation testing, even with noisy non-standard maps, the compression from abstraction is equally as effective, with a significant reduction in the number of data points whilst maintaining map features and coverage. Figure 9, which outlines a series of three real-world maps, each shows a significant reduction, with the whole lab loop showing a reduction of 99.94 percent from the full occupancy map size to the abstracted map. This is very useful when calculating multiple cost map layers and higher-level path planning in terms of computational power required. Each map shows a similar order of magnitude reduction in the compression of the occupancy map representation.

Overall, testing of both systems proved successful with abstraction being accomplished on both simulated and real-world maps. It should also be noted that an important part of the abstraction is to be computationally efficient enough to have a suitably short abstraction time. Typically occupancy maps change and update as they are explored and as such periodic re-abstraction of the current map will be needed to remain current. For this to be achievable in real time it was deemed that a new map should render before a robot is able to physically move into the area. During testing even the largest maps were capable of rendering in there entirety in less then 0.1 s. This execution time was taken from when the first node was defined to the entire node network being published by the node. Execution time was also tested on a low power all-in-one PC (Aaeon core board) with execution time still remaining under 0.5 s which is still performs suitably under testing of the largest maps.

7   Conclusion

The results shown in this paper have successfully demonstrated that the proposed algorithm is an effective method for abstracting occupancy map data into a significantly compressed representation to achieve several order-of-magnitude reductions in the quantity of data required to represent an environment. The algorithm has been shown to be capable of handling complex and noisy real-world maps whilst still maintaining the important features of the environment. Additionally it has been outlined that this algorithm is capable of running efficiently enough for even low computing power equipped robots. This will also allow for a significantly larger environment to be handled in a substantially more computationally efficient manner. Finally the aim of this work was to create a data form that could be used for higher level mission planning when assessing risk. Instead of conducting this on an occupancy map, application to a nodal map will allow significantly higher-level decisions in more complex environments to be computed much more efficiently.

References

1. Azpúrua, H., et al.: A Survey on the autonomous exploration of confined subterranean spaces: perspectives from real-word and industrial robotic deployments. Robot. Auton. Syst. **160**, 104304 (2023). https://doi.org/10.1016/j.robot.2022.104304
2. Bird, B., Nancekievill, M., West, A., Hayman, J., Ballard, C., Jones, W., Ross, S., Wild, T., Scott, T., Lennox, B.: Vega-A small, low cost, ground robot for nuclear decommissioning. J. Field Robot. (2021). https://doi.org/10.1002/rob.22048
3. Cheah, W., et al.: MIRRAX: a reconfigurable robot for limited access environments. IEEE Trans. Robot. **39**(2), 1341–1352 (2023). https://doi.org/10.1109/TRO.2022.3207095
4. David, J., Bridgwater, T., West, A., Lennox, B., Giuliani, M.: Internal state-based risk assessment for robots in hazardous environment. In: checo-Gutierrez, S., Cryer, A., Caliskanelli, I., Tugal, H., Skilton, R. (eds.) Towards Autonomous Robotic Systems. TAROS 2022. LNCS (including subseries LNAI and LNB), vol. 13546 LNAI, pp. 137–152. Springer Science and Business Media, Deutschland GmbH (2022). https://doi.org/10.1007/978-3-031-15908-4_12
5. De Geeter, J., Decréton, M., Colon, E.: Challenges of telerobotics in a nuclear environment. Robot. Auton. Syst. **28**(1), 5–17 (1999). https://doi.org/10.1016/S0921-8890(99)00025-1
6. Groves, K., Hernandez, E., West, A., Wright, T., Lennox, B.: Robotic Exploration of an unknown nuclear environment using radiation informed autonomous navigation. Robotics. **10**(2), 78 (2021). https://doi.org/10.3390/robotics10020078, https://www.mdpi.com/2218-6581/10/2/78
7. Nagatani, K., et al.: Emergency response to the nuclear accident at the Fukushima Daiichi Nuclear Power Plants using mobile rescue robots. J. Field Robot. **30**(1), 44–63 (2013). https://doi.org/10.1002/rob.21439, https://onlinelibrary.wiley.com/doi/10.1002/rob.21439
8. NDA: The NDA's 'Grand Challenges' for technical innovation - Cleaning up our nuclear past: faster, safer and sooner. https://nda.blog.gov.uk/the-ndas-grand-challenges-for-technical-innovation/
9. Nouri Rahmat Abadi, B., et al.: CARMA II: a ground vehicle for autonomous surveying of alpha, beta and gamma radiation. Front. Robot. AI. **31**,10 (2023). https://doi.org/10.3389/frobt.2023.1137750, https://www.frontiersin.org/articles/10.3389/frobt.2023.1137750/full
10. Robinson, T.: Challenges for robotics in nuclear decommissioning. Eng. Technol. Ref. (2016). https://doi.org/10.1049/etr.2016.0097
11. Smith, R., Cucco, E., Fairbairn, C.: Robotic development for the nuclear environment: challenges and strategy. Robotics. **9**(4), 94 (2020). https://doi.org/10.3390/robotics9040094, https://www.mdpi.com/2218-6581/9/4/94
12. Tominaga, A., Hayashi, E., Fujisawa, R., Mowshowitz, A.: Graph-Based Path Generation for Robot Navigation in a Forest Environment. Technical report (2022)
13. West, A., Knapp, J., Lennox, B., Walters, S., Watts, S.: Radiation tolerance of a small COTS single board computer for mobile robots. Nucl. Eng. Technol. (2021). https://doi.org/10.1016/j.net.2021.12.007
14. West, A., Wright, T., Tsitsimpelis, I., Groves, K., Joyce, M.J., Lennox, B.: Real-time avoidance of ionising radiation using layered costmaps for mobile robots. Front. Robot. AI. **9** (3 2022). https://doi.org/10.3389/frobt.2022.862067

Spiral Sweeping Protocols for Detection of Smart Evaders

Roee M. Francos$^{(\boxtimes)}$ and Alfred M. Bruckstein

Faculty of Computer Science, Technion- Israel Institute of Technology, Haifa, Israel
{roee.francos,freddy}@cs.technion.ac.il

Abstract. Consider a given planar circular region, in which there is an unknown number of smart mobile evaders. We wish to detect evaders using a line formation of sweeping agents whose total sensing length is predetermined. We propose procedures for designing spiral sweeping protocols that ensure the successful completion of the task, thus deriving conditions on the sweeping speed of the linear formation and its path. Successful completion of the task implies that evaders with a given limit on their speed cannot escape the sweeping agents. A simpler task for the sweeping formation is the confinement of evaders to a desired region. The feasibility of completing these tasks depends on geometric and dynamic constraints that impose a lower bound on the speed that the agents' formation must have. This speed is derived to ensure the satisfaction of the confinement task and increasing it above the lower bound enables sweepers to complete the full search task as well. We present two spiral line formation search processes for smart evaders, that address current limitations in search against smart evaders and present a quantitative and qualitative comparison analysis between the total search time of circular line formation sweep processes and spiral line formation processes. We evaluate the different strategies by using two metrics, total search time and the minimal critical speed required for a successful search.

Keywords: Motion and Path Planning for Multi Agent Systems · Mobile Robots · Applications of Multi Agent Systems

1 Introduction

The objective of this research is to develop efficient search policies for smart evaders. The proposed search policies are performed by a line formation of sweeping agents, or alternatively by a single agent with an equivalent sensing diameter. The formation's agents are referred to as sweepers. The goal of the sweepers is to ensure that all smart evaders that are originally inside a given circular region of radius R_0 are detected. The number of smart evaders and their precise locations are unknown to the sweepers. The only information known to the sweepers is the maximal speed of the evaders, V_T. The region where evaders might be located is referred to as the evader region. The line formation of sweepers moves at a speed $V_s > V_T$ and detects evaders by using sensors with a combined length of $2r$. The search protocols may also be performed by a single agent with a line

F. Iida et al. (Eds.): TAROS 2023, LNAI 14136, pp. 89–100, 2023.
https://doi.org/10.1007/978-3-031-43360-3_8

sensor of length $2r$. A line sensor with a length of $2r$ is has a rectangular shape with zero width and a length of $2r$.

Since the original circular domain does not contain boundaries, evaders attempt to move as far as possible from the original domain that is being scanned by the line formation in order to escape detection. Hence, the goal of the evaders is avoid being detected and the goal of the line formation of sweepers is to ensure the detection of all evaders. Therefore, in this work we propose search strategies that guarantee detection of all smart evaders in the region, regardless of the trajectories that the smart evaders choose to implement. Smart evaders are agents with superior sensing and planning capabilities compared to the line formation's agents that may attempt to devise a plan that allows some evaders to escape the region, thus resulting in the failure of the line formation's objective.

Implementing a search policy that guarantees detection of all smart evaders imposes a requirement on the minimal speed of the formation's sweepers. This speed is referred to as the critical speed, and it depends on the formation's trajectory. Evaders are detected immediately once a sweeper's sensor intersects their position. Figure 1 presents an illustration of the line formation's sensor. The developed protocols can be executed over a planar 2 dimensional region over which the formation moves or alternatively in 3 dimensional domain where the sweeping formation flies over an area containing evaders. The analysis of both scenarios is equivalent. The analysis of the mentioned $2D$ and $3D$ sweep protocols is follows a similar analysis.

Additionally, sweep protocols that are carried out by a line formation of sweepers or by a single sweeper (with equivalent sensing capabilities as the combined sensing capabilities of formation) are exactly the same. By assumption, the evader region has no obstacles.

Fig. 1. Line formation of spiral sweeping agents that has a combined sensor diameter length of $2r$. The line formation's speed, V_s, is measured with respect to the formation's center.

There may be two objectives that the line formation of agents may attempt to accomplish. The first is the confinement task and the second is the complete cleaning or detection task. The goal of the line formation of sweepers executing the confinement task is to prevent all evaders from leaving their original domain and escaping the line formation's agents without being detected. The result of a successful confinement task is keeping the evader region's size constant after each sweep around the region.

The ability to successfully complete the confinement task depends on a lower bound on the speed that the line formation's agents must have. This lower bound is named the critical speed and it depends on the applied search protocol. If the formation's agents move at a speed below the critical speed they will not be able to complete the confinement task.

If the line formation of sweepers speed exceeds the critical speed, the sweepers have the ability to also succeed in the complete detection task. Succeeding in the complete detection task implies that after the completion of a full sweep around the evader region, the evader region size decreases, until eventually its area is reduced to zero and all smart evaders are located.

The two metrics we use to evaluate a search protocol are the minimal sweeper's speed required to complete the confinement task and the search time needed to detect all smart evaders in the region. The obtained results depend on the radius of the initial evader region, the evader's maximal speed and the sensing range of the line formation of sweepers.

1.1   Overview and Comparison to Related Research

Several interesting search problems originated in the second world war due to the need to design patrol strategies for aircraft aiming to detect ships or submarines in the English channel, see [9]. Patrolling a corridor with multi agent teams whose goal is ensuring detection and interception of smart evaders was also investigated in [15] while optimally proven strategies were provided in [2]. A somewhat related, discrete version of the problem, was also investigated in [1]. In [3], Bressan et al. investigate optimal strategies for the construction of barriers in real-time aiming at containing and confining the spread of fire from a given initial area of the plane by determining a minimal barrier construction speed that enables the confinement of the spreading fire.

Another set of related problems are pursuit-evasion games, where the pursuers' objective is to detect evaders and the evaders objective is to avoid the pursuers. Pursuit-evasion games include combinations of single and multiple evaders and pursuers scenarios. Recent surveys on pursuit evasion problems are [4,10,16]. In [16], the authors present a recent survey on pursuit-evasion differential games and classify the papers according to the numbers of participating players: single-pursuer single-evader, one-pursuer multiple-evaders, and multiple pursuers and multiple evaders (MPME). In [7], a two-player differential game in which a pursuer aims to capture an evader before it escapes a circular region is investigated. In [11], pursuit-evasion problems involving MPME are studied.

This article provides an extension and a considerable improvement to our previous work [5], hence for a detailed discussion and overview regarding related research we refer the interested reader to [5] and mention in this article only the most closely related work. In [5], the confinement and cleaning tasks for a line formation of agents or alternatively for a single agent with a linear sensor are analyzed. Several methods are proposed on how to determine the minimal speed for a circularly sweeping agent, in order to shrink the evader region within a circle with a smaller radius than the searcher's sensor length. The results show that this speed equals more than twice the theoretical lower bound. Furthermore, a proof that a single agent or a line formation of agents with an equivalent sensing range, employing a circular search pattern around the evader region cannot completely cleaning it without modifying the search pattern is provided. Lastly, the paper describes a modification to the trajectory of the sweepers that is performed once the evader region is bounded in a circular region with a smaller radius than half the formation's sensing range, and allows to clean the region from all evaders.

An additional closely related work to ours is [12] which also investigates search protocols against smart evaders. Contrary to the line sensor used by the sweeping line formation in our work, searchers in [12] are equipped with disk shaped sensors having a radius of r to detect evaders. In this work, we provide a comprehensive analysis on the time it takes to detect all evaders in the region, whereas [12] only calculates the radius of the maximal circle that can be successfully searched and does not provide an algorithm on how to search the entire region or the time it takes to complete it. In [8], a related problem to ours is investigated as well, however as in [12], the searcher is also equipped with a disk shaped sensor that detects all evaders located at a distance of at most r from the searcher. Similarly to our setting, in [13], searchers move at a constant speed and the evaders maximal speed is known to the searchers as well. In [13], the searchers have disk shaped sensors as in [12] and [8].

The methodology in [13] resembles our approach in the sense that ensuring that if evaders cannot escape during the first sweep around the region, they will surely not be able to escape in following sweeps around a smaller evader region. In [13], the time it takes to completely clear the region from evaders is not explicitly calculated as in our work, however results of a simulation showing the probability to detect an evader that executes a random walk within a certain number of time steps are presented.

Furthermore, in contrast to our approach, in [12,13] the searchers do not form a linear formation and are distributed equally around the region. Moving in a linear formation allows the line formation to recover more quickly from a failure of one of the sweepers by replacing the malfunctioned sweeper with the sweeper closest to it, consequently requiring all sweepers that are closer to the center of the evader region to redistribute themselves equally again to a smaller linear array and continue the search protocol with a reduced sensing range.

In this work we combine ideas from our previous work [5] and from [12] in order to develop more efficient search protocols. The developed line formation spiral protocols in this work improve the search time by an order of magnitude compared to [5], while the improved spiral sweep protocol proposed in this work reduces the required critical speed of [5] to nearly half its value. The obtained results are applicable to practical robotic applications such as surveillance and monitoring applications such as security, search and rescue, wildlife tracking, emergency response, fire control and many more.

1.2   Contributions

We present a comparative study based on theoretical analysis that seeks to find optimal trajectories, critical speeds, and minimal sweep times for a line formation of sweepers that must ensure detection of all smart evaders originally situated inside a given circular domain. The initial circular domain that contains the evaders has no boundaries, hence the smart evaders attempt to devise a plan that will allow some of them to move out of the region that is searched by the sweepers and escape without being detected.

- We consider two novel line formation spiral sweep protocols:
  - Drifting Spiral Sweep Protocol
  - Improved Spiral Sweep Protocol
- For each sweep protocol, a critical speed required for the line formation of sweepers to succeed in confining the evaders is calculated. Moving at speeds above the critical speed allows the line formation of sweepers to decrease the evader region. We present results that are based on development of explicit formulas that allow to compute the number of required sweeps, and the time, to detect all evaders in the region.
- The constructed critical speed of the improved spiral sweep protocol allows to sweep the region at a nearly theoretically optimal speed and allows the detection of all smart evaders at a fraction of the time compared to previous approaches, as can be seen in Fig. 6.
- Figures that show results from empirical simulations performed with Matlab and NetLogo are embedded in the manuscript.
- A video attachment that graphically illustrates the dynamic evolution of the evader region and the areas detected by the line formation throughout the progression of the sweep protocols is provided as well.

2   Spiral Sweep Protocols

This work investigates the question of devising efficient search protocols that are carried out by a single agent or alternatively by a line formation of identical sweeping agents with an equivalent sensing range that must guarantee detection of all smart evaders originally location inside a circular region of radius R_0. The number of evaders and their locations is unknown to the sweeping agents, hence it is assumed that evaders can be originally located anywhere inside the evader region and that once the search protocol commences they may move out of the region at a maximal speed of V_T in all direction. The sweepers move in a way that the line formation advances, most often perpendicularly to the agents' linear array with a speed of V_s (measured at the center of the linear sensor). We assume that evaders move at a maximal speed of V_T, and do not have any maneuverability restrictions. The sweepers have two potential tasks they try to achieve. The sweepers' first goal is to ensure that no evader escapes the region being searched undetected, while keeping the size of the evader region constant after each sweep. If the line formation's speed exceeds the critical speed that allows to satisfy the confinement goal, then the goal of the formation is to implement a sweeping protocol that enables the fastest detection of all evaders in the region, by reducing to zero the evader region's area. This is achieved by iteratively reducing the radius of the circle bounding the evader region after the completion of each sweep.

Planning against smart evaders can be seen as solving the worst-case scenario of a given situation and hence the applied search protocols are preprogrammed and deterministic to ensure that the chosen search protocol allows to detect all evaders regardless of the escape plans they choose. The time it takes to completely detect all evaders naturally depends on the applied search protocol. In this work the line formation of sweepers performs spiral search protocols that track the advancing wavefront of potential evader locations. The line formation of sweepers starts the protocol when its entire sensor of length $2r$ is inside the evader region, thus allowing it to detect as many evaders as possible.

In order to compare the developed search protocols in this work and to compare them to previous methods as well, we use lower bound on the line formation's speed independent of the search protocol developed in [5]. Afterwards, we present two different spiral line formation search protocols that can be applied. For each protocol, we determine the minimal speed required by the line formation to confine all evaders.

The first spiral search protocol, the drifting spiral search protocol considers only spiral sweeps. After each sweep around the evader region, a new center for the evader region is computed and the next sweep is performed with respect to that center. This new evader region center is computed as the midpoint between the highest and lowest points the evader region spread to, after a completion of a sweep around the region. A completion of a full sweep around the evader region is called a cycle or an iteration. Changing the center of the evader region after each sweep enables the sweep protocol to consist of only spiral sweeps without linear inward advancements in which no cleaning occurs, as are performed in [5]. This protocol allows for a simpler search procedure that does not require any assumptions on the turning rates of the sweepers. This sweep protocol implies that after each sweep the center of the new evader region moves upwards by a positive distance. The drifting spiral search protocol yields that the minimal agent speed that ensures satisfaction of the confinement task is lower than the critical speed developed in [5], however it is still not close to the lower bound on a searcher speed, and hence is not optimal.

In order to improve the drifting spiral search protocol and reduce the critical speed that enables confinement as well as decreasing the complete sweep time required to detect all evaders, we present a different and improved spiral sweep protocol. This protocol does not allow for a derivation of analytical formulas for the entire search protocol, unlike the drifting spiral search protocol, however it yields nearly optimal results. In the improved spiral protocol the center of the evader region stays fixed throughout the search. Illustrative simulations that demonstrate the evolution of the search protocols were generated using NetLogo software [14]. For a full analytical analysis of the results presented in this paper see [6].

3   The Drifting Spiral Sweep Protocol

At the start of every circular sweep in the circular sweep protocol developed in [5], half of the line formation's sensor is outside of the evader region. Naturally, in order for the sweeping line formation to employ a more efficient motion throughout the search protocol, the footprint of the formation's sensor that overlaps the evader region should be maximal. This is obtained by performing a spiral trajectory, in which the formation's sensor tracks the expanding evader region's wavefront, while at the same time it attempts to preserve the evader region's shape to be nearly circular. The line formation of sweepers begins its spiral traversal with the upper tip of its sensor tangent to the edge of the evader region at point $P = (0, R_0)$. In order to keep its sensor tangent to the evader region, the formation must travel at angle ϕ to the normal of the evader region. ϕ is calculated by,

$$\phi = \arcsin\left(\frac{V_T}{V_s}\right) \tag{1}$$

An illustration of the initial placement of a line formation of agents that employs the drifting spiral sweep protocol is presented in Fig. 2. The line formation of agents has a sensor of length $2r$. We wish the sweepers to have the lowest possible critical speed, hence we propose a different search protocol compared to [5]. A lower critical speed enables sweepers to scan larger evader regions successfully and enables shorter cleaning times of the evader region, given an agent's speed. The line formation of sweeping agents starts with a sensor length of $2r$ inside the evader region. If the sweeper formation's speed is above the scenario's critical speed, the sweeper formation reduces the evader region's area after completing a traversal of 2π degrees around the evader region.

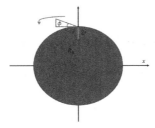

Fig. 2. Initial placement of a line formation of sweepers implementing a spiral sweep protocol. The formation's sensor is shown in green. Red areas indicate locations where potential evaders may be located. The angle ϕ is the angle between the tip of the formation's sensor and the normal of the evader region. ϕ is an angle given by the ratio of sweeper and evader velocities. (Color figure online)

An illustrative simulation that demonstrates the confinement task when the sweeper formation employs the drifting spiral sweep protocol is presented in Fig. 3. The sweeper line formation confines evaders to an area of the same size as initial evader region. The new evader region is an upwards shifted version of the initial evader region.

Fig. 3. Swept areas and evader region status for a scenario where the line formation of agents successfully confines evaders to an area of the same size as initial evader region with the drifting spiral sweep protocol. The new evader region is an upwards shifted version of the initial evader region. Green areas are locations that are free from evaders and red areas indicate locations where potential evaders may still be located. (Color figure online)

In the proposed line formation spiral sweep, the center of the evader region does not remain fixed. After the completion of each sweep it moves up by a positive distance. Therefore, as the sweepers progress in their search mission, the evader region shrinks while the region itself moves upwards. If the agents in the formation move at a speed greater than the critical speed for the corresponding scenario they can progress with the search task. An illustrative simulation that demonstrates the evolution of the search protocol when the sweeper formation employs the drifting spiral sweep protocol is presented in Fig. 4. Green areas are locations that are free from evaders and red areas indicate locations where potential evaders may still be located. After each sweep around the region, the evader region is bounded by a circle whose radius can be analytically calculated.

4   The Improved Spiral Sweep Protocol

Since our aim is to provide a sweep protocol that improves both the circular and drifting spiral sweep protocols, we would like sweepers to employ a more efficient motion throughout the sweep protocol so that they have the lowest possible critical speed. Similarly to the idea presented in the previous section, we wish that throughout the motion of the line formation of sweepers, its sensor's footprint will maximally overlap the evader region. An illustration of the initial placement of a line formation of employing the proposed improved spiral sweep protocol is presented in Fig. 2. It is the same as the initial placement of sweepers employing the drifting spiral sweep protocol. The line formation of sweepers

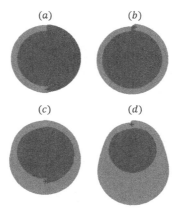

Fig. 4. Swept areas and evader region status for different times in a scenario where the line formation of agents employs the drifting spiral sweep protocol. Green areas are locations that are free from evaders and red areas indicate locations where potential evaders may still be located. (a) - After a sweep by an angle of π. (b) - Towards the end of the first sweep. (c) - Beginning of the third sweep. (d) - Beginning of the tenth sweep. (Color figure online)

starts with a sensor length of $2r$ inside the evader region. If the formation's speed exceeds the required critical speed of the given scenario, the line formation reduces the evader region's area after completing a full sweep around it. The line formation of sweepers begins its spiral traversal with the upper tip of its sensor tangent to the boundary of the evader region at point $P = (0, R_0)$. In order to keep its sensor tangent to the evader region, the formation must travel at angle ϕ to the normal of the evader region. ϕ is calculated in Eq. (1) in the previous section. This method of traveling at angle ϕ preserves the evader region's circular shape.

The first modification in this spiral protocol with respect to the drifting spiral sweep protocol is that the sweeper formation travels more than a full sweep of 2π at each iteration around the evader region in order to detect all escaping smart evaders. The additional angle, denoted by β, needs to be traversed in order to detect all evaders that may have spread from the "most dangerous point" at the beginning of the sweep. Evaders located at the "most dangerous point" have the maximum time to escape throughout the sweepers' movements. Consequently, if evaders attempting to escape from this location are detected, evaders attempting to escape from all other locations are detected as well.

After each iteration, the sweeper formation moves inwards towards the center of the evader region and the radius of the circle that bounds the region decreases. Consequently, the angle after which the formation moves inside after the next sweep changes as well. An illustrative simulation that demonstrates the cleaning progress of the evader region when the sweeper formation employs the improved spiral sweep protocol is presented in Fig. 5.

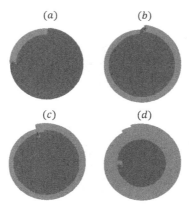

Fig. 5. Swept areas and evader region status for different times in which the line formation of agents employs the improved spiral sweep protocol. The sweepers' sensors are shown in green. (a) - After a sweep by an angle of $\frac{\pi}{2}$. (b) - Towards the end of the first sweep. (c) - Beginning of the second sweep. (d) - Beginning of the sixth sweep. (Color figure online)

5   Comparison of Line Formation Sweep Protocols

In this section we compare the time it takes line formations of sweepers that employ spiral sweeps versus circular sweeps to clean the evader region completely. Since the critical speeds of the drifting and improved spiral sweep protocols are lower than the circular critical speed, a comparison of sweep times is performed when line formations that employ the different sweep protocols are performed with equivalent sensing capabilities and move at equal speeds above the circular critical speed. In Fig. 6 we plot the times it takes a line formation of sweepers that employ the drifting spiral, improved spiral and the circular sweep protocols to clean the evader region when the sweeper formation moves with a speed of ΔV above the critical circular sweeper speed. The circular critical speed for the line formation scenario is derived in [5] and is given by,

$$V_c = \frac{2\pi R_0 V_T}{r} + V_T \qquad (2)$$

Figure 6 shows the reduction in sweep times that are obtained when using the spiral sweep protocols, and in particular the improved spiral sweep protocol favourable performance. If the user can choose for a given sweeper speed that is above the circular critical speed which sweep method to employ, the obvious choice is to sweep the area with a spiral protocol. It is to be noted that throughout the circular sweep protocol, as well as in the improved spiral protocol the center of the evader region does not change while in the drifting spiral protocol's setting the center of the region moves upwards as the search progresses.

From the results displayed in Fig. 6 it is clear that performing the improved spiral protocol is clearly best since it provides considerably shorter sweep times.

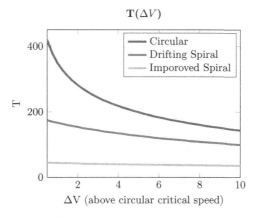

Fig. 6. Sweep times until complete cleaning of the evader region. The line formation of sweepers that employ the spiral and circular sweep protocols move with speeds that are ΔV above the circular critical speed. ΔV varies between $0.5V_T \leq \Delta V \leq 10V_T$. The other parameters values chosen for this plot are $V_T = 1$, $R_0 = 100$ and $r = 10$.

Furthermore, the improved spiral protocol requires a smaller critical speed compared to the circular and drifting spiral search protocols. Hence, with respect to both performance metrics performing the improved spiral protocol is best.

6 Conclusions

We investigate a search problem where a line formation of sweeping agents (or a single agent with equivalent sensing capabilities), must guarantee detection of all smart evaders that aim to escape from a given circular domain while evading the sweeping agents. We discuss and compare 2 types of spiral search protocols. The first protocol, the drifting spiral protocol, consists of only spiral sweeps and throughout it the center of the region moves upwards while the region shrinks until all evaders in the region are located. The second spiral protocol that is presented is an improved spiral sweep protocol around a fixed center that consists of spiral and inward linear motions.

We compare the developed critical speeds of both protocols to a lower bound on the critical speed that is independent of the search protocol the sweeper formation employs. Both spiral sweep protocols yield a lower critical speed than the circular line formation critical speed developed in [5], and thus the spiral sweep protocols enable the sweeper line formation to scan faster and more efficiently a given region. Furthermore, sweeping with spiral protocols also enables, given a limit on the sweepers speed, to sweep successfully larger regions compared to a line formation of agents that employs the circular sweep method.

We show that with respect to both considered performance metrics, critical speed and search time, performing the improved spiral protocol is clearly best and that compared to the circular sweep protocol, the improved spiral protocol's search time requires a fraction of the search time and that is also considerably better than the drifting spiral protocol.

References

1. Altshuler, Y., Yanovski, V., Wagner, I.A., Bruckstein, A.M.: Multi-agent cooperative cleaning of expanding domains. Int. J. Robot. Res. **30**(8), 1037–1071 (2011)
2. Altshuler, Y., Yanovsky, V., Wagner, I.A., Bruckstein, A.M.: Efficient cooperative search of smart targets using UAV swarms. Robotica **26**(4), 551–557 (2008)
3. Bressan, A., Wang, T.: On the optimal strategy for an isotropic blocking problem. Calc. Var. Partial. Differ. Equ. **45**(1–2), 125–145 (2012)
4. Chung, T.H., Hollinger, G.A., Isler, V.: Search and pursuit-evasion in mobile robotics. Auton. Robot. **31**(4), 299–316 (2011)
5. Francos, R.M., Bruckstein, A.M.: Search for smart evaders with sweeping agents. Robotica **39**(12), 2210–2245 (2021)
6. Francos, R.M., Bruckstein, A.M.: Spiral sweeping search for smart evaders. arXiv preprint (2023)
7. Garcia, E., Casbeer, D.W., Pachter, M.: Optimal strategies of the differential game in a circular region. IEEE Control Syst. Lett. **4**(2), 492–497 (2019)
8. Hew, P.C.: Linear and concentric arc patrols against smart evaders. Mil. Oper. Res. **20**(3), 39–48 (2015)
9. Koopman, B.O.: Search and screening: general principles with historical applications. Pergamon Press (1980)
10. Kumkov, S.S., Le Ménec, S., Patsko, V.S.: Zero-sum pursuit-evasion differential games with many objects: survey of publications. Dyn. Games Appl. **7**(4), 609–633 (2017)
11. Makkapati, V.R., Tsiotras, P.: Optimal evading strategies and task allocation in multi-player pursuit-evasion problems. Dyn. Games Appl. **9**(4), 1168–1187 (2019)
12. McGee, T.G., Hedrick, J.K.: Guaranteed strategies to search for mobile evaders in the plane. In: 2006 American Control Conference, p. 6. IEEE (2006)
13. Tang, Z., Ozguner, U.: On non-escape search for a moving target by multiple mobile sensor agents. In: 2006 American Control Conference, p. 6. IEEE (2006)
14. Tisue, S., Wilensky, U.: Netlogo: a simple environment for modeling complexity. In: International Conference on Complex Systems, vol. 21, pp. 16–21. Boston, MA (2004)
15. Vincent, P., Rubin, I.: A framework and analysis for cooperative search using UAV swarms. In: Proceedings of the 2004 ACM Symposium on Applied Computing, pp. 79–86. ACM (2004)
16. Weintraub, I.E., Pachter, M., Garcia, E.: An introduction to pursuit-evasion differential games. In: 2020 American Control Conference (ACC), pp. 1049–1066. IEEE (2020)

Investigation of Action Recognition for Improving Pedestrian Intent Prediction

Sarfraz Ahmed[1]([envelope]) [iD], Chitta Saha[2] [iD], and M. Nazmul Huda[3] [iD]

[1] School of Future Transport Engineering, Coventry University, Priory Street,
Coventry CV1 5FB, West Midlands, UK
ahmed157@uni.coventry.ac.uk
[2] School of Engineering and Built Environment, Millennium Point, Birmingham City
University, Birmingham, UK
Chitta.Saha@bcu.ac.uk
[3] Department of Electronic and Electrical Engineering, Brunel University London,
Kingston Lane, Uxbridge, London UB8 3PH, UK
MdNazmul.Huda@brunel.ac.uk

Abstract. Pose estimation has been a critical aspect for the recent improvements made in the field of pedestrian intent prediction. Current pose estimators are capable of providing highly accurate posture and head orientation information. In our previous work, we utilised posture information for predicting the crossing behaviour of pedestrians in urban environments. We referred to this as the multi-scale pedestrian intent prediction (MS-PIP) architecture. This technique yielded state-of-the-art results of 94% accuracy. It has been suggested from some previous works that head orientation information provides insight into the pedestrian's behaviours and intentions. Therefore, in this study, we investigate the benefits of implementing head orientation on top of the existing MS-PIP architecture. We found that the addition of head orientation information in fact decreases accuracy when compared to our previous works, in some cases by over 50%. Data augmentation and data generalisation techniques were also applied which slightly improved the accuracy. However, the accuracy was still lower than the original MS-PIP results.

Keywords: Pedestrians · Pose Estimation · Action Recognition

1 Introduction

Predicting the intentions of pedestrians is a crucial aspect of Autonomous Vehicles (AVs) and general road safety. The purpose of pedestrian intent prediction is to avoid and limit road-traffic incidents involving pedestrians. Accurately predicting the pedestrian's intentions provides useful information, such as the pedestrian's future trajectory and desired destination. Based on this information, vehicles can path plan with respect to the pedestrian as well as perform evasive manoeuvres (e.g., stopping, changing lanes, slowing down) to avoid the pedestrian in a safe and effective manner.

© The Author(s), under exclusive license to Springer Nature Switzerland AG 2023
F. Iida et al. (Eds.): TAROS 2023, LNAI 14136, pp. 101–113, 2023.
https://doi.org/10.1007/978-3-031-43360-3_9

Pose estimation has been a key aspect in the field of pedestrian intent prediction. Pose estimation provides pedestrian posture information [1]. This posture information over time provides speed and trajectory information that have been used for predictions, such as pedestrian crossing intentions. When a pedestrian crosses a road, they are entering the domain of road vehicles, which is particularly dangerous. For this reason, predicting pedestrian crossing intentions have been heavily researched in previous studies, such as, [5,7,11,13,15]. This has led to significant improvements made in the field of pedestrian intent prediction, with some methods achieving an accuracy of over 90%. However, the field requires further work to reach human-level performance.

More recently pedestrian action recognition (e.g., looking, nodding, waving) received significant attention for further improving upon existing pose estimation-based pedestrian intent prediction techniques. Pose estimation not only provides posture information but also provides head orientation information. Posture information was utilised for the MS-PIP architecture presented in [1]. According to [10], head orientation also provides insight into the pedestrian's behaviours and intentions. As discussed in [1], pose estimation (i.e., keypoints) can be used to calculate the trajectory and speed of a pedestrian to predict their future intentions. However, the direction in which a pedestrian is moving could be different to the direction the pedestrian is looking. This could mean that the pedestrian has not given their full attention to the road or the on-coming vehicle.

Therefore, in this paper, we investigate 'looking actions' based on head orientation for improving the results in the previously proposed MS-PIP architecture for pedestrian intent prediction [1]. An action classifier module is added to the existing MS-PIP. We focus on the looking actions (i.e., whether the pedestrian is looking or not looking at the vehicle). The JAAD [9] and PIE [8] datasets are utilised for training and evaluating the proposed architecture as they are both large-scale, widely available datasets which provide both pedestrian crossing and looking annotations.

2   Related Works

In [14], it is argued that pedestrian crossing intentions cannot be accurately predicted by trajectory information alone. Instead, using a combination of trajectory and body language (e.g., body posture, head orientation, hand gestures, etc.) is necessary for crossing intention prediction. In [6], it is discussed that when pedestrians are moving, their head orientations are typically in the same direction as their movement. Therefore, using the pedestrian's head orientation, their direction of movement could be inferred. They also mention that when a pedestrian maintains a head orientation and movement in the same direction typically crosses the road. However, when their head orientation is towards the vehicle instead of the movement of their body, they typically do not intend to cross. In this way, [6] used head orientation to predict pedestrian intentions. It seems that actions, head orientation, in particular, have been useful for pedestrian intent prediction. Therefore, in this paper, the effects of utilising head orientation information are investigated to improve the MS-PIP proposed in [1].

The MS-PIP architecture utilises keypoints to predict the crossing intentions of pedestrians by calculating pedestrians' trajectory and speed. This proposed approach achieved an accuracy of more the 90% using body posture information alone. However, previous works, such as [6,10,14], also use pedestrian actions, particularly head orientation to predict the crossing intentions of pedestrians. Because pedestrians are capable to make changes to their speed and trajectories very quickly [12], it is important to constantly predict the intention of pedestrians with a high level of accuracy, allowing the autonomous vehicle sufficient time to act, if required. Therefore, investigating the effects of head orientation for improving the results presented in [1] could be beneficial.

3   Methodology

Building upon the MS-PIP architecture proposed in [1], an additional module is added for classifying head orientation (see Fig. 1a). The actions utilised in this work are the *looking* and *not looking* actions. The update in the flowchart is subtle as it is simply an additional module. It should be noted and will be discussed in the next section, that due to the modular approach, action recognition is easily added to the existing MS-PIP architecture. The action classifier adds a layer of complexity to the MS-PIP architecture, however, if these actions improve the results presented in [1], this increased complexity would be considered justified. In terms of the methodology, the MS-PIP functions as in [1], but with an additional module. Therefore, the full architecture will not be discussed in this paper, and instead, the focus will be on that additional module, referred to as the action classifier. Overall, the MS-PIP with Action Recognition architecture consists of the following four key components:

1. Pose Estimation
2. Tracking-By-Detection
3. Intent Classification
4. Action Classification

3.1   Pose Estimation

Pose estimation can be categorised into two approaches; top-down or bottom-up [1]. The top-down approach typically consists of a off-the-shelf or fine-tuned pedestrian detector for predicting bounding boxes, such as in [3,4]. Pose estimation is applied within the predicted bounding boxes for predicting keypoints. Instead, the bottom-up approach predicts keypoints for the whole image and groups those keypoints into a group for each pedestrian. Thus, a standalone detector is not required, unlike the top-down approach. This leads the bottom-up approach better suited for real-time tasks [2]. For time-critical applications, such as Autonomous Vehicles (AVs), time consideration is a crucial aspect for path planning, particularly for the vehicle's occupants and those sharing the

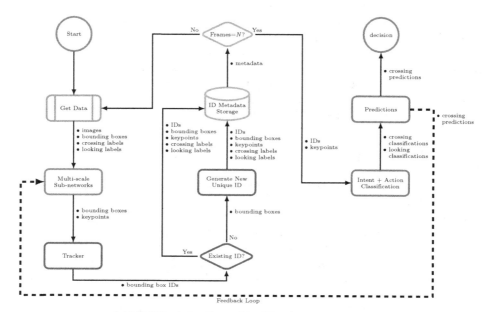

(a) MS-PIP+Action Recognition Flowchart

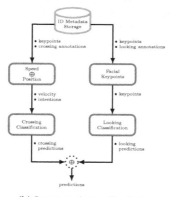

(b) Intent + Action Prediction

Fig. 1. The MS-PIP with Action Recognition adds an additional module to the MS-PIP architecture. As the original MS-PIP is a modular design, it is simply added to the existing design (see Fig. 1a). This approach combine posture information with head orientation/facial features for aiding in predicting pedestrian crossing intentions (see Fig. 1b).

roads. Therefore, the proposed approach employs the bottom-up pose estimation approach for this task. The run-time of the proposed method will be compared with other similar techniques later in this work to demonstrate it's effectiveness in real-time. It should be noted that the MS-PIP with Action Recognition is a multi-task approach. This means that multiple pedestrians are considered per image. Unlike previous methods that employ the top-down pose estimation approach, which only considers one pedestrian at a time.

3.2   Tracking-by-Detection

Tracking-by-detection refers to tracking pedestrians based on their bounding boxes. Therefore, the performance of the tracker is dependent on the quality of the bounding boxes. As the proposed approach is a multi-task approach, multi-pedestrian tracking was required. However, the JAAD and PIE datasets do not include ground-truth keypoint annotations. Because of this predicted keypoints cannot be evaluated. However, both datasets do include ground-truth bounding box annotations. Therefore, a method for using keypoint-based generated bounding boxes was proposed. For predicted keypoints, the first two rows represent the (x, y) coordinate of the predicted keypoint while the third row is the confidence score of each predicted keypoint (see Fig. 2). Any confidence score of less than 0.5 is omitted. This means only the highly accurate keypoints are used to generate the associated bounding boxes. Based on the (x, y) coordinates, associated bounding boxes can represent by (1). The values for $left, top, right, bottom$ is calculated via (2)-(5). In Fig. 3, there are two bounding boxes, ground truth and generated bounding boxes. Using the intersection-over-union (IoU) metric, the keypoint is evaluated. If the IoU value of these boxes is larger than the threshold value, then it is counted as a correct detection, whereas, if the value is lower than the threshold, it is considered a false detection.

$$\begin{bmatrix} x_1 & y_1 & score \\ x_2 & y_2 & score \\ \vdots & \vdots & \vdots \\ x_n & y_n & score \end{bmatrix}$$

Fig. 2. HigherHRNet Keypoint Predictions Format

$$box = [left, top, right, bottom] \tag{1}$$

$$left = \min([x_1, x_2 \ldots x_n]) \tag{2}$$

$$right = \max([x_1, x_2 \ldots x_n]) \tag{3}$$

$$top = \min([y_1, y_2 \ldots y_n]) \tag{4}$$

$$bottom = \max([y_1, y_2 \ldots y_n]) \tag{5}$$

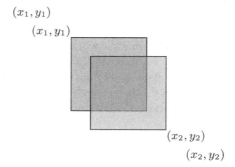

(x_1, y_1)

(x_1, y_1)

(x_2, y_2)

(x_2, y_2)

Fig. 3. IoU for two bounding boxes

3.3   Intent Classification

The stored keypoints are aggregated, which provides spatio-temporal information. This spatio-temporal information provides the location of the keypoints and the changes of those keypoints from frame to frame. The changes in these keypoints over time (i.e., along the frames) is used to calculate the trajectory, direction and speed of the pedestrian. Based on this information, the crossing intentions of the pedestrian can be classified.

3.4   Action Classifier

To better understand the action classification aspect in Fig. 1, refer to Fig. 1b. In [1], when the number of stored keypoints (i.e., *Keypoint Store* Fig. 1a) is equal to N, it is passed to the classifier. However, in the updated MS-PIP where head orientation is considered, the classifier not only calculates the speed and trajectory of the pedestrian, it also classifies the looking action. Due to the modular design of the MS-PIP architecture, these modules can be interchanged for classifying other actions. For example, action recognition can be replaced with a module for classifying waving or nodding actions. These are all actions that are acknowledging the vehicle and therefore should aid in the decision-making of the AV.

4   Experimentation

4.1   Datasets

Both the JAAD and PIE datasets include the looking actions, amongst other action annotations. However, there is a class imbalance for the looking annotations. In the JAAD dataset, the *looking* class only makes up 19% of the data while in PIE there is 18% for the *looking* class. As discussed in [1], this can lead to over-fitting/under-fitting issues, where the model has a bias towards the majority class. Overcoming the dataset imbalance issue is discussed in Sect. 4.2.

In Fig. 4, the *looking* and *not looking* actions are visualised to demonstrate the sheer amount of data imbalance that exists when considering the *looking* actions of the JAAD and PIE datasets. Due to the limited number of samples for the *reasonable (small)* and *heavily occluded* classes, the MS-PIP model struggled to learn enough useful features and generalise, leading to poor results during evaluation (as discussed throughout this Section).

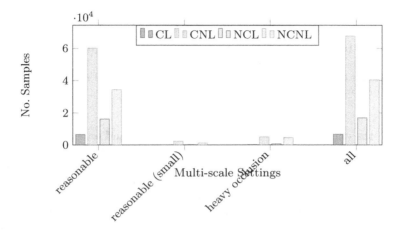

Fig. 4. Number of samples for multi-scale pedestrians with crossing behaviours and actions. Where C is crossing, NC is not crossing, L is looking and NL is not looking.

It was found that when a pedestrian is looking at the oncoming vehicle, the eyes and nose are typically visible, however, when a pedestrian is looking away from the vehicle, some of these keypoints are not visible. For example, when a pedestrian is looking away from the vehicle, only one of the eyes is showing as in Fig. 5a. The pose estimator attempts to predict the non-visible keypoints based on adjacent keypoints. This results in inaccurate keypoints, which negatively affected the performance of the model, as will be discussed in Sect. 5.1. When the pedestrian is looking directly at the on-coming vehicle, these keypoints are much more accurate (see Fig. 5b).

4.2 Training and Evaluation Protocols

For training and evaluation, the protocols set in [1] were implemented. This provided consistency between the works conducted in this paper with the original results presented in [1]. Please refer to [1] for further information.

4.3 Data Augmentation

In [9], an approach was implemented that used negative samples to overcome the dataset imbalance issue. In this approach, the training dataset consists of all the

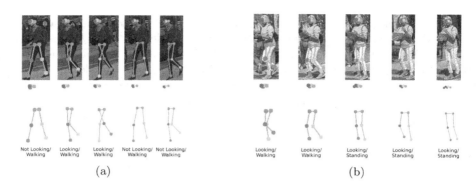

Fig. 5. Example of pedestrian not looking at on-coming vehicle (Fig. 5a) and pedestrian not looking at on-coming vehicle (Fig. 5b)

samples of the class with the least number of samples and an equivalent number of negative samples. However, this significantly reduces the number of overall samples, as the class with the least amount of samples was only 19% and 33% for the JAAD and PIE datasets, respectively. Therefore, it was found more useful to use data augmentation techniques, such as re-sampling (see [1]), to increase the number of samples for the least represented class. This technique would not only re-use the samples for the lesser class but also apply some transformations, particularly, flipping, and resizing. This method increased the overall number of samples. As mentioned in previous sections, the larger the number of data samples, the better the model can generalise features for accurate predictions.

Using these data augmentation techniques, a baseline was created to compare the MS-PIP with and without action recognition modules (see Table 1). However, this method initially leads to over-fitting, where the model performs well for the training set, but did not learn the features to make useful predictions for previously unseen samples in the test dataset (see Table 1). This occurs when the model sees too much of a particular class, such as the classes where the samples are re-used to match the number of samples for the majority classes. This led to poor performance for the test set, where the majority of the predictions

Table 1. MS-PIP with Action Recognition

Setting	JAAD	PIE
Reasonable	63%	64%
Reasonable (small)	21%	24%
Heavy Occlusion	17%	21%
All	34%	36%

This table presents the results for the MS-PIP with Action Recognition. These results will be used as a baseline for comparing with the original MS-PIP.

were *not looking*. In particular, the *reasonable (small)* and *Heavily Occluded* samples suffered. This may be due to the difficulty associated with localising the keypoints of the faces for smaller pedestrians. In the case of the heavily occluded, the face may not be visible to predict the keypoints.

To overcome the over-fitting challenge, for the JAAD dataset, the *not looking* samples were reduced by approximately 20% while re-sampling the 19% *looking* class samples. This led to approximately 60% and 40% ratio of *not looking* and *looking* classes. This method helped alleviate the bias and over-fitting issues as the dataset was more balanced. The same approach was applied to the PIE dataset. The results for this approach are presented in Table 3. Although the results were slightly improved when compared to the results in Table 1, they are still significantly worse than the original results presented in [1] (see Table 2).

Table 2. Performance of original MS-PIP [1]

Setting	JAAD	PIE
Reasonable	89%	92%
Reasonable (small)	78%	81%
Heavy Occlusion	40%	43%
All	87%	89%

This table presents the results for the original MS-PIP. When compared to the baseline in Table 1, the performance has decreased. As illustrated in Fig. 4, this could be due to the significant class imbalance.

Table 3. Improved Performance of MS-PIP with Action Recognition

Setting	JAAD	PIE
Reasonable	65%	67%
Reasonable (small)	22%	24%
Heavy Occlusion	17%	22%
All	35%	37%

Applying data augmentation techniques, the performance of the improved for the baseline from Table 1, however, the results are still significantly worse then the original MS-PIP.

4.4   Data Generalisation

The results in Table 3 indicate the addition of action recognition (i.e., looking behaviours) has negatively affected the performance of the MS-PIP when compared to results in [1]. However, this may not be due to the addition of the action recognition module alone. Due to the data augmentation techniques applied in Sect. 4.3, the overall number of samples was decreased, approximately by 20% for the JAAD dataset and 15% for the PIE dataset. This coupled with the re-sampling of such a small amount of samples could make it difficult for the model to learn useful features and generalise. Therefore, the data generalisation technique from [1] was applied in an attempt to improve the number of samples. The results are presented in Table 4. The results for all of the multi-scale settings were closer to Table 3. However, the purpose of this investigation was to determine if action recognition can improve the performance of the MS-PIP. Based on the results, the performance does not improve with the addition of the looking actions.

Table 4. Performance of Pre-trained MS-PIP with Action Recognition

Setting	JAAD	PIE
Reasonable	66%	67%
Reasonable (small)	24%	26%
Heavy Occlusion	19%	22%
All	36%	38%

These table presents the results of the MS-PIP with Action Recognition utilising the original MS-PIP model parameters. Unfortunately, the results do not see any significant improvements when compared to Table 3.

4.5 Run-Time Analysis

The run-time was calculated in the same manner as presented in [1], however, with the addition of the action classification layer. Again, this was for comparability purposes. As in [1], the run-time is calculated based on the average time taken for the MS-PIP to predict keypoints, generate bounding boxes, and classify behaviours and actions to make crossing predictions. It was found that the action classifier has a negligible effect on the average run-time of the MS-PIP model. This will be further discussed in Sect. 5.1.

5 Results and Discussions

5.1 Performance and Efficiency Improvements

Based on the results in Section, 4, the addition of the action recognition to the MS-PIP harms performance. By simply implementing the action recognition module to the existing MS-PIP model, the accuracy decreased for the *All* setting by over 50% and 30% for the JAAD and PIE datasets, respectively (see

Table 1). As there was a significant class imbalance for the *looking* and *not looking* actions, data augmentation techniques were applied. This led to improved accuracy results, however, the accuracy was still 25% lower for the PIE dataset and 24% for the JAAD dataset. Even applying the data generalisation techniques as in [1], the improvements were subtle and still underperformed when compared to the results in [1]. It should be noted that facial keypoints are more difficult to localise when compared to body keypoints. This, with the addition of the class imbalance issues discussed in Sect. 4.3, may have led to the decline in performance. The MS-PIP was designed to use posture information to calculate the speed and positioning of the pedestrian along frames. It was expected that adding head orientation would add further information for crossing behaviours. However, perhaps the current MS-PIP architecture prevented an association between the posture of the pedestrian and looking actions from being made.

According to the run-time analysis in Sect. 4.5, the run-time does not seem to be affected by the increased number of input data points. Initially, the MS-PIP uses 8 keypoints for posture information (i.e., shoulders, hips, knees and ankles). The action recognition adds a further 3 keypoints (i.e., eyes and nose) to represent the head orientation. The processing of these 3 extra keypoints does not increase the initial run-time found in [1]. This may be since the fine-tuned DEKR pose estimator used by the MS-PIP architecture predicts all 17 keypoints as per the COCO dataset, which was used to initially train the DEKR pose estimator. As the model is already predicting the head orientation keypoints, the run-time is not affected. Also, as the LSTM is using the data points as is (i.e., without any pre-processing), the extra 3 data points do not add to the run-time either. Based on this, the run-time may be improved further for the original MS-PIP by training the model to predict only the keypoints that are to be utilised. This could be an aspect for further improvement in future works.

6   Conclusions

Based on the results, it can be concluded that the addition of head orientation information harmed the initial results of the MS-PIP presented in [1]. The head orientation was determined by the keypoints representing the eyes and nose and based on those keypoints it was determined whether or not the pedestrian was looking in the direction of the vehicle. There may be several reasons why the head orientation was not effective for the MS-PIP model. One reason could be the lack of samples in certain classes. It was found that the *reasonable (small)* and *heavily occluded* had significantly fewer samples than the *reasonable* class when considering samples of *looking* and *not looking* actions. Although data augmentation and data generalisation techniques were applied, the results in this paper underperformed when compared to the MS-PIP results presented in [1]. Another aspect to consider is that facial keypoints are much more difficult to localise than body keypoints as the joints, such as eyes and nose, are smaller. It may also be that the facial keypoints do not provide enough information to generate useful features to improve MS-PIP. The MS-PIP in [1] utilises the changes in the keypoints with respect to each other. Unlike the body keypoints, such as knees and ankles, facial keypoints do not provide spatial information. The change in the knee and ankle keypoint along frames provides localisation data points, and the changes of these localised data points with respect to the data point from subsequent frames provide spatio-temporal information. However, facial keypoints do not provide the same level of spatio-temporal information that can be used by the existing MS-PIP architecture in the same manner. In future works, the MS-PIP utilising a 3D CNN will be explored. As the 3D CNN utilises the data points and images, perhaps the facial keypoint information may be more effective. This is further aspect that will be explored in future works.

References

1. Ahmed, S., Bazi, A.A., Saha, C., Rajbhandari, S., Huda, M.N.: Multi-scale pedestrian intent prediction using 3D joint information as spatio-temporal representation. Expert Syst. Appl. **225**, 120077 (2023)
2. Cheng, B., Xiao, B., Wang, J., Shi, H., Huang, T.S., Zhang, L.: HigherhrNet: scale-aware representation learning for bottom-up human pose estimation. In: Proceedings of the IEEE Computer Society Conference on Computer Vision and Pattern Recognition, pp. 5385–5394 (2020)
3. Fang, Z., López, A.M.: Is the pedestrian going to cross? Answering by 2D pose estimation. In: IEEE Intelligent Vehicles Symposium, Proceedings, vol. 2018-June, pp. 1271–1276 (2018)
4. Fang, Z., Vázquez, D., López, A., Fang, Z., Vázquez, D., López, A.M.: On-board detection of pedestrian intentions. Sensors. **17**(10), 2193 (2017)
5. Gesnouin, J., Pechberti, S., Bresson, G., Stanciulescu, B., Moutarde, F.: Predicting intentions of pedestrians from 2d skeletal pose sequences with a representation-focused multi-branch deep learning network. Algorithms **13**(12), 1–23 (2020)
6. Kwak, J.Y., Ko, B.C., Nam, J.Y.: Pedestrian intention prediction based on dynamic fuzzy automata for vehicle driving at nighttime. Infrared Phys. Technol. **81**, 41–51 (3 2017). https://doi.org/10.1016/J.INFRARED.2016.12.014
7. Liu, B., Adeli, E., Cao, Z., Lee, K.H., Shenoi, A., Gaidon, A., Niebles, J.C.: Spatiotemporal relationship reasoning for pedestrian intent prediction. IEEE Robot. Autom. Lett. **5**(2), 3485–3492 (2020)
8. Rasouli, A., Kotseruba, I., Kunic, T., Tsotsos, J.: PIE: a large-scale dataset and models for pedestrian intention estimation and trajectory prediction. In: Proceedings of the IEEE International Conference on Computer Vision 2019-October, pp. 6261–6270 (2019)
9. Rasouli, A., Kotseruba, I., Tsotsos, J.K.: Agreeing to cross: how drivers and pedestrians communicate. In: 2017 IEEE Intelligent Vehicles Symposium (IV), pp. 264–269. IEEE (2017)
10. Raza, M., Chen, Z., Rehman, S.U., Wang, P., Bao, P.: Appearance based pedestrians' head pose and body orientation estimation using deep learning. Neurocomputing. **272**, 647–659 (2018)
11. Razali, H., Mordan, T., Alahi, A.: Pedestrian intention prediction: a convolutional bottom-up multi-task approach. Transp. Res. Part C. Emerg. Technol. **130**(June), 103259 (2021)

12. Ridel, D., Rehder, E., Lauer, M., Stiller, C., Wolf, D.: A literature review on the prediction of pedestrian behavior in urban scenarios. In: IEEE Conference on Intelligent Transportation Systems, Proceedings, ITSC. vol. 2018, November, pp. 3105–3112. Institute of Electrical and Electronics Engineers Inc. (2018)
13. Samant, A.P., Warhade, K., Gunale, K.: Pedestrian intent detection using skeleton-based prediction for road safety. In: 2021 2nd International Conference on Advances in Computing, Communication, Embedded and Secure Systems (ACCESS), vol. 130(September), pp. 238–242 (2021)
14. Schmidt, S., Färber, B.: Pedestrians at the kerb - Recognising the action intentions of humans. Transp. Res. Part F. Traffic Psychol. Behav. **12**(4), 300–310 (2009). https://doi.org/10.1016/J.TRF.2009.02.003
15. Yang, B., Zhan, W., Wang, P., Chan, C., Cai, Y., Wang, N.: Crossing or not? Context-based recognition of pedestrian crossing intention in the urban environment. IEEE Trans. Intell. Transp. Syst. **23**(6), 5338–5349 (2022)

Evaluation of SLAM Algorithms for Search and Rescue Applications

Zhiyuan Yang[1], Nabila Naz[2], Pengcheng Liu[3], and M. Nazmul Huda[4](✉)

[1] Shanghai Huawei Technology Co., Ltd., Shanghai, China
[2] School of Engineering, Technology and Design, Canterbury Christ Church University, Canterbury, UK
[3] Department of Computer Science, University of York, York, UK
[4] Department of Electronic and Electrical Engineering, Brunel University London, London, UK
mdnazmul.huda@brunel.ac.uk

Abstract. Search and rescue robots have been widely investigated to detect humans in disaster scenarios. SLAM (Simultaneous Localisation and Mapping), as a critical function of the robot, can localise the robot and create the map during the rescue tasks. In this paper, prominent 2D SLAM algorithms are investigated and three of them (Gmapping, Hector, and Karto) are implemented on a low-cost search and rescue robot to demonstrate their feasibility. Moreover, experiments containing various ground surface scenarios are performed. Maps created by various SLAM algorithms are compared to identify the best SLAM algorithm for search and rescue tasks using a low-cost robot. The experimental results suggest that Karto SLAM performs best for low-cost search and rescue robots among the three SLAM algorithms.

Keywords: Search and Rescue · Low-cost robot · SLAM · Karto · Gmapping

1 Introduction

Robots are widely used in highly repeatable, dangerous and precise tasks in industry, service, military, healthcare, scientific research and so on. The search and rescue robots [1], have been employed in rescue tasks for more than 20 years [2]. However, performing rescue tasks in an extreme situation has many requirements [3]. Firstly, the size of the robot should be suitable. It should be small enough to enter the narrow area and big enough to move on the rough terrain without being stuck, which means the hardware of the robot is also required to be simplified [4]. Secondly, its operation should not be difficult so that ordinary humans can operate it. Thirdly, it should be low cost so that it can be widely used by people in various scenarios [5]. Fourthly, it should have basic functions, such as SLAM for map building and real-time video streaming [6].To keep the robot's cost down, the hardware, sensors (e.g., LIDAR) and computing resources need to be low-cost as well.

SLAM [7] (simultaneous localization and mapping) aims to implement the robot localization and map building in an unknown environment at the same time [8]. Many

F. Iida et al. (Eds.): TAROS 2023, LNAI 14136, pp. 114–125, 2023.
https://doi.org/10.1007/978-3-031-43360-3_10

SLAM algorithms have been developed and implemented on the ground mobile robots. Several studies have also been performed comparing the performance of various SLAM algorithms [9–13] either through simulations [9, 10, 12] or experiments [13] or both [11]. However, all of them aim to display the optimum performance of the algorithms. As a result, some high-cost hardware such as the high precision Lidar [14] and high-performance controller [11], have been employed. Besides, the environmental constraints have been ignored i.e., they assumed the ground to be a flat surface. Therefore, it is critical to implement the SLAM algorithms on a low-cost robot and explore the influence of various ground surfaces which are comparable to the rescue scenarios, to find the most effective and efficient SLAM algorithms for search and rescue robot to be applied in specific disaster scenarios. This research investigates three SLAM algorithms on a low-cost mobile robot and finds the algorithms' performance through a set of experiments including different types of ground surfaces.

This paper has the following structure. Section 2 presents the low-cost search and rescue robot platform; Sect. 3 investigates five popular SLAM algorithms and identifies three algorithms for further investigation; Sect. 4 presents the maps built by three selected SLAM algorithms and tests their feasibility for a low-cost robot; Sect. 5 presents experiments to investigate the impact of various ground surfaces on map building, to emulate the environment of real disaster scenarios; Sect. 6 analyses the findings of the research and Sect. 7 concludes the paper.

2 Low-Cost Search and Rescue Robot Platform

This research aims to evaluate the performance of various SLAM algorithms for a low-cost search and rescue robot (Fig. 1) in disaster scenarios. The software framework and hardware specifications of the low-cost robot platform are provided in this section.

For the software framework, ROS (Robot Operating System) is used on the robot, which is originated from the AI Lab project of Stanford University, developed by Willow Garage in 2010 [15]. The main hardware components of the robot are a tracked Chassis, an RPLidar A1M8-R5, a Raspberry Pi 3 Model B (main controller), a secondary control board based on STM32 (STM32F103RCT6), two DC brushed motor, a 9-DoF IMU (GY-85), a 12V 8400mAh li-po battery pack. The total cost of the robot is approximately £210 (£40 - Raspberry Pi, £20 - STM32 based secondary controller board, £90 - Lidar, £40-chassis with two motors, £20 - cables, screws, and others).

The Raspberry Pi is used as the main controller of the robot as it is stable and widely used to work as an embedded controller on robotics. Raspberry Pi 3B is based on Quad Cortex A53 chip with 1.2 GHz operating speed [16]. The RPLidar A1 is used because of its stable performance and low cost as an elementary laser range scanner. The parameters of the Lidar are 12 m distance range, 360° angular range, and 4000 Hz sample frequency [17].

Fig. 1. Low-Cost Search and Rescue Robot Platform

3 SLAM Algorithms and Discussions

Many 2D SLAM algorithms have been developed. The example includes Gmapping SLAM [18, 19], Hector SLAM [14, 20], Karto SLAM [11], Cartographer SLAM [21], Core SLAM [22] etc. This section briefly introduces the above-mentioned SLAM algorithms and identifies the algorithms that could be employed in low-cost search and rescue robots. The readers who want more details on the algorithms may read the review papers on 2D SLAM algorithms [11, 23, 24].

3.1 SLAM Algorithms

Gmapping SLAM is based on Rao-Blackwellized Particle Filters (RBPF) framework. It obtains the robot pose from localisation data first, then creates the map. The process of Gmapping SLAM has four main steps: sampling through Lidar, calculating the weight through the information carried by the particles, resampling according to the weight and finally, estimating the map [18]. This is the most widely used SLAM algorithm [11].

Hector SLAM implements the localisation and mapping at the same time. It uses the occupancy grid map, which is divided into limit grid cells, to estimate the map by each grid cell occupancy situation. During initialization, the data of the first frame will be mapped in the grid cell. Then, the data of the next frame will be matched to the previous one [20].

Karto SLAM, developed by Karto Robotics of SRI International, is a graph-based SLAM algorithm which uses highly optimized and non-iterative Cholesky matrix to calculate the solution of the sparse system. The Sparse Pose Adjustment (SPA) method is adopted to be responsible for scan matching and loop-closure procedures [11].

Cartographer SLAM, developed by Google in 2016, aims to provide the solution on map building for real-time obstacle-avoiding and path planning applications with limited computing ability such as in-door service robot (e.g. sweeping robot) [21]. The Cartographer SLAM can be located with low computing consumption, real-time optimization, but the precision is lower than other algorithms [25].

Core SLAM is an algorithm to minimize the loss of SLAM performance. The algorithm is simplified into two steps, distance calculation and map update process [22]. It is based on a simple particle filter algorithm to calculate distance and particle filter matching is used to laser and map matching. However, it requires high computing power [11].

3.2 Discussions

Trejos et al. [23] compared various 2D SLAM algorithms based on four metrics namely pose error, map accuracy, CPU usage, and memory usage. They reported that overall, Karto SLAM outperformed other 2D SLAM algorithms. Karto SLAM uses Sparse Pose Adjustment (SPA) method which has faster speed and better convergence on solving robot pose and large sparse graphs. It will have a great advantage on a large scene map building because only one pose graph needs to be maintained [26]. Therefore, we have selected Karto SLAM to further investigate it in a low-cost search and rescue robot.

The Gmapping SLAM is a good algorithm to build a map in a small scene. It can build a real-time map with high precision. Compared with Hector SLAM, it has low requirement on the Lidar precision as it uses odometer information to estimate the robot pose first. However, as the surface area increases, the particle number and information will rapidly increase, so Gmapping is not suitable for large scene map building. Yet we have selected Gmapping SLAM for further investigation as this is the most widely used SLAM algorithm in robots [11].

Trejos et al. [23] reported that Hector SLAM has the least CPU usage as it does not need to use odometer. However, compared with Gmapping, it has a high requirement of Lidar scanning frequency [27]. Yet, we have selected Hector SLAM for further investigation as it has the least CPU usage. However, through our investigation we will find out whether the scanning frequency of a typical low-cost LIDAR is sufficient for Hector SLAM.

As reported in [11], the maps built by Core SLAM are less impressive with higher error and CPU load. Therefore, Core SLAM will not be used in this research. Hess et al. [27] reported that the Cartographer SLAM was developed for indoor real-time map building, which means this algorithm may not meet the demand of search and rescue tasks because the flat and smooth indoor ground surface is different from the rough terrain formed by collapsed buildings. As a result, Cartographer SLAM will not be used in this research. We will investigate Gmapping SLAM, Hector SLAM and Karto SLAM for low-cost search and rescue applications.

4 Experimentation on Low-Cost Robot

In this section, the Gmapping SLAM, Hector SLAM, and Karto SLAM are implemented on the robot to build a 2D map for the office floor (Fig. 2) with a flat surface. This section aims to test the feasibility of these three algorithms for a low-cost robot. The robot was deployed at the same location of the office floor and remotely operated and followed identical trajectory. RViz was used to construct the map.

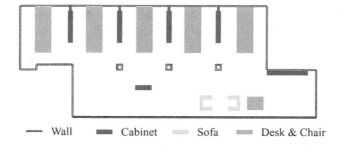

Fig. 2. 2D map of the office floor

4.1 Gmapping SLAM

From the map (Fig. 3) built by Gmapping SLAM, we see that error occurs at the top-right corner. The generated map rotates the wall about 45 ° counterclockwise. This error happens at the time when the robot makes a turn to avoid an obstacle, and the odometer posts incorrect data so that the orientation predicted by the robot is also incorrect which generates the incorrect edge of the wall.

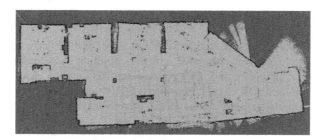

Fig. 3. Map built by Gmapping SLAM for the office floor of Fig. 2

4.2 Hector SLAM

From the map (Fig. 4) generated by the Hector SLAM, we see that most of the area is overlapped. This is because Hector SLAM is based on occupancy grid map without odometer i.e., this algorithm has a high requirement on the Lidar scanning frequency. The low-cost Lidar (RPLidar A1) used in this research has a maximum scanning frequency of 10 Hz which does not meet the demand of the Hector SLAM. Additionally, Hector SLAM has no ability to correcting the map so that all subsequent matches will have problems once the map makes an error [27].

Fig. 4. Map built by Hector SLAM for the office floor of Fig. 2

4.3 Karto SLAM

The map (Fig. 5) built by Karto SLAM has good precision and resolution. However, it can be found that the bottom of the map is not closed. The robot performed a rotation at the middle of the bottom area of the map to avoid an obstacle. The odometer may have had an erroneous reading at that time. The accumulation of odometer errors could have contributed to the error in mapping the wall.

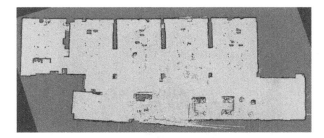

Fig. 5. Map built by Karto SLAM for the office floor of Fig. 2

4.4 Discussion

The experimental result of Fig. 4 shows that the Map built by Hector SLAM for the office floor of Fig. 2 is too far from accurate. Tee et al. [24] also reported failed map construction by Hector SLAM. Thus, Hector SLAM is not suitable for a low-cost robot with a low-cost Lidar. The experimental results of Fig. 3 and Fig. 5 suggest that the map generated using Gmapping and Karto SLAM for the low-cost robot has moderate accuracy. The next section will further investigate Gmapping and Karto SLAM for search and rescue applications.

5 Experimentation on Low-Cost Robot for Search and Rescue Applications

This experiment aims to find the best SLAM algorithm in search and rescue scenarios. Gmapping SLAM and Karto SLAM will be investigated to find the best SLAM algorithm. The experiment contains three different ground surfaces in the same room (Fig. 6), flat ground, slope ground (Fig. 8), and rough ground (Fig. 10). In each environment, two SLAM algorithms are employed to build the map. The area used is a rectangular room. The robot was deployed at the same location of the room and remotely operated and followed identical trajectory. RViz was used to construct the map.

5.1 Flat Ground

Figure 7 shows the maps built by Gmapping SLAM and Karto SLAM for a rectangular room when the surface is flat. The result shows that both Gmapping and Karto SLAM algorithm can build a map with a closed and clear edge in the flat ground surface. A little difference between them is that the map built by Gmapping SLAM is rough with a low resolution while the map built by Karto SLAM has a precise edge with a high resolution.

Fig. 6. Rectangular room

5.2 Slope Surface

The slope surface (Fig. 8) is made by two boxes in the lab and the gradient is about 37.5%. The maps are created using both algorithms while the robot moved within the room using the slope surface. From the two results (Fig. 9), we see that the map built by Gmapping SLAM is influenced by the slope, so the area overlap occurs in this map. On the other hand, the slope has very little influence on the map built by Karto SLAM. Therefore, in the slope scenario, the Karto SLAM is more adaptable than the Gmapping SLAM.

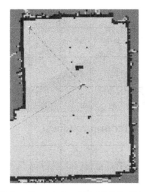
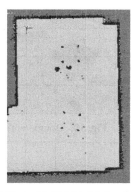

Fig. 7. Maps built by Gmapping SLAM (left) and Karto SLAM (right) for the rectangular room of Fig. 6 when the surface is flat.

Fig. 8. Slope surface used for map building.

Fig. 9. Maps built by Gmapping SLAM (left) and Karto SLAM (right) for the rectangular room of Fig. 6 when the surface has a slope (Fig. 8)

5.3 Rough Terrain

The rough ground (Fig. 10) is made of several components in the lab, which aims to move the robot up and down in a smaller range than the slope scenario. From the maps (Fig. 11) built by the algorithms, we see that there is still overlap in the map built by Gmapping SLAM, however, the result is better than the slope situation. On the other hand, the map built by Karto SLAM is still clear and precise.

Fig. 10. Rough terrain used for map building.

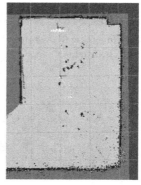

Fig. 11. Maps built by Gmapping SLAM (left) and Karto SLAM (right) for the rectangular room of Fig. 7 when the surface is rough (Fig. 10).

5.4 Discussion

Table 1 compares the performance of Gmapping and Karto SLAM for three different ground surfaces. Both Gmapping and Karto SLAM performed well in the flat ground scenario, however, in the slope and rough terrain scenarios, the advantage of Karto SLAM is obvious compared to Gmapping SLAM. As a result, Karto SLAM is more adaptable for the low-cost search and rescue robot in disaster scenarios.

Table 1. Performance Comparison of Gmapping and Karto SLAM

Scenarios	Gmapping SLAM	Karto SLAM
Flat ground	Constructed map has a closed edge but the resolution is low	Constructed map has a closed edge and the resolution is high
Slope surface	Constructed map has overlapped area	Constructed map has a closed edge
Rough ground	Constructed map has unidentified edge	Constructed map has a closed edge

6 Analysis

This paper investigates various SLAM algorithms for low-cost search and rescue applications and presents experimental results and comparison of various SLAM algorithms. The key findings of this research are provided below.

The experimental results show that the Hector SLAM generates an inaccurate map for the low-cost search and rescue robot even at the flat surface. It suggests that the Hector SLAM is inappropriate for low-cost applications. Hector SLAM is based on grid map which has a high requirement on Lidar scanning frequency. Lidar scanning frequency of the low-cost robot does not meet the requirement of Hector SLAM algorithm. This leads to an overlap of areas in the map generated using the Hector SLAM in this paper. The other two algorithms use odometer information as well. However, the Hector SLAM does not use odometer information. Thus, if Lidar provides noisy data Hector SLAM cannot recover from that whereas other two algorithms can.

This paper presents the results of map generation for three different ground surfaces. The results show that the worst influence on map building occurs in the slope scenario among the three situations. This is because the slope surface makes the Lidar out of the scan plane. The new plane formed by the slope surface has an angle with the original plane, which will change the distance scanned by the Lidar. When the robot is back to the flat ground and the original plane, the scan edge cannot be closed so that the area is overlapped.

Overall, Karto SLAM presents better performance than Gmapping SLAM. Thus, Karto SLAM is the best SLAM for the low-cost search and rescue robot in disaster scenarios. Gmapping SLAM relies on odometer and IMU to estimate the robot pose first, which highly depends on the hardware. The hardware of a low-cost robot may not be able to estimate the robot pose accurately for the Gmapping algorithm, which causes the error in the created map. However, the Karto SLAM is graph-based and thus the impact on the created map is low for various ground surfaces.

7 Conclusions

This paper implemented three SLAM algorithms on a low-cost search and rescue robot. The result shows that the Hector SLAM algorithm is not suitable for low-cost robots while the Gmapping SLAM and Karto SLAM can create map with acceptable accuracy in flat ground. The performance of Gmapping SLAM and Karto SLAM have been further compared in three different ground surfaces where Karto SLAM performed better over Gmapping on the map resolution, precision, and stability. The Gmapping SLAM is not good enough on complicated ground surface situation, such as slope and rough terrain.

References

1. Niroui, F., Zhang, K., Kashino, Z., Nejat, G.: Deep reinforcement learning robot for search and rescue applications: exploration in unknown cluttered environments. IEEE Robot. Autom. Lett. 4(2), 610–617 (2019)

2. Siciliano, B., Khatib, O. (eds.), Springer handbook of robotics. Springer, Berlin (2008). https://doi.org/10.1007/978-3-540-30301-5
3. Liu, J., Wang, Y., Li, B., Ma, S.: Current research, key performances and future development of search and rescue robots. Front. Mech. Eng. China 2(4), 404–416 (2007)
4. Priandana, K., et al.: Design of a task-oriented autonomous wheeled- robot for search and rescue. In: 2018 International Conference on Advanced Computer Science and Information Systems (ICACSIS), pp. 259–263, October 2018
5. Dang, L., Kwon, J.: Design of a new cost-effective head for a low-cost humanoid robot. In: 2016 IEEE 7th Annual Ubiquitous Computing, Electronics Mobile Communication Conference (UEMCON), pp. 1–7, October 2016
6. Uddin, Z., Islam, M.: Search and rescue system for alive human detection by semi-autonomous mobile rescue robot. In: 2016 International Conference on Innovations in Science, Engineering and Technology (ICISET), pp. 1–5, October 2016
7. Li, M., Zhu, H., You, S., Wang, L., Tang, C.: Efficient laser-based 3D SLAM for coal mine rescue robots. IEEE Access 7, 14124–14138 (2019)
8. Cadena, C., et al.: Past, present, and future of simultaneous localization and mapping: toward the robust-perception age. IEEE Trans. Robot. 32(6), 1309–1332 (2016)
9. Zhang, Y., Zhang, T., Huang, S.: Comparison of EKF based SLAM and optimization based SLAM algorithms. In: 2018 13th IEEE Conference on Industrial Electronics and Applications (ICIEA), pp. 1308–1313. IEEE (2018)
10. Qi, P., Wang, L.: On simulation and analysis of mobile robot SLAM using rao-blackwellized particle filters. In: 2011 IEEE/SICE International Symposium on System Integration (SII), pp. 1239–1244, IEEE (2011)
11. Santos, J.M., Portugal, D., Rocha, R.P.: An evaluation of 2D SLAM techniques available in Robot Operating System. In: 2013 IEEE International Symposium on Safety, Security, and Rescue Robotics (SSRR), pp. 1–6, October 2013
12. Tuna, G., Gulez, K., Cagri Gungor, V., Veli Mumcu, T.: Evaluations of different simultaneous localization and mapping (SLAM) algorithms. In: IECON 2012 - 38th Annual Conference on IEEE Industrial Electronics Society, Montreal, QC, Canada: IEEE, pp. 2693–2698, October 2012, Accessed 14 Sep 2019. http://ieeexplore.ieee.org/document/6389151/
13. da Silva, B.M.F., Xavier, R.S., do Nascimento, T.P., Gonsalves, L.M.G.: Experimental evaluation of ROS compatible SLAM algorithms for RGB-D sensors. In: 2017 Latin American Robotics Symposium (LARS) and 2017 Brazilian Symposium on Robotics (SBR), Curitiba, pp. 1–6. IEEE, November 2017, Accessed 14 Sep 2019. http://ieeexplore.ieee.org/document/8215331/
14. Khan, S., Wollherr, D., Buss, M.: Modeling laser intensities for simultaneous localization and mapping. IEEE Robot. Autom. Lett. 1(2), 692–699 (2016)
15. Quigley, M., et al.: ROS: an open-source robot operating system. In: ICRA Workshop Open Source Software, p. 6, January 2009
16. Shanavas, I.H., Reddy, P.B., Doddegowda, M.C.: A personal assistant robot using raspberry Pi. In: 2018 International Conference on Design Innovations for 3Cs Compute Communicate Control (ICDI3C), pp. 133–136, April 2018
17. Gong, Z., Li, J., Li, W.: A low cost indoor mapping robot based on TinySLAM algorithm. In: 2016 IEEE International Geoscience and Remote Sensing Symposium, pp. 4549–4552, July 2016
18. Grisetti, G., Stachniss, C., Burgard, W.: Improved techniques for grid mapping with rao-blackwellized particle filters. IEEE Trans. Robot. 23(1), 34–46 (2007)
19. Abdelrasoul, Y., Saman, A.B.S.H., Sebastian, P.: A quantitative study of tuning ROS gmapping parameters and their effect on performing indoor 2D SLAM. In: 2016 2nd IEEE International Symposium on Robotics and Manufacturing Automation (ROMA), pp. 1–6, September 2016

20. Yu, N., Zhang, B.: An improved hector SLAM algorithm based on information fusion for mobile robot. In: 2018 5th IEEE International Conference on Cloud Computing and Intelligence Systems (CCIS), pp. 279–284, November 2018
21. Filatov, A., Filatov, A., Krinkin, K., Chen, B., Molodan, D.: 2D SLAM quality evaluation methods. In: 2017 21st Conference of Open Innovations Association (FRUCT), pp. 120–126, November 2017
22. Steux, B., Hamzaoui, O.E.: tinySLAM: a SLAM algorithm in less than 200 lines C-language program. In: 2010 11th International Conference on Control Automation Robotics Vision, pp. 1975–1979, December 2010
23. Trejos, K., Rincón, L., Bolaños, M., Fallas, J., Marín, L.: 2D SLAM algorithms characterization, calibration, and comparison considering pose error, Map accuracy as well as CPU and memory usage. Sensors **22**(18), 6903 (2022)
24. Tee, Y.K., Han, Y.C.: LiDAR-based 2D SLAM for mobile robot in an indoor environment: a review. In: 2021 International Conference on Green Energy, Computing and Sustainable Technology (GECOST), pp. 1–7. IEEE (2021)
25. Hess, W., Kohler, D., Rapp, H., Andor, D.: Real-time loop closure in 2D LIDAR SLAM. In: 2016 IEEE International Conference on Robotics and Automation (ICRA), Stockholm, Sweden, pp. 1271–1278. IEEE, May 2016, Accessed 01 Sep 2019. http://ieeexplore.ieee.org/document/7487258/
26. Konolige, K., Grisetti, G., Kümmerle, R., Burgard, W., Limketkai, B., Vincent, R.: Efficient sparse pose adjustment for 2D mapping. In: 2010 IEEE/RSJ International Conference on Intelligent Robots and Systems, pp. 22–29, October 2010
27. Kohlbrecher, S., von Stryk, O., Meyer, J., Klingauf, U.: A flexible and scalable SLAM system with full 3D motion estimation. In: 2011 IEEE International Symposium on Safety, Security, and Rescue Robotics, pp. 155–160, November 2011

Developing an Integrated Runtime Verification for Safety and Security of Industrial Robot Inspection System

Elif Degirmenci$^{(\boxtimes)}$ (ID), Yunus Sabri Kırca (ID), Özlem Örnek (ID), Mert Bulut,
Serhat Kahraman, Metin Özkan (ID), and Ahmet Yazıcı (ID)

Eskisehir Osmangazi University, Eskisehir, Türkiye
{edegirmenci,yunussabri.kirca,ozlem.ornek,meozkan,
ayazici}@ogu.edu.tr

Abstract. Robotic systems are increasingly integrated into various industries, including manufacturing, transportation, and healthcare. So, it is essential to identify the vulnerabilities of these systems and take precautions. These systems are vulnerable to cyber-attacks compromising their safety and operations. In this study, we developed an integrated runtime verification for the safety and security of an industrial robot inspection system. Runtime verification is a lightweight technique that involves evaluating the behaviour of a system at runtime. The developed runtime verification system is named MARVer. In the experiments, firstly, the runtime verification is independently for safety and security using MARVer-R. Then, integrated runtime verification is realized to monitor the effects of security attacks on safety. The experiments are evaluated in a TRL5 laboratory environment designed for quality inspection of automotive-body-in-white. Our study highlights the importance of verifying safety and security at runtime.

Keywords: Runtime Verification · Safety · Security Attacks · Robotic Systems · Robot Operating System

1 Introduction

Robotic systems are becoming more widespread in various industries, including manufacturing, assembly, transportation, and healthcare. However, integrating these systems also poses security risks, as they may be susceptible to cyber-attacks that can disrupt their operation and compromise their safety. To address these risks, it is necessary to have reliable tools and technologies in place to safe and secure robotic systems.

Ensuring the tools and technologies safety and security in robotic systems is important since failures of these can cause harm to the environment or humans or any material damage to itself. In this context, verification can ensure that a system meets the requirements. The robotic systems can be verified by different formal verification approaches, such as model checking and Runtime Verification (RV) [1]. Formal verification is a process that involves evaluating whether a software system meets specified requirements

F. Iida et al. (Eds.): TAROS 2023, LNAI 14136, pp. 126–137, 2023.
https://doi.org/10.1007/978-3-031-43360-3_11

and behaves as intended [2]. However, due to the dynamic environment of robotic systems, it is hard to define all states in the model, and this is also leading to a problem known as the state explosion problem [3]. On the other hand, RV is a lightweight technique that evaluates the behavior of a system at runtime [4]. RV is a lightweight formal verification technique since it does not need a complex specification, like model checking. RV includes monitoring and controlling the system with predefined specifications and verifying unexpected situations at runtime. Also, in the literature, Huang et al. [5] state that while performing RV, reliable software components that should provide basic features can be written in a high-level programming language, and "systematic testing" is required interchangeably with "model checking" of the event-driven part. Moreover, Desai A. et al. [6] claim that combinations of software model checking and monitoring of RV can be used to provide a high level of assurance on the operation of robotic systems.

Security attacks can have devastating effects on the safety of industrial systems. A successful security attack on these systems can result in physical damage, environmental hazards, and even loss of life. One of the most well-known examples of security attacks on industrial systems are Stuxnet in 2010, email phishing/malware in 2015 targets to the German steel mill, Havex malware in 2014 targets to energy companies, and Wannacry ransomware targeting Taiwan chipmakers and many others [7]. All these attacks highlighted the importance of implementing effective security measures to protect against cyber threats. So, even highly protected systems need a verification system at runtime for constant monitoring and analysis of the system functioning as intended.

The main contribution of this paper is the development of an integrated RV for the safety and security of the industrial robot inspection system. This study allows monitoring of the effects of security attacks on the safety of robotic arms during operations. The MARVer tool is used for Robot Operating System (ROS) based verification of safety and security. The tool is flexible and can easily integrate new services, and the MARVer user interface provides flexibility in visualizing integrated services' results. Three MARVer services are used; an Online Distance Tracker (ODT), a security attacker, and anomaly detection for evaluating RV. Our experimental results involve three case studies: (1) RV of unexpected object detection approach when the robotic arm encounters an unexpected object, (2) RV of volumetric security attacks on anomaly detection service, and (3) integration of safety and security domains for RV of unexpected object detection of robotic arm behavior under a security attack.

The rest of this paper is as follows. Section 2 presents the literature review for Verification and Validation, RV, on safety and security domains and usage in a robotic system. In Sect. 3, the proposed system details are presented. Section 4 presents the experimental setup and discusses the experimental results. Section 5 summarizes the paper's results and potential future studies.

2 Literature Review

This work relates to the RV of robotic systems in both security and safety domains. This section gives the literature on RV for safety and security. RV is one of the lightweight approaches for verification. RV is effective in detecting a variety of different types of errors, including runtime errors and security vulnerabilities. In the literature, RV is generally used in safety-based applications for ROS [6, 8–11]. Interconnection between

RVs and safety can be clarified by guaranteeing RVs' secure and safe functioning. So, RVs involve considering both the upper and lower levels of the software stack and the external environment in which the robot operates [6]. To be responsive to input from the physical world and other software components, high-level controllers are designed as concurrent event-driven systems. However, testing and debugging these controllers can be challenging due to unpredictable interactions caused by the input scheduling of event handlers. Therefore, model checking is well-suited for verifying this type of software. Yang et al. [9] have described a formal approach for generating safe autonomous decision-making in ROS. They use formal verification as a static verification. In addition, they have explained how to improve existing static verification approaches to verify multi-goal multi-agent decision-making.

Researchers have demonstrated the transition from enhanced static verification to the proposed RV approach. Shivakumar et al. [10] introduced SOTER, a framework applied to multi-robot surveillance, highlighting its efficiency through the incorporation of RV safety modules. SOTER, using the domain-specific language P, enables the development of reactive robotic software and integrated runtime safety systems, providing safety guarantees even with unprotected components. Torfah et al. [11] discussed the application of VerifAI for creating runtime monitors that ensure the safe operation of AI/ML systems, which they illustrated through a case study in autonomous aviation. Further, Desai et al. [6] conducted practical tests to demonstrate the efficacy of a secure drone surveillance system, confirming that the runtime assurance incorporating SOTER ensures safety even when third-party elements malfunction. Lastly, Ferrando et al. [8] introduced ROSMonitoring, a new framework to support RV of ROS-based robotic applications. ROSMonitoring offers high portability across different ROS distributions without reliance on specific formalisms for specification. They validated its effectiveness and scalability through a Mars Curiosity rover simulation. However, there are few security studies, such as ROSRV. ROSRV is a framework for developers to ensure safety by implementing a user-specified access control policy, controlling the system's state and command execution in security problems [5]. In another study, an RV architecture is proposed for the ROS environment under the security attacks targets to the ROS network communication [12].

3   Proposed System

The proposed system is designed to verify safety and security of an industrial robot inspection system in ROS-based environments in real time. It helps identify vulnerabilities and threats in each domain with a holistic perspective at runtime.

3.1   Proposed Workflow for Runtime Verification

The proposed system uses a systematic workflow for integrated RV of robotic system, realizing safety, security and integration of safety and security domains (Fig. 1). This includes initializing MARVer toolchain [13], which can be used for model checking, RV, and several safety/security services. It begins with ROS complaints for robot communication and safety and security services execution. These services are used with

RV. In this study, among other services, three MARVer-S services are used. These are anomaly detection, ODT, and attack injector. The user can configure the RV rules using MARVer-R. After the configuration setting, the RV process is initiated.

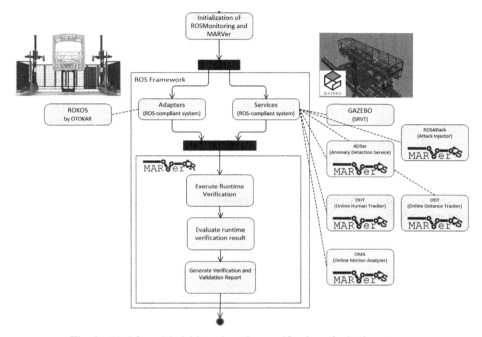

Fig. 1. Workflow: Model-based runtime verification of robotic systems.

3.2 Details of MARVer Tool for Implementation

MARVer is a model-aided RV tool designed to verify ROS-compatible systems (Fig. 2) [13]. It consists of three key subsystems: MARVer-M, MARVer-R, and MARVer-S. MARVer-M is utilized for system modeling and model-checking. MARVer-R is an RV tool designed to simplify the verification and validation process. MARVer-S incorporates services like ODT and Anomaly Detection (ADService), which can be adjusted any robot and specifications.

In this study uses three key services under MARVer-S: ODT, ADService, and ROS attack tool (ROSAttack). The ODT service is used for safety purposes, aiming to determine the minimum distances between the robotic arm and its surroundings. The ADService and ROSAttack services are utilized for security verification at runtime. The ODT uses cylinders to represent the robotic arm and occupancy maps for the environment [13]. And a bounding box approach is employed to improve the computational efficiency of calculating the minimum distances.

Anomaly detection is an important aspect of maintaining system security to detecting malicious events or unexpected behaviors in the system (Fig. 3) [12, 14]. ADService

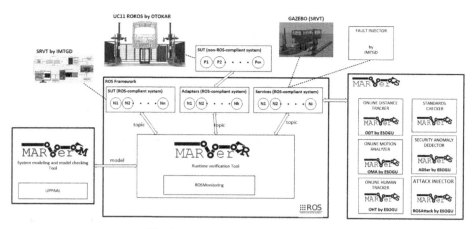

Fig. 2. General structure of MARVer.

is developed under MARVer-S. It uses a statistical approach for anomaly detection, monitors the ROS network and nodes traffic flow and visualizes the network traffic on GUI.

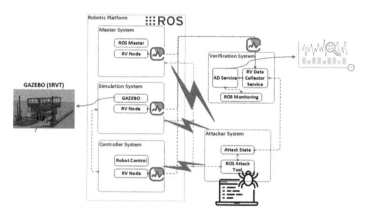

Fig. 3. Runtime verification architecture for anomaly detection service [12].

ROSAttack is another service in MARVer-S used for automated security attacks in this study [15]. The ROSAttack integrates several volumetric attacks and ensures users can automate the attack's schedule and duration using GUI. Users can see the history of the attacks on the user interface. And, this service could evaluate distributed attacks on the network traffic.

4 Experimental

The proposed system is tested for an automated robot inspection cell for quality control of automotive-body-in-white (ROKOS) [16] in the VALU3S project. The details of the experimental setup for the actual ROKOS system and the experimental results are given below.

4.1 Experimental Setup

A TRL5 experimental setup is built in an IFARLab-DIH [17] laboratory environment for the proposed ROKOS system, as given in Fig. 4(a). The laboratory environment comprises a test platform for the body in white, a robotic arm mounted on the mobile robot, and a depth camera that is mounted to a robotic arm (Fig. 4(a)). A robotic arm inspects existence of each part of the test platform using a depth camera. The controller system transmits missions to the robotic arm, which then proceeds to the specified object to perform the assigned tasks. The robotic arm follows the mission plan and navigates around the test platform, utilizing a depth camera to inspect the chassis for any absent components. The robotic arm follows a predefined trajectory during the controlling process. The RV of MARVer-S services (ODT, ADService and ROSAttack) and the resulting effects of security attacks on the robotic arm are realized in this experimental setup.

The MARVer-R interface design simplifies the control and verification mechanism using a single channel to record error outputs during RV. The interface requires configurations and properties created in the "Configuration and Property Files" to apply RV. The Configuration File includes four subheadings for creating the needed configurations: Monitor, Node, Topic, and Oracle. The Property File is divided into Define Property and Define Formula, where the nodes' names are automatically processed. An appropriate form related to types of published data is written. The defined formulas and properties can be saved as XML files and uploaded to the interface for RV. During RV, the uploaded properties monitor faults in the user interface, such as distance limits between the body and the robotic arm or anomaly detection on network/node traffic flow.

4.2 Experimental Results

The study includes three case studies: (1) Online Distance Tracker (ODT) for safety RV, monitoring robotic arm's distance from surrounding objects, (2) RV of anomaly detection during volumetric security attacks, and (3) Integration of safety and security domains, observing robotic arm behavior under security attack. All three cases study full video is given in [18].

In the first case, ODT service for RV is tested when an unexpected object appears near the robotic arm. Normally, the arm follows a set trajectory, controlling the test platform body parts. Encountering an unexpected object, it stops to prevent damage. At the same time, MARVer-R evaluates RV minimum distance requirements via ODT from MARVer-S. ODT tracks the robotic arm, maintaining a safe distance from unexpected objects (Fig. 4(b)). When an unexpected object is placed on the test platform (Fig. 4(c)),

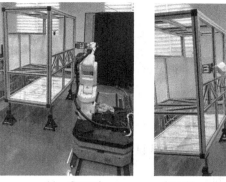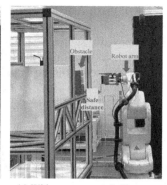

| (a) General perspective | (b) Without an unexpected object | (c) With an unexpected object encountered |

Fig. 4. Robotic arm inspects the automative-body-in-white parts.

the arm stops around 18–20 cm away from it using a camera sensor. ODT alerts if the distance falls below a safe level. After object removal, the arm continues its trajectory.

The MARVer-R user interface provides to monitor the ODT service verification results at runtime. In this case, the study of ODT verified the distance detection approach successfully for helping the ensuring safe distance. If the safe distance limit is exceeded, the text turns red on the MARVer-R user interface, as shown in Fig. 5.

Fig. 5. The MARVer-R runtime verification results for ODT service.

The ODT publishes four distance metrics for the robotic arm, one of which is the camera sensor distance. The robotic arm stops if the camera sensor distance calculated below 20 cm. For other body parts, the safe limit is under 0.5 cm. ODT computes these four metrics during test scenarios to measure minimum distances to surrounding objects.

Figure 6 presents the results of the minimum distances for the robotic arm. The robotic arm doesn't exceed the minimum distance thresholds in a normal scenario (Fig. 6(a)). However, in Fig. 6(b), the robotic arm exceeds these thresholds when encountering an unexpected object during its predefined trajectory.

Between the 85th and 95th seconds of Fig. 6(b), the robot arm exceeds due to an unexpected object encounter. The unexpected object encountered case test scenario (Fig. 6(b)) took longer as the system maintained a safe distance until the unexpected object was removed. Once removed, the robotic arm completed the task. While the normal scenario concluded at the 280th second, the unexpected object added scenario finished closer to the 300th second due to the unexpected object.

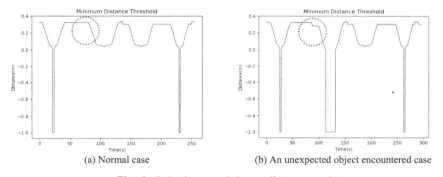

(a) Normal case   (b) An unexpected object encountered case

Fig. 6. Robotic arm minimum distance results.

In the second case study, security domain services RV is tested. ADService is tested under two conditions: normal and node traffic flow under a security attack. This test employs two MARVer-S services: ROSAttack and ADService. ROSAttack conducts automated security attacks on ROS camera node or network traffic. Figure 7(a) shows normal node traffic flow as stable and continuous, while Fig. 7(b) illustrates the effects of a volumetric attack on the ROS node traffic flow, causing a significant drop in communication at the 220th second.

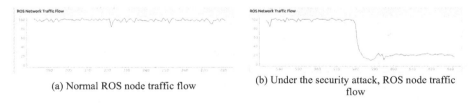

(a) Normal ROS node traffic flow   (b) Under the security attack, ROS node traffic flow

Fig. 7. Anomaly detection service GUI for ROS node traffic flow results.

ADService is designed to identify security issues in the ROS traffic flow. Anomaly detection parameters are set using ADService's GUI, selecting a statistical approach and a sensitivity of 10. Lowering sensitivity could make the system more responsive to minor attacks. ADService sends anomaly detection results to MARVer-R, which receives attack status data from ROSAttack as ground truth for RV. MARVer-R simultaneously reports negative RV results on the user interface (Fig. 8). If the anomaly detection fails or issues a warning in a non-anomalous situation, RV alerts the system with a message like "Property is not satisfied."

Online Monitor
```
The instrumentation is initialized successfully
 >>> Runtime verification setup is READY <<<
In case of any violation, an error message will appear
<< PROPERTY IS NOT SATISFIED >> TIME: 15501.399  CONTENT: adResult: 1 attackState: 0
<< PROPERTY IS NOT SATISFIED >> TIME: 15502.397  CONTENT: adResult: 1 attackState: 0
<< PROPERTY IS NOT SATISFIED >> TIME: 15503.399  CONTENT: adResult: 1 attackState: 0
<< PROPERTY IS NOT SATISFIED >> TIME: 15504.397  CONTENT: adResult: 1 attackState: 0
<< PROPERTY IS NOT SATISFIED >> TIME: 15505.397  CONTENT: adResult: 1 attackState: 0
<< PROPERTY IS NOT SATISFIED >> TIME: 15506.399  CONTENT: adResult: 1 attackState: 0
<< PROPERTY IS NOT SATISFIED >> TIME: 15507.399  CONTENT: adResult: 1 attackState: 0
<< PROPERTY IS NOT SATISFIED >> TIME: 15508.397  CONTENT: adResult: 1 attackState: 0
```

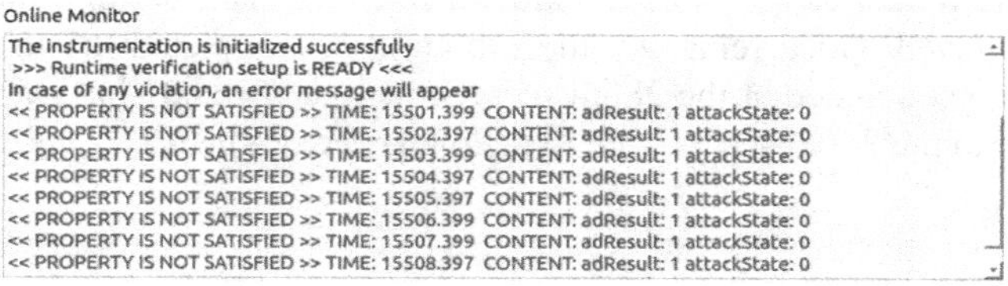

Fig. 8. MARVer-R runtime verification results for anomaly detection service under the security attack.

In the third case study, the security attack effects are tested on the safety of the robotic arm. Security attacks are evaluated on the ROS camera node when the robotic arm encounters an unexpected object. In Fig. 9(a) and Fig. 9(b), red rectangles point out the unexpected object when the automotive body-in-white is in the production process. In a normal situation, the robotic arm stops at a safe distance, as seen in Fig. 9(a) at runtime. For the normal situation, ODT verified that the safe distance works correctly, that the limits are within the threshold, and that there is no warning in Fig. 9(c). However, when the security attacks are started, the robotic arm loses communication with the controller system, which gives tasks to the robotic arm. So, the robotic arm could not communicate to stop at a safe distance or take its next task, and it still tried to finish its last task. And it tries to get inside to check the parts from the upper left body of the chassis. As seen in Fig. 9(b), the robotic arm collided with an unexpected object and entered the test platform, which could endanger its safety. The MARVer-R verification results for ODT under the security attack are shown in Fig. 9(d). The ODT verification result gave a warning about the safe limit being exceeded, as pointed out by the red arrow.

ODT publishes four distance metrics for a robotic arm. The unexpected object detection system takes a lower distance of four for the robotic arm's safety. In the normal system, safe distance limits change, given in Fig. 10(a). If the robotic arm is under security attack, communication with the controller system is lost since heavy network traffic is on ROS. And it is unable to control safe limits simultaneously. Therefore, the robotic arm continued its movement as there was no unexpected object in the way of the task. In Fig. 10(b), the robotic arm's minimum distance data flow is given when an unexpected object is encountered at 80th second, and the robotic arm stops its move. However, in Fig. 10(b), at the same time interval robotic arm, continues its movement at 100th second.

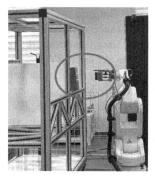

(a) Robotic arm at a safe distance with an unexpected object

(b) Robotic arm hits the unexpected object under the security attack

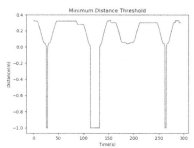

(c) A close scene of runtime verification results for ODT service with an unexpected object

(d) A close scene of runtime verification results for ODT service under the security attack

Fig. 9. Runtime verification of integrated case study results.

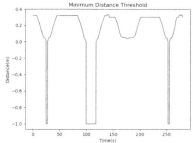

(a) Robotic arm at a safe distance with an unexpected object

(b) Robotic arm hits the unexpected object under the security attack

Fig. 10. The robotic arm's minimum distance results in a normal system and under the security attack.

5 Conclusion

This study investigated an integrated RV approach for ensuring the safety and security of industrial robot inspection systems. Three case studies are evaluated for the runtime verification (RV) on the safety and security of industrial robot inspection systems. In the first case study, the safety of a robotic arm is verified when encountering an unexpected object. The safety RV results of ODT gave a warning if the safe limits were exceeded on MARVer-R, which RV tool. The robotic arm safe distance approach was verified at runtime. The second case study verifies the ROS node-based anomaly detection approach at runtime under volumetric security attacks. The security RV results gave the warning when anomaly detection fails to detect anomalies as security attacks. Lastly, the integration of RV was examined for robotic arms safety under the volumetric security attack. In the integrated case study, the ODT for RV results showed that the RV warns the system even if the robotic arm fails to detect the unexpected object. Our experimental results provide valuable insights into our approach to individually detecting and warning the security and safety risks and highlight the importance of integrated considering verification of safety and security during the runtime of robotic systems.

Overall, our findings demonstrate the potential of RV techniques for ensuring the safety and security of robotic systems and highlight the need for further research and development in this area. In future studies, runtime enforcement should focus on taking immediate actions to correct behavior and enforce system safety situations.

Acknowledgement. This work was supported by the VALU3S project that has received funding from the ECSEL Joint Undertaking (JU) under grant agreement No 876852. The JU receives support from the European Union's Horizon 2020 research and innovation programme and Austria, Czech Republic, Germany, Ireland, Italy, Portugal, Spain, Sweden, Turkey (TUBITAK, under contract no:119N356).

This work is supported by the Scientific and Technical Research Council of Turkey (TUBITAK), Contract No 120N800, project title: "Verification and Validation of Automated Systems' Safety and Security".

The views expressed in this work are the authors' and do not necessarily reflect the views or position of the European Commission. The authors, the VALU3S Consortium, and the ECSEL JU are not responsible for the use which might be made of the information contained in here.

References

1. Farrell, M., Mavrakis, N., Ferrando, A., Dixon, C., Gao, Y.: Formal modelling and runtime verification of autonomous grasping for active debris removal. Front. Robot. AI. **8**, 425 (2022)
2. Gjondrekaj, E., et al.: Towards a formal verification methodology for collective robotic systems. In: Aoki, T., Taguchi, K. (eds.) ICFEM 2012. LNCS, vol. 7635, pp. 54–70. Springer, Heidelberg (2012). https://doi.org/10.1007/978-3-642-34281-3_7
3. Falcone, Y., Jaber, M., Nguyen, T.H., Bozga, M., Bensalem, S.: Runtime verification of component-based systems. In: Barthe, G., Pardo, A., Schneider, G. (eds.) Software Engineering and Formal Methods. SEFM 2011. LNCS, vol. 7041, pp. 204–220. Springer, Berlin (2011). https://doi.org/10.1007/978-3-642-24690-6_15
4. Bartocci, E., Falcone, Y. (eds.): Lectures on Runtime Verification. LNCS, vol. 10457. Springer, Cham (2018). https://doi.org/10.1007/978-3-319-75632-5
5. Huang, J., et al.: ROSRV: Runtime verification for robots. In: International Conference on Runtime Verification (2014)
6. Desai, A., Ghosh, S., Seshia, S.A., Shankar, N., Tiwari, A.: SOTER: a runtime assurance framework for programming safe robotics systems. In: 2019 49th Annual IEEE/IFIP International Conference on Dependable Systems and Networks (DSN) (2019)

7. Alladi, T., Chamola, V., Zeadally, S.: Industrial control systems: Cyberattack trends and countermeasures. Comput. Commun. **155**, 1–8 (2020)
8. Ferrando, A., Cardoso, R.C., Fisher, M., Ancona, D., Franceschini, L., Mascardi, V.: ROS-Monitoring: a runtime verification framework for ROS. In: Mohammad, A., Dong, X., Russo, M. (eds.) Towards Autonomous Robotic Systems: 21st Annual Conference, TAROS 2020, Nottingham, UK, September 16, 2020, Proceedings, pp. 387–399. Springer, Cham (2020). https://doi.org/10.1007/978-3-030-63486-5_40
9. Yang, Y., Holvoet, T.: Generating Safe Autonomous Decision-Making in ROS. arXiv preprint arXiv:2209.14042. (2022)
10. Shivakumar, S., Torfah, H., Desai, A., Seshia, S.A.: SOTER on ROS: a run-time assurance framework on the robot operating system. In: Deshmukh, J., Ničković, D. (eds.) Runtime Verification. RV 2020. LNCS, vol. 12399, pp. 184–194. Springer, Cham (2020). https://doi.org/10.1007/978-3-030-60508-7_10
11. Torfah, H., Junges, S., Fremont, D.J., Seshia, S.A.: Formal analysis of AI-based autonomy: from modeling to runtime assurance. In: Feng, L., Fisman, D. (eds.) Runtime Verification. RV 2021. LNCS, vol. 12974, pp. 311–330. Springer, Cham (2021). https://doi.org/10.1007/978-3-030-88494-9_19
12. Kirca, Y.S., et al.: Runtime verification for anomaly detection of robotic systems security. Machines. **11**, 166 (2023)
13. Guclu, E., Örnek, Ö., Ozkan, M., Yazici, A., Demirci, Z.: An online distance tracker for verification of robotic systems' safety. Sensors. **23**, 2986 (2023)
14. Chatterjee, A., Ahmed, B.S.: IoT anomaly detection methods and applications: a survey. Internet Things. **19**, 100568 (2022)
15. Kirca, Y.S., Değirmenci, E., Yazici, A., Özkan, M.: ROS based attack tool for verification of robotic system security (2022)
16. Kanak, A., et al.: Verification and validation of an automated robot inspection cell for automotive body-in-white: a use case for the VALU3S ECSEL project. Open Res. Europe **1**, 115 (2021)
17. Eskisehir Osmangazi university intelligent factory and robotics laboratory. https://ifarlab.ogu.edu.tr/
18. ESOGU corner case youtube video. https://youtu.be/hj8ekJUY50E (2023)

Collaborative and Service Robotics

Sonification of Ionising Radiation Data for Robot Operators

Andrew West[✉] ⓘ, Mia Chapman, and Barry Lennox ⓘ

Department of Electrical and Electronic Engineering, The University of Manchester,
Manchester M13 9PL, UK
andrew.west@manchester.ac.uk

Abstract. Deploying robots in extreme environments brings many hazards which an operator must avoid during teleoperation. In a nuclear setting, intensity of ionising radiation (alpha, beta, gamma, neutron) is not only important to monitor from a safety perspective, but also to protect robot systems which are susceptible to radiation induced damage. Therefore, robot operators must avoid ionising radiation whilst managing many other threats and information streams simultaneously. This work provides a non-visual method to communicate radiation dose rate, by imitating the clicking sound of a Geiger counter for the operator, using affordable and ubiquitous hardware. The operator is then free to use visual cues to monitor other important aspects. The system accurately emulates realistic clicks due to stochastic radioactive decay rather than use a steady repetitive tempo, with average rate of audio events governed by measured radiation dose rate on a remote robot. This system readily aids an operator to identify and avoid regions of elevated radiation intensity against background, and can be adopted by any ROS compatible robot platform.

Keywords: Teleoperation · Nuclear · ROS · Robot Operating System · Human-Robot Interaction

1 Introduction

Operators of robots in hazardous environments must contend with many pressures, often juggling many different control aspects and managing multiple possible threats to the robot platform. A clear case study from the nuclear sector is that of the Quince robot deployed into Fukushima Unit 2, to perform inspection missions as part of the initial response. Operators were faced with managing thermal stress on the motors, navigation, obstacle avoidance, tether management, damage assessment to the facility structure, image capture, and radiation dose monitoring and management. In total, operators had at least 5 camera feeds

This research was supported by UK Research and Innovation via the ALACANDRA project EP/V026941/1. BL acknowledges support from the Royal Academy of Engineering, UK, CiET1819\\13.

and as many readout values to manage simultaneously, including radiation dose rate from a detector mounted on the robot [9]. For operators deploying robots into hazardous nuclear environments they are likely overburdened with many simultaneous responsibilities, the majority relying on visual information.

Damage due to ionising radiation limits the effective lifetime of robot platforms in nuclear environments. For the previously mentioned Quince deployments, a limit of 100 Gy was chosen, meeting the mission requirements but also corresponds to the total ionising dose for common electronic components [8,12]. Though robots can be given autonomous behaviours to avoid radiation [15], for teleoperation by a human operator they must constantly monitor the dose rate and avoid unnecessary exposure. As the detector is on the robot, in a remote location, operators have been limited to only numeric value readout to assess dose rate, they cannot rely on the auditory cue of clicks to signify dose rate or a change in rate. A microphone on the robot could stream these clicks if the detector emits them, however, not all detectors provide this, such as the electronic personal dosimeters deployed into Fukushima [9], and it would still not be as clear as having the clicks emanating from hardware near the operator. If these units do provide an audible output, typically it is only for alarm conditions a set threshold value.

To alleviate the visual burden on operators, this work presents sonification of numerical radiation dose rate values, and converts them into physically realistic Geiger Counter like clicks. Radiation dose rate values are communicated via the robot operating system (ROS) [10] using standardised messages [13], and are interpreted by the hardware presented as short click-like chirps from a piezoelectric buzzer along with a flash of light from an LED.

Geiger counter clicks are a socially pervasive auditory cue, inherently signifying danger due to the association with ionising radiation. Though the same modality has been used to map other input parameters to a rate of chirps [4,7], the assessment for ionising radiation itself has not been widely explored. In Virtual Reality settings, it has been shown that the recognisable click of a Geiger counter is more effective than abstract sounds in reducing operator stress and increasing system usability, specifically in a robot teleoperation setting [1].

Typically for sonification, tempo is at a set rate proportional to the intensity of a measurand, for example the rear parking sensor of a car where the time between auditory icons is consistent, only changing with distance. However, this is in contrast to a true Geiger counter which has randomly occurring clicks, leading to a discrepancy between the expected behaviour and mimicked behaviour. This work differentiates itself from previous work by conveying radiation dose rate information via the recognisable stochastic clicks of a detector, and using dedicated ROS enabled hardware to generate realistic clicks, rather than use an audio or MIDI track [3], for remotely deployed robotics.

2   Hardware

To achieve realistic click like sounds, a piezoelectric buzzer is activated at 400 Hz for 4 ms duration via pulse width modulated square wave. This delivers a convincing sound reminiscent of a Geiger counter, though pitch and duration can be altered to preference. It should be stated that the shorter the chirp duration, the more pulses per second the system is capable of communicating as individual events. There is also an LED which flashes in sympathy with the buzzer, as there is a hardware switch to mute the buzzer if the operator desires, with LED colour changing if in the mute state.

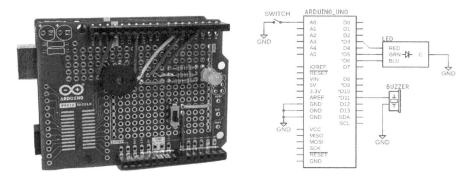

Fig. 1. Photograph of sonification hardware board mounted on an Arduino Uno (left). The circuit diagram (right) consists of a piezoelectric buzzer, tri-colour LED, and switch.

To control the buzzer, LED, and communicate with ROS, an Arduino Uno was selected. The Arduino Uno offers a ubiquitous, simple, well documented platform, and has ROS compatibility via ROSSerial. The additional components are connected via a daughter board, hosting the buzzer, tri-colour LED and switch as shown in Fig. 1. These are in a trivial arrangement which is easily replicated.

Algorithm 1 shows how the hardware uses simple internal timers to manage the intervals between random chirps and how new time intervals are generated. Once the time elapsed since the last chirp is greater than the time interval, the hardware emits a chirp and LED flash and generates a new time interval. The calculation of random intervals is explained in the next section. The microcontroller runs a continuous looping function until power off. Communication to the external ROS system is performed during every loop, with the ROSSerial link achieved over simple USB cable to a host PC.

Algorithm 1: Psuedocode of clicker hardware, with steps to generate random intervals in response to new radiation intensity observations.

Function GenerateRandomInterval(r):
  U = RandomNum()
  t = InverseTransformSample(U, r)
  return t

Function Loop():
  PerformROSUpdates()
  if *RadiationUpdate* **then**
    r = RadiationRateObservation()
    t = GenerateRandomInterval(r)
    Reset(*TimeElapsed*)
  end
  if *TimeElapsed* $\geq t$ **then**
    ChirpAndFlash()
    t = GenerateRandomInterval(r)
    Reset(*TimeElapsed*)
  end

3   Method

To generate stochastic clicks, rather than use fixed rate, it is necessary to consider the physical behaviour of radioactive decay. The rate of events measured by a detector is proportional to the intensity of ionising radiation (alpha, beta, gamma, neutron), however, not with a fixed time interval between events. Instead, timing between events will fluctuate due to the random nature of radioactive decay, but over a number of events yields an average value proportional to intensity. Typically, a radiation detector will present this averaged data in counts per second (cps) alongside any calibrated values such as Sv/hr, with an integration time on the order of seconds. This work takes the averaged value as measured by a real detector, and converts that back into randomly distributed click events, mimicking radioactive decay.

The probability distribution of times between events in a Geiger counter is expressed as an exponential distribution [5]. The average rate values, r in counts per second, are converted into randomly timed chirps, by sampling from an exponential distribution shown in Eq. 1.

$$P_{(t)} = \frac{1}{r}e^{-r} \tag{1}$$

$$t = -\frac{1}{r}\ln(1 - U) \tag{2}$$

Unfortunately, the Arduino Random package samples from a uniform distribution (U), therefore, inverse transform sampling is used to convert from a uniform distribution to an exponential distribution via Eq. 2. Once a chirp has been completed, a new random value is sampled from the uniform distribution (normalised to between $[0, 1)$), U, converted into a time interval, t, and the microcontroller waits to then chirp again. The counts per second value, r, is typically updated at 1 Hz from the remote radiation detector.

In the hypothetical scenario where the robot goes from a low dose area to a high dose area, possibly due to shielding materials or a collimated source, the dose rate can increase dramatically. However, the time interval for the next chirp may be long, and the operator is therefore left unaware of the new rate as the microcontroller is idle. Upon receiving a new rate measurement, as time intervals are independent of each other, it can be recalculated using the same exponential probability distribution in Eq. 1.

4   Results

To demonstrate the response from the hardware, both in the generation of stochastic time intervals and the response to measured radiation intensity, audio recordings were made of the hardware during operation. The system was connected to a ROS compatible PC, which published radiation_msgs/DoseRate messages on a topic subscribed to by the hardware. This rate, given in counts per second is what is interpreted and converted into stochastic click events.

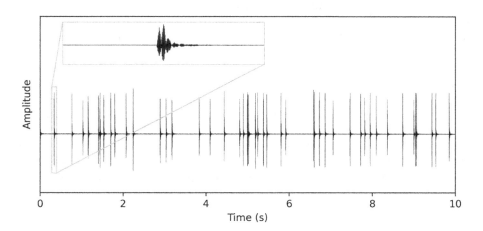

Fig. 2. Audio track of Geiger counter like click events generated by hardware, based on an average rate of 5.0 counts per seconds, provided via ROS. The inset region highlights the audio response from a single event.

Figure 2 shows an audio track of randomly distributed click events for an average rate of 5.0 cps, it is clear that the system does not produce events at a fixed rate, rather the delay and bunching expected of random radioactive decay is present.

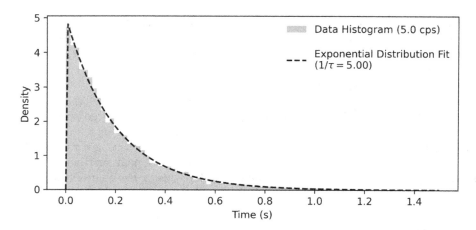

Fig. 3. Histogram of ≈15000 time intervals generated via inverse transformation sampling with an average rate of 5.0 counts per second, with a fit to the data using a true exponential distribution represented by a dashed line.

Though events do not have fixed time intervals, it must be assessed whether the use of inverse transformation sampling, and the uniform random distribution generation of the Arudino microcontroller, is suitable enough to reproduce a reasonable approximation of an exponential distribution as would be seen in radioactive decay. Figure 3 shows a histogram of generated time intervals, using the same average rate of 5.0 cps as Fig. 2, with an exponential distribution fitted to the data. The mean time interval for the raw data is around 0.2 sec, which is in line with 5.0 Hz average rate. This is further corroborated by the exponential fit, which reports a rate parameter $\tau \approx 0.2$ (the rate parameter is not to be confused with rate of events) equivalent to an expected mean value of 5.0 Hz.

This shows that the hardware is capable of mimicking the exponential distribution expected from radioactive decay, and therefore Geiger counter events. Furthermore, the average rate is the same as that reported by any radiation detection instruments reporting via ROS. Figure 4 shows how the number of click events will correctly increase as the rate increases, whilst remaining stochastically distributed.

To assess the utility of the device for a robot operator, a mock inspection task was undertaken. As a proxy for ionising radiation a partially collimated upward facing light sensor was used, made ROS compatible via ROSSerial, with ambient light providing an analogous background radiation level. Though reporting light intensity, the experiment had these interpreted as radiation intensity, mapping luminance to an increase in counts per second. Figure 5a shows the lightmeter attached to a Clearpath Jackal Uncrewed Ground Vehicle (UGV), a platform previously used for nuclear inspection [11,14]. In a small indoor arena, a lamp was fitted to one region of the arena to mimic a more intense radiation source. The operator had the sonification hardware connected to a PC, with remote ROS

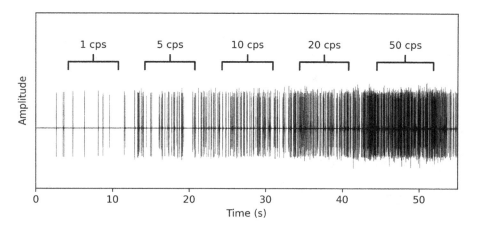

Fig. 4. Audio track of click events with varying rate in counts per second.

connection via WiFi to the robot platform. This PC also provided Lidar scan visualisation, SLAM (Simultaneous Localisation and Mapping) maps, camera streams and other visual information typically utilised by a robot operator. A schematic representation of the experiment is shown in Fig. 5b.

Whilst the robot was teleoperated, it was clear from the increase in clicks which region had increased "activity" compared to background levels observed elsewhere in the arena. This is a known benefit with sonification, to aid in navigation by providing another data stream for control and wayfinding [4]. This demonstrates how the device can be successfully used in conjunction with a remote robot to aid in identification and avoidance of regions with elevated radiation intensity. This experiment also highlighted some improvements which could be made to future iterations.

5   Discussion

The hardware has been demonstrated to be ROS compatible, and correctly produces click events in the same stochastic manner as would be seen for real radiation. This provides a robot operator with a realistic hardware recreation of a detector response as would be experienced if in the radioactive environment itself. Further study is necessary to ascertain whether the more realistic random events are more advantageous over a fixed pattern. Moreover, previous work usually provide audio stimulation through headphones or speakers, the use of an imitation click may improve or exacerbate user performance, particularly in high risk environments as those found in the nuclear sector.

Upper and lower thresholds on the rate could remove ambiguity whether an operator needs to take heed of distracting random intermittent clicks which would be present due to simple background radiation. These intermittent but unimportant auditory icons may be a distraction [6], or could contribute toward

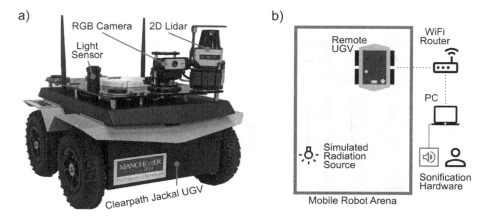

Fig. 5. Photograph of robot hardware and experimental schematic, a) Clearpath Jackal UGV with attached sensors including upward facing light sensor, b) schematic of the experiment with an operator piloting the robot remotely.

"alarm fatigue" a known phenomena in the medical sector [2]. Below a certain value, for example twice the expected background rate, the device could be made silent, removing the need for the operator to concern themselves with radiation dose rate. Furthermore, the upper limit could be made to produce a solid tone, or other pattern that distinguishes itself from the random clicks of a normal Geiger counter, representing a safety threshold may be approaching or reached.

From a user comfort perspective, volume control on the clicks by way of a simple potentiometer could be beneficial, whilst maintaining the flashing LED as a redundant indication. In this work, a tri-colour LED was utilised, changing from a white flash to a red flash when the device was fully muted. The device could be augmented with a readout value (e.g. a small LCD screen), providing more accurate information stream without the need for additional hardware or utilising important screen space for a visual indicator.

The code and circuit schematics for this work are available on GitHub via: https://github.com/EEEManchester/GeigerCounterClicker.

6   Conclusion

This work uses a hardware solution to replicate Geiger counter like clicks which would be heard from detectors in nuclear environments. By simulating click events on hardware this allows for remote radiation detectors, primarily deployed on mobile robots, to be audible to an operator rather than requiring a dedicated visual readout of the radiation intensity. The device is ROS compatible, and has been demonstrated to reproduce the stochastic time intervals as exhibited by radioactive decay, based on a reported average value from a remote instrument. This hardware solution can remove a visual data stream from already over-burdened robot operators, to improve their performance in extreme environments, whilst leveraging the association of Geiger counter like clicks with ionising radiation intensity.

References

1. Bremner, P., Mitchell, T.J., McIntosh, V.: The impact of data sonification in virtual reality robot teleoperation. Front. Virt. Reality **3** (2022). https://doi.org/10.3389/frvir.2022.904720
2. Cvach, M.: Monitor alarm fatigue: an integrative review. Biomed. Instrument. Technol. **46**(4), 268–277 (2012). https://doi.org/10.2345/0899-8205-46.4.268
3. Dubus, G., Bresin, R.: A systematic review of mapping strategies for the sonification of physical quantities. PLoS ONE **8**(12), e82491 (2013). https://doi.org/10.1371/journal.pone.0082491
4. Hermann, T., Hunt, A., Neuhoff, J.G.: The Sonification Handbook. Logos Verlag, Berlin (2011)
5. Knoll, G.F.: Radiation Detection and Measurement, 4th edn. Wiley, Hoboken (2010)
6. Lei, Z., Ma, S., Li, H., Yang, Z.: The impact of different types of auditory warnings on working memory. Front. Psychol. **13** (2022). https://doi.org/10.3389/fpsyg.2022.780657
7. Ludovico, L.A., Presti, G.: The sonification space: A reference system for sonification tasks. Int. J. Hum.-Comput. Stud. **85**, 72–77 (2016). https://doi.org/10.1016/j.ijhcs.2015.08.008
8. Nagatani, K., et al.: Gamma-ray irradiation test of electric components of rescue mobile robot quince. In: 2011 IEEE International Symposium on Safety, Security, and Rescue Robotics, pp. 56–60. IEEE, November 2011. https://doi.org/10.1109/ssrr.2011.6106756
9. Nagatani, K., et al.: Emergency response to the nuclear accident at the Fukushima Daiichi nuclear power plants using mobile rescue robots. J. Field Robot. **30**(1), 44–63 (2013). https://doi.org/10.1002/rob.21439
10. Quigley, M., et al.: ROS: an open-source robot operating system. In: ICRA Workshop on Open Source Software, vol. 3, p. 5. Kobe, Japan (2009)
11. Tsitsimpelis, I., et al.: Simultaneous, robot-compatible γ-ray spectroscopy and imaging of an operating nuclear reactor. IEEE Sens. J. **21**(4), 5434–5443 (2021). https://doi.org/10.1109/jsen.2020.3035147
12. West, A., Knapp, J., Lennox, B., Walters, S., Watts, S.: Radiation tolerance of a small COTS single board computer for mobile robots. Nucl. Eng. Technol. (2021). https://doi.org/10.1016/j.net.2021.12.007
13. West, A., Smith, A.: ROS messages for nuclear sensing. In: Proceedings of Decommissioning Environmental Science and Remote Technology 2021 (DESD/RRSD 2021), pp. 142–145. American Nuclear Society, November 2021
14. West, A., et al.: Use of gaussian process regression for radiation mapping of a nuclear reactor with a mobile robot. Sci. Rep. **11**(1) (2021). https://doi.org/10.1038/s41598-021-93474-4
15. West, A., Wright, T., Tsitsimpelis, I., Groves, K., Joyce, M.J., Lennox, B.: Real-time avoidance of ionising radiation using layered costmaps for mobile robots. Front. Robot. AI 9, March 2022. https://doi.org/10.3389/frobt.2022.862067

Automating a Telepresence Robot for Human Detection, Tracking, and Following

Nasiru Aboki$^{(\boxtimes)}$, Ilche Georgievski , and Marco Aiello

University of Stuttgart, 70569 Stuttgart, Germany
{nasiru.aboki,ilche.georgievski,marco.aiello}@iaas.uni-stuttgart.de

Abstract. The operation of a telepresence robot as a service robot has gained wide attention in robotics. The recent COVID-19 pandemic has boosted its use for medical uses, allowing patients to interact while avoiding the risk of contagion. While telepresence robots are designed to have a human operator that controls them, their sensing and actuation abilities can be used to achieve higher levels of autonomy. One desirable ability, which takes advantage of the mobility of a telepresence robot, is to recognize people and the space in which they operate. With the ultimate objective to assist individuals in office spaces, we propose an approach for rendering a telepresence robot autonomous with real-time, indoor human detection and pose classification, with consequent chaperoning of the human. We validate the approach through a series of experiments involving an Ohmni Telepresence Robot, using a standard camera for vision and an additional Lidar sensor. The evaluation of the robot's performance and comparison with the state of the art shows promise of the feasibility of using such robots as office assistants.

Keywords: Service-Oriented Robotic Systems · Autonomous Navigation · ROS · Service Robots · Human-Robot Interaction

1 Introduction

Social service robots are becoming increasingly accepted and used in workplaces and even homes. They have been integrated into living environments to perform various tasks, such as healthcare [9], energy saving [7], transportation [28], infotainment [25], smart home assistance [10], privacy awareness in offices [6], site inspection [20], and task planning in crowded environments [13]. For a social service robot to assist humans, it needs to have sufficient perception abilities to recognize the state of the world it is acting in, and actuating abilities to support the human or even take over some tasks.

Telepresence robots as social service robots are increasingly being used in the context of social interactions and assisting humans by enhancing the sense of (co-)presence via social robot mediation [1]. Telepresence robots are primarily

Partially supported by the German Academic Exchange Service (DAAD) and the Petroleum Technology Development Fund (PTDF) Nigeria.

© The Author(s), under exclusive license to Springer Nature Switzerland AG 2023
F. Iida et al. (Eds.): TAROS 2023, LNAI 14136, pp. 150–161, 2023.
https://doi.org/10.1007/978-3-031-43360-3_13

used as social agents by connecting people that cannot be physically in the same place, through videoconferencing and navigation abilities [1]. When mobility is required, such as healthcare visits, factory excursions, and office meetings, a telepresence robot can provide a physical presence for a remote participant. The participant teleoperates the robot in real-time by navigating it and using its cameras, microphones, and speakers to interact with the people near the robot.

More though seems that can be achieved with the control of a telepresence robot. Let us consider the Ohmni Telepresence Robot, a modern and physically appealing robot that is easily acceptable for social interactions [12] and is modular and easily extendable. Zand et al. improve the control of this robot with the aid of a mobile application on a smartphone [27]. This solves the initial constraint of controlling the robot with only a desktop application that confines the user to a PC thereby limiting mobility and the ability to control the robot when on the move. Also, the mobile application enables the user to take advantage of the gyroscope and accelerometer on their smartphone to aid in gesture-based control of the robot. Fitter et al. add a robotic arm to the Ohmni Telepresence Robot [4]. The arm is used to improve non-verbal communication with the aid of gestures, through gesture-based manipulation of the robotic arm by a human via onscreen, dial-based, and skeletal tracking methods. However, to the best of our knowledge, no work has been done to render the Ohmni Telepresence Robot autonomous. More generally, scarce are the works that make telepresence robots autonomous by giving them the ability to perceive their environment and be localized therein using multimodal sensing, thereby allowing the robots to independently determine their trajectory in order to perform tasks.

Thus, we propose an approach to automating a telepresence robot to improve its non-verbal social interactions with humans by implementing human detection, pose estimation, tracking, and following features that are independent of a human teleoperator. In particular, (1) we propose a system design of software components optimized for the Robotic Operating System and can be distributed on more than one processing unit; (2) we propose an algorithm that enables a telepresence robot to DEtect, TRAck and FOllow (DETRAFO) a person with the aid of our system design; (3) we implement all software components of our system on the Ohmni Telepresence Robot; (4) we experimentally evaluate the system in our own living lab and show that the Ohmni Telepresence Robot is able to autonomously navigate the entire course with 95% effectiveness and 98% efficiency while following a human, and with reasonable use of processing power for object recognition; and (5) we compare our approach with other approaches to detection, tracking, and following humans and show that our approach offers advantages in terms of consistent human detection, a smooth robot trajectory, and efficient path navigation.

The remainder of the paper is organized as follows. Section 2 lists and discusses the state of the art in related work. The system design, hardware setup, and DETRAFO algorithm are described in Sect. 3. The empirical evaluation is presented in Sect. 4. Section 5 is a discussion on our observations while carrying out the experiments, while concluding remarks are contained in Sect. 6.

2 State of the Art

Service robots have been used in various environments to assist humans with daily tasks at home, in an office, in a hospital, at a restaurant, in a supermarket, and in many other domains [18]. A component of supporting and collaborating with humans is the ability to detect and follow a person. The effectiveness and efficiency of DETRAFO a person by a robot are affected by several conditions, such as the topography of the environment, whether it is indoor or outdoor, the type of sensors used, the individual's distance from the robot [28], lighting conditions [21], available (local) computational resources [9,18], and also the number of dynamic objects in the environment.

An orthogonal but relevant aspect to classify DETRAFO approaches is the intended use of robots. Many previous works focus on a generic goal (e.g., [5,14,16–18,23,26]), while other examples are tailored to specific usages, such as office assistant [6], nurse assistant [9], social companion [21], video surveillance [15,20], and transportation [28]. Some existing algorithms require that a specific person be tracked within the field of perception of the robot using skeletal detection [9], face detection [18], color tag detection [14], or leg detection [26]. Others track a random person using a bounding box [5], leg detection [18], angle detection [21], or a 3D Point Cloud Human detection [20]. Some detection or position estimation algorithms require the individual to carry a device with radio frequency, such as RFID, WiFi Received Signal Strength Indication (RSSI), or Bluetooth RSSI [17]. High computational costs of implementation too can affect the overall performance of driving a robot as performance degradation can lead to a lag or start-stop following behavior of the robot, as observed in face recognition detection in the work presented in [18]. Also, computational costs are tied to battery life which in turn can affect the overall experience of the system.

Human tracking is usually done with the aid of a depth sensor, such as an Infra-red (IR) sensor, Laser-Range Finder (LFR), and Light Detection and Ranging (Lidar), so as to determine the distance between the robot and the target human. The use of an IR sensor to determine range is cheap but performs poorly (e.g. [20]). Knowing the range between a robot and a human is essential for the following functionality [26]. Also, the change in angular and linear velocities of the robot can be dependent on the distance between the robot and the human.

Table 1 shows a comparison and classification of related works, including this work, where we use the following abbreviations: Person Detection and Following Method (PDAFM), Maximum Range For Detection (MRFD), Sharp Turn Test (STT), Person Tracked in Motion or Standing (PTIMOS), and Purpose of Usage (POU). One can observe that our work is the only one that focuses on the Ohmni Telepresence Robot and on offices. We share a bounding box as a detection mechanism with [5], and our approach is in the minority of approaches where PTIMOS is random. Our approach to MRFD and STT is comparable to other works. Finally, our system design is modular, enabling the robot not only to operate using a composition of services but also to be easily adapted or extended with new functionality due to its loose coupling. For example, our system can be also applied to specific person detection if a suitable detection service is

Table 1. Characteristics and properties of the DETRAFO approaches.

Study	Robot	PDAFM	MRFD	STT	PTIMOS	POU
[18]	Prototype	Leg Det.	5.6 m, 240°	✓	Random	Generic
[18]	Prototype	Face Det.	3.5 m, 57°	X	Specific	Generic
[15]	Prototype	Blob Detection		X	Specific	Surveillance
[16]	Turtlebot2 (TurtlebotRex)	IR Beacon Det.	8 m, 60°	✓	Specific	Generic
[16]	Turtlebot2 (TurtlebotRex)	AR Marker Det.	8 m, 60°	✓	Specific	Generic
[14]	Simulated	Clothes Color Det.	6 m, 57°	✓	Specific	Generic
[28]	Prototype	Point Cloud Human Det.	2.5 m, 270°	✓	Random	Transport
[20]	Prototype	3D Point Cloud Human Det.	3.5 m, 57°	✓	Random	Surveillance
[5]	Ceci Telepresence	Bounding Box	8 m, 60°	✓	Random	Generic
[23]	ActivMedia Pioneer P3-AT	Sensor Fusion Based Det.	5 m, 60° 270°	✓	Specific	Generic
[21]	Adept Mobile Pioneer LX	Following Angle Det.	0° 30° 60°	✓	Specific	Social
[8]	Prototype	Color Tag Det.	4 m	✓	Specific	Generic
[17]	Prototype	Bluetooth RSSI and IMU		✓	Specific	Generic
[26]	Dr. Robot Jaguar 4 × 4 wheel	Leg Det. With Sensor Fusion	5.6 m, 90° 270°	✓	Specific	Generic
[9]	Prototype	Skeletal Det.	3.8 m, 57°	✓	Specific	Nursing
This work	Ohmni Telepresence	Human Bounding Box Det.	3.6 m, 140°	✓	Random	Office

integrated into the system. Another advantage is that the service-oriented design of the system promises scalability. Nevertheless, while our focus is on offices, the robot's tracking capabilities are generic and can be utilized in other use cases.

3 System Design

The system we propose uses the Ohmni Telepresence Robot which was initially built for the sole purpose of telepresence, Fig. 2. The robot has a Baselink or Baselink Controller which houses an AAEON UP Board CPU, 1 GB RAM, 16 GB Storage, USB Expansion Base, Wireless Modem, Ethernet Port, and many other peripherals which are wired to the robot. Given our application, we use the extension opportunity to add a LIDAR to the robotic platform. A customized version of Linux called OhmniOS is installed. We based our system design upon the Robotic Operating System (ROS) [24]. Resorting to ROS has advantages in the modularity and portability of the solution.

3.1 The DETRAFO Algorithm

Algorithm 1 shows the algorithm for detection, tracking, and following a human target. The algorithm requires as input, streams of data from the camera and Lidar sensors so as to generate values to drive the orchestration of the robot. Since we assume object detection from image frames and we aim at identifying a human within the image frame, we need to set a threshold as a truth value for positive human detection. An offset or offset angle is an angle of deviation from a defined central position, in this case, it is the horizontal mid-point of the field of view of the camera. We can use the offset angle as the angle at which a human is tracked from the center of the robot. To detect the offset angle of a human based on the midpoint of the camera's field of view, we can compute the angle

Algorithm 1. DETRAFO

Require: *Object*   ▷ detected object
Require: *goal_angle*   ▷ offset angle
Require: *goal_dist*   ▷ person distance
Require: *msg.y msg.z*   ▷ Odometry published messages
Require: *Twist*()   ▷ differential drive messages
   speed ← *Twist*()
   goal_angle ← *msg.y*   ▷ our calculated value
   goal_dist ← *msg.z*   ▷ data from laser scanner
   while True **do**
      if *Object* > .85 **then**   ▷ person probability
         Object ← *person*
      end if
   end while
   function *RobotMotion*
      if *goal_angle* > 7 **then**
         speed.angular.z ← $\frac{goal\_angle}{128}$ ▷ Rotate clockwise
      else if *goal_angle* > -7 **then**
         speed.angular.z ← $\frac{goal\_angle}{128}$ ▷ Rotate anticlockwise
      else
         speed.angular.z ← 0.0
         if *goal_dist* > 1 *and goal_dist* < 6 **then**
            speed.linear.x ← $\frac{goal\_dist}{11}$ ▷ Move forward
            if *speed.linear.x* > 0.4 **then**
               speed.linear.x ← 0.4   ▷ Limit linear speed
            else if *goal_dist* < 0.6 **then**
               speed.linear.x ← −0.15   ▷ Move backward
            end if
         else
            if *speed.linear.x* <= 0 **then**
               speed.linear.x ← 0
            else *speed.linear.x* ← *speed.linear.x* − 0.04   ▷ Stop
            end if
      end if
   end function

---

in the camera frames corresponding to the pixel position of the image. In other words, the image is mapped within a bounding box to the field of view of the camera. The offset angle, considering the horizontal field of view of the Ohmni Super camera is 140°, is given by $offset\_angle = \frac{140}{2} - camera\_angle$ where $camera\_angle = \frac{center\_x \times 140}{640}$ and $center\_x = xmin + \frac{(xmax - xmin)}{2}$. $center\_y$ is defined analogously. $xmin$ and $ymin$ are coordinates of the top left corner of the detected bounding box and $xmax$ and $ymax$ of the bottom right corner.

The robot has two tasks, to orient and to move. The Orient task performs a motion so as to align the root to the target human by rotating either clockwise or anticlockwise. So, it has two sub-tasks: rotate clockwise and rotate anticlockwise. The Move task has three sub-tasks: go forward, go backward, and stop.

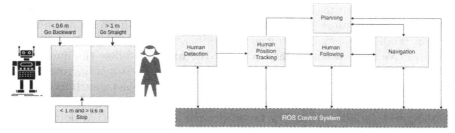

(a) Rules for robot's actions.   (b) Overview of the system architecture.

Fig. 1. Design details of the proposed system.

To enable the robot to perform these tasks, we can make use of the linear and angular velocities of the left and right wheels on the robot's Baselink. We assume both linear and angular velocities can be expressed in all three dimensions, that is, (x, y, z). The tasks are determined by the value of the offset angle. If the offset angle exceeds the margin range of values between $-7°$ and $7°$ in either direction, the robot will orient left or right towards a target human using either its left or right differential drives. If the value is a negative degree, the robot rotates in an anticlockwise direction; if it is a positive value, the robot rotates in a clockwise direction. If the offset angle is within the margin range, the robot is aligned toward the person and can start moving considering the distance to the human calculated using the Lidar. The robot goes forward if the length exceeds the safe distance, which we configure to be one meter. If the length is less than the safe distance and exceeds the critical distance of 0.6 m, the robot stops at its location. The robot moves backward if a person is at a distance less than the critical distance to itself. Figure 1a illustrates the definition of movement rules considering the robot's distance from a person. The threshold angles and the optimal linear and angular velocities of the robot were experimentally determined.

3.2 Software Architecture

The main components of our system are Human Detection, Position Tracking, Human Following, and Navigation. The Human Detection component is responsible for collecting image frames and detecting a human from those image frames. The Position Tracking component is where the information about the detected human is accepted and used to further determine the human's position in relation to the position and orientation of the robot. The Human Following component is the point where the distance of the robot arrives as input and is used to determine the actions the robot should take. The Navigation component is responsible not only for the localization and environment mapping but also robot's navigation. Its functionality includes controlling the wheels of the robot.

The architecture includes a secondary component called Planning. The functionality of this component is to generate plans consisting of actions related to the Move and Orient tasks of the robot. The component is based on AI planning and, therefore, requires a domain model and a problem instance as input. The domain model consists of predicates describing the robot, the target human, the objective to be accomplished (i.e., for the robot to follow the human), and actions describing moving forward, moving backward, stopping, rotating left, and rotating right. The problem instance consists of objects, such as the robot and target human, predicates instantiated with offset angle, minimum and maximum angles, and distance to the target person, and the goal. The domain model in combination with the problem instance constitutes a planning problem. The solution to the planning problem is a sequence of motion actions that are triggered in the robot navigation base.

The architecture is designed around ROS, which means that all components are nodes in a ROS network. The components communicate by sending messages to each other, while we assume the communication is managed over ROS distributed control system. The architecture is illustrated in Fig. 1b.

3.3   Implementation

Given the limitations of the hardware, we use an additional processing unit, a laptop with a 3 GHz processor, and an NVIDIA GPU capable of running Compute Unified Device Architecture (CUDA) [11].

The GPU is needed to accelerate the processing of the image frames from the robot's camera sensor. The robot and the laptop are connected over a wireless network, and they discover and communicate with each other using the ROS server network. The second addition to the Ohmni Telepresence Robot is the Lidar. We use the YDLIDAR X4 developed by EAI. It is a 360°2D Lidar system that consists of optics, electronics, and algorithms to measure distances with high precision [22]. Figure 2 shows the Ohmni Telepresence Robot with the hardware extensions.

We utilize an Ubuntu Linux 20.04 long-term support (LTS) distribution with a ROS Version 1, specifically, ROS Noetic Ninjemys. We created a catkin workspace which is a directory that we use to install and manage our ROS packages. Considering ROS packages, we use RViz, which is a graphical user inter-

Fig. 2. The Robot.

face (GUI) that is used to visualize data such as RGB and mono images, depth clouds, and depth maps, that are crucial for human detection, tracking, and robot localization [18]. We further use the YOLO ROS package for human detection, the ROS Adaptive Monte Carlo Localization (AMCL) package for localization, and the ROSPlan package for path planning. More details follow.

We implement the Human Detection component based on the You-Only-Look-Once version 2 (YOLOv2) model, which is a state-of-the-art and general-purpose model for real-time object and human detection from images [19]. It runs at up to 45 frames per second (FPS) or higher, making it a far faster algorithm than its competitors [19]. YOLOv2 is available as a ROS package, called YOLO ROS, which is what we adopt in the project. Due to the YOLOv2 model being capable of detecting false positive objects as a human, a threshold value of 86% or above is used as a truth value for positive human detection. Figure 3 is an illustration of an identified target person in a bounding box.

Fig. 3. Bounding box.

We implement position tracking of a human within the field of view of the robot's camera. Every point within an image frame is a pixel position composed of an x-axis and a y-axis. We take advantage of our knowledge of the horizontal field of view of the robot's camera and the dimension of the image captured by the camera to calculate the offset angle of the bounding box of a detected object from the center of projection of the camera sensor.

We implement the localization functionality of the Navigation component based on pose tracking of the robot on a grid map using particle filters. We use the ROS AMCL package to achieve this and localize the robot in a 2D environment. In addition, we utilize this package to determine if there are obstacles in the trajectory of a robot while it is in motion based on the sensor data coming from the Lidar module, thus collision avoidance is also implemented. We implement the motion functionality of the Navigation component by sending velocity commands and controlling the wheels of the robot.

Finally, for the Planning component, we use the ROSPlan package by providing a domain model and problem instance to the Knowledge Base of ROSPlan, which are then used by ROSPlan to generate a planning problem. ROSPlan also generates ROS topics that are equivalent to the actions defined in our domain model. These movement actions are triggered by the Navigation component [2].

4   Evaluation

Having in mind our ultimate objective of transforming the Ohmni Telepresence Robot into an intelligent office assistant, we perform experiments using our proposed approach and demonstrate its effectiveness in an office environment. In addition, we compare our approach with existing methods for object detection and human following to demonstrate the accuracy of our approach from our results. To that end, we first describe the experimental setup and the evaluation metrics of interest, followed by the results and discussion.

Experimental Setup. We deploy our system and the Ohmni Telepresence Robot in our own building, the Computer Science Building, at Universitätsstraße 38, Stuttgart, Germany. The building has four floors that house the Department

(a) Lab Photo   (b) Grid Map

Fig. 4. Photo and Grid Map Representation of The Living Lab

of Computer Science, four lecture halls, and several seminar rooms. We exploit
our own living lab as an environment for the deployment and testing of the
system and robot. The living lab is located on the ground floor and covers an
area of $140\,\mathrm{m}^2$. The living lab serves as a working space for several persons and
a place to perform tests and experiments. It is an open space equipped with
seven working desks with room for unrestricted movement. Figure 4a shows a
photo of the living lab, while Fig. 4b shows a grid map of the living lab which
we generated using a ROS Simultaneous and Mapping (SLAM) algorithm.

We conducted a series of experiments in the living lab with ambient lighting conditions. The experiments involved the robot detecting the position of a
human, and approaching the individual till it stops when it reaches a safe distance, or it follows the human if the individual is in motion. We performed 10
trials where the robot was to detect a human and follow the individual over
an approximate distance of 63 m composed of straight and curved pathways.
During each trial, we performed several measurements which are summarized in
Table 2, where DTBR stands for Distance Travelled By Robot, TD for Trajectory
Distance, and NOMFBR for Number of Minutes Followed By Robot.

Evaluation Criteria. We consider qualitative and quantitative metrics tied to
mobile robot navigation. In particular, we consider the following metrics when
conducting the experiments: computational cost, the effectiveness of automation,
the efficiency of travel by the robot, robustness in object detection and tracking
in narrow spaces, self-awareness of the robot, obstacle detection, and collision
avoidance, number of successful missions, path length traveled by the robot,
time taken to cover the path, robustness in object detection, human tracking in
a sharp and narrow space, and smoothness of trajectory [3].

Results. For every trial in our experiments, we recorded the time taken for the
human and robot to cover the trajectory, and also the number of interventions,
composed of losses of the target or safety precautions involving a third party that
the robot experienced. We also observed the smoothness of the robot's motion
while taking turns, and in particular, a stress test was performed involving sharp

Table 2. Living lab evaluation.

| No. of Trials | DTBR (m) | TD (m) | NOMFBR (mins) | Time taken by Person | Interventions | |
					Loss	Safety
1	62.4	62.4	4 min 56 s	4 min 53 s	5	0
2	62.4	62.4	5 min 2 s	4 min 59 s	6	0
3	62.4	62.4	4 min 7 s	4 min 4 s	1	3
4	62.4	62.4	4 min 48 s	4 min 45 s	2	2
5	62.4	62.4	5 min 11 s	5 min 8 s	3	3
6	62.4	62.4	5 min 3 s	4 min 59 s	4	1
7	62.4	62.4	4 min 34 s	4 min 31 s	4	2
8	62.4	62.4	4 min 9 s	4 min 6 s	2	1
9	62.4	62.4	5 min 13 s	5 min 10 s	4	0
10	62.4	62.4	4 min 54 s	4 min 51 s	4	0

Table 3. Performance comparison of the DETRAFO approaches.

Study	Detection Method	Average Load (%)	Following Effectiveness (%)	Distance Travelled (m)	Trajectory Distance (m)	Minutes Followed (mins)
[18]	Leg Detection	30.5CPU (low)	74.29	23.77	32	
[18]	Face Detection	98.9CPU (high)	25.71	8.22	32	
[15]	Blob Detection	low	85			
[14]	Clothes Color Detection	low	100			
[21]	Following Angle Detection	low		20	20	
[8]	Color Tag Detection	low				15
[17]	Bluetooth RSSI and IMU	low		3.47	4.87	
[9]	Skeletal Detection	low	100			8
This work	Human Bounding Box Detection	72.2GPU (moderate) 32.3CPU (low)	95	62.4	62.4	4 min 47 s

turns that the robot had to undertake. These results are shown in Table 2. We also recorded the average CPU and GPU load during each trial to observe their effect on the battery performance. We use these recordings and other measures to compare our approach with the most closely related works [8,9,14,15,17,18,21]. The result of the comparison is presented in Table 3.

5 Discussion

YOLOv2 can process between 90–120 image frames per second while making use of GPU which outperforms using a CPU that only achieves between 1–2 image frames per second. Thus, the efficiency of object detection helps the overall performance of our algorithm. Furthermore, the robot sometimes fails to come to a halt while being at a distance that is less than the critical distance and following a target individual. The critical distance is necessary to provide safety for a human while it is being trailed by the robot. The failure might be due to the robot not decelerating sufficiently fast and therefore bumping into a person in its path. In addition, the pace of the individual can also affect the motion of the robot and therefore the overall results of the experiments. Finally, our algorithm was built for the detection of random humans. If two people are in its field of view it occasionally stops tracking one and starts tracking the other one.

6   Conclusion

We investigated the automation of the movement of a telepresence robot using our proposed DETRAFO approach. The purpose of the implementation is to automate a robot that can act as an office assistant. Human detection and pose estimation is achieved with a vision sensor and Lidar. The field of view of the robot's camera is (140°) which gives advantages for tracking an individual. The trade-off for detection consistency is a higher computational cost for accurately detecting a bounding box with a human while making use of a camera. We performed experiments on the robot to measure the performance of its human position detection, and how effective the robot automation is based on following a human's trajectory and avoiding collision with obstacles. We plan to extend the abilities of the robot. In particular, we plan to use voice commands to control the robots' movement and to enable facial recognition, so that the robot can track and interact with an individual based on the specific person. From a computational point of view, we plan to explore ways to reduce the costs of human detection using the video camera. Image compression will play a role in such investigation. We plan also to explore the use of ROSPlan to dynamically create the motion paths of the robot. Finally, the integration of more sensors on the robot will be investigated.

References

1. Almeida, L., Menezes, P., Dias, J.: Telepresence social robotics towards co-presence: a review. Appl. Sci. **12**(11), 5557 (2022)
2. Cashmore, M., et al.: ROSPlan: planning in the robot operating system. In: ICAPS, vol. 2015, pp. 333–341 (2015)
3. Ceballos, N.D.M., Valencia, J.A., Ospina, N.L.: Quantitative performance metrics for mobile robots navigation. In: Barrera, A. (ed.) Mobile Robots Navigation. IntechOpen (2010)
4. Fitter, N.T., Joung, Y., Hu, Z., Demeter, M., Matarić, M.J.: User interface tradeoffs for remote deictic gesturing. In: IEEE RO-MAN, pp. 1–8 (2019)
5. Flores-Vázquez, C., Angulo, C., Vallejo-Ramírez, D., Icaza, D., Pulla Galindo, S.: Technical development of the CeCi social robot. Sensors **22**(19), 7619 (2022)
6. Georgievski, I., Jeyakumar, I.H.J., Kale, S.: Designing a system based on robotic assistance for privacy awareness in smart environment. In: IEEE UEMCON, pp. 427–432 (2021)
7. Gurguze, G., Turkoglu, I.: Energy management techniques in mobile robots. Int. J. Energy Power Eng. **11**(10), 1085–1093 (2018)

8. Hassan, S., Khan, M., Khan, A.: Design and development of human following robot. In: Student Research Paper Conference, Islamabad, July 2015
9. Ilias, B., Shukor, S., Yaacob, S., Adom, A., Razali, M.: A nurse following robot with high speed kinect sensor. ARPN J. Eng. Appl. Sci. **9**(12), 2454–2459 (2014)
10. Kaldeli, E., Warriach, E.U., Lazovik, A., Aiello, M.: Coordinating the web of services for a smart home. ACM Trans. Web **7**(2), 1–40 (2013)
11. Kirk, D.B., Wen-Mei, W.H.: Programming Massively Parallel Processors: A Hands-on Approach. Morgan Kaufmann, San Francisco (2016)
12. Kwak, S.S.: The impact of the robot appearance types on social interaction with a robot and service evaluation of a robot. Arch. Des. Res. **27**(2), 81–93 (2014)
13. Liu, Y., Palmieri, L., Georgievski, I., Aiello, M.: Human-flow-aware long-term mobile robot task planning based on hierarchical reinforcement learning. IEEE Robot. Autom. Lett. **8**, 4068–4075 (2023)
14. Megalingam, R.K., Anandu, R., HemaTejaAnirudhBabu, D., Sriram, G., YashwanthAvvari, V.S.: Implementation of a person following robot in ROS-gazebo platform. In: IEEE ICONAT, pp. 1–5 (2022)
15. Patoliya, J.J., Mewada, H.K.: Automated tracking and real time following of moving person for robotics applications. J. Autom. Mobile Robot. Intell. Syst. **13**, 31–37 (2019)
16. Pena, P., Albina, T.: Follow Pedro! An infrared-based person-follower using nonlinear optimization. arXiv Preprint 1912.06837 (2019)
17. Pradeep, B.V., Rahul, E., Bhavani, R.R.: Follow me robot using bluetooth-based position estimation. In: IEEE ICACCI, pp. 584–589 (2017)
18. Priyandoko, G., Wei, C.K., Achmad, M.S.H.: Human following on ROS framework a mobile robot. Sinergi **22**(2), 77–82 (2018)
19. Redmon, J., Divvala, S., Girshick, R., Farhadi, A.: You only look once: unified, real-time object detection. arXiv Preprint 1506.02640 (2015)
20. Sankar, S., Tsai, C.Y.: ROS-based human detection and tracking from a wireless controlled mobile robot using kinect. Appl. Syst. Innov. **2**(1), 5 (2019)
21. Shanee, H.S., Dror, K., Tal, O.G., Yael, E.: The influence of following angle on performance metrics of a human-following robot. In: IEEE RO-MAN, pp. 593–598 (2016)
22. Shenzhen: YDLIDAR—Focus on lidar sensor solutions (2015). https://www.ydlidar.com/. Accessed 20 Mar 2023
23. Sonoura, T., Yoshimi, T., Nishiyama, M., Nakamoto, H., Tokura, S., Matsuhira, N.: Person following robot with vision-based and sensor fusion tracking algorithm. In: Zhihui, X. (ed.) Computer Vision. IntechOpen (2008)
24. Stanford Artificial Intelligence Laboratory: Robotic Operating System (2020). https://www.ros.org
25. Tomoya, A., Nakayama, S., Hoshina, A., Sugaya, M.: A mobile robot for following, watching and detecting falls for elderly care. Procedia Comput. Sci. **112**, 1994–2003 (2017)
26. Wunderlich, S., Schmölz, J., Kühnlenz, K.: Follow me: a simple approach for person identification and tracking. In: IEEE ISIE, pp. 1609–1614 (2017)
27. Zand, G., Ren, Y., Arif, A.S.: TiltWalker: operating a telepresence robot with one-hand by tilt controls on a smartphone. Proc. ACM Hum. Comput. Interact. **6**(ISS), 381–406 (2022)
28. Zheng, K., Wu, F., Chen, X.: Laser-based people detection and obstacle avoidance for a hospital transport robot. Sensors **21**(3), 961 (2021)

Towards Multimodal Sensing and Interaction for Assistive Autonomous Robots

Emanuele De Pellegrin[1,3]([✉]) [iD], Ronnie Smith[2,3] [iD], Scott MacLeod[2] [iD],
Mauro Dragone[2] [iD], and Ronald P. A. Petrick[1] [iD]

[1] School of Mathematical and Computer Sciences, Heriot-Watt University,
Edinburgh, UK
`r.petrick@hw.ac.uk`
[2] School of Engineering and Physical Sciences, Heriot-Watt University, Edinburgh,
UK
`{ras35,scott.macleod,m.dragone}@hw.ac.uk`
[3] School of Informatics, University of Edinburgh, Edinburgh, UK
`ed50@hw.ac.uk`

Abstract. Assistive environments that combine sensors, actuators, and robotic devices have gained attention in recent years, with the potential to provide assistance and support to individuals with disabilities or to the ageing population. One key challenge in designing autonomous assistive environments is to accurately recognise and understand the user's goals and intentions. To address these challenges, we propose a system with a goal recognition and planning loop that uses data collected from sensors embedded in an assistive environment. We present the general architecture of the system, highlighting the key components available at the time of writing, plus the proposed extensions for the long-term goal of the project. We present data collected in a smart kitchen used by the activity recognition system, as well as a custom tool to simulate and test the data.

Keywords: Robotics · Ambient Intelligence · Proactivity

1 Introduction

Ambient Intelligence (AmI) assistive environments combining Internet of Things (IoT) sensors, actuators, and robotic devices have gained attention in recent years, with the potential to provide assistance and support to individuals with disabilities or to the ageing population [9]. Such environments enable real-time monitoring and autonomous assistance on everyday tasks, such as cooking, cleaning, and general assistance. One key challenge in designing autonomous assistive environments is to accurately recognise and understand the user's goals and intentions. Moreover, with robots involved, a constant revision of users' goals and intentions is required to plan autonomously useful interactions.

F. Iida et al. (Eds.): TAROS 2023, LNAI 14136, pp. 162–173, 2023.
https://doi.org/10.1007/978-3-031-43360-3_14

To be autonomous, robots require a base domain of knowledge in the environment where they operate. Planning for robotics also needs a reasoning method to cope with dynamic environments. When these interactions are simple enough, it is possible to analytically model such domains, and efficient planning methods exist to solve this problem. However, sometimes, this is not possible or the process is too difficult, time-consuming, and error-prone. The difficulties involved in modelling real-world domains is a well-known bottleneck in the planning community for the application of planning methods in robotics [2]. Furthermore, when deployed in a real-world environment, a robotic agent might not sense the environment completely due to limited view or can detect noisy and erroneous sensor readings [15, 17, 28].

To address these challenges, we propose a system with a goal recognition and planning loop that uses data collected from sensors embedded in an assistive environment. We primarily use the data to learn what effects an action can have on the environment by selecting specific activities that can be performed in a kitchen environment. The system aims to recognise the user's goals and intentions based on their interactions with various objects and appliances in the kitchen. We also incorporate a long-short-term memory (LSTM) based gesture recognition system to recognise a set of predefined gestures performed by the user from video data. The output of this gesture recognition system provides additional information to improve the accuracy of the goal recognition system. Moreover, catering for gestures during human-robot interaction has the potential to promote social engagement with the robotic agent.

We tested our components and approach in the METRICS HEART-MET competition [27], whose purpose is to tackle the growing problem of healthcare costs and quality of life for the elderly and the ageing population. The aim is to evaluate robotics solutions and functionalities such as object detection, activity recognition, object handover, and speech understanding that are needed to assess the status of the activity of a person.

The paper is organised as follows: (i) We provide an overview of related work on robotic assistance, proactivity, planning, and model acquisition for robotics; (ii) we then present the general architecture of our system, highlighting the key components available at the time of writing, plus the proposed extensions for the long-term goal of the project; (iii) we describe in detail components related to the METRICS HEART-MET competition entry where the single components have been tested; and (iv) we present results from the competition, and (v) we conclude with future work planned for the project.

2   Related Work

Ambient Intelligence. Cook et al. define AmI as solutions which are: sensitive, responsive, adaptive, transparent, ubiquitous, and intelligent. Specifically, an AmI environment is "a digital environment that proactively, but sensibly, supports people in their daily lives" [6]. Another common term is Ambient Assisted Living (AAL), which can be thought of as a realisation of AmI focusing on the needs of older adults and their carers [4].

Assistive robots fit naturally into AmI as they afford a mutually beneficial relationship between the robot and other AmI services. Robots can take advantage of existing sensors to augment their own sensing capabilities (a.k.a. distributed perception), vastly expanding their sensing modality space. On the other hand, robots can endow other services with a physical embodiment, providing manipulation capabilities and increasing opportunities for advanced interaction [9].

Assistive Robotics. Assistive Robots (ARs), in a home context, refers to robots which aim to support the user in their daily life. It is common for assistive robots to also be social agents, i.e., they are Socially Assistive Robots (SARs), as effective interaction with the user is central to providing effective assistance [10]. Assistive robots often demonstrate proactive behaviour, i.e., they make autonomous decisions to assist the user at home. Proactive robots are those that *anticipate* the needs (i.e., *goals*) of the user, *plan* how to provide effective assistance, and *act* by taking actions that will bring them closer toward achieving their goals [11]. Proactive assistive robots have a range of applications, such as: helping the user while cooking [18]; ensuring the environment is kept the way the user likes it [12]; or helping the user during specific activities through Human-Robot Collaboration (HRC) [13].

Learning for Planning. A robot should be a proactive agent in the assistive environment. From the agent's perspective, the environment can be noisy and uncertain given the nature of the interaction with humans. Human actions are unpredictable, durative and sometimes incomplete. To improve its understanding of other agents (i.e. humans) and their beliefs, a planning agent should integrate knowledge representation and behaviour learning. This falls down in the field of active goal recognition [3,22] where the robot agent needs to infer the goal or the plan the human is currently executing, and perhaps starts cooperative tasks or engage to provide assistance if recognize the goal is not achievable. Recent work aims to use automated planning solutions to proactively provide assistance to humans in everyday situations. Additionally, it can proactively engage with humans, continuously updating its internal knowledge of the world and other agent's beliefs, and recognise human goals in order to help achieve them [8,19,21].

3 Conceptual Architecture

The high-level architecture of our proposed system is shown in Fig. 1. The diagram shows the functional building blocks of the system, i.e. components which provide specific services and/or behaviours, such as person recognition. We divided these into 3 main characteristics: perception, robot actions, and Human-Robot Interaction (HRI). The perception block accounts for the computer vision and sensor low-level data acquisition. This gives the robot access to infer gestures, current activity, and localization of the human and objects in the environment. The robot actions block concerns the robot navigation stack and

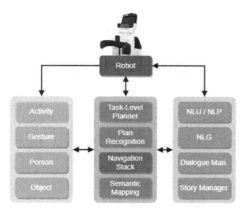

Fig. 1. Conceptual system architecture diagram. Yellow blocks (left) show perception functions, purple blocks (center) show robot-related functions, and green blocks (right) represent HRI-related functions. Parts that are still in development and were not used in the METRICS HEART-MET competition. (Color figure online)

the automated planning for decision-making processes. Finally, the HRI block deals with all the language and dialogue management to promote social interactions with the human, such as asking questions about current activity and giving guidance. These building blocks can then be used to create more complex behaviours, which require high-level task planning and orchestration of various functions. Complex tasks in competitions such as RoboCup@Home [29] or METRICS HEART-MET [26] typically involve navigation, human-robot interactions (verbal and physical), vision-based classification, and manipulation. We continue to work towards the completion of our full architecture.

4   Methodology

4.1   Dataset

Participants were required for the purposes of collecting data on how different individuals perform the same activities in their daily lives. Participants in this study were healthy adults, without any special access requirements. Data was collected at the Robotic Assisted Living Testbed (RALT) at Heriot-Watt University.[1] We are making this data publicly available.[2]

The activities included were: (i) prepare a cup of tea; (ii) prepare a sandwich; (iii) prepare a bowl of cereal; (iv) set the table; (v) wash the dishes; and (vi) clean the kitchen.

One participant at a time was invited to the testbed to take part in the data collection campaign. Five participants each performed three runs of the set of

---

[1] https://ralt.hw.ac.uk/.
[2] https://care.hw.ac.uk/datasets/multimodal_adls_2022.zip.

Table 1. Excerpt of semantic events recorded with Signalman. Sensor names are abbreviated: DC = Dinnerware Counter, KMS = Kitchen Motion Sensor, KWC = Kitchen Wall Cabinet, KP = Kettle Pressure, and KTP = Kitchen Tap Power.

Predicate	x	y	Predicate(x,y)	Event	Origin	Raw	Timestamp
move	user	kitchen	move(user,kitchen)	Presence	KMS 2	ON	1643729000
alter	cabinet	TRUE	alter(cabinet,true)	DC	KWC 1	OFF	1643729001
alter	cabinet	FALSE	alter(cabinet,false)	DC	KWC 1	ON	1643729003
take	user	kettle	take(user,kettle)	Kettle	KP	OFF	1643729005
alter	tap	TRUE	alter(tap,true)	Tap	KTP	ON	1643729008
...	...	...	...	...	...	...	...

activities, for a total of 15 runs. For each participant, two runs were 'free form' where participants could perform activities in any order they wished, while one run was carried out in a prescribed order.

Data were collected from around the environment,[3] from the following sources: (i) three video cameras focusing on the kitchen worktops and dining table; (ii) video from two robots within the environment; (iii) 52 semantically tagged fixed sensors from around the environment (e.g. motion, cupboards, furniture and objects); (iv) power usage about appliances (e.g. watts); (v) non-visual robot sensors data, such as point clouds and LIDAR; (vi) RSSI and phase measurements of RFID tags from objects tagged throughout the environment (36 objects) were collected using a UHF RFID system installed in the testbed [24]; and (vii) inertial measurement data from a wrist-worn Apple Watch. An excerpt of sensor data collected from the smart home is shown in Fig. 1.

The data set was labelled for the activity that was being performed (e.g., preparing a cup of tea), in addition to all of the objects that the user interacted with and where.

4.2   Smart Home and Plan Simulator

The dataset recorder from the smart home can be visualised and replayed in the custom simulator using a plan visualisation system called PDSim [7]. PDSim is an existing simulator for automated planning that uses visual cues and animations to translate the output of a plan into a 3D environment. Although primarily focused on simulating classical plans, PDSim can be modified and adapted to display 3D animation of the changes in the environment. In this case, a sensor is a single semantic representation of the current state of the world (the smart home). The simulator can show the changes in the state of the sensors by, for example, opening and closing cabinets, playing sounds and particles when the kettle is on, etc. (see the possible sensors and states in the dataset). Figure 2 shows this visual output of the data being simulated in PDSim and the virtual User Interface that tells the current state of a particular object in the kitchen.

---

[3] Data from smart home, cameras, and robots captured via OpenAAL *Signalman* [23].

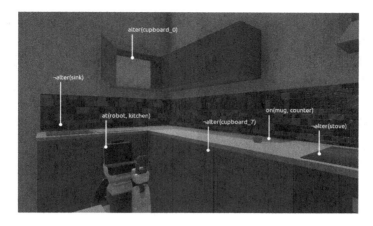

Fig. 2. Smart Home and Plan simulation

4.3   Person and Object Detection

The person and object detection module is used to identify the person engaged in the interaction with the robot, to approach or to get the attention of the human and to identify which objects are present in the environment. Person detection works by inferring from a 2D image the key points of the human joints and deriving a bounding box. This will be used later as input for the gesture recognition module. Similarly, the object detection module returns a bounding box and a list of all the objects detected from the robot camera's point of view.

Model. The detectron2 platform provides pre-trained models using the COCO (Common Objects in Context) dataset [16]. The building block of the model used for both person and object detection is a faster recursive convolutional neural network [20]. The dataset include objects of everyday use, but was not enough for the purpose of the competition. We have used the data provided by the METRICS [27] competition to retrain the last layer of the existing model to incorporate the detection of more objects that can be found in a household.

Examples. Figure 3 shows an example of how the person- and object-detection models performed in the competition. In particular, the left-hand side shows the correct detection of a sponge object requested by the referee. The right-hand side shows the correct identification of a person by identifying the key points of the body joints, particularly useful for detecting the whole figure of a person if it is partially hidden, such as the right image where the person is sitting behind the table.

4.4   Gesture Detection

The gesture detection module was implemented on the day of the competition in conjunction with data collection. Although it was not accurate enough for

Fig. 3. Examples of object (left) and person (right) detection results. The object in question is a sponge. The person is standing being a table, and is partially occluded. The green overlay indicates ground truth data, while the red overlay indicates what our model detected. (Color figure online)

the competition, in this section we will present the latest and updated development and scores. The module works in parallel to the conversation module to get non-verbal cues from the human; in particular, it focuses on the following gestures: Calling, Nodding, Pointing, Shaking, Stopping, ThumbsDown, ThumbsUp, WaveAway, and Waving.

Dataset. The data is a collection of max 30 s videos where the participant executes the gesture listed above. After the video was collected a derived dataset was created by extracting the key points from each frame using the detectron person recognition model. Every keypoint and bounding box coordinate was normalised by the video width and height, and every keypoint is recalculated by taking its inner position inside the bounding box. The data is prepared by grouping frames 30 by 30 and discarding the remaining. For example: for a 112 frames video, the key points are collected in 3 groups of 30 frames each and leave 22 frames out. Finally, the dataset was split using 60% for training and 40% for validation.

Model. The model used for gesture recognition is a Long-Short-Term Memory (LSTM) network [14]. For reproducibility sake, Table 2 shows the parameters used to train the network. Figure 4 shows the latest training scores for the gesture recognition network, which outperforms the model that was deployed for the METRICS competition. The model outputs scores on the certainty of which gesture is being executed in a span of 30 frames. A threshold value can be passed to get the second most certain gesture. For example, if the value set is 50%, if the model predicts a class with a confidence greater than 50%, then the output will be only that particular class, however, if the prediction is less than the threshold, the output will be the 2 most confident predictions.

Examples. Figure 5 shows examples of the gesture recognition model. In particular, the left image shows accurate recognition of the human doing a stop sign,

Table 2. LSTM Network Parameters

Batch Size	Epochs	Learning Rate	Hidden Layers	N. Layers
50	1500	10e−4	350	1

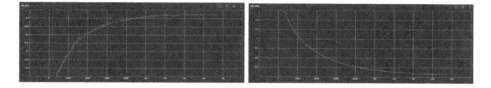

Fig. 4. LSTM model validation accuracy (left) and loss (right)

while the right image shows the 2 most confident predictions as the threshold value was set to 50%, the network predicted the thumbs-up and wave someone away with almost identical scores for the selected 30 frames.

Fig. 5. Gesture Recognition Examples

4.5 Activity Recognition

The 'Assess Activity State' task benchmark laid out in the METRICS HEART-MET competition rulebook dictates that the robot should be able to assess a person's activity state visually and verbally, using conversation as an additional layer of assessment on top of vision-based methods [27]. As such, our approach combines both methods as shown in Fig. 6.

Model. For the activity recognition portion of the task, we have used a model published by the METRICS HEART-MET competition organisers which is pre-trained on classes from the competition [26]. The model is an Inflated 3D Network (I3D) video classifier, that consists of two main components: a feature

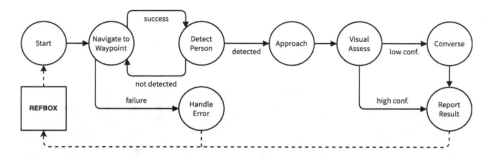

Fig. 6. Task flow for the 'assess activity state' task benchmark.

extractor and a classifier [5]. The last layer of the model has been retrained to account for the competition activities classes. This was the model in place when taking part in the competition, as described in 5.

Dialogue. We utilise an existing general-purpose conversational annotation interface designed for end-user labelling of ADLs [25]. The approach involves extracting an 'ADL descriptor' from a user utterance, matching it to a set of common ADL labels, and then to a set of labels for the target domain. We map to the labels used in the METRICS competition. For example, if the user says *"At the moment, I am reading a magazine"* then the descriptor 'reading a magazine' is extracted, and then mapped to the common ADL 'reading'.

In this case, when the model is unable to confidently detect the activity of the human (i.e. $T_{conf} < 0.5$ for the highest ranked predicted class), the conversational interface is activated. To begin extracting a label from the user via conversation we send an empty annotation request (the interface supports preloading of potential labels, but we do not use this feature) to the conversational interface. If the interface successfully extracts a label, we take this as ground truth, otherwise if this process fails the original model prediction is used instead.

5   Experience at METRICS HEART-MET

As discussed in the introduction, assistive robots for the home are commonly evaluated through benchmarking competitions. We had the opportunity to attend the METRICS HEART-MET Field Campaign in October 2022 [1] at the University of Nottingham, which allowed us to perform some preliminary evaluation of our work.

The competition focuses on assisting an individual while living independently in their home, e.g. the robot is their live-in companion who can assist with physical tasks. The competition is divided into *functional* (e.g. specific discrete behaviours) and *task* (e.g. composite behaviours), as outlined in Table 3. The same table also indicates which benchmarks we took part in on this occasion (Table 4).

Table 3. METRICS HEART-MET Functional and Task Benchmarks [27]

Functional Benchmarks

Description	Participation
Object Detection	Yes
Person Detection	Yes
Gesture Recognition	Yes
Activity Recognition	Yes
Cluttered Pick	No
Handover	No
Receive Object	No

Task Benchmarks

Description	Participation
Assess Activity State	Yes
Item Delivery	No

Table 4. Summary of our results from the METRICS HEART-MET Field Campaign in October 2022 at the University of Nottingham.

Benchmark	Score	Rank	Measure
Object Detection	73.5%	1 / 4	$(TP + TN)/Total$
Person Detection	74.5%	2 / 4	TP
Gesture Recognition	16.7%	2 / 3	TP
Activity Recognition	20.0%	2 / 3	TP
Assess Activity State	N/A	1 / 3	See Rulebook

6   Conclusion and Future Work

This work shows the progress of a robotic architecture that aims to be deployed in a smart home environment for care and assistive scenarios. We presented the vision building blocks used by the HSR robot such as the persons and objects detection and gesture recognition. The persons and objects detection systems are able to precisely perform the detection request. The gesture recognition system tested in the competition differs from the one presented in the paper that correctly categorizes the gesture, however, gestures that have similar movements such as 'pointing' or 'stop sign' are detected incorrectly sometimes. This might be improved in future work, where we plan to collect additional data and use different approaches to detect human poses. We also plan to test data generation and enhancement for the smart home environment. The digital twin simulator will be of great help in the case to test and validate generated data. Given the modularity of the simulator, we plan to use it to test if generating virtual data can further help the detection systems. Also, while Social Interaction is tested and integrated into the pipeline, there will also be tests and integration of the plan recognition module to help the human perform the activity if it is detected that help is needed.

Acknowledgements. Emanuele De Pellegrin and Ronnie Smith are supported by EPSRC Centre for Doctoral Training in Robotics and Autonomous Systems (EP/S023208/1 and EP/L016834/1) at Heriot-Watt University and the University of Edinburgh. Ronnie Smith and Mauro Dragone are also supported by METRICS (European Union Horizon 2020 agreement No. 871252).

References

1. 2022 Oct Field Campaign - METRICS. https://metricsproject.eu/healthcare/2022-oct-field-campaign/
2. Aineto, D., Celorrio, S.J., Onaindia, E.: Learning action models with minimal observability. Artif. Intell. **275**, 104–137 (2019)
3. Amato, C., Baisero, A.: Active goal recognition. arXiv:1909.11173 [cs], September 2019
4. Calvaresi, D., Cesarini, D., Sernani, P., Marinoni, M., Dragoni, A.F., Sturm, A.: Exploring the ambient assisted living domain: a systematic review. J. Amb. Intell. Hum. Comput. **8**(2), 239–257 (2017). https://doi.org/10.1007/s12652-016-0374-3
5. Carreira, J., Zisserman, A.: Quo vadis, action recognition? A new model and the kinetics dataset. In: Proceedings of the IEEE Conference on Computer Vision and Pattern Recognition, pp. 6299–6308 (2017)
6. Cook, D.J., Augusto, J.C., Jakkula, V.R.: Ambient intelligence: technologies, applications, and opportunities. Pervasive Mob. Comput. **5**(4), 277–298 (2009). https://doi.org/10.1016/j.pmcj.2009.04.001. https://linkinghub.elsevier.com/retrieve/pii/S157411920900025X
7. De Pellegrin, E., Petrick, R.P.: What plan? Virtual plan visualization with PDSim. In: 32nd International Conference on Automated Planning and Scheduling (2022)
8. Dissing, L., Bolander, T.: Implementing theory of mind on a robot using dynamic epistemic logic. In: Proceedings of the Twenty-Ninth International Joint Conference on Artificial Intelligence, pp. 1615–1621. International Joint Conferences on Artificial Intelligence Organization, Yokohama, Japan, July 2020. https://doi.org/10.24963/ijcai.2020/224. https://www.ijcai.org/proceedings/2020/224
9. Dragone, M., Saunders, J., Dautenhahn, K.: On the integration of adaptive and interactive robotic smart spaces. Paladyn J. Behav. Robot. **6**(1) (2015). https://doi.org/10.1515/pjbr-2015-0009. https://www.degruyter.com/document/doi/10.1515/pjbr-2015-0009/html
10. Feil-Seifer, D., Mataric, M.: Socially assistive robotics. In: 9th International Conference on Rehabilitation Robotics, 2005, ICORR 2005, Chicago, IL, USA, pp. 465–468. IEEE (2005). https://doi.org/10.1109/ICORR.2005.1501143. http://ieeexplore.ieee.org/document/1501143/
11. Grant, A.M., Ashford, S.J.: The dynamics of proactivity at work. Res. Org. Behav. **28**, 3–34 (2008). https://doi.org/10.1016/j.riob.2008.04.002. https://linkinghub.elsevier.com/retrieve/pii/S0191308508000038
12. Grosinger, J., Pecora, F., Saffiotti, A.: Robots that maintain equilibrium: proactivity by reasoning about user intentions and preferences. Pattern Recogn. Lett. **118**, 85–93 (2019). https://doi.org/10.1016/j.patrec.2018.05.014. https://linkinghub.elsevier.com/retrieve/pii/S0167865518301843, direct
13. Harman, H., Simoens, P.: Action graphs for proactive robot assistance in smart environments. J. Amb. Intell. Smart Environ. **12**(2), 79–99 (2020). https://doi.org/10.3233/AIS-200556. https://www.medra.org/servlet/aliasResolver?alias=iospress&doi=10.3233/AIS-200556

14. Hochreiter, S., Schmidhuber, J.: Long short-term memory. Neural Comput. **9**(8), 1735–1780 (1997)
15. Kaiser, P., Lewis, M., Petrick, R.P., Asfour, T., Steedman, M.: Extracting common sense knowledge from text for robot planning. In: 2014 IEEE International Conference on Robotics and Automation (ICRA), pp. 3749–3756. IEEE (2014)
16. Lin, T.Y., et al.: Microsoft COCO: Common objects in context, February 2015. https://doi.org/10.48550/arXiv.1405.0312. http://arxiv.org/abs/1405.0312
17. Mourao, K., Zettlemoyer, L.S., Petrick, R., Steedman, M.: Learning strips operators from noisy and incomplete observations. arXiv preprint arXiv:1210.4889 (2012)
18. Neumann, A., et al.: "KogniChef": a cognitive cooking assistant. KI - Künstliche Intelligenz **31**(3), 273–281 (2017). https://doi.org/10.1007/s13218-017-0488-6. http://link.springer.com/10.1007/s13218-017-0488-6, direct
19. Pantaleoni, M., Cesta, A., Umbrico, A., Orlandini, A.: Learning user habits to enhance robotic daily-living assistance. In: Cavallo, F., et al. (eds.) Social Robotics. ICSR 2022. LNCS, vol. 13817, pp. 165–173. Springer, Cham (2022). https://doi.org/10.1007/978-3-031-24667-8_15
20. Ren, S., He, K., Girshick, R., Sun, J.: Faster R-CNN: towards real-time object detection with region proposal networks (2015)
21. Shvo, M., Hari, R., O'Reilly, Z., Abolore, S., Wang, S.Y.N., McIlraith, S.A.: Proactive robotic assistance via theory of mind. In: 2022 IEEE/RSJ International Conference on Intelligent Robots and Systems (IROS), pp. 9148–9155, October 2022. https://doi.org/10.1109/IROS47612.2022.9981627
22. Shvo, M., McIlraith, S.A.: Active goal recognition. In: Proceedings of the AAAI Conference on Artificial Intelligence, vol. 34, no. 06, pp. 9957–9966 (2020). https://doi.org/10.1609/aaai.v34i06.6551
23. Smith, R.: GitHub - care-group/RALT-Signalman-Container-ROS-Deps (2022). https://github.com/care-group/RALT-Signalman-Container-ROS-Deps
24. Smith, R., Ding, Y., Goussetis, G., Dragone, M.: A COTS (UHF) RFID floor for device-free ambient assisted living monitoring. In: Novais, P., Vercelli, G., Larriba-Pey, J.L., Herrera, F., Chamoso, P. (eds.) ISAmI 2020. AISC, vol. 1239, pp. 127–136. Springer, Cham (2021). https://doi.org/10.1007/978-3-030-58356-9_13
25. Smith, R., Dragone, M.: A dialogue-based interface for active learning of activities of daily living. In: 27th International Conference on Intelligent User Interfaces, Helsinki Finland, pp. 820–831. ACM, March 2022. https://doi.org/10.1145/3490099.3511130
26. Thoduka, S.: GitHub - HEART-MET/activity_recognition_ros (2022). https://github.com/HEART-MET/activity_recognition_ros
27. Thoduka, S., Nair, D., Hochgeschwender, N., Caleb-Solly, P., Dragone, M., Cavallo, F.: METRICS HEART-MET field evaluation campaign rulebook. Technical report (2022)
28. Wang, A., Kurutach, T., Liu, K., Abbeel, P., Tamar, A.: Learning robotic manipulation through visual planning and acting. arXiv preprint arXiv:1905.04411 (2019)
29. Wisspeintner, T., Zant, T.v.d., Iocchi, L., Schiffer, S.: RoboCup@Home: scientific competition and benchmarking for domestic service robots. Interact. Stud. Soc. Behav. Commun. Biol. Artif. Syst. **10**(3), 392–426 (2009). https://doi.org/10.1075/is.10.3.06wis. http://www.jbe-platform.com/content/journals/10.1075/is.10.3.06wis

Locomotion and Manipulation

CPG-Based Locomotion Control of a Quadruped Robot with an Active Spine

Yunlong Lian$^{(\boxtimes)}$ [ID], Tianyuan Wang[ID], Joe Ingham[ID], Mark A. Post[ID], and Andy Tyrrell[ID]

School of Physics, Engineering and Technology, University of York, York YO105DD, UK
`yunlong.lian@york.ac.uk`

Abstract. Central pattern generators (CPGs) are neural networks responsible for producing rhythmic behaviours and are commonly found in both vertebrate and invertebrate animals. This paper proposes a novel internal feedback mechanism for a CPG model designed to generate leg-spine coordinated locomotion in a quadruped robot with an active spine. This mechanism enables the CPG to independently control the frequency and amplitude of the stance and swing durations while also modifying the definition of stance and swing phases to generate more gaits. The CPG model's results are demonstrated on a simulated "tensegrity quadruped robot" called TQbot, which features a flexible spine with 3 degrees of freedom (DOF). By adjusting the parameters, the CPG model can generate gaits with leg-spine coordination and uses the spine for turning.

Keywords: Quadruped robot · CPG · Tensegrity spine · Spine control

1 Introduction

In nature, a supple spine plays a crucial role in maintaining gait stability and facilitating agility for quadrupedal animals. Utilising spinal motion to generate equally agile gaits for quadruped robots has always been an exciting and challenging goal. Many research institutes and commercial organizations have developed state-of-the-art quadruped robots to achieve animal-like performance. However, due to the development cost, design and control difficulties, most quadruped robots use a rigid body [1,10,13,17,19,20,23].

Robotic spine studies are often found in crawling [11], snake [14], salamander [12] and modular robots [2]. A salamander robot with an active spine is able to perform a walking gait on the ground and swimming motion in water. The locomotion that synchronises the spine and legs is determined by coupled phase oscillators [4]. Another biologically inspired sprawling posture robot can

Supported by a University Research Priming Funding Grant from the University of York.

perform agile turning behaviours with its active spine [8]. Their controller also achieves precise control and synchronises leg and spine motion by solving the inverse kinematics of the spine. Other studies investigated the influence of the spine on quadruped robots. MIT Cheetah explored the flexible spine impact on energy efficiency and high-speed running [21]. The differentially actuated spine can be actuated in the sagittal plane when the rear legs are in-phase. Serval is a quadruped robot with an active spine that has 3 DOF [5]. It was developed for utilising its spine to perform agile turning behaviours that are achieved by simply adding an offset to the spinal joint. Another study built a rat-like robot with a soft active spine to explore the effect of spine motion in the sagittal plane on the speed [9]. The results have shown a lateral flexion of an actuated spine benefit on robot's velocity.

On the other hand, the spine function of different robots depends significantly on the spine structures that require it to be specially designed. The incorporation of additional actuators at the waist of a quadruped robot with a spine can lead to an increase in overall weight. Thus, it poses a challenge to design a spine with 3 DOF while minimising weight gain. Furthermore, special mechanism design causes the control methods to be robot-specific. In the case of a rigidly connected spine, its motion can be effectively generated by solving inverse kinematics. However, employing this method to manipulate a flexible spine precisely would be difficult. Furthermore, the coordination of leg and spine movements poses an additional challenge in generating efficient and dynamic locomotion for quadruped robots with a spine. The survey revealed three main methods used to control the spinal motion of quadruped robots: modelling the robot and defining desired spine movement in Cartesian space, then using robot kinematics to fit it [7,24]; using a parameterised wave function to generate spinal motion but the cooperation of leg and spine is a problem [22]; Combining a bio-inspired method, CPG, with inverse kinematics can achieve precise control of the spine and coordinate it with legs, but this method is limited to control one of the orientations of the spine [8].

A quadruped robot with an actuated spine has the potential to improve the stability and speed of the whole body during movement [16]. Thus, a quadruped robot with an active spine to investigate leg-spine coordination and demonstrate in simulation is the core of this paper. Its spine joint mechanism is described in the next section. Section 3 introduces the modified CPG model in detail; in Sect. 4, the gaits generation results of the CPG in a simulation will be demonstrated. Section 5 completes the paper with conclusions and suggestions for future work.

2   TQbot Structure

The quadruped robot used in this paper is called TQbot, which stands for a tensegrity quadruped robot, shown in Fig. 1(a). The robot with a flexible spine and has 15 DOF, with 3 DOF for each leg and the spine.

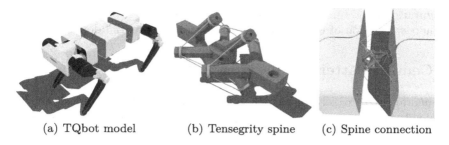

(a) TQbot model   (b) Tensegrity spine   (c) Spine connection

Fig. 1. TQbot structure: The robot body comprises three parts shown in (a). Two tensegrity spines are passive components that connect neighbouring body segments (b). Four braided wires around the passive spine are used to drive the spinal joints (c).

2.1   Spinal Joint

Existing studies on quadruped robots with a spine typically have one or two actuated DOF in the lumbar region, and a few have 3 DOF [5,8,9]. Others research passive elastic soft spine to improve its energy efficiency while the weight of the body also increases [21]. However, the tensegrity structure as a robot spine has the following advantages compared with existing rigid actuated spines:

(1) Its independent three degrees of rotational freedom can be simultaneously actuated. The overall workspace of the robot is thus extensively increased to realise more advanced and agile manoeuvres.
(2) Tensegrity structures have higher structural efficiency compared with rigid structures, which allows a greater payload ratio of the robot.
(3) The inherent compliance of the tensegrity spine improves the robustness of the robot for situations such as external impacts and hazards.
(4) The flexibility of the tensegrity spine can potentially improve the energy efficiency of the robot and deal with external perturbation.

The spine structure has passive and active parts. The passive part is two identical tensegrity spines that only provide a connection between body segments, shown in Fig. 1(b). Each is composed of one tensegrity vertebra and two half-vertebrae as the rigid elements to imitate its biological counterparts. They are continuously pretensioned in a passive manner for structural integrity and to constrain the translational displacement to a certain extent. To actuate three degrees of rotational freedom allowed by the tensegrity spine in roll, pitch and yaw orientation, the active part adopts the completely constrained parallel manipulator (CPRM) configuration. It imitates the muscles around the vertebrate to drive spinal joints to generate spinal motions. The CPRM configuration consists of eight 2 mm diameter braided polyethene lines with a load capacity of 250 kg. Adjacent body segments are connected by four wires, shown in Fig. 1(c). Four motors are placed in the middle body segment, and each controls two wires simultaneously and is connected to the front and rear body, respectively. Such configuration allows fewer actuators to actuate three DOF but also results in a symmetrical motion of the two spines in the time and spatial domain.

3 Central Pattern Generators

As a neural circuit widely found in vertebrate and invertebrate animals, the CPG has a natural advantage in coordinating and synchronizing the motion of the spine and legs. A modified CPG model with an internal feedback mechanism is proposed to generate diverse locomotion for a quadruped robot with an actuated spine. The improved CPG model is capable of independently controlling the stance and swing phases of a gait. Moreover, adjusting a specific parameter can modify the definition of stance and swing phases to produce more behaviours. The mathematical equations utilised in the CPG will be elaborated, followed by a presentation of the CPG topology structure and reference oscillator.

3.1 The Modified Phase Oscillator and Internal Feedback Mechanism

The modified oscillators that composed the CPG model are based on [4], which is a set of differential equations. Due to the special mechanical design, the robot has two symmetric spine joints, which can only simultaneously be in a symmetrical orientation. Thus an oscillator is used to drive one orientation of the spine joint, a total of three oscillators controlling the spine of the robot, which are responsible for controlling the rotation in transverse, sagittal and coronal planes separately. The equations of the modified phase oscillators used for all joints are given in Eqs. 1–7:

$$\dot{\phi} = 2\pi * f(v_i) + \sum_j (\omega_{ij} sin(\phi_j - \phi_i - \varphi_{ij})) \tag{1}$$

$$\dot{r}_i^{st} = a_r(R_i^{st} - r_i^{st}) \tag{2}$$

$$\dot{r}_i^{sw} = a_r(R_i^{sw} - r_i^{sw}) \tag{3}$$

$$\dot{x}_i = a_x(X_i - x_i) \tag{4}$$

$$\theta_i = x_i + f(r_i)cos(\phi_i) \tag{5}$$

with

$$f(r_i) = \lambda_i(r_i^{st} + r_i^{sw}) + r_i^{sw} \tag{6}$$

$$f(v_i) = \lambda_i(v_i^{st} + v_i^{sw}) + v_i^{sw} \tag{7}$$

where ϕ_i and v_i are the phase and frequency of the i-th oscillator separately. The parameters w_{ij} are the coupling weights that are zero if oscillators i and j do not have a connection while φ_{ij} represents the phase difference between oscillator i and j. θ_i is the set-point generated by the oscillator that can be regarded as an angle, torque or angular of a joint. It varies with time, and the unit can be determined according to the actual application. In this study, θ_i represents a joint angle, and a PD controller is used to follow it. X_i and x_i are target and current offset of i-th oscillator. a_r and a_x are constant positive gains that represent the convergence speed of amplitude and offset.

However, the amplitude and frequency of some quadruped gaits vary in the stance and swing phases. The independent control of the amplitude and frequency allows for the potential generation of more dynamic and stable gaits. To achieve this, Eqs. 2 and 3 are used to generating target amplitude for the i-th oscillator in the stance and swing phase. R_i^{st} and R_i^{sw} control the desired stance and swing amplitudes, and the current amplitudes are r^{st} and r^{sw}. The stance and swing frequency, v^{st} and v^{sw}, will be directly input and each set to the same in the same gait. For the automatic selection of parameters corresponding to the phase in gaits, an internal feedback mechanism is proposed in the CPG model (as shown in Fig. 3). The Eq. 6–7 utilises the mechanism to dictate the amplitude and frequency in each leg's stance and swing phases. λ_i is an internal feedback signal obtained from the k-th hip joint oscillator ($k \in (8, 9, 10, 11)$). It is used to determine the stance and swing phases for the shoulder and knee joint oscillators of the same leg. Figure 2 shows the value of λ_k varies with the k-th hip joint phase and how μ_k's value to affect the definition of stance and swing phase.

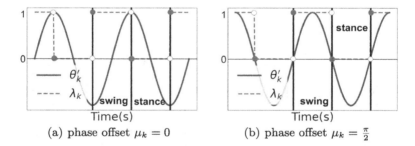

(a) phase offset $\mu_k = 0$ (b) phase offset $\mu_k = \frac{\pi}{2}$

Fig. 2. Internal feedback signal: The dashed red line is the signal (λ_k), and the blue line is the trajectory of θ'_k. In (a), The definition of swing phase is defined as a rising edge of the blue line, while the stance phase is the falling edge. In (b), the swing phase corresponds to θ'_k value greater than 0, and the stance phase is the opposite. The red solid point indicates that the λ_k is defined, while the hollow point is not defined. (Color figure online)

The λ_k is calculated using Eqs. 8–9:

$$\lambda_k = \begin{cases} \frac{|\dot{\theta}'_k| - \dot{\theta}'_k}{2|\dot{\theta}'_k|}, & \dot{\theta}'_k \neq 0 \\ 1, & \dot{\theta}'_k = 0, \ddot{\theta}'_k \leq 0 \\ 0, & \dot{\theta}'_k = 0, \ddot{\theta}'_k > 0 \end{cases} \tag{8}$$

with

$$\theta'_k = cos(\phi_k + \mu_k) \tag{9}$$

Equation (8) is a linear piecewise function that only has two values: 0 and 1, which represent the swing and stance phases respectively. According to the definition of hip joint angle, the stance phase is a falling edge from the highest point to the lowest point during movement, while the swing phase is the opposite. Hence, determining whether the leg is in the swing or stance phase can be achieved by calculating the first and second-order differential of (5). Moreover, the stance and swing phase definition should be changeable, considering those are different in some behaviours, for instance, walking on the spot. To achieve this, Eq. (9) is introduced, which takes the k-th hip joint phase, ϕ_k, and a phase offset, μ_k, as the input. The θ'_k has the same phase as the k-th oscillator and the parameter μ_k is used to change the definition of stance and swing phase in gaits.

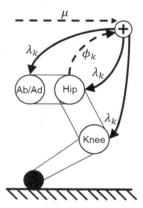

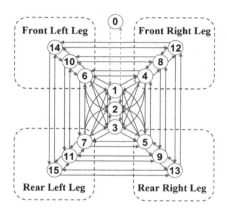

Fig. 3. Internal feedback mechanism in a leg: μ_k is an user input and ϕ is obtained from a hip joint. Output λ_k value to shoulder (Ab/Ad), hip and knee joint to independent control of swing and stance amplitude and frequency.

Fig. 4. Topology structure of the CPG: The red lines indicate spinal oscillators connected to other joints, and the blue lines are leg joint oscillators' connections. The arrow shows the connection direction between each oscillator. (Color figure online)

3.2 CPG Model Structure

The CPG model can easily generate rhythmic patterns for robots. However, as robots have different structures and DOF, it is necessary to design a suitable topology for a particular robot to generate its desired pattern.

Fish and salamander-shaped robots usually use chain CPGs [3,4,11,12], while quadrupedal robots usually use mesh structures [6,15,18]. The purpose of the CPG model is to synchronize the movement of the limbs with the spine for TQbot. To achieve this, the CPG consists of 15 oscillators, each of which corresponds to a single DOF. The topology of the CPG model is a network with a complicated coupling, shown in Fig. 4. The oscillators of spinal joints are connected to each other and have a full connection with the oscillators of shoulder joints. The oscillators of the shoulder, hip and knee joints in one leg are connected to each other in turn, and each oscillator is interconnected with adjacent oscillators. Owing to the complexity of the CPG network, the coupling weights for spinal joints to shoulder joints are double those of the other joints to ensure fast convergence of the phase among the oscillators towards the desired value (i.e., $\omega_{ij} = 8$ where $i \in (1, 2, 3)$, otherwise, $\omega_{ij} = 4$.). This emphasizes the significant influence that the phase of the spinal joint exerts on the shoulder joint to a certain degree.

In Fig. 4, 0 is a reference oscillator that does not correspond to any joints. 1–3 are spinal joint oscillators responsible for generating reference trajectories in roll, pitch, and yaw orientation. 4–7, 8–11, and 12–15 oscillators are shoulder joints, hip joints and knee joints respectively.

3.3   Reference Oscillator

For CPG models with a limited number of oscillators and simple connection relationships, the phase matrix utilises relative phase to determine the phase difference between oscillators. However, as the number of oscillators grows and the topology structure becomes increasingly complex, identifying the relative phase is challenging. For example, a fully connected CPG network comprising four oscillators necessitates at least six relative phases to derive a complete phase matrix. In our 15-oscillator CPG network, a minimum of 27 relative phases between oscillators must be determined due to the specified connection way.

Although it is possible to calculate the entire phase matrix from the relative phase of any one of the oscillators to the others, this approach leads to modifying the phase difference with all other oscillators when the phase of that oscillator needs to be altered. This undoubtedly complicates the process of adjusting the phase difference matrix. For instance, if the oscillator that controls the roll motion of the spine joint is employed as a reference oscillator, adjusting its phase in a specific gait would require changing the phases of all other oscillators. Consequently, using the relative phase to obtain the entire phase difference matrix can be troublesome for complex CPG models.

To resolve this issue, a reference oscillator is introduced to acquire the phase difference from others and calculate the relative phase between oscillators, thereby obtaining the entire phase matrix. The reference oscillator in the CPG is labelled as zero and is connected solely to the second oscillator, marked as one, that controls the roll orientation of the spinal joint(as shown in Fig. 4). The reference oscillator does not output externally and maintains an unchanged phase.

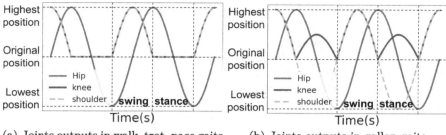

(a) Joints outputs in walk, trot, pace gaits   (b) Joints outputs in gallop gaits

Fig. 5. Single leg joints trajectories shaped by the internal feedback mechanism: phase and amplitude relationships in gaits.

4   Simulation

Currently, CPG is not the main gait generation method for quadruped robots because its ability to generate dynamic gaits is limited. One of the reasons for this is that the mechanism utilising feedback to shape locomotion is unknown in biology. The conventional CPG model with phase oscillators can only generate rhythmic but unnatural gaits for quadruped robots [4]. Other modified CPG models usually use hard-code programs to control the amplitude and frequency in the stance and swing phases, but it is difficult to generate different patterns [6]. However, the proposed internal feedback mechanism provides a way to shape more natural and various gaits that are difficult for other models. In this section, several gaits are analysed for tuning the parameters of the CPG to generate different frequencies and amplitude in the stance and swing phases. Especially trot in place gait, which other CPG models can hardly generate. The results of the diversity and effectiveness of gait patterns shaped by the internal feedback mechanism are verified by conducting experiments in a simulation called Isaac Sim[1].

4.1   Gaits Shaped by the Internal Feedback Mechanism

Basic Gaits. Following the gaits often observed in quadruped mammal walking videos, the phase difference between each joint can be determined. As illustrated in Fig. 5(a), during the swing phase, the leg must be lifted off the ground to allow for effective forward motion. To achieve this, the knee and shoulder joints are contracted and lifted separately during this phase. Then as the hip joint swings back to its original position from the highest position, the shoulder and knee joints are raised to their highest points. At the start of the stance phase, the shoulder and knee joints return to their original positions, and the hip joints reach the lowest position. The knee and shoulder joints generally remain stationary during the stance phase to ensure the stability of the robot while in

---

[1] All experimental results can be found at https://youtu.be/NJrMatc6PwU.

motion unless the swing of the hip joint is too large, in which case the knee and shoulder joints need to be extended until they hit the ground and then bent back into their original position. In the walk, trot and pace experiment, the swing of the hip joint was kept at small angles.

Figure 5(b) shows the leg joints phase in the gallop gait. The shoulder joint did not remain in position in the stance phase but continued to swing to obtain a greater stride length to increase speed. The phase of the knee joint is also slightly different from other gaits in the gallop gait due to the hip joint swinging at big angles. In order to maintain stability during the run, the knee joint in the stance phase will, the same as in the swing phase, contract slightly at first, reaching its highest position at the original position of the hip swing and then gradually extending back to its original position.

Trot in Place Gait. Except for the four basic gaits mentioned above, the gait of the trot in place is another commonly used gait for quadruped robots. The swing phase is when the hip joint swings backwards from the original position to the lowest position and back to the original position, while the whole leg does not move in the stance phase, as shown in Fig. 6. It can be easily generated by adjusting the phase offset ($\mu_k = \frac{\pi}{2}$) in the internal feedback mechanism.

The Usage of Spinal Motion. Typically, spine flexion at the coronal plane increases the length of the stride to improve speed, while flexion in the transverse plane helps with turning. In these experiments, all four basic gaits except the pace gait utilise the spine to varying extents. Walk and trot gaits incorporate the spine movements in the coronal and transverse planes. As the robot's front leg swings forward, the curvature of the spine in the coronal plane is toward the side of the front swinging forward leg. The movement of the spine in the transverse plane serves as a functional equivalent to the shoulder joint, lifting the leg during the swing phase. In the gallop gait, the spine bends downwards in the sagittal plane as the two front legs swing forward and upwards in the stance phase of the front legs, increasing the stride and speed of the robot. The results of the CPG output and gait transition of five basic gaits are shown in Fig. 6.

4.2   Multi-direction Movement in the Trot Gait

Move Backwards. In addition to implementing the basic gait for forward movement, a trot gait to enable the robot to move backwards has been developed. Notably, opposite to the forward gait, the hip joint in the backward gait enters the stance phase while swinging forward and the swing phase while swinging backwards. Thanks to the reference oscillator, the new phase difference matrix can be obtained by swapping the phase of the hip joints of the left and right legs. Other parameters and phase differences are the same as the forward trot gait parameters.

186   Y. Lian et al.

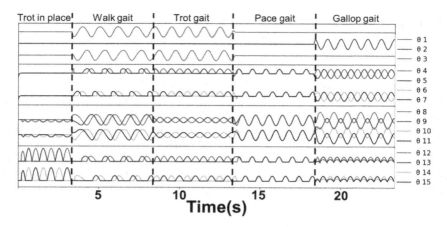

Fig. 6. Gait transitions: Achieved by replacing the parameter configurations of different gaits. In a real application, using a spline function can achieve a smooth transition. Changed at 3, 8, 13 and 18 s. Initial positions of all joints are 0. θ 1 to 3 are spinal joints corresponding to the movement in the transverse, sagittal and coronal planes. 4–7, 8–11, and 12–15 are shoulder, hip and knee joints that follow the RF-RR-LF-LR leg sequence.

Sideways Movement. Additionally, sideways movements are implemented based on the trot gait, which allows the robot to move laterally to the left or right. In this gait, the shoulder joints of the left and right legs are in phase, while that of the front and rear legs are in phase for half a cycle. In other words, the shoulder joints of the left front and right front legs are simultaneously extended to their highest position while the shoulder joints of the left rear and right rear legs are simultaneously contracted to their lowest position. It is important to note that the hip joint does not move during this gait; also, the stance/swing phase of shoulder and knee joints is different when moving left and right. For translating to the left, the shoulder joint of the left front leg is abduction in the swing phase, and that of the right rear leg is adduction simultaneously. Meanwhile, the knee joints of the left front leg and right rear leg rotate to the highest position, while that of the right front and left back legs are rotated to the lowest position. The shoulder joint is in the opposite phase when moving to the right, which can be achieved by swapping the phase difference between the right and left shoulder joints.

Turn in Circles. Regarding turning encircles gaits, the quadrupedal robots use the spine to make turns by simply giving it a bias in the coronal plane without modifying the trajectory of the leg joints. In this gait, the spine is not moved in the transverse and sagittal planes. The results in the simulation showed that the robot could generate efficient and stable turning gaits when the curvature of the spine in the coronal plane is within plus or minus 0.3 radians. Figure 7

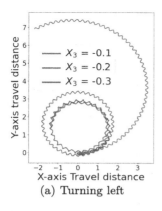
(a) Turning left

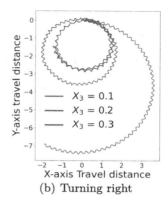
(b) Turning right

Fig. 7. Turning by bending the spinal joint in the coronal plane: The robot started to walk at $(0, 0)$ coordinates and moved for $50\,\mathrm{s}$. X_3 is the offset of the spinal joint in the coronal plane, which is negative to turn left and positive to turn right.

shows the travel trajectories using the turning gait with a bending spine in the simulation.

5 Conclusion

This paper presents a modified CPG model with an internal feedback mechanism, which is capable of coordinating a quadruped robot's legs with a 3-DOF spine to generate more natural and dynamic gaits. Additionally, the spinal motion employed in the trot gait is beneficial for executing circular turns. A reference oscillator is incorporated to adjust the phase difference matrix based on the absolute phase difference, simplifying the modification of oscillator phases and enhancing interpretability.

However, generating gait patterns using CPG models requires prior knowledge of the gaits and then tuning parameters by hand, making it challenging for robots to generate dynamic and robust gaits on rough terrains. In conclusion, future research should focus on the following aspects: (1) conducting parametric learning to enable robots to explore gaits autonomously; (2) developing a reflex system that integrates sensory information to generate dynamic gaits on unstructured terrains; and (3) combining other learning methods to achieve self-balancing in various terrains.

References

1. BostonDynamics: Spot. https://www.bostondynamics.com/products/spot. Accessed 17 Apr 2023
2. CH, S.S.R., et al.: 2DxoPod-a modular robot for mimicking locomotion in vertebrates. J. Intell. Robot. Syst. **101**, 1–16 (2021)

3. Crespi, A., et al.: Controlling swimming and crawling in a fish robot using a central pattern generator. Auton. Robot. **25**(1), 3–13 (2008)
4. Crespi, A., et al.: Salamandra Robotica II: an amphibious robot to study salamander-like swimming and walking gaits. IEEE Trans. Rob. **29**(2), 308–320 (2013)
5. Eckert, P., et al.: Towards rich motion skills with the lightweight quadruped robot serval - a design, control and experimental study. In: Manoonpong, P., Larsen, J.C., Xiong, X., Hallam, J., Triesch, J. (eds.) SAB 2018. LNCS (LNAI), vol. 10994, pp. 41–55. Springer, Cham (2018). https://doi.org/10.1007/978-3-319-97628-0_4
6. Gay, S., et al.: Learning robot gait stability using neural networks as sensory feedback function for central pattern generators. In: 2013 IEEE/RSJ International Conference on Intelligent Robots and Systems, pp. 194–201. IEEE (2013)
7. Hatton, R.L., Choset, H.: Generating gaits for snake robots: annealed chain fitting and keyframe wave extraction. Auton. Robot. **28**, 271–281 (2010)
8. Horvat, T., et al.: Spine controller for a sprawling posture robot. IEEE Robot. Autom. Lett. **2**(2), 1195–1202 (2017)
9. Huang, Y., et al.: Enhanced quadruped locomotion of a rat robot based on the lateral flexion of a soft actuated spine. In: 2022 IEEE/RSJ International Conference on Intelligent Robots and Systems (IROS), pp. 2622–2627. IEEE (2022)
10. Hutter, M., et al.: ANYmal-a highly mobile and dynamic quadrupedal robot. In: 2016 IEEE/RSJ International Conference on Intelligent Robots and Systems (IROS), pp. 38–44. IEEE (2016)
11. Ijspeert, A.J., et al.: From swimming to walking with a salamander robot driven by a spinal cord model. Science **315**(5817), 1416–1420 (2007)
12. Ijspeert, A.J., et al.: Online trajectory generation in an amphibious snake robot using a lamprey-like central pattern generator model. In: Proceedings 2007 IEEE International Conference on Robotics and Automation, pp. 262–268. IEEE (2007)
13. Kenneally, G., et al.: Design principles for a family of direct-drive legged robots. IEEE Robot. Autom. Lett. **1**(2), 900–907 (2016)
14. Liljeback, P., et al.: Snake robot locomotion in environments with obstacles. IEEE/ASME Trans. Mechatron. **17**(6), 1158–1169 (2011)
15. Liu, C., et al.: CPG driven locomotion control of quadruped robot. In: 2009 IEEE International Conference on Systems, Man and Cybernetics, pp. 2368–2373. IEEE (2009)
16. Pouya, S., et al.: Spinal joint compliance and actuation in a simulated bounding quadruped robot. Auton. Robot. **41**, 437–452 (2017)
17. Raibert, M., et al.: BigDog, the rough-terrain quadruped robot. IFAC Proc. Vol. **41**(2), 10822–10825 (2008)
18. Righetti, L., Ijspeert, A.J.: Pattern generators with sensory feedback for the control of quadruped locomotion. In: 2008 IEEE International Conference on Robotics and Automation, pp. 819–824. IEEE (2008)
19. Semini, C.: HyQ-design and development of a hydraulically actuated quadruped robot. Doctor of Philosophy (Ph. D.), University of Genoa, Italy (2010)
20. Semini, C., et al.: Design of HyQ-a hydraulically and electrically actuated quadruped robot. Proc. Inst. Mech. Eng. Part I J. Syst. Control Eng. **225**(6), 831–849 (2011)
21. Seok, S., et al.: Design principles for highly efficient quadrupeds and implementation on the MIT cheetah robot. In: 2013 IEEE International Conference on Robotics and Automation, pp. 3307–3312. IEEE (2013)
22. Tesch, M., et al.: Parameterized and scripted gaits for modular snake robots. Adv. Robot. **23**(9), 1131–1158 (2009)

23. UnitreeRobotics: B1 robot. https://www.unitree.com/b1. Accessed 17 Apr 2023
24. Yamada, H., Hirose, S.: Study on the 3d shape of active cord mechanism. In: Proceedings 2006 IEEE International Conference on Robotics and Automation, 2006, ICRA 2006, pp. 2890–2895. IEEE (2006)

Low-Resolution Sensing for Sim-to-Real Complex Terrain Robots

Dexter R. Shepherd$^{(\boxtimes)}$ ⓘ and James C. Knight ⓘ

University of Sussex, Brighton, UK
d.r.shepherd@sussex.ac.uk
https://www.sussex.ac.uk/

Abstract. Here we employ evolutionary approaches to enable robotic agents to learn strategies for energy-efficient navigation through complex terrain, consisting of water and different heights. Simulated agents, equipped with a low-resolution depth sensor, must learn how to navigate between randomly chosen locations in a procedurally generated world, along a path which minimises energy usage. The solution that consistently emerged, was an agent that followed the contours of the map, resulting in near-optimal performance in little evolutionary time. Furthermore, initial experiments showed that neural networks trained in simulation were able to successfully predict the movements required to follow contours from real Kinect sensor data. This demonstrates that this approach is able to transfer from simulation to the real world (known as the 'reality gap') and suggests that the evolved strategies are robust to noise. We suggest that this robustness is due to the use of a low-resolution sensor.

Keywords: Robotics · low-resolution · evolution

1 Introduction

Nearly all organisms are limited at some point when it comes to movement and environmental conditions. For example, leaf cutter ants avoid wet leaves to prevent themselves being washed away [1]. Such environmental factors constrain an organism's ability to traverse terrain. When a path looks too hazardous, organisms will often choose an easier route. While robots can use path planning algorithms to solve this problem [2], these require an accurate terrain model of the world. If there is no map, or the world is dynamic, the path must be decided using local information. Such approaches are particularity relevant for planetary exploration where, due to long communication delays, autonomy is required but a robot getting stuck could result in billions of dollars wasted.

Here, we use a genetic algorithm to evolve a controller for a simulated agent equipped with a low-resolution depth sensor to enable it to navigate within complex, unmapped terrain. The agent is given a desired destination it has to reach while avoiding impassable areas within the environment. Success was

© The Author(s), under exclusive license to Springer Nature Switzerland AG 2023
F. Iida et al. (Eds.): TAROS 2023, LNAI 14136, pp. 190–201, 2023.
https://doi.org/10.1007/978-3-031-43360-3_16

defined as reaching the goal while expending as little energy as possible. If the agent gets stuck it will receive no reward and if it makes unnecessary movements the amount of reward it received will be reduced. The agent is controlled by a two layer neural network, which receives inputs from a depth sensor and produces outputs representing the desired direction of movement. Following a straight path to the goal is the obvious solution, but even with such low resolution and a small network, agents that perform contour following were consistently evolved through trials.

Genetic approaches have been previously used for successful navigation in simulated environments [3] but, bridging the gap between simulation and real world (known as the reality gap), poses challenges with real world noise and complexity [4]. However, by using our trained networks with input from a real Kinect sensor, our preliminary results suggest that the low-resolution sensor enables robust behaviour in the face of noise and crucially allows the successful transfer of the solution to the real robot.

Finally, as well as being able to avoid treacherous terrain, some organisms also have additional strategies for overcoming obstacles. For example cockroaches bend their backs and bring their limbs into phase to climb over obstacles as illustrated in Fig. 1. Inspired by this strategy, we developed a robot with claw-like wheel-leg hybrid actuators known as 'whegs' [5–7] and had an additional motor which could be used to bend its 'back' [8]. Again, using genetic algorithms we develop controllers for the back-bending actuator based on motor current and accelerometer sensors.

Fig. 1. (left) How a cockroach rotates its limbs to climb an obstacle. (right) A robot with wheg's inspired by this strategy (after [8]).

Our genetic approach used a simulated environment for training and successfully avoided hazardous terrain in the real world. We believe this is down to the low resolution sensing in both simulation and real life that helps abstract from unnecessary detail. The model is deploy-able within an unknown environment, unlike many SLAM techniques which can require prior exploration to the navigation.

2 Methods

2.1 Simulated Environment

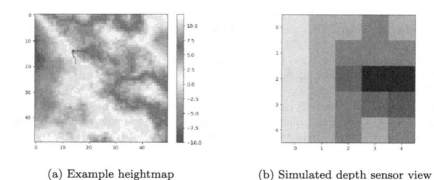

(a) Example heightmap   (b) Simulated depth sensor view

Fig. 2. Example procedural terrain with agent looking towards bottom of the map. This is recognisable by the increased climb in the in the bottom-right corner of the map. This corresponds to the hill climb facing the agent. The darker values represent a greater height than a lower value. The orientation of b is as the robot is looking at it. From a first person view b would be rotated $180°$ within the agent perception. The agent was viewing parallel to the ground, therefore would not view sky in order to reduce the complexity of the simulation.

We set up the simulated environment shown in Fig. 2a using Python by generating a 2D heightmap from 10 octaves of Perlin noise [9]. We generated a first person depth view by casting rays outwards from the agent at $20°$ intervals across a field-of-view of $100°$ in azimuth, at 5 different height levels. This generates a 5×5 image of the terrain within 5 units of the front of the robot as shown in Fig. 2b. The energy consumed (E) by an agent in a given trial can calculated from the number of steps taken (S) and the accumulated terrain value of each place (P). The difference between movement is the step S up, down, or across from the current height. This is called the terrain value. More energy is used going uphill than downhill, so these state transitions are valuable for calculating fitness. The Manhattan distance [10] is used as a measure of how far the agent has travelled, as fitness is measured at the end of a trial from start and end positions and we need to approximate the distance travelled. To add additional complexity, we defined any regions below a set height as water, which acted as an in-penetrable obstacle.

2.2 Neural Network

Our network architecture consisted of one 2D convolutional layer with a single 3×3 filter, followed by a linear layer which also had two additional input nodes providing the direction vector towards the end goal, supplying the model with the direction the agent *should* be travelling. Both of these hidden layers use of a Sigmoid activation function

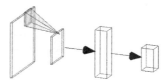

Fig. 3. Network architecture with one convolutional filter being flattened into a linear layer. This linear layer takes in additional data which is not seen in the diagram.

Finally, the linear layer was densely connected to an output layer with 8 nodes, representing movements in worldspace that the agent could take. At each timestep, the agent moves in the direction specified by the output node with the largest value. These output nodes represent each of the movements in worldspace as a vector $(1,1)$, $(1,0)$, $(0,1)$, $(-1,-1)$, $(-1,0)$, $(0,-1)$, $(-1,1)$, and $(1,-1)$ applied over the eight nearest neighbour gridspace (Fig. 3).

2.3   Strategies

We used a genetic algorithm (GA) to train the parameters of the neural network described above. The GA made use of mutation, crossover, and fitness evaluation where parameters were sampled from Gaussian distributions. The evolutionary encoding for these parameters would take the concatenated flattened shapes of all the weights and biases of the network, and generate a random Gaussian array of floating point values. A population of these would be formed at the beginning of each trial. When a genotype was selected it was broken down by a number of indices to be reshaped into the matrices that formed the neural network.

Mutation was implemented by applying another Gaussian distribution over the top of a genotype. We explored different standard deviation and mean parameters and constrained values between -4 and 4 to prevent values getting too high or too low and biasing the performance of the network.

The first GA was a simple microbial algorithm. This generated a population of varied sizes and the optimal was found to be between 10–20 genotypes. Two genotypes would be selected from the sample and trialled on three different random maps starting from randomly generated coordinates, and then fitness calculated. The winner would copy over to the losing gene with a crossover between a mutation of the winning genotype and the current genotype.

2.4   Evolutionary Training

In each trial, a start position and end goal were placed at random locations in the environment, 10 units apart. We optimised the neural network described above

using the Microbial genetic algorithm [11] and a fitness function $((100-\text{energy})\times$
$0.003+(10-\text{endDist})\times 0.007)\times 100$ such that minimising distance is worth 70%
of the fitness, and minimising energy 30%. Additionally, if the agent collides with
water or ends up further away from the target than it started, fitness is set to
0. As it is only possible to get 100% energy efficiency by travelling down hill, it
is likely that most trials are only able to get a top fitness within the 90% range.
Each genotype is trialled three times on random coordinates, and the fitness is
averaged. This is to make sure the genotype isn't biased to a specific point which
would result in a unrepresentative high fitness.

2.5   Physical Robot

Fig. 4. Robotic chassis used for physical trials.

We developed the robot chassis shown in Fig. 4 which is driven by continuous
rotation servos, attached to claw-style wheels known as 'whegs', inspired by
the cockroach locomotion strategy previously described [8]. The whegs were 3D
printed using our own novel bi-directional design which allows the robot to go
backwards and forwards over obstacles. The robot had a bendable back driven
by two servos on a pan-tilt mechanism. We used a simple hill climber to evolve a
feed forward neural network of two hidden layers (each of size 3) that would bend
the back of the robot when it became stuck. The network made use of sigmoid
activation functions. The neural network received tilt input from a MPU050 6-
axis IMU, servo angle from the back joint and servo current measured with a
Raspberry Pi powerHat. The output makes use of two nodes where the maximum
predicted value out of the two nodes represents whether the servo should move
up $20°$, or move down $20°$.

2.6   Visual Processing

In order to provide a similar depth image to that provided in our simulation, we
used an Xbox Kinect sensor. We cropped out the central 200×400 pixels of the
depth image to obtain the correct field-of-view and downsampled this to 5×5
using area interpolation to match the input resolution of our simulated agent.

(a) Distances and Raw image   (b) Pre-processed

Fig. 5. Xbox Kinect sensor output with measured distances of objects including: A solder coil, a sofa, the back of a sofa/the wall. in a e have labelled the distance from the camera to each object.

Figure 5b shows that images produced in this way closely resemble those obtained from the simulation (see Fig. 2b) – the nearest object is highlighted clearly, while the background gets further distant. The sofa and wall are recognisable but smaller details are abstracted from view.

A   B

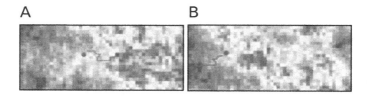

Fig. 6. Example trials in simulated environment. Red and blue circles show agent start and end positions respectively and lines show path taken. (Color figure online)

3 Results

3.1 Performance of Simulated Agents

We evolved 20 agents for 500 generations using the baseline microbial algorithm and evaluated their performance by averaging the fitness across three trials with random start and end positions. The mean fitness of successful agents was 89% and this was always achieved in <100 generations. Figure 6 shows typical behaviour and it is interesting to see that contour-following has emerged – a strategy which avoids energy loss *and* water. This is clearly visible in Figs. 6A and Fig. 6B where the agent avoids water and overly steep terrain. We also explored a 'group' GA [12], inspired by groups of genes within a larger population. Research has showed that such approaches can outperform microbial algorithms due to a higher diversity of genes within winning groups which

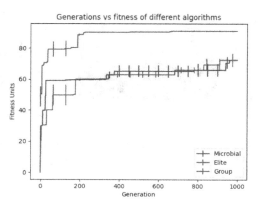

(a) Comparing evolutionary algorithms

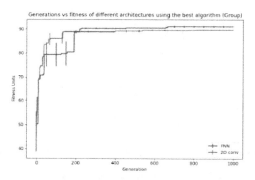

(b) Comparing network architectures

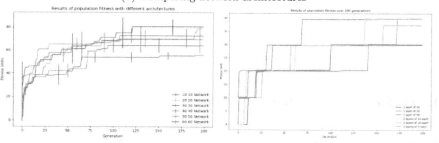

(c) Comparing hyperparameters CNN   (d) Comparing hyperparameters FNN

Fig. 7. Mean fitness across generations over three trials. Error bars indicate standard deviations. Networks in b and c were evolved using the group algorithm. In b the FNN uses two densely-connected layers with 10 units each and the convolutional neural network uses a kernel size 3×3 followed by two densely-connected layers with 10 units each. The kernel is preset therefore does not need to evolve this (meaning parameters are the same size within the genotypes). In c, the values within the legend are encoded as "numInLayer1 numInLayer2 hidden layer" i.e. "10 10" means there were 10 nodes in layer one and 10 nodes in layer two. When using a convolutional layer, this refers to the linear layers that proceed the fixed convolution. d demonstrates the same evaluation but on an FNN.

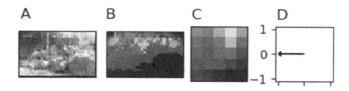

Fig. 8. (**A**) RGB & (**B**) depth image from Kinect. (**C**) Depth image downsampled to 5×5 (yellow = far, black = near). (**D**) Movement direction from model. (Color figure online)

prevents convergence on sub-optimal solutions. Fitness was measured by the summation of the fitness of all genes within a group $\sum_{i=1}^{n}(\text{fitness}(\text{gene}_i))$.

The theory is that the group strategy would result in more internal diversity and thus provide better solutions and prevent premature convergence on sub-optimal solutions, as Fig. 7b shows. The group algorithm within these trials significantly outperformed the other algorithms and landed with a high fitness. We averaged separate random start positions and end positions of the same agent. This prevented fluke results of agents biased to specific routes. Maximum fitness would converge in the 80% range which is seen in the results. This inspired the creation of the 'elitist' GA algorithm which would use a microbial strategy for a fixed number of generations, then repopulate the population with mutations of the top gene. The most effective, according to the tests within Fig. 7a was the group of microbial with re-selection of the best genes.

The fitness units in Fig. 7 are not optimal averaging different trials of the same network. The population is regenerated randomly each time which leads to some trials having a low fitness bearing population by default. The use of standard deviations helped evaluate the spread of fitnesses each trial to assist in picking the best architecture for this task. In our baseline experiments the agent achieved 89% fitness with a microbial algorithm. It is likely this was an outlier, as multiple trials showed significant difference between the algorithms used.

In Fig. 7b we compare the performance of a densely connected feedforward network and a convolutional architecture with the same number of parameters. While the FNN appears to out-perform the convolutional network, by a few percent, qualitative inspection showed more interesting contour following behaviour emerged with the CNN. The interest in particular arose from a higher diversity in movement from the convolutional network. In Fig. 7c we also show the result of an exploration of different network hyper parameters such as numbers of nodes and numbers of layers. We found that more larger layers did not result in any significant accuracy improvement over smaller networks. This is probably due to the larger number of parameters there was to evolve.

3.2 Preliminary Evaluation of Models on Real-World Data

To determine if our trained models are robust enough to cross the reality gap, we provided agents with a random goal direction and a real-world depth image from the Kinect sensor (preprocessed as previously described). As Fig. 8A-C illustrates, our preprocessing successfully extract a low-resolution depth map of the scene. Furthermore, as Fig. 8D shows, when confronted with this scene the agent would move left – which would skirt the steepest area of rocks. Although inspection of the depth maps suggests that real world noise *can* lead to erroneous depth estimates (See Fig. 9), the model appears robust to this. Indeed, comparing against human labelling of 150 images, the robot picked a sensible direction 74% of the time suggesting that the solution will cross the reality gap.

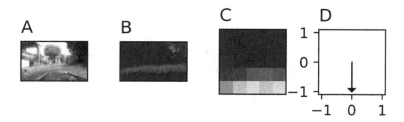

Fig. 9. The issue of objects being too far away and the depth camera registering as too close.

3.3   Evolved Back-Bending Controllers

Back-bending was used when the robot was stuck, in order to redistribute weight and find a way out of its stuck position. Being stuck was detected through current monitoring of the servo motors. If a motor is driven but, due to environmental constraints is prevented from turning, then the current would spike as shown in Fig. 11. Based on the measurements shown in Fig. 11 we determined that the robot was stuck if the motor current exceeded 400mA in more than 30% of the last three current readings.

Back actuation improved the robots ability to traverse terrain, which can be seen in the qualitative example shown in Fig. 10. Redistribution of weight allowed more torque to the front Whegs. The physical agent was trailed over different terrain. In order to prove the concept of back-bending and obstruction detection, the robot was placed on a flat surface and it would be physically held onto the floor to detect being stuck. Once detected the robot would be released. When we placed the robot over rocks to trial this same principle. When the robot detected being stuck, the neural network would be activated and would keep predicting back bending instructions until the robot detects that it is no longer stuck.

Fig. 10. How the angle on the robot changes with back actuation. The first image is where the robot got stuck going over a barrier. The second image shows the distribution of weight to the centre of the robot, which allowed more torque to be focused on the back wheel rotation rather than holding the weight of the robot. The final image shows the robot having climbed over the obstacle. Outlined in Fig. 10 is a drawn axis in blue to demonstrate the movement undertaken by the robot.

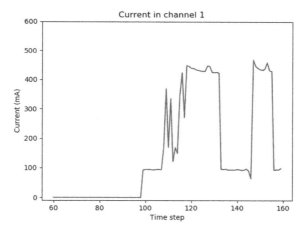

Fig. 11. Current draw from the device to each individual servo motor attached to the robotic chassis. At timestep 98, power is provided to free-spinning servo. At timestep 110, some resistance is applied. At timestep 120, robot is placed fully on the ground with weight preventing it from moving. Between timesteps 120 and 135, the robot was picked up, and placed back down.

4 Conclusion

In this paper, we have shown that agents using a low-resolution depth sensor can successfully avoid collision with environmental hazards and find paths across complex terrain that minimise energy usage through emergent contour following. Using such a low resolution depth image not only reduced the computation required to train and use the model but – as has been demonstrated in insect-inspired visual navigation research [13] – improves robustness to noise by only retaining low-frequency information. We demonstrated this by taking models evolved in simulation across the reality gap and showing that they were able to avoid obstacles in the real world. The success of this approach suggests that low-resolution sensing might be an interesting alternative to other more complex Sim2real approaches [14] and we also believe is key to how insects are able to navigate robustly despite very large restrictions on energy and neural resources. Next steps: smaller sensor and live running robot. If it is the low-resolution that is improving this, this perhaps suggests how insects are able to perform robustly despite very large restrictions on energy and neural resources, perhaps suggesting low-resolution sensing should be more widely investigated/is an alternative to other Sim2real approaches (e.g. radical envelope of noise/minimal simulation). Limitations of this research was only the depth sensor was trialled as input to the robot. The depth imaging was reduced to remove noise, something that could be trialled with other sensors, which could be the study of future work. Using a biologically inspired chassis improved the robot's ability to traverse terrain, which was expected. The locomotion features of cockroaches were successfully implemented using 3D printed Whegs and a bendable back. This allowed the chassis to climb over rocks and redistribute weight to improve torque at separate parts of the robot.

References

1. Farji-Brener, A.G., et al.: Working in the rain? Why leaf-cutting ants stop foraging when it's raining. Insectes Sociaux **65**, 233–239 (2018)
2. Delling, D., Sanders, P., Schultes, D., Wagner, D.: Engineering route planning algorithms. In: Lerner, J., Wagner, D., Zweig, K.A. (eds.) Algorithmics of Large and Complex Networks. LNCS, vol. 5515, pp. 117–139. Springer, Heidelberg (2009). https://doi.org/10.1007/978-3-642-02094-0_7
3. Tsai, C.-C., Huang, H.-C., Chan, C.-K.: Parallel elite genetic algorithm and its application to global path planning for autonomous robot navigation. IEEE Trans. Industr. Electron. **58**(10), 4813–4821 (2011)
4. Jakobi, N., Husbands, P., Harvey, I.: Noise and the reality gap: the use of simulation in evolutionary robotics. In: Morán, F., Moreno, A., Merelo, J.J., Chacón, P. (eds.) ECAL 1995. LNCS, vol. 929, pp. 704–720. Springer, Heidelberg (1995). https://doi.org/10.1007/3-540-59496-5_337
5. Martin-Alvarez, A., De Peuter, W., Hillebrand,J., Putz, P., Matthyssen, A., De Weerd, J.F.: Walking robots for planetary exploration missions. In: Proceedings of the of 2nd World Automation Congress (1996)
6. Quinn, R.D., Offi, J.T., Kingsley, D.A., Ritzmann, R.E.: Improved mobility through abstracted biological principles. In: IEEE/RSJ International Conference on Intelligent Robots and Systems, vol. 3, pp. 2652–2657 (2002)
7. Schwendner, J., et al.: CESAR: a lunar crater exploration and sample return robot. In: 2009 IEEE/RSJ International Conference on Intelligent Robots and Systems, pp. 3355–3360 (2009)
8. Schroer, R.T., Boggess, M.J., Bachmann, R.J., Quinn, R.D., Ritzmann,R.E.: Comparing cockroach and whegs robot body motions. In: IEEE International Conference on Robotics and Automation. Proceedings, ICRA 2004, vol. 4, pp. 3288–3293 (2004)
9. Perlin, K.: Improving noise. In: Proceedings of the 29th Annual Conference on Computer Graphics and Interactive Techniques, SIGGRAPH 2002, New York, NY, USA, pp. 681–682. Association for Computing Machinery (2002)

10. Malkauthekar, M.D.: Analysis of euclidean distance and Manhattan distance measure in face recognition. In: Third International Conference on Computational Intelligence and Information Technology (CIIT 2013), pp. 503–507 (2013)
11. Harvey, I.: The microbial genetic algorithm. In: Kampis, G., Karsai, I., Szathmáry, E. (eds.) ECAL 2009. LNCS (LNAI), vol. 5778, pp. 126–133. Springer, Heidelberg (2011). https://doi.org/10.1007/978-3-642-21314-4_16
12. Tomko, N., Harvey, I., Virgo, N., Philippides, A.: Many hands make light work: further studies in group evolution. Artif. Life **20**(1), 163–181 (2014)
13. Wystrach, A., Dewar, A., Philippides, A., Graham, P.: How do field of view and resolution affect the information content of panoramic scenes for visual navigation? A computational investigation. J. Comp. Physiol. A Neuroethol. Sens. Neural Behav. Physiol. **202**(2), 87–95 (2016)
14. Kadian, A., et al.: Sim2real predictivity: does evaluation in simulation predict real-world performance? IEEE Robot. Autom. Lett. **5**(4), 6670–6677 (2020)

Towards Wait-and-Catch Routine of a Dynamic Swinging Object Using a Prototype Robotic Arm Manipulator

Catalin Stefan Teodorescu[1]([✉]) [ID], Steve Vandenplas[2] [ID],
and Bruno Depraetere[2] [ID]

[1] Department of Electrical and Electronic Engineering, The University of
Manchester, Manchester M13 9PL, UK
`s.teodorescu@manchester.ac.uk`
[2] Flanders Make, Gaston Geenslaan 8, 3001 Heverlee, Belgium
{`steve.vandenplas,bruno.depraetere`}`@flandersmake.be`

Abstract. A robotic ball-catcher test demonstration built from a unique prototype manipulator is presented. Other than in previous work, the gripper catches a dynamic object moving within the workspace of the robot. The challenge is to be able to use a slow vision system yielding deficient measurements. We present theory for deriving the explicit (analytical) solution of the forward and inverse kinematics for the 5 degrees-of-freedom robotic manipulator. A dynamical model of the swinging object is used to predict its future trajectory, including the intercept point, algorithm tested in simulation and partly on the real experimental setup.

Keywords: prototype · robotic manipulator · kinematics

1 Introduction

Catching an object moving in the air is a challenging task for both humans (e.g. players of baseball, cricket) as well as for robots. This requires careful integration of mechatronic components with visual sensing algorithms [1,11,13]. The value of such applications resides in developing and testing key robotic algorithms that can be transferred to the industry [13]. Although perceived as a toy problem, the underlying method presented in this article has the potential to meet specific needs found in the agriculture sector [3]. It can also be used as a future education enabler [5].

In all works, the workflow is the same: a vision system tracks a moving object and sends the current location to a prediction algorithm able to anticipate the future trajectory of the flying object. This is then used to define an intercept point in Cartesian space. Using inverse kinematics, it is transformed to joint coordinates, sent as references to motors actuating the robotic arm and gripper. The general theory that enables such test demonstrators to be built is well developed [12] and can be applied to the particular case of the prototype robotic

This research was partially supported by Flanders Make, the strategic research centre for the manufacturing industry.

manipulator in Fig. 1. However there are still some practical challenges that need to be carefully addressed.

1.1 Previous Work

In [15] we introduced a prototype robot (an open, modular research platform).

It was designed to meet requirements of a robotic arm for fruit picking operations, with better capabilities than human operators. Emphasizing a more general use, we presented a test demonstrator of a repetitive pick-and-place operation involving static round objects as illustrated in Fig. 1a: the robot awaits the operator's command to start collecting the randomly distributed yellow balls, which will be automatically placed inside a cardboard box (positioned on the far end of the table on which the yellow balls sit).

1.2 Contributions

Regarding the practical developments, this work differs significantly from previous work [15] in two aspects. First, in this paper we present a second test demonstrator, where the robot manipulator gripper should catch a dynamic object while it moves within the workspace of the robot. One yellow ball is attached to one end of a string, while the other end of the string is fixed to the ceiling: this forms a pendulum. The aim is to be able to grab the ball using the robotic arm's gripper. The manipulator in Fig. 1 being one of a kind, some fundamental problems (theory) needed to be addressed, including the forward kinematics and inverse kinematics.

The second aspect is that new algorithms are needed to cope with a rather slow vision system, originally designed to detect *static* objects (not *dynamic* objects) at low frequency, about 2 Hz. This means that only two measurements can be taken during one period of the pendulum (a complete swing motion takes about 1 s). Consequently, because little information about the exact location of the ball is known, this poses a challenge to the prediction algorithm that needs to extrapolate this information to future locations of the ball.

In this paper, we: (i) derive the explicit (analytical) solutions of the forward and inverse kinematics problems for this particular 5 degrees-of-freedom robotic arm in Sect. 3; (ii) design a physical dynamical model of the swinging ball, represented as a 3D pendulum, in Sect. 4. This is used first to compute the best estimate of the *current location* of the ball using an extended Kalman filter, and then second, to predict the *future trajectory* of the ball, given its current estimated location; (iii) test results in simulation in Sect. 5.

2 Vision System Performance

The visual ball tracking is often the limiting factor in robotic ball-catcher applications [1]. The test rig in Fig. 1 uses a rather slow vision system, which sends out the position of the yellow ball: (i) asynchronously, (ii) time-delayed and (iii)

(a) in the so-called *homing position*, awaiting decision to start pick-and-place of the static yellow balls sitting on the table. Adapted from [15]

(b) approaching a swinging ball hanging up in the air, attached at the end of a string

Fig. 1. Prototype robotic arm manipulator (Color figure online)

at low frame rate (about 2 Hz) i.e. operates at low bandwidth. The histogram in Fig. 2 illustrates the distribution of the elapsed time between requesting and receiving a new measurement from the vision system. It shows an overall non-Gaussian behavior [4], with possibly two main effects. The x-axis data is quite spread (one can think of, e.g. the standard deviation) emphasizing the non-deterministic nature of the vision system measurements.

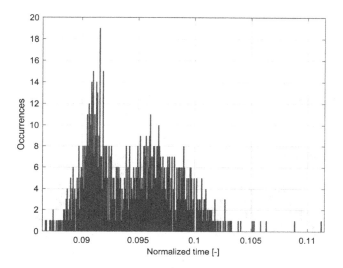

Fig. 2. Histogram of the time elapsed between requesting and receiving a new measurements from the vision system

The vision system algorithm relies on stereovision [6] and its working principle is depicted in Fig. 3a drawn using *OpenCV Viz*: two cameras attached on a fixed frame pointing towards a yellow object to be identified in the real world, take pictures synchronously (one per camera), then find (identify) the object on each picture, and next do the reconstruction of the 3D location of the object. The green lines in Fig. 3a connect the cameras' center of projection to the center of mass of the object and then, extend into the real environment. The reconstructed location of the object is where the two lines intersect. Figure 3b shows a screenshot from the actual system.

The motivation for this works follows. The motion of the swinging ball is fast compared to the capabilities of the vision system. Since we cannot rely on good temporal resolution for the location of the ball (i.e. measure quickly and with less delay), we need to combine those slow measurements and thus reconstruct the actual location. Moreover, in view of working towards a wait-and-catch demonstration, we need to be able to anticipate its location in the future.

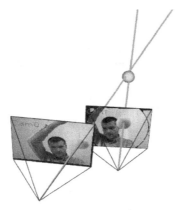

(a) Stereovision: reconstructing the 3D position of a moving object (a yellow ball) using two low-cost webcams located a few cm apart

(b) The hanging yellow ball was correctly identified and marked accordingly; the setup uses two professional cameras located a few meters apart

Fig. 3. Vision system (Color figure online)

3   Modeling the Robotic Arm

The manipulator has 5 degrees-of-freedom (dof), denoted by the linear displacement z_{0b}, and the angular displacements α, β, γ, Ω, illustrated in Fig. 4a: the robotic arm is capable of moving up-down on a vertical plane with angle α; rotates left-right around a vertical axis with angle β; rotates around two perpendicular axes with angles γ and Ω; slides forward-backward with linear distance z_{0b}.

In this section we address the forward and the inverse kinematics problems.

3.1 Forward Kinematics

The forward kinematics problem can be formulated as follows: given $(z_{0b}, \alpha, \beta, \gamma, \Omega)$, find the Cartesian coordinates vector of the gripper $p^0 = (x_0, y_0, z_0)$. The notation "0" stands for the inertial frame in Fig. 5; all conventions regarding the subscript or superscript used in this paper are consistent with [12]. Using the notations from Fig. 4b, where "H" stands for *height* and "L" stands for *length*, simple geometric calculations [12] give the following relations:

$$z_0 = z_{0b} + (L_c + L_t \cos\alpha + L_{gj}) \cos\beta - H_{ee} \sin\gamma \sin\beta \tag{1}$$

$$y_0 = (H_c + L_t \sin\alpha + H_{gj}) + H_{ee} \cos\gamma \tag{2}$$

$$x_0 = (L_c + L_t \cos\alpha + L_{gj}) \sin\beta + H_{ee} \sin\gamma \cos\beta \tag{3}$$

Note that Eqs. (1)–(3) are independent of Ω, so we will add it next. Assuming the more general case of an object that has a dominant dimension (say, the length) and which needs to be grabbed with a gripper, we shall impose the condition that, viewed from above, the gripper jaws should be positioned perpendicular to the axis of the dominant dimension of the object. Then, the following relation is obtained:

$$\Omega + \Lambda - \beta = \pi \tag{4}$$

where Λ is the angle between $-o_0 z_0$ and $o_{obj} x_{obj}$. The notation *obj* stands for the object frame, which will be presented in the next Sect. 3.3. To summarize, Eqs. (1)–(4) define the forward kinematics of this robotic arm manipulator.

3.2 Inverse Kinematics

The inverse kinematics problem can be formulated as follows: given $p^0 = (x_0, y_0, z_0)$, find $(z_{0b}, \alpha, \beta, \gamma, \Omega)$. The following physical restrictions apply to our experimental setup:

$$z_{0b} \in [0, 1] \text{ meter}, \quad \alpha \in [0°, 90°] \quad \beta \in [-180°, 180°],$$
$$\gamma \in [-90°, 270°], \quad \Omega \in [-180°, 180°] \tag{5}$$

In this work we are interested in the analytic explicit relations, readily used for code generation purpose (Matlab/Simulink to C/C++). Below, we show how to derive them in 5 steps. First, we fix the value of γ, motivated by the fact that we want to grab the swinging balls at a specific angle.

Second, with γ known, one can extract the value of α from (2):

$$\alpha = (-1)^k \arcsin \frac{y_0 - H_c - H_{gj} - H_{ee} \cos\gamma}{L_t} + k\pi$$

with $k \in \mathbb{Z}$. This relation has an infinite number of mathematical solutions, however by close inspection one will notice that only $k = 0$ allows to obtain a physical solution where $\alpha \in [0°, 90°]$ in order to comply with (5). All other solutions where $k \neq 0$ are disregarded.

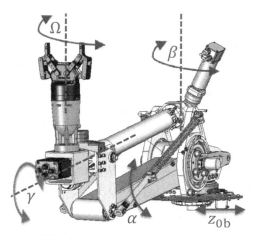

(a) CAD drawing emphasizing the 5-dof

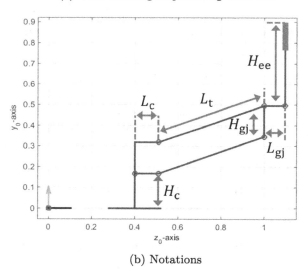

(b) Notations

Fig. 4. Robotic arm manipulator

Third, with γ and α known, one can use (3) in order to extract β:

$$\beta = (-1)^k \arcsin \frac{x_0}{\sqrt{(L_c + L_t \cos\alpha + L_{gj})^2 + (H_{ee}\sin\gamma)^2}}$$
$$+ k\pi - \varphi$$

where $\varphi = \text{atan2}\,(H_{ee}\sin\gamma,\ L_c + L_t\cos\alpha + L_{gj})$ and $k \in \mathbb{Z}$. Again, we are faced with an infinite number of mathematical solutions that are candidates for the physical solutions. Actually there are only two values $k \in \{-1, 0\}$ that allow to derive values for $\beta \in [-180°, 0°]$ in order to comply with (5). Each of these two solutions corresponds to a different kinematic configuration: while an object is grabbed with the gripper, the body of the robotic arm can be located either towards the left or the right of the object, respectively. A decision will need to be made based on the location of the swinging object.

Fourth, with (α, β, γ) known, z_{0b} can be extracted from (1):

$$z_{0b} = z_0 - (L_c + L_t \cos \alpha + L_{gj}) \cos \beta + H_{ee} \sin \gamma \sin \beta$$

Fifth, the gripper angle is calculated from (4):

$$\Omega = \pi - \Lambda + \beta \tag{6}$$

where the angle $\Lambda = \text{atan2}(R^0_{obj}(3,2), -R^0_{obj}(1,2))$. Here we used the notation $R^0_{obj}(i,j)$ which stands for the matrix element situated on the i-th row and the j-th column of the rotation matrix R^0_{obj}. A close inspection of (6) reveals that the result $\Omega \in [-\pi, 2\pi]$. Since the gripper can physically turn between $[-\pi, \pi]$ according to (5), in case a value exceeding π is obtained, it then needs to be subtracted by 2π.

We end this section by mentioning that for other, more complex manipulators, involving a larger number of (possibly redundant) dof, where deriving inverse kinematics eqs. analytically (explicitly) can be challenging, this task can be pursued, e.g. numerically [2] or by making use of machine learning tools like the Gaussian processes [9].

3.3 Coordinate Frames. Transformations

Figures 5 illustrates the relations between the following frames: the robotic arm inertial frame (o_0, x_0, y_0, z_0), the vision system or camera frame (o_c, x_c, y_c, z_c), the object frame $(o_{obj}, x_{obj}, y_{obj}, z_{obj})$ having its origin at the center of mass of the object to be picked, and the pendulum inertial frame (o_p, x_p, y_p, z_p).

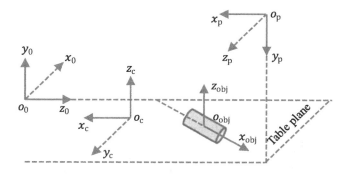

Fig. 5. Frames defined using the right-hand convention

For example, the position of an object defined in the camera frame P^c can be expressed in the pendulum inertial frame P^p using:

$$P^p = H^p_c \, P^c \tag{7}$$

where H^p_c is a transformation matrix containing a rotation and a translation [12].

4 Modeling a Swinging Object

A 1-dof pendulum can be used to represent the motion of a ball moving on a 2D plane. Instead of that, we are interested in the free motion happening in Cartesian space (3D space), and thus an extra dof is needed.

We used the robotics textbook approach [12] to create 3D motion by moving 2 rigid links on orthogonal 2D planes. The forward and inverse kinematics, and the dynamical model are straightforward. The resulting 2-dof system was used: (i) to compute the best estimate of the *current location* of the ball using an extended Kalman filter; (ii) to predict the *future trajectory* of the ball, given its current estimated location. Although not considered here, the *spherical pendulum* [7] is an alternative to the dynamical model used here.

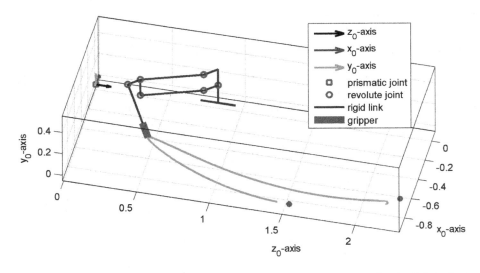

Fig. 6. Simulating wait-and-catch: after receiving two measurements (teal solid circles), the robot predicts the trajectory (green) of a dynamic swinging object, and takes the zero velocity position to be adequate for grabbing the object; the robot also computes how long it needs to wait there before closing the gripper. Note $\beta = -145°$ (Color figure online)

5 Simulations

All the theoretical results from the previous sections were used to build a wait-and-catch simulator, see Fig. 6. Because measurements coming from the vision system are scarce, it relies on an observer to reconstruct the *current location* of the yellow ball, given: (i) the slow measurements from the vision system; (ii) the time-variable but otherwise known time-delay, as explained in Sect. 2.

5.1 An Observer

To compute the best estimate of the *current location* of the yellow ball, a continuous-time extended Kalman filter (EKF) with asynchronous discrete-time measurements [8, Sect. 5.3.3] was implemented. The details are presented in [14]. The overall algorithm relies on the chain of actions depicted in Fig. 7: the vision system's output, a time-delayed asynchronous measurement p^c is converted using the transformation (7) into p^p; applying the inverse kinematics eqs., the vector q is extracted and then fed into the EKF; the *internal model* of this EKF relies on the dynamic model of the pendulum; using the joint coordinates estimates $\hat{q}$ and the forward kinematics eqs. of the pendulum, the estimate of the *current location* of the yellow ball $\hat{p}^p$ is computed.

Fig. 7. Estimating the current location of the swinging ball using an extended Kalman filter (EKF)

Although not considered here, in the same setting other observer designs are possible, like the unscented Kalman filter [8], the *particle filter* [10], or the simplified kinematic model [10], etc., some of which will be used in future work to benchmark our proposed EKF.

5.2 Predicting the Wait-and-Catch Location

At each sampling time, the EKF computes an estimate of the current location of the swinging ball $\hat{p}^p$ as well as a confidence. After sufficiently many measurements, the confidence becomes high enough to exceed an arbitrary threshold, and next, a predictor algorithm uses $\hat{p}^p$ as initial location to compute the future trajectory of the swinging ball. Specifically, the point where the future velocity vanishes becomes a reference location where the robot is positioned with its gripper wide open, awaiting the arrival of the ball between its fingers (see Fig. 6). To transform the reference location into reference joint coordinates, the inverse kinematics eqs. from Sect. 3.2 are used. These steps are reiterated at each sampling period, and the robotic arm keeps on repositioning itself until finally it grabs (catches) the ball by closing its gripper.

The accompanying video, available on https://youtu.be/w6gRV3Hz1y8 shows experimental validation of the forward and inverse kinematics equations from Sect. 4, and ongoing progress with the wait-and-catch demonstration. Figure 8 shows the setup during operation.

Fig. 8. Robotic arm during operation. The screen on the right is connected to the vision PC running ROS. The other two screens are connected to a laptop running the EKF and motion controllers in Matlab/Simulink. The green lamp is on, indicating the robot is in active operation mode (lower right corner of the photo) (Color figure online)

6   Conclusions

This paper presented theory and simulations for running a wait-and-catch demonstration. The prediction algorithm of the intercept point of the swinging object, relying on solving the direct and inverse kinematics problems of the 5-dof robotic arm and on a dynamical model of the swinging object, was shown to be reliable and robust. The algorithm was tested successfully in simulation and partly on the experimental rig.

References

1. Bäuml, B., Wimböck, T., Hirzinger, G.: Kinematically optimal catching a flying ball with a hand-arm-system. In: 2010 IEEE/RSJ International Conference on Intelligent Robots and Systems (IROS), pp. 2592–2599, Taipei, Taiwan, October 2010

2. Chitta, S.: MoveIt!: an introduction. In: Koubaa, A. (ed.) Robot Operating System (ROS). SCI, vol. 625, pp. 3–27. Springer, Cham (2016). https://doi.org/10.1007/978-3-319-26054-9_1

3. De Preter, A.: Autonomous navigation for park maintenance and greenhouse horticulture. Robot driveability, ultra wideband positioning and calibration, semantic navigation. Ph.D. thesis, KU Leuven (2021)

4. Kallenberg, O.: Foundations of Modern Probability, 3rd edn. Springer, Cham (2021). https://doi.org/10.1007/978-3-030-61871-1

5. Kizilkaya, B., Zhao, G., Sambo, Y.A., Li, L., Imran, M.A.: 5G-enabled education 4.0: enabling technologies, challenges, and solutions. IEEE Access **9**, 166962–166969 (2021). https://doi.org/10.1109/ACCESS.2021.3136361

6. Laganiere, R.: OpenCV 3 Computer Vision Application Programming Cookbook, 3rd edn. Packt Publishing, Birmingham (2017)

7. Lemons, D.S.: Perfect Form: Variational Principles, Methods, and Applications in Elementary Physics. Princeton University Press, Princeton (1997)

8. Lewis, F.L., Xie, L., Popa, D.: Optimal and Robust Estimation. With an Introduction to Stochastic Control Theory, 2nd edn. CRC Press, New York (2008)

9. Rasmussen, C.E., Williams, C.K.I.: Gaussian Processes for Machine Learning (2nd Print). MIT Press, Cambridge (2006)

10. Ridolfi, M., et al.: Experimental evaluation of UWB indoor positioning for sport postures. Sensors **18**(1), 168 (2018). https://doi.org/10.3390/s18010168

11. Sato, M., Takahashi, A., Namiki, A.: Kinematically optimal catching a flying ball with a hand-arm-system. In: 2020 IEEE/RSJ International Conference on Intelligent Robots and Systems (IROS), pp. 9131–9136, Las Vegas, USA, October 2020

12. Spong, M.W., Hutchinson, S., Vidyasagar, M.: Robot Modeling and Control, 2nd edn. Wiley, Hoboken (2020)

13. Stoev, J., Gillijns, S., Bartic, A., Symens, W.: Badminton playing robot-a multidisciplinary test case in mechatronics. IFAC Proc. Volumes **43**(18), 725–731 (2010). https://doi.org/10.3182/20100913-3-US-2015.00028

14. Teodorescu, C.S., Caplan, I., Eberle, H., Carlson, T.: Model-based sensor fusion and filtering for localization of a semi-autonomous robotic vehicle. In: European Control Conference, Rotterdam, The Netherlands, 29 June–2 July 2021

15. Teodorescu, C.S., Vandenplas, S., Depraetere, B., Anthonis, J., Steinhauser, A., Swevers, J.: A fast pick-and-place prototype robot: design and control. In: IEEE Multi-conference on Systems and Control, Buenos Aires, Argentina, September 2016

Simultaneous Base and Arm Trajectories for Multi-target Mobile Agri-Robot

Joshua Davy[1,2(✉)] and Charles Fox[2,3]

[1] STORM Lab, School of Electronic and Electrical Engineering, University of Leeds, Leeds, UK
[2] School of Computer Science, University of Lincoln, Lincoln, UK
el17jd@leeds.ac.uk
[3] Ibex Automation Ltd, Sheffield, UK

Abstract. Many agricultural robotics tasks require an end effector to hold stationary above individual plants in the field for short periods. Examples include precision harvesting, imaging and spraying. This effector may be mounted on a mobile base such as a large tractor or small robot, driving in the field. We consider how to optimise control of the base and the end actuator together, to minimise total time taken to visit the plants. Our approach is based on low level combination of simple motion primitives, with mid level target clustering, and higher level planning. For the high level, three strategies are compared and evaluated in simulation: baseline stop-and-spray, constant velocity, and variable velocity. The baseline strategy is common in existing systems, and is shown to be outperformed by the new methods. The application considered here is weed spraying, but the methods are applicable to many tasks.

1 Introduction

Precision Agriculture is the differential rather than aggregate treatment of crops. Ideally, it aims for per-plant precision, treating each plant as an individual. This allows time and resources to be utilised more efficiently compared to aggregate treatments. It is well suited to robotics, due to their accuracy and non-reliance on human labour time [1]. Mobile robots used in agriculture usually fall into two classes: automated large tractors, and small human-size robots. Small robots equipped with arms are being applied to precision agriculture processes such as crop harvesting [2], imaging, data collection, [3,4], and chemical treatments [5,6]. Such applications require an end effector to be accurately positioned over each plant or region of interest, and held there for a period of time to performs its work, such as spraying or collecting data. Agricultural systems typically have tens of thousands of plants per hectare, so visiting each plant can be prohibitively time-consuming even for autonomous robots. More usually, a subset of plants in need of actuation can be identified in advance, then visited.

In most systems [6–9], robots with arms drive from one plant of interest to the next, stopping near each one. They then move their arm to accurately

F. Iida et al. (Eds.): TAROS 2023, LNAI 14136, pp. 214–226, 2023.
https://doi.org/10.1007/978-3-031-43360-3_18

position an end effector over the plant, then activate the effector, all with the base stationary. This appears inefficient compared to a system where motion of robot base and arm take place simultaneously, and without the base needing to stop. The present study thus considers generation of simultaneous trajectories for the base and arm in to improve this efficiency.

The duration the effector is required to be held over the plant must be specified for each application. Any arm has a upper limit on its movement speeds [10], which must accounted for along with the speed and maneuverability of the base. The order to visit targets is an important consideration. The optimum order would maximise the number of weeds visited within available time (and roughly equivalently, energy use) subject to the above motion constraints. Computational efficiency is also important for systems to be practically deployed.

We consider only cases where the base is constrained to drive in predefined straight, parallel rows (swathing), but is able to adjust its speed. This is usually required if crops are planted in rows, so that the wheels drive between rather then over crops. Where crops are not in rows, as in grassland, swathing is still often used to ensure coverage of a field. Large tractors with boom style arms are usually most efficient when swathing. Small robots could however drive directly from target to target. Optimising for that case is a larger problem beyond the present study, though the present study might provide a first step towards its solution. Even when driving is constrained along rows, finding an optimal ordering of targets for the arm to visit forms an NP-hard travelling salesman problem [6], so heuristics may be needed.

The only previous work to consider arm motion planning for agri-robots with continuous base movement [11] uses potential field methods to dynamically calculate the motion of a mounted manipulator in real time. However, it assumes approaching crops are linearly spaced and therefore no choice of optimum spray order is needed. An analogous problem exists in industrial manipulation scenarios such as the interception of items on a conveyor belt [12]. Here instead of a moving robot base, objects move towards the manipulator which must intercept the objects as they come into the arm's workspace. As the aim is to maximise the number of objects intercepted by the manipulator, the motion must take place at the upper limits of the arm in order to reduce trajectory time. This upper limit is defined by the dynamic constraints of the system which involve solving complex differential equations numerically in order to find the fastest trajectory [10]. The application considered here is precision weed spraying, but the methods are applicable to many precision agriculture and other tasks. Weed detection from ground platforms [13] and UAV [14] platforms has been demonstrated, so we assume that such detections are available as input. We use a heuristic which considers paths between and within clusters of nearby targets.

2   Methods

Generation of appropriate trajectories for the weed spraying task is here considered at three abstraction levels. The lowest is the formulation of individual weed spraying arm motions where the goal is to generate kinematically feasible trajectories which intercept and match the weed's position and relative velocity with the arm sprayer. This is achieved by a fast, piecewise combination of joint space polynomial and Cartesian space linear segments. The middle level is that of choosing the optimum weed spray ordering in advance in order to simplify the planning process. This is approximated via a K-means based clustering of upcoming weeds in order to group weeds which should be sprayed together in sequence. The highest level chooses the points in the arm workspace at which weeds should be sprayed, together with planning the base velocity to maximise performance.

The focus is on generating arm trajectories and base speeds given known positions of upcoming weeds in the robot's fixed direction of travel. As the robot moves along the field these weed relative positions move closer to the robot. The end effector must be held above the weed as the pesticide is released and therefore must match the Cartesian velocity of the ground relative to the robot.

2.1   Demonstrator Platform

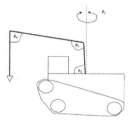

Fig. 1. Demonstrator platform - Kinematic structure and joint parameters.

Our demonstrator robot platform (Fig. 1) consists of a 4DOF manipulator mounted to a mobile base. The final joint in the arm is constrained to always point the pesticide sprayer vertically down. This means motion generation is simplified to consider only the first three joints of the system. Inverse kinematic solutions can then be found analytically due to the simplified structure.

Here we solve inverse kinematics for the particular demonstrator robot, by constraining motion of the arm and considering the its position in cylindrical coordinates. Figure 1 shows the kinematic structure of the arm with four joint angles $\{\theta_1, \theta_2, \theta_3, \theta_4\}$ and three linkages of lengths $\{l_1 = 0.5\,\text{m}, l_2 = 1.0\,\text{m}, l_3 = 0.5\,\text{m}\}$. The position of the end effector is considered in a 3D cylindrical coordinates system (r, θ, z). Forward kinematics can be solved to determine position of the end effector given the joints,

$$\begin{bmatrix} r \\ \theta \\ z \end{bmatrix} = \begin{bmatrix} l_1 \cos(\theta_2) + l_2 \cos(\theta_2 + \theta_3) + l_3 \cos(\theta_2 + \theta_3 + \theta_4) \\ \theta_1 \\ l_1 \sin(\theta_2) + l_2 \sin(\theta_2 + \theta_3) + l_3 \sin(\theta_2 + \theta_3 + \theta_4) \end{bmatrix} \quad (1)$$

The inverse solution, $\theta_1 = \theta$, is trivial given its direct correspondence with the cylindrical coordinate angle θ. The end linkage is constrained to point the end effector vertically downwards, to direct the spray correctly. θ_4 therefore is set by compensating for the other joints, $\theta_4 = -\theta_2 - \theta_3$. Substituting Eq. 1,

$$\begin{bmatrix} r \\ \theta \\ z \end{bmatrix} = \begin{bmatrix} l_1 \cos(\theta_2) + l_2 \cos(\theta_2 + \theta_3) \\ \theta_1 \\ l_1 \sin(\theta_2) + l_2 \sin(\theta_2 + \theta_3) - l_3 \end{bmatrix}. \tag{2}$$

The inverse solution for θ_2 and θ_3 can be determined by trigonometric identities, as shown in [15], which gives,

$$\theta_3 = -\mathrm{acos}(\frac{r^2 + (z + l_3)^2 - l_1^2 - l_2^2}{2l_1 l_2}), \tag{3}$$

$$\theta_2 = \mathrm{atan2}(z + l_3, r) + \mathrm{atan2}(l_2 \sin(\theta_3), l_1 + l_2 \cos(\theta_3)). \tag{4}$$

Maximum platform base velocity is $1\,\mathrm{m/s}$. Maximum joint velocities are $\dot{\theta}_{1,max} = \dot{\theta}_{2,max} = \dot{\theta}_{3,max} = \dot{\theta}_{4,max} = 3\mathrm{rads}^{-1}$, and maximum accelerations are $\ddot{\theta}_{1,max} = 5\mathrm{rads}^{-2}$, $\ddot{\theta}_{2,max} = \ddot{\theta}_{3,max} = \ddot{\theta}_{4,max}\} = 4\mathrm{rads}^{-2}$.

Kinematic solutions for other robot configurations may vary but will have a similar structure to our example. The rest of the methods are general to any mobile base with any arm.

2.2   Low Level Motion

The low level motion generates smooth trajectories for the arm joints given the relative velocity of a single weed, a required point for the sprayer and weed to first meet, and a required duration for the sprayer to be held above the weed t_{spray}. This level consists of two phases. The *intercept* phase is getting the effector above the weed and matching its relative velocity. The *tracking* phase is holding it in place during the spraying.

Trajectories for the arm are formed by piecewise combination of two phases. To reduce computational complexity, only kinematic joint limits such as maximum angular velocity and acceleration – as opposed to dynamic limits such as maximum angular momentum and torque – are considered (this heuristic often works in industrial manipulation [10]).

In the *intercept* phase, the trajectory is defined by a 5th degree polynomial generated in joint space. For each of the robot joints, j, its pose q at time t is:

$$q_j(t) = a_j + b_j t + c_j t^2 + d_j t^3 + e_j t^4 + f_j t^5 \tag{5}$$

and the six polynomial parameters $a_j - f_j$ can be found analytically as the solution to six simultaneous equations, formed by imposing a target initial and final constraint on the position, velocity and acceleration of each joint, $(\theta_0, \dot{\theta}_0, \ddot{\theta}_0, \theta_f, \dot{\theta}_f, \ddot{\theta}_f)$ found by inverse kinematics to match the position and velocity of the weed, and the trajectory start and end time t_0, t_f. The six equations are formed by differentiating Eq. 5 twice, for both the start and end times:

$$
\begin{bmatrix} \theta_{j,0} \\ \dot{\theta}_{j,0} \\ \ddot{\theta}_{j,0} \\ \theta_{j,f} \\ \dot{\theta}_{j,f} \\ \ddot{\theta}_{j,f} \end{bmatrix} = \begin{bmatrix} 1 & t_0 & t_0^2 & t_0^3 & t_0^4 & t_0^5 \\ 0 & 1 & 2t_0 & 3t_0^2 & 4t_0^3 & 5t_0^4 \\ 0 & 0 & 2 & 6t_0 & 12t_0^2 & 20t_0^3 \\ 1 & t_f & t_f^2 & t_f^3 & t_f^4 & t_f^5 \\ 0 & 1 & 2t_f & 3t_f^2 & 4t_f^3 & 5t_f^4 \\ 0 & 0 & 2 & 6t_f & 12t_f^2 & 20t_f^3 \end{bmatrix} \begin{bmatrix} a_j \\ b_j \\ c_j \\ d_j \\ e_j \\ f_j \end{bmatrix}
\tag{6}
$$

These can be solved via the Moore-Penrose pseudoinverse. To find the maximum joint velocities and accelerations – which tells higher levels if the trajectory is feasible – an analytic method can be used. The first and second derivatives of the trajectory form quintic and cubic polynomials respectively. These represent the velocity and acceleration during the trajectory. Differentiating them gain, and solving for their roots, gives their maxima and minima.

For the *tracking* phase, a simple linear trajectory for the end effector is found in Cartesian space, $p(t) = v(t - t_0) + c$, where v is the relative velocity and c is the intercept point. This motion is formed by keeping the effector at a constant velocity, compensating for base motion. To calculate if the kinematic limits are being satisfied (for use by higher levels), the inverse kinematic solution is calculated at discrete points in order to check against the joint limits.

After the tracking phase, the final state of the manipulator is used as the initial state of the next intercept phase as the arm intercepts the next weed. By alternating intercept and tracking motions, multiple weeds can be visited, if the arm can intercept them while maintaining joint kinematics limits, as shown in Fig. 2. After this relatively computationally cheap stage the full sets of joint angles over time that form the trajectory can be calculated by Eqs. 5 and 6 (Fig. 3).

Calculating Validity of Weed Spraying. By generating a full trajectory, the validity of a weed to be sprayed by the system can be calculated at a given intercept point. To determine the intercept point for the weed, trajectories could be generated at each time step until the first successful trajectory is found. This however, is computationally inefficient. Most trajectories will be invalid, for not yet entering the arm range, or being beyond the point where the weed can be successfully sprayed. We thus use an initial system to reject weeds by determining a smaller range of intercept points to evaluate with the full trajectory generation system. The reach of the arm is treated as a constant radius around the arm base on the 2D weed plane. As a weed enters this circle, then it is at a valid point of interception. The weed will stay in a valid interception pose until the point at which there will be not enough time to track the weed whilst the pesticide is released. Figure 4 shows how this valid range is calculated. Consider a weed at a current position (x, y). The first point at which the weed enters a valid intercept point is (x_0, y_0). This point is given as $(x, +\sqrt{r^2 - x^2})$ where r is the radius of valid intercepts. This occurs at time $t_0 = \frac{y - y_0}{v}$ where v is the forward velocity of the robot. The point at which the weed is no longer in a valid state

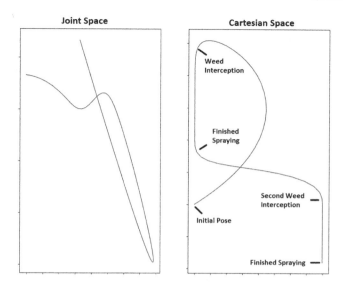

Fig. 2. Example generated trajectories for a two joint arm for spraying two weeds. Consisting of joint space polynomial segments for matching the weed position and velocity followed by Cartesian space linear segments for tracking the weed whilst the sprayer is activated.

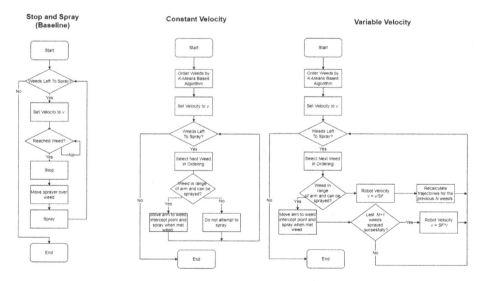

Fig. 3. Flowcharts showing the three proposed spraying strategies.

is given by (x_1, y_1). Any point after this, there is no longer time to intercept the weed and spray without going beyond the range of the arm. This point is given as $(x, -\sqrt{r^2 - x^2} + vt_{spray})$ where t_{spray} is the time needed to hover

over the weed and release the pesticide. The time of intercept here is given as $t_1 = \frac{y - y_1}{v}$. Between t_0 and t_1 the intercept is valid. This range can then be used with the full trajectory generator to determine kinematic viability. Areas at the horizontal extremes of the circle have no valid intercept points meaning weeds crossing these points cannot be sprayed without a decrease in velocity. Higher velocities increase this area so limit the range of valid weeds.

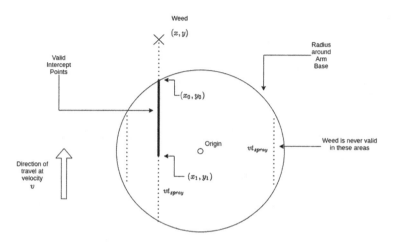

Fig. 4. How the range of valid intercepts is calculated based on a constant radius range. Note the areas at the extremes of the circle form areas where no weed can be sprayed. These areas grow with velocity v.

2.3   Middle Level - Weed Spray Ordering

The middle level takes the locations of all the weeds as input, and creates an ordering in which to visit them as output. This ordering is passed to the low level to generate a trajectory connecting them together. The spray ordering is decided in advance of the high level strategy.

Optimally visiting n weeds with distances between them is a Travelling Salesman Problem which is NP-hard. However, in addition to the distances, we have extra information about their metric positions in space, which simplifies the problem, so a heuristic based ordering algorithm can be utilised. The heuristic is based on the principle that weeds close together should be sprayed together. K-means clustering of the weeds in space is first performed to cluster close weeds. The *distortion* [16] property, α, is then measured as the average Euclidean distance between all weeds in each cluster and its respective centroid. A maximum distortion α_{max} is imposed, and the number of clusters (K) is increased until the maximum distortion requirement is satisfied.

The clusters are ordered by proximity to the robot base. Then within each cluster, the weeds are ordered again by proximity to the robot base. The final ordering is made by concatenating each of the intra-cluster orderings in the order of the inter-cluster ordering as in Algorithm 1.

Algorithm 1: K-Means weed ordering

Input *weedArray* - Array of Weed Poses, α_{max} - Maximum Distortion
Output *weedOrder* - Index of Weed Ordering
distortion = +inf;
k := 2;
while α ¿ α_{max} **do**
   | clusters, α = kMeans(weedArray, k);
   | k:=k+1;
end
orderedClusters = orderByX(clusters);
closestCluster = assign(weedArray, orderedClusters);
weedOrder = array();
for *cluster* **in** *orderedClusters* **do**
   | weedsInCluster = closestCluster[cluster];
   | weedOrder.append(orderByX(weedsInCluster));
end
return weedOrder;

2.4 High Level Spraying Strategies

The task of the high level is to plan the motion of the mobile robot base. It takes as input the mid level's target ordering, and it interacts with the low level's trajectory generation to links base motion plans to arm motion plans.

In general this is a hard problem, with an infinite possible search place of arbitrary, continuous, curved paths available to both the base and the arm. The present study thus considers only a limited subset of solutions which all constrain the base to drive in straight rows, but with the ability to control its velocity. We consider three strategies of increasing velocity control complexity within this directional constraint: stop-and-spray, constant velocity, and variable velocity, shown in Fig. 5.

Stop and Spray (SAS). This simple strategy as used by most existing systems so is considered as the baseline for our more advanced strategies. The base drives forward at a constant velocity until a weed enters the arm workspace. The base then slows to a halt. The arm then performs a point to point movement to position the effector above the weed. The spray is released for the required t_{spray} seconds. Any other weeds in the workspace are also be sprayed from the same stationary base location. Once all weeds in the workspace have been sprayed the

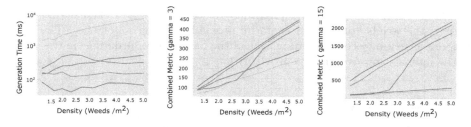

Fig. 5. Graph showing Performance on a 10 m by 3 m row of uniformally distributed weeds at varying densities.

robot will continue at the given velocity. For the point to point movements, the above low level intercept trajectory is used. For finding the minimum movement time, the trajectory is recalculated at increasing time intervals until the joint limits are satisfied.

Constant Velocity (CV). In this strategy, the base drives forward at fixed speed, without stopping, and the arm moves to match the weed's position and relative velocity. This is more complex due to decisions on spray order and where and when to intercept the weeds as they pass through the arm's range of motion. As discussed in Sect. 2.3, firstly the spray order is determined. From there, the trajectory generation begins by determining the validity of spraying each weed in the order, skipping those that a viable trajectory cannot be found for. The robot begins to move at a constant velocity v and a trajectory is generated to match the first weed's velocity and acceleration at the earliest point of entering the reach of the arm. If this trajectory is not feasible then later intercept points within the arm range is considered until either a feasible trajectory is found or the weed cannot be sprayed. If a feasible trajectory is found then it is added to the plan; if not the weed is dismissed from the trajectory.

Variable Velocity (VV). In this strategy, the speed – but not the direction – of the mobile base is adapted during interactions with the low level trajectory system, to reduce the number of weeds missed at high densities, and to reduce execution times at low weed densities. The strategy is similar to the constant velocity strategy but with two velocity update rules based on constants N and SF. The first update rule is that to re-plan the previous N weed spray trajectories using the current velocity divided by the scaling factor SF. This is triggered by a weed being unable to be feasibly sprayed. The reason for going back and re-planning for the previous N weeds as well as the weed that was unable to be sprayed is that if a weed was unable to be sprayed then the intercept points will be relatively late in the range of possible intercepts. Re-planning allows these intercept points to be earlier and therefore improve the overall trajectory execution time. The second update rule is the choice to increase the robot velocity. This is triggered by $N + 1$ weeds being successfully sprayed in a row. Here the velocity is then multiplied by SF as long as it is below the maximum velocity v_{max} of the base. This also reduces execution time by allowing the robot base to move faster along the row at low densities of weeds.

3   Evaluation

To evaluate the methods, a 3D simulation was used, with a 10 m by 3 m row containing weeds placed at random locations drawn from a uniform distribution over the area, at a given parameterised density. The simulation, as shown in Fig. 6 and a Video Demo (https://youtu.be/sKV4pRKN5DA), models the pose of the sprayer arm and the position of upcoming weeds to the robot. For the maximum permitted distortion a_{max} a value of 0.5 m was used for the K-means spray ordering. For the Variable Velocity strategy, the two constants N and SF, 3 and 1.2 were used for their respective value after initial experimentation.

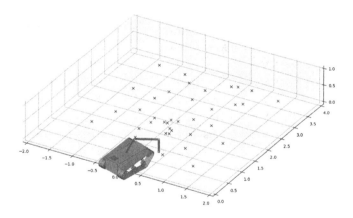

Fig. 6. Simulation setup.

Each strategy was evaluated in the simulation for a range of densities from 0.1 to 5.0 weeds per m^2. Performance for each of these experiments was averaged over three runs with different random seeds. A Combined Metric is defined which weights the cost of time against the cost of missing weeds, $M(t_r, w_m) = t_r + \gamma w_m$, where t_r is the trajectory runtime and w_m is the amount of weeds missed. γ is a constant representing the cost of missing one weed measured in units of seconds (value of time). For example a value of $\gamma = 10$ would represent that is worth a extra 10 s of time in order to spray an extra weed. Lower values of the metric correspond to better strategy performance. Farmers currently pay around 10 USD/hr = 0.002 USD/sec for human sprayers, who walk around 1.8 m/s and hit around 95% of weeds. For a typical row density of 1 weed/meter, this costs 0.001 USD/weed to spray, equivalent to $\gamma = 0.5$. Robots have a negligible cost of time compared to their human operators. If the human changes role to monitoring 6 robots on a small farm, then $\gamma = 3$; if they monitor 30 robots on a large farm then $\gamma = 15$.

Table 1. Generation time, execution time and weeds sprayed by weed density.

Density (weeds/m^2)	Strategy	Generation Time (ms)	Execution Time (ms)	Weeds Sprayed (%)
0.5	SAS	47.0	49.6	100
	CV $v = 0.1\,\mathrm{ms}^{-1}$	43.3	100.0	100
	CV $v = 0.2\,\mathrm{ms}^{-1}$	48.4	50.0	100
	CV $v = 0.5\,\mathrm{ms}^{-1}$	47.5	20.0	66.6
	VV	323.7	**30.9**	**100**
2	SAS	218.0	138.0	100
	CV $v = 0.1\,\mathrm{ms}^{-1}$	423.1	100.0	98.3
	CV $v = 0.2\,\mathrm{ms}^{-1}$	151.3	50.0	26.6
	CV $v = 0.5\,\mathrm{ms}^{-1}$	59.0	20.0	6.6
	VV	2058.9	**110.0**	**100**
5	SAS	455.8	288.7	100
	CV $v = 0.1\,\mathrm{ms}^{-1}$	290.5	100.0	16.0
	CV $v = 0.2\,\mathrm{ms}^{-1}$	155.1	50.0	4.6
	CV $v = 0.5\,\mathrm{ms}^{-1}$	75.4	20.0	2.6
	VV	6130.3	**241.4**	**100**

4 Discussion

It is possible to construct smooth low-level trajectories from polynomial segments with low computational costs (Fig. 6a), to fit to selected weed orderings from a clustering heuristic, and to combine these with the high level strategies.

Switching from the commonly used high-level stop and spray method to the more advanced constant velocity and variable velocity methods improves time and costs of weed spraying, when weighted with typical agricultural costs (Fig. 6b, c) and may deliver similar gains in related tasks.

At low densities (0.5 weeds/m^2), performance between the strategies is similar, but as density increases, performance of both stop and spray and constant velocity strategies begins to drop off due to long execution times and poor spray success rates (Table 1). At higher densities, even at very low base velocities (0.1 ms^{-1}), the constant velocity strategy struggles achieving just 16% of weeds sprayed successfully (Table 1). The variable velocity strategy however continues to do well, achieving 100% weed coverage (Table 1), though at the cost of slowing down and taking more time (Table 1). Stop and Spray and Constant Velocity strategies require much lower computational cost then the Variable velocity strategies (Fig. 6a). This is due to the re-planning phase of the variable velocity strategy that leads to a greater number of evaluations of the low level trajectory generator. For the large farm, $\gamma = 15$, the gap in performance between Stop and Spray and Variable Velocity reduces (Fig. 6c.) representing that the improved execution times of the Variable Velocity strategy representing less importance in the overall system performance. For the small farm, $\gamma = 3$ (Fig. 6b), the improvement is more noticeable.

References

1. Duckett, T., et al.: Agricultural robotics: the future of robotic agriculture. arXiv preprint arXiv:1806.06762 (2018)
2. Bac, C.W., Hemming, J., Van Tuijl, B., Barth, R., Wais, E., van Henten, E.J.: Performance evaluation of a harvesting robot for sweet pepper. J. Field Robot. **34**(6), 1123–1139 (2017)
3. Mueller-Sim, T., Jenkins, M., Abel, J., Kantor, G.: The robotanist: a ground-based agricultural robot for high-throughput crop phenotyping. In: IEEE International Conference on Robotics and Automation (2017)
4. Raja, R., Nguyen, T.T., Slaughter, D.C., Fennimore, S.A.: Real-time weed-crop classification and localisation technique for robotic weed control in lettuce. Biosys. Eng. **192**, 257–274 (2020)
5. Sabanci, K., Aydin, C.: Smart robotic weed control system for sugar beet. J. Agric. Sci. Technol. **19**(1), 73–83 (2017)
6. Lee, J.J.H., Frey, K., Fitch, R., Sukkarieh, S.: Fast path planning for precision weeding. In: Australasian Conference on Robotics and Automation, ACRA (2014)
7. Xiong, Y., Ge, Y., Liang, Y., Blackmore, S.: Development of a prototype robot and fast path-planning algorithm for static laser weeding. Comput. Electron. Agric. **142**, 494–503 (2017)
8. Raja, R., Nguyen, T.T., Slaughter, D.C., Fennimore, S.A.: Real-time robotic weed knife control system for tomato and lettuce based on geometric appearance of plant labels. Biosyst. Eng. **194**, 152–164 (2020)
9. Martin, J., et al.: A generic ROS-based control architecture for pest inspection and treatment in greenhouses. IEEE Access **9**, 94 981–94 995 (2021)
10. Kim, J.Y., Kim, D.H., Kim, S.R.: On-line minimum-time trajectory planning for industrial manipulators. In: ICCAS 2007 - International Conference on Control, Automation and Systems, pp. 36–40 (2007)
11. Zhao, D., Zhang, B., Zhao, Y., Sun, Q., Li, C., Wang, C.: Research on motion planning for an indoor spray arm based on an improved potential field method. PLoS ONE **15**(1), e0226912 (2020)
12. Park, T., Lee, B.: Approach to robot motion analysis and planning for conveyor tracking. IEEE Syst. Man Cybern. **22**(2), 378–384 (1992)
13. Binch, A., Fox, C.: Controlled comparison of machine vision algorithms for Rumex and Urtica detection in grassland. Comput. Electron. Agric. **140**, 123–138 (2017)
14. Binch, A., Cooke, N., Fox, C.: Rumex and Urtica detection in grassland by UAV. In: Proceedings of International Conference on Precision Agriculture (2018)

15. Tokarz, K., Kieltyka, S.: Geometric approach to inverse kinematics for arm manipulator. Int. Conf. Syst. **1**(26), 682–687 (2010)
16. Pham, D.T., Dimov, S.S., Nguyen, C.D.: Selection of K in K-means clustering. Proc. Inst. Mech. Eng. C **219**(1), 103–119 (2005)

Design and Kinematic Analysis of a 3D-Printed 3DOF Robotic Manipulandum

Ian S. Howard$^{(\boxtimes)}$

SECAM, University of Plymouth, Plymouth PL4 8AA, UK
ian.howard@plymouth.ac.uk

Abstract. Robotic manipulanda are often used to investigate human motor control of arm movements, as well as for tasks where haptic feedback is useful, e.g., in computer-aided design and in the teleoperation of robotic arms. Here we present the design and implementation of a small, low-cost, torque controlled 3DOF revolute manipulandum which supports translational movement in three-dimensions. All bespoke structural components are 3D printed and the arm lengths are constructed from carbon fiber tubes, which exhibit high stiffness but are very light, resulting in a design that exhibits a low intrinsic endpoint mass at the handle. We use rare-earth BLDC motors employing built-in low-ratio planetary-gearboxes, so the system is back-drivable and arm endpoint force can be controlled. We provide an analysis and simulation in MATLAB of the arm's forward and inverse kinematics, as well as its static motor torque and endpoint force relationships. We used a microcontroller to operate the motors over their CAN interfaces. Finally, we demonstrate the use of the manipulandum as a robot for general point-to-point movement tasks using a microcontroller implementation of its inverse kinematics.

Keywords: Haptic interface · Revolute arm · 3DOF · Torque control · BLDC motors · Manipulandum · 3D-printing · Cobot

1 Introduction

1.1 Existing Robotic Manipulanda

Robotic manipulanda are devices often used to investigate the sensori-motor control of human arm movements. To do so, a participant will typically hold and move the handle of the device, which is located at the endpoint of its robotic arm. The position of the handle is calculated from arm joint angle measurements, so its movement can be tracked, much like a computer mouse can record its location in a plane. However, unlike a computer mouse, force can also be applied to the handle by the robot's actuators, so endpoint dynamics can, within limits, be set as desired. Often, visual feedback of movement is provided by means of a calibrated virtual reality environment. Typical experimental paradigms investigate how participants adapt to novel dynamics, or rotations of the visual field, whilst performing reaching movements between locations in space [1].

Many studies make use of manipulanda with planar arms that only permit movement in a plane [2–4]. However several commercial 3D manipulanda exist, such as

F. Iida et al. (Eds.): TAROS 2023, LNAI 14136, pp. 227–239, 2023.
https://doi.org/10.1007/978-3-031-43360-3_19

the Phantom robot platforms, which were developed as haptic interfaces [5], and high performance units that can exert considerable force, such as the haptic master [6] and the BioMotionBot [7]. Force Dimension builds a range of haptic devices that use a unique delta-based parallel kinematics mechanical design [8], developed at the EPFL [9]. Using a similar design structure, Novint Technologies manufactures a very low-cost haptic device aimed for the consumer market. MPB Technologies is a Canadian company that makes two haptic devices. The Freedom6 is a haptic interface that uses a serial mechanism [10]. Quanser supplies various haptic devices including the 3DOF pantograph and 5 DOF twin-pantograph [11]. Haptic pens, based on twin-pantographs have also been constructed [12]. More recently low-cost units have also been developed in order to broaden access to the technology [13].

1.2 Overview and Requirements

There are many factors to be considered in the design of a haptic device [14–16]. The key responsibilities of a 3D robotic manipulandum are to measure a participant's hand position during movement tasks in 3-dimensional space and simultaneously apply appropriate translational forces to the participant's hand (including a null force condition, during which no force should be applied). Ideally, a robotic manipulandum would therefore use actuation that was fully back-drivable and free from backlash; employ arm construction that was very stiff, so its arm does not deflect under load; exhibit low intrinsic dynamics, so movement of the handle is not dominated by the robotic arm itself; measure endpoint position to a high precision in both time and space; have the ability to exert reasonable force from its endpoint onto the participant's hand; and finally, have a useful workspace area. Of course, an overall compromise between these requirements needs to be found. In particular, the workspace of the robot needs to be kept as small as possible to ensure the arm mechanism remains both stiff and lightweight at the same time.

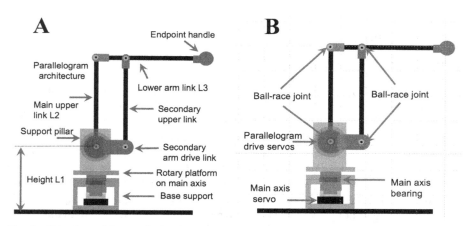

Fig. 1. Side view of the manipulandum. **Panel A:** Main base components and parallel arm links. **Panel B:** Locations of bearings and drive actuators.

2 RRR Arm Mechanism

2.1 Design and Construction Methods

Here we present the design of a low-cost 3D-printed robotic manipulandum that takes the form of a revolute 3DOF robotic arm which operates in a 3D workspace. Due to space limitations, our analysis only focuses on its kinematic relationships. Autodesk Fusion 360 was used to design all custom parts, which were 3D-printed in PLA+ using a Creality CR-6 SE. Arm joint forks and bearing holders were printed with 100% infill to ensure a high level of stiffness and strength. Other parts were printed at 35% infill to reduce their overall weight and material usage.

2.2 Rotating 2-DOF Parallelogram Design

The design is illustrated in Fig. 1 and its standard configuration and physical realization is shown in Fig. 2. The design follows the general principle that to achieve low effective mass at the handle, the mass and moment of inertia of all moving parts must be kept to a minimum, whereas stationary parts, and parts close to the axes of rotation, can be made sturdy and heavier. Care was taken to ensure that distal parts of the upper parallelogram mechanism were low mass, including arm links and joints, and relevant component weights are provided in the description below.

The base of the manipulandum consists of a box structure constructed from two 20 mm thick 3D printed plates at the top (215 g each of 35% infill PLA+), supported by side pillars (111 g each of 35% infill PLA+). This provides a rigid support to hold the arm rotor assembly. The vertical axis of the arm mechanism consists of a large diameter 3D printed shaft, realizing the 1st degree of freedom of the arm. The shaft is clamped around a 50 mm bore deep groove ball bearing mounted in the base top plate assembly, to provide both axial and radial support. The lower end of the shaft is driven directly by a servo motor attached to the base of the robot (254 g 35% infill PLA+). Its upper end consists of a mounting plate for the upper planar arm mechanism which is constructed using carbon fibre (CF) tubes. The latter is based on a recent previous design [17], and takes the form of a 2 DOF parallelogram structure.

The arm joints form a critical part of the design of the arm mechanism and use small ball bearings to ensure low joint friction. See Figs. 1 and 2 for details of the arm structure. The design of one of the link joints of the arm is shown in Fig. 3A and its assembly in Fig. 3B. Each joint contains two miniature low weight (1.5 g) 3 mm internal diameter ball bearing races located in a 3D printed bearing holder assembly. Bearing holders were constructed from solid PLA+. The secondary upper links and lower link bearing holders used 19 g, 16 g and 24 g of PLA+ respectively.

The bearings rotate around lightweight m3 bolt shafts that are held in place by a 3D printed fork. The latter makes use of two lightweight (4.4 g) aluminium flanges per fork to support the shaft that passes through the bearings, since aluminium offers superior mechanical properties to PLA+. The m3 bolt is firmly secured to the fork using a locknut. Stainless steel washers are placed between the flanges and the bearings to achieve suitable joint clearance (in total each bolt assembly weighs 3.5 g with washers and locknut). The main lower parallelogram arm linkage is driven directly using a servomotor using a 3D printed structure that holds the main lower CF arm link (112 g of solid PLA+). Similarly, the secondary lower CF arm, is driven directly by a 3D printed mini-arm structure attached to a servomotor (170 g solid PLA+). Since the latter two components are located close to their axes of rotation, their larger masses do not contribute much to endpoint effective mass. An upper CF arm link forms the upper part of the parallelogram and is connected to the ends of the lower arm via the two fork joints. The main and secondary arm solid PLA+ forks used 47 g and 52 g of material respectively. A lightweight handle knob was used as an end-effector (25 g, 35% infill PLA+). The lower and upper arm links themselves were constructed from 16 × 14 mm diameter carbon fibre tubing (wall thickness 1 mm, length 250 mm, weight 18 g) to achieve high stiffness with a light weight. The CF tubes were attached to their 3D printed joint components using Loctite Precision superglue. Including joint components and the knob, the 3 CF links that comprise the parallel arm mechanism have a combined mass of 380 g.

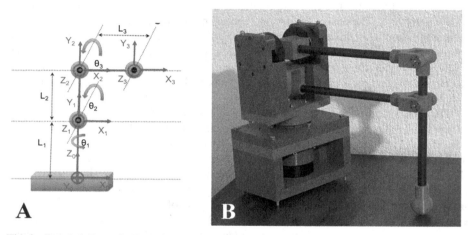

Fig. 2. Panel A Denavit-Hartenberg co-ordinate frames for 3-link planar arm defined in terms of link lengths L_1, L_2 and L_3 and corresponding joint angles θ_1, θ_2, θ_3. Default configuration is shown with $\theta_1 = 0°$, $\theta_2 = 90°$, $\theta_3 = -90°$. **Panel B** 3D manipulandum revolute arm. The base section implements a rotary joint around the vertical axis, and needs to be firmly attached to a suitable table. An upper 2DOF arm mechanism, which takes the form of a parallelogram, is mounted onto this rotary platform. A round knob is attached to the end of the arm to provide a suitable grip point for human operators.

Minimizing mass was also important in the design of the parallel arm support pillars and platform assembly, since they rotate during operation. The two pillars and rotating platform used 35% infill PLA+ and weighed 214 g each and 187 g respectively. The main axis shaft needed to be structurally strong and used 298 g solid PLA+. In total, 2.47 kg of PLA+ was used in the construction of the entire robot arm mechanism.

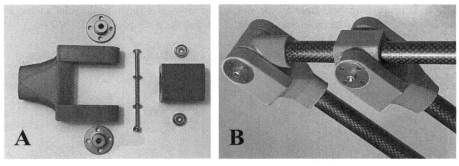

Fig. 3. Arm joints. **Panel A:** Secondary arm fork joint components showing two fork flanges, an m3 bolt, two bearings and a bearing holder. **Panel B:** Showing the two fork joints mounted in situ on the lower arm link.

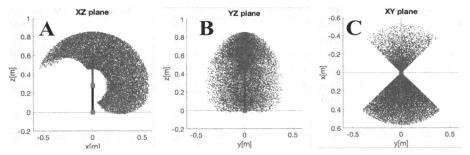

Fig. 4. Panel A: Side view from XZ plane of workspace cloud of the robot's endpoint, which is also shown in its canonical configuration. **Panel B:** Front YZ plane view of workspace cloud. **Panel C:** XY plane top view of workspace cloud.

2.3 BLDC Motor Actuation

We make use of BLDC planetary gear servo actuation (MY ACTUATOR RMD-X6 Brushless DC Gear Motor 1:6, MC300A). Their low 1:6 gearing ratio ensures the motors are back-drivable and exhibit low backlash (0.083°). Each unit delivers a nominal torque of 3.5 Nm, has a nominal speed of 190 rpm ($\approx$20 Rad/s) and operates from a 48 v supply. The servos incorporate 16-bit absolute magnetic encoders so their rotational angle can be precisely sensed. They are controlled over a CAN bus interface [18]. One servo motor directly drives the main vertical revolute joint shaft. An additional two servo motors are mounted in pillars attached to the rotating table baseplate and directly drive the lower main and secondary parallelogram arm links. Each motor weighs 335 g.

Table 1. Denavit-Hartenberg table for the arm, with conservative limits on the joint angles. In practice the θ_1 and θ_2 limits could be increased, expanding the workspace.

Link	Angle θ [°]	Min θ [°]	Max θ [°]	Angle α [°]	Radius a [mm]	Offset d [mm]
1	θ_1	$-45°$	$45°$	90	0	280
2	θ_2	$0°$	$180°$	0	300	0
3	θ_3	$-145°$	$-35°$	0	300	0

3 Kinematic Analysis

3.1 Denavit-Hartenberg Analysis

Although the analysis of forward and inverse kinematics of revolute arm mechanisms are available in many textbooks on robotics, e.g. [19, 20], derivations are included here for the convenience of the reader. Suitable frames for Denavit-Hartenberg (DH) analysis are shown in Fig. 2A. This leads to the classical DH parameter table shown in Table 1. The link lengths for the current design are $L_1 = 280$ mm, $L_2 = 300$ mm and $L_3 = 300$ mm (L_3 includes the distance to the end of the spherical knob). A classical DH-frame can be represented by the homogeneous transformation matrix, written here in shorthand, where c refers to cosine and s to sine:

$$A_i = \begin{bmatrix} c\theta_i & -s\theta_i c\,\alpha_i & s\theta_i s\,\alpha_i & a_i c\theta_i \\ s\theta_i & c\theta_i c\,\alpha_i & -c\theta_i s\,\alpha_i & a_i s\theta_i \\ 0 & s\,\alpha_i & c\,\alpha_i\,d_i \\ 0 & 0 & 0 & 1 \end{bmatrix} \tag{1}$$

3.2 Forward Kinematics

The mapping from frame 3 to base frame 0 is calculated using the product of homogeneous matrices for the three links:

$$_3^0H = {}_1^0H\,{}_2^1H\,{}_3^2H \tag{2}$$

We make use of MATLAB symbolic toolbox to simplify the matrix equations. This leads to the overall homogeneous transformation

$$_3^0H = \begin{bmatrix} c_{23}c_1 & -s_{23}c_1 & s_1 & c_1(L_3c_{23} + L_2c_2) \\ c_{23}s_1 & -s_{23}s_1 & -c_1 & s_1(L_3c_{23} + L_2c_2) \\ s_{23} & -c_{23} & 0 & L_1 + L_3s_{23} + L_2s_2 \\ 0 & 0 & 0 & 1 \end{bmatrix} \tag{3}$$

where L_1, L_2, and L_3 represent the 3 link lengths, and we use the further following simplifying notation: $c_1 = \cos(\theta_1)$, $s_1 = \sin(\theta_1)$, $c_{23} = \cos(\theta_2 + \theta_3)$, $s_{23} = \sin(\theta_2 + \theta_3)$.

By inspection it can be seen that the endpoint position at the 3rd link is given by the expression:

$$\begin{bmatrix} x_{end} \\ y_{end} \\ z_{end} \end{bmatrix} = \begin{bmatrix} c_1(L_3c_{23} + L_2c_2) \\ s_1(L_3c_{23} + L_2c_2) \\ L_1 + L_3s_{23} + L_2s_2 \end{bmatrix} \tag{4}$$

Using 20,000 samples drawn from a uniform distribution of permitted joint angles of the arm joints, corresponding endpoints were calculated using forward kinematics, resulting in a cloud of reachable endpoint locations indicative of the arm's workspace (see Fig. 4.).

3.3 Velocity and Force Relationships

To calculate the velocity and torque/force relationships between the control joints and endpoint and orientation, we form the 3×3 Jacobian matrix by partially differentiating the endpoint position with respect to the joint angles θ_1, θ_2 and θ_3:

$$J = \begin{bmatrix} \frac{\partial x}{\partial \theta_1} & \frac{\partial x}{\partial \theta_2} & \frac{\partial x}{\partial \theta_3} \\ \frac{\partial y}{\partial \theta_1} & \frac{\partial y}{\partial \theta_2} & \frac{\partial y}{\partial \theta_3} \\ \frac{\partial z}{\partial \theta_1} & \frac{\partial z}{\partial \theta_2} & \frac{\partial z}{\partial \theta_3} \end{bmatrix} \tag{5}$$

This leads to the 3×3 Jacobian matrix:

$$J = \begin{bmatrix} -s_1(L_3c_{23} + L_2c_2) & -c_1(L_3s_{23} + L_2s_2) & -c_1L_3s_{23} \\ c_1(L_3c_{23} + L_2c_2) & -s_1(L_3s_{23} + L_2s_2) & -s_1L_3s_{23} \\ 0 & L_3c_{23} + L_2c_2 & L_3c_{23} \end{bmatrix} \tag{6}$$

We use the Jacobian to compute the endpoint linear velocities from the joint velocities:

$$\begin{bmatrix} \dot{x} \\ \dot{y} \\ \dot{z} \end{bmatrix} = J \begin{bmatrix} \dot{\theta}_1 \\ \dot{\theta}_2 \\ \dot{\theta}_3 \end{bmatrix} \tag{7}$$

Provided we avoid singularities of the arm, we can use the inverse Jacobian to rearrange Eq. (7) and calculate the joint angular velocities from the endpoint velocities.

$$\begin{bmatrix} \dot{\theta}_1 \\ \dot{\theta}_2 \\ \dot{\theta}_3 \end{bmatrix} = J^{-1} \begin{bmatrix} \dot{x} \\ \dot{y} \\ \dot{z} \end{bmatrix} \tag{8}$$

In addition, the transpose of the 3×3 Jacobian can be used to relate static joint torques, written as $\begin{bmatrix} \tau_1 & \tau_2 & \tau_3 \end{bmatrix}^T$, to static endpoint forces $\begin{bmatrix} f_x & f_y & f_z \end{bmatrix}^T$ using the relationships:

$$\begin{bmatrix} \tau_1 \\ \tau_2 \\ \tau_3 \end{bmatrix} = J^T \begin{bmatrix} f_x \\ f_y \\ f_z \end{bmatrix} \tag{9}$$

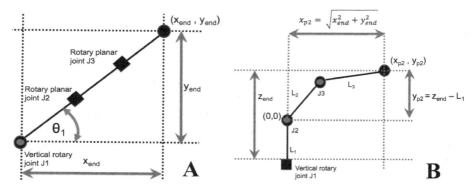

$$x_{p2} = \sqrt{x_{end}^2 + y_{end}^2}$$

Fig. 5. Panel A: Looking down on the robot arm from above. It is simple to relate control angle θ_1 to the end-effector position, defined as (x_{end}, y_{end}) with respect to origin located at J_1. **Panel B:** Looking at arm in plane of parallelogram mechanism, with the planar arm frame end position defined as (x_{p2}, y_{p2}) with respect to origin located at J_2.

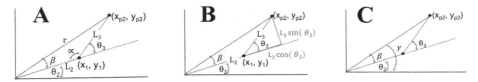

Fig. 6. Schematics of 2D revolute planar arm that is useful for the derivation of inverse kinematics, showing relevant positions, angles and lengths.

3.4 Inverse Kinematics

To derive the inverse kinematics for the arm, we first define the endpoint location as $(x_{end}, y_{end}, z_{end})$. We note that the first joint of the mechanism is a rotation around the z-axis of the base frame co-ordinate system, and it rotates the planar arm mechanism which it supports by an angle θ_1. In the base frame coordinate system, rotation is the only cause of displacement of the end-effector in the y-axis (Fig. 5A). Consequently, by inspection, we can calculate θ_1 using the simple relationship

$$\theta_1 = atan\left[\frac{y_{end}}{x_{end}}\right] \tag{10}$$

To analyze the remainder of the arm, namely the planar arm mechanism, we define a new 2D coordinate frame in the plane of the parallelogram arm mechanism (Fig. 5B). To account for the base rotation of the planar arm, in the coordinate frame of the base of the planar arm, we define the end effector location by the 2D point (x_{p2}, y_{p2}). The x-displacement x_{p2} is equal to the length of hypotenuse of the right-angled triangle formed by the distances x_{end} and y_{end} from the overall arm origin at its base.

$$x_{p2} = \sqrt{x_{end}^2 + y_{end}^2} \tag{11}$$

The planar arm y-axis is aligned with the base frame 3D z-axis, and to account for height of the base in planar arm y-direction, the 2D end-effector location y_{p2} is given by:

$$y_{p2} = z_{end} - L_1 \tag{12}$$

Inverse kinematics for a 2-link arm mechanism can be derived analytically using the cosine rule. Here, we wish to find arm angles (θ_2, θ_3) given endpoint locations (x_{p2}, y_{p2}) of the 2-link section of the arm. From Fig. 6A, the elbow of the planar arm mechanism is located at $(x_{p1}\ y_{p1})$ and the upper arm end at (x_{p2}, y_{p2}). Pythagoras' theorem gives:

$$r^2 = x_{p2}^2 + y_{p2}^2 \tag{13}$$

Using the cosine rule equation, we can write an expression for $cos(\alpha)$ in terms of known quantities (x_{p2}, y_{p2}) and $L_2, L_3.$

$$r^2 = L_2^2 + L_3^2 - 2L_2L_3cos(\alpha) \tag{14}$$

$$\Rightarrow cos(\alpha) = \frac{L_2^2 + L_3^2 - x_{p2}^2 - y_{p2}^2}{2L_2L_3} \tag{15}$$

To derive the expression for $cos(\theta_3)$ again from Fig. 6A we note that:

$$\theta_3 = \pi - \alpha \tag{16}$$

We also note that:

$$cos(\pi - \alpha) = -cos(\alpha) \tag{17}$$

$$\Rightarrow cos(\theta_3) = \frac{x_{p2}^2 + y_{p2}^2 - L_2^2 - L_3^2}{2L_2L_3} \tag{18}$$

From Fig. 6B from the right-hand triangle that has angle β we see that

$$tan(\beta) = \frac{L_3 \sin(\theta_3)}{L_3 \cos(\theta_3) + L_2} \tag{19}$$

$$\Rightarrow \beta = atan\left[\frac{L_3 \sin(\theta_3)}{L_3 \cos(\theta_2) + L_2}\right] \tag{20}$$

We now make use of angle β to derive the expression for angle θ_2. As indicated by geometric considerations as shown on Fig. 6C we also see that:

$$\theta_2 = \gamma - \beta \tag{21}$$

$$\gamma = atan\left[\frac{y_{p2}}{x_{p2}}\right] \tag{22}$$

$$\Rightarrow \theta_2 = atan\left[\frac{y_{p2}}{x_{p2}}\right] - atan\left[\frac{L_3 \sin(\theta_3)}{L_3 \cos(\theta_3) + L_2}\right] \tag{23}$$

Finally, writing the planar arm end effector location in terms of (x_{end}, y_{end}):

$$\begin{bmatrix} x_{p2} \\ y_{p2} \end{bmatrix} = \begin{bmatrix} \sqrt{x_{end}^2 + y_{end}^2} \\ y_{end} - L_1 \end{bmatrix} \tag{24}$$

We now substitute these values into Eqs. (23) and (18)

$$\Rightarrow \theta_2 = atan\left[\frac{y_{end} - L_1}{\sqrt{x_{end}^2 + y_{end}^2}}\right] - atan\left[\frac{L_3 \sin(\theta_3)}{L_3 \cos(\theta_3) + L_2}\right] \tag{25}$$

$$\Rightarrow \theta_3 = \pm acos\left[\frac{\left(\sqrt{x_{end}^2 + y_{end}^2}\right)^2 + (y_{end} - L1)^2 - L_2^2 - L_3^2}{2L_2L_3}\right] \tag{26}$$

We notice that Eq. (26) has two solutions, and that the value of θ_3 is used to calculate θ_2 using Eq. (25). Here we use the negative solution for θ_3 since it corresponds to the default configuration of our arm design (as shown in Fig. 2A).

4   Results

4.1   Simulating Forward, and Inverse and Differential Kinematics

To test both forward, inverse, and differential kinematics, and to predict the joint and end-point speed relationships, we simulated the robot arm moving around a circle of radius 20 cm at 1 Hz in the YZ plane (see Fig. 7A). To do so, target trajectory points were generated every 10 ms and the inverse Jacobian was used to compute the corresponding joint velocities. This leads to a constant endpoint speed of 1.26 m/s, and a corresponding

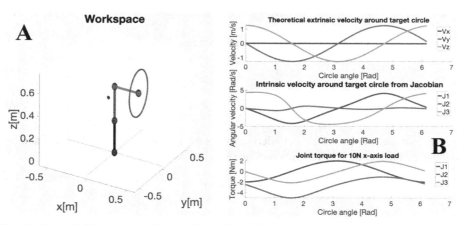

Fig. 7. Panel A: Target circle of radius 20 cm. **Panel B Upper:** Arm extrinsic endpoint velocity components during simulated movement of arm endpoint around target circle in YZ plane at a constant speed of 1.26 m/s. **Middle:** Corresponding arm joint angular velocities. **Lower:** Simulated torques at the three joints needed to generate 10 N force along x-axis.

maximum motor angular speed of 4.4 Rad/s (see Fig. 7B upper & middle plots). This is less than the maximum speed of rotation of the arm joints ($\approx$20 Rad/s). In the same movement task, neglecting the low intrinsic dynamics of the arm, we simulated the effect of exerting a 10N force in the x-direction using the transposed Jacobian. This resulted in a peak motor torque of 5 Nm (see Fig. 7B lower plot). This value slightly exceeds the continuous rating of the motors of 3.5 Nm but is possible for short durations. Since motor temperature measurements are available in the RMD X6, motor damage can be avoided using an appropriate motor-off strategy if temperature rises too high.

4.2 CAN Bus Operation Using a Microcontroller

The BLDC servo motors were operated over their CAN bus interfaces [18]. A simple C++ application program was developed on an Arduino Mega, which has more memory than the Arduino Uno. The microcontroller communicated with the CAN bus inputs of the servo motors via an MCP2515 CAN bus driver board. Inverse kinematics were implemented on the microcontroller based on Eqs. (10), (25) and (26) so the manipulandum was able to operate as a robot and perform extrinsic trajectory tracking tasks in real time, using the simple PID position controller built into the motor units.

4.3 Demonstrations of Robotic Operation

To showcase the utility of the arm as Cobot, a class of collaborative robot that is designed to work alongside humans in a shared workspaces [21, 22], we demonstrated operation in point-to-point and trajectory tracking movement tasks. Such tasks could be used, for example, pick and place tasks. To view demonstrations of the manipulandum, as well as a MATLAB simulation of the arm, please follow the YouTube channel link provided here:

https://youtube.com/playlist?list=PLjKvJX8cBCKVEfg1WxYSB7kiomAq1qZp0.

5 Discussion

5.1 Summary

We presented a back-drivable 3DOF manipulandum primarily intended for use as a haptic interface that can be used for sensorimotor research. The device is relatively low-cost compared to many commercial designs and is easy to manufacture using 3D printing and commercially available carbon fibre tubes and machine parts. As well as operating as a manipulandum, the arm is also well suited for use as a Cobot in simple point-to-point movement tasks, as it is lightweight thus limiting the kinetic energy stored in the arm during movement, minimizing the danger of an impact arising due to a collision. In addition, although not demonstrated here, even in position control mode the arm controllers can monitor motor torque and thus force output can be estimated, making it possible to detect unexpected arm loading arising from collisions, and to stop moving.

5.2 Future Work

Work is in progress to implement torque control, which is needed to generate arbitrary endpoint dynamics. A dynamic model of the robot is also currently under development to ensure the intrinsic dynamics of the arm, as well as gravity, can be compensated. This will also include the calculation of all joint forces for a given endpoint load.

At present a round knob is attached to the end of the arm to provide a suitable holding point, but a 3DOF gimbal handle will be developed to support experiments in which the use of a power grip is more appropriate. The current manipulandum design was implemented in PLA+, but PETG may provide a better alternative and would make the arm more robust for general use, as it is a material that can better resist wet, warm, and sunny environmental conditions. Furthermore, the current CF tubes used for the arm had rather thin walls. Increasing their wall thickness to 2 mm would increase arm stiffness and robustness with only a slight increase in link weight (by only 18 g per link).

The present version of the design uses small RMD-X6 servo drives. And larger motors from the same range would permit the generation of much larger forces at the endpoint. Finally, we note that the robot can currently (in 2023) be built with a components cost of £1000, with most cost arising from the relatively expensive RMD-X6 servomotors. Much cheaper high-torque large diameter low-kv BLDC drone motors, operating with in-house developed belt transmission and controllers, could be employed in future versions of the robot, which would reduce overall cost by at least half.

References

1. Shadmehr, R., Mussa-Ivaldi, F.A.: Adaptive representation of dynamics during learning of a motor task. J. Neurosci. **14**(5), 3208–3224 (1994)
2. Hogan, N., Krebs, H.I.: Interactive robots for neuro-rehabilitation. Restor. Neurol. Neurosci. **22**(3–5), 349–358 (2004)
3. Krebs, H.I., Hogan, N., Aisen, M.L., Volpe, B.T.: Robot-aided neurorehabilitation. IEEE Trans. Rehabil. Eng. **6**(1), 75–87 (1998)
4. Howard, I.S., Ingram, J.N., Wolpert, D.M.: A modular planar robotic manipulandum with end-point torque control. J. Neurosci. Methods **181**(2), 199–211 (2009). https://doi.org/10.1016/j.jneumeth.2009.05.005
5. Massie, T.H., Salisbury, J.K.: The phantom haptic interface: a device for probing virtual objects. In: Proceedings of the ASME Winter Annual Meeting, Symposium on Haptic Interfaces for Virtual Environment and Teleoperator Systems, vol. 55, no. 1, pp. 295–300, Chicago, IL (1994)
6. Van der Linde, R.Q., Lammertse, P., Frederiksen, E., Ruiter, B.: The HapticMaster, a new high-performance haptic interface. In: Proceedings of Eurohaptics, Edinburgh University, pp. 1–5 (2002)
7. Bartenbach, V., et al.: The biomotionbot: a robotic device for applications in human motor learning and rehabilitation. J. Neurosci. Methods **213**(2), 282–297 (2013)
8. Clavel, R.: Conception d'un robot parallèle rapide à 4 degrés de liberté. In: EPFL (1991)
9. Grant, D.: Two new commercial haptic rotary controllers. In: Proceedings of Eurohaptics, p. 451. Citeseer (2004)
10. Demers, J.-G., Boelen, J., Sinclair, I.: Freedom 6s force feedback hand controller. IFAC Proceedings Volumes **31**(33), 115–120 (1998)

11. Salcudean, S.E., Stocco, L.: Isotropy and actuator optimization in haptic interface design. In: Proceedings 2000 ICRA. Millennium Conference. IEEE International Conference on Robotics and Automation. Symposia Proceedings (Cat. No. 00CH37065), vol. 1, pp. 763–769. IEEE (2000)

12. Stocco, L.J., Salcudean, S.E., Sassani, F.: Optimal kinematic design of a haptic pen. IEEE/ASME Trans. Mechatron. **6**(3), 210–220 (2001)

13. Forsslund, J., Yip, M., Sallnäs, E.-L.: Woodenhaptics: a starting kit for crafting force-reflecting spatial haptic devices. In: Proceedings of the Ninth International Conference on Tangible, Embedded, and Embodied Interaction, pp. 133–140 (2015)

14. Hayward, V., Choksi, J., Lanvin, G., Ramstein, C.: Design and multi-objective optimization of a linkage for a haptic interface. In: Lenarčič, J., Ravani, B. (eds.) Advances in Robot Kinematics and Computational Geometry, pp. 359–368. Springer, Dordrecht (1994). https://doi.org/10.1007/978-94-015-8348-0_36

15. Hayward, V., Astley, O.R.: Performance measures for haptic interfaces. In: Giralt, G., Hirzinger, G. (eds.) Robotics research: The Seventh International Symposium, pp. 195–206. Springer, Cham (1996). https://doi.org/10.1007/978-1-4471-1021-7_22

16. Tan, H.Z., Srinivasan, M.A., Eberman, B., Cheng, B.: Human factors for the design of force-reflecting haptic interfaces. Dyn. Syst. Control **55**(1), 353–359 (1994)

17. Howard, I.S.: Design and prototyping of a low-cost light weight fixed-endpoint orientation planar Cobot. In: 2022 International Conference on System Science and Engineering (ICSSE), pp. 047–054. IEEE (2022)

18. Di Natale, M., Zeng, H., Giusto, P., Ghosal, A.: Understanding and Using the Controller Area Network Communication Protocol: Theory and Practice. Springer, Cham (2012). https://doi.org/10.1007/978-1-4614-0314-2

19. Siciliano, B., Sciavicco, L., Villani, L., Oriolo, G.: Motion control. Robot. Model. Plann. Control 303–361 (2009)

20. Lynch, K.M., Park, F.C.: Modern Robotics. Cambridge University Press, Cambridge (2017)

21. Wannasuphoprasit, W., Gillespie, R.B., Colgate, J.E., Peshkin, M.A.: Cobot control. In: Proceedings of International Conference on Robotics and Automation, vol. 4, pp. 3571–3576. IEEE (1997)

22. Colgate, J.E., Wannasuphoprasit, W., Peshkin, M.A.: Cobots: robots for collaboration with human operators. In: Proceedings of the 1996 ASME International Mechanical Engineering Congress and Exposition (1996)

Sim-to-Real Deep Reinforcement Learning with Manipulators for Pick-and-Place

Wenxing Liu[1,2(✉)] [ID], Hanlin Niu[1,2] [ID], Robert Skilton[1] [ID],
and Joaquin Carrasco[2] [ID]

[1] Remote Applications in Challenging Environments (RACE), United Kingdom
Atomic Energy Authority, Culham, UK
{wenxing.liu,hanlin.niu,robert.skilton}@ukaea.uk
[2] Department of Electrical and Electronic Engineering, The University of
Manchester, Manchester, UK
joaquin.carrasco@manchester.ac.uk

Abstract. When transferring a Deep Reinforcement Learning model from simulation to the real world, the performance could be unsatisfactory since the simulation cannot imitate the real world well in many circumstances. This results in a long period of fine-tuning in the real world. This paper proposes a self-supervised vision-based DRL method that allows robots to pick and place objects effectively and efficiently when directly transferring a training model from simulation to the real world. A height-sensitive action policy is specially designed for the proposed method to deal with crowded and stacked objects in challenging environments. The training model with the proposed approach can be applied directly to a real suction task without any fine-tuning from the real world while maintaining a high suction success rate. It is also validated that our model can be deployed to suction novel objects in a real experiment with a suction success rate of 90% without any real-world fine-tuning. The experimental video is available at: https://youtu.be/jSTC-EGsoFA.

Keywords: Deep Reinforcement Learning · Sim-to-real · Vision · Pick-and-place · Manipulators

1 Introduction

Robotic technology has resulted in significant advancements in various areas such as goal attainment [8], object manipulation [9,27], formation tracking [28,29], human-robot interaction [23], collision avoidance [12,13], and path planning [14]. Deep reinforcement learning (DRL) has become an essential element in robotic

Supported by EPSRC project No. EP/S03286X/1, EPSRC RAIN project No. EP/R026084/1, EPSRC RNE project No. EP/P01366X/1 and UKAEA/EPSRC Fusion Grant 2022/2027 No. EP/W006839/1.

F. Iida et al. (Eds.): TAROS 2023, LNAI 14136, pp. 240–252, 2023.
https://doi.org/10.1007/978-3-031-43360-3_20

control, where an agent gradually develops a particular strategy through inter-action with the environment to receive maximum rewards. However, transferring DRL models from simulation to the real world is challenging due to the discrepancy between the two environments. It takes considerable time to fine-tune the model parameters to adapt to the real-world environment. The use of robotic arms in a real environment is time-bound, raising the crucial question of reducing the real-world fine-tuning duration while maintaining high accuracy in picking and placing objects.

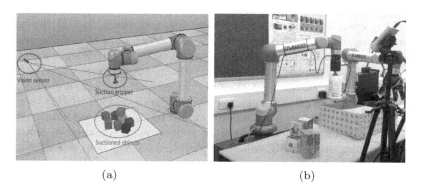

(a)   (b)

Fig. 1. (a) The training environment in simulation; (b) Pick-and-place objects with the proposed method in the real world

In comparison to conventional methods for object manipulation, using DRL poses certain challenges, including the need for feature extraction through neural networks to enable suctioning of objects, the ability to generalize to novel objects with different shapes and heights, developing self-supervised approaches to avoid the need for pre-labelled training data, and adapting to challenging environments such as crowded and stacked objects. This paper proposes a self-supervised end-to-end DRL approach that enables robots to effectively and efficiently pick and place objects by directly transferring the training model from simulation to the real world, see Fig. 1. The key contributions of the paper can be summarized as follows:

1. A fully self-supervised DRL method that utilizes visual information to enable manipulators to learn how to pick and place objects is proposed. By encouraging the Universal Robot 5 (UR5) robot arm to suction the area near the centre of the target object in simulation, the proposed training model can directly be applied to pick and place trained objects in the real world with a 90% suction success rate.
2. In particular, a height-sensitive action policy is developed to facilitate the proposed self-supervised vision-based DRL method for suctioning in a challenging environment where objects are crowded and stacked.
3. The efficacy of the proposed method is evaluated in both simulated and real environments, demonstrating its robustness and applicability to a variety of

scenarios. The approach is also shown to achieve a 90% suction success rate on novel objects without requiring any fine-tuning in the real world.

2 Related Work

Sim-to-Real: The concept of Sim-to-real training has been extensively researched to minimize the gap between simulation and real-world environments [6]. The central concept is to modify simulated environments using real-world samples [24]. In [25], a novel domain adaptation approach was proposed for robot perception to close the reality gap between simulation and the real world by searching common features of synthetic and real data. In [17], an end-to-end pipeline was developed to generate realistic depth data from 3D simulation models by accurately modelling vital real-world factors such as sensor noise and surface geometry. In recent years, there have been publications where only simulation was used for training, yet they performed well in the real environment. A grasp quality convolutional neural network was developed in [11] to configure the robustness of grasp from a point cloud. In [26], a closed-loop controller was trained with only simulation to make robots tackle unexpected changes in objects. Switching from RGB images to depth data can help reduce the sim-to-real gap, as depth images carry less information than RGB images. Due to limitations in physical properties, such as the inability to accurately capture dark-coloured or thin objects, depth cameras may struggle to measure certain objects, thereby hindering the real-world performance of robotic arms. The proposed method is capable of suctioning objects of various shapes and heights, making it more versatile.

Pick-and-Place: Pick-and-place is a crucial concept in the field of robotic manipulators [5,7,16]. In recent times, there has been an increasing focus on the manipulation of objects through picking and placing. For instance, an industrial robot system with several stationary cameras was mentioned in [3] to ensure safe human-robot cooperation. In [18], an application of visual serving to a 4 degree-of-freedom (DOF) robot manipulator was proposed to pick and place a target using the edge detection method as visual input. A remote-controlled mobile robot was developed and designed in [1] to deal with the pick-and-place task. In [20], the software development for a vision-based pick-and-place robot was presented to provide the computational intelligence required for its operation. In order to eliminate human intervention or error and work more precisely, a pick-and-place robot using Robo-Arduino was developed in [4] for any pick-and-place functions. A pick-and-place robot which offered sensing, control and manufacturing assistance was present in [21], which improved productivity and reduced the risk of injury because of repetitive tasks. However, the studies mentioned above are primarily focused on model-based grasping using certain types of robotic manipulators, which could be seen as a constraint. The approach presented in this paper emphasizes end-to-end and pixel-to-pixel suctioning, which can be readily adapted to other robotic systems.

3 Methodology

The proposed method is trained entirely through self-supervision, which involves the interaction between the UR5 robot arm and the simulated environment.

3.1 System Overview

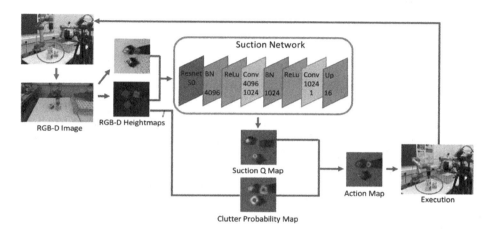

Fig. 2. Overview of the proposed framework. BN stands for Batch Normalization. Conv represents convolution. Up stands for upsampling. The red circle denotes pixel-wise best suction position. More details can be found from Algorithm 1.

The overview of the proposed DRL framework is shown in Fig. 2. The RGB-D image g_t, captured by a fixed camera, is orthographically projected in the gravity direction to construct the colour heightmap c_t and the depth heightmap d_t. Then both heightmaps are fed into the suction network to generate a suction Q map q_t. By detecting different heights from d_t, a clutter probability map l_t can be obtained. The position with the highest probability in the action map denotes the pixel-wise best suction position $[x_t, y_t]$. The suction height z_t is obtained from d_t.

3.2 Reward Space and State Space

Reward Space. During iteration t, the centre distance ψ_t between the suctioned object and the pixel-wise best suction position $[x_t, y_t]$ can be computed by

$$\psi_t = \sqrt{(x_t - \sigma_t)^2 + (y_t - \iota_t)^2} \tag{1}$$

where σ_t and ι_t denote x, y positions of the centre of the suctioned object.

The reward function can be defined as follows:

$$r = \frac{r_p}{(\psi_t + \delta)} r_g \tag{2}$$

where r_p is a positive constant reward, δ is a small positive number which prevents zero division, $r_g = 1$ if the object is successfully suctioned, otherwise $r_g = 0$. As a result, the reward stimulates agents to suction the area close to the centre of the expected suctioned object during each iteration, which increases the suction success rate.

State Space. The state s_t contains the colour heightmap c_t and the depth heightmap d_t.

3.3 Network Structure

As shown in Fig. 2, the input of the suction network passes data through ResNet-50 [22] to extract features from both heightmaps. Then the aforementioned features are fed into a Batch Normalization layer [15] with 4096 input features, a ReLu layer [15], a Convolution layer [15] with 4096 input channels and 1024 output channels. After passing data through another Batch Normalization layer [15], ReLu layer [15] and Convolution layer [15], data are processed by a bilinear upsample layer [15] with a scale factor of 16. The output of the suction network shares the same image size as the heightmap input, which is a dense pixel-wise Q map. The pixel with the highest probability in the action map denotes the best suction position.

3.4 Height-Sensitive Action Policy

To effectively suction in a challenging environment, a height-sensitive action policy is proposed. As can be seen from Fig. 2, q_t can be acquired from c_t and d_t. However, the information contained in q_t is not enough to make the proposed framework sensitive to the heights of the grasped objects. As a result, we introduce the clutter probability map l_t. The depth heightmap is shifted along one axis for 60 pixels to generate a translated map. By contrasting the depth difference between the translated and the original depth heightmap, the pixel with enough depth difference is counted as 1 otherwise 0, which builds the clutter probability map l_t. The action space a_t can be computed as follows:

$$a_t = \arg\max_a (q_t l_t) \tag{3}$$

where q_t and l_t depend on the action.

4   Experiments and Results

The feasibility of the proposed method is validated in both simulated and real environments. The proposed approach is implemented on a desktop with Nvidia GTX 2080 and Intel Core i9 CPU with 64 GB RAM.

4.1   Training Details

The proposed method is trained in Coppeliasim [19] using Python [10] and Pytorch [15]. The UR5 robot arm is connected with a suction gripper [2] to pick and place objects, as shown in Fig. 1 (a). During each training iteration, a vision sensor captures RGB-D images of the UR5 robot arm in a 0.448×0.448 m^2 workspace. The resolution of the RGB-D images is 640×480. The UR5 robot arm motion planning task can be accomplished using Coppeliasim [19] internal inverse kinematics. The suctioned objects are $5 \times 5 \times 5$ cm^3 cubes.

Algorithm 1 Vision-based DRL for Pick-and-place

1: Initialize training parameter ϕ_t, learning rate α, RGB-D image g_t, discounted factor γ, training steps parameter T, replay buffer R_p.
2: **while** $t < T$ **do**
3:    Generate c_t and d_t from g_t.
4:    Generate l_t from d_t.
5:    **if** object number $b_t <$ empty threshold **then**
6:        Feed c_t and d_t into the suction network with the height-sensitive action policy to get action-value function $Q(\phi_t, s_t, a_t)$.
7:        **if** $t > 2$ **then**
8:            Use $Q(\phi_{t-1}, s_{t-1}, a_{t-1})$ to generate r_t.
9:            Minimize the temporal difference error ξ_{t-1}:
10:               $$y_{t-1} = r_t + \gamma \max_a (Q(\phi_{t-1}^-, s_t, a)).$$
11:               $$\xi_{t-1} = Q(\phi_{t-1}, s_{t-1}, a_{t-1}) - y_{t-1}.$$
12:            Sample a minibatch from R_p for experience replay.
13:        **end if**
14:        Suction objects.
15:        Store (c_t, d_t, a_t) in R_p.
16:    **else**
17:        Reposition objects.
18:    **end if**
19: **end while**

Depending on the size of the suction gripper and the intrinsic of the vision sensor, we set $r_p = 15$ and $\delta = 0.00001$ in (2). For other robotic platforms, these values can also be reconfigured. In Algorithm 1, the learning rate α is set to 0.0001. The discounted factor γ has a fixed value of 0.5. The training steps parameter T is set to 400. The training is considered to be successful if the UR5 robot arm is able to pick and place target objects which are randomly dropped into the workspace.

4.2   Evaluation Metrics

We design two metrics to evaluate the suction performance of the UR5 robot arm. For all these metrics, a larger value leads to better performance.

The suction success rate S_r is given by:

$$S_r = \frac{N_s}{N_i} \times 100\% \qquad (4)$$

where N_s stands for the number of successful suctions, N_i represents the number of training steps.

The distance rate D_r is defined as follows:

$$D_r = \frac{N_d}{N_i} \times 100\% \qquad (5)$$

where N_d is the number of times when $\psi_t < 0.015$ m.

4.3   Baseline Method

The performance of our system is compared with the following baseline approach: **Visual Grasping method** shares the same input as our proposed method to generate the probability maps for best suction positions. However, it takes binary classification for the reward space design in which 1 stands for successful grasp and 0 otherwise. This baseline method is analogous to the Visual Pushing Grasping (VPG) method [30]. Nevertheless, we extend this method to our suction framework for a fair comparison.

4.4   Simulation Evaluation

To confirm the validity of our design, we train both methods in simulation for 400 steps. Overall the proposed method outperforms the Visual Grasping method in terms of both suction success rate and distance rate by large margins. It can be obtained from Fig. 3 (a) that the proposed method arrives at around 97% suction success rate at 150 training steps, while the Visual Grasping method shows only 52%. Removing the height-sensitive action policy from both methods leads to a longer time to achieve the same suction success rate. As can be seen from Fig. 3 (b), the distance rate of the proposed method reaches around 80% at 400 training steps, whereas the Visual Grasping method shows only 58%. When the height-sensitive action policy is separated from both methods, the distance rates decrease by 20% and 33%, respectively. These simulation results confirm the validity of the proposed reward space design in improving the suction success rate by encouraging robots to suction the area close to the centre of the expected suctioned object.

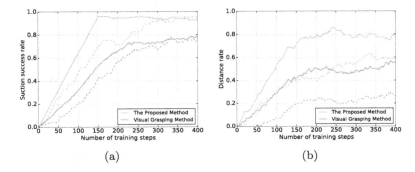

(a)   (b)

Fig. 3. (a) Suction success rates; (b) Distance rates of both methods. The dotted lines represent methods without the height-sensitive action policy.

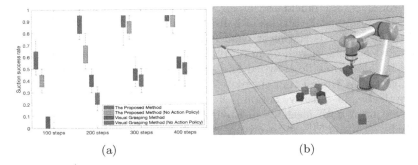

(a)   (b)

Fig. 4. (a) Real-world evaluation of both methods; (b) Edge suctioning with the Visual Grasping method. Although the suctions are considered successful in simulation, they will cause real-world failures.

4.5   Real-World Evaluation

We evaluate both methods directly in the real environment using the models trained in Fig. 3 without any real-world fine-tuning. The UR5 robot arm is connected to a Robotiq EPick vacuum gripper for real-world evaluation. A fixed Azure Kinect camera is used to capture RGB-D images with a resolution of 1280×720. The suctioned objects are $7 \times 7 \times 7$ cm^3 cubes. Figure 4 (a) depicts the box plot of real-world evaluation with both methods. The proposed method achieves a 90% suction success rate at 200 training steps in real-world evaluation, while the Visual Grasping method shows only 40%. When the height-sensitive action policy is separated from both methods, the suction success rates drop to 65% and 30%, respectively. By implementing the proposed method, the suction success rate gap between the simulation and the real environment is only 6%, much smaller than the gap using the Visual Grasping method (26%). Although the suctions are considered successful in Fig. 4 (b), they will result in real-world failures because of edge suctioning, which enlarges the gap between the simulation and the real world. The proposed method boosts the suction success rate of the UR5 robot arm by motivating it to suction the region in proximity to the centre of the intended object, outperforming the Visual Grasping method.

4.6 Suction in Challenging Environments

The performance of the height-sensitive action policy in our proposed method is validated in this section. The common practice among humans when picking and placing crowded or stacked objects is to first grasp the objects on the top and then those at the bottom, as it is deemed to be a safer approach. Inspired by this, we have developed a height-sensitive action policy that instructs the UR5 robot arm to take the heights of objects into consideration, thus minimizing the risk of potential collisions when applying the presented approach. The testing environments are elucidated in Fig. 6. Environment 1 contains fully stacked objects. Environment 2 consists of half-stacked objects, which is more challenging. Environment 3 is the most challenging environment which contains both half-stacked objects as well as novel objects. As shown in Fig. 5, the proposed method is able to handle crowded and stacked objects in a safe manner. It can be obtained from Table 1 that the more challenging the environment is, the more effective the height-sensitive action policy is. If the height-sensitive action policy is removed from both methods in Environment 3, the collision probability will increase by 45% and 51%, respectively. Some failed examples are shown in Fig. 7, which are due to the fact that the UR5 robot arm tries to suction the object below first rather than the object above, thus colliding with the object above. This confirms the necessity of the proposed height-sensitive action policy which ensures safety during the entire movement of the UR5 robot arm.

Fig. 5. The demonstration of suctioning in Challenging Environment 3

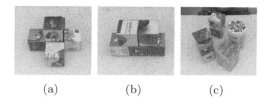

(a)   (b)   (c)

Fig. 6. Suctioning in challenging environments: (a) Environment 1; (b) Environment 2; (c) Environment 3

Table 1. Average performance in challenging environments

Collision rate (%)	Env 1	Env 2	Env 3
The proposed method	0	0	5
The proposed method (No Policy)	0	45	50
Visual Grasping method	0	1	9
Visual Grasping method (No Policy)	5	55.5	60

* No Policy means without the height-sensitive action policy.

4.7 Real-World Unseen Objects Challenge

In this section, we validate the generalisation capability of our proposed vision-based DRL method. As shown in Fig. 8, novel objects contain cylinders of different heights as well as irregularly shaped objects. The proposed method can generalise to novel objects with a suction success rate of 90% without any real-world fine-tuning. More details can be seen in Fig. 9.

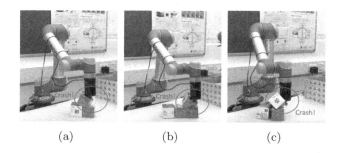

(a)   (b)   (c)

Fig. 7. Examples of collisions without the height-sensitive action policy

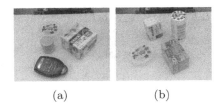

Fig. 8. Novel objects for real-world suctioning: (a) Environment 1; (b) Environment 2

Fig. 9. Pick-and-place novel objects with the proposed method

5   Conclusion

In this paper, we introduce a self-supervised DRL approach using vision-based methods to reduce the gap between simulated and real environments. Our proposed approach shows significant improvement over the Visual Grasping method in terms of suction success rate and distance rate. The suction success rate of the proposed approach reaches 90% after 200 training steps, while the Visual Grasping method only achieves 40%. By implementing a height-sensitive action policy, our method can safely pick and place crowded and stacked objects in challenging environments. Our model can be directly applied to real-world experiments and is capable of generalizing to new objects with a success rate of 90% without any fine-tuning. In the future, an exploration of optimizing the proposed method to handle more complicated scenarios will be carried out.

References

1. Abdulkareem, A., Ladenegan, O., Agbetuyi, A., Awosope, C.: Design and implementation of a prototype remote-controlled pick and place robot. Int. J. Mech. Eng. Technol. **10**(2), 235–247 (2019)
2. Ge, J., Saeidi, H., Kam, M., Opfermann, J., Krieger, A.: Supervised autonomous electrosurgery for soft tissue resection. In: 2021 IEEE 21st International Conference on Bioinformatics and Bioengineering (BIBE), pp. 1–7. IEEE (2021)
3. Gecks, T., Henrich, D.: Human-robot cooperation: safe pick-and-place operations. In: ROMAN 2005. IEEE International Workshop on Robot and Human Interactive Communication, pp. 549–554. IEEE (2005)

4. Harish, K., Megha, D., Shuklambari, M., Amit, K., Chaitanya, K.J.: Pick and place robotic arm using Arduino. Int. J. Sci. Eng. Technol. Res. (IJSETR) **6**, 1568–1573 (2017)
5. Huang, P.C., Mok, A.K.: A case study of cyber-physical system design: autonomous pick-and-place robot. In: 2018 IEEE 24th International Conference on Embedded and Real-time Computing Systems and Applications (RTCSA), pp. 22–31. IEEE (2018)
6. Kaushik, R., Arndt, K., Kyrki, V.: SafeAPT: safe simulation-to-real robot learning using diverse policies learned in simulation. IEEE Robot. Autom. Lett. **7**, 6838–6845 (2022)
7. Kumar, R., Lal, S., Kumar, S., Chand, P.: Object detection and recognition for a pick and place robot. In: Asia-Pacific World Congress on Computer Science and Engineering, pp. 1–7. IEEE (2014)
8. Liu, W., Niu, H., Jang, I., Herrmann, G., Carrasco, J.: Distributed neural networks training for robotic manipulation with consensus algorithm. IEEE Trans. Neural Netw. Learn. Syst. 1–15 (2022). https://doi.org/10.1109/TNNLS.2022.3191021
9. Liu, W., Niu, H., Pan, W., Herrmann, G., Carrasco, J.: Sim-and-real reinforcement learning for manipulation: a consensus-based approach. In: 2023 IEEE International Conference on Robotics and Automation (ICRA), pp. 3911–3917 (2023). https://doi.org/10.1109/ICRA48891.2023.10161062
10. Lutz, M.: Programming Python. O'Reilly Media, Inc., Sebastopol (2001)
11. Mahler, J., et al.: Dex-Net 2.0: deep learning to plan robust grasps with synthetic point clouds and analytic grasp metrics. arXiv preprint arXiv:1703.09312 (2017)
12. Na, S., Niu, H., Lennox, B., Arvin, F.: Bio-inspired collision avoidance in swarm systems via deep reinforcement learning. IEEE Trans. Veh. Technol. **71**(3), 2511–2526 (2022)
13. Na, S., et al.: Federated reinforcement learning for collective navigation of robotic swarms. IEEE Trans. Cogn. Dev. Syst. 1–1 (2023). https://doi.org/10.1109/TCDS.2023.3239815
14. Niu, H., Ji, Z., Savvaris, A., Tsourdos, A.: Energy efficient path planning for unmanned surface vehicle in spatially-temporally variant environment. Ocean Eng. **196**, 106766 (2020)
15. Paszke, A., et al.: PyTorch: an imperative style, high-performance deep learning library. In: Advances in Neural Information Processing Systems, vol. 32 (2019)
16. Perumaal, S.S., Jawahar, N.: Automated trajectory planner of industrial robot for pick-and-place task. Int. J. Adv. Rob. Syst. **10**(2), 100 (2013)
17. Planche, B., et al.: DepthSynth: real-time realistic synthetic data generation from CAD models for 2.5D recognition. In: 2017 International Conference on 3D Vision (3DV), pp. 1–10. IEEE (2017)
18. Qul'am, H.M., Dewi, T., Risma, P., Oktarina, Y., Permatasari, D.: Edge detection for online image processing of a vision guide pick and place robot. In: 2019 International Conference on Electrical Engineering and Computer Science (ICECOS), pp. 102–106. IEEE (2019)
19. Rohmer, E., Singh, S.P., Freese, M.: V-REP: a versatile and scalable robot simulation framework. In: 2013 IEEE/RSJ International Conference on Intelligent Robots and Systems, pp. 1321–1326. IEEE (2013)
20. Sharan, R.V., Onwubolu, G.C.: Client-server control architecture for a vision-based pick-and-place robot. Proc. Inst. Mech. Eng. Part B J. Eng. Manuf. **226**(8), 1369–1378 (2012)
21. Smys, S., Ranganathan, G.: Robot assisted sensing control and manufacture in automobile industry. J. ISMAC **1**(03), 180–187 (2019)

22. Szegedy, C., Ioffe, S., Vanhoucke, V., Alemi, A.A.: Inception-v4, inception-ResNet and the impact of residual connections on learning. In: Thirty-First AAAI Conference on Artificial Intelligence (2017)

23. Thabet, M., Patacchiola, M., Cangelosi, A.: Sample-efficient deep reinforcement learning with imaginary rollouts for human-robot interaction. In: 2019 IEEE/RSJ International Conference on Intelligent Robots and Systems (IROS), pp. 5079–5085 (2019). https://doi.org/10.1109/IROS40897.2019.8967834

24. Tobin, J., Fong, R., Ray, A., Schneider, J., Zaremba, W., Abbeel, P.: Domain randomization for transferring deep neural networks from simulation to the real world. In: 2017 IEEE/RSJ International Conference on Intelligent Robots and Systems (IROS), pp. 23–30. IEEE (2017)

25. Tzeng, E., et al.: Adapting deep visuomotor representations with weak pairwise constraints. In: Algorithmic Foundations of Robotics XII. SPAR, vol. 13, pp. 688–703. Springer, Cham (2020). https://doi.org/10.1007/978-3-030-43089-4_44

26. Viereck, U., Pas, A., Saenko, K., Platt, R.: Learning a visuomotor controller for real world robotic grasping using simulated depth images. In: Conference on Robot Learning, pp. 291–300. PMLR (2017)

27. Wang, F., Olvera, J.R.G., Cheng, G.: Optimal order pick-and-place of objects in cluttered scene by a mobile manipulator. IEEE Robot. Autom. Lett. **6**(4), 6402–6409 (2021)

28. Wu, K., Hu, J., Ding, Z., Arvin, F.: Finite-time fault-tolerant formation control for distributed multi-vehicle networks with bearing measurements. IEEE Trans. Autom. Sci. Eng. 1–12 (2023). https://doi.org/10.1109/TASE.2023.3239748

29. Wu, K., Hu, J., Lennox, B., Arvin, F.: Mixed controller design for multi-vehicle formation based on edge and bearing measurements. In: 2022 European Control Conference (ECC), pp. 1666–1671. IEEE (2022)

30. Zeng, A., Song, S., Welker, S., Lee, J., Rodriguez, A., Funkhouser, T.: Learning synergies between pushing and grasping with self-supervised deep reinforcement learning. In: 2018 IEEE/RSJ International Conference on Intelligent Robots and Systems (IROS), pp. 4238–4245. IEEE (2018)

Machine Vision

Fast 3D Semantic Segmentation Using a Self Attention Network and Random Sampling

Sandeep Babu[1] , Majid Jegarian[2]([✉]) , Dirk Fischer[1] ,
and Bärbel Mertsching[1]

[1] GET Lab, Department of Electrical Engineering and Information Technology,
Paderborn University, Pohlweg 47–49, 33098 Paderborn, Germany
{babu,fischer,mertsching}@get.uni-paderborn.de
[2] IPEK-Institute of Product Engineering at Karlsruhe Institute of Technology (KIT),
Kaiserstrasse 10, 76131 Karlsruhe, Germany
majid.jegarian@kit.edu

Abstract. For many use cases, reliable autonomous behavior of mobile robots can only be achieved if semantic information about the environment is available together with a topological map. However, current techniques either rely on costly sampling methods or involve computationally heavy pre- or post-processing steps, making them unsuitable for real-time systems with limited resources. In this paper, we propose an optimized approach for 3D point cloud processing that uses a self attention network combined with random sampling to directly infer the semantics of individual 3D points. The approach achieves competitive results on large scale point cloud data sets, including Semantic KITTI and S3DIS.

Keywords: Semantic segmentation · 3D Point cloud processing · Self attention

1 Introduction

Autonomous navigation and exploration of unknown environments are fundamental tasks in the field of mobile robots and require that a robot is capable of interpreting the data obtained from the environment. For many applications, a plain point cloud that only provides information about the obstacles in the environment may be sufficient, but for more complex tasks, understanding the scene is critical; for example, it must be possible to distinguish a closed door from a wall. Here, the semantic segmentation of point clouds is an indispensable tool, and several methods already give remarkably good results. However, their use of mobile robots is not without problems due to the limited resources and real-time constraints of these systems. Therefore, our goal is to develop a memory and computationally efficient approach for processing 3D point clouds directly.

Our analysis of different approaches shows that especially the utilized point sampling methods are inadequate for large point clouds and heavily impede real-time processing. From our point of view, random sampling is a more appropriate

F. Iida et al. (Eds.): TAROS 2023, LNAI 14136, pp. 255–266, 2023.
https://doi.org/10.1007/978-3-031-43360-3_21

method to process large point clouds due to its speed and scalability. However, important features may be omitted, especially for objects with few points. To address this, we draw from the success of transformers in natural language processing (NLP) [22] and computer vision [16,24]. In NLP tasks, transformers can identify appropriate relationships and dependencies between source and target words. Hence, we leverage the attention mechanism to design a local feature transformation layer to capture the relationships in point cloud processing. Moreover, a local self attention based U-shaped network is used that naturally builds a feature hierarchy without manual grouping. It allows the collection of rich geometric representations and exhibits fast inference times, even for large scenes.

The rest of this paper is organized as follows: In Sect. 2, recent developments in the area of 3D semantic segmentation are discussed. The proposed approach is presented in Sect. 3, followed by the experimental setup and detailed results in Sect. 4. Finally, in Sect. 5, we conclude and suggest possible ideas for future work.

2   Related Work

Several techniques have been proposed to address the challenges in processing and analyzing point cloud data. This section reviews the most relevant work on learning-based point cloud segmentation, i.e., projection-based, point-based, and attention-based networks.

2.1   Projection-Based Networks

These approaches employ projection techniques to transform unstructured point clouds into regular structures, such as 2D images or 3D voxel grids. They have become popular in recent years due to their effectiveness in processing point clouds and their ability to leverage advancements in computer vision and convolutional neural networks (CNN). Several works use spherical projection, which is usually dense, but causes distortion of physical dimensions. RangeNet++ [13] makes use of DarkNet [17] and applies an accelerated k-nearest neighbor search (k-NN) on the projection result, while SalsaNext [6] introduces an uncertainty-aware mechanism for point feature learning. Systems like these provide state-of-the-art inference times (up to 50 fps) with reasonable prediction rates for outdoor driving scenes, but face problems such as blurred CNN outputs and quantization errors. Decisive is the fact that geometric information in point clouds collapses during the projection phase and the choice of projection planes can notably impact recognition performance, with 3D occlusion potentially affecting accuracy.

2.2   Point-Based Networks

Unlike projection-based networks, point-based methods operate on raw points and maintain geometric accuracy. PointNet [3] introduces a multi-layer perceptron (MLP) for 3D scene understanding, which is enhanced in PointNet++ [15]

by using hierarchical sampling. Recent studies attempt to apply convolution on point clouds as local sampling and grouping, which is challenging due to the sparsity and disorder of 3D points. KPConv [21] performs convolution using kernel points defined in a continuous space and employs a k-d tree for point-wise convolution of query points. RandLA-Net [9] uses random sampling and local feature aggregation to minimize the loss of information from the random operation, which speeds up the point network but still results in accuracy loss. Although random sampling reduces memory usage and enhances learning of local patterns, neighborhood search, such as k-NN or k-d tree construction, results in significant computational overhead when processing large-scale 3D scenes.

2.3   Attention-Based Networks

Various networks, e.g., Ramachandran et al. [16], already use self attention for image classification and object detection tasks. Zhao et al. [24] developed vector self attention for image recognition, leading researchers to explore self attention transformer-based architectures for point cloud understanding. Xie et al. [23] presented dot-product self attention techniques for capturing shape and geometry information in point clouds. Point Cloud Transformer [8] proposed offset attention to calculate the difference between self attention and input features through element-wise subtraction. Recently, Zhao et al. [26] improved the point cloud analysis with a vector-based self attention network and k-NN search, resulting in noteworthy performance gains. However, most previous studies have used global attention and scalar dot-product attention, which are unsuitable for large scale 3D scene understanding.

As 3D point clouds consist of point sets with positional attributes, a self attention model seems appropriate for this type of data. Therefore, to achieve high accuracy, we propose to use local self attention and vector attention to be able to process large scenes with millions of points. In addition, sampling methods considerably affect the processing of large scale point clouds. We demonstrate that well-designed self attention networks can handle large, complex 3D scenes and advance the state-of-the-art in segmenting large scale point clouds.

3   Methodology

Our approach aims to provide accurate yet fast semantic segmentation of raw point clouds for mobile robotic systems. To achieve this, we propose a transformer based encoder-decoder architecture that successively increases the receptive field and downsamples the number of points quickly and effectively. Figure 1 shows the extraction of per-point semantic labels from the input point cloud. This is done by passing the point cloud through a shared MLP layer and five encoding and decoding blocks, consisting of multiple point self attention modules and random sampling layers. Per-point semantic labels are then predicted using fully-connected layers.

Note that the number of layers, blocks, and the down sampling can be varied to according to the use case. However, larger models require additional computation and may lead to overfitting. We perform random point sampling with a ratio of four, i.e., (N, N/4, N/16, N/64, N/256) where N is the number of points. Simultaneously, the per-point feature dimensions is increased in each block to preserve information, i.e., (8, 64, 128, 256, 512). The three core blocks of our method are explained in detail below: 1. An efficient point down sampling layer, 2. A point self attention layer as an encoder, and 3. Shared MLPs as the decoders with interpolation layers.

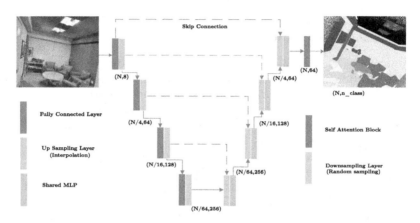

Fig. 1. Detailed architecture of our network, Where (N, D) represents the number of points and feature dimensions respectively.

3.1   Point Downsampling Layer

Processing large scale point clouds with millions of points covering a huge area consumes a lot of memory and time. Hence, it is necessary to downsample the points successively without loosing useful point features. State-of-the-art semantic segmentation methods typically use Furthest Point Sampling (FPS) [7,15]. Although FPS provides a good coverage of the entire point cloud, it is computationally expensive with a complexity of $\mathcal{O}(KN)$. In contrast, Random Sampling (RS) randomly selects k out of N points and has a computational complexity of only $\mathcal{O}(K)$. Among all the sampling methods random sampling has the highest computational efficiency [9]. We therefore rely on random sampling, which appears to be more suitable than other approaches for efficient processing of large point clouds. At the same time, random sampling can result in useful point features being dropped. Therefore, a self attention-based feature aggregation module is used to address this issue.

This module captures complex local features around each point by progressively increasing the receptive field in each layer. Additionally, a vector self attention block explicitly captures robust features due to the interactions among features, which helps to preserve the local geometry. The attention mechanism is able to automatically retain prominent features. These blocks are implemented as shared MLPs so that the network can achieve a good trade-off between efficiency and computation time.

3.2 Point Self Attention Block

As shown in Fig. 2, the point self attention block comprises a self attention layer and a learnable position encoding, including an embedding operation on the input point cloud's coordinates. In addition to spatial coordinates, the input point cloud may contain features, such as RGB color and normal vectors. The additional features are concatenated (coordinates and additional features) and used as initial features. First, the shared MLPs generate three linear projection matrices, namely query, key, and value of the input features. Then, the k-NN algorithm generates local neighborhoods for each key and value feature. The position encoding block encodes the relative position and Euclidean distance around each neighborhood center point.

Due to the large amount of dot product operations, standard transformers incur high computation costs and memory consumption. The computation and memory complexities of the standard self attention layer for N input points are quadratic, i.e., $\mathcal{O}(N^2)$. To address this, we follow the work of Zhao et al. [26], which utilizes relational functions like subtraction and a feed-forward network to consider feature interactions. An attention map is then produced using a mapping function like *Softmax*. However, we further reduce the complexity by using only shared MLPs for the entire block, thus making the attention block lightweight. At last, an element-wise product is formed between the value vector and the attention map, and a residual connection is added. The self attention layer learns the feature vectors' content and their geometric relationships. The following sections describe the self attention layer and the position encoding block in detail.

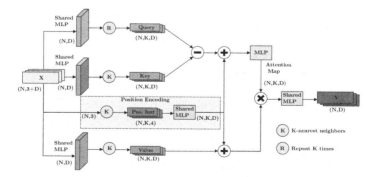

Fig. 2. Point self attention block with the position encoding module.

Point Self Attention Layer. To enhance interactions among feature vectors and to extract robust local features, the vector self attention layer from [26] is used which allows to apply the attention mechanism patch-wise. However, since feature vectors are not arranged in order, vector attention is not permutation invariant. Therefore, a position encoding ϕ is added, resulting in

$$y_i = \sum_{j \in \mathcal{R}(i)} \rho\left(\gamma\left(\delta\left(\mathbf{x}_i, \mathbf{x}_j\right) + \phi\right)\right) \odot \left(\beta(\mathbf{x}_j) + \phi\right), \tag{1}$$

where

$$\delta\left(\mathbf{x}_i, \mathbf{x}_j\right) = \varphi(\mathbf{x}_i) - \psi(\mathbf{x}_j) \tag{2}$$

is the subtraction relational operation performed between query $\varphi(\mathbf{x}_i)$ and key $\psi(\mathbf{x}_j)$ feature transformations. The subset $\mathcal{R}(i)$ is a set of k-nearest-neighbor points in a local neighborhood of $\mathbf{x}_i$. γ enables interactions between the features in the subset $\mathcal{R}(i)$ to generate the attention vectors and ρ applies a normalization function, such as *softmax*, on the attention features. An element-wise multiplication $\odot$ taken between the resulting attention map and the value feature transformation $\beta(\mathbf{x}_j)$.

Position Encoding. A local neighborhood is generated for each point p_i in the point cloud using k-nearest neighbors. Then, the relative distances between the points in the neighborhood $(p_i - p_i^k)$ and their Euclidean distances $\| p_i - p_i^k \|$ are concatenated for each point. Our position encoding function ϕ is defined as follows:

$$\phi = \theta\left(\left[(p_i - p_i^k) \oplus (\| p_i - p_i^k \|)\right]\right). \tag{3}$$

where, p_i^k is the kth neighbour point centered around p_i. θ is a trainable function which also generates position embeddings and ensures that the dimensions of the position encoding matches those of the feature vectors. The position encoding function is implemented with two linear layers and Gaussian Error Linear Unit (GELU) non-linearity.

3.3   Decoder Block

The decoder block consists of an upsampling layer and a shared MLP layer. For efficiency and simplicity, we use nearest neighbor interpolation as in [9]. The coordinates of downsampled points are retained for reference, and k-NN is used to find the nearest neighboring point from the previous layer. Features of the nearest points are copied to the target point and concatenated with the features from the corresponding encoder block, provided via a skip connection. The decoder block feeds the concatenated feature vectors to a shared MLP layer to reduce memory and time requirements. The final decoder stage produces a feature vector for each point in the input point cloud. By passing the feature vectors through shared fully-connected layers (N, 64), (N, 32), and (N, n_{class}) with a dropout layer, the semantic label for each point is obtained.

4   Experiments

For the evaluation we have chosen the datasets Stanford Large Scale 3D Indoor Spaces (S3DIS) [1] and SemanticKiTTI [2] due to their rich diversity and densely annotated labels. The results and a comparison with the current state-of-the-art are given using the metrics mean of class-wise accuracy (mAcc), and mean intersection over union (mIoU).

The network is implemented in PyTorch [14]. The Stochastic Gradient Descent (SGD) optimizer is applied with momentum and weight decay set to 0.9 and 10^{-6}, respectively. Based on the ablation study in Sect. 4.3 the number of nearest neighbor points k is set to 16. During training, a fixed number of points (80,960) is sampled from each point cloud and fed into the model. During testing, several sub-clouds are iteratively inferred with sufficient overlap until all the points are covered. Since several points are inferred more than once, we follow the voting scheme given in [9,21] and perform a soft update to the predictions for better accuracy.

4.1   S3DIS Dataset

The S3DIS dataset has 271 rooms in six areas across three buildings, with 3D points and color information for semantic scene understanding. The proposed model is evaluated by following a common protocol [9,26] in two approaches, i.e., Area 5 is used for validation, and the rest of the areas are used for training and 6-fold cross-validation. The model is trained for 200 epochs with an initial learning rate of 0.02, dropped by 10x at epochs 140 and 180.

The results are presented in Table 1 and 2. On Area 5, our model achieved a mAcc of 76.0% and a mIoU of 60.0%. The performance of our model is competitive with the existing state-of-the-art models, but it falls short of the best-performing model, PointTransformer [26]. Nonetheless, our model shows promising results in terms of accurately segmenting certain classes, such as windows, doors, and chairs. Table 2 reports the average wall-time latency of each method when processing S3DIS Area 5 point clouds. For a fair comparison of the inference time, each model's latency is measured on a machine with a single NVIDIA Geforce GTX 1080TI GPU using their official code. Our method achieves a mAcc of 79.7% and mIoU of 61.8% during 6-fold cross-validation which is still close to the best performing methods, i.e., PointTransformer [26] and RandLA-Net [9]. However, our inference time of 2.67 s is significantly lower and outperforms all other evaluated methods. The observed improvement in inference time can be attributed to the absence of a pre-processing stage and the adoption of a more efficient downsampling approach.

Figure 3 shows the visualization results of our model predictions. We can see that the predictions are consistent with the ground truth across all classes. However, some classes like posters, windows, and boards are under-oversegmented which may be due to the random sampling process the objects' three-dimensional shape is destroyed.

Table 1. Semantic segmentation results for Area 5 from the S3DIS dataset. Scores are taken from the respective work.

Method	OA	mAcc	mIoU	ceiling	floor	wall	beam	column	window	door	table	chair	sofa	bookcase	board	clutter
PointNet [3]	−1	49.0	41.1	88.8	97.3	69.8	0.1	3.9	46.3	10.8	59.0	52.6	5.9	40.3	26.4	33.2
SegCloud [20]	−1	57.4	48.9	90.1	96.1	69.9	0.0	18.4	38.4	23.1	70.4	75.9	40.9	58.4	13.0	41.6
TangentConv [19]	−1	62.2	52.6	90.5	97.7	74.0	0.0	20.7	39.0	31.3	77.5	69.4	57.3	38.5	48.8	39.8
PointCNN [11]	85.9	63.9	57.3	92.3	98.2	79.4	0.0	17.6	22.8	62.1	74.4	80.6	31.7	66.7	62.1	56.7
SPGraph [10]	86.4	66.5	58.0	89.4	96.9	78.1	0.0	42.8	48.9	61.6	84.7	75.4	69.8	52.6	2.1	52.2
PCCN [11]	−1	67.0	58.3	92.3	96.2	75.9	0.3	6.0	69.5	63.5	66.9	65.6	47.3	68.9	59.1	46.2
PointWeb [25]	87.0	66.6	60.3	92.0	98.5	79.4	0.0	21.1	59.7	34.8	76.3	88.3	46.9	69.3	64.9	52.5
MinkowskiNet [5]	−1	71.7	65.4	91.8	98.7	86.2	0.0	34.1	48.9	62.4	81.6	89.8	47.2	74.9	74.4	58.6
KPConv [21]	−1	72.8	67.1	92.8	97.3	82.4	0.0	23.9	58.0	69.0	81.5	91.0	75.4	75.3	66.7	58.9
PCT [4]	−1	67.7	61.3	92.5	98.4	80.6	0.0	19.4	61.6	48.0	76.6	85.2	46.2	67.7	67.9	52.2
PointTransformer [26]	90.8	76.5	70.4	94.0	98.5	86.3	0.0	38.0	63.4	74.3	89.1	82.4	74.3	80.2	76.0	59.3
Ours	86.5	76.0	60.0	90.0	98.0	79.0	0.0	24.0	55.0	58.0	74.0	84.0	59.0	66.0	56.0	44.0

[1] values not available.

Table 2. Semantic segmentation results on the S3DIS dataset, evaluated on 6-fold cross validation. Shows the average inference time in seconds for each method. Scores are taken from the respective work.

Method	OA	mAcc	mIoU	Latency(Seconds)	GPU
PointNet [3]	78.5	66.2	47.6	18.16	RTX 3090
SPGraph [10]	85.5	73.0	62.1	8.28	RTX 3090
PointCNN [11]	88.1	75.6	65.4	−1	RTX 3090
PointWeb [25]	87.3	76.2	66.7	11.62	RTX 3090
RandLA-Net [9]	88.0	**82.0**	70.0	−1	−1
KPConv [21]	−1	79.1	70.6	105.15	RTX 3090
PointTransformer [26]	**90.2**	81.9	**73.5**	80.0	GTX 1080TI
Ours	86.9	79.7	61.8	**2.67**	GTX 1080TI

[1] values not available.

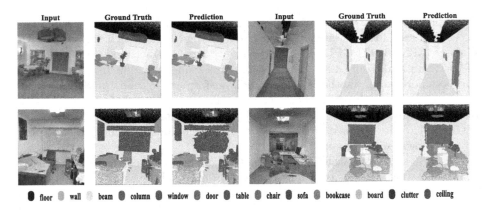

Fig. 3. Visualization of semantic segmentation results on S3DIS dataset.

4.2   SemanticKITTI Dataset

The SemanticKITTI dataset includes over 43,000 densely annotated lidar scans across 22 sequences. Each 3D point cloud contains point coordinates and is labeled with 19 categories, including moving objects. The model is trained for 50 epochs with the initial learning rate set to 0.02 and is dropped by 10x at epochs 30 and 40.

Table 3 presents the results of various semantic segmentation methods evaluated on Sequence 08 of the SemanticKITTI dataset. Our proposed method achieved a mIoU of 53.8%, which is slightly lower than the state-of-the-art method, SPVNAS [18], with a mIoU of 66.4%. Compared to the point-based methods such as PointNet [3], PointNet++ [15], and RandLA-Net [9], our method achieves competitive results, while having a lower latency of 400ms on a NVIDIA Geforce GTX 1080TI GPU. Among the voxel and graph-based methods such as PVCNN [12], MinkowskiNet [5], and SPGraph [10] our method achieves comparable performance, albeit with a moderately higher latency. This must be due to the much smaller point cloud size in the SemanticKITTI dataset, making the impact of pre-processing less significant. This shows that our method can easily be used for point clouds of different sizes without critical performance degradation.

Table 3. Semantic segmentation results on the SemanticKITTI dataset, evaluated on Sequence 08.

Method	mIoU	Latency (ms)	GPU
PointNet [3]	14.6	500[1]	–[2]
SPGraph [10]	17.4	5200[1]	–[2]
PointNet++ [15]	20.1	5900[1]	–[2]
TangentConv [19]	40.9	3000[1]	–[2]
RandLA-Net [9]	53.9	880	GTX 1080TI
MinkowskiNet [5]	63.1	294[1]	GTX 1080TI
PVCNN [12]	39.0	**146**[1]	GTX 1080TI
SPVNAS [18]	**66.4**	259	GTX 1080TI
Ours	53.8	400	GTX 1080TI

[1]results are taken from Behley et al. [2], [2]values not available.

4.3   Ablation Studies

To verify our design choices, ablation studies are performed on the point self attention module. All the studies are conducted on the S3DIS dataset and tested on Area 5, to understand what is effectively learned by the model.

Number of Neighbors. In the self attention block, k determines the local neighborhood around each point. The results of the ablation study on the values of k are shown in Table 4. The results demonstrate that the choice of k significantly impact the performance. The method achieves the best performance when k is 16, with an mIoU of 60.0% and an mAcc of 76.0%. This suggests that a moderate number of neighbors provides a good balance between capturing local details and preserving global context. When k is small (k=4), the method struggles to capture enough local context, resulting in a drop in performance. On the other hand, when k is large (k=32), the method captures a wider global context, leading to confusion between classes and a decreased performance. Overall, the results indicate that the proposed method is sensitive to the choice of k.

Table 4. Ablation study on number of neighbors k.

k	mIoU	mAcc
4	44.4	63.1
8	54.0	72.1
16	**60.0**	**76.0**
32	56.5	73.4

Position Encoding. To select a suitable position encoding ϕ, four encoding schemes have been tested: no encoding, relative position encoding, distance encoding, and a combination of relative position and distance encoding. The results in Table 5 show that using position encoding improves the model's performance. When no encoding was used, the model achieved a mIoU of 52.3% and a mAcc of 69.6%. This may be due to the loss of local geometric structure around each point. When relative position encoding was used, the mIoU increased to 57.0%, and the mAcc increased to 74.5%. Distance encoding also led to an improvement in performance, with a mIoU of 54.6% and a mAcc of 71.0%. However, using both the encoding methods together resulted in the best performance, with a mIoU of 60.0% and a mAcc of 76.0%. These results suggest that incorporating information about the positions of points relative to each other can help the model better understand the spatial relationships between points, leading to improved semantic segmentation performance. Additionally,

Table 5. Ablation study on position encoding scheme.

Position encoding	mIoU	mAcc
none	52.3	69.6
relative position	57.0	74.5
distance	54.6	71.0
all	**60.0**	**76.0**

using multiple encoding schemes simultaneously may provide complementary information and further improve performance.

5   Conclusion

We have developed a fast 3D semantic segmentation approach for large-scale point clouds which combines the advantages of self attention architectures and random point downsampling. This combination provides a balance between accuracy and inference time without any pre-processing stages. The complexity of the network is further reduced by applying self attention only in the encoder block. Experiments show that our method significantly reduces computational costs, performs well on various benchmarks, and is suitable for a wide range of point cloud sizes. Compared to the state-of-the-art PointTransformer [26], our network achieves a 30 times faster inference time on the S3DIS dataset. However, the mIoU of the proposed method is slightly lower than the one of the state-of-the-art approaches which could be attributed to the loss of valuable features during random point downsampling. Therefore, our future work will first investigate a faster and more effective point-sampling approaches combined with point-voxel representations to preserve these valuable features.

References

1. Armeni, I., et al.: 3D semantic parsing of large-scale indoor spaces. In: IEEE Conference on Computer Vision and Pattern Recognition (CVPR) (2016)
2. Behley, J., et al.: SemanticKITTI: a dataset for semantic scene understanding of LiDAR sequences. In: IEEE/CVF International Conference on Computer Vision (ICCV) (2019)
3. Charles, R.Q., Su, H., Kaichun, M., Guibas, L.J.: PointNet: deep learning on point sets for 3D classification and segmentation. In: IEEE Conference on Computer Vision and Pattern Recognition (CVPR) (2017)
4. Chen, S., Niu, S., Lan, T., Liu, B.: PCT: large-scale 3D point cloud representations via graph inception networks with applications to autonomous driving. In: IEEE International Conference on Image Processing (ICIP) (2019)
5. Choy, C., Gwak, J., Savarese, S.: 4D spatio-temporal convnets: minkowski convolutional neural networks. In: IEEE/CVF Conference on Computer Vision and Pattern Recognition (CVPR) (2019)
6. Cortinhal, T., Tzelepis, G., Erdal Aksoy, E.: SalsaNext: fast, uncertainty-aware semantic segmentation of lidar point clouds. In: Advances in Visual Computing: 15th International Symposium, ISVC (2020)
7. Eldar, Y., Lindenbaum, M., Porat, M., Zeevi, Y.: The farthest point strategy for progressive image sampling. In: 12th IAPR International Conference on Pattern Recognition, vol. 2 - Conference B: Computer Vision & Image Processing (1994)
8. Guo, M.H., Cai, J.X., Liu, Z.N., Mu, T.J., Martin, R.R., Hu, S.M.: PCT: point cloud transformer. Comput. Vis. Media (2021)
9. Hu, Q., et al.: RandLA-Net: efficient semantic segmentation of large-scale point clouds. In: IEEE/CVF Conference on Computer Vision and Pattern Recognition (CVPR) (2020)

10. Landrieu, L., Simonovsky, M.: Large-scale point cloud semantic segmentation with superpoint graphs. In: IEEE/CVF Conference on Computer Vision and Pattern Recognition (2018)
11. Li, Y., Bu, R., Sun, M., Wu, W., Di, X., Chen, B.: PointCNN: convolution on X-transformed points. In: Neural Information Processing Systems (2018)
12. Liu, Z., Tang, H., Lin, Y., Han, S.: Point-voxel CNN for efficient 3D deep learning. In: Advances in Neural Information Processing Systems (2019)
13. Milioto, A., Vizzo, I., Behley, J., Stachniss, C.: RangeNet ++: fast and Accurate LiDAR Semantic Segmentation. In: IEEE/RSJ International Conference on Intelligent Robots and Systems (IROS) (2019)
14. Paszke, A., et al.: PyTorch: an imperative style, high-performance deep learning library. In: 33rd International Conference on Neural Information Processing Systems. Curran Associates Inc (2019)
15. Qi, C.R., Yi, L., Su, H., Guibas, L.J.: PointNet++: deep hierarchical feature learning on point sets in a metric space. In: 31st International Conference on Neural Information Processing Systems (2017)
16. Ramachandran, P., Parmar, N., Vaswani, A., Bello, I., Levskaya, A., Shlens, J.: Stand-alone self-attention in vision models. In: 33rd International Conference on Neural Information Processing Systems. Curran Associates Inc (2019)
17. Redmon, J., Farhadi, A.: YOLOv3: an incremental improvement (2018). Technical Report, preprint arXiv:1804.02767
18. Tang, H., et al.: Searching efficient 3D architectures with sparse point-voxel convolution. In: Vedaldi, A., Bischof, H., Brox, T., Frahm, J.-M. (eds.) ECCV 2020. LNCS, vol. 12373, pp. 685–702. Springer, Cham (2020). https://doi.org/10.1007/978-3-030-58604-1_41
19. Tatarchenko, M., Park, J., Koltun, V., Zhou, Q.Y.: Tangent convolutions for dense prediction in 3D. In: IEEE/CVF Conference on Computer Vision and Pattern Recognition (2018)
20. Tchapmi, L., Choy, C., Armeni, I., Gwak, J., Savarese, S.: SEGCloud: semantic segmentation of 3D point clouds. In: International Conference on 3D Vision (3DV) (2017)
21. Thomas, H., Qi, C.R., Deschaud, J.E., Marcotegui, B., Goulette, F., Guibas, L.: KPConv: flexible and deformable convolution for point clouds. In: IEEE/CVF International Conference on Computer Vision (ICCV) (2019)
22. Vaswani, A., et al.: Attention is all you need. In: 31st International Conference on Neural Information Processing Systems. Curran Associates Inc (2017)
23. Xie, S., Liu, S., Chen, Z., Tu, Z.: Attentional ShapeContextNet for point cloud recognition. In: IEEE/CVF Conference on Computer Vision and Pattern Recognition (2018)
24. Zhao, H., Jia, J., Koltun, V.: Exploring self-attention for image recognition. In: IEEE/CVF Conference on Computer Vision and Pattern Recognition (CVPR) (2020)
25. Zhao, H., Jiang, L., Fu, C.W., Jia, J.: PointWeb: enhancing local neighborhood features for point cloud processing. In: IEEE/CVF Conference on Computer Vision and Pattern Recognition (CVPR) (2019)
26. Zhao, H., Jiang, L., Jia, J., Torr, P., Koltun, V.: Point transformer. In: IEEE/CVF International Conference on Computer Vision (ICCV) (2021)

An Assessment of Self-supervised Learning for Data Efficient Potato Instance Segmentation

Bradley Hurst[1]([✉]) [iD], Nicola Bellotto[1,2] [iD], and Petra Bosilj[1] [iD]

[1] University of Lincoln, Lincoln, UK
{brhurst,pbosilj}@lincoln.ac.uk
[2] Università di Padova, Padua, Italy
nbellotto@dei.unipd.it

Abstract. This work examines the viability of self-supervised learning approaches in the field of agri-robotics, specifically focusing on the segmentation of densely packed potato tubers in storage. The work assesses the impact of both the quantity and quality of data on self-supervised training, employing a limited set of both annotated and unannotated data. Mask R-CNN with a ResNet50 backbone is used for instance segmentation to evaluate self-supervised training performance. The results indicate that the self-supervised methods employed have a modest yet beneficial impact on the downstream task. A simpler approach yields more effective results with a larger dataset, whereas a more intricate method shows superior performance with a refined, smaller self-supervised dataset.

Keywords: Self Supervised Learning · Instance Segmentation · Small Datasets · Agriculture · Agri-robotics

1 Introduction

Advances in technology have contributed to the growing development of robotic and autonomous systems (RAS) in the agricultural domain [22]. However, the organic nature of agriculture poses a number of challenges, one of which is the perception of the environment in which RAS must operate. NIR, RGB, and RGB-D cameras [22], offer a range of hardware imaging solutions while machine vision approaches are used to process the captured data.

Deep learning has revolutionised machine vision by providing more robust solutions than hand crafted approaches. The large amounts of required annotated data, which is costly to produce for specialised (e.g. agricultural) applications, often poses a barrier to adoption. Transfer learning [33] and data augmentation

This work was supported by the Engineering and Physical Sciences Research Council [EP/S023917/1] as part of the AgriFoRwArdS CDT.

(a)   (b)   (c)

Fig. 1. Examples of Semantic Segmentation (a), Object Detection (b), and Instance Segmentation (c)

[30] aim to effectively re-use labelled data and are considered standard in training deep learning models. However, using only labelled data can be limiting.

Self-supervised learning (SSL) offers an alternative approach, instead using unlabelled data to learn useful semantic representations on an auxiliary (upstream) task. This is then fine tuned to the main (downstream) task using labelled data. This is appealing if they can be effectively used in the agricultural domain, as data collection is often far more cost effective relative to annotating the data in the production of a task-specific dataset alone.

In agricultural applications, generative and contrastive SSL is more frequent, while we employ spatially representative SSL as it is more efficient with smaller datasets such as the ones used in this study [34]. They have been used in classification [3] and object detection [20] in agriculture but not, to our knowledge, in instance segmentation tasks. The key contributions of this work are as follows:

- the novel application of Jigsaw [21] and RotNet [5] SSL approaches to an instance segmentation task in the agri-robotics domain,
- an exploration of the effect of Jigsaw and RotNet SSL when trained on a limited dataset,
- an investigation into the influence of the quality versus the quantity of data for training the self-supervised tasks on the downstream task performance.

Section 2 reviews related work on instance segmentation and self-supervision. Sections 3 and 4 detail the datasets and methodology, respectively. Section 5 outlines the experimental setup and evaluation metrics. The results are presented and discussed in Sect. 6, and Sect. 7 concludes the paper, highlighting future work.

2   Related Works

This section reviews related work in instance segmentation and self-supervised learning within agriculture and agri-robotics, and their relevance to this work.

2.1   Instance Segmentation

Instance segmentation identifies and precisely delineates individual objects in image data, similar to a blend of semantic segmentation and object detection (Fig. 1). Mask R-CNN [8], a seminal work in the field of instance segmentation, is extensively used in agricultural applications, such as crop [36] and cattle monitoring [20], and crop harvesting [11]. It is representative of two-stage approaches. Examples of single-stage approaches, known for their higher inference speeds, include YOLACT++ [1] and SOLOv2 [32]. YOLACT++ was used for maize crop lesion segmentation [9] and paired with Tiny-YOLOv4 for tomato crop harvesting [28]. SOLOv2 was used in the segmenting of fish and grapes [29,35].

Custom methods are typically developed to enhance model performance while working within the constraints of the domain. U-Net based models have been developed for crop leaf instance segmentation [27,31]. FoveaMask is another customised method developed for green fruit instance segmentation that outperforms general architectures, including Mask R-CNN and YOLACT++ [12]. Mask R-CNN is disproportionately utilised in agriculture and agri-robotics applications, likely due to its robustness when applied to real-world tasks. It is commonly used as a starting point for many works, including this one.

2.2   Self-supervised Learning

SSL uses unannotated data to learn an upstream task during pretext training, which embeds useful features into the model. The model is then fine tuned to the downstream task using an annotated dataset. In machine vision, SSL approaches are classified as contrastive, generative, and spatially representative [19].

Contrastive approaches maximise the distance between positive (similar) pairs and minimise it between negative (dissimilar) ones. Positive pairs are selected from the input image and negative pairs from other images in the training batch. These approaches are effective, but require large amounts of unlabelled data and large batch sizes. SimCLR [2] makes use of batch sizes between 256 and 8192. MoCo [7] improves performance and reduces the hardware requirements but still uses batch sizes between 256 and 4096. **Generative** approaches use Generative Adversarial Networks [16] and Variational Auto Encoders [23] to embed representations at the individual pixel level into the feature extractor. Additionally, generative self-supervised tasks often train models with partially complete inputs, requiring the models to complete the input, with examples including colourisation [37] and inpainting [25] based tasks. **Spatially representative** approaches use classification tasks to embed semantic information into the feature extractor. The tasks are designed such that the semantic information is required to solve them, but the labelling is automatic. Examples are rotation classification [5], jigsaw solving [21], and sample position prediction [4].

In the agricultural domain, contrastive approaches have been applied to classification based phenotyping tasks [6], generative approaches integrated to leaf segmentation [18], and spatially representative approaches to cattle detection [20] and fruit anomaly detection [3]. However, no conclusive trend can be found in the adoption and application of approaches in the domain yet.

Fig. 2. Example images from the dataseset collected in the **lab** in (a), **outdoor** (b), and during **planting** (c).

Fig. 3. Unlabelled data examples. All are used for full self supervised training. (e) and f) images are used in the refined dataset

3 Datasets

Our data collection is detailed in Subsect. 3.1. The curation of collected images into the datasets used in this work is described in Subsect. 3.2.

3.1 Data Collection

The work involved imaging potato tubers provided by the Jersey Farmers Union (JFU) during their planting operation. Images were collected in three stages (shown in Fig. 2): (1) in a **lab** environment, (2) **outdoors** under varying natural lighting conditions (direct/indirect sunlight, diffused/overcast light, shade), and (3) during **planting** under similar natural lighting. Table 1 provides key stage details. Due to poor weather, additional data was captured from **storage** and packing houses. These less ideal, synthetically lit, out-of-context images (shown in Fig. 3) formed a large part of the unlabelled dataset.

Table 1. Data collection approach parameteres

Stage	Samples	Camera	Resolution	Capture Method	Lighting Conditions
Lab	70	RealSense D435	640 × 480	Hand Held, Manipulator Held	Synthetic
Outdoor	300	Huawei P20 Lite	1920 × 1080	Hand Held	Sunlight, Direct Light, Shade, Overcast
Planting	—	Nikon D3300	6000 × 4000	Hand Held	Overcast

Table 2. Break down of images instances captured in the lab, in an outdoor environment, and during planting operations.

Stage	Instance Count	Image Count	Average Instances	Train, Test, Val Split
Lab	1716	138	12.4	100:0:0
Outdoor	1123	20	56.2	64:16:20
Planting	3170	59	53.7	64:16:20
Total	6009	217	—	87:06:07

3.2 Dataset Curation

Table 2 shows the amount of annotated data per stage in terms of images and instances. We chose not to include lab-collected data in the test and validation dataset due to the synthetic lighting condition, which we were not interested in testing for. In addition to the labelled dataset, a further 1105 images remain unlabelled and comprising both **outdoor** and **planting** images, along with the additional **storage** data. Examples are shown in Fig. 3. Dataset curation is important for SSL, so a third reduced dataset was put together comprising only 235 in-context images (examples in Figs. 3e and 3f).

4 Methodology

This section outlines the SSL and instance segmentation models used in this work, specifically RotNet, Jigsaw, and Mask R-CNN, which will be applied to the datasets previously described. ResNet50 [15] serves as the feature extractor in all experiments.

4.1 Mask R-CNN Instance Segmentation Model

Mask R-CNN [8] is developed from the Faster R-CNN [26] object detection architecture, adding a mask head alongside the classification and bounding box generation heads. In the architecture the feature extractor is paired with a Feature Pyramid Network (FPN) [17], which forwards its outputs to the first stage,

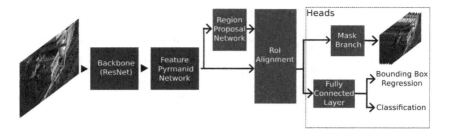

Fig. 4. Mask R-CNN architecture.

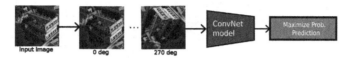

Fig. 5. RotNet architecture.

a region proposal network. The second stage is a region of interest alignment module that also receives input from the first stage. This stage incorporates the patch classification, bounding box regression, and mask heads to process the output from multiple layers, thereby producing the outputs.

4.2 Self Supervised Pretext Approaches

Two spatially representative models, RotNet [5] and Jigsaw [21], were selected for evaluation in this study.

RotNet takes a sample image and rotates it by either 0°, 90°, 180°, or 270°. The rotation of the image is recorded and returned as the ground truth that the model must predict. The image is passed into the feature extractor, and the classification head produces the prediction.

Jigsaw requires the model to classify the correct sequence of scrambled tiles that collectively make up an image. A sample of the input image is taken and split into a 3 × 3 grid, forming the nine tiles to be scrambled. There are 9! potential permutations the 9 tiles could be arranged into. This is too high for the model to practically classify so maximum Hamming distance between all permutations are calculated and used to select the 100 most distinct. The tiles

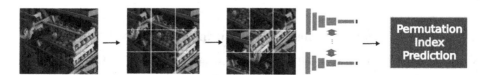

Fig. 6. Jigsaw Architecture.

are re-ordered to one of the randomly selected permutations and passed to the model along with the index of the randomly selected permutation as the ground truth. The model passes each tile into the backbone separately before a fully connected layer aggregates the features from the nine tiles to predict the correct permutation class.

5   Experimental Setup

In this Section, the experimental setup, including the details of the specific experiments and the software and hardware configurations for running them, are detailed in Subsec. 5.1. Subsection 5.2 provides details on the evaluation.

5.1   Experimentation Details

Three experiments were devised with the goal of assessing the performance of the instance segmentation approach and the effects of the self-supervised learning approaches. The designed experiments are as follows:

- **Experiment 1 (Baseline):** Training Mask R-CNN on the annotated dataset only, to provide a baseline result for comparing the effects of self-supervision.
- **Experiment 2 (Full Pretext Training):** Training using all available unla-belled data to evaluate the self-supervised models on the largest available quantity of data.
- **Experiment 3 (Reduced Pretext Training):** Training using a refined unlabelled dataset to assess the performance of SSL when data quality is prioritized over data quantity.

The pipeline for this work was implemented using PyTorch 1.8 and Python 3.8. The pipeline used a desktop computer with an Nvidia GeForce RTX 2080 GPU. Preliminary experiments to find the optimum learning rate for the Adam optimizer were carried out over a range of 5e-3 to 1e-7 in steps of 0.5, finding the best learning rate to be 5e-5.

In all the experiments, ResNet was initialised with ImageNet pre-trained weights. The pretext training pipeline had a train, validation, and test split of 64:16:20. For pretext training images were resized as to allow for optimum batch size training of both the Jigsaw and RotNet based approaches on the available hardware. Images were resized to a minimum dimension was 500 pixels, and then a 500×500 pixel center crop of the image taken. RotNet used a batch size of 8 whilst Jigsaw used a batch size of 4. Experiments with batch sizes of 1, 2, 4, 8, and 16 found a batch size of 1 to work best for Mask R-CNN with the available data along with an input image size of 800×1333 pixels. Table 3 details the augmentations used in both upstream pretext training and downstream instance segmentation training. Table 3 also shows the number of epochs used in training; note that Mask R-CNN makes use of a step scheduler adjusting the learning rate to 5e-6 at the 50th epoch. Finally both Jigsaw and RotNet based approaches made use of dropout layers with a probability of 0.2

Table 3. Approach Epochs and Augmentations. The probability with which the augmentation is applied (p) is displayed in brackets.

	Mask R-CNN	RotNet	Jigsaw
Epochs	80	50	50
Augs (p)	Grayscale (0.3), Brightness Contrast (0.1), Rotation (0.2), Horizontal Flip (0.5)	Horizontal Flip (0.5), Grayscale (0.2), Downscaling (0.1), Color Jitter (0.2), Brightness Contrast (0.2), Cropping and Resize (0.1)	Horizontal Flip (0.5), Grayscale (0.2), Downscaling (0.1), Color Jitter (0.2), Brightness Contrast (0.2)

5.2   Evaluation Metrics

The effectiveness of SSL approaches will be determined by their effect on the downstream Mask R-CNN model performance. The metric used in this work to assess the performance of the instance segmentation model is the mean average precision of the predicted instances when compared to the test set ground truth instances. Specifically, we use the pycocotools implementation of the metric (for a single class), as used for the COCO benchmarking dataset evaluation:

$$mAP = \frac{1}{N} \sum_{\substack{k=1 \\ i=0.5(k+9)}}^{N} AP_i. \tag{1}$$

Equation (1) describes the pycocotools implementation, with $N = 10$ signifying our range of IoU thresholds (0.5 to 0.95 at 0.05 steps). Here, AP represents the class's average precision, derived from the precision recall curve's area.

6   Results and Discussion

The results from all three experiments are depicted in Fig. 7. Each of the five columns presents the average and standard deviation of the performance of 10 models, derived by repeating the corresponding experiment. The model variation arises from the non-deterministic nature of PyTorch [24], which makes repeatability impossible in this case. Compared to the baseline, SSL using both the datasets containing all available unlabelled data and the reduced set for training positively influenced the downstream instance segmentation performance.

RotNet showed a 0.50% improvement in mAP over the baseline when using all unlabelled data, and a 0.25% improvement when employing the reduced dataset. Whilst Jigsaw showed a 0.49% mAP improvement over the baseline when using all the available unlabelled data and a notable 0.82% improvement when trained with the reduced data set. This is in line with the improvements achieved by these approaches for other applications, e.g. in human embryo classification of

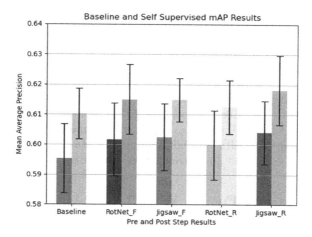

Fig. 7. Comparison of models obtained in experiments 1 (Baseline), 2 (RotNet_F, Jig-Saw_F), and 3 (RotNet_R, Jigsaw_F). The error bars represent the standard deviation over 10 repetitions.

(a)   (b)   (c)

Fig. 8. Qualitative results of full crate in (a), over segmented region in (b), and under segmented region in (c). (b) and (c) are zoomed in regions of (a).

1226 images the Jigsaw approach improved performance by 0.33%, and RotNet by 0.11% over a baseline accuracy of 91.00%. [34].

Our findings indicate that the Jigsaw approach was able to more effectively utilise the reduced dataset, and may have even been adversely affected by the out-of-context images when using all available data. This could be because, even with only 235 images, it could produce 23,500 pseudo images with the 100 potential permutations, compared to the 87,000 out-of-context pseudo images of the 110500 pseudo images using all available data. RotNet, on the other hand, only has 4420 pseudo-images when using all available data and had 940 pseudo-images when using the reduced dataset.

The importance of high quality data and well curated datasets in self supervised learning applications cannot be overstated, and the Jigsaw results may provide further evidence for this. However, considering the results achieved by RotNet, this approach may have been able to leverage the out of context images to learn useful features, or it may have simply not received enough data to achieve optimal results. This suggests future work should focus on collecting a larger, high-quality dataset for further investigation into the effects of the quality and quantity of data for this approach.

Figure 8 provides examples of what an average performing model is able to achieve at around 61% mAP. In Fig. 8a, we can see that the model is able to segment the tuber well. However, adhering to the boundaries of the tuber and the detection of tuber sprouts is less consistent. Zooming in we observe cases of both over- (Fig. 8b) and under-segmentation (Fig. 8c), with tuber being missed, and areas of some tuber being split or repeatedly segmented. In summary, these results suggest that even with limited amounts of data, the approaches seem to have a positive effect on the downstream task performance.

7   Conclusion and Future Work

This work shows that SSL has a positive effect on the downstream instance segmentation performance in all performed experiments. This confirms that Jigsaw approach is well suited to such situations where small amounts of unlabelled data are available to assist in instance segmentation approaches, as it had the biggest impact on the downstream task using only 235 high quality images. Though RotNet also has a positive effect on the downstream tasks, we can only conclude that it requires a larger quantity of data before the effects of data quality can be fully analysed.

Therefore, future work will focus on experiments using a larger amount of higher quality data under broader lighting condition. This will also allow evaluating the performance of generative and contrastive approaches which require more unlabelled data during training, hence they where not evaluated in this work. Dataset design is important but attention will also focus on how the data is used. The work on curriculum-based learning [14] shows that self SSL are prone to learning problematic heuristics to the tasks and suggesting how to address these. Another direction is to explore multi-tasks learning approaches, which have been shown to help the model learn features that are beneficial to both tasks, in contrast to the sequential approach employed in this work which is prone to learning features useful for the upstream task only [10,13].

References

1. Bolya, D., Zhou, C., Xiao, F., Lee, Y.J.: YOLACT++: better real-time instance segmentation. IEEE Trans. Pattern Anal. Mach. Intell. (2020)
2. Chen, T., Kornblith, S., Norouzi, M., Hinton, G.: A simple framework for contrastive learning of visual representations. In: International Conference on Machine Learning, pp. 1597–1607. PMLR (2020)
3. Choi, T., Would, O., Salazar-Gomez, A., Cielniak, G.: Self-supervised representation learning for reliable robotic monitoring of fruit anomalies. In: 2022 International Conference on Robotics and Automation (ICRA), pp. 2266–2272. IEEE (2022)

4. Doersch, C., Gupta, A., Efros, A.A.: Unsupervised visual representation learning by context prediction. In: Proceedings of the IEEE International Conference on Computer Vision, pp. 1422–1430 (2015)
5. Gidaris, S., Singh, P., Komodakis, N.: Unsupervised representation learning by predicting image rotations. arXiv preprint arXiv:1803.07728 (2018)
6. Güldenring, R., Nalpantidis, L.: Self-supervised contrastive learning on agricultural images. Comput. Electron. Agric. **191**, 106510 (2021)
7. He, K., Fan, H., Wu, Y., Xie, S., Girshick, R.: Momentum contrast for unsupervised visual representation learning. In: Proceedings of the IEEE/CVF Conference on Computer Vision and Pattern Recognition, pp. 9729–9738 (2020)
8. He, K., Gkioxari, G., Dollár, P., Girshick, R.: Mask R-CNN. In: Proceedings of the IEEE International Conference on Computer Vision, pp. 2961–2969 (2017)
9. Huang, M., Xu, G., Li, J., Huang, J.: A method for segmenting disease lesions of maize leaves in real time using attention YOLACT++. Agriculture **11**(12), 1216 (2021)
10. Ilteralp, M., Ariman, S., Aptoula, E.: A deep multitask semisupervised learning approach for chlorophyll-a retrieval from remote sensing images. Remote Sens. **14**(1), 18 (2022)
11. Jia, W., Tian, Y., Luo, R., Zhang, Z., Lian, J., Zheng, Y.: Detection and segmentation of overlapped fruits based on optimized mask R-CNN application in apple harvesting robot. Comput. Electron. Agric. **172**, 105380 (2020)
12. Jia, W., et al.: FoveaMask: a fast and accurate deep learning model for green fruit instance segmentation. Comput. Electron. Agric. **191**, 106488 (2021)
13. Kendall, A., Gal, Y., Cipolla, R.: Multi-task learning using uncertainty to weigh losses for scene geometry and semantics. In: Proceedings of the IEEE Conference on Computer Vision and Pattern Recognition, pp. 7482–7491 (2018)
14. Keshav, V., Delattre, F.: Self-supervised visual feature learning with curriculum. arXiv preprint arXiv:2001.05634 (2020)
15. Krizhevsky, A., Sutskever, I., Hinton, G.E.: ImageNet classification with deep convolutional neural networks. Commun. ACM **60**(6), 84–90 (2017)
16. Ledig, C., et al.: Photo-realistic single image super-resolution using a generative adversarial network. In: Proceedings of the IEEE Conference on Computer Vision and Pattern Recognition, pp. 4681–4690 (2017)
17. Lin, T.Y., Dollár, P., Girshick, R., He, K., Hariharan, B., Belongie, S.: Feature pyramid networks for object detection. In: Proceedings of the IEEE Conference on Computer Vision and Pattern Recognition, pp. 2117–2125 (2017)
18. Lin, X., et al.: Self-supervised leaf segmentation under complex lighting conditions. Pattern Recogn. **135**, 109021 (2023)
19. Liu, X., et al.: Self-supervised learning: generative or contrastive. IEEE Trans. Knowl. Data Eng. (2021)
20. Nakamura, K., Taniguchi, Y.: Detecting mounting behaviors of dairy cows by pre-training with pseudo images
21. Noroozi, M., Favaro, P.: Unsupervised learning of visual representations by solving jigsaw puzzles. In: Leibe, B., Matas, J., Sebe, N., Welling, M. (eds.) ECCV 2016. LNCS, vol. 9910, pp. 69–84. Springer, Cham (2016). https://doi.org/10.1007/978-3-319-46466-4_5
22. Oliveira, L.F., Moreira, A.P., Silva, M.F.: Advances in agriculture robotics: a state-of-the-art review and challenges ahead. Robotics **10**(2), 52 (2021)
23. Van den Oord, A., et al.: Conditional image generation with PixelCNN decoders. In: Advances in Neural Information Processing Systems, vol. 29 (2016)

24. Paszke, A., et al.: PyTorch: an imperative style, high-performance deep learning library. In: Advances in Neural Information Processing Systems, vol. 32, pp. 8024–8035. Curran Associates, Inc. (2019). http://papers.neurips.cc/paper/9015-pytorch-an-imperative-style-high-performance-deep-learning-library.pdf
25. Pathak, D., Krahenbuhl, P., Donahue, J., Darrell, T., Efros, A.A.: Context encoders: feature learning by inpainting. In: Proceedings of the IEEE Conference on Computer Vision and Pattern Recognition, pp. 2536–2544 (2016)
26. Ren, S., He, K., Girshick, R., Sun, J.: Faster R-CNN: Towards real-time object detection with region proposal networks. In: Advances in Neural Information Processing Systems, vol. 28 (2015)
27. Roggiolani, G., Sodano, M., Guadagnino, T., Magistri, F., Behley, J., Stachniss, C.: Hierarchical approach for joint semantic, plant instance, and leaf instance segmentation in the agricultural domain. arXiv preprint arXiv:2210.07879 (2022)
28. Rong, J., Dai, G., Wang, P.: A peduncle detection method of tomato for autonomous harvesting. Complex Intell. Syst. 8(4), 2955–2969 (2022)
29. Shen, L., et al.: Identifying veraison process of colored wine grapes in field conditions combining deep learning and image analysis. Comput. Electron. Agric. **200**, 107268 (2022)
30. Shorten, C., Khoshgoftaar, T.M.: A survey on image data augmentation for deep learning. J. Big Data **6**(1), 1–48 (2019)
31. Vayssade, J.A., Jones, G., Gée, C., Paoli, J.N.: Pixelwise instance segmentation of leaves in dense foliage. Comput. Electron. Agric. **195**, 106797 (2022)
32. Wang, X., Zhang, R., Kong, T., Li, L., Shen, C.: SOLOv2: dynamic and fast instance segmentation. Adv. Neural. Inf. Process. Syst. **33**, 17721–17732 (2020)
33. Weiss, K., Khoshgoftaar, T.M., Wang, D.D.: A survey of transfer learning. J. Big Data **3**(1), 1–40 (2016). https://doi.org/10.1186/s40537-016-0043-6
34. Wicaksono, R.S.H., Septiandri, A.A., Jamal, A.: Human embryo classification using self-supervised learning. In: 2021 2nd International Conference on Artificial Intelligence and Data Sciences (AiDAS), pp. 1–5. IEEE (2021)
35. Yu, G., Luo, Y., Deng, R.: Automatic segmentation of golden pomfret based on fusion of multi-head self-attention and channel-attention mechanism. Comput. Electron. Agric. **202**, 107369 (2022)
36. Yu, Y., Zhang, K., Yang, L., Zhang, D.: Fruit detection for strawberry harvesting robot in non-structural environment based on mask-R-CNN. Comput. Electron. Agric. **163**, 104846 (2019)
37. Zhang, R., Isola, P., Efros, A.A.: Colorful image colorization. In: Leibe, B., Matas, J., Sebe, N., Welling, M. (eds.) ECCV 2016. LNCS, vol. 9907, pp. 649–666. Springer, Cham (2016). https://doi.org/10.1007/978-3-319-46487-9_40

Automated 3D Mapping, Localization and Pavement Inspection with Low Cost RGB-D Cameras and IMUs

N'zebo Richard Anvo[1,2]([✉]), Thomas George Thuruthel[3], Hussameldin M. Taha[2,4], Lavindra de Silva[4], Abir Al-Tabbaa[4], Ioannis Brilakis[4], and Fumiya Iida[1]

[1] The Bio-Inspired Robotics Lab, Department of Engineering, University of Cambridge, Cambridge, UK

[2] Costain Group PLC, Maidenhead, UK
nzra2@cam.ac.uk

[3] Department of Computer Science, University College London, London, UK

[4] Department of Engineering, University of Cambridge, Cambridge, UK

Abstract. Roads play a critical role in a country's infrastructure by facilitating the transportation of people and goods. The Department for Transport in Great Britain revealed 297.6 billion vehicle miles on Great Britain's roads in 2021. As traffic volume and road age increase, a range of irregularities can emerge on the road surface. Although numerous studies have already focused on the state of road pavements, there is still potential for the use of low-cost technology for the swift inspection of road pavements. This study aims to bring low-cost technology to help road inspection to be more efficient and accurate. To this end, a fast real-time condition monitoring approach is proposed for road pavements using an RGB (Zed 2i) stereo camera with IMUs mounted on a car. The algorithm used for road pavement reconstruction is based on Structure from Motion (SfM) and requires no calibration of the sensor data. The experiment uses two types of roads to compare the pavement reconstruction and IMU data. The findings indicate that the method effectively reproduces pavement distress, promoting a preliminary approach to enhance pavement management.

Keywords: Road inspection · Autonomous inspection · SfM · Photogrammetry · IMU

1 Introduction

Pavement deterioration affects road users in various dimensions such as increased cost, delays, accidents, and pollution. The conventional approach of manually inspecting roads is widely recognized as a process that demands significant amounts of labour and time, and tends to be impractical in areas where traffic closure is impossible or costly. This paper proposes a semi-automated low-cost technique for assessing road conditions, with accelerometers, laser sensors, and cameras, which provides a non-disruptive way of understanding road conditions and the repairs needed. This paper also develops a preliminary methodology to accommodate these sensors in future road surveys.

© The Author(s), under exclusive license to Springer Nature Switzerland AG 2023
F. Iida et al. (Eds.): TAROS 2023, LNAI 14136, pp. 279–291, 2023.
https://doi.org/10.1007/978-3-031-43360-3_23

Previous work

There are several approaches for pavement condition detection, where the surveys involved low- or high-performance methodologies. The traditional manual inspection is highly time-consuming, labour-intensive, and prone to the subjectivity of the inspector [2]. The methodology requires the inspector's full attention, which may sometimes be subject to fatigue and distraction. Conversely, high-performance procedures provide automated or semi-automated detection solutions that reduce subjectivity and enhance productivity. High-performance mobile mapping systems with vision-based sensors provides a great opportunity for road distress detection, location, and classification but are associated with the cost of running on a large-scale implementations on the road network [5]. Many of the systems combine multiple sensors to provide robust information on the asset under inspection.

The last few decades have seen a significant increase in research for road condition detection via regular data collection and evaluation with different techniques in order to improve maintenance and repair. The methods for detecting road distress can be classified into three categories: vibration-based techniques, two-dimensional (2D) image-based techniques, and three-dimensional (3D) model-based techniques [10]. The vibration methods use sensors, such as accelerometers or gyroscopes, to measure the vibration of the vehicle as it travels over the road surface; with further data analysis the irregularity in the road surface may indicate distresses [6]. Alternatively, 2D image-based methods use cameras mounted on a vehicle or a drone to capture images of the road surface. The images are then analyzed using computer vision techniques to detect distresses such as cracks, potholes, or other surface irregularities [15, 19]. However, obtaining depth information on road distress is difficult, if not impossible, due to the lack of vertical geometry. This limitation is addressed through the use of 3D model-based methods. These methods use laser scanners or other sensors to create a 3D model of the road surface. The model is then analyzed to identify distresses such as cracks, potholes, or other surface irregularities [20]. Each approach has its own strengths and weaknesses, and the choice of method will depend on factors such as the type of road being monitored, the level of detail required, and the available resources. In the work of [21], the application of high-resolution 3D line laser imaging technology was utilized to identify cracks on a road, exhibiting durability against various lighting conditions and low-intensity contrast situations. Additionally, this technology demonstrated the ability to effectively handle diverse contaminants such as oil stains.

Recent advances in high-resolution optical cameras and image processing techniques has made it possible to derive 3D models from 2D images with sufficient accuracy and high efficiency, which makes image-based 3D models a possible cheaper substitute for or a supplement to 3D laser scanning. Numerous photogrammetry software options exist that can automatically generate 3D models from unmanned aerial vehicle (UAV) images. These models have been utilized in a variety of research studies. Regarding the use of 3D models for road health evaluation, [16] manually identified ruts and potholes from a 3D model and verified their accuracy using the Global Mapper software. An effective algorithm for pothole detection utilizing stereo vision was suggested by [23]. Additionally, various other techniques combining 2D image processing and 3D model-based methods have been developed to leverage the efficiency of 2D image-based methods and the accuracy of 3D model-based methods. Examples include the research carried out by [9,17].

There has been an increasing focus on developing low-cost monitoring systems that are progressively more advanced and effective, with the aim to enable regular assessment of pavement conditions across the road network. Work from [14] used mobile smartphones equipped with various sensors, including GPS, accelerometers, and microphones to monitor roads and traffic conditions. Real-time traffic information data recorded by black boxes were collected from all vehicles on the road network to localize road pavement distress [12,13], whenever a vehicle travels over an irregularity on the road surface, such as a bump or pothole. The accelerometers installed on the vehicle captured the occurrence by associating it with positional data received from the GPS receiver. Although the detection algorithm allows the understanding of some information from the recorded signal, it does not allow the distresses on the road pavement surface to be classified. In contrast, tools based on vision are capable of analyzing image features such as texture, size, and shape. Indeed, the severity of road pavement irregularities plays a crucial role in determining the current condition of road segments and identifying the most suitable maintenance solutions. From a cost-effectiveness standpoint, it was discovered that there are several limitations in detecting fatigue cracking irregularities using inexpensive techniques. The road pavement inspection methods depend on the type of road distress [3,11], e.g. cracks can be detected and classified using imaging techniques or ground-penetrating radar and infrared, and vision-based techniques or vibration analysis can be used to detect and classify potholes or patches.

Detecting and classifying multiple types of road surface distresses can be achieved through a 3D vision-based approach, or by utilizing a combination of various techniques. The SfM approach does not need prior information about the target position, as it simultaneously and automatically estimates the camera's intrinsic and extrinsic parameters and the 3D geometry of the scene from a series of overlapping images [22]. This technique has its origins in the computer vision community. A variety of SfM approaches have been proposed including incremental [1,7], hierarchical [8], and global approaches [4]. Incremental SfM is the most widespread strategy for unordered image-based 3D reconstruction [18].

This paper on road pavement distresses detection such as cracks, road surface unevenness, and potholes uses the SfM algorithm to reconstruct a 3D model from the 2D images and IMU data collected with the car. The aim is to propose a cost-effective technique to help the inspector to capture every element of the road surface during the inspection for better maintenance planning. The rest of the paper is organized as follows. Section 2 presents an overview of data collection and the methodology employed for road pavement reconstruction. An example of pavement reconstruction is then given in Sect. 3, and Sect. 4 presents a discussion and conclusion.

2   Methodology

2.1   Data Acquisition and Processing

The camera used in this work to collect road pavement photos was a Zed 2i stereo camera. Its specifications and configuration settings are shown in Table 1.

Table 1. Zed 2i camera parameters.

Resolution	*2x(1920x1080)@30fps*
Field view	*Max. 110(H)x70(W)x120(D)*
Depth range	*0.3m to 20m(10 to 65.6ft)*
Depth accuracy	*1% up to 3m and 5% up to 15m*

The camera is mounted on the car via a suction cup that can withstand up to an 80km/h drive with a maximum payload of 3kg (Fig. 1). The reason for using a car rather than a drone is to avoid traffic and driver distraction hazards and to prove that any ordinary car with a camera can collect good data for 3D reconstruction. The data was collected with a two-speed drive of 20–25km/h with a max speed limit of 30km/h, and 7–10km/h with a max speed limit of 15km/h.

Fig. 1. Car equipped with a Zed 2i stereo camera.

The camera was set up to meet the image overlapping requirement (of image processing software) as follows: 60% overlap for side-facing images and 80% overlap for forward-facing images. A multi-trip survey was performed to overcome lighting condition changes during the day, which could result in failing to find a common point between overlapping photos. The two lenses on the right and left of the camera took overlapping photos of the road pavement at the same time. Images were collected at a rate of 50 images/s to achieve the desired overlap in images, and at the resolution shown in the table in order to achieve the desired 3D model precision, which is affected by image resolution. Each lens of the camera captured images at the same sample rate with IMU data associated with the images. The reconstruction of the 3D road pavement did not make use of Ground Control Points (GCPs); therefore, the overlaps between images needed to be high enough to produce the 3D model using photogrammetry.

The software that was trialled as part of this work is commercially available. The trialled software included Agisoft Metashape, 3D Survey, Bentley ContextCapture, Pix4Dmapper, and Meshroom, the last of which is open source. The final decision was to use Agisoft Metashape as it allows to generate georeferenced, dense point clouds, textured polygonal models, digital elevation models, and orthomosaics from a set of overlapping images with the corresponding referencing information. The software is low-cost for researchers and has high accuracy in 3D model reconstruction.

2.2   Photogrammetry Pipeline from 2D to 3D Reconstruction

The following steps were carried out to reconstruct the road pavement in 3D from 2D images. Each of these steps will be discussed next (Fig. 2).

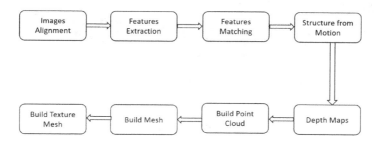

Fig. 2. Photogrammetry Pipeline.

Image Alignment. Image alignment is used to filter the photos that will be used for 3D reconstruction. Alignment of the images was done using the 'highest' parameter in Metashape, with the 'generic preselection' option. The 'key point limit' and 'tie point limit' values were set to zero. This latter setting uses high computational resources but provides high accuracy. After alignment is completed (see Fig. 3), the generated sparse point cloud and camera position results can be used to inspect the alignment and remove incorrectly positioned cameras.

Feature Extraction. This step aims to identify unique clusters of pixels that remain relatively consistent across different camera viewpoints during photo acquisition. As a result, the visual attributes present in the scene should have comparable feature descriptors in all images. To ensure that SfM can accurately identify features across multiple images, it is necessary for the features to remain invariant under both radiometric and geometric changes. This means that the quality of the photos and the features extracted must be able to withstand variations in lighting conditions and camera viewpoints, while still being identifiable and distinct enough to be recognized consistently.

Fig. 3. Sparse point cloud and camera positions.

Feature Matching. This process is to match all features between pairs of images. SfM leverages distinctive features to discover images that capture the same part of a scene. The photogrammetric match is limited to a set of overlapped photos in the selection to avoid redundancy. The naive approach is to use every image pair to detect scene overlap; SfM instead searches for feature correspondences by finding the most similar feature for every feature in the image, using a similarity metric comparing the appearance of the features. This process required high computational resources and enabled the creation of a 3D model from multiple 2D images.

Structure from Motion. This stage verifies the potentially overlapping image pairs, since the feature matching is based on the overlapping and appearance of the photos and there is no guarantee that the corresponding feature maps to the same scene points (Fig. 4).

SfM utilizes projective geometry to estimate a transformation that maps feature points between images in order to verify the matches. The method estimates the 3D structure and camera pose of 2 cameras based on their relative pose. To ensure high-quality reconstructions and avoid drift, bundle adjustment is repeatedly performed as more cameras are added.

Depth Maps. A depth map refers to an image or image channel that stores information about the distance of objects' surfaces from a specific viewpoint in the scene. The

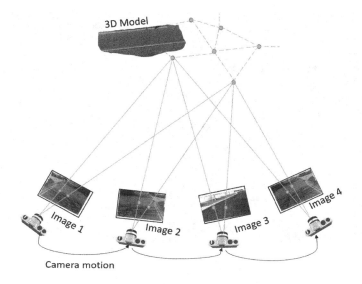

Fig. 4. Incremental SfM pipeline.

method aims to obtain the depth values of every pixel for all the cameras that have been processed by SfM, by employing the Semi-global Matching technique.

Build Point Cloud. The SfM estimates the motion of the camera and recovers a three-dimensional scene from a two-dimensional image taken from two or multiple different views of one camera. Figure 5 is the point cloud reconstructed from 2D image capture. A point cloud is a collection of data points that are defined in a 3D coordinate system, typically using the XYZ axes. Each point represents a single spatial measurement of the surface of an object.

Build Mesh. The objective of this step is to create a geometric model that represents the detailed surface of the scene. A 3D mesh, also known as a polygonal mesh or a polyhedral mesh, is a collection of vertices, edges, and faces that together define the shape of a three-dimensional object. The face consists of triangles that are connected by their common edges or vertices.

Build Textured Mesh. The purpose of this step is to apply textures onto 3D mesh objects. If the mesh has no associated UVs, Metashape will calculate the UV map automatically. Creating a textured mesh involves dividing the surface of a 3D object into smaller polygons or triangles, which are then individually assigned a portion of a texture map. Additionally, it can be used to optimize the performance of 3D models by reducing the number of polygons needed to achieve a particular level of detail. Overall, a textured mesh is an essential tool for creating high-quality, realistic 3D graphics. The texture feature allows the building of different types of textures for a model. The

Fig. 5. Dense point cloud from images.

texture types supported by Metashape are: a diffuse map (the basic texture that stores the colors of the model surface), a normal map (a texture map that allows calculating the illumination of the model parts from different light sources in the post-processing workflow), an occlusion map (a texture that contains pre-calculated shading information from background lighting), a displacement map (a black-and-white texture where each pixel has a value from 0 to 255; these values are used to determine the height of each point on the surface of the object). The images allow for building a colored texture map based on the aligned images of the model.

IMU Data Processing. The IMU sensor provides acceleration in three axes along with the 3-axis orientation of the camera. For our experiments, we are only using the acceleration information to infer the road surface quality. The raw sensor data obtained with the IMU over a test run is shown in Fig. 6. The observed acceleration data is a function of the road surface parameters, particularly in the direction of gravity (Y-axis). Hence, this information can be used to infer surface properties of the pavement, which are otherwise difficult to be determined using visual data. To obtain a rough estimate of the road surface property, we first pre-process the accelerometer data. We hypothesize that the variance in the acceleration data is an estimate of the road roughness, for a given vehicle. Hence, the standard deviation of the acceleration in the Y-axis is first calculated and scaled using an exponential function to obtain our road roughness estimate.

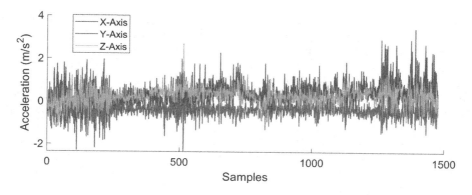

Fig. 6. Normalized raw acceleration data from the IMU over the course of a test run.

3   Experimental Results

The experiment was set up using two different datasets. The first dataset was collected at JJ Thomson Avenue, close to the Civil Engineering Building, West Cambridge and the second dataset was part of Madingley Road A13303. This survey explores asphalt pavements due to the road network of the UK being mostly asphalt.

Fig. 7. SfM 3D model of the road pavement.

Flexible pavements do require regular maintenance to keep them in good condition after a certain number of years in service. It is important to note that regular maintenance is key to prolonging the life of flexible pavements and reducing the need for costly repairs and replacements in the future. This work provides a low-cost survey to help a road maintenance operator to take appropriate maintenance decisions. The first survey took approximately 7 min to drive with 2000 images taken with right and left camera lenses with IMU data associated with each image taken. The photos were then processed using Metashape, and the images reconstructed with the SfM algorithm. Figure 7 shows the SfM reconstruction of the 3D model of the road pavement. The reconstruction highlights the degradation of the structures and the need for attention by the maintenance team. Most of the pavement distresses are potholes and cracks. The second survey data collection took approximately 5 min and 1500 images. After SfM 3D model reconstruction, Fig. 8 shows the road pavement in a 3D model. This portion of the pavement shows some features, such as an uneven surface, that may be missed during the manual inspection. This highlights the importance of using SfM for further analysis to identify subtle variations in the road surface. Using the reconstructed 3D map, we can further localize and measure the surface defects. This can help automate the subsequent maintenance process without further overhead.

Fig. 8. An uneven pavement surface.

The inertial measurement unit (IMU) on its own for surveys can sometime give uncertain information about the condition of the road surface. To make use of the IMU data in our survey, we develop an algorithm to tag each image with timestamps and corresponding IMU data such as translation, orientation, and acceleration. Combining this with the visual data can not only provide further information about road conditions, but also help with localization and calibration. We use accelerometer data to estimate the road roughness as described in the previous section. Figure 9 shows a qualitative analysis of how this data can be used for monitoring road surface condition. Two test runs over the same road section was done with our vehicle and the corresponding visual data and IMU measurements were registered. Our proposed estimate of road roughness and surface defects are overlayed with visual data. Road roughness and rider comfort is challenging to be measured using just visual data. Hence, the inertial measurement data can be combined with the visual data to provide a holistic overview of a road's conditions.

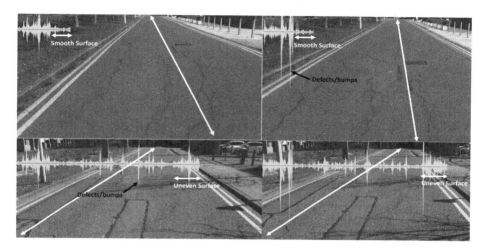

Fig. 9. Road roughness evaluation using IMU data. For newly paved smooth surfaces, the vertical acceleration components would have lesser variations and this can be used to estimate road condition and rider comfort. Additionally, unevenness and defects can also be clearly detected using just the IMU data.

4   Discussion and Conclusion

In this paper, we proposed a low-cost automated road pavement inspection approach using a RGB-D camera and an integrated IMU. The survey captured 3500 overlapping stereo images with associated IMU data with two types of asphalt roads. The 3D model of the road pavement was reconstructed using the Structure from Motion algorithm in Agisoft Metashape. The approach to using SfM for road survey pavement reconstruction allows us to visualize the overall health of the pavement with cost-effective equipment. From the experimental results, the model obtained from SfM allows the identification of the presence of distresses on the road pavement and the condition of the road in detail. The inertial measurement unit data associated with the image provides clear details of the road pavement condition. The 3D maps generated by stitching can then localize defects and hazards. Our approach can thus be used by road maintenance management teams in their decision-making processes for road maintenance. Future work includes the geometric representation of the distresses and their severity and looking into other types of road pavements such as concrete pavements.

Acknowledgments. This work was supported by the UK Engineering and Physical Sciences Research Council (EPSRC) [grant number EP/V056441/1]. The authors would like to thank Costain Group PLC and National Highways as the partners in this Prosperity Partnership.

Data Availability Statement. The datasets for this study would be provided upon request.

References

1. Agarwal, N.S., Snavely, I., Simon, S.S., Szeliski, R.: Building Rome in a day. ICCV, Kyoto, Japan 1 (2009)
2. Attoh-Okine, N., Adarkwa, O.: Pavement condition surveys-overview of current practices. Delaware Center for Transportation, University of Delaware, Newark, DE, USA (2013)
3. Coenen, T.B., Golroo, A.: A review on automated pavement distress detection methods. Cogent Eng. **4**(1), 1374822 (2017)
4. Crandall, D., Owens, A., Snavely, N., Huttenlocher, D.: Discrete-continuous optimization for large-scale structure from motion. In: CVPR 2011, pp. 3001–3008. IEEE (2011)
5. Elhashash, M., Albanwan, H., Qin, R.: A review of mobile mapping systems: from sensors to applications. Sensors **22**(11), 4262 (2022)
6. Eriksson, J., Girod, L., Hull, B., Newton, R., Madden, S., Balakrishnan, H.: The pothole patrol: using a mobile sensor network for road surface monitoring. In: Proceedings of the 6th International Conference on Mobile Systems, Applications, and Services, pp. 29–39 (2008)
7. Frahm, J.-M., et al.: Building Rome on a cloudless day. In: Daniilidis, K., Maragos, P., Paragios, N. (eds.) ECCV 2010. LNCS, vol. 6314, pp. 368–381. Springer, Heidelberg (2010). https://doi.org/10.1007/978-3-642-15561-1_27
8. Gherardi, R., Farenzena, M., Fusiello, A.: Improving the efficiency of hierarchical structure-and-motion. In: 2010 IEEE Computer Society Conference on Computer Vision and Pattern Recognition, pp. 1594–1600. IEEE (2010)
9. Jog, G., Koch, C., Golparvar-Fard, M., Brilakis, I.: Pothole properties measurement through visual 2D recognition and 3D reconstruction. In: Computing in Civil Engineering (2012), pp. 553–560 (2012)
10. Kim, T., Ryu, S.K.: Review and analysis of pothole detection methods. J. Emerg. Trends Comput. Inf. Sci. **5**(8), 603–608 (2014)
11. Martinelli, A., et al.: Road surface anomaly assessment using low-cost accelerometers: a machine learning approach. Sensors **22**(10), 3788 (2022)
12. Meocci, M., Branzi, V., Begani, F.: Le black box per il monitoraggio delle pavimentazioni stradali. Strade & Autostrade 10 (2019)
13. Meocci, M., Branzi, V., Sangiovanni, A.: An innovative approach for high-performance road pavement monitoring using black box. J. Civil Struct. Health Monitor. **11**(2), 485–506 (2021). https://doi.org/10.1007/s13349-020-00463-8
14. Mohan, P., Padmanabhan, V.N., Ramjee, R.: Nericell: rich monitoring of road and traffic conditions using mobile smartphones. In: Proceedings of the 6th ACM Conference on Embedded Network Sensor Systems, pp. 323–336 (2008)
15. Ryu, S.K., Kim, T., Kim, Y.R.: Image-based pothole detection system for its service and road management system. Math. Probl. Eng. **2015**, 1–10 (2015)
16. Saad, A.M., Tahar, K.N.: Identification of rut and pothole by using multirotor unmanned aerial vehicle (UAV). Measurement **137**, 647–654 (2019)
17. Salari, E., Bao, G.: Automated pavement distress inspection based on 2D and 3D information. In: 2011 IEEE International Conference on Electro/Information Technology, pp. 1–4. IEEE (2011)
18. Schonberger, J.L., Frahm, J.M.: Structure-from-motion revisited. In: Proceedings of the IEEE Conference on Computer Vision and Pattern Recognition, pp. 4104–4113 (2016)
19. Siriborvornratanakul, T., et al.: An automatic road distress visual inspection system using an onboard in-car camera. Adv. Multimedia **2018**, 1–10 (2018)

20. Tan, Y., Li, Y.: UAV photogrammetry-based 3D road distress detection. ISPRS Int. J. Geo-Inf. **8**(9), 409 (2019)
21. Tsai, Y., Jiang, C., Wang, Z.: Pavement crack detection using high-resolution 3D line laser imaging technology. In: 7th RILEM International Conference on Cracking in Pavements: Mechanisms, Modeling, Testing, Detection and Prevention Case Histories, pp. 169–178. Springer, Dordrecht (2012). https://doi.org/10.1007/978-94-007-4566-7_17
22. Westoby, M.J., Brasington, J., Glasser, N.F., Hambrey, M.J., Reynolds, J.M.: 'structure-from-motion' photogrammetry: a low-cost, effective tool for geoscience applications. Geomorphology **179**, 300–314 (2012)
23. Zhang, Z., Ai, X., Chan, C., Dahnoun, N.: An efficient algorithm for pothole detection using stereo vision. In: 2014 IEEE International Conference on Acoustics, Speech and Signal Processing (ICASSP), pp. 564–568. IEEE (2014)

Optimized Custom Dataset for Efficient Detection of Underwater Trash

Jaskaran Singh Walia[1](✉) and Karthik Seemakurthy[2]

[1] Vellore Institute of Technology, Chennai, India
karanwalia2k3@gmail.com
[2] University of Lincoln, Lincoln, UK
kseemakurthy@lincoln.ac.uk

Abstract. Accurately quantifying and removing submerged underwater waste plays a crucial role in safeguarding marine life and preserving the environment. While detecting floating and surface debris is relatively straightforward, quantifying submerged waste presents significant challenges due to factors like light refraction, absorption, suspended particles, and color distortion. This paper addresses these challenges by proposing the development of a custom dataset and an efficient detection approach for submerged marine debris. The dataset encompasses diverse underwater environments and incorporates annotations for precise labeling of debris instances. Ultimately, the primary objective of this custom dataset is to enhance the diversity of litter instances and improve their detection accuracy in deep submerged environments by leveraging state-of-the-art deep learning architectures. The source code to replicate the results in this paper can be found at GitHub.

Keywords: Deep Learning · Computer Vision · Visual Object Detection · Artificial Intelligence · Robotics · Marine Debris · Trash Detection · Dataset Generation · Data Pre-processing

1 Introduction

Over the past few years, the increase in underwater debris due to poor waste management practices, littering, and international industry expansion has resulted in numerous environmental issues, such as water pollution and harm to aquatic life [1,2]. The debris, which remains in the epipelagic and mesopelagic zones (Fig. 1) for years after it is dumped into the water, not only pollutes the water but also harms aquatic animals [3]. However, removing debris from beneath the aquatic surface is challenging and expensive. Thus, there is a need for a cost-effective solution that can operate effectively and efficiently in a wide range of environments.

Recent advances in robotics, artificial intelligence, and automated driving [5,6] have made it feasible to use intelligent robots for underwater debris removal. Nevertheless, existing approaches are costly, and computationally demanding. Additionally, publicly available datasets are environment-specific, which limits their ability to produce a generalized and robust model. Therefore, we propose a

© The Author(s), under exclusive license to Springer Nature Switzerland AG 2023
F. Iida et al. (Eds.): TAROS 2023, LNAI 14136, pp. 292–303, 2023.
https://doi.org/10.1007/978-3-031-43360-3_24

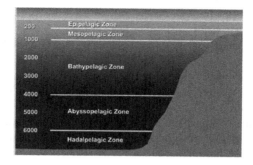

Fig. 1. Zones of the Oceans [4].

new dataset where the main focus is to increase the diversity of litter instances and enhance the generalization ability of state-of-the-art object detectors.

Autonomous underwater vehicles (AUVs) are a crucial component of a successful strategy for removing debris from maritime ecosystems. Therefore, the primary requirement for Autonomous Underwater Vehicles (AUVs) is the detection of underwater debris, specifically plastic debris. To address this challenge, we evaluated the dataset using advanced computer vision techniques to establish a baseline for litter detection. Our goal is to replace resource-intensive, time consuming algorithms with more efficient ones that will aid in real-time underwater debris detection. In this regard, we explore various deep learning based visual object detection networks that are trained and tested using the proposed dataset. The effectiveness of these detectors is evaluated using multiple metrics to validate their performance accurately.

The following are the main contributions of this paper:

– Proposed a new dataset with a focus to increase the diversity of litter instances under different environments.
– Trash, Rover and Bio are the three classes in the proposed dataset.
– Benchmarked the litter detection by using various deep learning-based object detectors.

2 Related Work

The literature in underwater robotics has focused on the development of multi-robot systems for surface and deep water natural aquatic environment applications such as marine monitoring using learning-based recognition of underwater biological occurrences by the National Oceanic and Atmospheric Administration [7]. Underwater robots have also been utilized for environmental monitoring, environmental mapping [8], maritime robotics for guidance and localization [9–12].

Underwater debris, particularly plastic waste, has become a significant environmental concern due to its detrimental effects on marine ecosystems. Plastic debris can persist in the marine environment for long periods, posing threats to marine organisms through entanglement, ingestion, and habitat destruction [13,14]. It can also disrupt marine food webs and alter the biodiversity of marine ecosystems.

Efforts have been made to address the issue of underwater debris removal. Various methods have been employed, including manual clean-up operations, the use of remotely operated underwater vehicles (ROVs) equipped with gripping arms to physically capture debris, and the development of autonomous robotic systems specifically designed for marine debris removal. However, these approaches often face challenges in terms of efficiency, cost-effectiveness, and the vast scale of the problem. Researchers and organizations continue to explore innovative strategies and technologies to effectively tackle underwater debris and minimize its impact on the marine environment [15,16].

Recently, underwater robotics (ROVs) is considered as a popular alternative over the harmful manual methods to remove the marine debris. The vision system of a robot will aid in localising the debris and provide appropriate feedback to physically control a gripper limb to capture the objects of interest. A non-profit group for environmental protection and cleaning, Clear Blue Sea [17], has proposed the FRED (Floating Robot for Eliminating Debris). However, the FRED platform is not autonomous. In order to find garbage in marine habitats, another nonprofit, the Rozalia project, has employed underwater ROVs fitted with multibeam and side-scan sonars [3]. Autonomous garbage identification and collection for terrestrial settings have also been studied, such as in the case of Kulkarni et al. [18], who employed ultrasonic devices and applied them to interior garbage. However, a vision-based system can also be envisioned.

In a study on at-sea tracking of marine detritus by Mare [19], various tactics and technological possibilities were addressed. Following the 2011 tsunami off the shore in Japan, researchers have examined the removal of detritus from the ocean's top [20] using advanced Deep Visual Detection Models. In the study by M. Bernstein [21], LIDAR was used to locate and record beach garbage.

In recent research by Valdenegro-Toro[22], it was shown that a deep convolutional neural network (CNN) trained on forward-looking sonar (FLS) images could identify underwater debris with an accuracy of about 80%. This study made use of a custom made dataset created by capturing FLS images of items frequently discovered with marine debris in a water tank. Data from water tanks were also used in the assessment.

As mentioned above, the majority of the literature which dealt with debris detection used either sonar or lidar sensors. However, visual sensors have superior resolution over sensors such as sonars or lidar. A sizable, labeled collection of underwater detritus is required to allow visual identification of underwater litter using a deep learning-based model. This collection needs to include information gathered from a broad variety of underwater habitats to accurately capture the various looks across wide-ranging geographic areas. There are very few datasets that are publicly available and majority of them are unlabeled. The Monterey Bay Aquarium Research Institute (MBARI) has amassed a dataset over 22 years to survey trash strewn across the ocean floor off the western coast of the United States of America [23], specifically plastic and metal inside and around the undersea Monterey Canyon, which traps and transports the debris in the deep oceans. The Global Oceanographic Data Center, a division of the Japan Agency for Marine-Earth Science and Technology (JAMSTEC), is another example of a publicly available large dataset. As part of the larger J-EDI (JAMSTEC E-Library of Deep-sea Images) collection, JAMSTEC has made a dataset of deep-sea detritus available online [11]. This dataset provides type-specific debris data in the form of short video clips and images dating back to 1982. The annotated data was utilized to construct deep learning-based models for the work discussed in this paper.

In summary, various studies have been conducted on the use of autonomous robots for underwater monitoring and debris collection. The development of multi-robot systems for environmental monitoring, environmental mapping, maritime robotics, and other applications have utilized undersea robots. Researchers have also explored learning-based recognition of underwater biological occurrences for marine monitoring. Additionally, the use of remotely operated underwater vehicles (ROVs) and autonomous garbage identification and collection for terrestrial settings has been studied. A significant labeled collection of underwater trash is necessary for accurate identification using deep learning-based models.

3   Dataset

3.1   Existing Datasets

Although several publicly available datasets, including JAMSTEC, J-ED, Trash-CAN 1.0, and Trash-ICRA19, exist for automatic waste detection, they are highly domain-specific and restricted to very limited environmental variations [24]. Table 1 and 2 shows the statistics of existing detection and classification datasets, respectively. This limits the generalisation ability for using the vision based debris detectors across wide variety of water bodies. Also, lack of diversity in the existing datasets can induce bias into the object detection networks. The main aim of the proposed dataset is to increase the diversity of images in identifying three classes, namely Trash, Rover, and Bio, which are most useful for classifying submerged debris.

The Bio class provides an aspect of marine life in the environment and how much trash has affected it relative to nearby environments which can be used to further prioritise the trash cleaning. The Rover class helps differentiate the rover from being misclassified as trash in some input imagery. Finally, the Trash class helps to detect and quantify the amount of trash present in the input image/video. The dataset was curated by collecting inputs from various open-source datasets and videos across different oceans and water bodies with varying conditions and environments. We manually annotated marine debris in frames of images, focusing on selecting images with tricky object detection conditions

Table 1. Comparison of existing litter detection datasets.

Type	Dataset	# classes	# images	Annotation type	Environment
Detection	Wade-AI	1	1396	instance masks	outdoor
Detection	Extended TACO	7	4562	bounding box	outdoor
Detection	UAVVaste	1	772	instance masks	outdoor
Detection	TrashCan	8	7212	instance masks	underwater
Detection	Trash-ICRA	7	7668	bounding box	underwater
Detection	Drinking waste	4	4810	bounding box	indoor
Detection	MJU-Waste	1	2475	instance masks	indoor
Detection	MJU-Waste	1	2475	instance masks	indoor

Table 2. Comparison of existing litter classification datasets.

Type	Dataset	Images	Classes	Instances	Environment	Annotation type
Classification	Open Litter Map	$> 100k$	> 100	$> 100k$	outdoor	multilabels
Classification	Waste pictures	23633	34	23633	outdoor	labels
Classification	TrashNet	2194	5	2194	indoor	labels

like occlusion, noise, and illumination. We used an annotation tool [25] to create the final dataset, which comprises of 9625 images.

3.2 Data Preparation

The first step to create this dataset is to collect inputs from various open-source datasets and videos with varying ocean environments from different countries. We manually annotated the marine debris in frames of images, focusing on selecting images with difficult object detection conditions such as occlusion, noise, and illumination. The annotations were done using a free annotation tool [25], resulting in 9,625 images in the dataset. A few of the sample images from our dataset are shown in Fig. 2. It can be seen that the diversity of objects and the environments that were considered in this paper.

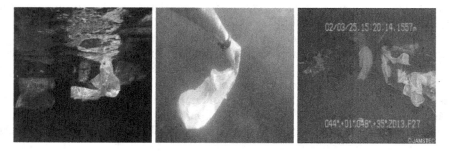

Fig. 2. Representative images from proposed dataset.

A Deep learning analysis was also performed on the pre-existing datasets, which can be viewed on our paper's source repository. While the models performed well on training, they failed to accurately detect classes when tested on unseen data from a slightly varying environment. Our dataset comprises of bounding box labels and image annotations and is available in more than ten different formats, making it readily importable for use with different algorithms. The dataset was prepared using the following steps.

1. **Data collection**: The input images were selectively picked manually, comprising of varying environments across different regions of the world.
2. **Annotation**: The unlabelled raw images were annotated and the annotations of labelled images were merged and renamed into three final categories, Trash, Rov and Bio which stands for underwater debris, rover (autonomous vehicle) and biological marine life respectively.
3. **Pre-processing**: These images were then rescaled to 416×416. A total of 26 classes were dropped and mapped into the final three classes. Clear water images that comprised of no annotations were also added to make the model more robust towards different environments. The dataset was further improved by randomly distorting the brightness and saturation of the images using PyTorch's built-in Transforms augmentation tool. This was done in order to mitigate the effects of spurious correlations on the model and to replicate variable underwater conditions such as illumination, occlusion, and coloring.

The total dataset consisted of 9625 images which were split into approximately 7300 for training, 1800 for validation and 473 for test. The Labels of the dataset were as follows:

- **Trash**: All sorts of marine debris (plastics, metals, etc.).
- **Bio**: All naturally occurring biological material, marine life, plants, etc.
- **Rover**: Parts of the rover such as a robotic arm, sensors, or any part of the AUV to avoid misclassification.
  The main objective behind choosing these three particular classes is that the trash class will contain all forms of trash, this increases the model's robustness when encountering unseen/new form of trash. The Bio class provides an aspect of current marine life in the environment and how much trash has affected it relative to nearby environments which can be used to prioritise the trash cleaning based on the quality of the marine life present. The Rover class helps the rover's components from being misclassified as trash in some input imagery.

4   Benchmarking

This section presents the latest trash detection and classification models, followed by benchmarks for the proposed dataset and statistical evaluation of the training metrics.

4.1 Object Detection Algorithms

The various architectures selected for this project were chosen from the most recent, efficient, and successful object detection networks currently in use. Each has its advantages and disadvantages, with different levels of accuracy, execution speeds, and other metrics. We utilized several state-of-the-art neural network architectures, including YOLOv7, YOLOv6s, YOLOv5s, and YOLOv4 Darknet, using their respective repositories. We also trained a custom FasterR-CNN and Mask R-CNN.

4.2 GPU Hardware

In this project, we utilized an Nvidia K80 GPU with a memory of 12 GB and a memory clock rate of 0.82GHz. This GPU was released in 2014 and has two CPU cores with 358 GB of disk space.

4.3 Models

In this section, we discuss the latest models used and the results produced.

You Only Look Once (YOLO). You Only Look Once, or YOLO, is a popular object detection technique that can recognize multiple items in a real-time video or image. In one evaluation, it utilizes a single neural network to predict bounding boxes and class probabilities straight from the complete image. Due to this approach, YOLO is faster and more accurate than other object detection systems and therefore it can provide fast inference speeds for the real-time application of this research.

- **YOLOv7 tiny** [26]: The YOLOv7 algorithm outperforms its older versions in terms of speed and accuracy. It requires significantly less hardware than conventional neural networks and can be trained much more quickly on small datasets with no pre-learned weights.
- **YOLOv5s small** [27] **and YOLOv6s (small)** [28]: Both of these algorithms have similar performances and results.

Faster R-CNN and Mask R-CNN. Faster R-CNN and Mask R-CNN are two popular region-based object detection models that use a two-stage approach for object detection. The first stage generates region proposals, and the second stage predicts the class and refines the bounding box of each proposal.

Mask R-CNN. [28]: Mask R-CNN extends Faster R-CNN by adding a branch to predict segmentation masks for each object. This allows the model to also segment the detected objects in addition to predicting their bounding boxes and class probabilities.

4.4 Evaluation Metrics

After the model has been trained, we utilize the testing and validation datasets, which comprise images that are mutually exclusive from the training dataset, as input to analyze the network's accuracy. The model generates a bounding box around correctly recognized items with a confidence value of .50 or higher. The amount of true positive bounding boxes drawn around marine plastic waste and true negatives serves as the basis for evaluation.

The following performance metrics were used to validate and compare the performance of the detectors used:

- **True positive and True negative values.**
- **Precision and Recall:** Reflects whether the model predicted debris in the input image.

$$Recall = \frac{TP}{TP + FN}, \quad Precision = \frac{TP}{TP + FP} \tag{1}$$

- **Mean Average Precision:** - Determines how frequently the network can correctly identify plastic. After gathering the true and false positive data, use the Intersection over Union (IoU) formula to build a precision-recall curve:

$$IOU = \frac{BBox_{pred} \cap BBox_{GroundTruth}}{BBox_{pred} \cup BBox_{GroundTruth}} \tag{2}$$

where $BBox_{Pred}$ and $BBox_{GroundTruth}$ are the expected areas under the curve for predicted and ground truth bounding boxes. To maximize accuracy, a high threshold for confidence and IoU must be specified, with a correct prediction, indicated by the threshold being exceeded. After that, the mAP can be calculated by integrating the precision-recall curve. obtained by integrating the precision-recall curve [29]:

$$mAP = \int_0^1 p(x)dx \tag{3}$$

5 Results

The results obtained for debris localization on our custom-curated dataset outperform previous models that used individual datasets for training. In this study, we tested the individual components of two frameworks by conducting exhaustive research on publicly available waste data in various contexts, including clean waters, natural or man-made lakes/ponds, and ocean beds. The broad range of baseline results for different contexts and diverse object dimensions will assist future researchers in this field. The tested models exhibit high average precision, mAP, and F1 scores compared to their inference speed.

The outcomes of a comprehensive study comparing several architectural networks are presented in Table 3. These trade-offs suggest that the results reported in this study better reflect long-term performance in a wider range of marine conditions, enabling a more comprehensive evaluation of the object identification model's performance in the field. Our findings suggest that YOLOv5-Small and YOLOv6s both achieve strong debris localization metrics in the real-time detection of epipelagic plastic. However, YOLOv7 yields a notably higher F1 score despite a slight reduction in inference performance. The results of a comprehensive research comparing several architectural networks is shown in the table below.

Table 3. Comparison between various algorithms for the purpose of benchmarking.

Network	mAP 0.5	Precision	Recall	Epochs
YOLOv7	0.96	0.96	0.93	120
YOLOv5s	0.96	0.95	0.93	110
YOLOv6s	0.90	0.94	0.92	180
Faster R-CNN	0.81	0.88	–	100
Mask R-CNN	0.83	0.85	–	100

The trade-offs observed in our study demonstrate that the reported outcomes reflect the long-term performance of the object identification model in a wider range of marine conditions, thereby facilitating a more comprehensive evaluation of the model's performance in the field. Our findings suggest that YOLOv5-Small and YOLOv6s achieve excellent debris localization metrics in real-time detection of epipelagic plastic. However, YOLOv7 achieves a significantly higher F1 score despite a slight decrease in inference performance.

After evaluating multiple advanced algorithms within the same family, including YOLOv5x, v7E6E, and v8x, it was determined that the nano/small/tiny network architecture demonstrated the highest performance in evaluations, had a smaller parameter count, and required less computational power. As a result, this architecture was selected for the study. These algorithms outperformed classic Faster-RCNN and Mask-RCNN algorithms in terms of both speed and F1 score.

The performance of the model in real-world scenarios was found to be consistent with the evaluation results presented in Table 3, with only slight variations observed in a near-real-time setting. These results demonstrate the model's efficacy in identifying and categorizing underwater debris in practical applications. Furthermore, the proposed research can serve as a crucial baseline and benchmark for future investigations focused on the identification and classification of marine debris.

$$ImgCord_k = BoxScore_i^j * Width \qquad (4)$$

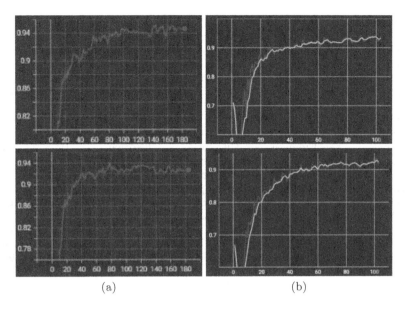

(a)   (b)

Fig. 3. Quantitative Analysis. (a) Yolov5 and (b) Yolov8. First row: Precision curves. Second row: Recall curves.

where k belongs to the top, down, right and left corners, i is the box index, $j \in 0, 1, 2, 3$, and $Width$ is the image width. In the test photos, these image coordinates were utilized to illustrate the results of predicted bounding boxes.

6   Conclusion

In this research, our objective was to improve object detection models by reducing dependence on environment-specific datasets. By employing our mixed, curated dataset and the latest state-of-the-art computer vision models, we were able to evaluate the feasibility of monitoring submerged marine debris in near-real-time for debris quantification. Through the use of robotic arms within Autonomous Underwater Vehicles (AUVs), our rapid inference speeds achieved a high level of performance, making real-time object detection of marine plastic litter in the ocean's epipelagic and mesopelagic layer possible, as well as the automatic detection, classification, and sorting of various submerged objects, including the collection of debris in locations such as sea-beds that are inaccessible to humans due to high pressure and other environmental factors. This application has the potential to automate trash recycling in the extreme aquatic environment with the help of deep learning. Furthermore, our proposed research serves as a fundamental baseline and benchmark for future research involving the identification and classification of underwater debris.

References

1. Coyle, R., Hardiman, G., Driscoll, K.O.: Microplastics in the marine environment: A review of their sources, distribution processes, uptake and exchange in ecosystems. Case Stud. Chem. Environ. Eng. 2, 100010 (2020). https://doi.org/10.1016/j.cscee.2020.100010, https://www.sciencedirect.com/science/article/pii/S2666016420300086
2. Derraik, J.G.B.: The pollution of the marine environment by plastic debris: a review. Marine Pollution Bull. **44**(9), 842–52 (2002)
3. Honingh, D., van Emmerik, T., Uijttewaal, W., Kardhana, H., Hoes, O., van de Giesen, N.: Urban river water level increase through plastic waste accumulation at a rack structure. Front. Earth Sci. **8**. https://doi.org/10.3389/feart.2020.00028
4. Layes of the oceans. https://www.sas.upenn.edu/msheila/biolumevolution.html
5. Xiao, Y., et al.: A review of object detection based on deep learning. Multimedia Tools Appl. **79**(33–34), 23729–23791 (2020). https://doi.org/10.1007/s11042-020-08976-6
6. Andreu-Perez, J., Deligianni, F., Ravi, D., Yang, G.-Z.: Artificial Intelligence and Robotics (2018). https://doi.org/10.48550/ARXIV.1803.10813. https://arxiv.org/abs/1803.10813
7. N Oceanic, A Administration: What is marine debris?. https://oceanservice.noaa.gov/facts/marinedebris.html
8. Yuan, X., Martínez-Ortega, J.-F., Fernández, J.A.S., Eckert, M.: Aekf-slam: A new algorithm for robotic underwater navigation. Sensors **17**(5), 1174 (2017)
9. Torrey, L.A., Shavlik, J.W.: Chapter 11 transfer learning (2009)
10. Drever, M.C., Provencher, J.F., O'Hara, P.D., Wilson, L., Bowes, V., Bergman, C.M.: Are ocean conditions and plastic debris resulting in a 'double whammy' for marine birds? Marine Pollution Bull. **133**, 684–692 (2018). https://doi.org/10.1016/j.marpolbul.2018.06.028, https://www.sciencedirect.com/science/article/pii/S0025326X18304259
11. Tensorflow "tensorflow object detection zoo. https://github.com/tensorflow/models/blob/master/research/objectdetection/g3doc/detectionmodelzoo.md
12. Derraik, J.G.: The pollution of the marine environment by plastic debris: a review. Marine Pollution Bull. **44**(9), 842–852 (2002). https://doi.org/10.1016/S0025-326X(02)00220-5, https://www.sciencedirect.com/science/article/pii/S0025326X02002205
13. Thompson, R., et al.: Lost at sea: where is all the plastic? Science (New York) **304**, 838 (2004). https://doi.org/10.1126/science.1094559
14. Jambeck, J., et al.: Marine pollution. plastic waste inputs from land into the ocean. Science (New York) 347, 768–771 (2015) . https://doi.org/10.1126/science.1260352
15. Jia, T., et al.: Deep learning for detecting macroplastic litter in water bodies: A review. Water Res. **119632** (2023)
16. Zocco, F., Lin, T.-C., Huang, C.-I., Wang, H.-C., Khyam, M.O., Van, M.: Towards more efficient efficientdets and real-time marine debris detection. IEEE Robotics Autom. Lett. **8**(4), 2134–2141 (2023)
17. Fred cars. https://www.sandiego.edu/news/detail.php?_focus=72984
18. Kulkarni, S., Junghare, S.: Robot based indoor autonomous trash detection algorithm using ultrasonic sensors, pp. 1–5 (2013). https://doi.org/10.1109/CARE.2013.6733698
19. Girdhar, Y., et al.: MARE: marine autonomous robotic explorer. In: Proceedings of the 2011 IEEE/RSJ International Conference on Intelligent Robots and Systems (IROS 2011), San Francisco, USA, pp. 5048–5053 (2011)

20. Fulton, M., Hong, J., Islam, M., Sattar, J.: Robotic detection of marine litter using deep visual detection models

21. Bernstein, M., Graham, R., Cline, D., Dolan, J.M., Rajan, K.: Learning-Based Event Response For Marine Robotics, pp. 3362–3367 (2013)

22. Singh, D., Valdenegro-Toro, M.: The marine debris dataset for forward-looking sonar semantic segmentation, arXiv: 2108.06800

23. Stutters, L., Liu, H., Tiltman, C., Brown, D.J.: Navigation technologies for autonomous underwater vehicles. IEEE Trans. Syst. Man Cybern. Part C (Appli. Rev.) **38**(4), 581–589 (2008). https://doi.org/10.1109/TSMCC.2008.919147

24. Majchrowska, S., et al.: Learning-based waste detection in natural and urban environments. Waste Manag. **138**, 274–284 (2022). https://doi.org/10.1016/j.wasman.2021.12.001, https://www.sciencedirect.com/science/article/pii/S0956053X21006474

25. Alexandrova, S., Tatlock, Z., Cakmak, M.: Roboflow: a flow-based visual programming language for mobile manipulation tasks In: 2015 IEEE International Conference on Robotics and Automation (ICRA), pp. 5537–5544 (2015). https://doi.org/10.1109/ICRA.2015.7139973

26. Wang, C.-Y., Bochkovskiy, A., Liao, H.-Y.M.: Yolov7: Trainable bag-of-freebies sets new state-of-the-art for real-time object detectors (2022). https://doi.org/10.48550/ARXIV.2207.02696, https://arxiv.org/abs/2207.02696

27. Jocher, G. et al.: Ultralytics/yolov5: v7.0 - YOLOv5 SOTA Realtime Instance Segmentation (Nov 2022). https://doi.org/10.5281/zenodo.7347926

28. He, K., Zhang, X., Ren, S., Sun, J.: Deep residual learning for image recognition (2015). https://doi.org/10.48550/ARXIV.1512.03385, https://arxiv.org/abs/1512.03385

29. Boyd, K., Eng, K.H., Page, C.D.: Area under the precision-recall curve: point estimates and confidence intervals. In: Blockeel, H., Kersting, K., Nijssen, S., Železný, F. (eds.) ECML PKDD 2013. LNCS (LNAI), vol. 8190, pp. 451–466. Springer, Heidelberg (2013). https://doi.org/10.1007/978-3-642-40994-3_29

A Geometric Algebra Solution to the $3D$ Registration Problem

Charalampos Matsantonis$^{(\boxtimes)}$ (iD) and Joan Lasenby (iD)

Signal Processing and Communications Group, University of Cambridge, Cambridge, UK
{cm2128,jl221}@cam.ac.uk

Abstract. In 1992 Besl and McKay proposed the ICP algorithm, one of the most well known geometry-based registration algorithms, for solving the $3D$-$3D$ registration problem. This problem plays a crucial role for computer vision applications in robotics and automation, and it poses an active research topic in many scientific fields, such as object recognition and tracking. Conventionally, it is solved using Linear Algebra. This work presents the development, implementation and evaluation of a fairly simple closed-form solution to the $3D$-$3D$ registration problem by calculating the rotation using Geometric Algebra objects, i.e. *rotors*. The proposed solution effectively follows the standard steps of the ICP algorithm but replaces the rotation matrix calculation step with a *rotor-calculation step*. The solution is extensively evaluated through various test cases and it is shown that it can reach the same level of accuracy as well-known iterative Linear Algebra methods.

Keywords: $3D$ Registration · Robotics · Computer Vision · Geometric Algebra · Rigid Body Transformation

1 Introduction

The purpose of this study is to explore the potential use of Geometric Algebra, an extension of vector algebra in reformulating and solving the $3D$-$3D$ registration problem. The efficient and safe movement of mobile robotic platforms in their environment was always an area of great importance in the fields of robotics and automation. Robotic platforms must be able to successfully recognize objects in their environment by merging visual sensing techniques and computer technology. There are many open problems for efficient vision-driven robotic systems and each has its own particular application areas associated with it that must be resolved for successful operation. One such an important problem is the $3D$-$3D$ registration problem with unknown point correspondences.

The most commonly used algorithm to solve the $3D$-$3D$ registration problem is the Iterative Closest Point (ICP) Algorithm. It was proposed by Besl and McKay [1] and it operates on two point sets. It transforms the points in a

F. Iida et al. (Eds.): TAROS 2023, LNAI 14136, pp. 304–314, 2023.
https://doi.org/10.1007/978-3-031-43360-3_25

measured (transformed) point-set X^b so they can be matched with a model point-set X^a. The two point-sets X^a and X^b are related by an isometric transformation described by a rotation matrix $\mathbf{R}$ and a translation vector $\mathbf{t}$. Without loss of generality, we assume that the transformation is applied to the point-set X^b and the centroids of the point-sets $\overline{X^a}, \overline{X^b}$, have been subtracted, i.e. $X^a = X^a - \overline{X^a}, \quad X^b = X^b - \overline{X^b}$. In light of this, the ICP algorithm assumes that one of the two sets is the model point-set (X^a) and then for each point $X_i^a \in X^a$ it searches for the closest point $X_i^b \in X^b$ in a measured set with the ultimate goal to minimize the following cost function:

$$\mathfrak{C}(\mathbf{R}, \mathbf{t}) = \sum_{i=1}^{N} \|X_i^a - (\mathbf{R}X_i^b + \mathbf{t})\|^2 \tag{1}$$

where N denotes the total number of points in the point-sets X^a and X^b. At each iteration, after calculating the correspondences, the optimal Euclidean transformation can be found by one of the following methods, i.e. Horn's unit quaternions [2], Horn's orthonormal matrices [3] or Arun's SVD solution [4]. Although all methods result in the same solution, Besl and McKay [1] used the method of unit quaternions to match $3D$ points-shapes.

The ICP algorithm can be used in computer vision systems and SLAM (Simultaneous Localization and Mapping) applications, where a mobile robotic platform moves in space and has no prior knowledge of the environment map. SLAM is an essential component in the autonomy of robotic vehicles [5,6]. However, a problem arises, i.e. the measurements from sensors of the robot can be noisy and they are dependent on the position of the vehicle. If the real map of the environment was known, then the vehicle trajectory would be included in the localization problem [7–9]. Accordingly, if the real trajectory of the robotic vehicle was given then the creation of the map would be part of the mapping problem [10,11]. Thus, ICP-based point cloud matching is often used to estimate the movement of the robotic vehicle sequentially. This involves matching the point clouds and calculating the traveled distance, which can then be used for vehicle localization. Typically, grid maps or voxel maps are common representations for $2D$ or $3D$ point cloud maps.

The main contributions of this paper are summarized in the following:

1. We develop one Geometric Algebra algorithm to be compared with Arun's solution based on the SVD of the cross-correlation matrix (ICP-SVD) and with MATLAB's in-built function for the point-to-point ICP algorithm, namely *pcregistericp*.
2. We develop one Geometric Algebra algorithm to be compared with the SVD solution (Colour ICP-SVD) based on the geometry and the colour of the point clouds. In this case, both algorithms also exploit the RGB colour information in the data.
3. We evaluate and test the Geometric Algebra alogrithms extensively compared to Arun's SVD solution and MATLAB's in-built function, showing that they

have the same level of accuracy. We also indicate how our Geometric Algebra solution might be used in the future where the Geometric Algebra calculations are performed in spaces other than Euclidean.

The remainder of this paper is organized as follows. Section 2 gives an overview of Geometric Algebra. In Sect. 3 the two Geometric Algebra algorithms are presented and evaluated. Conclusions and future perspectives arising from the present research are examined in Sect. 4.

2   Geometric Algebra

Introduction: Geometric Algebra as developed by David Hestenes in the 1960's and detailed in [13] is a unified language for mathematics and physics. Due to limited space, we shall give a brief introduction. A very detailed introduction to Geometric Algebra is given in [14]. Geometric Algebra is formally a Clifford Algebra 'enhanced' with a geometrical interpretation and its elements are called *multivectors*.

Geometric Product: The most fundamental product is the *geometric product*. The geometric product of two vectors a and b is $ab = a \cdot b + a \wedge b$, where $a \cdot b$ denotes the *inner product* and $a \wedge b$ denotes the *outer product*[1].

Multivectors: These are combinations of geometric elements of different kinds – they encompass scalars and vectors. These different elements are characterised by their *grade*. Scalars are *grade-0*, vectors are *grade-1*, bivectors (directed areas) are *grade-2*, trivectors (directed volumes) are *grade-3*, and so on. Thus, a *multivector* A is a linear combination of objects of different grades:

$$A = \langle A \rangle_0 + \langle A \rangle_1 + \ldots = \sum_r \langle A \rangle_r \qquad (2)$$

where $\langle A \rangle_r$ denotes projecting out the grade r components of A.

r-vectors: A multivector which is of grade r only is called an *r-vector*. If an r-vector A_r can be expressed as an outer product of r-vectors $a_1, a_2, \ldots, a_r$ as:

$$A_r = a_1 \wedge a_2 \wedge \cdots \wedge a_r \qquad (3)$$

then it is called an *r-blade*. Any r-vector can be expressed as a sum of r-blades.

---

[1] The main limitation of the cross product lies in its existence only in $3D$, i.e. in higher dimensions, the direction becomes ambiguous. This issue was addressed by Grassmann, who devised a geometric encoding of a plane that does not depend on the concept of a vector perpendicular to it.

Reversion: If $a = a_1 \wedge \cdots \wedge a_r$, then the reversion of a is:

$$(a_1 \wedge \cdots \wedge a_r)^{\sim} = a_r \wedge \cdots \wedge a_1 \tag{4}$$

Rotations: One of the most important contributions of the Geometric Algebra is its handling of rotations. They are composed of two successive reflections and denoted by $\mathcal{R}$. A vector a is rotated as:

$$a' = \mathcal{R}a\tilde{\mathcal{R}} \tag{5}$$

where

$$\mathcal{R} \equiv mn \tag{6}$$

We call the multivector $\mathcal{R}$ a *Rotor* and it satisfies the relation $\mathcal{R}\tilde{\mathcal{R}} = 1$.

Reciprocal Frame: A *reciprocal frame* is defined as the set of vectors $\{e^i\}$ such that:

$$e^k \cdot e_j = \delta_j^k \quad (\,\cdot \text{ denotes the inner product}) \tag{7}$$

where δ_j^k is the Kronecker delta.

3   The Proposed Geometric Algebra ICP Algorithms

The implementations of the experiments for both algorithms, namely *ICP-Geomeric Algebra (GA)* (Algorithm 1) and *ICP-Geomeric Algebra (GA) Colour algorithm* (Algorithm 2) were done in MATLAB R2023a and the Clifford Multivector Toolbox was used [15]. We should note two things:

1. We compare the ICP-GA algorithm on artificial data[2] with the ICP-SVD algorithm and MATLAB's in-built function (*pcregistericp*). The ICP-GA algorithm uses an orthogonal basis and the point clouds do not carry any colour information. We coloured them for better visualization results.
2. We compare the Colour ICP-GA algorithm on real data[3] with the Colour ICP-SVD algorithm (as there isn't an equivalent function in MATLAB). The Colour ICP-GA algorithm uses reciprocal frames and the point clouds carry colour information in the RGB format.

The *Geodesic Distance* was used as quantification of the rotational convergence. For two rotation matrices R_1 and R_2, it is defined as:

$$dist_\angle(R_1, R_2) = dist\angle(R_1 R_2^T, I) = \frac{1}{\sqrt{2}} \| \log(R_1 R_2^T) \|_2 \ \in [0, \pi] \tag{8}$$

where $\|.\|_2$ is the Euclidean norm. All numerical values in the experiments have been calculated by normalizing both model (point-set X^a) and transformed (point-set X^b) point clouds to be within the unit sphere.

---

[2] The artificial data obtained from the Department of Scientific Computing at FSU, https://people.sc.fsu.edu/~jburkardt/data/ply/ply.html.

[3] The real data obtained from the 3D modeling platform website Sketchfab, https://sketchfab.com/feed.

Algorithm 1 - Theory: In situations where two sets of vectors (e.g. coordinates of point-sets) are related through rotor (Geometric Algebra) or an orthogonal transformation (Linear Algebra), it is frequently required to determine this rotor. One commonly encountered scenario is finding a rotor or an orthogonal matrix that represents a rotation (e.g. rotation component of the ICP - rotations have a fixed axis and they preserve the vector cross product, i.e. orientation) when the initial and transformed points are known. For ease of implementation, the algorithm is presented in pseudocode format (Algorithm 1).

Algorithm 1. ICP-GA Algorithm

Require: Model Point-set $\mathbf{X^a}$ and Measured Point-set $\mathbf{X^b}$, *error, tolerance*
1: Start Iterating: $k \leftarrow 1$
2: **repeat**
3:     Subtract the centroids $\overline{X^a}, \overline{X^b}$, from the point-sets $\mathbf{X^a}$ and $\mathbf{X^b}$

$$\mathbf{X^a} = \mathbf{X^a} - \overline{X^a}, \quad \mathbf{X^b} = \mathbf{X^b} - \overline{X^b}$$

4:     Calculate the closest points $\mathbf{C}_{X_a}$ based on the Euclidean Distance of $\mathbf{X^a}, \mathbf{X^b}$
5:     Form the correlation matrix M using $\mathbf{C}_{X_a}, \mathbf{X^b}$
6:     Estimate optimum transformation $\mathcal{R}^k$ and $\mathbf{t^k}$:
    – Calculate the Rotor using Eq. (10):

$$\mathcal{R}^k = (\tilde{\mathcal{R}})^{\sim}$$

    – Calculate the translation as:

$$\mathbf{t^k} = \overline{X^a} - \mathcal{R}\overline{X^b}\tilde{\mathcal{R}}$$

7:     $k \leftarrow k + 1$
8: **until** *error < tolerance*
9: **return** $\mathcal{R}^k, \mathbf{t^k}$

Therefore, if we have an initial frame of vectors $\{u_i\}$ and a final frame of vectors $\{v_i\}$ that are related by a rotor $\mathcal{R}$ (i.e. $v_i = \mathcal{R}u_i\tilde{\mathcal{R}}$) in $3D$ Euclidean space, then:

$$\mathcal{R} = \mu\left(1 + v_i u^i\right) \tag{9}$$

where μ is a constant that guarantees $\mathcal{R}\tilde{\mathcal{R}} = 1$. This has been well known for many years [13]. Recently, Lasenby et al. [16] presented a new method for calculating the rotor $\mathcal{R}$ in spaces of any dimension and any signature. The authors started with an n-dimensional frame $\{u_i\}$, $i = 1, \ldots, n$ and they assumed that $f(u_i) = \mathcal{R}u_i\tilde{\mathcal{R}}$, with $\mathcal{R}\tilde{\mathcal{R}} = 1$, and also $v_i = f(u_i) = \mathcal{R}u_i\tilde{\mathcal{R}}$ to show that:

$$\tilde{\mathcal{R}} = s\sum_{r=0}^{n} \partial_{(r)} f_{(r)} \tag{10}$$

where s is a real scalar, and the $\partial_{(r)} f_{(r)}$ is given by:

$$\partial_{(r)} f_{(r)} = \frac{1}{r!} \left(\partial_{u_{j_r}} \wedge \ldots \wedge \partial_{u_{j_1}} \right) \left(f\left(u_{j_1}\right) \wedge \ldots \wedge f\left(u_{j_r}\right) \right) \qquad (11)$$

where $\partial_{(r)} f_{(r)}$ is called the rth *Characteristic Multivector* of the linear function f. This recovers the rotor when n points are mapped to n points in an nD space. In [16], the authors did not extend to the N points mapping to N points, where $N > n$. We will examine this case next. Let us start with an orthogonal basis $\{u_i\}, i = 1, 2, \ldots N$ in $3D$ space. Then, a rotor $\mathcal{R}$ is sought that takes u_i to the columns m_j, $j = 1, 2, \ldots N$ of the correlation matrix M. If we apply equation (10) on Eq. (9) we can recover $\mathcal{R}$ as:

$$\tilde{\mathcal{R}} \propto 1 + [u_1 m_1 + u_2 m_2 \ldots] + [(u_2 \wedge u_1)(m_1 \wedge m_2) + \ldots ..] +$$
$$[(u_3 \wedge u_2 \wedge u_1)(m_1 \wedge m_2 \wedge m_3)] \qquad (12)$$

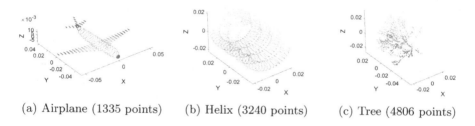

(a) Airplane (1335 points)   (b) Helix (3240 points)   (c) Tree (4806 points)

Fig. 1. Model Point Clouds

Algorithm 1-Experimental Results: Two of the major weakness of the ICP algorithm are:

1. Its sensitivity to the initialization of the parameters of the geometric transformation, i.e. how 'good' the correspondences between the point-sets are in the first iteration. The basis of the problem is that incorrect matches will occur, which will eventually lead the ICP algorithm to be trapped in a *local minimum*. For an objective evaluation, 200 random rotations and 200 random translations were generated along every direction with $\mathbf{R} \in [0°, 90°]$ and $\mathbf{t} \in [0, 1]$ for different point cloud geometries as shown in Fig. 1. We observe in Fig. 2 that all algorithms produce similar results and the differences between them are hardly noticeable. As far as the run-time is concerned, it is noticeable that the ICP-SVD algorithm and MATLAB's in- built function are faster than the ICP-GA algorithm. However, this is not entirely true as the ICP-SVD algorithm is based on MATLAB's in-built function for calculating the SVD which uses LAPACK (Linear Algebra PACKage) routines written in

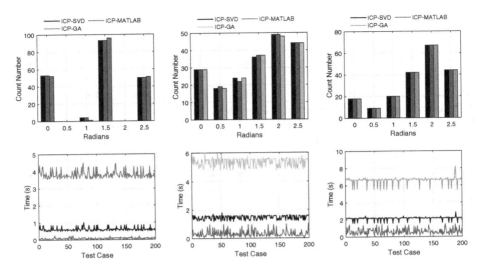

Fig. 2. • Airplane ○ Helix • Tree. *Top:* Rotational Convergence for 200 tests with random initial positions. *Bottom:* Computation Time for the ICP to be completed for 200 tests with random initial positions. (Color figure online)

FORTRAN. Similarly, MATLAB's function for the ICP is based on the low-level nature of C/C++ which along with their compilers produce extremely high execution speeds. On the other hand, the ICP-GA algorithm uses the Clifford Multivector Toolbox which is developed solely in MATLAB.

2. Its sensitivity to noise. Normally data scanned from geometrically unstable regions will contain high levels of noise, causing slower convergence and higher registration error. For this reason we added different levels of Gaussian Noise in the data, i.e. its amplitude can be modeled with a normal probability distribution. The highest levels of noise amplitudes are illustrated in Fig. 3. The ranges of rotation and translation for the three point clouds were selected again as $\mathbf{R} \in [0°, 90°]$ and $\mathbf{t} \in [0, 1]$ along every direction. Once again, the algorithms produced very similar results in the presence of noise as shown in Fig. 4.

Algorithm 2 -Theory: The ICP algorithm by Besl and McKay and the proposed ICP-GA algorithm do not utilize other information that the data may have. We propose a new algorithm based on the *Characteristic Multivector* method (as in Algorithm 1), but now it uses the point cloud geometry and the colour information of the point clouds to calculate more accurately the point correspondences between the model and the measured point clouds. Specifically:

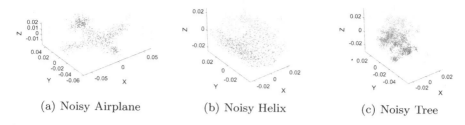

Fig. 3. Noisy Point Clouds under the Highest Noise Amplitude. *From Left to Right:* *Airplane Noise Amplitude*: 0.0039, *Helix Noise Amplitude*: 0.0012, *Tree Noise Amplitude*: 0.0015.

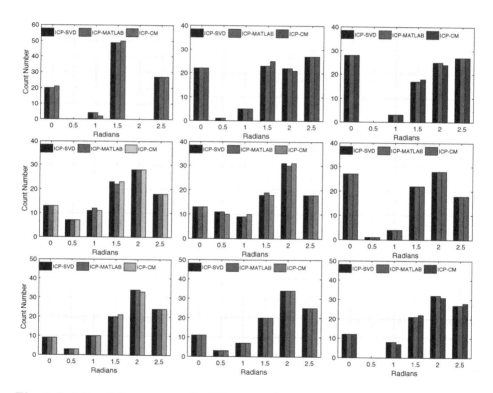

Fig. 4. Rotational Convergence for 100 tests with random initial position of the three algorithms for different Noise Levels. *Top*: Airplane - From Left to Right: *Noise Amplitude*: 0.0001, 0.0024, 0.0039. *Middle*: Helix - rom Left to Right: *Noise Amplitude*: 0.0003, 0.0008, 0.0012. *Bottom*: Tree - From Left to Right: *Noise Amplitude*: 0.0001, 0.0008 0.0015.

1. We modify the steps 4-6 of Algorithm 1 (we keep all other steps) as shown in Algorithm 2. Now, the distance between two points of the point-sets X^a and X^b is calculated as in Algorithm 1 + the differences in values of the RGB channels.
2. We do not use an orthonormal basis as Algorithm 1. Instead, we use *reciprocal frames*.

Algorithm 2. Modified Steps of Algorithm 1

4: Modify the Euclidean metric distance by also taking into account the difference in the RGB channels to improve the nearest neighbour search in order calculate the closest points $\mathbf{C}_{X_a}$ of $\mathbf{X^a}, \mathbf{X^b}$
5: Calculate the correlation matrix $M_{\alpha\beta}$ and auto-correlation matrix $G_{\alpha\beta}$ and form the reciprocal frames g^1, g^2, g^3
6: Calculate the Rotor using Eq. (15) (and not (12) as in Algorithm 1)

It is proved in [18] that for an orthonormal basis $\{e_i\}$ the *correlation matrix* $M_{\alpha\beta}$ and *auto-correlation matrix* $\mathbf{G}_{\alpha\beta}$ can be expressed in Geometric Algebra as:

$$M_{\alpha\beta} = \sum_{i=1}^{n}(e_\alpha \cdot X_i^a)(e_\beta \cdot X_i^b) \tag{13}$$

$$\mathbf{G}_{\alpha\beta} = \sum_{i=1}^{N}(e_\alpha \cdot X^b)(e_\beta \cdot X^b) \tag{14}$$

and then, the rotor $\mathcal{R}$ can be recovered as:

$$\tilde{\mathcal{R}} \propto 1 + \left[m^1 g_1 + m^2 g_2 \ldots\right] + \left[\left(m^2 \wedge m^1\right)\left(g_1 \wedge g_2\right) + \ldots..\right] + \left[\left(m^3 \wedge m^2 \wedge m^1\right)\left(g_1 \wedge g_2 \wedge g_3\right)\right] \tag{15}$$

Algorithm 2-Experimental Results: Since the Characteristic Multivector algorithm is not restricted to orthonormal sets of vectors, we used the reciprocal frames instead of an orthogonal basis based on the fact that when extra information is added[4] the correspondences are 'closer' to being 1-1. When the correspondences are known (point-sets are related via 1-1 correspondence), the reciprocal frames produce more robust results than the orthogonal basis. Details of this mathematical formalism can be found in [18]. Since the ICP-SVD algorithm and MATLAB's in-built function for the ICP produce similar results in the following experiment we will use the ICP-SVD algorithm for comparisons with the ICP-GA algorithm (Figs. 5, 6 and 7).

---

[4] SVD performs better than the Characteristic Multivector algorithm when colour information is added and an orthogonal basis is used.

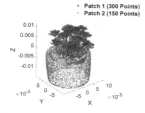
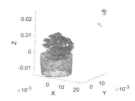
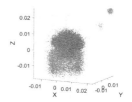

(a) Model Point Cloud with Model Patches

(b) No Noise. Point Clouds for Registration

(c) Noise Amplitude:0.0008. Point Clouds for Registration

Fig. 5. Plant Model Point Cloud (26161 points) with Selected Patches (Model and Measured [*Rotation (x,y,z-axes)*: $\pi/6°, \pi/4°, \pi/3°$. *Translation (x,y,z-axes)*: 0.0210] under no noise and highest noise amplitude.

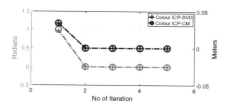

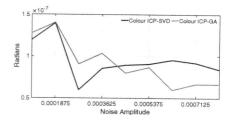

Fig. 6. Rotational Convergence (•) and Translation Error (•) of the algorithms.

Fig. 7. Rotational Convergence of the algorithms for 9 noise levels. *Noise Amplitude range*: 0.0001-0.0008.

4   Conclusion

We developed two Geometric Algebra algorithms and compared them with the standard solutions of the ICP algorithm. The results revealed that Geometric Algebra can provide equally robust solutions with Linear Algebra when the calculations are performed in Euclidean space. The knowledge gained through this work can provide a stable basis upon which even better results may be achieved. This may lead to:

– Extend the calculations to a non-Euclidean (curved) space, where the rotations and translations will be calculated concurrently in the ICP algorithm. In some cases, the ICP algorithm fails with both the CM method and the SVD method. We suspect that the ICP algorithm fails and does not converge if the positions of the point clouds are not close enough due to the decoupling of the rotation from the translation. Specifically, since the Characteristic Multivector method works in any dimension and signature, we believe that the use of Conformal Geometric Algebra [19], i.e. a new covariant approach to geometry where Euclidean, hyperbolic and spherical geometries are put on the same footing, might be beneficial to 3D registration algorithms.

Acknowledgements. This work was supported by the Engineering and Physical Sciences Research Council under reference number EP/S023917/1 and the MathWorks.

References

1. Besl, P.J., McKay, N.D.: A method for registration of 3-D shapes. IEEE Trans. Pattern Anal. Mach. Intell., 239–256 (1992)
2. Horn, B.K.: Closed-form solution of absolute orientation using unit quaternions. J. Opt. Soc. Am. A **4**(4), 629–642 (1987)
3. Horn, B.K., Hilden, H.M., Negahdaripour, S.: Closed-form solution of absolute orientation using orthonormal matrices. J. Opt. Soc. Am. A **5**(7), 1127–1135 (1988)
4. Arun, K.S., Huang, T.S., Blostein, S.D.: Least-squares fitting of two 3-D point sets. IEEE Trans. Pattern Anal. Mach. Intell., 698–700 (1987)
5. Sasiadek, J.Z., Monjazeb, A,, Necsulescu, D.: Navigation of an autonomous mobile robot using EKF-SLAM and FastSLAM. In: 16th Mediterranean Conference on Control and Automation, pp. 517–522 (2008)
6. Thrun, S.: Probabilistic robotics. Commun. ACM **45**(3), 52–57 (2020)
7. Fox, D., Burgard, W., Thrun, S.: Markov localization for mobile robots in dynamic environments. J. Artifi. Intell. Res. **11**, 391–427 (1999)
8. Dissanayake, M.W., Newman, P., Durrant-Whyte, H.F., Clark, S., Csorba, M.: An experimental and theoretical investigation into simultaneous localisation and map building, pp. 265–274 (1999)
9. Thrun, S., Fox, D., Burgard, W., Dellaert, F.: Robust Monte Carlo localization for mobile robots. Artifi. Intell. **128**(1–2), 99–141 (2001)
10. Nuchter, A.: 3D robotic mapping: the simultaneous localization and mapping problem with six degrees of freedom. Springer, Germany (2009). https://doi.org/10.1007/978-3-540-89884-9
11. May, S., et al.: Three-dimensional mapping with time-of-flight cameras. J. Field Robotics **26**(11–12), 934–65 (2009)
12. Umeyama, S.: Least-squares estimation of transformation parameters between two point patterns. IEEE Trans. Pattern Anal. Mach. Intell. **13**(04), 376–80 (1991)
13. Hestenes, D., Sobczyk, G.: Clifford Algebra to Geometric Calculus: A Unified Language for Mathematics and physics. Springer Science & Business Media, Germany (1984). https://doi.org/10.1007/978-94-009-6292-7
14. Doran, C., Lasenby, A.: Geometric Algebra For Physicists. Cambridge University Press, UK (2003)
15. Sangwine, J.S., Hitzer, E.: Clifford multivector toolbox (for MATLAB). Adv. Appli. Clifford Algebras **27**(1), 539–558 (2016)
16. Lasenby, A., Lasenby, J., Matsantonis, C.: Reconstructing a rotor from initial and final frames using characteristic multivectors: with applications in orthogonal transformations. Mathematical Methods in the Applied Sciences (2022)
17. Lasenby, J., et al.: New geometric methods for computer vision: an application to structure and motion estimation. Int. J. Comput. Vision **26**, 191–213 (2004)
18. Matsantonis, C., Lasenby, J.: A Geometric Algebra Solution to the Absolute Orientation Problem. Advanced Computational Applications of Geometric Algebra. Springer Proceedings in Mathematics & Statistics (2023), (submitted)
19. Lasenby, A.: Recent applications of conformal geometric algebra. In: Li, H., Olver, P.J., Sommer, G. (eds.) GIAE/IWMM -2004. LNCS, vol. 3519, pp. 298–328. Springer, Heidelberg (2005). https://doi.org/10.1007/11499251_23

Active Anomaly Detection
for Autonomous Robots: A Benchmark

Dario Mantegazza[1]([⊠]) [iD], Alind Xhyra[2,3] [iD], Alessandro Giusti[1] [iD],
and Jérôme Guzzi[1] [iD]

[1] Dalle Molle Institute for Artificial Intelligence (IDSIA), USI-SUPSI,
Lugano, Switzerland
`dario.mantegazza@idsia.ch`
[2] Constructor University, Schaffhausen, Switzerland
[3] Università della Svizzera Italiana, Lugano, Switzerland

Abstract. Autonomous robots require well-trained Anomaly Detection
systems to detect unexpected hazardous events in unknown deployment
scenarios. Such systems are difficult to train when data is scarce. During deployment, lots of data are collected but it is not apparent how
to efficiently and effectively use that data. We propose to use Active
Learning to select samples to improve the detection system performance.
We benchmark 8 different query strategies, of which 2 are novel, using
normalizing flow over image embeddings. While our results show that
our approach has the best performance overall, choosing the right query
strategy strongly depends on external factors.

Keywords: Visual Anomaly Detection · Model Benchmark · Deep
Learning for Visual Perception · Robotic Perception

1 Introduction

Industrial use of autonomous robots for inspection or patrolling is increasing;
more robots are now facing unexpected unknown events in new environments.
At the same time, robust sensors and deep learning models allow a better understanding of a robot's surroundings. In this context, Anomaly Detection has seen a
new breath of research [7,26,27,40] focused on applications for robotics, becoming an important feature of a vision system for robots. One overlooked question
regards the improvement of such models deployed on robots using data collected
over time.

In other fields a tried approach is to use Active Learning to efficiently use
data collected for model performance improvements [34,35]; to the best of our

This work was supported as a part of NCCR Robotics, a National Centre of Competence in Research, funded by the Swiss National Science Foundation (grant number
51NF40 185543) and by the European Commission through the Horizon 2020 project
1-SWARM, grant ID 871743.

F. Iida et al. (Eds.): TAROS 2023, LNAI 14136, pp. 315–327, 2023.
https://doi.org/10.1007/978-3-031-43360-3_26

knowledge, Active Learning has never been applied to a robot's Visual Anomaly detection system.

We focus on a specific scenario, an autonomous robot that explores underground tunnels where communication with the outside world is not available. While we expect the tunnels to be traversable, unexpected events can happen at any time; these events can become hazardous, impairing the robot or destroying it altogether. We emulate this scenario using a dataset [29] in which a ground robot traverses university corridors. Similarly to recent research [12,27,40], the robot uses a Visual Anomaly Detection Deep Learning model to detect anomalies in frames coming from the front-facing camera. In the scenario, we expect the training data to be limited to a set of nominal frames of the first safely-traversable meters of a tunnel.

To circumvent the limited availability of training samples, we propose to apply Active Learning to the data collected during the mission and carefully ask an expert to label only the most informative frames; then add these labeled samples, retrain the detector, and measure its performance using AUC and Average Precision on the testing set.

Our contribution is a benchmark of 8 active learning approaches to see which is the most efficient, from a sample labeling point of view, at improving the AUC and Average Precision. Our second contribution is two new query strategy approach that exploits our model's prediction.

2   Related Work

2.1   Anomaly Detection in Robotics

Anomaly Detection concerns finding anomalous patterns in data given a model of normality [10,31]; its application covers diverse fields: surveillance [9], intrusion detection [6], medical imaging [32], fault detection [20], agriculture [12] and autonomous robot [26,27,40].

In robotics, Anomaly Detection is used to detect anomalies in the environment [12,27,40] or in the robot itself [6,20] before they become hazards. In literature this is done using low-dimensional data [20,21] or high-dimensional one [9,12]; we focus on the latter by looking for anomalies in images coming from the robot's front-facing camera.

Visual Anomaly Detection for robotics is gaining traction. Early attempts concerned with autonomous patrolling [9] applied image-matching algorithms to identify unexpected differences. More advanced and recent approaches detect anomalies for autonomous agricultural robots using custom CNNs [12]; Wellhausen et al. [40] use anomaly detection to solve the task of safe traversability for legged robots in unknown environments. In our previous works [26,27] we also tackle Visual Anomaly Detection for both ground wheeled robots and flying drones; we use Autoencoders and Normalizing Flow models to detect anomalies in the robot's surroundings captured from the robots' camera.

2.2   Models and Approaches

Reconstruction-based methods - The use of Autoencoders trained only on nominal data is a reliable and tested [11,23,27,31,40] approach to solving Anomaly Detection. This approach works at the input image level, by calculating the reproduction error between input and output of the autoencoder, it is possible to extract an anomaly score to identify anomalies.

Normalizing Flows - Another approach uses Normalizing Flow models. Originally designed for generative purposes [1,17,22], in the context of anomaly detection [7,40] are used not at the input image level but at a latent features-level. After extracting latent features from the image, it is possible to train a Normalizing Flow model to learn a mapping between the features-space and a Normal distribution on the same dimensions. Models like Real-NVP [14] and NAF [18] can be used to detect anomalies by directly estimating the likelihood of a sample with respect to the distribution of non-anomalous samples used for training. In this paper, we use Real-NVP [14], a type of Normalizing Flow model.

Outlier Exposure - Outlier Exposure is a novel approach that allows the training of Anomaly Detection models also on anomalous samples [16]. In a recent work of ours [26], we explore a combination of Real-NVP and Outlier Exposure; in this paper, we use what found in our previous research to fully exploit Active Learning approaches.

2.3   Active Learning

Active Learning is an iterative process that aims at finding efficient ways to improve model performance by adding selected samples from an unlabeled set $\mathcal{U}$ to the training set $\mathcal{T}$. In Active Learning approaches the model selects the K unlabeled samples to be labeled by an expert/oracle. For us, $\mathcal{U}$ is the data collected during missions.

Settles [34] identify three settings that define the general query strategies one can use.

Memebership Query Synthesis - Introduced by Angluin et al. [2], in this setting the model asks generation of new samples that are not part of $\mathcal{T}$; the samples are then labeled by an oracle, but it could happen that the generated samples were unintelligible for a human expert [4]. New samples are generated by Generative Adversarial Networks $GANs$ [8,15].

Stream-Based Selective Sampling - Here it is assumed that continuous inexpensive or free streams of data are available [13]. After collection, the learner decides for the annotation or not. Labeling is made in isolation for each sample; thus we cannot exploit contextual information for choosing which samples to annotate.

Pool-Based Sampling - In this scenario the samples are selected from a large pool of unlabeled data $\mathcal{U}$ [25]. Using an acquisition function the learner makes a greedy selection of samples to be labeled by the oracle; the learner can exploit the sample surroundings and neighborhood to make a decision.

Pool-based sampling requires evaluation of each sample of $\mathcal{U}$; this process can become expensive, however, it has become the most studied approach for real-world scenarios [8, 24, 34, 36, 39].

2.4   Active Anomaly Detection

While there is a plethora of research on active learning [8, 34] and even recent efforts on active learning for anomaly detection on small-scale tabular data [36, 38, 39, 41], no research exists at the intersection of visual deep anomaly detection and active learning in a robotic context.

3   Method

We aim to compare, under a set of realistic assumptions, 8 different approaches of Active Learning to improve the performance of an Anomaly Detection system of a robot. We compare approaches with an automated pipeline that trains a custom Real-NVP model on the image's feature embeddings. The embeddings are part of Hazards&Robots [28] a dataset for studying Visual Anomaly Detection in the robotic context; the embeddings are extracted from images by a pre-trained CLIP [30] model. To trace the performance of the detector we use AUC and AP over the test set of the dataset.

3.1   Anomaly Detection

The embedding we use are 512-sized vectors; these are passed in input to our custom Real-NVP. The model learns to map the vectors to latent multivariate Normal distribution with the same dimensions. There we measure the probability of a sample being normal or anomalous. The model setup is similar to [26] but adapted to the larger embedding size; both the input and hidden layers have 512 neurons. For the outlier exposure loss($\mathcal{L}_{OE}$) component we use the original paper values of $\lambda = 1$ and $\gamma = 100$.

3.2   Active Learning

Assumptions. We follow [39] and set the following assumptions for our benchmark. **General Assumptions** - We focus on label *feedback* with a fixed *budget* of 64 samples to be *interpreted* by our perfect oracle.

Specific Assumptions - For *class distribution* we assume that anomalies are unusual observations with no underlying distribution. Our *learning objective* is to improve the AUC and Average Precision of our model on a test set. Our *initial pool* is an unlabeled pool of assumed nominal samples.

Query Strategies Overview. Trittenbach et al. [39] in their overview, propose a categorization of query strategies based on the *informativness* sources: *data-based* use statistical approaches on the samples, *model-based* rely on functions based on the learned model and, *hybrid* strategies that combine the two above; we propose an extension to the *data-based* category to consider strategies that extract information from the data itself (i.e. using spatial or geometrical [5] information).

We implement 8 different strategies: three are model-based (DB, HC, IHC), two are data-based (MM CLIP, MM RNVP), two are hybrids (HMM, HMM RNVP) and one is a baseline (RAN).

Decision Boundary - We base our implementation of *Decision Boundary*(DB) on the marginal strategy defined by Zhang et al. [41]; they use Neural Autoregressive Flow (NAF) [18] to detect anomalies and to select new samples. In the paper, the samples chosen are those that are closer to a decision boundary set as the α-quantile ($\alpha \in [0.9, 0.95]$) of the log-likelihood distribution of samples generated with NAF. We avoid that and set the decision boundary as $b = icdf(\alpha)$ where α is set to 0.95, thus $b = 1.96$, and *icdf* is the inverse cumulative density function. To select samples u_{DB}^* to be labeled we use:

$$u_{DB}^* = \arg\min_{u_{\mathcal{N}} \in \mathcal{U_N}} |(||u_{\mathcal{N}}||_2 - b)| \tag{1}$$

where $u_{\mathcal{N}}$ corresponds to the Real-NVP latent representation of an unlabeled sample.

High-Confidence - Another model-based strategy is *High-Confidence* [3](HC); HC selects the most anomalous samples of $\mathcal{U}$ as follows:

$$u_{HC}^* = \arg\max_{u \in \mathcal{U}} \mathcal{L}(u) \tag{2}$$

where $\mathcal{L}$ is the negative log-likelihood of the samples u of $\mathcal{U}$.

We also implemented *Inverse High-Confidence* (IHC) that consists in selecting the least anomalous samples from $\mathcal{U}$. Note that both HC and IHC in Unsupervised Anomaly Detection are special cases of DB; HC is DB where the boundary is set at an infinite distance from the nominal distribution and IHC corresponds to DB with a boundary at the center of the distribution.

Minimax - Under the data-based category we implement two strategies that explore the data space; inspired by Sener [33], Minimax (MM) select those samples from $\mathcal{U}$ that have the largest minimum distance from any sample t of $\mathcal{T}$.

We apply MM both on the CLIP space (MM CLIP) and on the RNVP latent space (MM RNVP).

$$u_{MM}^* = \arg\max_{u \in \mathcal{U}} dist(u, t), \forall t \in \mathcal{T} \tag{3}$$

where *dist* is the $\mathcal{L}_2$ distance in the chosen data-space.

Hybrid Minimax - We propose a novel Active Learning Pool-based hybrid query strategy called Hybrid Minimax.

Inspired by MedAL [35], it combines MM and HC. Differently than MedAL, we first select a set of $K \times m$ samples using MM, from these HC selects the K most anomalous samples. m is a hyperparameter and is set to 3; if set to 1 Hybrid Minimax would match MM on the same data space, on the opposite a large enough m would result in a Hybrid Minimax behaving like HC.

We propose two versions of Hybrid Minimax, depending on the data space of the first $K \times m$ samples selection; if selected in the CLIP-space we call it HMM, if the selection is made in the Real-NVP latent space then it is called HMM RNVP.

Our approach combines the coverage of distance-based selection with the informativeness of the model prediction, resulting in a different selection than the two parts alone.

Random - We also considera a naive baseline where K random samples are selected from the unlabeled set.

4 Experiments Setup

Dataset

The dataset we use is Hazards&Robots v3 [28]. This dataset is collected from a ground-wheeled robot traversing, under normal circumstances, tidy and empty university corridors. The dataset, purposely built for visual anomaly detection in robotics, contains situations that are considered anomalous.

The dataset contains 324'408 512×512 pixel RGB frames recorded from the robot's front-facing camera; additionally, the dataset provides features embeddings for each frame; these are used in the paper. In total, 145k samples are normal while 178k are anomalous; the dataset is not limited to a single anomaly class but differentiates between 20 classes.

The dataset provides four non overlapping sets: *training* ($\sim$ 47k frames), *training mixed*($\sim$ 144k frames), *validation* ($\sim$ 2.8k frames) and *test* ($\sim$ 129k frames). The *test* and *training mixed* sets contain both 35% of normal samples and 65% of anomalous samples, while *validation* and *training* contain only normal samples. To match the dataset to our Active Learning scenario we use *training mixed* as our $\mathcal{U}$ and part of *training* as the initial $\mathcal{T}$.

4.1 Implementation

We release the code to replicate our results[1]. We implemented everything using Python 3.8 and PyTorch 1.13 and we run our experiment on an NVIDIA 2080 Ti.

---

[1] code is available on GitHub https://github.com/idsia-robotics/ActiveAnomaly Detection.

Models Training - We run parallel training[2] of models on a single GPU; each model is trained for 100 epochs in 2 min. More than 6500 experiments are run amounting to 17 d of computation time.

Query Strategy Computation - For model-based query strategies, the computation is done on GPU, and predictions for the entirety of $\mathcal{U}$ take less than 1 s. For data-based query strategies, distance computation between data samples is done with Faiss [19] from FAIR. The library can compute distances on GPU using large tensors already in VRAM; the result is an almost instantaneous distance computation.

4.2 Metrics and Tracking

Evaluation of each model detection performance is done over the dataset test set with the following metrics. We use Area Under the ROC Curve (AUC)as it is robust to data imbalance and is threshold-independent; AUC has a probabilistic meaning, and the value (between 0 and 1.0) can be seen as the probability that the prediction of a positive (anomalous) sample is higher than the one of a negative (normal) sample. An AUC value of 0.5 corresponds to a random classifier and a value near 1.0 indicate good performance with 1.0 indicating an ideal detector. Following [36], we consider the Average Precision (AP) of a model; AP describes the precision-recall curve as the weighted average of precisions at consecutive thresholds using recalls of preceding thresholds as weights.

We trace both *progress curves* [39] of AUC and AP and their averages along 10 Active Learning cycles.

4.3 Experiment Run

An experiment is defined by a query strategy, an initial size of $\mathcal{T}$, and a $\mathcal{U}$ with a fixed percentage of anomalous samples. An experiment corresponds to 10 Active Learning cycles of a query strategy; the samples of $\mathcal{T}$, $\mathcal{U}$, and the u^* are traced. In a learning cycle we train and test the Real-NVP on $\mathcal{T}$ and the u^* samples selected before; then using the query strategy we select the next u^* from $\mathcal{U}$. We use four initial sizes for $\mathcal{T}$ (64, 512, 1024, 4096) and four percentage of anomalies in $\mathcal{U}$ (0%, 0.1%, 1%, 10%). We fix the number of samples chosen by the query strategies (K) to 64. These values are chosen to resemble realistic scenarios and other datasets [36].

Each experiment setup is run 5 times and each time the initial training sample, the anomalous one available in the unlabeled are randomly chosen and are fixed for the rest of the run.

5 Experiment Results

5.1 Overall Performance

In Tables 2, 3 we collect the query strategies metrics averaged across learning cycles and experiment repetitions. We highlight the best performance of each

---

[2] using GNU Parallel [37].

Table 1. AUC and AP of the initial models trained only on the initial training size.

Initial Size	64	512	1024	4096
AUC	0.9126	0.9342	0.9390	0.9434
AP	0.9583	0.9693	0.9719	0.9741

Table 2. Average AUC

Initial Size	64				512				1024				4096
% of Anom in $\mathcal{U}$	0.0	0.01	1.0	10	0.0	0.01	1.0	10	0.0	0.01	1.0	10	10
DB	0.912	0.914	0.913	0.914	0.934	0.934	0.933	0.934	0.938	0.938	0.939	0.939	0.943	0.943	0.943	0.943
HC	0.935	0.936	0.925	0.913	0.943	0.943	0.938	0.935	0.944	0.944	0.942	0.939	0.946	0.946	0.945	0.943
IHC	0.911	0.914	0.913	0.914	0.934	0.934	0.913	0.934	0.938	0.938	0.939	0.939	0.943	0.943	0.943	0.943
MM CLIP	0.936	0.936	0.927	0.913	0.943	0.943	0.938	0.935	0.945	0.944	0.942	0.939	0.946	0.947	0.945	0.943
MM RNVP	0.935	0.936	0.925	0.913	0.943	0.944	0.937	0.935	0.944	0.945	0.942	0.939	0.946	0.946	0.944	0.943
HMM	0.911	0.915	0.926	0.924	0.943	0.945	0.945	0.947	0.938	0.938	0.948	0.949	0.943	0.944	0.950	0.951
HMM RNVP	0.910	0.914	0.925	0.922	0.933	0.934	0.943	0.946	0.938	0.937	0.946	0.949	0.943	0.943	0.947	0.950
RAN	0.936	0.936	0.937	0.940	0.942	0.942	0.942	0.945	0.944	0.943	0.945	0.946	0.946	0.946	0.946	0.947

Table 3. Average AP

Initial Size	64				512				1024				4096
% of Anom in $\mathcal{U}$	0.0	0.01	1.0	10	0.0	0.01	1.0	10	0.0	0.01	1.0	10	10
DB	0.958	0.959	0.958	0.959	0.969	0.970	0.970	0.970	0.971	0.971	0.972	0.972	0.974	0.974	0.974	0.974
HC	0.971	0.971	0.965	0.959	0.974	0.975	0.972	0.970	0.975	0.975	0.974	0.972	0.976	0.976	0.975	0.974
IHC	0.958	0.960	0.958	0.959	0.969	0.970	0.969	0.970	0.972	0.971	0.972	0.972	0.974	0.974	0.974	0.974
MM CLIP	0.971	0.971	0.966	0.959	0.974	0.975	0.972	0.970	0.975	0.975	0.971	0.972	0.976	0.976	0.975	0.974
MM RNVP	0.971	0.971	0.966	0.959	0.974	0.975	0.971	0.970	0.975	0.975	0.971	0.972	0.976	0.976	0.975	0.974
HMM	0.958	0.960	0.966	0.964	0.969	0.970	0.975	0.975	0.971	0.971	0.977	0.977	0.974	0.974	0.978	0.978
HMM RNVP	0.958	0.960	0.966	0.963	0.969	0.970	0.974	0.975	0.971	0.971	0.976	0.976	0.974	0.974	0.976	0.977
RAN	0.970	0.970	0.971	0.974	0.973	0.973	0.973	0.975	0.974	0.974	0.975	0.975	0.975	0.975	0.975	0.976

query strategy in italics; we color grade the values across all experiments where the better the performance the darker the color, note that the grading is also local to each subset of runs relative to a certain percentage of anomalies. In Table 1 we report the average performance of a Real-NVP model trained only on the initial $\mathcal{T}$. While not reported in a Table, on average a model that sees the whole $\mathcal{T}$ and $\mathcal{U}$ sets achieve AUC 0.960 and AP 0.982.

In terms of AUC and AP, the most performing query strategy is HMM (AUC 0.951, AP 0.978).

5.2 Initial Training Size and Unlabeled Anomaly Presence

When data is scarce, i.e. few samples are available initially or anomalies are scarce in $\mathcal{U}$, it is better to explore the unlabeled set than to exploit what is learned; explorative strategies such as MM CLIP, MM RNVP, and HC lead to higher metrics than exploitative ones like DB and HMMs; note that if the initial size is very limited (64) the best strategy is RAN. Conversely, large initial $\mathcal{T}$ or high percentage of anomalies in $\mathcal{U}$, lead to better performances from hybrid queries(HMM, HMM RNVP). Since DB and IHC do not improve the performance of the model over the initial model (Table 1 we will exclude these two query strategies for the rest of the experiment analysis. We assume that the decision boundary of DB is set regardless of the learned model, thus not

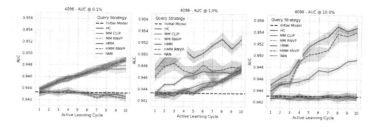

Fig. 1. Progress curves of query strategies with 4096 initial samples.

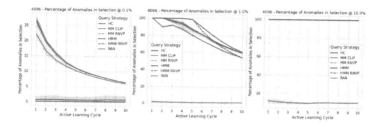

Fig. 2. 4kpercanom

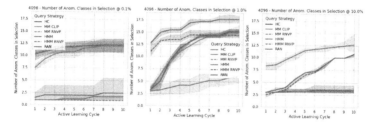

Fig. 3. 4kvaranom

providing a meaningful selection of samples; instead, IHC by sampling only the least anomalous data do not provide useful information to the model.

5.3 Anomaly Selection

In Fig. 1 we plot the progress curves of HMMs, MMs, HC, and RAN. In Fig. 2 we see the percentage of anomalies selected by each query strategy along the learning cycles. In Fig. 3 instead, we see the number (variety) of anomaly classes in selection. For these Figures we focus only on the 4096 initial size. From the Figures, we observe that the learning model benefits from selecting anomalies; in all percentages of Fig. 2, the model with a larger anomalies selection produced the better models (see Fig. 1). When the selection size is matched (see the central plot of Fig. 2 and 3 and 1) the variety of anomalies is dominant; in the plot the variety is expressed as number of unique anomaly classes selected).

It is safe to say that the resulting performance differences between query strategies, in the context of anomaly detection, do not only depend on the source of informativeness - as classic strategy classification implies - but also on the way a certain strategy selects anomalies, both in number and variety. We think that this later observation is novel to the Active Learning field and should be explored more in future research.

6   Conclusions and Future Work

In this paper, we benchmarked 8 different Active Learning strategies for the task of Visual Anomaly detection in a robotic scenario. Two strategies are novel and are proposed as an alternative to other approaches. In our benchmark, we compare how the selected strategies improve the AUC and AP when tested on a large-scale dataset for anomaly detection.

Our experiments show that at the beginning of a deployment cycle of an Anomaly Detection model, it is better to explore the data space, for example with a distance-based query strategy. Later when more data is collected and anomalies are found, it is better to move to a hybrid model like the one we propose, to improve the detection performance.

In this work, we used CLIP as a feature extractor for the RGB images collected with the robot's camera; this setup might not work for other robots' sensory configurations, thus, a limitation of this study is the input constraint that CLIP imposes. Future work will focus on exploring multimodal data-compatible backbones to explore active learning for anomaly detection with diverse sensory information, e.g. point clouds.

References

1. Abdelhamed, A., Brubaker, M.A., Brown, M.S.: Noise flow: noise modeling with conditional normalizing flows. In: International Conference on Computer Vision (ICCV) (2019)
2. Angluin, D.: Queries and concept learning. Mach. Learn. **2**(4), 319–342 (1988). https://doi.org/10.1023/A:1022821128753
3. Barnabé-Lortie, V., Bellinger, C., Japkowicz, N.: Active learning for one-class classification. In: 2015 IEEE 14th International Conference on Machine Learning and Applications (ICMLA), pp. 390–395 (2015). https://doi.org/10.1109/ICMLA.2015.167
4. Baum, E.B., Lang, K.: Query learning can work poorly when a human oracle is used. In: International Joint Conference on Neural Networks, Beijing, China, vol. 8, p. 8 (1992)
5. Beluch, W.H., Genewein, T., Nürnberger, A., Köhler, J.M.: The Power of Ensembles for Active Learning in Image Classification, pp. 9368–9377 (2018). https://openaccess.thecvf.com/content_cvpr_2018/html/Beluch_The_Power_of_CVPR_2018_paper.html

6. Birnbaum, Z., et al.: Unmanned aerial vehicle security using behavioral profiling. In: 2015 International Conference on Unmanned Aircraft Systems (ICUAS), pp. 1310–1319 (2015). https://doi.org/10.1109/ICUAS.2015.7152425
7. Blum, H., et al.: The fishyscapes benchmark: measuring blind spots in semantic segmentation. Int. J. Comput. Vis. **129**(11), 3119–3135 (2021)
8. Budd, S., Robinson, E.C., Kainz, B.: A survey on active learning and human-in-the-loop deep learning for medical image analysis. Med. Image Anal. **71**, 102062 (2021). https://doi.org/10.1016/j.media.2021.102062
9. Chakravarty, P., Zhang, A., Jarvis, R., Kleeman, L.: Anomaly detection and tracking for a patrolling robot. In: Proceedings of the Australiasian Conference on Robotics and Automation 2007, pp. 1–9 (2007)
10. Chandola, V., Banerjee, A., Kumar, V.: Anomaly detection: A survey. ACM Comput. Surv. **41**(3) (2009). https://doi.org/10.1145/1541880.1541882
11. Cho, K., et al.: Learning phrase representations using RNN encoder-decoder for statistical machine translation. In: Proceedings of the 2014 Conference on Empirical Methods in Natural Language Processing (EMNLP), pp. 1724–1734 (Oct 2014). https://doi.org/10.3115/v1/D14-1179
12. Christiansen, P., et al.: Deepanomaly: combining background subtraction and deep learning for detecting obstacles and anomalies in an agricultural field. Sensors **16**(11), 1904 (2016). https://doi.org/10.3390/s16111904
13. Cohn, D., Atlas, L., Ladner, R.: Improving generalization with active learning. Mach. Learn. **15**(2), 201–221 (1994)
14. Dinh, L., Sohl-Dickstein, J., Bengio, S.: Density estimation using real nvp (2016). https://doi.org/10.48550/ARXIV.1605.08803
15. Goodfellow, I.J., et al.: Generative adversarial networks (2014). https://doi.org/10.48550/ARXIV.1406.2661
16. Hendrycks, D., Mazeika, M., Dietterich, T.: Deep anomaly detection with outlier exposure (2018)
17. Ho, J., et al.: Flow++: improving flow-based generative models with variational dequantization and architecture design. In: International Conference on Machine Learning, pp. 2722–2730. PMLR (2019)
18. Huang, C.W., Krueger, D., Lacoste, A., Courville, A.: Neural autoregressive flows. In: Dy, J., Krause, A. (eds.) Proceedings of the 35th International Conference on Machine Learning. Proceedings of Machine Learning Research, vol. 80, pp. 2078–2087. PMLR (10–15 Jul 2018). https://proceedings.mlr.press/v80/huang18d.html
19. Johnson, J., Douze, M., Jégou, H.: Billion-scale similarity search with GPUs. IEEE Trans. Big Data **7**(3), 535–547 (2019)
20. Khalastchi, E., Kalech, M., Kaminka, G.A., Lin, R.: Online data-driven anomaly detection in autonomous robots. Knowl. Inf. Syst. **43**(3), 657–688 (2014). https://doi.org/10.1007/s10115-014-0754-y
21. Khalastchi, E., et al.: Online anomaly detection in unmanned vehicles. In: The 10th International Conference on Autonomous Agents and Multiagent Systems, AAMAS 2011, Richland, SC, vol. 1, pp. 115–122 (2011)
22. Kingma, D.P., Dhariwal, P.: Glow: generative flow with invertible 1x1 convolutions. In: Advances in Neural Information Processing Systems 31 (2018)
23. Kramer, M.: Autoassociative neural networks. Comput. Chem. Eng. **16**(4), 313–328 (1992). https://doi.org/10.1016/0098-1354(92)80051-A, neutral network applications in chemical engineering
24. Kumar, P., Gupta, A.: Active learning query strategies for classification, regression, and clustering: a survey. J. Comput. Sci. Technol. **35**(4), 913–945 (2020). https://doi.org/10.1007/s11390-020-9487-4

25. Lewis, D.D., Gale, W.A.: A sequential algorithm for training text classifiers. In: Proceedings of the 17th Annual International ACM SIGIR Conference on Research and Development in Information Retrieval, SIGIR 1994, pp. 3–12. Springer-Verlag, Berlin (Aug 1994). https://doi.org/10.1007/978-1-4471-2099-5_1

26. Mantegazza, D., Giusti, A., Gambardella, L.M., Guzzi, J.: An outlier exposure approach to improve visual anomaly detection performance for mobile robots. IEEE Robotics Automation Lett., 1–8 (2022). https://doi.org/10.1109/LRA.2022.3192794

27. Mantegazza, D., Redondo, C., Espada, F., Gambardella, L.M., Giusti, A., Guzzi, J.: Sensing anomalies as potential hazards: Datasets and benchmarks. In: Pacheco-Gutierrez, S., Cryer, A., Caliskanelli, I., Tugal, H., Skilton, R. (eds.) Towards Autonomous Robotic Systems. pp. 205–219. Springer International Publishing (2022). https://doi.org/10.1007/978-3-031-15908-4_17

28. Mantegazza, D., Xhyra, A., Gambardella, L.M., Giusti, A., Guzzi, J.: Hazards&Robots: A Dataset for Visual Anomaly Detection in Robotics (Apr 2023). https://doi.org/10.5281/zenodo.7859211, V3.1 of the Corridor scenario is released as the revised principal material for a Data in Brief paper

29. Mantegazza, D., Xhyra, A., Gambardella, L.M., Giusti, A., Guzzi, J.: Hazards&Robots: a dataset for visual anomaly detection in robotics. Data in Brief **48**, 109264 (2023). https://doi.org/10.1016/j.dib.2023.109264, https://www.sciencedirect.com/science/article/pii/S2352340923003839

30. Radford, A., et al.: Learning Transferable Visual Models From https://doi.org/10.48550/arXiv.2103.00020,arXiv: 2103.00020 [cs]

31. Ruff, L., et al.: A unifying review of deep and shallow anomaly detection. Proc. IEEE **109**(5), 756–795 (2021). https://doi.org/10.1109/JPROC.2021.3052449

32. Schlegl, T., Seeböck, P., Waldstein, S.M., Schmidt-Erfurth, U., Langs, G.: Unsupervised anomaly detection with generative adversarial networks to guide marker discovery. In: Niethammer, M., et al. (eds.) IPMI 2017. LNCS, vol. 10265, pp. 146–157. Springer, Cham (2017). https://doi.org/10.1007/978-3-319-59050-9_12

33. Sener, O., Savarese, S.: Active learning for convolutional neural networks: A core-set approach. In: International Conference on Learning Representations (2018). https://openreview.net/forum?id=H1aIuk-RW

34. Settles, B.: Active Learning Literature Survey. Technical Report, University of Wisconsin-Madison Department of Computer Sciences (2009). https://minds.wisconsin.edu/handle/1793/60660

35. Smailagic, A., et al.: Medal: Accurate and robust deep active learning for medical image analysis. In: 2018 17th IEEE International Conference on Machine Learning and Applications (ICMLA), pp. 481–488 (2018). https://doi.org/10.1109/ICMLA.2018.00078

36. Tang, X., Astle, Y.S., Freeman, C.: Deep anomaly detection with ensemble-based active learning. In: 2020 IEEE International Conference on Big Data (Big Data), pp. 1663–1670 (Dec 2020). https://doi.org/10.1109/BigData50022.2020.9378315

37. Tange, O., et al.: Gnu parallel-the command-line power tool. USENIX Mag. **36**(1), 42–47 (2011)

38. Trittenbach, H., Böhm, K.: One-class active learning for outlier detection with multiple subspaces. In: Proceedings of the 28th ACM International Conference on Information and Knowledge Management, CIKM 2019, pp. 811–820. Association for Computing Machinery, New York (Nov 2019). https://doi.org/10.1145/3357384.3357873

39. Trittenbach, H., Englhardt, A., Böhm, K.: An overview and a benchmark of active learning for outlier detection with one-class classifiers. Expert Syst. Appli. **168**, 114372 (2021). https://doi.org/10.1016/j.eswa.2020.114372, https://www.sciencedirect.com/science/article/pii/S0957417420310496

40. Wellhausen, L., Ranftl, R., Hutter, M.: Safe robot navigation via multi-modal anomaly detection. IEEE Robotics Automation Lett. **5**(2), 1326–1333 (2020). https://doi.org/10.1109/LRA.2020.2967706

41. Zhang, J., Saleeby, K., Feldhausen, T., Bi, S., Plotkowski, A., Womble, D.: Self-Supervised Anomaly Detection via Neural Autoregressive Flows with Active Learning (Oct 2021). https://openreview.net/forum?id=LdWEo5mri6

Multi-robot Systems

Hardware Validation of Adaptive Fault Diagnosis in Swarm Robots

James O'Keeffe$^{(\boxtimes)}$ and Alan G. Millard

Department of Computer Science, University of York, York, UK
{james.okeeffe,alan.millard}@york.ac.uk

Abstract. Robot swarms are vulnerable to faults and failures in individual agents. This can be particularly disruptive where an individual has only partially failed and remains in communication with the swarm. There have been a number of approaches to implementing active fault tolerance in swarms, where robots attempt to resolve faults autonomously. Fault diagnosis is an essential component of active fault tolerance that has thus far only been studied in simulation. This paper presents a hardware validation of an immune-inspired adaptive fault diagnosis system for swarm robots. The experiments detailed in this paper show that our system correctly diagnoses faults in the majority of cases when deployed in hardware, and that the same trends observed in software simulation hold true for hardware experiments.

Keywords: Swarm Robotics · Fault Tolerance · Fault Diagnosis

1 Introduction

Robustness – the ability to tolerate faults and failures – is given as an innate property of swarm robotic systems arising from their hardware redundancy [19]. However, partial failures - e.g. faults or failures that does not prevent a robot from attempting to interact with the swarm as if it were normally functioning - in individual robots can be detrimental to overall swarm performance, becoming increasingly severe with larger swarm sizes [22]. An active approach to fault tolerance in robot swarms is therefore necessary in order to enable long-term autonomy [2].

Our earlier work [17] demonstrated and characterised a novel adaptive online fault diagnosis system for swarms of marXbot robots [3] using Autonomous Robots Go Swarming (ARGoS) [18], a physics-based discrete-time swarm robot simulation software. Our approach drastically improved swarm performance when individual robots were subjected to faults during a beacon photo-taxis task - the same scenario used by Winfield and Nembrini [22]. However, it cannot be taken for granted that a system that performs well in software simulation will perform correspondingly well in hardware [9] - particularly in the case of swarms where there are many interacting hardware components.

© The Author(s), under exclusive license to Springer Nature Switzerland AG 2023
F. Iida et al. (Eds.): TAROS 2023, LNAI 14136, pp. 331–342, 2023.
https://doi.org/10.1007/978-3-031-43360-3_27

In this paper we demonstrate and validate our novel immune-inspired approach to fault diagnosis in hardware robot swarms, and compare our results to those previously obtained in simulation. This work represents the first implementation of fault diagnosis for swarm robotic systems in robot hardware.

2   Related Work

Swarm fault tolerance is generally understood to consist of fault detection, diagnosis and recovery (FDDR) [13,17]. Fault detection in robot swarms has been approached in a number of ways - e.g. Christensen et al. use a firefly-inspired approach to communicate the presence of faults to other robots in swarm [6], Millard compares a robots behaviour with an internal simulated model of itself [13], Khadidos et al. compare multiple observations of a robot's state by its neighbours [10], whilst Lee et al. focus instead on determining the most effective metrics by which faults can be detected [12]. Of particular relevance to this work, Tarapore et al. [21] use behavioural feature vectors (BFVs) to encode a robot behaviour as a vector of Boolean features - where 1 and 0 indicate a present or absent behavioural feature, respectively. Fault detection is implemented such that BFVs possessed by a majority of the robots in a local swarm are interpreted as normal, whilst BFVs that are possessed by only a minority of robots are indicative of a fault present in those robots. An advantage of this approach is that BFVs can be used to detect faults without the need for an *a priori* model of normal behaviour.

Daigle et al. [7] and Carrasco et al. [5] diagnose faults in multi-robot systems by formulating *a priori* models of the robot behaviours associated with various faults. One limitation of such approaches is the lack of capability to learn or adapt to dynamic fault signatures, and reliance on detailed – assumed to be unchanging – models of normal functioning robot behaviour. Faults can also be diagnosed through more explicit assessment. Kutzer et al. [11] implement diagnosis such that faulty robots perform diagnostic manoeuvres, consisting of various tests designed to isolate the root-cause of a fault. So far, the only research to specifically address fault diagnosis in robot swarms has been our own work in software simulation [15–17].

3   Immune-Inspired Fault Diagnosis

The vertebrate immune system protects its host from illness and is seemingly able to *remember* solutions, allowing for more a efficient response to a given pathogen on subsequent exposure [4]. Our approach to swarm fault diagnosis attempts to mimic this function, in this case where a fault is analogous to a pathogen [15,17]

Our fault diagnosis system encodes robot behaviours as BFVs, as in the work by Tarapore et al. [21] towards fault detection. When a robot is faulty, its behavioural 'signature' will be encoded in its BFV over time. We use a very simple method of fault-detection whereby a fault is detected when there is a persistent mismatch between a robot's proprioceptive reading of its own control state and its BFV state as observed exteroceptively by a neighbouring robot. This is necessary to ensure that our diagnosis system operates on BFV data that encodes faults. When this occurs, the neighbouring robot that detected the fault declares itself as an assessing robot. The assessing robot then observes the faulty robot as it performs a series of tests, similar to the diagnostic manoeuvres used by Kutzer et al. [11].

Faults are identified with corresponding diagnostic tests. For example, a robot is instructed to turn on each wheel to identify a motor failure. When a robot fails to perform a diagnostic test, the corresponding type of fault is associated with the BFV signature that prompted its detection. Our diagnosis system remembers this information so that, the next time a fault is detected in a robot, the BFV signature can be compared for similarities with the remembered BFV signatures of previous faults. If two BFV signatures are observed to be similar, the new fault can be diagnosed as belonging to the same category without having to run diagnostic tests. The system's representation of each fault type is therefore dynamic and can evolve in real time, making our system adaptive.

This approach to fault diagnosis was demonstrated to improve swarm fault tolerance in software simulation [17]. In the following section we detail our experimental setup for software simulation and hardware experiments, highlighting the differences between the two.

4   Methods

The hardware experiments described in this work were conducted using the Psi-swarm robot [8], a two-wheeled, 10.8 cm diameter swarm robot with on-board proximity sensors. The lack of range-and-bearing (RAB) sensor hardware on the Psi-swarm necessitated the use of range-limited virtual sensing. This was implemented using the ARDebug tool [14], which tracks a fiducial marker mounted on top each Psi-swarm via an overhead camera, allowing distances between each robot to be calculated, along with their respective linear and angular velocities, and transmitted to robots within sensing range of each other.

A swarm of 5 robots performed an obstacle avoidance behaviour in a $2.2 \, \text{m}^2$ enclosed arena (see Fig. 1). We examined a subset of the faults that we previously examined in our simulated experiments [17], as we found that some simulated faults could not be readily implemented in our hardware setup. The faults examined in this paper are power failure, complete sensor failure and complete motor failure.

- **Power failure** (H_1): The robot completely stops moving and is unresponsive to its surroundings.
- **Complete Sensor failure** (H_2): The robot is unable to detect the presence of neighbours or obstacles.
- **Complete Motor failure** (H_3): One of the robot's motors stops and becomes unresponsive to its controller.

In our simulated experiments each robot had some probability of being injected with a fault at each control-step, and an average of 30 faults were encountered by the swarm during one hour of simulated time [17]. We therefore set each hardware experiment to last for as long as it took the system to resolve an equivalent amount of faults. In this case, we consider a hardware swarm of half the size with half the potential fault types we examined in simulation, so 15 faults were injected per experiment. Each robot had a 1% probability of being injected with a random fault at each control-step (i.e. a robot would very likely have been injected with a fault after 100 control-steps had passed), where a maximum of two robots could be faulty at one time. The experiment ended once 15 faults were resolved - i.e. the time duration of each experimental replicate was variable.

Robot behaviour is encoded as BFVs, where the binary vector $BFV(t) = [F_1(t), F_2(t), F_3(t), F_4(t), F_5(t)]$, is defined as the following set of features:

- $F_1(t) = 1$ if $N_R(t) > 0$, otherwise $F_1(t) = 0$
  where $N_R(t)$ is the total number of neighbours in sensing range (approximately 60cm) of the robot at time t.
- $F_2(t) = 1$ if $N_C(t) > 0$, otherwise $F_2(t) = 0$
  where $N_C(t)$ is the total number of neighbours at a distance less than the close proximity threshold (approximately 3 cm), C, from the robot at time t.
- $F_3(t) = 1$ if $|v(t)| > 7.5 \text{ cms}^{-1}$, otherwise $F_3(t) = 0$
  where $|v(t)|$ is the magnitude of linear velocity at time t.
- $F_4(t) = 1$ if $|v(t)| > 1.5 \text{ cms}^{-1}$, otherwise $F_4(t) = 0$
- $F_5(t) = 1$ if $|\theta(t)| > 75° \text{ s}^{-1}$, otherwise $F_5(t) = 0$
  where $|\theta(t)|$ is the magnitude of angular velocity at time t.

These features were chosen with respect to the robot hardware, behaviours and potential fault types. $F_{1-2}^{e,p}$ (where e, p denote exteroceptive and proprioceptive feature estimations, respectively) for each robot are estimated using the ARDebug virtual RAB. Faults will only affect the proprioceptively sensed features. F_{3-5} are estimated proprioceptively by the robot monitoring its own controller output, and exteroceptively by the rate of change in readings from the ARDebug virtual RAB. Features are updated at an approximate frequency of 1.5 Hz. Faults are detected according to Eq. 1.

Faults are detected when discrepancy is observed between proprioceptively estimated features, F_{1-5}^p, and exteroceptively estimated features, F_{1-5}^e, according to Eq. 1

$$\text{Fault detected} = \begin{cases} true \text{ if } \sum_{t=T-W}^{T} d(t) \geq \rho W \text{ for } T > W \\ false \text{ otherwise} \end{cases} \quad (1)$$

Where T indicates the discrete number of control-steps since a robot began observation of a neighbour. The binary value d is set according to Eq. 2, where $d = 0$ if there is agreement between exteroceptively and proprioceptively estimated robot BFVs. A robot will make W discrete observations of its neighbour, once per control-step, before a fault can be detected. t indicates the number of control-steps since the start of an experiment - i.e. the current control-step at any point during an experiment. The value of ρ indicates what proportion of the W observations must prompt the value of d to be equal to 1 in order for a fault to be detected.

$$d(t) = \begin{cases} 0 \text{ if } F_i^p(t) = F_i^e(t) \text{ for } i = 1, .., 5 \\ 1 \text{ otherwise} \end{cases} \quad (2)$$

When a fault is detected in a robot by another member of the swarm, the set of W proprioceptively and exteroceptively estimated BFVs that prompted the fault to be detected are used as the BFV signature for that particular fault. The assessing robot – the robot that detected the fault – then stops and initiates a diagnostic test routine. The tests are arranged as follows, where failing the test indicates the presence of its associated fault:

- **Power Failure (T_1):** The assessing robot pings the faulty robot and instructs it to stop moving.
- **Complete Sensor failure (T_2):** The assessing robot, whilst in sensing range, observes the faulty robot's feature F_1^p, which should return 1.
- **Complete Motor failure (T_3):** The faulty robot is instructed to move forward in a straight line whilst its feature F_5^e, which should return 0 is monitored.

When a fault is diagnosed, the system then carries out a corresponding recovery action[1]:

- **Power Cycle (R_1):** This recovery action resolves power failure (H_1) faults.
- **Sensor Replacement (R_2):** Replacement of robot sensors resolves complete sensor failures (H_2).
- **Motor Replacement (R_3):** Replacement of robot motors resolves complete motor failures (H_3).

The assessing robot then makes another W observations of the faulty robot. If the faulty robot's exteroceptively and proprioceptively estimated BFVs match during this period, the fault is considered to be resolved.

If a robot's fault persists after having attempted diagnostic tests T_{1-3}, the system is considered to have failed to isolate the fault. In this case, the faulty robot is shut down, at which point it becomes an inanimate object in the environment.

When a fault is successfully resolved, the BFV signature for that fault and the respective diagnosis are stored in the assessing robot's memory, which is then shared with other members of the swarm via a simulated *ad-hoc* network

---

[1] Autonomous fault recovery is relevant to swarm fault tolerance, but is beyond the scope of this work. Recovery actions are simulated here for the purpose of validating the fault diagnosis system.

facilitated by ARDebug (psi-swarms do not have peer-peer communication capabilities). When subsequent faults occur, the BFV representations of those faults can be checked for similarity against the BFV representation of previous faults by finding the Pearson correlation coefficient [1] between their BFV signatures (Eq. 3):

$$r = \frac{\sum_m \sum_n (F_{mn} - \overline{F})(F_{0_{mn}} - \overline{F_0})}{\sqrt{(\sum_m \sum_n F_{mn} - \overline{F})^2 (\sum_m \sum_n F_{0_{mn}} - \overline{F_0})^2}} \tag{3}$$

Where r is the correlation coefficient between a current and previous fault signature, F and F_0, respectively, where F and F_0 are two dimensional binary data sets consisting of W observations at discrete consecutive times of a robot's $BFV(t)$. $\overline{F}$ and $\overline{F_0}$ are the mean values of sets F and F_0, respectively, and m and n indicate positional index within the 2D binary data set.

When attempting to diagnose a new fault from memory, the previously stored fault that produces the greatest r-value (Eq. 3) is considered the most likely fault type and the corresponding recovery action is initiated. To be eligible for this process $|r| > s$ is required, where s represents the threshold above which two BFV signatures are considered similar. The BFV signatures for different faults are therefore dynamic, and the system can adapt to changes in the effects of different faults in real time.

The parameter sensitivity analysis performed in [17] suggested that optimum parameter values for experiments in software simulation were $s = 0.56$, $W = 29$ and $\rho = 0.88$. We used these values as our initial experimental parameters.

We examined our system's performance during these experiments on the following criteria:

- P_1: The proportion of faults the system is able to diagnose from memory
- P_2: The proportion of attempts to diagnose a fault from memory that fail or are unrecognised by the system
- P_3: The total number of faulty robots the system is unable to resolve and are shut down during the experiment
- P_4: The average r-value between faults, using Eq. 3, when diagnosing from memory

For each experiment in software simulation, we conducted 10 replicates, from which a median of each metric P_{1-4} was taken.

5   Results and Discussion

The performance (P_{1-4}), of our diagnosis system implemented in robot hardware, where $s = 0.56$, $W = 29$ and $\rho = 0.88$, is displayed in Table 1, as well as the results obtained in software simulation [17] for comparison.

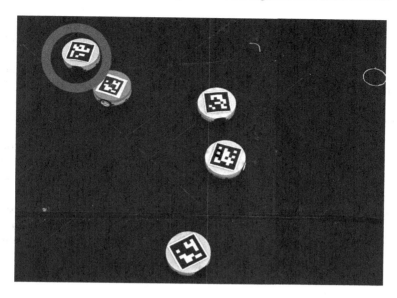

Fig. 1. Five Psi-swarm robots performing obstacle avoidance in an arena. The robot with a green hat suffers from power failure (H_1), whilst its assessing robot in this case is circled in blue. (Color figure online)

Table 1. Comparison of the performance of our diagnosis system in software simulation and hardware experiments. Data for software simulation experiments is taken from [17].

	P_1	P_2	P_3	P_4
Simulation	0.68	0.04	0	0.87
Hardware	0.27	0.41	1.5	0.75

Table 1 shows that, using the parameters that gave optimal performance in software simulation, performance in hardware suffers considerably on all metrics. The primary cause of this is that setting $W = 29$ does not allow enough time for the faulty robot to react, this is especially true for T_3. To illustrate, the assessing robot will instruct the faulty robot to demonstrate its motor function. The faulty robot receives this request over Bluetooth and returns a message to the assessing robot, instructing it to begin its observations. Between the assessing robot making its 1st and 29th observation, the faulty robot is often unable to accelerate quickly enough and maintain velocity for long enough to satisfy the assessing robot that the fault is resolved.

A challenge in implementing this system in hardware arises from the latency between proprioceptively and exteroceptively sensed features updating. When a robot turns to avoid an obstacle or neighbour, its controller state reflects this immediately. However, it takes longer for the ARDebug system to observe and report this change in linear and angular velocity. This was often to the extent that, by the time the exteroceptively sensed features reflect the robot turning, the turn has already occured and the robot is back to moving in a straight line, which is now what is being reported by its internal control state. This means that for short turning periods, which account for the vast majority of occasions in which a robot turns during these experiments, there is consistent discrepancy between proprioceptively and exteroceptively sensed features. As we do not examine instances of false-positive fault detection in this work, this does not pose a significant problem to detecting faults or their BFV signatures. However, when observing a faulty robot post-diagnosis, the greater the proportion of time it spends exhibiting avoidance behaviour, the greater the likelihood that it will be assessed as having its fault persisting, even if the fault has been resolved. The solution to this, given that avoidance is commonly exhibited but generally only for short periods of time, is to observe how increasing the value of W affects the proportion of faults diagnosable from memory. We repeated the same experiments, changing only the value of W. The results are shown in Table 2.

Table 2. Comparison of system performance for varying values of W (where $s = 0.56$ and $\rho = 0.88$).

W	P_1	P_2	P_3	P_4
29	0.27	0.41	1.5	0.75
58	0.5	0.1	0	0.78
87	0.53	0.15	0.5	0.79

The trends observed in Table 2 are very similar to those we observed in simulation. We previously observed a step-like relationship between W and $P_{1,2}$, where values below a threshold ($W < 5$ in simulation) severely reduced performance [17]. Above this threshold, however, there was no observable correlation as W increased. Table 2 demonstrates that increasing the value of W from 29 to 58 drastically improves overall performance on metrics P_{1-3}, after which point performance does not change substantially.

We also observed in [17] that as W increased, P_3 decays exponentially to optimum $P_3 = 0$. However, continuing to increase W eventually causes P_3 to increase proportionately, a trend that is followed by the data in Table 2. Table 2 shows that the best overall performance was obtained for $W = 58$. This is the value we therefore use for all remaining experiments.

We previously observed in software simulation that, the longer an experiment went on, the more frequently the system was able to diagnose faults from memory [15]. This effect can be seen in Fig. 2, and is a result of the system establishing a more comprehensive repertoire of BFV signatures for different types of faults such that it eventually becomes very probable when a fault is encountered that the system will have already diagnosed and resolved the fault under similar circumstances. Table 3 compares performance where the system encounters 15 faults and 25 faults during an experiment.

Table 3. Comparison of system performance where the system encounters 15 and 25 faults in an experiment (where $s = 0.56$, $W = 58$, and $\rho = 0.88$).

Num. Faults	P_1	P_2	P_3	P_4
15	0.5	0.1	0	0.78
25	0.6	0.14	1	0.75

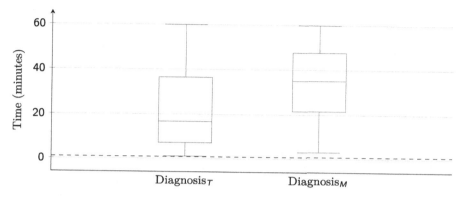

Fig. 2. The times at which a fault is classified using diagnostic tests (Diagnosis$_T$) or from memory (Diagnosis$_M$) in each experiment replicate (1 h total run-time). Dashed line indicates the point at which the first fault is injected in each experiment. [15]

Table 3 shows that our results in hardware follow the trend observed in Fig. 2: As the system is subjected to more faults, it becomes increasingly likely that future instances will be diagnosable from memory.

The last trend we investigated in our hardware experiments is how altering the value of s affects performance, shown in Table 4. The trends between s and system performance observed in Table 4 are very similar to those we observed in our software simulations. We observed in [17] that P_1 is largely unresponsive to s until a critical point, presumed to be the average r-value between faults, after which P_1 begins to decline with increasing s. The data in Table 4 generally fits this trend, but suggests that the critical point for s is lower in hardware, which is supported by the lower value of P_4 we observe. We also observed in software simulation that P_2 decreases for increasing values of s, which can also be observed in Table 4.

We were able to achieve $P_1 = 0.63$ in our hardware experiments, comparable to the value we obtained in software simulation ($P_1 = 0.68$). A reduction in performance is to be expected when implementing a system in hardware [9]. That we were able to achieve 93% performance on what we consider the most fundamental performance metric, combined with the fact we observed the same general trends in hardware experiments as we did in software, is evidence of our system's feasibility for deployment in real-world scenarios, and that the results

Table 4. Comparison of system performance for varying values of s (where $W = 58$ and $\rho = 0.88$).

s	P_1	P_2	P_3	P_4
0.28	0.6	0.34	1	0.72
0.42	0.63	0.19	0	0.72
0.56	0.5	0.1	0	0.78

obtained in software simulation should translate proportionately into real-world systems.

6   Conclusion

This work has validated our swarm fault diagnosis approach in robot hardware, and demonstrated that our system displayed similar trends in hardware and software simulation. Although performance was reduced in hardware, our system was able to diagnose faults from memory in the majority of cases ($P_1 = 0.63$) when set with appropriate parameter values, and was also able to maintain a comparatively low rate of misclassification ($P_2 = 0.19$ for the same parameter values, although by adjusting these we were able to get this as low as $P_2 = 0.1$). There were very few instances in which our system was unable to diagnose a fault (P_3).

Although we believe the results discussed in this work demonstrate our system's viability as a solution to improving fault tolerance in hardware robot swarms, they also highlight some of the present limitations. Most prominent of these is our system's dependence on reliable fault detection. When conducting the work described in this paper, we took the view that false-positives were a problem within the realm of fault detection, and that including them in this study would not meaningfully test our fault diagnosis system beyond what we have presented. Whilst we found no evidence to suggest that false-positive fault detection would impact the performance of our diagnostic mechanism positively or negatively, the fact that low values of W result in such degradation in performance is indicative that, without a reliable means of assessing the presence or absence of faults and failures autonomously, our system cannot be expected to demonstrate learning and memory functionality as we would like. Our results suggest that it is not practical to separate the process of diagnosis from detection, as we have demonstrated that the two processes are intrinsically linked.

In future work we will seek to integrate our method of fault diagnosis with a mature approach to fault detection. The CRM approach demonstrated by Tarapore et al. [20], or another BFV-based alternative, is an obvious candidate for this integration. We predict that improved fault detection mechanisms would allow our system to achieve competitive performance with our simulated experiments when implemented in hardware.

References

1. Benesty, J., Chen, J., Huang, Y., Cohen, I.: Pearson correlation coefficient. In: Noise Reduction in Speech Processing. Springer Topics in Signal Processing, vol. 2, pp. 1–4. Springer, Heidelberg (2009). https://doi.org/10.1007/978-3-642-00296-0_5

2. Bjerknes, J.D., Winfield, A.F.T.: On fault tolerance and scalability of swarm robotic systems. In: Martinoli, A., et al. (eds.) Distributed Autonomous Robotic Systems. Springer Tracts in Advanced Robotics, vol. 83, pp. 431–444. Springer, Heidelberg (2013). https://doi.org/10.1007/978-3-642-32723-0_31

3. Bonani, M., et al.: The marXbot, a miniature mobile robot opening new perspectives for the collective-robotic research. In: IEEE/RSJ International Conference on Intelligent Robots and Systems (IROS), pp. 4187–4193 (2010)

4. Capra, J.D., Janeway, C.A., Travers, P., Walport, M.: Inmunobiology: The Inmune System in Health and Disease. Garland Publishing (1999)

5. Carrasco, R.A., Núñez, F., Cipriano, A.: Fault detection and isolation in cooperative mobile robots using multilayer architecture and dynamic observers. Robotica **29**(4), 555–562 (2011)

6. Christensen, A.L., O'Grady, R., Dorigo, M.: From fireflies to fault-tolerant swarms of robots. IEEE Trans. Evol. Comput. **13**(4), 754–766 (2009)

7. Daigle, M.J., Koutsoukos, X.D., Biswas, G.: Distributed diagnosis in formations of mobile robots. IEEE Trans. Rob. **23**(2), 353–369 (2007)

8. Hilder, J., Horsfield, A., Millard, A.G., Timmis, J.: The Psi swarm: a low-cost robotics platform and its use in an education setting. In: Alboul, L., Damian, D., Aitken, J.M.M. (eds.) TAROS 2016. LNCS (LNAI), vol. 9716, pp. 158–164. Springer, Cham (2016). https://doi.org/10.1007/978-3-319-40379-3_16

9. Jakobi, N., Husbands, P., Harvey, I.: Noise and the reality gap: the use of simulation in evolutionary robotics. In: Morán, F., Moreno, A., Merelo, J.J., Chacón, P. (eds.) ECAL 1995. LNCS, vol. 929, pp. 704–720. Springer, Heidelberg (1995). https://doi.org/10.1007/3-540-59496-5_337

10. Khadidos, A., Crowder, R.M., Chappell, P.H.: Exogenous fault detection and recovery for swarm robotics. IFAC-PapersOnLine **48**(3), 2405–2410 (2015)

11. Kutzer, M.D.M., Armand, M., Scheid, D.H., Lin, E., Chirikjian, G.S.: Toward cooperative team-diagnosis in multi-robot systems. Int. J. Robot. Res. **27**(9), 1069–1090 (2008)

12. Lee, S., Milner, E., Hauert, S.: A data-driven method for metric extraction to detect faults in robot swarms. IEEE Robot. Autom. Lett. **7**(4), 10746–10753 (2022)

13. Millard, A.G.: Exogenous Fault Detection in Swarm Robotic Systems. Ph.D. thesis, University of York (2016)

14. Millard, A.G., et al.: ARDebug: an augmented reality tool for analysing and debugging swarm robotic systems. Front. Robot. AI **5**, 87 (2018)

15. O'Keeffe, J., Tarapore, D., Millard, A.G., Timmis, J.: Fault diagnosis in robot swarms: an adaptive online behaviour characterisation approach. In: 2017 IEEE Symposium Series on Computational Intelligence (SSCI), pp. 1–8. IEEE (2017)

16. O'Keeffe, J., Tarapore, D., Millard, A.G., Timmis, J.: Towards fault diagnosis in robot swarms: an online behaviour characterisation approach. In: Gao, Y., Fallah, S., Jin, Y., Lekakou, C. (eds.) TAROS 2017. LNCS (LNAI), vol. 10454, pp. 393–407. Springer, Cham (2017). https://doi.org/10.1007/978-3-319-64107-2_31

17. O'Keeffe, J., Tarapore, D., Millard, A.G., Timmis, J.: Adaptive online fault diagnosis in autonomous robot swarms. Front. Robot. AI **5**, 131 (2018)

18. Pinciroli, C., et al.: ARGoS: a modular, multi-engine simulator for heterogeneous swarm robotics. In: 2011 IEEE/RSJ International Conference on Intelligent Robots and Systems (IROS), pp. 5027–5034 (2011)
19. Şahin, E.: Swarm robotics: from sources of inspiration to domains of application. In: Şahin, E., Spears, W.M. (eds.) SR 2004. LNCS, vol. 3342, pp. 10–20. Springer, Heidelberg (2005). https://doi.org/10.1007/978-3-540-30552-1_2
20. Tarapore, D., Christensen, A.L., Timmis, J.: Generic, scalable and decentralized fault detection for robot swarms. PLoS ONE **12**(8), e0182058 (2017). https://doi.org/10.1371/journal.pone.0182058
21. Tarapore, D., Timmis, J., Christensen, A.L.: Fault detection in a swarm of physical robots based on behavioral outlier detection. IEEE Trans. Rob. **35**(6), 1516–1522 (2019)
22. AFT Winfield and Julien Nembrini: Safety in numbers: fault-tolerance in robot swarms. Int. J. Model. Ident. Control **1**, 30–37 (2006)

Mobile Robots for Collaborative Manipulation over Uneven Ground Using Decentralised Impedance Control

Myles Flanagan$^{(\boxtimes)}$ ⓘ, Niels Lohse ⓘ, and Pedro Ferreira ⓘ

Wolfson School of Robotics, Intelligent Automation, Loughborough University, Loughborough, UK
{m.flanagan,N.Lohse,p.ferreira}@lboro.ac.uk

Abstract. A novel approach to model collaborative mobile robots carrying a shared payload over uneven ground is proposed. This approach considers the manipulators as a 'Passive Suspension' system, utilizing an impedance control law. Detailed modelling and experimental results are presented to support the proposed method. The experiments involve a team of robots traversing various floor disturbances commonly found in industry, which can lead to undesired forces on the shared object. The focus of the results is on how the forces are distributed among the robots in the team. The experiments show that implementing impedance control enables the team to distribute the forces more effectively, reducing stress on the object. However, the performance of the controllers varies across different disturbances due to the passive suspension method not being optimized for any specific use case, which is a limitation discussed in this paper.

Keywords: Collaborative · Mobile Robots · AMR · Impedance Control · Shared Payload

1 Introduction

Industry is forever moving towards higher levels of automation and autonomy. Furthermore, areas of manufacturing are shifting away from high volume standardised products to more personalised and customised products [1]. Whilst current systems are designed for traditional high volume standardised products, they are not capable of the flexibility and adaptability required for the uncertain production volumes, variant updates and shorter production cycles which are associated with personalised and customised products [2,3]. Generally, typical material and product handling systems work with standardised fixtures and jig. With the increase of bespoke products these fixtures and jigs may no longer be suitable. Therefore, another solution is needed which offers a higher degree of flexibility and adaptability for transporting goods.

By mounting manipulators on Autonomous Mobile Robots (AMRs), a high degree of flexibility in grasping objects can be achieved, facilitating handling of various bespoke products and transporting them to desired locations. However, individual

This work was supported in part by EPSRC for the IRaaS project, funding code [EP/V050966/1].

F. Iida et al. (Eds.): TAROS 2023, LNAI 14136, pp. 343–355, 2023.
https://doi.org/10.1007/978-3-031-43360-3_28

manipulators may have limited payload capacity, necessitating the formation of teams of multiple AMRs with smaller manipulators. This distribution of weight enables the manipulation of otherwise impossible objects. Additionally, this approach enhances manufacturers' scheduling flexibility, as AMRs can be assigned to different tasks around the factory as needed.

The main challenge of this approach is controlling and coordinating the AMRs as a whole system. Instead of focusing solely on individual manipulator controllers [4–11], a holistic consideration of the system is vital, as combining manipulators can lead to unpredictable reactions and emergent behaviors. This complexity makes it difficult to model the dynamics of collaborative manipulation effectively, despite existing research [12] across multiple fields for individual manipulation tasks.

Previous research on Collaborative Mobile Transportation Systems (CMTS) has primarily focused on controlling manipulators through position or force control, overlooking the dynamics of the mobile platforms. The assumption of perfectly flat flooring ignores the reality of floor disturbances commonly encountered in workplaces like warehouses and factories. To accurately model CMTS for practical use in industry, the effects of uneven flooring must be considered.

Industrial environments, such as factories and warehouses, present stochastic and unpredictable conditions for AMRs due to the variable nature of flooring. Unevenness and disturbances like potholes and anti-slip flooring pose challenges for current CMTS controllers that haven't accounted for these factors.

The challenge of using multiple AMRs to transport an object lies in their individual behaviour as separate systems. When a single AMR is rigidly connected to an object and encounters a floor bump, (Fig. 1a), the object remains unaffected since any platform pose change is replicated in the object. However, when two AMRs hold the object, (Fig. 1b), kinematic constraints apply stress at both grasping points, potentially causing the object to break under excessive stress from the disturbance. Moreover, most AMRs lack suspension, making it difficult to keep the object level. For semi-rigid objects or those with a shifting Centre of Mass (CoM), this could lead to the AMR exceeding its weight capacity and causing damage to both the object and the AMR.

When considering positional displacement due to floor disturbances there is already a wealth of literature and knowledge to address this issue within another field of engineering, **Automotive engineering**. The automotive industry has developed several models which consider floor disturbances (known as road profile in the automotive field), and its effect on the vehicles. One such model is a full vehicle model [13]. It is a model which has a wealth of literature and has been extensively used throughout both academia and industry.

In this paper a novel approach to modelling CMTS is proposed by adapting and building upon the full vehicle model that exists within the automotive industry. By modelling each manipulator as a 'suspension' system the system model becomes a stacked version of the full vehicle model. The model presented in this paper considers disturbances in the floor and the impact it has on the forces and position of the shared object. The work in this paper takes a proof of concept approach and experiments are performed to identify if this approach is a suitable method of modelling CMTS.

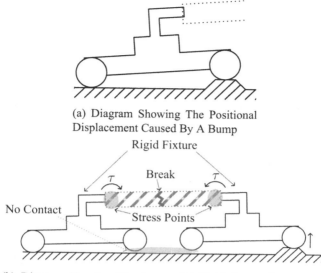

(a) Diagram Showing The Positional Displacement Caused By A Bump

(b) Diagram Showing The Impact Of Rigid Connections When Travelling Over A Bump

Fig. 1. Diagrams Showing The Difference Between A Single AMR & Two AMRs Travelling Over A Bump

The remainder of this paper is arranged as follows; Sect. 2 states the approach to modelling the manipulator as a suspension system; Sect. 3 details the dynamics of the mobile platform with the integrated manipulator and the object dynamics; Sect. 4 explains the experimental design used in the paper; Sect. 5 states the results of the experiments and Sect. 6 concludes the findings of this paper and states potential future work.

2 Modelling the Manipulator as a Suspension System

To model the manipulators as a 'suspension' system, a common impedance control law is used. The compliant behaviour of the i_{th} manipulator in task space is given by:

$$M_i(\ddot{\chi}^{des} - \ddot{\chi}^{act}) + D_i(\dot{\chi}^{des} - \dot{\chi}^{act}) + K_i(\chi^{des} - \chi^{act}) = h_i \tag{1}$$

Were $M, D, K \in \mathbb{R}^{6\times6}$ represent the apparent inertia, damping and stiffness, and are represented through diagonal matrices. $\chi \in \mathbb{R}^{6\times1}$ is a 6 element vector representing the translational and rotational elements of the end-effector. *des* & *act* represent the desired and actual pose of the end-effector. $h \in \mathbb{R}^{6\times1}$ represents the wrench being applied at the end-effector, which is comprised of a two 3 element vectors, force and torque, in the form $[F, \tau] = [F_x, F_y, F_z, \tau_x, \tau_y, \tau_z]$

Remark 1. Equation 1 only considers displacement at the end-effector. It does not consider movement at the manipulator base. Therefore, this would mimic a passive suspension system.

In order to implement an active suspension system the displacement at the manipulator base would need to be considered. This can be achieved by implementing the following:

$$\chi^{des} = \overrightarrow{Target} - \overrightarrow{mb} \tag{2}$$

Where $\overrightarrow{Target} \in \mathbb{R}^{6 \times 1}$ is the target pose the end-effector aims to reach. $\overrightarrow{mb} \in \mathbb{R}^{6 \times 1}$ is the positional displacement of the manipulator base, which is dependant on the mobile platform displacement due to a rigid connection.

3   CMTS Modelling

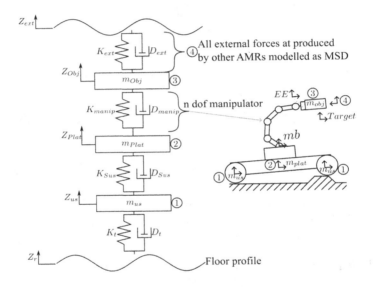

Fig. 2. Simplified 4 D.O.F Quarter Vehicle Model For An AMR In A CMTS

To begin, we simplify the entire CMTS model, taking inspiration from the quarter vehicle model [13] and consider each AMR as a 4 Degree of Freedom (DoF) Mass Spring Damper (MSD) system, (Fig. 2). Simplifying the model in this way helps visualise the movements and forces occurring at each stage, whilst also serving as a foundation to describe the non-simplified version of the model. Figure 2 can be described using the following equations:

$$
\begin{aligned}
m_{us}\ddot{Z}_{us} = &-K_t(Z_{us} - Z_r) - D_t(\dot{Z}_{us} - \dot{Z}_r) \\
&- K_{sus}(Z_{plat} - Z_{us}) - D_{sus}(\dot{Z}_{plat} - \dot{Z}_{us})
\end{aligned} \tag{3}
$$

$$m_{plat}\ddot{Z}_{plat} = -K_{sus}(Z_{plat} - Z_{us}) - D_{sus}(\dot{Z}_{plat} - \dot{Z}_{us})$$
$$- K_{manip}(Z_{obj} - Z_{plat}) - D_{manip}(\dot{Z}_{obj} - \dot{Z}_{plat}) \tag{4}$$

$$m_{obj}\ddot{Z}_{obj} = -K_{manip}(Z_{obj} - Z_{plat}) - D_{manip}(\dot{Z}_{obj} - \dot{Z}_{plat})$$
$$- K_{ext}(Z_{ext} - Z_{obj}) - D_{ext}(\dot{Z}_{ext} - \dot{Z}_{obj}) \tag{5}$$

where the subscripts $us, plat$ & obj represent the unsprung mass, platform and object respectively. Subscripts $t, sus, manip$ & ext represent the tyre, suspension, manipulator and external respectively. m represents the mass. $Z_r, Z_{us}, Z_{plat}, Z_{obj}$ are the floor profile, unsprung mass, platform and object displacements in the Z direction, respectively. K & D are the spring stiffness and damping coefficient respectively.

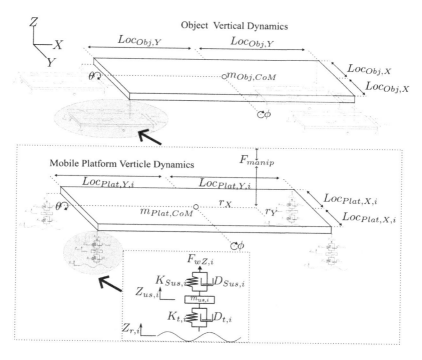

Fig. 3. Full CMTS Vertical Dynamic Model, With 4 AMRs

When considering the entire system, an object and n AMRs, it is possible to represent each element using the full vehicle model, resulting in a tiered vehicle model, (Fig. 3). For this paper, the system has four AMRs and each AMR is considered a 20 D.O.F system, 6 D.O.F for the manipulator, 6 D.O.F for the platform move in and about each axis, 4 D.O.F for each of the unsprung masses and 4 D.O.F for the spin of each wheel. The object is considered a 6 D.O.F system as it can move in and about each axis. Therefore, with a team of four AMRs the system has 86 D.O.F. The full vehicle model is typically split into a vertical and horizontal model, we continue this trend in this paper. By expanding Eqs. 3–5, the horizontal, vertical and dynamic model for the mobile platform integrated with the manipulator as a 6 D.O.F suspension system, gives the following set of equations:

$$F_{wZ,i} = -K_{t,i}(Z_{us,i} - Z_{r,i}) - D_{t,i}(\dot{Z}_{us,i} - \dot{Z}_{r,i}) \\ - K_{sus,i}(Z_{plat,i} - Z_{us,i}) - D_{sus,i}(\dot{Z}_{plat,i} - \dot{Z}_{us,i})$$

(6)

$$m_{plat}\ddot{Z}_{plat} = \sum_{i=0}^{n=nw} F_{wZ,i} + F_{manip,Z}$$

(7)

$$I_{Plat,X}\ddot{\theta} = \sum_{i=0}^{n=nw} (\pm F_{wZ,i} Loc_{Plat,Y,i}) + F_{manip,Z} r_Y$$

(8)

$$I_{Plat,Y}\ddot{\phi} = \sum_{i=0}^{n=nw} (\pm F_{wZ,i} Loc_{Plat,X,i}) + F_{manip,Z} r_X$$

(9)

$$F_{manip} = M_i(\ddot{\chi}^{des} - \ddot{\chi}^{act}) + D_i(\dot{\chi}^{des} - \dot{\chi}^{act}) + K_i(\chi^{des} - \dot{\chi}^{act})$$

(10)

$$F_{wX,i} = (F_{X,i} * \sin \delta_i) - F_{fric,X,i}$$

(11)

$$F_{wY,i} = (F_{Y,i} * \cos \delta_i) - F_{fric,Y,i}$$

(12)

$$m_{plat}\ddot{X}_{plat} = \sum_{i=0}^{n=nw} F_{wX,i}$$

(13)

$$m_{plat}\ddot{Y}_{plat} = \sum_{i=0}^{n=nw} F_{wY,i}$$

(14)

$$I_{Plat,Z}\ddot{\psi} = \sum_{i=0}^{n=nw} (\pm F_{wY,i} Loc_{Plat,X,i})$$

(15)

The vertical and horizontal dynamics of the object can then be described by combining n AMR dynamics equations where $n \in 1,2,\dots nr$, using the following set of equations:

$$m_{obj}\ddot{X}_{obj} = \sum_{i=0}^{n=nr} F_{manip,X,i}$$

(16)

$$m_{obj}\ddot{Y}_{obj} = \sum_{i=0}^{n=nr} F_{manip,Y,i}$$

(17)

$$m_{obj}\ddot{Z}_{obj} = \sum_{i=0}^{n=nr} F_{manip,Z,i}$$

(18)

$$I_{Obj,X}\ddot{\theta} = \sum_{i=0}^{n=nr} (\pm F_{manip,Z,i} Loc_{Obj,Y,i})$$

(19)

$$I_{Obj,Y}\ddot{\phi} = \sum_{i=0}^{n=nr} (\pm F_{manip,Z,i} Loc_{Obj,X,i})$$

(20)

$$I_{Obj,Z}\ddot{\psi} = \sum_{i=0}^{n=nr} (\pm F_{manip,Y,i} Loc_{Obj,X,i})$$

(21)

Were the subscript i represents the i_{th} wheel were $i \in 1, 2, \ldots n$. nw is the total number of wheels on the mobile platform. $F_{wZ,i}$ represents the force produced in the Z direction at the i_{th} wheel. $F_{manip,Z}$ represents the manipulator dynamics using the impedance control law. $r_{X/Y}$ represent the distance from the platforms centre of gravity to the manipulator base in the X and Y direction respectively. $I_{Plat,X/Y}$ represents the platforms inertia tensor about the X and Y direction respectively. $Loc_{Plat,X/Y}$ represents the location of the i_{th} wheel in the X/Y direction relative to the platforms centre. Sign is dictated by direction of rotation and location of the i_{th} wheel relative to the platforms centre. The subscript $fric$ represent the friction force acting at the i_{th} wheel. $F_{X/Y}$ represent the forces produced by the i_{th} wheel in the X/Y direction. δ is the angle the wheel has turn from its origin. Were nr is the number of AMRs transporting the object. $nr \in 1, 2, \ldots n$. $Loc_{Obj,X/Y}$ represents the location of the i_{th} AMR in the X/Y direction relative to the objects centre. Sign is dictated by direction of rotation and location of the i_{th} AMR relative to the objects centre.

Using this approach to modelling AMRs enables the dynamics of the end-effector to be calculated whilst also considering the effects of positional displacement due to disturbances in the floor and considering the effects of positional displacement at the object. By modelling the AMRs in this manner it opens up a wealth of knowledge that is used within academia and industry that is being applied in the automotive industry. This allows for several well tested suspension models, (Passive suspension, Semi-active suspension and Active suspension [14]), and controllers to be applied to the manipulator.

4 Experimental Design

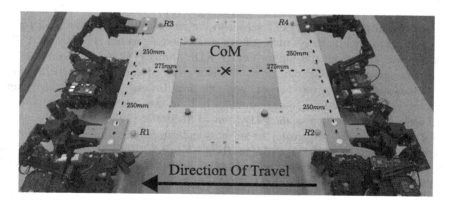

Fig. 4. Team Of Mobile Robots, Gripper Location w.r.t CoM Stated & Direction Of Travel

The aim of the experiments were to identify if the approach of modelling the manipulators as suspension systems using the impedance control law stated in Sect. 2, gives a better force distribution amongst the team, thus reducing the stress that the shared object is under. Experiments were conducted using a team of four homogenous AMRs, Fig. 4. Each AMR consisted of a turtlebot3 conveyor [15] for the platform and a OPENMANIPULATOR-X [16] for the manipulator. The object used was an MDF board with uniform mass distribution, with a mass of 1.55 Kg and dimensions $600 \times 600 \times 9$ mm. Five disturbances were used within the experiments. These were; **Flat**; **Cable Cover**; **Gap**; **Pitting** and a combination of the previous four referred to as **All**. Each of the disturbances was chosen to emulate a disturbance that is common place within an industrial setting. The parameters of the disturbances can be seen in Table 1. For each disturbance the CMTS had to travel from a starting pose to a goal pose. Five iterations of each experiment was conducted to account for variations in the way the AMRs contacted the disturbance. Due to drift in the mobile platforms, it cannot be guaranteed that the wheels of the platforms will contact the disturbance in the exact same manner each run. To limit the impact of drift, a simple bang bang controller was used to adjust the speed of the platforms and ensure that they stay in the same position relative to the objects centre during the experiment. The desired speed of the platforms was 0.1 m/s and the bang bang controller would adjust the speed by ± 0.025 m/s. An external camera system (Vicon) was used to measure the platforms positions relative to the objects centre, which served as the input to the bang bang controller.

To identify if using the manipulators as suspension provides better force distribution, a benchmark (BM) is needed. The BM was collected using the exact same experiments, but instead of using an impedance controller the manipulators were set to the target pose and unable to move, creating a rigid system without suspension. The results of the experiments are compared to a target force value, which is considered to be an ideal outcome. The target value was set to the force due to gravity acting on the object, divided by the number of AMRs in the team, $\therefore F_Z = (1.55 \text{ Kg} * -9.81 \text{ m/s})/4 \approx -3.8$ N, for the Z direction. In the experiments only the forces in the Z direction are considered. Whilst forces in the X & Y direction and torques will have an impact on the stress being placed onto the object, the focus is on the Z forces as they are thought to be more indicative. Due to the specific weight capacity of the OPENMANIPULATOR-X it was unrealistic to attach a F/T sensor to the end-effector to measure the forces being applied to the object. As such, a force estimation algorithm [17] was used. The algorithm was implemented using the Orocos KDL library [18] and its solvers. As the experiments uses small research robots and is a proof of concept idea, the absolute force values are not the focus when analysing the data. Instead the general patterns and trends are examined, and the forces estimator had the same trends and patterns when tested against a force estimator, the FTD-Mini-45 SI-580-20 [19].

For the manipulator suspension the stiffness and damping coefficients were chosen such that $K = Diag[25, 0, 25, 0, 0, 0]$ & $D = Diag[2.5, 0, 2.5, 0, 0, 0]$. Four of the elements were set to 0 due to the OMX only being 4 D.O.F. Furthermore, it is further constrained when working in the system limiting its D.O.F to 2, hence only X & Z having values. The stiffness and damping co-efficient's were chosen based on results gathered in simulation using a step and sine function to test the controllers performance. The impedance controller values were not optimised for any of the disturbances. As the manipulators have been implemented as a passive suspension system for this research it was seen as unrealistic to tune and optimise the controller for each specific use case.

Remark 2. It must be noted that the floor the experiments were conducted on was not level. There is an incline in both the X and Y direction. There was a ≈ 21 mm increase in the X direction and a ≈ 6 mm increase in the Y, resulting in a $\approx 4°$ & $\approx 0.07°$ incline, for X & Y respectively. This means that end-effectors of each manipulator will be at different heights, causing the forces to vary between AMRs. Due to this difference in height, the 'Flat' experiment can be considered as a smooth ramp.

Table 1. Disturbance Parameters

Flat	Workspace - $5 \times 4m$	
Cable Cover (CC)	$\approx 50mm$ Width, $\approx 25mm$ Height	
Gap	$49mm$ Wide, $6mm$ Deep	
Pitting (Pit)	Randomly cut grooves of varying depths, $8mm$ thick, depth ranging from $0mm$ - $2mm$	Random
All	Combination of all disturbances	

5   Results

The results of the experiments are summarised in Table 2. They show the range and minimum and maximum Average (AVG) forces and AVG Standard Deviation (STD) for each experiment across all four AMRs. The results only consider the forces measured when the wheels of the AMRs contact the disturbances with a $\pm 0.25\,$s tolerance, (Fig. 6). Due to the different parameters of each disturbance the time period that the

Table 2. Experimental Results, Minimum, Maximum & Range for the AVG Forces and AVG STD W.R.T Target Value

		AVG Forces			AVG STD		
		Min	Max	Range	Min	Max	Range
Flat	BM	−1	0.35	1.35	0.12	0.14	0.02
	Cont	−0.22	0.29	0.51	0.05	0.14	0.09
CC	BM	−1.28	0.77	2.05	0.14	0.33	0.21
	Cont	−0.24	0.27	0.51	0.05	0.20	0.18
Gap	BM	−0.84	0.28	1.12	0.04	0.19	0.16
	Cont	−0.35	0.33	0.67	0.03	0.13	0.12
Pit	BM	−0.60	0.19	0.78	0.02	0.12	0.11
	Cont	−0.26	0.39	0.65	0.02	0.07	0.05
All	BM	−0.43	0.22	0.65	0.09	0.21	0.14
	Cont	−0.81	−0.09	0.71	0.08	0.17	0.09

forces are recorded at vary between experiments. Additionally, the amount the AMRs contact the disturbances changes as well. The AMRs contact each disturbance a different amount, **Flat** = 1; **Cable Cover** = 4; **Gap** = 4; **Pitting** = 2 and **All** = 10. The focus of the results will be on the range value for both the AVG forces and STD. The range provides good insight into the variation of forces at each contact and for each individual AMR. The target outcome for the controller is that the range for both the forces and STD is smaller then the BM, which would suggest that the forces are more evenly distributed across the team and that there is less variation or spikes at the point of contact. Figure 5, shows the CableCover AVG forces across the 5 iterations for each contact with the disturbance.

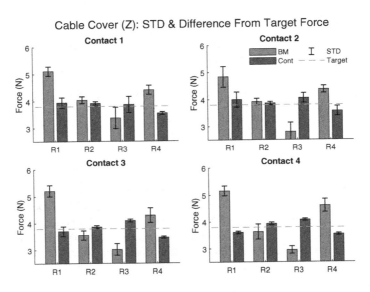

Fig. 5. Robot Forces With STD & Difference From Target Value

From the results in Table 2 we see a large reduction in AVG force range when examining the 'Flat', 'CableCover' and 'Gap' experiments with 'Gap' having the smallest reduction of ≈40% and the 'CableCover' experiment having a ≈75% reduction in range. Furthermore, the minimum and maximum AVG forces are closer to 0 when compared to the BM. Additionally, for 'Gap' and 'CableCover' the STD range also reduces. This shows that each AMR is attempting to reach the target value providing a better distribution of forces, whilst having less variation in forces implying there was less spikes in force at the point of contact. The STD for 'Flat' was higher then the BM, however, the variation in force is so small that minimal impact would be made to the forces being applied to the object across the AMRs.

'Pitting' has a very small reduction in the range which suggests that there was not much improvement in force distribution. However, when examining the minimum and maximum values it can be seen that the values are more evenly distributed around the target value when compared to the BM which had both a lower minimum and maximum value. The AVG STD range was smaller for the controller which shows that even though the range was similar that the amount of variation in the forces was smaller when using the controller which suggests the forces were more consistent.

The 'All' experiment is the only one to have a larger range then the BM and to have the minimum and maximum values be skewed to a single side of the target value. In each iteration of this experiment, R2 consistently measured much higher forces then the other AMRs. This behaviour is assumed to be caused by the AMRs attempting to compensate for multiple different disturbances at any one time causing R2 to become unstable and work against the team. It must be noted that the other AMRs in the team are actively attempting to distribute the forces.

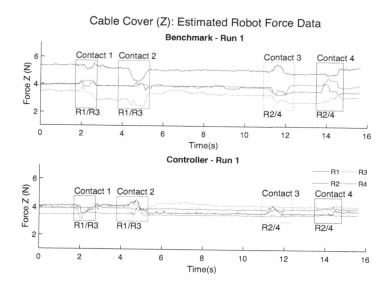

Fig. 6. Force Data For Robots Highlighting Contact Points

6 Conclusion and Future Work

This paper presents a novel approach to modelling CMTS by applying the full vehicle model used in vehicle control to a team of AMRs. The experimental results show that implementing an impedance control law on manipulators to act as suspension improves the distribution of forces in the Z direction in most cases. For scenarios with single or consistent disturbances, such as 'CableCover'/'Gap' and the ramp in the 'Flat' experiment, the controller effectively distributes forces, reducing stress on the object at each AMR's grasping points.

The controller also performs well in cases with a high frequency of small disturbances, like 'Pitting,' though the improvement is minimal compared to other disturbances. The main challenge arises when multiple disturbances are present simultaneously, as seen in the 'All' case. In such situations, a single AMR may counteract the others, possibly due to different behaviour caused by the combined disturbances.

In conclusion, implementing impedance control has achieved the desired outcome of better force distribution. However, the passive nature of the 'Suspension' system used in CMTS means it is not optimised for specific cases but tuned for general performance. Future work will explore an improved version of the controller incorporating semi-active suspension to adapt to varying environments. Additionally, the study will investigate the controller's performance when carrying objects with non-uniform mass distribution, as the current use of a simple square object with uniform mass distribution may not reflect real-world scenarios accurately.

References

1. Hu, S.J.: Evolving paradigms of manufacturing: from mass production to mass customization and personalization. Procedia CIRP **7**, 3–8 (2013)
2. Tan, J.T.C., Duan, F., Zhang, Y., Watanabe, K., Kato, R., Arai, T.: Human-robot collaboration in cellular manufacturing: design and development. In: 2009 IEEE/RSJ International Conference on Intelligent Robots and Systems, IROS 2009, pp. 29–34, December 2009
3. Hagele, M., Schaff, W., Helms, E.: Robot assistants at manual workplaces: effective co-operation and safety aspects (2002)
4. Al-Shuka, H.F.N., Leonhardt, S., Zhu, W.-H., Song, R., Ding, C., Li, Y.: Active impedance control of bioinspired motion robotic manipulators: an overview. Appl. Bionics Biomech. **1–19**, 2018 (2018)
5. Salehi, M., Vossoughi, G.: Impedance control of flexible base mobile manipulator using singular perturbation method and sliding mode control law. Int. J. Control Autom. Syst. **6**, 677–688 (2008)
6. Salehi, M., Vossoughi, G.R.: High-precision impedance control method for flexible base moving manipulators. Adv. Robot. **23**, 65–87 (2009)
7. Dietrich, A., Bussmann, K., Petit, F.P., Ott, C., Lohmann, B., Albu-Schäffer, A.: Whole-body impedance control of wheeled mobile manipulators: stability analysis and experiments on the humanoid robot rollin' justin. Auton. Robot. **40**, 505–517 (2016)
8. Grant, P.W., Jobling, C.P., Ko, Y.W.: A comparison of rule-based and algebraic approaches to the computer-aided manipulation of linear dynamic system models (1988)
9. Ding, F., Huang, J., Wang, Y., Mao, L.: Vibration damping in manipulation of deformable linear objects using sliding mode control. In: Proceedings of the 31st Chinese Control Conference (2012)
10. Yin, Y., Hosoe, S.: MLD modeling and optimal control of hand manipulation. In: 2005 IEEE/RSJ International Conference on Intelligent Robots and Systems, IROS, pp. 838–843 (2005)
11. Sun, Y., Fang, F., Qian, K., Gan, Y., Zhou, B.: Active compliance force control based on an iterative learning strategy for multi-task manipulation of robots. In: Chinese Control Conference, CCC, vol. 2022, pp. 3786–3791 (2022)
12. Erhart, S., Hirche, S.: Model and analysis of the interaction dynamics in cooperative manipulation tasks. IEEE Trans. Rob. **32**, 672–683 (2016)

13. Desai, R., Guha, A., Seshu, P.: A comparison of quarter, half and full car models for predicting vibration attenuation of an occupant in a vehicle. J. Vibr. Eng. Technol. **9**, 983–1001 (2021)

14. Lajqi, S., Pehan, S.: Designs and optimizations of active and semi-active non-linear suspension systems for a terrain vehicle. Strojniški vestnik - J. Mech. Eng. **58**, 732–743 (2012)

15. ROBOTIS: Turtlebot3 e_manual. https://emanual.robotis.com/docs/en/platform/turtlebot3/features

16. ROBOTIS: Openmanipulator-x e_manual. https://emanual.robotis.com/docs/en/platform/openmanipulator_x/specification/

17. Orocos: Force Estimation Algorithm. https://github.com/orocos/orocos_kinematics_dynamics/issues/304

18. Orocos: KDL wiki — The Orocos Project. https://www.orocos.org/kdl.html

19. FTD-Mini-45 SI-580-20. https://schunk.com/br_en/gripping-systems/product/30852-ftd-mini-45-si-580-20/

Multi-agent Collaborative Target Search Based on Curiosity Intrinsic Motivation

Xiaoping Zhang[1,2], Yuanpeng Zheng[1(✉)], Li Wang[1], and Fumiya Iida[2]

[1] School of Electrical and Control Engineering, North China University of Technology, Beijing 100144, China
zyp1416@163.com
[2] Department of Engineering, University of Cambridge, Cambridge CB2 1PZ, UK

Abstract. Multi-agent target search is an important research direction in the multi-agent field, and deep reinforcement learning has become one of the popular methods to study it. In the process of multi-agent collaborative target search using deep reinforcement learning, the agents face the sparse reward problem, which makes the learning difficult to converge. Therefore, this paper proposes a multi-agent collaborative target search method based on MADDPG with curiosity intrinsic motivation (MADDPG-C). Multi-agent curiosity intrinsic motivation module is designed and added to the MADDPG algorithm. The curiosity reward is taken as the intrinsic reward of the agent to make up for the lack of motivation of the agent to explore. A global reward function based on curiosity reward and environment reward is designed to solve the problem of sparse reward. We designed a simulation experiment to verify our algorithm, and the simulation results show that the agent can learn a good search strategy, and at the same time, the algorithm in this paper has great advantages in convergence speed and stability, as well as improving the target search efficiency.

Keywords: Multi-agent · Target search · Curiosity · Deep reinforcement learning

1 Introduction

In recent years, due to the development of biology, computer science, artificial intelligence, control science, sociology and other disciplines, multi-agent system has attracted more and more attention from many scholars, and has become a research hotspot in the field of control and artificial intelligence. Due to its characteristics of self-adaptability, decentralization and self-organization [1], multi-agent system has been widely used in traffic control [2], smart grid [3], complex environment target search [4], UAV formation [5] and other fields.

Supported by Natural Science Foundation of China (grant no. 61903006), Beijing Natural Science Foundation (grant no. 4202022, 4204096), R&D Program of Beijing Municipal Education Commission(KM202210009012); Beijing Municipal Great Wall Scholar Program (grant no. CIT&TCD 20190304); China Scholarship Council and Beijing Association for Science and Technology Young Talent Promotion Project.

© The Author(s), under exclusive license to Springer Nature Switzerland AG 2023
F. Iida et al. (Eds.): TAROS 2023, LNAI 14136, pp. 356–366, 2023.
https://doi.org/10.1007/978-3-031-43360-3_29

Different from a single agent system, the multi-agent system can share information, learn better cooperative strategies [6], and complete complex tasks that a single agent cannot complete. Multi-agent target search is essentially a collaborative competition problem in which agents learn the optimal strategy through collaborative. Traditional multi-agent target search methods mostly use probability map and swarm intelligence decision making method. Ru et al. [7] proposed a novel distributed Multi-UAVs cooperative search control method for moving target, which used Bayesian theory to update the probability map and transformed the cooperative search problem into a central optimization problem. Yao et al. [8] modeled the target search problem of multi-agent in an urban environment, using the model predictive control and an improved gray wolf optimizer to solve the problem. In addition, many improved group optimization algorithms had been proposed to solve the multi-agent target search problem. For example, the adaptive robotic particle swarm optimization (A-RPSO) algorithm [9] developed from the particle swarm optimization (PSO) algorithm, the swarm robot search algorithm based on pedestrian behavior [10], and the improved ant colony optimization (ACO) UAV formation search method [11]. However, the traditional multi-agent target search method is easy to fall into local optimal problem and is not suitable for complex scenes. At the moment, more and more researchers use machine learning method to seek the optimal target search strategy.

In recent years, deep reinforcement learning (DRL) provides a new way to solve the multi-agent target search problem. DRL combines the perceptual ability of deep learning with the decision-making ability of reinforcement learning [12], and constantly interacts with the environment. It is very suitable for multi-agent collaborative target searching task. Lowe et al. [13] proposed the multi-agent deep deterministic policy gradient (MADDPG) by improving the DDPG algorithm, and adopted the strategy inference and strategy set mechanism to enhance the robustness of the algorithm, which was widely used in the competition and cooperation among multi-agent. Although DRL adopts the end-to-end strategy and has more advantages than traditional methods, it is easy to fall into the problem of sparse rewards in the multi-agent target search scenario, resulting in difficult convergence of the model. Solving the sparse reward problem can accelerate the learning process of agents and reduce the interaction times between agents and environment. Therefore, in recent years, researchers had proposed curiosity-based exploration methods, which combine curiosity as intrinsic motivation with DRL method to effectively solve the problem of sparse rewards [14–16]. Pathak et al. proposed an intrinsic curiosity model (ICM) [17], designed an inverse dynamic model, combined with a forward model, trained in a self-supervised way, and modeled curiosity as the error of the predicted state. Burda et al. [18] further studied curiosity-based exploration, used random network distillation (RND) instead of environmental model, designed curiosity-based intrinsic incentives, and solved the sparse reward problem to a certain extent. Curiosity can be mapped as intrinsic reward signals in deep reinforcement learning. When there is a significant difference between the future state and the expected state, curiosity will drive the agent to explore this phenomenon and form a highly enlightening exploration strategy.

In this paper, we propose an improved deep reinforcement learning method, which uses MADDPG algorithm as the basic algorithm to solve the multi-agent collaborative target search problem. In order to solve the problem of sparse rewards caused by limited environmental rewards, we design the curiosity intrinsic motivation module inspired by the curiosity in creature, and add it to the MADDPG algorithm. The combination of curiosity intrinsic reward and environment reward makes up for the lack of exploration motivation of the agent. The remaining structure of this paper is shown as follows. The improved MADDPG algorithm and the design of curiosity intrinsic motivation module are introduced in Sect. 2. Section 3 introduces the design of simulation experiment and result analysis. Section 4 concludes the paper.

2   Methodology

Our work is to carry out multi-agent collaborative target search task in a continuous environment with continuous action space, so we take multi-agent deep deterministic policy gradient (MADDPG) algorithm as the basis of this method. We set up two reward signals to train multi-agent, one is environmental reward $r^e(t)$, the other is curiosity intrinsic motivation reward $r^C(t)$.

This paper transform the multi-agent collaborative target search problem into a Markov Decision Process (MDP). In each time step t, the agent i takes an action $a_i(t)$ and receives a reward $r_i(t)$ according to the observation of its current state $s_i(t)$. And the current state $s_i(t)$ is transformed into the next state $s_i(t+1)$ according to the transition dynamics $p_i(s_i(t+1)|s_i(t),a_i(t))$ of the environment. The purpose of each agent is to maximize its final expected reward. The reward of agent i at time t is designed as follows:

$$r_i(t) = -0.1 \times \sqrt{(x_i(t) - x_{tar}(t))^2 + (y_i(t) - y_{tar}(t))^2} + r_i^e(t) + r_i^C(t) \quad (1)$$

Here, $(x_i(t), y_i(t))$ and $(x_{tar}(t), y_{tar}(t))$ represent the positions of the agent i and the target at time t respectively. Here, $r_i^e(t)$ and $r_i^C(t)$ respectively represent the environmental reward and the curiosity intrinsic motivation reward obtained by the agent i at time t.

The environment reward $r^e(t)$ in this paper is set as follows:

$$r^e(t) = \begin{cases} +10 & \text{If the agents search for the target} \\ -1 & \text{If the agents collide} \\ -2 & \text{If the agents move out of bounds} \end{cases} \quad (2)$$

2.1   The MADDPG-C Algorithm

Multi-agent deep reinforcement learning is an effective method to solve the problem of multi-agent collaborative target search. Therefore, the algorithm baseline in this paper is the MADDPG algorithm proposed by Lowe et al. [13]. Its basic idea is the framework of centralized training with decentralized execution. That is, in the training stage, the Critic network can obtain the observation state of all agents to guide the Actor network training. In the execution stage, the agent only uses the *actor* network to take actions.

However, due to the sparse reward problem, the agent exploration motivation is insufficient, resulting in the MADDPG model is difficult to converge. Therefore, this paper introduces the intrinsic curiosity motivation module on the basis of the MADDPG algorithm (MADDPG-C), and the algorithm framework is shown in Fig. 1. By introducing the intrinsic curiosity motivation module, the agent i generates an intrinsic curiosity reward $r_i^C(t)$ based on the current state $s_i(t)$. We take the intrinsic curiosity reward $r_i^C(t)$ and the environment reward $r_i^e(t)$ together as the overall reward in the target search process of agent i. In this way, the exploration motivation of the agent is increased, the sparse reward problem is solved, and the excessive behavior is prevented. Multi-agent training is a process of searching for strategies that generate maximum average total reward expectation ,which is described in Eq. (3).

$$\max \mathbb{E}_{s_i \sim p^\mu, a_i \sim \pi_i} \left[\frac{1}{N} \sum_{i=1}^{N} \sum_t r_i(t) \right] \tag{3}$$

Here p^μ is the state distribution. N represents the total number of agents. π_i indicates the search policy of agent i.

As a whole, the actor-critic framework is still adopted in the improved MADDPG. Each agent is training by Actor network, Critic network, Target Actor network, and Target Critic network. Each agent trains its policy π_i with parameters θ_i using the respective gradient. The gradient update formula is shown as follows:

$$\nabla_{\theta_i} J(\theta_i) = \mathbb{E}_{s \sim p^\mu, a_i \sim \pi_i} [\nabla_{\theta_i} \log \pi_i(a_i | o_i) Q_i^\pi(x, a_1, ..., a_N)] \tag{4}$$

where $Q_i^\pi(x, a_1, ..., a_N)$ is a centralized action-value function, it takes the actions $(a_1, ..., a_N)$ of all agents and some state information x as input. $x = (o_1, ..., o_N)$ is the observed value of all agents. The output is the Q value of the agent i.

Centralised critics for deterministic action policies are optimised according to the following loss function.

$$\mathcal{L}(\theta_i) = \mathbb{E}_{x, a_i, r_i, x'} \left[\left((r_i + \gamma Q_i^{\pi'}(x', a_1', ..., a_N') |_{a_i' = \pi_i'(o_i)} - Q_i^\pi(x, a_1, ..., a_N) \right)^2 \right] \tag{5}$$

where x' is the updated state information. γ is the discount factor. Q_i^π and $Q_i^{\pi'}$ respectively represent the centralized action-value and the updated the centralized action-value. π_i' is the updated policy of agent i. o_i represents the observation of agent i.

The MADDPG-C algorithm adds an intrinsic curiosity motivation module, the design of which is described in Sect. 2.2. The current state of the agent is input into the internal curiosity module to generate a curiosity reward. By optimizing the reward calculation method of the agent's target search process, the

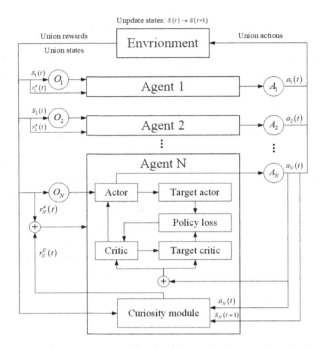

Fig. 1. The MADDPG-C algorithm framework.

improved MADDPG algorithm will give the agent a more appropriate reward, so as to adopt a better search strategy, and guide the agent to search the target faster and more accurately.

2.2 The Curiosity Intrinsic Motivation Module

In DRL, models are trained to maximize expected rewards and perform well in reward-intensive environments. However, in the collaborative target search environment, the rewards are sparse, and it is difficult for agents to form an effective search strategy. But inspired by the act of curiosity, DRL agents are encouraged to observe and explore something new. Therefore, Random Network Distillation (RND) is extended to multi-agent system as an intrinsic curiosity motivation module in this paper, and it is added to MADDPG algorithm framework. The design of curiosity module is shown in Fig. 2.

The curiosity intrinsic motivation module consists of three neural networks: one is a target network for setting prediction questions, one is a prediction network trained according to the data collected by agents, and the other is a strategy network. The target network generates constant output for a given state, the prediction network is used to predict the output of the target network, and the policy network determines the next action of the agent. The structure of target network and prediction network is the same. Both use Convolutional Neural

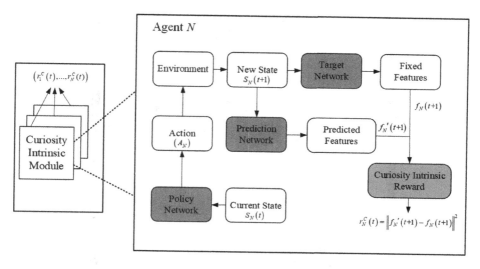

Fig. 2. The curiosity intrinsic motivation module.

Network (CNN) and full connection layer to perform feature transformation, and feature expressions are represented by $f_N(t+1)$ and $f_N'(t+1)$ respectively. We take the prediction error between the feature coding of the target network and the prediction network at time $t+1$ as the intrinsic curiosity reward $r_N^C(t)$ at time t, and the formula is as follows:

$$r_N^C(t) = \left\| f_N'(t+1) - f_N(t+1) \right\|^2 \tag{6}$$

By calculating the difference between the output of the target network and the output of the predicted network, the curiosity intrinsic motivation module generates greater intrinsic reward for unfamiliar states. It drives agents to minimize the error between the actual state and the predicted state, effectively solves the problem of sparse reward, and enables the agent to explore the environment more quickly as well as speed up the target searching.

3 Simulation Experiment

In order to verify the effectiveness of our algorithm, the Multi-agent Particle Environment (MPE) provided by OpenAI [13] is used. The multi-agent collaborative target search scenario is shown in Fig. 3. The blue balls represent the three agents, the red ball represents the target being searched, and the three black balls represent obstacles. In each episode of training, the obstacle position is fixed, but the agent and target position are randomly generated. We set that the target moves faster than the agents, so the agents must learn a good collaborative strategy to search for the target.

In the scenario shown in Fig. 3, the algorithm proposed in this paper (MADDPG-C) is adopted to train multi-agent. The results of multi-agent target

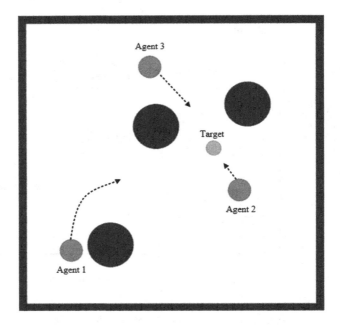

Fig. 3. The multi-agent collaborative target search scenario.

search process are shown in Fig. 4. It can be seen from the figures that the agent can learn a good collaborative strategy to search the target.

In order to evaluate the effectiveness of our algorithm in further, MADDPG-C, MADDPG and Independent Q-Learning (IQL) are all tested to train the multi-agent. The average rewards during different episodes are recorded, as shown in Fig. 5. It can be seen from the curve that MADDPG-C converges at about 12,000 episodes, while MADDPG and IQL converge at about 17,000 and 24,000 episodes. According to the curves, the convergence speed of MADDPG-C algorithm is significantly faster than the other two algorithms, and the reward value after convergence increases significantly.

In this paper, on the basis of MADDPG, intrinsic motivation of curiosity is added as intrinsic reward, which speeds up the search process of agents and improves the convergence speed and stability of the model. In order to better test the performance of the algorithm model, we designed a score evaluation index. In each episode of training, the agent gets five points if they successfully search the target, and zero points if they do not. The average score value and average reward value of the three algorithms in the whole training process of the agents are shown in Fig. 6 and Fig. 7. The results show that, compared with the other two algorithms, the algorithm proposed in this paper has higher average reward value and average score, indicating that the agents search the target more times and learn a better collaborative search strategy.

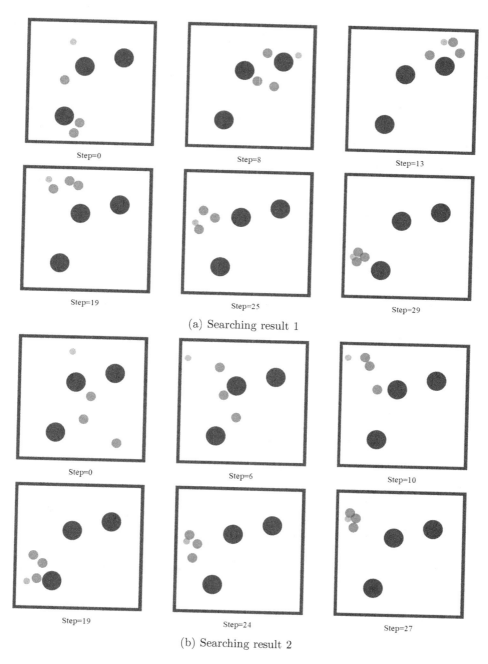

(a) Searching result 1

(b) Searching result 2

Fig. 4. The results of the multi-agent target search.

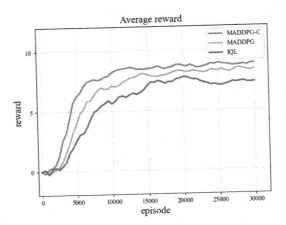

Fig. 5. Average rewards of MADDPG-C, MADDPG, IQL.

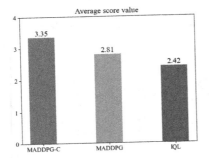

Fig. 6. Average score value.

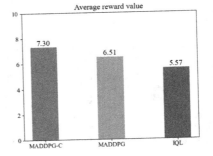

Fig. 7. Average reward value.

4   Conclusion

In this paper, the MADDPG algorithm based on intrinsic motivation of curiosity which named as MADDPG-C is proposed to solve the problem of low search efficiency caused by sparse rewards in the process of multi-agent collaborative target search. A new kind of curiosity intrinsic motivation module is designed. Therefore, the agent can generate an intrinsic curiosity reward according to the current state, and together with the environmental reward as the overall reward of the agent to solve the reward sparsity problem. In this paper, MADDPG-C algorithm is verified and compared with MADDPG and IQL algorithms in the multi-agent target search scenario. The results show that the proposed model has faster convergence speed, higher agent target search efficiency.

References

1. Shi, P., Yan, B.: A survey on intelligent control for multiagent systems. IEEE Trans. Syst. Man Cybern. Syst. **51**(1), 161–175 (2020)
2. Xu, M., An, K., Vu, L.H., et al.: Optimizing multi-agent based urban traffic signal control system. J. Intell. Transp. Syst. **23**, 357–369 (2019)
3. Roesch, M., Linder, C., Zimmermann, R., et al.: Smart grid for industry using multi-agent reinforcement learning. Appl. Sci. **10**(19), 6900 (2020)
4. Zhou, Y., Chen, A., Zhang, H., et al.: Multitarget search of swarm robots in unknown complex environments. Complexity **2020**, 1–12 (2020)
5. Zhu, X., Liang, Y., Yan, M.: A flexible collision avoidance strategy for the formation of multiple unmanned aerial vehicles. IEEE Access **7**, 140743–140754 (2019)
6. Zhou, X., Zhou, S., Mou, X., et al.: Multirobot collaborative pursuit target robot by improved MADDPG. Comput. Intell. Neurosci. **2022**, 1–10 (2022)
7. Ru, C.J., Qi, X.M., Guan, X.N.: Distributed cooperative search control method of multiple UAVs for moving target. Int. J. Aerosp. Eng. **2015**, 317953.1-317953.12 (2015)
8. Yao, P., Wang, H., et al.: Multi-UAVs tracking target in urban environment by model predictive control and improved grey wolf optimizer. Aerosp. Sci. Technol. **55**, 131–143 (2016)
9. Dadgar, M., Jafari, S., Hamzeh, A.: A PSO-based multi-robot cooperation method for target searching in unknown environments. Neurocomputing **177**, 62–74 (2016)
10. Shi, H., Li, J., Li, Z.: A distributed strategy for cooperative autonomous robots using pedestrian behavior for multi-target search in the unknown environment. Sensors **20**(6), 1606 (2020)
11. Perez-Carabaza, S., Besada-Portas, E., et al.: Ant colony optimization for multi-UAV minimum time search in uncertain domains. Appl. Soft Comput. **62**, 789–806 (2018)
12. Li, Y.: Deep reinforcement learning: an overview (2017)
13. Lowe, R., Wu, Y.I., Tamar, A., et al.: Multi-agent actor-critic for mixed cooperative-competitive environments. In: Advances in Neural Information Processing Systems, vol. 30 (2017)
14. Shi, X., Li, J., Li, J., et al.: Random curiosity-driven exploration in deep reinforcement learning. Neurocomputing **418**, 139–147 (2020)

15. Chen, W., Shi, H., Li, J., Hwang, K.-S.: A fuzzy curiosity-driven mechanism for multi-agent reinforcement learning. Int. J. Fuzzy Syst. **23**(5), 1222–1233 (2021). https://doi.org/10.1007/s40815-020-01035-0
16. Zhelo, O., Zhang, J., Tai, L., et al.: Curiosity-driven exploration for mapless navigation with deep reinforcement learning (2018)
17. Pathak, D., Agrawal, P., Efros, A.A., et al.: Curiosity-driven exploration by self-supervised prediction. In: 2017 IEEE Conference on Computer Vision and Pattern Recognition Workshops (CVPRW). IEEE (2017)
18. Burda, Y., Edwards, H., Storkey, A., et al.: Exploration by random network distillation (2018)

Simulation of Collective Bernoulli-Ball System for Characterizing Dynamic Self-stability

Fan Ye$^{(\boxtimes)}$, Arsen Abdulali , and Fumiya Iida

Bio-Inspired Robotics Lab, Department of Engineering, University of Cambridge, Cambridge CB2 1PZ, UK
aa2335@cam.ac.uk

Abstract. Collective behavior that is widely observed in nature, e.g., schools of fish and society of ants, has been serving as a primary source of inspiration in swarm robotics. This kind of behavior emerges when each individual in the group follows a simple set of rules of local interaction. However, it is still not trivial to apply local interactions to perform complicated tasks. In this work, by employing Bernoulli's Principle and local interaction rules, we developed a multi-ball simulator that can reproduce complex collective behaviors observed in real-world experiments. We believe the proposed simulation system is advantageous for augmenting the collective behaviors in swarm robotics.

Keywords: Collective behavior · Swarm intelligence · Bernoulli-Ball system · Swarm robotics

1 Introduction

Collective behavior plays an important role in the animal world by saving energy during the group motion [1], e.g., the schools of fish, the swarms of ants, and the flocks of birds [2]. For instance, to reduce the effort, birds fly in V-formation [3], lobsters queue in lines [4], and fish exploit vortices produced in their schools [5]. On one hand, individuals in these groups decide their movements based on locally acquired cues like the position or the motion of others [6]. On the other hand, one individual can in turn influence the group's behavior by adjusting how it interacts with other group members [7]. Since these collective behaviors result from local interactions between individuals without commands given by a leader [6], the group of animals is called a self-organizing system [8], which is the prototype that swarm robots refer to.

Swarm robotics focuses on designing large groups of robots that exchange information in a centralized or decentralized way to corporately solve a problem [9], for example, ant-like robots allocate tasks to collect resources and recruit

This work was supported by a Huawei HiSilicon Scholarship.

another robot when they identify an area with plenty of resources [10], and flocks of autonomous drones avoid collision without central control [11]. The interaction rule governs robots and hence determines their ability to fulfilling tasks. The Boids simulation proposed an interaction rule of birds in flocks by providing every single bird with an independent actor that decides the orientation according to its local dynamic environment [2]. However, challenges lie in designing interaction rules that can solve complicated problems. Although animals' interaction rules are eligible enough to fulfill complicated missions, there is no practical way to simulate animals' brains to make a similar decision. Therefore, alternatively, we propose the collective Bernoulli-Ball system that has complicated behavioral modes, and the interactions among Bernoulli-Balls are incidental and governed by physical laws instead of animals' brains. In this case, a simulator of the collective Bernoulli-Ball system can be built to solve complicated problems.

The Bernoulli-Ball system is based on Bernoulli's principle, in which a ball stabilizes itself in an upward stream, as shown in Fig. 1. The system becomes complicated when multiple balls are introduced to this system, where one ball changes the field of the airflow affecting the other balls. This interaction among balls causes the emergence of various collective behaviors. Unfortunately, although the interaction force between two spheres was evaluated in static experiments [12], there is no practical way to measure interaction forces directly in a dynamic physical experiment. There have been several attempts to simulate the dynamics of the fluid-sphere interaction on the Venturi nozzle [13]. Or in [14], the authors employed Computational Fluid Dynamics (CFD) simulation to visualize the flow and vorticity fields of fluid during interaction with a static sphere. Another research direction related to the approximation of the drag coefficient in fluid-sphere interaction under various Reynolds numbers [15,16], and to control the position of the sphere [17]. However, modeling a realistic collective Bernoulli-Ball system with multi-ball remains open for investigation.

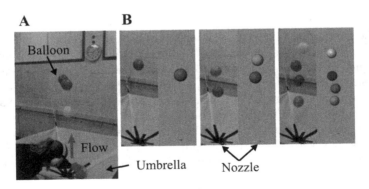

Fig. 1. The collective Bernoulli-Ball system in real-world experiment and simulation. A researcher is putting a balloon into the setup of the collective Bernoulli-Ball system (A). A vertical airflow comes out from the nozzle and lifts balloons. The umbrella is used to collect falling balloons and put them back into the airflow. Simulation of the collective Bernoulli-Ball system is conducted with 1,2 and 4 balloons, compared with the experiment correspondingly (B).

In this paper, we proposed a simulator incorporating models of Bernoulli's Principle, turbulence, and multi-ball interaction to simulate the physics model of the collective Bernoulli-Ball system. To reproduce a real-like phenomenon, we referred to the motion trajectories of balls in the physical Bernoulli-Ball setup recorded in our previous research [18], shown in Fig. 1A, and optimized the simulation parameters using Bayesian optimization. The accuracy of the simulator was validated by comparing the position distribution of Bernoulli-Balls observed in the physical experiment and simulation, the behavioral states of Bernoulli-Balls were defined and compared between experiments and simulation, and the scalability of the simulator was tested by extending the simulator from optimized situations to non-optimized situations.

2   Multi-ball Bernoulli Model

The proposed framework consists of three models: the Bernoulli-Ball model, the interaction model, and the turbulence model. The simulation software is written in Matlab (Simulink), and is freely available on Github at https://github.com/ Kyushudy/collective_bernoulli_ball_simulation.

2.1   Bernoulli-Ball Model

The dynamics system of the Bernoulli-Ball can be generally expressed as a balloon floating in a vertical stream of air with self-stability. As shown in Fig. 2A, the balloon balances at a certain height where vertical forces due to air drag and gravity compensate for each other. The flow velocity is usually faster near the nozzle and slows down with the distance from it. Since drag force correlates with the flow velocity, this effect leads to the vertical self-stability of the balloon at a certain height. Horizontally, the balloon is affected by forces due to Bernoulli's Principle. The flow velocity is faster at the center of the flow leading to a low-pressure area there. This difference in the pressure level induces forces stabilizing a ball horizontally.

The Bernoulli-Ball model estimates drag, damping, and vertical forces that individual balloon experiences due to airflow. The drag force due to the airflow can be defined as follow:

$$F_{Drag} = \frac{1}{2}\rho v_{VR}^2 C_{Drag} A, \quad v_{VR} = v_F - v_{VB}, \tag{1}$$

where ρ indicates the air density, v_{VR} denotes the vertical relative velocity between a balloon and airflow, C_{Drag} is the drag coefficient of the balloon, taken as 0.418 under estimated Reynolds number of real-world experiments [16], A indicates the area of the balloon in vertical view, v_F indicates flow speed, and v_{VB} is the vertical velocity of the balloon.

To get v_F, a flow field is introduced as a normal distribution on a horizontal circular-type surface. All the flow velocity is vertically upward. The radius of the horizontal circle is given by

$$R_{Flow} = R_{Nozzle} + z \cdot tan(\alpha), \tag{2}$$

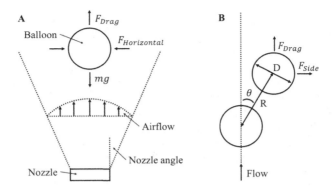

Fig. 2. Dynamics of the Bernoulli-Ball system. Dynamics system of Bernoulli-Ball (A). Schematic plot of drag/side force, R, D and θ (B).

where R_{Nozzle} is the radius of the nozzle, z is the vertical position of the circle, and α is the outlet angle of the nozzle. Given that the quantity of flow is constant through the horizontal surface, we have that:

$$v_C = v_{Nozzle}\frac{R^2_{Nozzle}}{R^2_{Flow}}, \qquad v_F = v_C \cdot F(p_{xy}), \qquad (3)$$

where v_C is the flow speed of the circle, v_{Nozzle} is the flow speed of the nozzle, F returns the probability density of a two-dimensional normal distribution function with a mean equals to 0, and a standard deviation σ, p_{xy} is the position of the balloon on the x-y plane. According to Bernoulli's Principle and drag force model, the horizontal force can be evaluated as:

$$F_H = F_P + F_{HD}, \qquad F_P = \frac{1}{2}\rho(v^2_{Inner} - v^2_{Outer})A, \qquad F_{HD} = \frac{1}{2}\rho v^2_{HR}C_D A, \quad (4)$$

where F_H indicates the horizontal force, F_P indicates the pressure force under Bernoulli's Principle, aiming to the horizontal center of the flow, F_{HD} indicates the horizontal drag force, aiming opposite to the x-y velocity of the balloon, v_{Inner} indicates the flow speed at the inner edge of the balloon, v_{Outer} indicates the flow speed at the outer edge of the balloon, and v_{HR} indicates the horizontal relative speed between the balloon and flow.

2.2   Interaction Model

Two balloons could interact via mechanical contact, so a spatial contact force model between every two balloons is introduced to the simulator. This has three parameters to be tuned: normal force stiffness, damping, and transition region width.

When there is no mechanical contact, interaction force through the flow occurs: the lower balloon has an effect on the airflow incident on the upper balloon and vice versa. Some empirical research on the aerodynamic interaction between two spheres at Reynolds numbers around 10^4 have already been conducted [12], while the Reynolds number in our system is:

$$Re = \frac{\rho v d}{\mu} = \frac{1.22 \times 2 \times 0.16}{1.825 \times 10^{-5}} = 2.1 \times 10^4 = \mathcal{O}(10^4), \tag{5}$$

which makes the result of previous empirical research applicable to our system.

In the empirical research [12], the author formed plots of $C_{Interacted}/C_D$ against R/D and θ, where $C_{Interacted}$ is the drag/side force coefficient of the trailing sphere when interacted with the leading sphere, C_D is the original drag coefficient without interaction, R is the distance between the sphere centers, D is the sphere diameter, θ is the angle of attack of balloons (deg), whose schematic plot is in Fig. 2B. The interaction forces between two balls are available in Fig. 3.

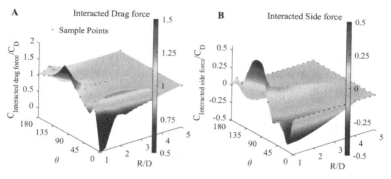

Fig. 3. Drag/side force model. Interacted drag force (A) and interacted side force (B) between two balloons related to R/D and θ, whose schematic plot is in Fig. 2B. A positive side force indicates a separating potential movement of two spheres on the horizontal plane.

An interaction exists between two balloons in the system. However, when another balloon is introduced into this two-balloon system, the third balloon may affect the interaction between the first and second balloon. There is no existing model to couple this kind of multi-agent interaction in fluid dynamics. Inspired by the three-body problem, we assume that the third balloon will build interaction separately with the first and second balloon, and has no effect on the interaction between the first and second balloon. Similarly, this happens when the fourth balloon is introduced.

2.3 Turbulence Model

Turbulence and uncertain environment input make the balloon vibrate around its balanced position. In this case, to increase the randomness of the model, a noise input could be added, allowing the simulated system to better approximate the real-world case. Three Gaussian distributed random signals were input for x, y, and z directions with a mean equal to zero and an adjustable variance separately. Then they were combined with the dynamical forces of balloons to simulate the uncertainty. Every balloon has its distinct seed of random noise, but they share the same horizontal variance and vertical variance. This noise model introduces three governing parameters to the model: horizontal variance, vertical variance, and noise sampling time.

3   Model Identification

Real-world experiments for the collective Bernoulli-Ball system were conducted to track the trajectories of balloons under different conditions, for example, the number of balloons shifted from 1 to 4, the fan power adjusted from low to high, and the balloon mass varied from 1 g to 7 g. One part of the real-world trajectories was used as a sample to optimize the simulator for its better accuracy, while another part of them was used to investigate the scalability of the simulator that had already been optimized in the first part. The dataset can be accessed at https://github.com/hcrisp98/IIB-Project. Bayesian optimization was used to train the model to match the real-world system. Adjustable parameters and their bounds are shown in Table 1.

Table 1. Parameters and their bounds for optimization.

Model	Parameter	Lower limit	Upper limit	Unit
Airflow	Outlet velocity	1	5	m/s
	Normal scaling	0.25	1	1
	Damping coefficient	0	0.05	N/(m/s)
	Nozzle angle	1	10	degree
Noise	Vertical variance	0	0.03	m
	Horizontal variance	0	0.03	m
	Sampling time	0.05	0.1	s
Contact	Stiffness constant	0.5e7	1.5e7	N/m
	Damping constant	10	1000	N/(m/s)
	Transition width	0.5e-4	1.5e-4	m

For the sake of the randomness in this collective Bernoulli-Ball system, the simulated trajectory of balloons cannot match that of the experiment frame-by-frame, so we defined their global system characteristics for the cost function as follows:

$$e = (e_z^\mu + e_z^{\sigma^2} + e_{xy}^{\sigma^2})/3, \tag{6}$$

where e_z^μ, $e_z^{\sigma^2}$ and $e_{xy}^{\sigma^2}$ denote the error between simulation and experiment in the mean z position, the variance of z position, and the variance of x-y position. The overall error is noted as e.

Models with different adjustable parameter sets were optimized under various circumstances. Parameter sets of Bernoulli-Ball models with one, two, and four balloons are shown in Table 2. Model a and a* verify the airflow model in exhibiting the stability of the balloon. Model d, e, and f are non-interaction versions of model g, h, and i correspondingly, to show the significance of the interaction model. Other models with parameter inheritance investigate whether our proposed model can extend to non-optimized cases.

Table 2. Trial models for the Bernoulli-Ball system.

Parameter set	Models without interaction/interaction applied		
One-balloon system	a(a*)/−	b/−	c(c*)/−
Airflow	Optimized	Inherited from a*	Optimized
Noise	−	Optimized	Optimized
Two-balloon system	d/g	e/h	f/i(i*)
Airflow	Inherited from b	Inherited from b	Optimized
Noise	Inherited from b	Optimized	Optimized
Contact	Optimized	Optimized	Optimized
Four-balloon system	−/j	−/k	m/l(l*)
Airflow	Inherited from i*	Inherited from i*	Optimized
Noise	Inherited from i*	Optimized	Optimized
Contact	Inherited from i*	Inherited from i*	Optimized

1 Model a* used e_z^μ as its cost function to ignore the variances of position.
2 Model c*,i*,l* completed 1000 iterations to get an ideally optimal result.

4   Results and Discussion

4.1   Optimization Result

To visualize e_z^μ, $e_z^{\sigma^2}$ and $e_{xy}^{\sigma^2}$, a boxplot of z position for balloons was drawn together with an x-y variance figure to show the difference between our simulator and real-world cases, as in Fig. 4.

As shown in Fig. 4, under the noise-free circumstance, $\bar{\mu}_z$ of model a* ($e_z^\mu = 0.18\%$) matches the real-world experiment better than model a ($e_z^\mu = 9.56\%$). This happened because model a considers $e_z^{\sigma^2}$ and $e_{xy}^{\sigma^2}$ as its extra cost function, making it have more outliers to match the σ_z^2 of the real-world experiment. However, in such a non-noise environment, it was obvious that model a and a* should have a very low $\bar{\sigma}_z^2$ and $\bar{\sigma}_{xy}^2$, so a more proper aim for these models was to reduce the e_z^μ, as optimized in the model a*. Then, the flow parameters of model a* could be inherited by model b to optimize the noise parameters. In comparison, model b had a similar $\bar{\mu}_z$ as model a*, whilst exhibiting $\bar{\sigma}_z^2$ and $\bar{\sigma}_{xy}^2$ similar as a

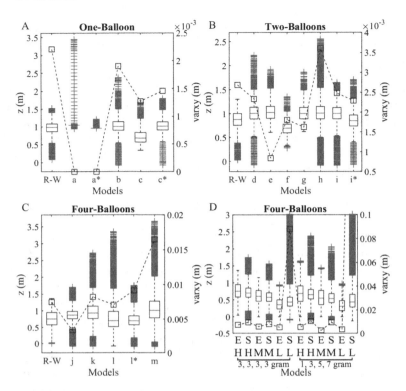

Fig. 4. Comparison between models in the Bernoulli-Ball system. Comparison of boxplots for the real-world (R-W) case and simulation models optimized with a position-based cost function. The boxplot shows its z position distribution, while the dotted line chart reveals the variance of the x-y position, marked as $\bar{\sigma}_{xy}^2$. The one-balloon system (A), the two-balloon system (B), the four-balloon system (C), and the four-balloon system with different fan power (H for 0.22 PWM, M for 0.20 PWM, L for 0.18 PWM, E for experiment, S for simulation) and balloon mass (D).

real-world experiment, stressing the importance of the noise model. Compared with model b, model c was optimized without parameter inheritance. After completing 100 iterations, the result was very significant: inheriting parameters from model a*, model b showed great ability to simulate μ_z, σ_z^2 and σ_{xy}^2 of the real-world experiment, better than model c. Although 1000 iterations were optimized in model c* with the same adjustable parameters of model c, $\bar{\sigma}_{xy}^2$ still could not match the real world. In all, model b with parameter inheritance was the best model among all one-balloon models, which reveals that parameter inheritance had a significant effect on increasing the accuracy and reducing the number of iterations needed for optimization, thus saving time spent in optimization. Besides, model b had an overall error ($e = 11.7\%$) against the real-world experiment, which showed the success of our simulator in reproducing the position of the one-balloon system.

For the two-balloon system, in general, models which had interaction matched the experiment better than non-interacted models, which reveals the effect of the interaction model in reducing errors. Model g inherited airflow patterns and noise patterns from model b, while model h only inherited airflow patterns. It was commonly thought that the noise of the system would change when the model transferred from one-balloon to two-balloon, so model h might have a better performance. However, the result reveals that model g and h shared similar e_z^{μ} and $e_{xy}^{\sigma^2}$. Meanwhile, model g matched the real-world experiment better than model h in $\bar{\sigma}_z^2$. Without inheritance, model i got rid of the influence of previous optimizations, which helped it to find its own suitable condition and make it perform better than model g and h. After completing 1000 iterations, model i* showed the best performance ($e = 5.9\%$) among all two-balloon models. This reduced error shows that our interaction model works well in the collective Bernoulli-Ball system.

For the four-balloon system, model j matched the real-world well in $\bar{\mu}_z$ and $\bar{\sigma}_z^2$, stressing the scalability of our simulator from the two-balloon system to the four-balloon system. Model m was a non-interaction version of model l, which had the worst performance among all four-balloon models. This stressed the necessity of the interaction model, especially in a multi-balloon system. After completing 1000 iterations, model l* showed the best performance ($e = 12.5\%$) among all four-balloon models. In all, our simulator successfully reproduces the position distribution of balloons in the one/two/four-balloon system and shows good scalability when the number of balloons varies.

4.2   Model Validation

To claim that our simulator is applicable, we need to validate the four-balloon simulation in exhibiting the collective behavior of the collective Bernoulli-Ball system. To specify it, we first defined four behaviors of balloons based on the observation of experiments:

1. Falling: when the balloon is far from the flow center and falls vertically downward to the ground, the falling behavior is detected.
2. Interaction: as shown in Fig. 3, drag/side force is significant when the distance is less than 1.1 times of ball diameter, where the interaction is detected.
3. Moving: the moving behavior can be defined as the balloon moving at a speed faster than $0.1\,(m/s)$ vertically when it is not falling or interacting.
4. Stable: the stable behavior can be defined as all other cases when the balloon is not falling, interacting, or moving.

The experiment result was from the real-world four-balloon system, while the simulation result was from model l*. The trajectory of z position in Fig. 5AC was filtered using a moving average filter to make the trajectory more readable, while Fig. 5BD shows the unfiltered trajectory in a short period of time. As shown in Fig. 5, in both experiment and simulation, four balloons took turns to do falling behavior. The pie chart of Fig. 5 shows that balloons spent a similar proportion of time in falling behavior both in the experiment and simulation, but interacted less, moved, and behaved stably more frequently in the experiment compared to the simulation. This might be caused by the dynamic turbulence flow between balloons: when two balloons approach each other, they indeed tend to bond with each other in a steady state, which is shown in Fig. 3, but in a dynamic system, the turbulence flow around one balloon tends to resist another balloon, which may reduce the frequency of interaction behavior. In addition, this effect will also increase the noise between balloons, breaking their bonds. As a result, the frequency of the interaction mode increased, and the frequency of the moving and stable modes decreased in the simulation. Except for the turbulence effect introduced above, our simulator works well in reproducing the behaviors of balloons. Especially, one typical behavior of the collective Bernoulli-Ball system was observed in both experiment (Fig. 5B) and simulation (Fig. 5D).

4.3 Model Scalability

For optimized cases our simulator shows great accuracy in the position and the state change of balloons, revealing collective behaviors in the collective Bernoulli-Ball system, but the robustness of the simulator is still uncertain: can it be extended to other non-optimized cases with great accuracy? Further simulations and experiments are conducted with different fan power or balloon mass. Under the same parameters from optimization, the scalability of the simulator was verified through comparison against reality in non-optimized cases.

Experiment results with fan power 0.22 PWM and four similar balloons having 3 g of weight were used for the optimization of the model 1*. Similarly, we conducted the experiments by setting the power of the fan to 0.18 PWM and 0.20 PWM with balloons having masses of 1, 3, 5, and 7 g, in comparison with simulation 1* with the same set of parameters. When the fan power was changed, the outlet velocity was accordingly adjusted. However, the relationship between fan power and outlet velocity is nonlinear and depends highly on other parameters, like pulse width [19]. In this case, a series of model a* was optimized using the outlet velocity as its only adjustable parameter, compared to one-balloon experiments with the fan power 0.18, 0.20, and 0.22 PWM. The result shows that, given the outlet velocity as v_{Out} under fan power 0.22 PWM, the outlet velocity of fan power 0.20 PWM was $0.6464 \cdot v_{Out}$, and that of fan power 0.18 PWM was $0.3744 \cdot v_{Out}$. When conducting a simulation of model 1* under different fan power, the outlet velocity was adjusted by the corresponding factors.

Figure 4 shows the scalability of the simulator under non-optimized circumstances. Our simulator could accurately be extended to high power (0.22 PWM, 1.4 m/s outlet velocity) or mid-power (0.20 PWM, 0.9 m/s outlet velocity) systems with four balloons having masses 3 g each, as well as with different masses, i.e., 1, 3, 5, 7 g. When the situation switch to a low power system, our simulator showed significantly high $\bar{\sigma}_z^2$ and $\bar{\sigma}_{xy}^2$. Due to the low fan power, the fluid field was not able to support the four-balloon system. In experiments, balloons tended to frequently fall to the ground, while in simulation balloons tend to bond together to get stronger flow support without the turbulence that separated them. When

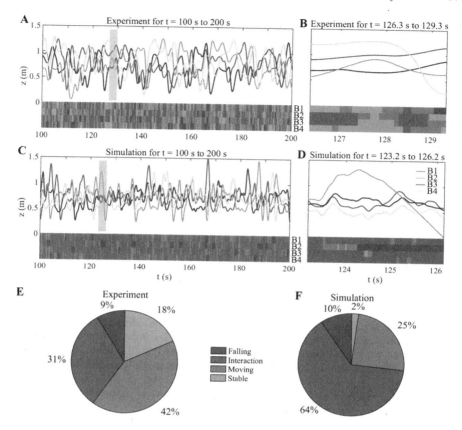

Fig. 5. Trajectory of z position and behavioral proportion for the four-balloon system. The trajectory of z position and corresponding classified behaviors of four balloons (AC) for $t = 100\ s$ to $200\ s$, with a specified period of time separately (BD). The proportion of time spent in each behavioral mode (EF) for 300 s in experiment and simulation. The mass of all four balloons is 3 g.

several balloons gathered together, one left balloon would suffer a significant side force tearing it apart from other balloons. This resulted in the relatively high $\bar{\mu}_z$, extremely high $\bar{\sigma}_{xy}^2$, and some outliers in simulation.

5   Conclusion

In our work, we built a scalable simulator to accurately reproduce the behavioral diversity of the real collective Bernoulli-Ball system with a various number of balloons. Without changing any other parameters, our simulator can be extended from a two-balloon system to a four-balloon system, from 1 g balloon weight to 7 g balloon weight, and from $0.9\ m/s$ outlet velocity to $1.4\ m/s$ outlet velocity, while keeping a good accuracy compared to the real-world experiment. Besides, the quantitative evaluation of our simulator suggests that three physics models of our framework, i.e., the Bernoulli-Ball model, the interaction model, and the stochastic turbulence model can jointly reproduce complicated behaviors of collective Bernoulli-Balls observed in the real world.

References

1. Vicsek, T.: Fluctuations and Scaling in Biology. Oxford University Press, New York (2001)
2. Reynolds, C.W.: Flocks, herds and schools: a distributed behavioral model. In: Proceedings of the 14th annual conference on Computer graphics and interactive techniques, pp. 25–34
3. Lissaman, P.B., Shollenberger, C.A.: Formation flight of birds. Science **168**(3934), 1003–1005 (1970)
4. Bill, R.G., Herrnkind, W.F.: Drag reduction by formation movement in spiny lobsters. Science **193**(4258), 1146–1148 (1976)
5. Liao, J.C., Beal, D.N., Lauder, G.V., Triantafyllou, M.S.: Fish exploiting vortices decrease muscle activity. Science **302**(5650), 1566–1569 (2003)
6. Couzin, I.D.: Collective cognition in animal groups. Trends Cogn. Sci. **13**(1), 36–43 (2009)
7. Schaerf, T.M., Dillingham, P.W., Ward, A.J.W.: The effects of external cues on individual and collective behavior of shoaling fish. Sci. Adv. **3**(6), e1603201 (2017)
8. Camazine, S., Deneubourg, J.L., Franks, N.R., Sneyd, J., Theraula, G., Bonabeau, E.: Self-Organization in Biological Systems. Princeton University Press, Princeton (2020)
9. Dorigo, M., Theraulaz, G., Trianni, V.: Swarm robotics: past, present, and future [point of view]. Proc. IEEE **109**(7), 1152–1165 (2021)
10. Krieger, M.J.B., Billeter, J.B., Keller, L.: Ant-like task allocation and recruitment in cooperative robots. Nature **406**(6799), 992–995 (2000)
11. Vasarhelyi, G., Viragh, C., Somorjai, G., Nepusz, T., Eiben, A.E., Vicsek, T.: Optimized flocking of autonomous drones in confined environments. Sci Robot. **3**(20), eaat3536 (2018)
12. Lee, K.C.: Aerodynamic interaction between two spheres at Reynolds numbers around 104. Aeronaut. Q. **30**(1), 371–385 (1979)
13. Faulkner, B.E., Ytreberg, F.M.: Understanding Bernoulli's principle through simulations. Am. J. Phys. **79**(2), 214–216 (2011)
14. Johnson, T., Patel, V.: Flow past a sphere up to a Reynolds number of 300. J. Fluid Mech. **378**, 19–70 (1999)
15. Massey, B.: Mechanics of fluids dynamics (1968)
16. Flemmer, R.L.C., Banks, C.L.: On the drag coefficient of a sphere. Powder Technol. **48**(3), 217–221 (1986)
17. Howison, T., Giardina, F., Iida, F.: Augmenting self-stability: height control of a Bernoulli ball via bang-bang control. In: 2020 IEEE International Conference on Robotics and Automation (ICRA), pp. 3974–3980. IEEE (2020)
18. Howison, T., Crisp, H., Hauser, S., Iida, F.: On the stability and behavioral diversity of single and collective bernoulli balls. Artif. Life **29**(2), 1–19 (2022)
19. Pipan, M., Heraković, N.: Volume flow characterization of PWM-controlled fast-switching pneumatic valves. Strojniški vestnik-J. Mech. Eng. **62**(9), 543–550 (2016)

Soft Robotics

Casting vs Injection Moulding: A Comparison Study for In-Lab Low-Cost Soft Robot Fabrication

Kedar Suthar, Nicholas Lesseps, Ruth Mackay, and Mingfeng Wang[✉] [iD]

Department of Mechanical and Aerospace Engineering, Brunel University London,
London UB8 3PH, UK
Mingfeng.Wang@brunel.ac.uk

Abstract. This paper investigates the efficacy of silicone moulding methods using casting and injection moulding in a laboratory environment. The production of soft material components involves a variety of techniques, including both low-cost, in-house practices and high-level methods that require specialized training and expensive equipment. This paper focuses on two in-lab low-cost techniques: the casting method, which is commonly employed for shaping simple geometries, and the injection moulding process that produces highly intricate parts easily. To carry out the comparison study, a special shape was designed and three silicon materials (i.e., Ecoflex 00–50, Ecoflex 00–30 and DragonSkin-10) were selected first. Secondly, a mould was created using low-cost standard SLA and poly jet 3D printers. Thirdly, an effective in-lab fabrication process was proposed. Finally, a series of silicon parts were fabricated and compared.

Keywords: Casting · injection moulding · soft robotics

1 Introduction

Body parts made from Polydimethylsiloxane (PDMS) have been widely applied in the field of soft robotics, due to the elastomer's excellent optical, electrical, and mechanical properties [1]. To fabricate effective PDMS based soft robots in a low-volume laboratory, many studies have been carried out in the last two decades including material mixing (by hand, turbine, stand or planetary mix), mould design and manufacturing, directly 3D printing, and so on.

Creating intricately shaped and designed objects requires moulds, a crucial part of the casting process. They are essential for the finished product's quality and accuracy. Constructing the geometry, putting together the mould, and preparing the materials are all functions required in casting. The final product's strength, precision, and general quality depend on the type of mould employed. Many methods are used in the industry, such as sacrificial moulds [2] and reusable moulds [3]. Different types of additive manufacturing create moulds quickly and accurately, such as Fused Deposition Modelling (FDM) [4], stereolithography (SLA) [5] and material-jetting (MJ).

F. Iida et al. (Eds.): TAROS 2023, LNAI 14136, pp. 381–392, 2023.
https://doi.org/10.1007/978-3-031-43360-3_31

Research has been conducted on fabricating soft robots and different methods for shaping soft structures. PDMS material parts are cast by pouring silicone into two open portions of a two-part mould. The top and bottom of a simple two-part mould are set with their contents facing up. Another method used to mould the PDMS part is spin casting. Instead of relying solely on gravity, spinning the mould, and applying centrifugal forces can raise the pressure gradient and degas more efficiently [6]. Using a vacuum to key mould regions while the polymer is poured could also force degassing. Vacuum casting enables detail replication down to sub-millimetre levels [7]. Functional interfaces, reinforcement, actuators, or even electronic components may be over-moulded in multi-step moulding [8–10]. These extra parts must adhere to the newly added material and be properly positioned, secured, and fastened to the mould. Moulding the part into many subparts that can be bonded together by gluing or dipping the pieces in uncured material is the simplest method for producing internal volumes and undercuts [11]. However, due to the seams created by this process, the part may be structurally weak. When moulding complex structures, an internal core is necessary, which can pose a challenge when extracting it after setting. In some cases, the core may consist of several parts that can be disassembled and removed through an access hole [12, 13]. Alternatively, the core can be made of fusible or soluble material and destroyed after moulding the part. Soft cores can also be used, which can be removed from the moulded part using a vacuum to simplify the process [14]. Additionally, internal volumes can be moulded from a single side. Rotational moulding can be used if interior geometry accuracy is not a top concern [7]. This process involves filling and sealing a mould before spinning it around two axes to uniformly coat every surface with the polymer.

Injection moulding, widely used in industrial silicone parts manufacturing, usually requires specific and costly liquid silicone injection moulding machines. In recent studies, researchers have tried to develop a low-cost injection moulding method for lab use [15]. However, this method requires machines to inject silicone into the mould with 8–25 MPa of pressure. Inspired by this method, in this paper, a simplified injection moulding method has been proposed without machinery and compared with the traditional casting method.

This paper compares the casting method for a complex PDMS component to the in-lab injection moulding method for the same shape. In Sect. 2, the moulding methodology is presented along with the shape geometry and the mould design for both the casting and injection methods. This will be used to compare the process and the material characteristics of the silicone used. Section 3 analyses the results of both fabrication methods, including the part wall thickness. Section 4 presents the discussion and conclusion.

2 Methodology

In this section, the design of the geometry used to test the moulds is presented following with the designs of the mould, and the fabricating protocol for silicone material.

2.1 Geometry Used for Testing

To test moulding methods a complex shape is needed. The shape will consist of three differently sized rings stacked vertically, resulting in complex geometry. The part walls will have varying thicknesses, ranging from 1 mm for SI-1 to SI-9 and 2 mm for SII-1 to SII-4 (see Fig. 1). This thickness variation could cause warping during curing if the mould is not manufactured correctly. The part will also have several overhangs and curves, making it challenging to mould using silicone. In addition to the angles and fillets, the geometry will include straight edges and sharp turns. This will test how both moulding methods deal with straight and curved edges. Ensuring high dimensional accuracy is crucial, as any defects could cause part failure. Surface finish is also a critical factor in part quality and performance, as imperfections can lead to weak spots or structural issues. Therefore, it is essential to choose a moulding method capable of producing a smooth, defect-free surface while handling the different thicknesses and shapes of the part.

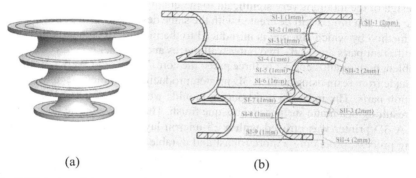

(a)   (b)

Fig. 1. CAD design of the proposed geometry: (a) Isometric view of the part and (b) Section view of the geometry to show the internal wall thickness.

2.2 Materials Used for Testing

Silicone is lightweight, flexible, and resistant to chemicals and heat. It also has an excellent strength-to-weight ratio, making it an ideal application choice for soft robotics. Silicone is also easy to work with, making it possible to create complex shapes with high accuracy. Three distinct types of silicone were used: DragonSkin-10, Ecoflex 00–50 and Ecoflex 00–30, which have a varying range of physical properties (see Table 1). The stiffest silicone is the DragonSkin-10 and the least stiff is the Ecoflex 00–30. The DragonSkin-10 has a higher Shore Hardness rating, meaning it is the most rigid material of the three. The Ecoflex 00–50 has a middle rating, and the Ecoflex 00–30 has the lowest rating and is considered the softest of the three materials. When working with silicone materials, it's important to keep in mind that the mixing ratio should always be 1:1. However, a slight variance of 5% can be tolerated without having a significant impact on the final material properties. It is critical to consider the material's viscosity. Material viscosity between parts A and B may lead to limited injection pressures.

Table 1. Physical properties of investigated silicones

Silicone	Tensile Strength (MPa)	Modulus 100 (MPa)	Mixed Viscosity (cps)	Shore hardness	Pot Time (minutes)
Ecoflex 00–50	2.171	0.0827	8,000	00–50	18
Ecoflex 00–30	1.378	0.0689	3,000	00–30	45
DragonSkin-10	3.275	0.1517	23,000	10 A	45

2.3 Design of the Moulds

The design of the mould is very significant to the quality of the part. The casting mould and the injection mould will be created with the same design but with a small difference in the method by which silicone is introduced to the mould. To create the final mould, three different parts are used - two outer wall pieces and an inner core piece that can be assembled, both moulds consist of three parts: the core, Wall 1, and Wall 2. Both moulds were made from resin using an SLA 3D printer, producing extremely accurate and high-resolution parts. The injection and pouring moulds were printed using Formlabs grey resin, resulting in a matte surface and opaque finish. The highly precise Formlabs Form 3L SLA 3D printer was utilized with a 25-micron layer thickness resolution for the printing process, producing a more robust and durable mould. This allows for a much more precise and accurate mould, resulting in a significantly better product. Additionally, the SLA printer allows for more intricate and complex designs. This makes it ideal for creating moulds of complex shapes and patterns that would otherwise be impossible to replicate with traditional manufacturing methods.

Silicone is evenly poured on top of the mould for the casting method (see Fig. 2). It will make a slow way through the mould and fill the cavity between the walls and the mould's core. Once the silicone has cooled and solidified, the mould is opened, and the silicone part is removed. The mould is then ready to be reused to create more pieces. This process is cost-effective and creates a replica of the desired shape. It is also much faster than other methods, such as machining, which takes longer to produce parts.

The silicone can be injected into the mould through the bottom of the mould by hand, like injection moulding (see Fig. 2). The core had to be redesigned to attach a syringe to inject silicone into the mould. One end of an attachment had a Luer lock thread, and the other had a syringe. The 3D-printed part can be tapped with a hand drill tap to create a thread in the mould. This will create a thread that connects to the mould. The user can control the syringe completely, allowing precise silicone injection. Silicone must be evenly distributed throughout the mould for a good part. This is done with a cavity at the bottom of the core with five channels for silicone to flow. The channels will ensure that the silicone is evenly distributed throughout the mould and that there are no air bubbles.

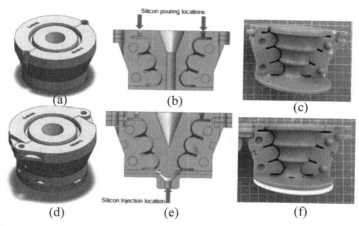

Fig. 2. Casting mould: (a) CAD design with isometric view of the mould and (b) CAD design with section view of the mould to show the pouring location of the silicone and (c) Mould core and Wall 1. Injection mould: (a) CAD design with isometric view of the mould and (b) CAD design with section view of the mould to show the pouring location of the silicone and (c) Mould core and Wall 1.

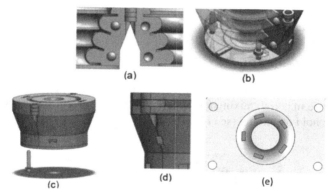

Fig. 3. CAD design of the mould with focused view of (a) mould keys, (b) guiding slides, (c) cut-outs on the side where hex nuts fit into, (d) ejector location and (e) vent location on the core of the mould.

Mould keys were also added to the mould outer walls (see Fig. 3a). Adding the mould keys makes it easier to ensure that the two mould walls are correctly aligned when the mould is closed. This helps to ensure the casting quality and reduce the chances of the walls shifting during the casting process. This minimises the risk of the casting being deformed and improves the overall accuracy of the casting process. The moulds have guiding slides to help align the core and the mould walls (see Fig. 3b).

The mould also features cut-outs on the side where hex nuts fit into (see Fig. 3c). This ensures that the screws are not driven in too deep and that the thread is strong. Hex nuts also provide more surface area for screws to grip, making them more secure and reliable. This reduces the stress on the part and makes it less likely to deform or weaken from over-tightening. The hex nuts form a more secure connection and ensure screws are held in place stronger.

Many different aspects of the mould were carefully considered. The first aspect to consider is the clamping force of the mould; this is done by the two bolts at the hinge. These bolts provide a force to ensure no silicone escapes the mould during moulding and curing. The mould parts could misalign and separate if the clamping force is insufficient. As the mould is a three-part mould, there will be a parting line where the different parts meet. The mould is made using SLA 3D printing, which has a layer height of only 25 microns. The mould's tolerance is significant when making parts, so the tolerances are ±0.2 mm for both moulds. There is also a vent at the bottom of the mould where trapped air can escape as silicone is being cast/injected into the mould. But this vent must be covered once the air has escaped and the silicone begins to come out. The mould also has an ejector location where once the silicone has cured (see Fig. 3d), the mould can be easily disassembled with a simple prying motion. These points are placed in areas with more structural support to minimise mould damage risk. This is so that the force applied during the disassembly process will be distributed evenly, and the mould will not be damaged. Special tools should be used to pry the mould apart to ensure that the force applied is distributed evenly and the mould is not damaged. The hinges of the moulds allow them to be opened and closed quickly when assembled and disassembled easily. There are also some vents in the mould's core (see Fig. 3e), where the silicone is injected, and air can escape.

2.4 Silicone Fabrication Process

The in-lab fabrication system is setup for this study, consists of the mould, vacuum chamber, silicone material, mixing tool, weighting scale, container to hold the mixture and a clamp to hold the mould (see Fig. 4.).

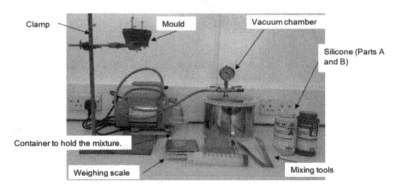

Fig. 4. Equipment required to mould silicone.

To make the silicone part the detailed process presented below will be followed (see Fig. 4):

Step 1: Clean the mould thoroughly using All-Purpose Cleaner (APC) to remove any stains, dirt, and grease from any surface of the mould. It is an effective cleaning product that removes stubborn stains, dirt, and oil from various surfaces. It is essential to thoroughly clean the mould before further steps are taken.

Step 2: Carefully stir both parts A and B ensuring there are no clumps.

Step 3: Parts A and B should be added to the mixing container in the specified amounts (1A:1B by weight).

Step 4: The mixture should be well mixed for 3 min, scraping the sides and bottom of the mixing container as necessary.

Step 5: Vacuum degassing is required to remove trapped air in liquid rubber after combining parts A and B. Vacuum pump must draw twenty-nine inches of mercury (or 1 bar/100 kPa). Allow space in the container for expansion. Vacuum the material until it rises, breaks, and falls, then vacuum for one minute after it falls.

Step 6: Pour the silicone into the mould without spilling it/Inject the silicone into the mould using a syringe by hand. Use a spatula to spread the silicone over the entire mould. Fill until the silicone fills the mould, then tap the mould edges to remove air bubbles.

Step 7: Clamp the mould, ensuring the top silicone is level. Allow the silicone to cure as prescribed at room temperature (73°F/23 °C) before removing it from the moulding. Do not cure silicone at less than 65°F/18 °C.

Step 8: Carefully remove the silicone part from the mould and inspect the piece for imperfections. Cut away excess silicone if necessary.

Step 9: The mould must be thoroughly cleaned with soap and dried before storage. Moulds with two or more parts should be assembled. Moulds should be kept on a level surface in a cold, dry place. Store the mould in a protective case or container to remove dust and debris. Check the mould periodically for signs of wear and tear. Replace the mould if it is damaged or worn.

3 Results and Discussion

3.1 Analysis Setup

To compare the manufacturing methods, measurements of the dimensional accuracy of each process were taken. Five parts were fabricated, two were cast and three through injection. It was not possible to manufacture the Ecoflex 00–50 with the casting method due to the significantly shorter pot time. The thickness of the silicone wall was measured at various locations (see Fig. 1) and compared to the target dimensions. This process was carried out by cutting the finished silicone part along its radial axis of symmetry (see Fig. 6) to enable access. Measurements were taken with digital vernier callipers at each of the detailed locations. Using a vernier calliper to measure soft silicone material instead of a micrometre is better. Micrometres can compress the material, causing incorrect measurements. On the other hand, vernier callipers can hold materials without causing damage. Minor deformation is still possible. The procedure for measuring thickness

388   K. Suthar et al.

is as follows: the vernier calliper is adjusted to a specific thickness and then wrapped around the silicone. Next, the calliper should be slowly tightened away from the silicone and then placed over the silicone until it no longer fits inside the jaws. This will give the final measurement. These locations were selected at key points in the geometry that contributed to its function. The parts were divided into 2 segments, SI and SII, with different desired dimensions (1 mm and 2 mm respectively). SI was further separated into 9 points, 3 on each ring of the geometry. Whilst SII was separated into 4 points, one for each protrusion. Table 2 shows the values collected for the points outlined separated by segment.

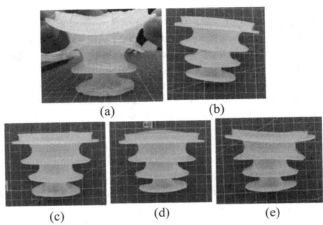

Fig. 5. Images of silicone part made from (a) casting of Ecoflex 00–30, (b) casting of DragonSkin-10, (c) injection of Ecoflex 00–30, (d) injection of Ecoflex 00–50, (e) injection of DragonSkin-10.

3.2 Analysis Results

Figure 6 shows the results gathered through measurement of the silicone parts cross-sections. The casting method displayed significantly more thickness variation (error) that the injection method. There were several points (SI-3, SI-7) where taking a value was not possible due to failure of the part for the Ecoflex 00–30 casting. Discounting these, the average error of the casting method was still significantly greater than the injection method. The maximum thickness variation for the casting method was 25% for SI-6 for the Ecoflex 00–30 casting, whereas 12% was the maximum for the injection method (Ecoflex 00–50 SI-8).

When compared, the casting method, on average, provided a lesser wall thickness than the target value. The inverse is true for the Injection method which, on average, provided a thicker wall value. There is also a general trend (when considering the SI values) of the injected parts thinning towards the top of the model, again the inverse is true for the casting method although to a lesser extent. There is no clear difference between the silicones of the same method.

Table 2. Table of the thicknesses measured from the different silicone parts.

Points on geometry	Thickness measurement (mm)					
	Desired thickness	Casting-EF30	Casting-DS10	Injection-EF30	Injection-EF50	Injection-DS10
SI-1	1	1.10	1.10	0.98	1.01	0.94
SI-2	1	1.00	1.07	0.97	0.96	0.92
SI-3	1	0.00	1.00	0.95	0.99	1.00
SI-4	1	1.05	0.86	0.96	1.09	1.06
SI-5	1	1.00	1.01	1.08	1.00	1.10
SI-6	1	0.75	1.04	1.10	1.08	0.95
SI-7	1	0.00	0.84	1.09	1.06	1.07
SI-8	1	0.90	0.99	1.10	1.11	1.04
SI-9	1	1.05	1.04	1.03	1.12	1.08
Avg error (mm)		0.08*	0.07	0.06	0.06	0.06
SII-1	2	2.06	2.08	2.03	1.97	1.98
SII-2	2	1.85	2.08	1.97	2.04	2.02
SII-3	2	1.96	2.05	2.00	2.01	1.99
SII-4	2	2.08	2.03	1.95	2.05	1.91
Avg error (mm)		0.08	0.06	0.03	0.03	0.04

* Average error calculated excluding outliers of SI-3 and SI-7

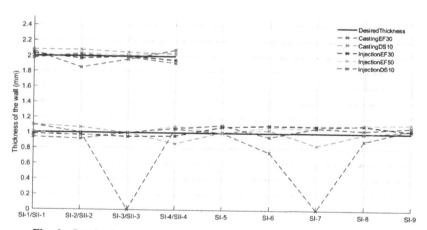

Fig. 6. Graph of the thicknesses measured from the different silicone parts.

3.3 Analysis Observations

Figure 5 (a) and (b) display the results of the casting method. The silicones used are Ecoflex 00–30 and DragonSkin-10 respectively. There are extensive imperfections in the parts structures likely resulting in impaired function. Large internal cavities are visible in (a) where air did not escape during the pouring process and was trapped within the curing silicone. It is also the case that significant warping occurred to the part. This appears to be caused by partial curing during the pouring process, and by the trapped air caused by pouring in the silicone from the top of the mould. Visible in (b) are less extensive yet larger holes completely through the walls of the part. These would likely impair the function of the part. These differences in mould failures are suspected to be the result of the varied viscosities and pot times of different silicones used. Extensive effort was made to ensure the part was manufactured as quickly as possible. Despite this, the preparation (pre-pour) process represents a large amount of time, and the silicone was beginning to cure before the entire mould was poured, this likely contributed significantly to the large imperfections visible with this method. These results indicated that this method is not viable for the manufacturing of this part, with these dimensions and wall thickness, and as such the injection method was developed with the aim of reducing the time to get the silicone into the mould minimising the effect of premature curing. It is unexpected that visibly there was more trapped air in the casted EF 30 than the DS10 due to the reduced viscosity. It is suspected that small variation in the procedure or ambient conditions, particularly temperature, may have resulted in the discrepancy.

The injection moulding method was used to mould all three silicone types, DragonSkin-10, Ecoflex 00–50 and Ecoflex 00–30, visible in Fig. 5 (c), (d) and (e) respectively. There are much fewer visible imperfections to the parts structure. During the injection process, as the silicone is subjected to high pressure, it can evade the mould's seals and leak from the joins. This was most significant with the Ecoflex 00–30 silicone due to its significantly lower mixed viscosity. This typically does not significantly affect the quality of the part, as extra silicone is injected to account for this. However, this effect is more pronounced lower in the mould due to the upright position. This is a suspected cause of the slightly higher wall thickness in the lower rings.

Viscosity was a significant factor in the injection process. DragonSkin-10 is the stiffest silicone, and the most viscous when mixed (see Table 1). As such, the pressure required to inject the silicone was significantly greater than the other silicones and likely approaching the limit of what was achievable with the current apparatus. The Ecoflex 00–50 only had a workable pot time of 18 min which after the preparation (mixing, degassing etc.) allowed for a short amount of time for the injection process, however despite this, it proved to be quick and effective to manufacture the part using this method. Another noted observation was that all the injected silicone parts have a small bubble in the top ring. This is likely caused by the air being trapped at the top layer as it fills up. To prevent this air bubble from forming, the injection mould could be improved so air can escape during the injection process. This can be achieved by adding vents to the mould or using a slow injection speed or by adding a draft angle on the top layer of the mould. The bubble is a result of the manufacturing process and will not affect the function of the part. Both moulds have identical vents at the bottom to release air during pouring and injection. However, the small wall thickness of the test geometry restricted the silicone flow through the mould. This was due to its high viscosity. This coupled with limited pot life caused uneven curing, contributing to wall thickness variation. To address this, silicone thinner was considered. However, its effect on shore hardness made it unsuitable for this test, which required specific shore hardness values.

Based on these results, it appears that this manufacturing method can be used with a variety of silicone types, from viscous silicone to silicone with a low pot life, allowing users to manufacture silicone parts with the desired properties. Additionally, the injection moulding method was efficient, with the silicone part being moulded with significantly reduced handling and an overall lesser process time. This method also allowed bubbles to rise, resulting in a more successful and dimensionally accurate final product.

4 Conclusion

In this work, a comparison study has been carried out between casting and injection moulding methods by fabricating complex shape parts with three different silicon materials (i.e., Ecoflex 00–50, Ecoflex 00–30 and DragonSkin-10). It has been proposed that a silicone-based soft part fabrication process can be easily switched between casting and injection moulding by modifying the material input port to the minimum extent possible. Table 2 shows that injection moulded parts exhibit increased precision in achieving the desired thickness by measuring the part's wall thickness at different locations. The Casting-EF30 and Casting-DS10 have demonstrated accuracy with average errors of 0.08 mm and 0.07 mm on SI-1 to SI-9 and 0.08 mm and 0.06 mm on SII-1 to SII-4, respectively. The Injection-EF30, Injection-EF50, and Injection-DS10 parts have been highly accurate, with an average error rate of only 0.06 mm, 0.06 mm and 0.06 mm for SI-1 to SI-9 and 0.03mm, 0.03 mm and 0.04 mm for SII-1 to SII-4, respectively. These preliminary results show that with this minimised modification to the mould, the proposed injection moulding method surpasses the casting method in producing complex parts. More samples may be necessary to consolidate the results and is a possible avenue for future work.

Acknowledgement. This work was supported by Brunel Research Initiative & Enterprise Fund (BRIEF) and EPSRC Impact Acceleration Account (EP/X525510/1).

References

1. Miranda, I., et al.: Properties and applications of PDMS for biomedical engineering: a review. J. Funct. Biomater. **13**, 2 (2021). https://doi.org/10.3390/jfb13010002
2. Mohanty, S., et al.: Fabrication of scalable and structured tissue engineering scaffolds using water dissolvable sacrificial 3D printed moulds. Mater. Sci. Eng., C **55**, 569–578 (2015). https://doi.org/10.1016/j.msec.2015.06.002
3. Alderighi, T., Malomo, L., Auzinger, T., Bickel, B., Cignoni, P., Pietroni, N.: State of the art in computational Mould design. Comput. Graph. Forum **41**, 435–452 (2022). https://doi.org/10.1111/cgf.14581
4. Mwema, F.M., Akinlabi, E.T.: Basics of fused deposition modelling (FDM). Fused Deposition Model. 1–15 (2020).https://doi.org/10.1007/978-3-030-48259-6_1
5. Mohd Fuad, N., Carve, M., Kaslin, J., Wlodkowic, D.: Characterization of 3D-printed moulds for soft lithography of Millifluidic devices. Micromachines. **9**, 116 (2018). https://doi.org/10.3390/mi9030116
6. Mazzeo, A.D., Hardt, D.E.: Centrifugal casting of microfluidic components with PDMS. J. Micro Nano-Manufact. **1**(2), 021001 (2013). https://doi.org/10.1115/1.4023754

7. Zhao, H., Li, Y., Elsamadisi, A., Shepherd, R.: Scalable manufacturing of high force wearable soft actuators. Extreme Mech. Lett. **3**, 89–104 (2015). https://doi.org/10.1016/j.eml.2015.02.006

8. Polygerinos, P., et al.: Towards a soft pneumatic glove for hand rehabilitation. In: 2013 IEEE/RSJ International Conference on Intelligent Robots and Systems (2013). https://doi.org/10.1109/iros.2013.6696549

9. Roche, E.T., et al.: A bioinspired soft actuated material. Adv. Mater. **26**, 1200–1206 (2013). https://doi.org/10.1002/adma.201304018

10. Deimel, R., Brock, O.: A compliant hand based on a novel pneumatic actuator. In: 2013 IEEE International Conference on Robotics and Automation (2013). https://doi.org/10.1109/icra.2013.6630851

11. Onal, C.D., Rus, D.: A modular approach to soft robots. In: 2012 4th IEEE RAS & EMBS International Conference on Biomedical Robotics and Biomechatronics (BioRob) (2012). https://doi.org/10.1109/biorob.2012.6290290

12. Schumacher, C.M., Loepfe, M., Fuhrer, R., Grass, R.N., Stark, W.J.: 3D printed lost-wax casted soft silicone monoblocks enable heart-inspired pumping by internal combustion. RSC Adv. **4**, 16039–16042 (2014). https://doi.org/10.1039/c4ra01497a

13. Marchese, A.D., Katzschmann, R.K., Rus, D.: A recipe for soft fluidic elastomer robots. Soft Rob. **2**, 7–25 (2015). https://doi.org/10.1089/soro.2014.0022

14. Galloway, K.C., et al.: Soft robotic grippers for biological sampling on deep reefs. Soft Rob. **3**, 23–33 (2016). https://doi.org/10.1089/soro.2015.0019

15. Bell, M.A., Becker, K.P., Wood, R.J.: Injection molding of soft robots. Adv. Mater. Technol. **7**, 2100605 (2021). https://doi.org/10.1002/admt.202100605

Estimation of Soft Body Deformation by Using Light

Chapa Sirithunge[1(✉)], Ryman Hashem[2], and Fumiya Iida[1]

[1] Bio-Inspired Robotics Laboratory, Department of Engineering, University of Cambridge, Cambridge CB2 1PZ, UK
{csh66,fi224}@cam.ac.uk

[2] Department of Medical Physics and Biomedical Engineering, University College London, London WC1E 6BT, UK
r.hashem@ucl.co.uk

Abstract. Soft robots are becoming increasingly popular due to their ability to mimic the flexibility and adaptability of biological systems. However, they still face challenges in terms of sensing and feedback methods. Elastomers can absorb light when exposed to a light source, and the absorption intensity can be varied when elastomers are on dynamic behaviour. In this paper, we explore the potential of using different light absorption properties of elastomers as a sensing and feedback technique in soft robots. We present experimental results that show the response of two most commonly encountered deformations of soft robots: linear and spherical, towards light absorption upon deformation. This concept can be used for assisting soft robotic sensing through freely available forms of light in the surrounding. Our findings suggest that using elastomers with different light absorption properties can significantly enhance the sensing performance of soft robots and open up new avenues for research in this field.

Keywords: Soft robots · light sensing · deformation of materials

1 Introduction

Nature is a constant source of inspiration for scientists developing devices and robots. Among these, soft robots mimic living organisms' physical properties and capabilities, such as flexibility, adaptability, and resilience [1]. Hence nature can provide various sources of information and energy to make soft robots more life-like. Unlike traditional rigid robots, soft robots are highly deformable and can change shape in response to forces or pressure. This makes them particularly useful for applications where delicate interactions with the environment are necessary [2]. Sensing is essential for soft robots to function effectively and

This work is supported by Engineering and Physical Sciences Research Council (EPSRC) RoboPatient grant EP/T00519X/1.

efficiently in dynamic and unstructured environments [3]. By providing real-time information about the robot's surroundings and internal state, sensors can enable soft robots to perform complex tasks with greater accuracy, precision and higher safety and reliability. Providing autonomy and advancing beyond open-loop control requires multimodal sensors in soft-bodied systems for adequate sensory feedback [4]. This can be particularly important for applications where precision and accuracy are critical, such as in surgical procedures or industrial manufacturing processes.

A significant challenge to establishing adequate sensing in soft robots is flexibility, which gets disturbed when multiple sensors are used [5]. Therefore natural sources of information provide a simple sensing method where only a limited number of sensors or limited space is available in a robot. Living organisms can sense and respond to environmental changes through reflex-driven pathways based on light [6]. Such capabilities can improve the somatosensory capabilities of robots at a later stage. Natural light is an example of a free source of information that exists in the surrounding. Light creates information in a soft robot through reflection, refraction, and penetration. Unlike rigid robots, deformation is part of the actuation process in soft robots. Hence it is essential to track the deformation with sensors for feedback, actuation and control [7]. Optical properties of materials such as refraction, absorption and dispersion change under deformation. As natural light is freely available in the environment, it can be used to measure at least one of the above properties. We explored how natural light can be used to measure the deformation of soft bodies during actuation. This can be investigated by analysing light intensity over an elastic object with changing deformation.

Sugiura et al. designed a method of detecting the deformed shape of soft robots without spoiling their softness through directional photo-reflectivity measurement that uses IR light [8]. Although this requires no physical connection with any object, this is hand-sized and hence not appropriate for measuring the deformation of small-scale objects. There are simulation techniques to estimate the soft body deformation through visual and depth information [9]. However, IR-based approaches must be more accurate for outdoor applications of soft bodies. Liquid crystalline polymers (LCPs) programmed to undergo three-dimensional shape changes in response to light are promising materials for light sensing. The successful development of autonomous, highly controlled light-driven soft robots calls for understanding light-driven actuation [10,11]. In addition, there are applications where it is possible to tailor photoluminescence, optical properties of materials, or both [12]. Furthermore, soft robots make use of light for locomotion using photo-responsive materials [13,14]. However, still light is an underexplored aspect in soft robotics in terms of sensing.

We present an experiment conducted on soft elastomers to explore how the penetration of natural light through elastomers can be used to improve soft robotic sensing. As soft robots are made of materials combining several substances and mostly handcrafted, it is challenging to model their behaviour using the existing equations and coefficients. Therefore we analysed the possibility of using light from surrounding light sources to acquire information regarding the deformation of soft objects, using existing mathematical models to explain light penetration of highly elastic materials.

2   Methods

When light penetrates a soft material, it can be absorbed or scattered by the material, depending on its optical properties. The amount of light absorbed or scattered depends on the thickness and composition of the material, as well as the wavelength of the light. In general, the deeper the light penetrates the material, the greater the amount of energy absorbed or scattered, and therefore, the greater the potential for deformation [15].

The extent of deformation also depends on the properties of the material, such as its elasticity and viscosity. Soft materials with high elasticity and low viscosity are more likely to deform in response to light penetration. Therefore, the relationship between light penetration and the deformation of soft material is complex and depends on various factors, including the material's properties, the light's intensity and wavelength, and the material's geometry. However, light penetration can play a significant role in sensing the degree of deformation in soft materials. This paper explores how this fact can be used to improve soft robotic sensing and response towards environmental stimuli.

2.1   Light Penetration Through Elastic Materials

Light can penetrate elastic materials to varying degrees, depending on the optical properties of the material and the wavelength of the light. Elastic materials such as rubber, silicone, and elastomers are highly transparent to visible light. Still they can absorb or scatter light at certain wavelengths, such as ultraviolet (UV) or infrared (IR) light. The amount of light absorbed or scattered depends on the composition and thickness of the material, as well as the wavelength of the light.

The penetration depth of light into elastic materials also depends on the optical properties of the material [16]. For example, if the elastic material has a high refractive index, the light will be refracted more and will penetrate deeper into the material. On the other hand, if the elastic material has a low refractive index, the light will be reflected more and will not penetrate as deeply.

In addition to absorption and scattering, light can cause elastic deformation. This is because light can generate a gradient of light intensity within the material, leading to a non-uniform distribution of forces that can cause the material to deform. The extent of deformation depends on various factors, including the light's intensity and wavelength, the material's properties, and the material's geometry.

2.2   Modelling Optical Behaviour of Materials

The penetration of light into elastic materials can be described mathematically using several equations, including the Beer-Lambert law and the Fresnel equations [17]. The Beer-Lambert law describes light absorption as it passes through a medium, such as an elastic material. It can be expressed as:

$$I = I_0 * e^{-\alpha * L} \tag{1}$$

where I is the intensity of the light after passing through the material, I_0 is the initial intensity of the light, α is the absorption coefficient of the material, and L is the thickness of the material. The absorption coefficient, α, depends on the properties of the material and the wavelength of the light.

From 1, it can be derived that

$$ln(I/I_0) = -\alpha * L \tag{2}$$

While Hooke's law can be applied to materials which behave linearly within its elastic limit and for nonlinear highly deformable materials, more constructive equations might be required to accurately describe their behaviour. Hence, L is inversely proportional to $ln(I)$. However, when an elastic material stretches, its thickness decreases, increasing the light permeability. Hence $d \propto 1/L$, where d is the deformation in length. In other words, $d \propto ln(I)$.

The Fresnel equations describe the reflection and refraction of light as it passes from one medium to another, such as from air to an elastic material. The equations are different for light polarized parallel to the plane of incidence (s-polarized) and light polarized perpendicular to the plane of incidence (p-polarized).

These equations can be used to model the behaviour of light as it passes through elastic materials and interacts with the material's properties, such as its absorption and refractive indices. However, it is worth noting that the actual behaviour of light in elastic materials can be complex and depend on various factors. These equations provide simplified models for the interactions between light and elastic materials. Therefore, to analyse the optical properties of elastomers used in soft robotics, we used 2 materials and shapes: Ecoflex 00–10 (a rectangular membrane) and a rubber balloon (spherical shape when inflated). This is because linear and spherical deformations are commonly used in soft robotic actuation.

The relationship between pressure or volume inside elastomers and their light absorption depends on the specific material and its properties. In general, elastomers are materials that can be deformed and return to their original shape when the deformation is removed. When an elastomer is compressed, the distance between the molecules is reduced, which can affect the material's optical properties. The deformation of a balloon due to light penetration depends on various factors, including the thickness and composition of the balloon material, the intensity and wavelength of the light, and the properties of the balloon material, such as its elasticity and viscosity.

When light penetrates through a balloon, it can be absorbed or scattered by the material, causing a transfer of energy. The amount of energy transfer depends on the amount of light absorbed or scattered, which in turn depends on the thickness and composition of the balloon material and the wavelength of

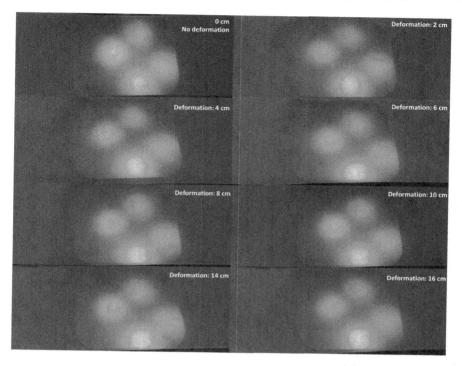

Fig. 1. How a light source appears on the other side of the membrane at different levels of deformation when stretched is shown here.

the light. Figure 1 shows how the light passes through a soft membrane upon various stages of deformation appearing to the camera. It can be seen that, it is hard to visually differentiate if a deformation was present at certain amounts of deformations.

3   Experiment and Results

3.1   Experimental Setup

There are many different geometries associated with soft robots such as elongation, contraction, bending, and twisting motions [18]. Out of them, we used two commonly used deformations by soft robots in our experiments: linear and volumous elongation. There were two experiments to observe the deformation of soft elastomers by using light.

Experiment 1: The setup for experiment 1 is shown in Fig. 2. We used this setup to test the light penetration through an elastomer (Ecoflex 0010) which undergoes linear deformation. A rectangular piece of elastomer of thickness 5 mm thickness was clamped from opposite sides. A light source was fixed above it and an ambient light sensor (B-LUX-V30B) was below. The light source, sensor and

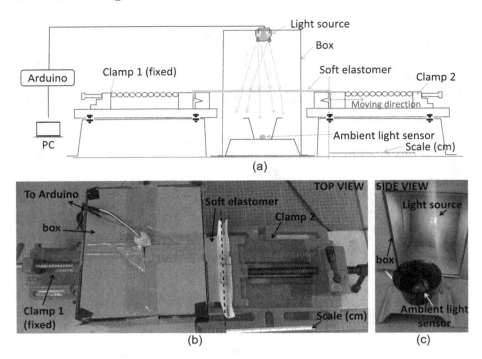

Fig. 2. The setup for experiment 1 is shown here. (a) As most part of the actual experiment setup is covered by the box, the experiment setup is illustrated together with the components which are not visible to the outside (b) The experiment setup with the box and the two clamps holding the elastomer on either sides: top view (c) The ambient light sensor covered by the box and the light source attached on the top of the box are shown.

elastomer were covered with a box to avoid the effect of background light. One clamp was fixed on the ground and the other was free to move horizontally in the direction shown in Fig. 2(a). The light source was lit throughout the experiment, and the ambient light sensor reading was taken at different displacements of the movable clamp. The displacement of the clamp resulted in stretching the elastomer in an equal amount and this ranged from 0 to 20 cm. This was repeated at three different levels of light intensities (145, 232 and 302 lx) from the light source to observe the optical properties of the elastomer.

Experiment 2: The setup for experiment 2 is shown in Fig. 3. In this experiment, we tested the spherical shape of an elastomer and its optical properties under deformation. We replaced the clamped elastomer in experiment 1, with a pneumatically actuated balloon (rubber). We used a separate pneumatic input to inflate the balloon in equal volumes each time (SMC ITV 0030 pneumatic regulator). The balloon was put around the ambient light sensor so the sensor could read the light penetrated through the balloon upon inflation. As the flow rate of the pneumatic regulator was constant, the regulator was operated throughout a constant time (1 s in the experiment) to inflate the balloon with

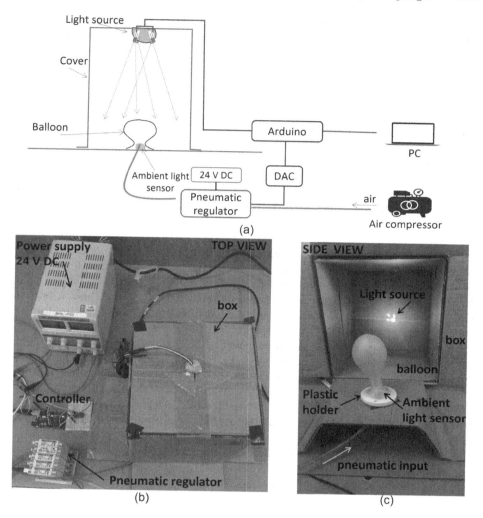

Fig. 3. The setup for experiment 2 is shown here. (a) Complete experiment setup is illustrated including the equipment covered by the box (b) The experiment setup with the box, pneumatic supply, control circuitry and the power supply: top view (c) The ambient light sensor attached to the balloon and the light source attached on top of the box are shown.

a constant volume of air. Readings of the ambient light sensor were recorded at the controller and analysed by the PC as shown in the figure. The volume of the balloon was increased by the same amount each time and the light intensity inside the balloon was recorded.

Each experiment was conducted under four different strengths of the lights source. Light intensity was varied by varying the number of LEDs lit at each stage. For instance, we used two, three and four LEDs to vary the light intensity. This step is intended to closely observe the effect of light intensity towards the optical penetration of the elastomer.

3.2   Results and Discussion

Results of experiment 1 are shown in Fig. 4. For all three light intensities from the source, the intensity received at the ambient light sensor through the elastomer was proportional to its displacement as seen from Fig. 4(a). Although this relationship is not linear, the luminosity increased with the deformation. It could be observed that the rate at which the concentration of light increased or decreased when the displacement exceeded a certain value. Hence an exponential increment of lux level could be deduced from the light intensity vs deformation plot.

We discussed in Sect. 2.2 that $d \propto ln(I)$ from Eq. 2. Even so, it is difficult to establish the mathematical relationship between the thickness and the deformation of elastomers. However it can be seen from Fig. 4(b), that the deformation of the membrane behaves similar to that in 2. Hence it can be observed that ln(I) is proportionate to the deformation of the soft body. From these results it can be seen that the regression curve obtained from experiment 1 resembles the relationship between the parameters stated in the Eq. 2.

Results of experiment 2 are shown in Fig. 5(a) and (b). For all three light intensities from the source, light intensity received at the ambient light sensor through the elastomer, was proportional to its displacement as illustrated in Fig. 5(a). In addition, it could be observed from Fig. 5(b) that ln(I) is proportionate to the volumetric deformation of the soft body. Although there is no established relationship between the volume and the deformation of an elastomer, it can be observed that ln(I) is proportional to the volumetric deformation of the body. According to Fig. 5(a), although the luminosity kept increasing with the balloon's volume, there was a considerable nonlinearity between the light intensity and the deformation compared to experiment 1. A possible reason for this is the shape of the balloon which is not entirely spherical at the opening. To elaborate, the shape of the balloon at each stage: when it is under-inflated, properly-inflated and over-inflated, is different. From these results it can be seen that the regression curve obtained from experiment 2 resembles the relationship between the parameters stated Eq. 2.

As a whole, there is an observable relationship between a soft material's optical properties and its deformation and it resembles Eq. 2. This has been true for both the uniform (sheet of soft elastomer) and nonuniform shapes considered in the experiments. As soft robots undergo different types of nonlinear deformations, it is worth looking at this to increase the somatosensory capabilities of a robot and its response to environmental stimuli similar to natural organisms. Furthermore, when casting soft robots, several materials are mixed to acquire the intended softness/flexibility of soft robots. Hence it is worth analysing the optical behaviours of these new substances in order to improve their sensing capacity.

The experiment conducted in this study aimed to investigate how the deformation of a soft phantom affects the penetration of light through it. The results showed that there is a clear correlation between the degree of deformation and the amount of light that passed through the phantom. Specifically, as the phantom deformed more, the amount of light that was able to penetrate through it increased. These findings have important implications for various applications in which the deformation of soft materials can impact light transmissions,

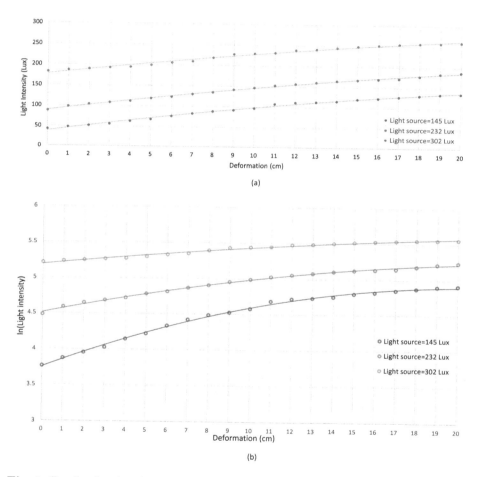

Fig. 4. Graphs showing the relationship between the light intensity and deformation of a soft elastomer as observed in experiment 1 (a) Light intensity received at the ambient light sensor is plotted against the deformation of the soft elastomer. The deformation of the elastomer was measured as the change in length. (b) Logarithmic value of the light intensity: ln(I) received at the ambient light sensor is plotted against the deformation of the soft elastomer. The deformation of the elastomer was measured as the change in length.

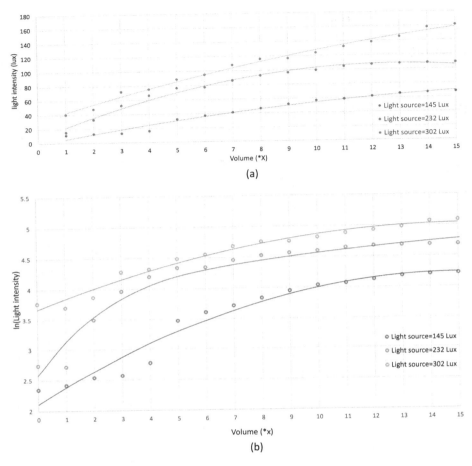

Fig. 5. Graphs showing the relationship between the light intensity and deformation of a balloon as observed in experiment 2 (a) Light intensity received at the ambient light sensor is plotted against the deformation of the soft elastomer. The deformation of the elastomer was measured as the change in length. (b) Logarithmic value of the light intensity: ln(I) received at the ambient light sensor is plotted against the deformation of the balloon. The deformation of the balloon was measured as the change in volume. Note: Volume of the balloon was increased by factors of 1,2,3,.., 15.

such as in medical imaging or optical sensing. in medical imaging, soft tissue deformation can affect the quality of images produced by X-rays or ultrasound. Understanding how this deformation impacts light penetration could improve sensing technologies. The measurement of light using an ambient light sensor on one side of the phantom provided a simple and effective method for quantifying the amount of light that was able to pass through the material. However, it is important to note that this method may limit its application in some scenarios as the properties of the ambient light and the orientation of the sensor could influence the results.

The intensity of natural light can be insufficient for some sensing applications, especially in low-light conditions. This is considered a limitation of using natural light for sensing. Although an alternative can be using an artificial light source, this can be space-consuming and can affect the flexibility of a soft robot. In addition, directionality of light might affect measurements. In such situations, measures should be taken to provide uniform illumination to sensors. Natural light can be subject to interference from other sources of light which can affect the accuracy and reliability of sensing measurements. Therefore, measures must be taken to avoid unnecessary forms of light from the environment.

As a whole, this study provides valuable insights into the relationship between the deformation of soft materials and light penetration. It highlights the importance of considering this relationship in a range of applications. We wanted to prove that these relationships are possible without having to model by using the established equations, such as in Sect. 2. Going forward, we plan to develop a genera model to use light in measuring irregular deformations in actuating soft robots. Thus making soft actuators and sensors more versatile, adaptable and operate safely and effectively in various environments. Future research could further explore this relationship by investigating the effects of different deformation types or exploring alternative measurement methods.

4   Conclusions

In this study, we investigated the relationship between light absorption of elastomers and their deformation. Our results indicate a proportionality between these two variables even when irregular shapes of soft body deformations are considered, which suggests that the light absorption of elastomers can be used to measure a substance's degree of deformation. Specifically, we found that both linear and volumous elongation of elastomers exhibit changes in their light absorption properties as they undergo deformation, which allows the development of soft robots that are highly responsive to light and can be efficiently controlled through feedback from light stimuli. Our findings have important implications for soft robotics, which suggest using elastomers with different light absorption properties to enable the development of soft robots with more responsiveness and adaptability. Additionally, the ability to measure deformation through changes in light absorption could be useful in a variety of applications, such as in monitoring the structural integrity of materials and in the development of smart materials that respond to external stimuli. Overall, our study highlights the potential of using the light absorption of elastomers as a tool for measuring deformation and controlling soft robots especially where irregularly shaped bodies are utilised. Further research is needed to explore the full range of applications and implications of this relationship, but our findings provide a promising starting point for future studies in this field.

References

1. Whitesides, G.M.: Soft robotics. Angew. Chem. Int. Ed. **57**(16) 4258–4273 (2018)
2. Lee, C., et al.: Soft robot review. Int. J. Control Autom. Syst. **15**(1), 3–15 (2016). https://doi.org/10.1007/s12555-016-0462-3
3. Navarro, S.E., et al.: A model-based sensor fusion approach for force and shape estimation in soft robotics. Robot. Autom. Lett. **5**(4), 5621–5628 (2020). IEEE
4. Wang, H., Massimo, T., Lucia, B.: Toward perceptive soft robots: progress and challenges. Adv. Sci. **5**(9), 1800541 (2018). Nature
5. Rus, D., Michael, T.: Tolley: Design, fabrication and control of soft robots. Nature **521**(7553), 467–475 (2015)
6. Wang, X.-Q., et al.: Somatosensory, light-driven, thin-film robots capable of integrated perception and motility. Adv. Mater. **32**(21), 2000351 (2020). Wiley
7. El-Atab, N., et al.: Soft actuators for soft robotic applications: a review. Adv. Intell. Syst. **2**(10), 2000128 (2020)
8. Yuta S., et al: Detecting shape deformation of soft objects using directional photo reflectivity measurement. In: Proceedings of the 24th Annual ACM Symposium on User Interface Software and Technology, pp. 509–516. ACM (2011)
9. Kang, D., Moon, J., Yang, S., Kwon, T., Kim, Y.: Physics-based simulation of soft-body deformation using RGB-D data. Sensors **22**(19), 7225 (2022). MDPI
10. Da Cunha, M.P., Debije, M.G., Schenning, A.P.H.J.: Bioinspired light-driven soft robots based on liquid crystal polymers. Chem. Soc. Rev. **49**(18), 6568–6578 (2020)
11. Yang, X., et al.: Bioinspired light-fueled water-walking soft robots based on liquid crystal network actuators with polymerizable miniaturized gold nanorods. Nano Today **43**, 101419 (2022)
12. Jiang, F., et al.: Synergistically tailoring mechanical and optical properties of diblock copolymer thermoplastic elastomers via lanthanide coordination. Chem. Mater. **34**(4), 1578–1589 (2022)
13. Yang, Y., Li, D., Shen, Y.: Inchworm-inspired soft robot with light-actuated locomotion. Robot. Autom. Lett. **4**(2), 1647–1652 (2019). IEEE
14. Zhang, P., et al.: Integrated 3D printing of flexible electroluminescent devices and soft robots. Nature Commun. **13**(1), 4775 (2022). Nature
15. Calloway, D.: Beer-lambert law. J. Chem. Educ. **74**(7), 744 (1997). ACS
16. Tilley, R.J.D.: Colour and the optical properties of materials. John Wiley & Sons (2020)
17. Lvovsky, A.I.: Fresnel equations. In: Encyclopedia of Optical and Photonic Engineering (Print)-Five Volume Set, pp. 1–6. CRC Press (2015)
18. Chen, F., Wang, M.Y.: Design optimization of soft robots: a review of the state of the art. Robot. Autom. Mag. **27**(4), 27–43 (2020). IEEE

Reduced-Order Modeling of a Soft Anthropomorphic Finger for Piano Keystrokes

Huijiang Wang$^{(\boxtimes)}$, Yuyi Zhang , and Fumiya Iida

Bio-inspired Robotics Lab, Department of Engineering, University of Cambridge, Trumpington Street, Cambridge CB2 1PZ, UK
hw567@cam.ac.uk

Abstract. The soft-bodied robotic hand provides a new paradigm for developing intelligent robotic systems with omnidirectional flexibility. This paper presents a novel approach to modeling the behavior of a soft anthropomorphic finger used in piano keystrokes. The proposed reduced-order model aims to capture the essential dynamics and characteristics of the finger's motion during piano playing. By leveraging the particle jamming technique, we design and fabricate a variable stiffness finger to achieve soft-bodied touch on a piano. The interaction between the soft finger and the piano keys is approximated using a high-dimensional linear time-invariant system, with state-space model parameters identified. To facilitate rapid computation and efficient keystroke control, we apply frequency-limited balanced truncation for model order reduction in the context of single-note piano playing. Our experimental results demonstrate the effectiveness of frequency-limited balanced truncation in compressing the high-dimensional state-space model while accurately representing the finger's kinematics during piano keystrokes under various stiffness conditions.

Keywords: Soft robot modeling · Variable stiffness · Balanced truncation

1 Introduction

The unparalleled adaptability and flexibility of soft materials are paving the way for the rise of soft robotics, a rapidly emerging field boasting an extensive array of applications, from sensing to locomotion, human-robot interaction, and even to the nuanced task of musical instrument playing [1–4]. Among these developments, anthropomorphic soft robotic hands deserve particular attention. Characterized by their inherent structural compliance, these entities are instrumental in humanizing the interactions between humans and machines, thus making complex and dexterous manipulation tasks like adaptive grasping and in-hand manipulation feasible [3–6].

Parallel to these advancements, researchers have made remarkable strides in the development of innovative materials, design methods, and fabrication techniques for soft robots [7–9]. However, the accurate modeling of soft robots remains a daunting challenge, compounded by the highly non-linear and time-variant nature of soft materials, their infinite degrees of freedom (DoF), and the intricacy of blending various materials [10].

Modeling is a crucial component for developing controllers adept at managing complex dynamic tasks involving soft robots and their interactions with the environment. The research conducted thus far on soft robot modeling largely oscillates between two primary paradigms: physics-based approaches and data-driven methods [7,11].

Physics-based models, anchored in rigorous physical principles, strive to encapsulate the inherent physical essence of the robot. A variety of methods, including the piecewise constant curvature (PCC), Cosserat rod theory, and beam models have been proposed and tested [12–15]. Despite their utility in modeling soft robot locomotion and electromechanical behavior [2,16], these models present several limitations. Their infinite DoFs become insurmountable when dealing with soft robots integrating multiple materials [17], and their specificity to certain robot geometries inhibits their ability to provide a high-fidelity approximation for new morphologies [18]. Alternatively, data-driven methods model the system directly from input-output data. These methods are direct and unambiguous; however, they heavily lean on experimental data for model identification. This reliance necessitates substantial computational resources and can occasionally compromise the accuracy of the model [10,11,19,20].

To date, the Finite Element Method (FEM) emerges as a promising solution for modeling soft robots. FEM provides a systematic methodology for high-fidelity modeling of the physics of soft robots [5,21,22]. It has been extensively utilized for the visualization of nonlinear deformation in soft robots, contact analysis, and design optimization. Further, derivative techniques from FEM, like differentiable simulation, have been introduced to ameliorate the simulation-to-reality gap engendered by the non-linearity of soft materials [1,10]. However, the high-dimensional nature of FEM limits its application to simple structured robots [11,23]. Additionally, the complex matrix inverse operations that FEM necessitates significantly increase the computational cost, thus hampering its application in real-time control tasks [23,24].

To address this challenge, the Model Order Reduction (MOR) has been proposed to streamline high-dimensional FEM models while preserving modeling accuracy [25]. MOR has found applications in constrained optimal control with linearized FEM models and in inverse kinematics-based control with nonlinear FEM models [26–29]. However, these applications still struggle with addressing the dynamic control challenges of variable-stiffness soft robots, especially in tasks such as piano playing.

To this end, our study introduces a new MOR approach for controlling a variable-stiffness soft finger in passive piano playing. The proposed framework comprises three stages: first-principles modeling, parameter identification, and MOR based on frequency-limited balanced truncation. We model the variable stiffness soft finger as a high-dimensional mass-spring-damper system and express the keystroke for passive piano playing as a state-space model with parameters

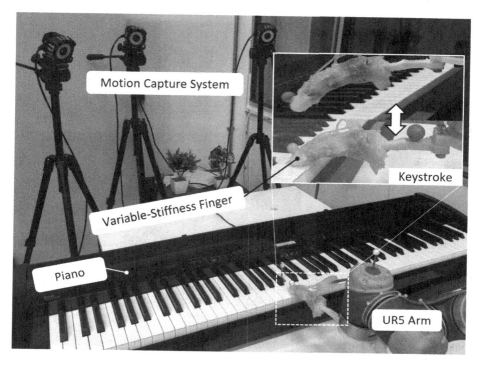

Fig. 1. Anthropomorphic keystroke action with a variable-stiffness finger for robotic piano playing.

identified through data-based approximation. By analyzing the energy contributions of each state and formulating a finite-frequency model order reduction (FF-MOR) problem, we are able to compress the high-dimensional state-space model into a more manageable low-dimensional representation. Consequently, our work contributes a systematic framework for developing reduced-order models of soft robots, a semi-physical model for a soft finger with variable mechanical properties, a model order reduction methodology based on energy contribution analysis, and a specially designed controller for soft-bodied piano playing within a specific frequency spectrum (Fig. 1).

2   Materials and Fabrication

2.1   Fabrication of Soft Finger

We designed the soft finger as a hybrid system, combining both soft and rigid components. The finger structure comprises a 3D printed skeleton (Rigur RGD450) enveloped in a silicone skin (Ecoflex^{TM} 00–30), achieving a balance between structural integrity and adaptability (Fig. 2). Ground coffee, serving as the particle jamming medium, fills the finger joints, creating discrete areas of

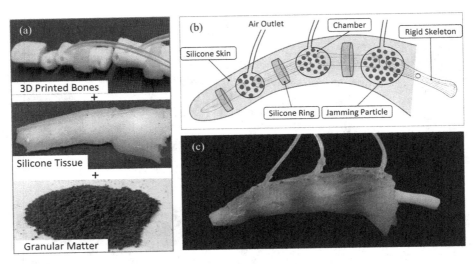

Fig. 2. The fabrication of the variable stiffness finger. (a) Materials include the 3D printed skeleton with silicone ring and tubing, silicone skin, and granular ground coffee; (b) Schematic of the particle jamming; (c) Fabricated soft finger.

localized rigidity. To prevent the cross-transition of granular particles between adjacent joints, silicone rings are situated around the skeleton. This configuration establishes an independent vacuum chamber at each joint. Subsequent to assembly, the complete finger is immersed in liquid silicone, enhancing the airtightness.

To control the particle-jammed joints, PVC tubes are inserted into preexisting holes on the skeleton, connecting the joints to a pneumatic regulator. At the end of each air tube, we attach a small piece of cloth to prevent the coffee powder from being inhaled and subsequently clogging the tube. The pneumatic regulator is linked to a compressed air valve through a vacuum pump (SMC ZH10B). By manipulating the pneumatic regulator, we can adjust the stiffness of the soft finger by modulating the vacuum pressure (between $-80\,kPa$ and $0\,kPa$) within the particle chambers.

2.2 Experimental Setup

In our experimental setup, we affixed the manufactured particle-jammed soft finger to a UR5 robotic arm. To test its performance, we programmed the UR5 to execute a repetitive motion where the finger presses a piano key by alternating the vertical acceleration, velocity, depth of the arm, and stiffness of the finger. Each set of parameters was tested three times to ensure consistency and reliability of the results.

For this study, we utilized the Kawai ES8 digital piano to conduct one-note piano key pressing tests. Our main interest was the MIDI $OnVelocity$, a metric produced by the piano with each keystroke that represents the velocity of the keypress [17]. To capture the intricate movements of the piano key and the soft finger, we implemented a 3D infrared motion capture system (OptiTrack). This allowed us to record in detail the trajectory of the soft finger throughout each keystroke action. By positioning reflective markers on the UR5 end-effector, the soft finger's center of mass, the soft finger's tip, and the surface of the piano key, we managed to capture the displacements in a 3D space at a frame rate of 120 Hz.

3   Theoretical Framework

3.1   First-Principles Model

The challenge of anthropomorphic piano playing lies in the need for exceptional dexterity and adaptability of the soft finger. While the soft finger is theoretically assumed to have infinite degrees of freedom, in this study, given the limited deformation and reachability constraints in the context of robotic piano playing, we assume that the entire soft finger can be represented by a finite number of mass-spring-damping systems (Fig. 3). It is noteworthy that the input and output are exclusively on a single-degree vertical axis, which simplifies the model as the experiments preclude lateral movement, and the extension is not measured. We assume that the deformation-dependent material parameters minimally impact control within a specific system's behavior of interest. Thus, we model the piano keystroke with a variable stiffness finger as a high-dimensional mass-spring-damper system, incorporating the physical principles of the passive finger. A mathematical model for this physical system can be represented using a set of input, output, and state variables.

The quality of the resulting music, typically characterized by the MIDI protocol, is fundamentally influenced by the timing and velocity of the fingertip during repetitive keystroke actions [17]. For achieving real-time dynamic control of piano playing, a model that approximates the kinematics of the fingertip is required.

In this context, the non-linearity of the soft-finger contact is represented by a high-order steady-states model (as shown in Eq. 1), where the trajectory of the fingertip (denoted as x_1) is the output and the trajectory of the UR5 (denoted as x_0) is the input. The behavior of the keystroke under varying stiffness conditions is approximated as a single-input single-output (SISO) high-order system, represented generally as:

$$\dot{z}(t) = A(t)z(t) + B(t)x_0(t) + Ke(t),$$
$$x_1(t) = C(t)z(t) + D(t)x_0(t) + e(t),$$
$$z(0) = z_0,$$

(1)

where $A \in \mathbb{R}^{r \times r}$, $B \in \mathbb{R}^{n \times m}$, $C \in \mathbb{R}^{p \times n}$ and $D \in \mathbb{R}^{p \times m}$ in the state-space representation of the model contain elements that capture the physical characteristics of the system. $z(t)$ is the state vector of variables representing the state of the system. The initial states are specified by z_0. K and $e(t)$ represent coefficients for an output-error model. Nevertheless, the high-order nature of the state-space representation with large matrices A, B, C, and D can pose a substantial computational burden in the control process.

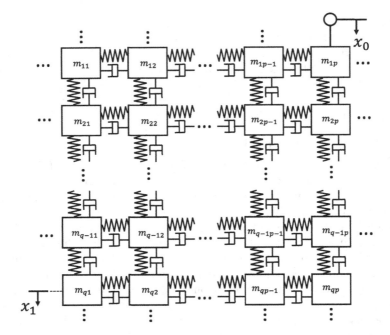

Fig. 3. The mass-spring-damping representation of the physics-based model.

3.2 System Identification

To address the computational challenges associated with high-dimensional state-space models, a data-driven approach is employed to capture the essential system parameters. This hybrid modeling process combines both first principles and data-driven modeling techniques, resulting in a quasi-physical method. Unlike traditional data-driven approaches that require a large amount of data, the proposed model leverages a small dataset to capture the fundamental mechanical characteristics of the soft finger-key interaction.

In modeling the variable stiffness of the soft finger, instead of using a linear parameter-varying (LPV) model [30], the linear variation of stiffness is considered as the input to the system. The collected dataset from actual robotic piano playing is used for system identification, allowing for the development of a state-space model that closely approximates the dynamics of real-world soft piano playing.

3.3 Model Order Reduction

The modeling of the soft finger in piano playing presents a challenge due to the high order of the theoretical model. To address this, we approach the problem as a finite-frequency model order reduction (FF-MOR) problem. The objective is to reduce the order of the state-space model to improve computational efficiency while retaining the essential behavior of the system. To achieve this, we utilize balanced truncation, which effectively captures the dominant dynamics of the system while reducing the number of degrees of freedom. The approach involves performing a coordinate transformation that balances the system's energy distribution and then truncating the model based on its contribution to the system's behavior of interest.

By reducing the model's order, we simplify the computational requirements while still preserving the essential characteristics of the system within the specific frequency range of interest. The reduced order model allows for more efficient computations, making it feasible to implement real-time control algorithms for piano playing. Despite the reduction in complexity, the model retains the key characteristics that are necessary for accurately representing the interaction between the soft finger and the piano keys. For the control problem, we have the system as:

$$
\begin{cases}
\frac{d}{dt}\begin{bmatrix} \widetilde{X} \\ Z_t \end{bmatrix} = \begin{bmatrix} \Phi^* A\Psi & \Phi^* AT_t \\ S_t A\Psi & S_t AT_t \end{bmatrix}\begin{bmatrix} \widetilde{X} \\ Z_t \end{bmatrix} + \begin{bmatrix} \Phi^* B \\ S_t B \end{bmatrix} u \\
y = \begin{bmatrix} C\Psi & CT_t \end{bmatrix}\begin{bmatrix} \widetilde{X} \\ Z_t \end{bmatrix}
\end{cases}
\tag{2}
$$

Here the matrices represent the captured essence from the model using the system identification with a state space method. Note that the matrices are high-order in dimension, which is challenging for online or real-time control for soft robots. The matrices obtained after balanced truncation represent a compressed representation of the original system. They retain the key characteristics and behavior of the soft finger-piano interaction but with a significantly reduced dimensionality compared to the high-order model. The state space model is described as follows:

$$
\begin{cases}
\frac{d}{dt}\widetilde{X} = \Phi^* A\Psi\widetilde{X} + \Phi^* Bu \\
y = C\Psi\widetilde{X}
\end{cases}
\tag{3}
$$

In Eq. 2 and 3, matrices A, B and C denote the original state-space matrices before MOR while $\widetilde{X}$ denotes the essential states capturing the dominant patterns of the input-output data. Φ^* and Ψ denote the MOR transformation imposed on the original state-space matrices. Z_t depicts the states discarded after the balanced truncation. The balanced truncation approach targets to find states that jointly balance the controllability of that state with the observability.

4   Results

4.1   Model Output

The first experiment conducted in this study is aimed at evaluating the accuracy of the quasi-physical model in approximating the variable stiffness of the soft finger-piano interaction. We scrutinize the vertical displacement of the fingertip in response to the UR5 robot's input under three distinct stiffness conditions.

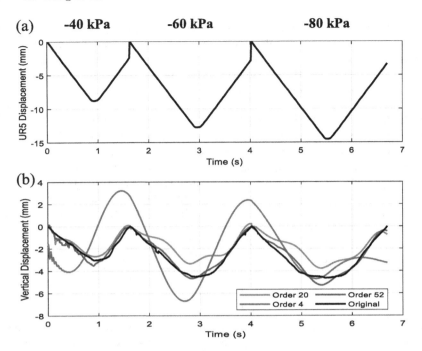

Fig. 4. The approximation of variable stiffness finger for models with different orders. (a) System input signals; (b) Comparison of three different order models' approximated system outputs and the original output.

Figure 4 portrays the results of the experiment, highlighting the vertical displacement of the fingertip for each stiffness condition. We juxtapose the original output, derived from the first-principles model of the soft finger, with the outputs of three state-space (SS) models of varying orders. The results demonstrate the efficacy of the proposed model in providing a robust approximation of the input-output kinematics for the soft finger-piano interaction. It was discerned that the low-order SS models, such as the Order 4 and Order 20, fell short in encapsulating the input-output relationship for a soft-bodied finger with real-time stiffness tunability. In contrast, the Order 52 model, despite its relatively high order for a Single-Input-Single-Output (SISO) system, managed to effectively capture the intrinsic characteristics of the system's behavior. This high-order model bears a strong resemblance to the original output, thereby signifying its competence in approximating the intricate dynamics of the soft finger-piano interaction.

4.2   Frequency-Limited Balanced Truncation

The original state-space (SS) model is characterized by a high order with 52 states, resulting in significant computational complexity and making it challenging to achieve real-time dynamic control. However, in the context of human

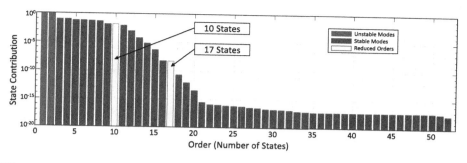

Fig. 5. Energy contribution of each state in the high-order system with limited frequency range.

piano keystrokes, there are inherent constraints in terms of the upper bound of keystroke speed due to the constraints imposed by the musculoskeletal system [31,32]. For the single-note keystroke system, there is no need to consider the system's response in an infinite frequency range. Focusing on the relevant frequency range allows for a more targeted and efficient analysis and control of the system.

Energy Contribution. In order to build a computationally efficient controller, we perform MOR for the original SS model. We need to discard superfluous states from the original high-order system based on their contribution to the model. The system's limited frequency range is considered in line with the real physical constraints.

The established SS model has 52 states, but not all of them contribute significantly to the resultant approximation performance. Considering all 52 orders into the controller can result in a significant computational burden. As a result, we examined the Hankel Singular Value to determine the energy contribution of each state. Figure 5 depicts the model's state contribution for the specific frequency spectrum. Even while the 52-state model achieves a decent approximation of the system, not all states contribute significantly to the model. Following orders with 10 and 17 states, significant declines in energy contribution have been observed for the remaining states. As a result, we chose those two reduced models and truncated the remaining states.

Model Response. We have two reduced models based on the examination of each state's energy contribution (10 states and 17 states). To evaluate the performance of these reduced models, we compare their Bode diagrams with the original model in Fig. 6. Because of the biomechanical constraints, a finite frequency system is considered in a single-note piano-playing scenario. From the Bode diagrams, we observe that both reduced models closely approximate the original high-order model in the frequency range of 0.1–6 Hz. However, the 10-state model deviates from the original model outside this frequency range,

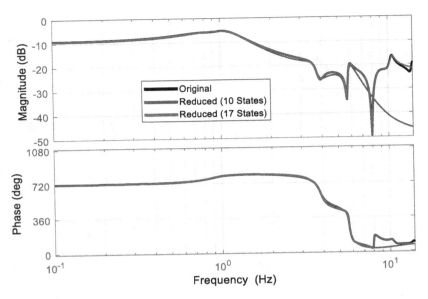

Fig. 6. Responses of the original model (52 states) and two reduced models for frequency of interest.

while the 17-state model provides a high-fidelity approximation for the entire frequency of interest.

5   Conclusion and Discussions

A systematic framework for reduced order modeling of a soft finger with variable mechanical properties has been proposed. A variable stiffness finger based on particle jamming has been fabricated to enable the soft-bodied touch with a piano. The soft-bodied finger-piano interaction is modeled based on a physics-based way and depicted as a mass-spring-damper system with multiple degrees of freedom. A state-space model, whose parameters are identified using a data-driven approximation, is proposed to capture the nonlinearity and compliance of the soft robot. In line with the ground truth that humans can only perform piano playing within a limited frequency due to musculoskeletal constraints, a frequency-limited balanced truncation approach is exploited to generate reduced models.

This work demonstrates that the behaviors of high-order, non-linear and soft-bodied interactions can be approximated by a reduced-order model. The framework is promising to serve as a general approach to representing a category of soft-bodied manipulation tasks that can occur repeatedly, such as mouse clicking, keyboard typing, and doorbell pressing. Several compromises have been made for the purpose of physics-based representation, e.g., the soft finger is considered with finite degrees of freedom. Future work could include substituting the coefficient matrices in the state-space model with time-variant deformation-dependent coefficients to improve approximation performance.

Acknowledgment. This work was supported by the EU-funded Marie Skłodowska-Curie SMART project (grant No. 860108).

References

1. Tao, D., Hughes, J., Wah, S., Matusik, W., Rus, D.: Underwater soft robot modeling and control with differentiable simulation. IEEE Robot. Autom. Lett. **6**(3), 4994–5001 (2021)
2. Goldberg, N.N., et al.: On planar discrete elastic rod models for the locomotion of soft robots. Soft Robot. **6**(5), 595–610 (2019)
3. She, Yu., Li, C., Cleary, J., Hai-Jun, S.: Design and fabrication of a soft robotic hand with embedded actuators and sensors. J. Mech. Robot. **7**(2), 021007 (2015)
4. Wang, H., Thuruthel, T.G., Gilday, K., Abdulali, A., Iida, F.: Machine learning for soft robot sensing and control: a tutorial study. In: 2022 IEEE 5th International Conference on Industrial Cyber-Physical Systems (ICPS), pp. 1–6. IEEE (2022)
5. Runge, G., Wiese, M., Günther, L., Raatz, A.: A framework for the kinematic modeling of soft material robots combining finite element analysis and piecewise constant curvature kinematics. In: 2017 3rd International Conference on Control, Automation and Robotics (ICCAR), pp. 7–14. IEEE (2017)
6. Gupta, A., Eppner, C., Levine, S., Abbeel, P.: Learning dexterous manipulation for a soft robotic hand from human demonstrations. In: 2016 IEEE/RSJ International Conference on Intelligent Robots and Systems (IROS), pp. 3786–3793. IEEE (2016)
7. Ilami, M., Bagheri, H., Ahmed, R., Skowronek, E.O., Marvi, H.: Materials, actuators, and sensors for soft bioinspired robots. Adv. Mater. **33**(19), 2003139 (2021)
8. Paik, J.: Soft robot design methodology for 'push-button' manufacturing. Nat. Rev. Mater. **3**(6), 81–83 (2018)
9. Onal, C.D., Rus, D.: A modular approach to soft robots. In: 2012 4th IEEE RAS & EMBS International Conference on Biomedical Robotics and Biomechatronics (BioRob), pp. 1038–1045. IEEE (2012)
10. Bern, J.M., Schnider, Y., Banzet, P., Kumar, N., Coros, S.: Soft robot control with a learned differentiable model. In: 2020 3rd IEEE International Conference on Soft Robotics (RoboSoft), pp. 417–423. IEEE (2020)
11. Tonkens, S., Lorenzetti, J., Pavone, M.: Soft robot optimal control via reduced order finite element models. In: 2021 IEEE International Conference on Robotics and Automation (ICRA), pp. 12010–12016. IEEE (2021)
12. Webster III, R.J., Jones, B.A.: Design and kinematic modeling of constant curvature continuum robots: a review. Int. J. Robot. Res. **29**(13), 1661–1683 (2010)
13. Della Santina, C., Katzschmann, R.K., Bicchi, A., Rus, D.: Model-based dynamic feedback control of a planar soft robot: trajectory tracking and interaction with the environment. Int. J. Robot. Res. **39**(4), 490–513 (2020)
14. Renda, F., Boyer, F., Dias, J., Seneviratne, L.: Discrete cosserat approach for multisection soft manipulator dynamics. IEEE Trans. Rob. **34**(6), 1518–1533 (2018)
15. Gravagne, I.A., Rahn, C.D., Walker, I.D.: Large deflection dynamics and control for planar continuum robots. IEEE/ASME Trans. Mechatron. **8**(2), 299–307 (2003)
16. Li, W.-B., Zhang, W.-M., Zou, H.-X., Peng, Z.-K., Meng, G.: A fast rolling soft robot driven by dielectric elastomer. IEEE/ASME Trans. Mechatron. **23**(4), 1630–1640 (2018)

17. Wang, H., Howison, T., Hughes, J., Abdulali, A., Iida, F.: Data-driven simulation framework for expressive piano playing by anthropomorphic hand with variable passive properties. In: 2022 IEEE 5th International Conference on Soft Robotics (RoboSoft), pp. 300–305. IEEE (2022)
18. Renda, F., Giorelli, M., Calisti, M., Cianchetti, M., Laschi, C.: Dynamic model of a multibending soft robot arm driven by cables. IEEE Trans. Rob. **30**(5), 1109–1122 (2014)
19. Gillespie, M.T., Best, C.M., Townsend, E.C., Wingate, D., Killpack, M.D.: Learning nonlinear dynamic models of soft robots for model predictive control with neural networks. In: 2018 IEEE International Conference on Soft Robotics (RoboSoft), pp. 39–45. IEEE (2018)
20. Thuruthel, T.G., Falotico, E., Renda, F., Laschi, C.: Model-based reinforcement learning for closed-loop dynamic control of soft robotic manipulators. IEEE Trans. Robot. **35**(1), 124–134 (2018)
21. Coevoet, E., Escande, A., Duriez, C.: Optimization-based inverse model of soft robots with contact handling. IEEE Robot. Autom. Lett. **2**(3), 1413–1419 (2017)
22. Elsayed, Y., et al.: Finite element analysis and design optimization of a pneumatically actuating silicone module for robotic surgery applications. Soft Robot. **1**(4), 255–262 (2014)
23. Largilliere, F., Verona, V., Coevoet, E., Sanz-Lopez, M., Dequidt, J., Duriez, C.: Real-time control of soft-robots using asynchronous finite element modeling. In: 2015 IEEE International Conference on Robotics and Automation (ICRA), pp. 2550–2555. IEEE (2015)
24. Della Santina, C., Duriez, C., Rus, D.: Model based control of soft robots: a survey of the state of the art and open challenges. arXiv preprint arXiv:2110.01358 (2021)
25. Thieffry, M., Kruszewski, A., Guerra, T.-M., Duriez, C.: Reduced order control of soft robots with guaranteed stability. In: 2018 European Control Conference (ECC), pp. 635–640. IEEE (2018)
26. Lorenzetti, J., Pavone, M.: Error bounds for reduced order model predictive control. In: 2020 59th IEEE Conference on Decision and Control (CDC), pp. 2521–2528. IEEE (2020)
27. Thieffry, M., Kruszewski, A., Guerra, T.-M., Duriez, C.: Trajectory tracking control design for large-scale linear dynamical systems with applications to soft robotics. IEEE Trans. Control Syst. Technol. **29**(2), 556–566 (2019)
28. Katzschmann, R.K., et al.: Dynamically closed-loop controlled soft robotic arm using a reduced order finite element model with state observer. In: 2019 2nd IEEE International Conference on Soft Robotics (RoboSoft), pp. 717–724. IEEE (2019)
29. Goury, O., Duriez, C.: Fast, generic, and reliable control and simulation of soft robots using model order reduction. IEEE Trans. Rob. **34**(6), 1565–1576 (2018)
30. Tóth, R.: Modeling and Identification of Linear Parameter-Varying Systems, vol. 403. Springer, Heidelberg (2010). https://doi.org/10.1007/978-3-642-13812-6
31. Bernays, M., Traube, C.: Investigating pianists' individuality in the performance of five timbral nuances through patterns of articulation, touch, dynamics, and pedaling. Front. Psychol. **5**, 157 (2014)
32. Bresin, R., Battel, G.U.: Articulation strategies in expressive piano performance analysis of legato, staccato, and repeated notes in performances of the andante movement of Mozart's sonata in g major (k 545). J. New Music Res. **29**(3), 211–224 (2000)

Tactile Sensing

Multi-directional Force and Tactile Sensor Sleeves for Micro Catheters and Cannulas

Joelle Sogunro, Xiaochong Wu, Carlo Saija, Basma Alabdullah, Joseph Rowell, Anhao Liu, Cristina Sanchez Fernandez, Kawal Rhode, Christos Bergeles, and S. M. Hadi Sadati$^{(\boxtimes)}$

School of Biomedical Engineering and Imaging Sciences, King's College London, London, UK
smh_sadati@kcl.ac.uk

Abstract. Robot-assisted minimally invasive surgery with catheters and steerable cannulas such as Concentric Tube Robots can improve the postoperative patient experience. Haptic sensing for tooltip can reduce the chance of complications in such procedures, such as vessel irritation, vasospasm, perforation, and aneurysm rupture. This paper investigates the design of an affordable multi-directional micro force and tactile sensor by comparing two sensing modalities: (i) Electrical Impedance sensing (EIS) via tissue impedance and electrical noise measurement, and (ii) Force Sensitive Resistance (FSR) measurement. For both of these techniques, we successfully developed two bi-directional sensor sleeves that were designed to envelope cannulas of varying dimensional configurations. In in-vitro phantom experiments with realistic mechanical and electrical proprieties, We showcased that the proposed designs have the potential to be used as an affordable disposable multi-modal bi-directional tactile and force sensor for off-the-shelf vascular intervention catheters.

Keywords: Sensor Sleeve · Force · Tactile · Medical robot · Vascular intervention · Thrombectomy

1 Introduction

Cardiovascular disease is the leading cause of death worldwide accounting for a staggering 32.2% in 2019, which is a 4.3% increase since the year 2000 [1]. To reduce the mortality rates, currently available procedures must be made more accessible at minimal cost and with as little mechanical complexity possible [5]. Procedures typically involve inserting catheters and guidewires into small incisions in the skin and guiding them through blood vessels to target regions in the body, such as the heart.

Operations involving steerable instruments rely heavily on pre-operational images taken with CT and/or MRI to calculate the path trajectory of the tooltip. However, commonly used 2D imaging techniques with no depth perception are not reliable enough to navigate a complex yet fragile 3D space with little to no

---

J. Sogunro, X. Wu—Co-first authors.

F. Iida et al. (Eds.): TAROS 2023, LNAI 14136, pp. 419–430, 2023.
https://doi.org/10.1007/978-3-031-43360-3_34

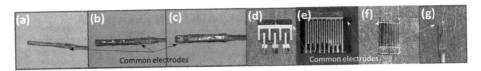

Fig. 1. Different structural design and dimensions for the Electrical Impedance-based (a–c) and Force Sensitive Resistor-based sensor sleeves (d–g).

reliable haptic feedback. Most surgeons rely on this feedback to some extent to comprehend the bodily environment of the tooltip in real time [10].

Currently, there are very few force feedback systems available commercially for steerable catheters [4,8,15]. Several transductive sensing techniques have been introduced in literature such as: capacitive, piezoresistive, piezoelectric, magnetic, optoelectric, strain gauges and hybrid sensors. However, each of these methods come with their own challenges whether that is bulkiness, susceptibility to humidity, temperature, noise, hysteresis, or inconsistency in the results [12].

Electrical Impedance is the measure of opposition that a circuit has to an alternating current, and measurement relies primarily on the frequency of sinusoidal voltage applied [2]. Su et al. [10] utilised this property to create a sensor for a biopsy needle that could distinguish tissue type using electrical impedance sensing, but does not provide peri-operational force readings. All conductive materials - including body tissue - have an innate resistivity that varies if distorted or deformed. Similar to the common large-size EIT-based tactile interfaces in the literature [6], we hypothesise that there might be a meaningful relationship between the force applied to living tissue and its impedance. Also, a bi-directional sensor design can provide directional tactile feedback as well as tissue type detection. However, sensing designs based on Impedance and resistance measurement suffers from micro fabrication challenges, measurement inconsistency, and lack of repeatability. In this paper, we try to address these issues by introducing a multi-layered sleeve design that can be wrapped around a micro catheter or steerable cannula.

On the other hand, Force Sensitive Resistors (FSR) are a form of haptic force feedback technology, where two flat (usually comb-shaped) conductors intertwine with a minuscule air gap between the electrode teeth. These conductors are then sandwiched between two flexible polymer-based FSR films that insulate and preserve the structure of the sensor with the thickness typically being 0.25 mm [14]. The FSR film has a high resistance (*approx* 1 MΩ) when no force is applied. When the FSR surface is pressed, the resistance will fall exponentially, revealing an inversely proportional relationship between the applied force and resistance [14]. In medical research, they have been seen often in prosthetics and bionics for pressure sensing [3,11], or even as a bending sensor in a robotic catheter system [16]. Unlike the FSR bending sensor placed at the actuation side of a catheter robot in [16], we attempted to attach an FSR to the tooltip of a catheter and tackle the micro-fabrication challenges that came with it.

In this paper, for the first time, we present the proof-of-concepts for two affordable micro-sized multi-directional tactile sensing sleeves that can be attached to off-the-shelf micro catheters and guidewires with diameters as small as 0.75 mm. The sensors should be designed to cover the medically relevant forces experienced during catheter vascular interventions, e.g. in the range of 0.02–1.7 N for interaction forces with silicon phantom of subclavian and common carotid arteries [9] and about 1.72 ± 0.59 N perforation forces for porcine cardiac perforation [7]. The goal is to provide surgeons with bi-directional tooltip tactile feedback to further improve tracking of catheters and steerable cannulas within the body. The implementation of this technology could possibly reduce the reliance of perioperative imaging through CT and MRI.

Section 2 explains the sensor structure, experimental setup, and phantom designs and variations. The experimental results and discussions are presented in Sect. 3. The paper is concluded in Sect. 4.

2   Materials and Methods

Catheters used in Cardiovascular interventions must fulfil certain criteria to be suitable for insertion into the body, and so we designed the sensors in a way to be complementary to them. The sensor size must be compatible with micro-scale steerable tube robots. This is why we used hollow steel rods with diameters of 0.75 mm, 1.10 mm, 1.20 mm and 3.00 mm to model the sensors on. We also stripped enamelled wire with a diameter of 70 μm to act as thin electrodes and connect the circuitry. We then used commercially manufactured FSR units (Akozon flexible thin film Pressure sensor, 0–500 g, and Hilitand RP-S40-ST thin film pressure sensor, 20–1000 g) that we cut to form electrodes with widths ranging from 0.1 mm to 0.5 mm. Another method we used to develop EIT sensor electrodes of varying size was to use adhesive copper foil with a thickness of 20 μm which was wrapped around a stripped wire. Thin double-sided/single-sided tape and super glue were used to hold the sensors together. Images of these electrode can be seen in Fig. 1.

The sensors produced in this paper express lateral force feedback in 3 different directions around the steel rod, each $\approx 120°$ apart. The sensor versatility will come from the simplicity of the designs. Using a simple design will not only make it easier to implement, but also reduce manufacture cost. This is why we decided to explore the use of EIS- and FSR-based deigns as they are relatively simple concepts that can be made bio-compatible, although it is not directly investigated in this paper. The price of the materials used to formulate these sensors were minute considering what and how little we used to fabricate them; however, this price mark may change in the future as we develop these sensors further and make them safe for the body.

2.1   Sensors' Design and Fabrication

EI-Based Sensors. Figure 1a–c show images of the four EI-based sensors that were created to investigate how the sensor's structural design and dimensions can affect force readings and sensitivity of the sensors. EI Sensors 1–3 (Fig. 1a–b) are modelled on a 0.75 mm steel rod whilst Sensor 4 (Fig. 1c) is on a 1.1 mm steel rod to investigate the effects of catheter radius and stiffness. Sensor 1 electrodes consist of 70 µm stripped solder-coated wires whilst sensors 2, 3, and 4 have copper-foil electrodes with lengths of 7.77 mm, 15.54 mm and 7.77 mm respectively to analyse the effects of electrode surface area. Sensor 4 has a common electrode above the input electrodes whilst the others have them below to find the optimum electrode arrangement for the force sensing tip.

During experimentation, it was observed that the sensors were responsive when in contact with moisturised or wet hands even when there was no voltage from the common electrode being supplied (there was no response to dry hands). This prompted us to design additional experiments that would allow us to compare single signal electrode noise readings compared to the impedance measurement between a pair of common and signal electrodes as a means to interpret the exerted force [2].

FSR-Based Sensors. In total, five distinct FSR-based sensors were designed, some of which can be seen in Fig. 1d–g. The comb-shape electrodes for sensor variations 1–3 (Fig. 1d–e) were taken from an off-the-shelf FSR sensor from Hilitand but with different electrode thicknesses that we cut to suit our design (see Fig. 2). Sensor variations 4–5 (Fig. 1f–g) were created from 70 µm diameter striped enameled wires as the common and signal electrodes, giving each of the electrodes a much smaller surface area than the sensors 1–3, but still keeping the same layout for sensor 5, we used electrically insulative enamelled wires between the common and signal electrodes to prevent short circuiting from occurring between the electrodes. We used single- and double-sided tapes to maintain an insulated air layer between each of the electrodes (Fig. 2).

FSR sensor designs 1–3 were to evaluate the sensors' directional accuracy, and how consistent the voltage-pressure relationship would be in controlled dry and wet conditions including in a saline solution (table salt and distilled water at

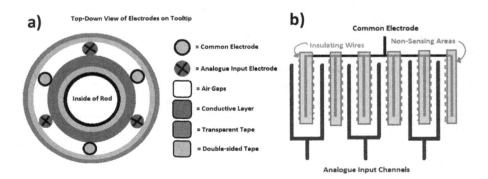

Fig. 2. The FSR-based sensor Electrode layout: (a) from a cross sectional view when wrapped around a tube, (b) in the flat state with the additional insulating wire elements, highlighting in blue the areas that are not detected by the electrodes. The overall sensor sensitivity can be increased by reducing the blue zone via moving the insulating wires closer to the common electrodes. (Color figure online)

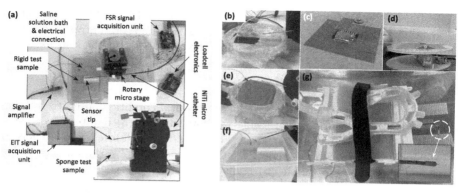

Fig. 3. (a) Top down view of experimental setup. The inset figure shows the way the rotary micro-stage allows the sensor electrodes to make contact with a phantom submerged in a saline bath. Snapshots of experimental studies on the different sensors and phantoms. (b) EIT sensor on rigid phantom with conductive Paint, (c) FSR sensor wet flat tests, (d) wrapped FSR sensor on a micro catheter in dry tests on a silicon tube round surface, (e) EIT sensor on conductive sponge phantom, (f) EIT sensor on a phantom with realistic electrical properties, (g) EIT sensor deployment and navigation feasibility in an in-vitro aortic arch phantom navigation study.

a concentration of 10%) with realistic biological electrical properties. They also tested the effects of having multiple electrodes connected to a single analogue input channel and whether that improves the signal output. FSR sensor designs 4 and 5 were later developed to miniaturize the designs with more flexibility. They were deployed onto a micro-catheter, analysed to compare different electrode sizes, and evaluated to measure the reliability when affixed to different materials, i.e. a stainless-steel rod versus a soft plastic catheter.

2.2   Experimental Setup Design

To test the sensors, voltage readings were taken from the input electrodes when they were pressed against a phantom atop of a load cell. The setup for all the experiments can be seen in Fig. 3, which is used for tests on different phantoms. The setup has the following components. A load cell with a sensitivity of 3 kg is connected to an Arduino and HX-711 amplifier board to record the force data. Above of the load cell is a stage to place the phantom. Seven Different Phantoms and experimental conditions were used to test the sensors. A Custom-made sensor holder was attached to a rotary micro-stage which is used to have control and consistency over the movement of the sensor during experiments. The stage rotation allowed the sensors to make accurately controlled contact with the phantom surface.

The EI sensors were connected to an data acquisition unit (NI-DAQ USB-6000) through 3 analogue input channels, and the data is collected via the MAT-LAB application "Analogue Input signal Recorder". The common electrode is connected to the 5 v output of the device when needed. The FSRs connect to an Arduino and the data is collected though the Arduino serial graph plotter. A simple pull-down circuit is used to stabilise the signals for all the sensors.

2.3   Experimental Phantom Models

In total, the were seven phantoms and experimental conditions used to test the sensors: (1) dry flat surface; (2) saline wet flat surface; (3) dry tests against a silicon tube; (4) sponge phantom covered by a conductive fabric layer submerged in saline; (5) 3D printed PLA rigid Phantom coated in a silver based conductive paint and submerged in saline, (6) realistic phantom of a generic blood vessel, and (7) navigation through a realistic aortic arch phantom. The phantoms in experiments 6-7 were 3D printed according to the method presented in [13] to achieve a porous flexible structure with realistic mechanical and electrical properties when soaked and submerged in a saline bath. Figure 3 shows some of the experiment cases.

2.4   Experimental Procedure

All of the sensors had three analogue input channels. The sensor was rotated 120° after every trial to test the different direction. All trials, except the ones explicitly stating otherwise, consist of pressing the sensor against a phantom five times using the rotary micro-stage.

Note that the EI measurement relies on the conductivity of the target material while a FSR sensor is solely depended on the contact forces. As a result, during the EI sensor experiments, the saline solution and the phantom surface were supplied with a 3.3 V current to simulate the small current in the human body. This also enabled us to measure electrical noise variation due to tissue contact and deformation as a means of measuring the contact forces.

2.5   EIS Experiments

For this sensing modality, we designed five experiments to test the consistency of results (cases 1–2), the directional ability, and overall performance of the sensors (cases 3–5). **Exp 1:** Using the conductive sponge submerged in saline, while the common electrode is not in use. **Exp. 2:** Same as **Exp. 1** with the common electrode is connected to a 5 V power supply. **Exp. 3:** The painted PLA phantom was used without the sensor common electrode connected. Three different sensor sizes were tested. **Exp. 4:** Same as **Exp. 3** except with the common electrode connected to 5 V. **Exp. 5:** Only the noise was measured, and the common electrode was not connected.

2.6   FSR Experiments

Below is an explanation of each experiment used to test the FSR sensors. **Exp. 1:** Flat versions of sensors 1–3 were fixed to the stage above the load cell and each channel was pressed individually with a small tube to sense its responsiveness (Dry flat test). **Exp. 2:** The same as in **Exp.** 11 except with a drop of saline solution applied to the flat sensor (Wet flat test). **Exp 3:** A dry silicon tube is attached to the stage and the rotary micro stage is used to push the sensor onto the tube curved surface (Dry tube test). **Exp. 4:** The conductive sponge phantom is used (Submerged sponge test). **Exp. 5:** The sensor sleeve on an off-the-shelf catheter was tested using the aortic arch phantom (Submerged Phantom test).

3   Results and Discussions

This section presents the results and discussions for our experimental studies.

3.1   EI-Based Sensors

We found all of the EI sensors being responsive when submerged in saline, and three out of four of the sensor variations could sense direction consistently. The voltage-time-force plots in Fig. 4a–b show sample raw voltage data for the sensor three electrode channels in two experimental trials in **Exp.** 1.

For **Exp.** 1, sensor 1 was shown to be consistently responsive to submersion in saline and strongly correlates to the force being applied. For sensor 2 during **Exp.** 1 & 2, we observed consistent and responsive signals with the active sensor having the largest voltage peaks. **Exp.** 3 & 4 only revealed significant readings when the sensor was removed from the saline solution. **Exp.** 4 for this sensor design showed consistency between sensors 2 and 3 design variations as they could detect submersion in the saline, but with insignificant changes in the electrode signal values. In **Exp.** 5, the active area showed a direct proportional relationship between the measured voltage and the applied force of 0–200 mN.

Sensor 3 was the most consistently responsive design across all the experiments, showing distinguishable proportionality between noisy signal readings and the force (see Fig. 4c). Sensor 4 showed a reasonable but inconsistent output only in **Exp.** 1 & 4. One point to note however is that it requires much more force than the other sensors in order to trigger an output response.

Data Acquisition Performance. From the plots generated for the EI Sensing Modality, it can be seen that the noise measurements performed better than the Vcc experiments on average (see Fig. 4a, b), Vcc referring to the use of a 5 V current. A jump in the noise signals were observed by the insertion of the sensor in the saline bath. The same jump was not present during the Vcc (impedance) measurements as the sensor remains wet outside of the saline. We did not investigate the use of Alternating Current (AC) as commonly used for EIT applications in medicine. The use of an AC in a future work can make the experimental conditions more realistic and may alter the observed results.

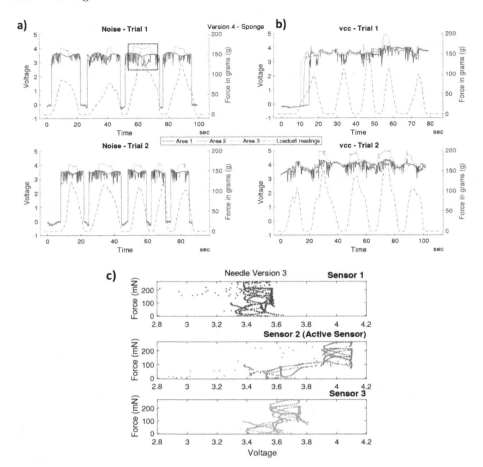

Fig. 4. EIT-based sensor results. The voltage-time-force graph for sensor 4 in (a) **Exp. 1**, and (b) **Exp. 2**. VCC indicates the sensor impedance measurement. The dotted box highlights a distinguishable relationship between the force and voltage. (c) Force-voltage plot for Experiment 1 - trial 2 results with electrode two of the sensor activated (pushed against the phantom) with the practitioners average reaction speed taken into consideration.

Sensor Structural Design. All of the sensors were mounted on stainless steel rods, with similar bending constants for sensors 1–3 (similar rod dimensions) which is smaller than the bending stiffness of sensor 4 due to its larger rod outer diameter the rod larger bending stiffness only increased the amount of force needed to trigger a response in the sensors. A more elastic rod meant that a larger contact surface was needed to achieve similar force sensitivity to a sensor on a stiffer rod.

Sensor 1 (electrodes with the smallest surface area) had the worst performance overall in terms of signal directionality and consistency. Meanwhile sen-

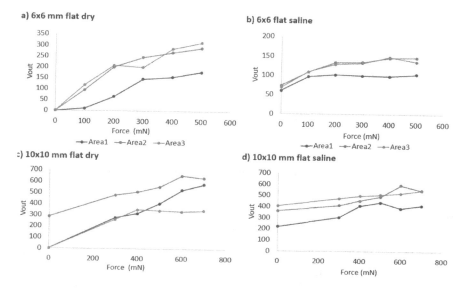

Fig. 5. FSR sensor experiments in flat state and in dry (a & c) and wet (b & d) with saline droplet conditions with different dimensions: (a, b) 6 × 6 mm, (c, d) 10 × 10 mm.

sor 3 (largest surface area) performed the best in terms of sensing direction and force-voltage proportionality.

Comparing sensors 2 and 4 as they were the same except for the common electrode placement, sensor 2 performed better on the PLA phantom. This indicates that it's better to have the common electrode below the analogue input sensors. The sensor initial contact possibly played a significant role in force sensing as there was a larger surface area in direct contact with the phantom. Both sensors were able to sense the applied force direction, with sensor 2 being more responsive in noise measurements despite the fact that the common electrode was not needed for noise measurement case.

3.2   FSR-Based Sensors

All of the sensor design successfully showed directional responses to the force applied. As a result, Fig. 5 & 6 only presents the signal for the activated channel toward the applied force direction.

During **Exp. 1**, voltage readings for sensor 1 increased with force applied with one electrode channel being more responsive. This lack of uniformity in electrode signals was common across all electrodes and sensors in all of the experiments. Sensors 2 and 3 indicated a similar trend as sensor 1, except that the signals generated by the active signals were more consistent and better aligned.

During **Exp. 2**, the sensors showed the same trend as in **Exp. 1**, except with a slight reduction of sensitivity, revealing that wet conditions have little effect on the quality of the results for the FSR sensors. The only notable difference

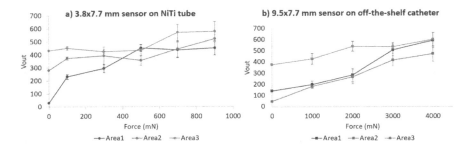

Fig. 6. Results for the FSR sensor final design wrapped around (a) a NiTi tube, and (b) an off-the-shelf cardiovascular intervention catheter in tests against a silicon tube in dry condition. The error bars show the standard deviation between the different experiment trials.

between **Exp. 1 & 2** was that saline exposure cased a bias voltage reading when there was no fore applied.

Results for sensor 3 in **Exp. 3** showed some proportionality between force and pressure values for smaller force (<1 N). We noticed that different electrode channels could have different sensitivities, mainly due to the manual fabrication process. For sensor 5 in **Exp. 3**, a clear relationship was seen.

There were a few factors that affected the sensitivity of the FSR sensors which are discussed below. Force sensitivity seemed to grow with the number of electrodes used to form a channel. This is seen comparing sensors 1–3 as they showed a gradual increase in the force-signal relation slope with sensor 3 showing the steepest relation. Connecting multiple electrodes to one channel possibly increased the effective area of the electrodes and improved the overall sensitivity of the sensors. More experimentation should be done to evaluate this effect using thin wire electrodes.

Sensors 5 which was fabricated with coated enamelled wire to insulate the adjacent electrodes had better sensor performance in terms of consistency, but at the cost of reduced overall sensitivity. We suspect that the highlighted regions in blue in Fig. 2b were less sensitive to pressure. In the scenario that the circumference of the base rod is much larger than the electrode widths, the insulating wires can be placed much closer to the common electrodes to reduce these less sensitive areas. Sensors 1–3 used larger electrodes than sensors 4–5. The advantage of the electrode larger size on the force sensitivity was evident from the graphs in Fig. 5.

The FSR sensor better covered the force range of a vascular intervention procedure, e.g. 0.02–1.7 N for interaction forces with silicon phantom of subclavian and common carotid arteries [9] and $\approx 1.72 \pm 0.59$ N perforation forces for porcine cardiac perforation [7]. However, when sensor 5 was affixed to a soft catheter during **Exp. 4 & 5**, a reasonable force measurement was not possible, since the catheter bending forces were smaller than the sensor activation (minimum measurable) forces. To overcome this, we inserted a small metal rod into the catheter sensor in order to stiffen the catheter tip. The catheter soft material affected the sensor sensitivity significantly. It can be seen based on the change in the force sensing range between the plots in Fig. 6. The same issue was observed for an EI sensor too. We concluded that to maintain the force sensor sensitivity, the force sensors must be attached on a non-flexible base.

Using off-the-shelf FSR layers was a challenge, as the film was too stiff to be properly wrapped around a micro catheter or needle. It is much more reliable to make silicon-base FSR layers in a future research.

4   Conclusion

it is extremely beneficial for practitioners to have force feedback information during surgical interventions. In this paper, we explored the viability of two cost-effective force sensing modalities, i.e. Electrical Impedance (EI) and Force Sensitive Resistance (FSR) measurement techniques, to address this problem. In different experiments with realistic environments and phantoms, we observed that both sensor modalities can provide outputs with adequate directionality and proportionality with the extorted force.

FSR sensors were successful in delivering a consistent proportional relationship for forces in the range of 0.1–1 N when attached to a stiff base. FSR sensors required a tight waterproof design to perform in wet conditions. The EI sensors based on environment noise measurement were more advantages to detect directional contact incidents, as a contact sensor, and for small force in the range of 0–200 mN. The EI sensors were more robust in wet conditions. We observed that the sensor sensitivity decreases with surface area for both sensor modalities. Finally, we showcased the feasibility of deploying both sensors on an off-the-shelf cardiovascular catheter in a realistic in-vitro vessel navigation task.

Both of the tested sensing modalities showed promising results as cost-effective disposable tactile and force sensing solutions that can be easily integrated on the available miniature medical robots and catheters. As the next step, we are going to investigate measuring axial forces as well as combining these two technologies to fabricate a Multi-modal tactile sensor sleeve for forces and tissue identification.

Acknowledgment. This work was supported by an ERC Starting Grant [714562], the Wellcome/EPSRC Centre for Medical Engineering [WT 203148/Z/16/Z], and an NIHR Cardiovascular MIC Grant.

References

1. Global health estimates: leading causes of death. https://www.who.int/data/gho/data/themes/mortality-and-global-health-estimates/ghe-leading-causes-of-death
2. Bayford, R.: Basic electrical impedance tomography. In: Simini, F., Bertemes-Filho, P. (eds.) Bioimpedance in Biomedical Applications and Research, pp. 29–44. Springer, Cham (2018). https://doi.org/10.1007/978-3-319-74388-2_3

3. Castellini, C., Ravindra, V.: A wearable low-cost device based upon force-sensing resistors to detect single-finger forces. In: 5th IEEE RAS/EMBS International Conference on Biomedical Robotics and Biomechatronics, pp. 199–203 (2014). ISSN 2155-1782
4. Chi, C., Sun, X., Xue, N., Li, T., Liu, C.: Recent progress in technologies for tactile sensors. Sensors 18(4), 948 (2018)
5. Mensah, G.A.: Eliminating disparities in cardiovascular health. Circulation 111(10), 1332–1336 (2005)
6. Nagakubo, A., Alirezaei, H., Kuniyoshi, Y.: A deformable and deformation sensitive tactile distribution sensor. In: 2007 IEEE International Conference on Robotics and Biomimetics (ROBIO), pp. 1301–1308 (2007)
7. Perna, F., Heist, E.K., Danik, S.B., Barrett, C.D., Ruskin, J.N., Mansour, M.: Assessment of catheter tip contact force resulting in cardiac perforation in swine atria using force sensing technology. Circ. Arrhythm. Electrophysiol. 4(2), 218–224 (2011)
8. Puangmali, P., Althoefer, K., Seneviratne, L.D., Murphy, D., Dasgupta, P.: State-of-the-art in force and tactile sensing for minimally invasive surgery. IEEE Sens. J. 8(4), 371–381 (2008)
9. Rafii-Tari, H., et al.: Objective assessment of endovascular navigation skills with force sensing. Ann. Biomed. Eng. 45(5), 1315–1327 (2017). https://doi.org/10.1007/s10439-017-1791-y
10. Su, B., et al.: Biopsy needle system with a steerable concentric tube and online monitoring of electrical resistivity and insertion forces. IEEE Trans. Biomed. Eng. 68(5), 1702–1713 (2021)
11. Swanson, E.C., Weathersby, E.J., Cagle, J.C., Sanders, J.E.: Evaluation of force sensing resistors for the measurement of interface pressures in lower limb prosthetics. J. Biomech. Eng. 141(10), 101009 (2019)
12. Tiwana, M.I., Redmond, S.J., Lovell, N.H.: A review of tactile sensing technologies with applications in biomedical engineering. Sens. Actuators A Phys. 179, 17–31 (2012)
13. Wang, S., et al.: Cardiac radiofrequency ablation simulation using a 3D-printed bi-atrial thermochromic model. Appl. Sci. 12(13), 6553 (2022)
14. Yaniger, S.: Force sensing resistors: a review of the technology. In: Electro International, pp. 666–668 (1991)
15. Zhang, T., Ping, Z., Zuo, S.: Miniature continuum manipulator with 3-DOF force sensing for retinal microsurgery. J. Mech. Robot. 1–34 (2021)
16. Zhou, J., et al.: A remote-controlled robotic system with safety protection strategy based on force-sensing and bending feedback for transcatheter arterial chemoembolization. Micromachines 11(9), 805 (2020)

Towards Smooth Human-Robot Handover with a Vision-Based Tactile Sensor

Prasad Rayamane⬛, Francisco Munguia-Galeano⬛, Seyed Amir Tafrishi⬛, and Ze Ji(✉)⬛

School of Engineering, Cardiff University, Cardiff, UK
jiz1@cardiff.ac.uk

Abstract. Cooperative human-robot interaction often requires successful handovers of objects between the two entities. However, the assumption that a human can reliably grasp an object from a robot is not always valid. To address this issue, we propose a vision-based tactile sensor for object handover framework that utilises a low-cost sensor with variable sensitivity and pressure. The sensor comprises a latex layer that makes contact with the object and a tracking marker that registers the resulting changes in position. By pre-processing this information, a robot can determine whether it is necessary to open the gripper. Our approach is validated through an exploratory user study involving ten participants who completed handover tasks involving eight objects of varying shapes and stiffness, including rigid and deformable objects like raspberries and dough. The study results demonstrate the effectiveness of our approach, with a success rate of 94%. Additionally, users reported less difficulty performing the handover tasks when the sensitivity value was decreased. Overall, our vision-based tactile sensor framework offers a promising solution for the challenging problem of human-robot handover in cooperative settings.

Keywords: Tactile sensing · Human-robot handover · Robotics

1 Introduction

In recent years, there has been remarkable progress towards more direct collaboration between humans and robots, enabled by technological advances in robot hardware [1]. The current trend of Industry 4.0 envisions shared environments, where robots interact with their surroundings, humans, and other agents [2]. In addition, the recent COVID-19 pandemic has increased the demand for autonomous and collaborative robots in environments such as care homes and hospitals [3]. Human workers can potentially benefit from robotic assistants due to several advantages, such as transferring repetitive, low-skill, and ergonomically unfavourable tasks to robots. In this context, robot handover is of great significance [4].

We would like to thank all the individuals who participated in our experiments. Your time and effort are greatly appreciated.

F. Iida et al. (Eds.): TAROS 2023, LNAI 14136, pp. 431–442, 2023.
https://doi.org/10.1007/978-3-031-43360-3_35

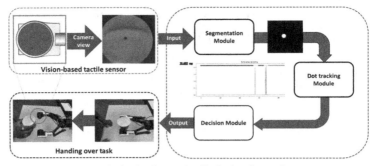

Vision-based tactile sensor for object handover framework

Fig. 1. Vision-based tactile sensor for handover framework

The human-robot handover task has been studied in several works. One of these pioneering works is [5], in which the authors proposed a system that comprises a three-finger gripper attached to a robot that makes decisions regarding when to open the gripper, close it or adjust one of the fingers in case the contact between the gripper and the object is lost. This approach uses a combination of information regarding joint angles, contact with the object, and kinematics to assess the grasping stability. The authors showed that handover is closely related to grasp stability since the robot must hold the object until the human is ready to receive it. In contrast, Edsinger and Kemp demonstrated that humans adapt how they hand objects over to a specific configuration of the robot's gripper [6].

There are handover approaches based on using the user's hand velocity to determine when the robot should release an object [7]. However, visual information can be unreliable if the object is occluded or the lighting conditions are not appropriate. Besides that, some objects, such as soft or irregularly shaped objects, may be challenging to hand over. On the contrary, tactile sensors provide more precise and accurate information to the robot, enabling it to adapt according to the object's physical properties. This allows the robot to perform the handover of a broader range of objects with varying shapes, sizes, and textures and ensures a more robust grasp of an object whose surface friction is unknown [8]. Despite the benefits of tactile sensing and its implementation under various operation principles (e.g., pressure, vibration, temperature, texture, or shape), the use of vision-based sensors for human-robot handover tasks has not yet reached its full potential.

In this paper, we present a vision-based tactile sensor for object handover framework[1], aiming to solve the problem of coordination and timing in human-robot handover. The framework is based on a sensor comprising a latex rubber layer with a marker on the interior surface, a camera, and a chamber with variable pressure. The contact movement is estimated by tracking the marker on the

---

[1] https://github.com/FranciscoMunguiaGaleano/TactileSensorHandover
Demo available at https://www.youtube.com/watch?v=w4grAJL-h6Y.

latex skin's surface. This information is then used to decide if opening the robot's gripper is required. We investigate several aspects of the framework, such as success rate with an exploratory user study in which ten participants complete the task of handing over eight objects. Each object has a different size, shape, and stiffness. For our experiments, we built an interface for experiments that allows the user and the robot to interact during the handover tasks. Our contributions are summarised as follows: (i) a framework that allows human-robot handover with a vision-based tactile sensing principle and (ii) a method for calibrating the sensor's sensitivity based on the user's experience.

The rest of the paper is organised as follows. Section 2 discusses related work on tactile sensors and human-robot handover. Then, Sect. 3 presents our vision-based tactile sensor for the object handover framework. In Sect. 4, we explain the experimental setup used to validate the framework. Section 5 discusses the results. Finally, we conclude this paper and propose potential future work in Sect. 6.

2   Related Work

A handover is defined as a collaborative joint action in which one agent (the giver) gives an object to another agent (the receiver). The physical exchange begins when the receiver first touches the object held by the giver and ends when the giver completely hands over the object to the receiver. Human-robot handover, a frequent collaborative action among humans, requires a concerted effort of prediction, perception, action, learning, and adjustment by both parties. Implementing an object handover that is as efficient and fluent as the exchange among humans is an open challenge in robotics [9].

There is a significant amount of literature on human-robot object handover with the potential to enhance robot capabilities performed from a range of aspects, such as visualising robot intent [10], adaptiveness to user preference [11], visual perception for handover [12], affordance-based handover [13], and gripper effort control [7]. These approaches are based on specific aspects, such as the human hands, objects, contact points, and contact pressure. On the other hand, our framework does not depend on contact force estimation. Instead, it utilises the direct measurement of the object's movement by tracking the dot placed on the internal face of the layer.

Among the different robotic applications and tactile sensing types, slip detection is a typical application [14]. An important early approach in this area was proposed in [15], where the authors describe grasping behaviours and grip forces. Similar vision-based optical tactile sensors have been studied in [16,17], with the purpose of detecting slip. For example, the sensor proposed in [18], covered with an opaque surface skin made of latex, provides slip detection by producing high-resolution force arrays. Another popular device for tactile sensing is the BioTac sensor [19]. For example, in [20], two BioTac sensors are used to detect slip. BioTac sensors are also used in [21], where the authors defined three types of tactile estimation: finger forces-based, slip detection-based, and slip classification-based.

Despite the success of the aforementioned approaches, the most commonly used object shapes to test are cylindrical (i.e. bottle) or rectangular (i.e. box). These objects are easier to hand over than deformable and fragile objects; Hence, the generalisation of handovers to a variety of objects with different shapes and stiffness has not yet reached its full potential.

3   Vision-Based Tactile Sensor for Object Handover Framework

In this section, we present the vision-based tactile sensor for object handover framework (Fig. 1), which aims to solve the problem of human-robot handover. The framework comprises the following modules: segmentation, dot tracking, and decision.

The **segmentation module**'s input is the video stream image captured by the camera inside the sensor. This module is in charge of segmenting the dot printed at the centre of the latex layer. For this purpose, the original image is transformed into a negative version of it and then into grayscale. This module is implemented using Python and OpenCV.

The **dot tracking module** utilises the output of the segmentation module as input and transforms the image into coordinates of the white dot's centre. First, the dot tracking module sets an initial position once the gripper has closed and is holding an object. Then, the centre coordinates of the dot moving with respect to the initial position are stored in the vector v, which is the output of this module.

The **decision module** controls the sensitivity-pressure pair of the sensor and the open and close actions of the gripper. The accumulated displacement of the object being pulled by the user while the gripper holds it is given by the following :

$$M = \sum_{i=T-n}^{T} \left| \frac{||v_i - v_{(i-1)}||}{(t_i - t_{(i-1)})} \right|, \tag{1}$$

where t_i and $t_{(i-1)}$ denote the current and past time, and v_i and $v_{(i-1)}$ are the current and past positions of the dot, respectively. Here, i takes values within the range $(T-n, ..., T)$. The value of M increases proportionally to the accumulated displacement of the dot, and the bigger the value of n, the more past information is considered. The decision module can decide if opening the gripper is necessary based on the following:

$$Gripper_{action} = \begin{cases} \text{Open,} & M > S \\ \text{No action,} & \text{otherwise} \end{cases} \tag{2}$$

where S is the sensitivity and acts as a threshold that determines when the robot should release an object.

Fig. 2. The image displays the experimental setup in which the robot is handing over a cup to a user.

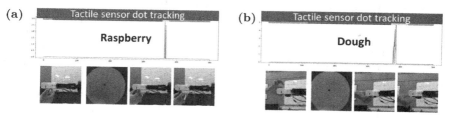

Fig. 3. A human and a robot are performing a handing-over task with raspberry (a) and dough (b) during the experiments. In (a) and (b), when the colour of the line is red, the gripper is closed. The yellow colour indicates that the user is trying to get the object. The green colour indicates that the gripper is open. (Color figure online)

4 Methodology

To investigate the optimality of the sensitivity-pressure pair that is more comfortable from the user's perspective when using our framework, we conducted an experiment in which users rated how easy or difficult it was to hand over an object from the robot. Additionally, users rated the degree of damage the object sustained after completing the task. The time taken by the user to attempt to take the object from the gripper until it was released (sensing time) was also measured for all the handover tasks. The experimental setup (Fig. 2) consisted of a KUKA® LBR IIWA 14 robot arm with 7 degrees of freedom and a Robotiq® 2-finger gripper with a vision-based optical tactile sensor attached to its fingers. Moreover, the user followed instructions displayed on a screen placed next to the robot, indicating when to place or take the object from the gripper.

4.1 Participants

We asked 10 participants from Cardiff University, including eight males and two females aged 24–30, to do the experiments. There was no compensation for the participants. Among them, 2 participants had previous experience with robots, while 8 participants had never interacted with a collaborative robot.

Table 1. Parameters used for the sensitivity-pressure pairs during the experiments.

Parameter	Sensitivity-pressure pair								
	S_1P_1	S_1P_2	S_1P_3	S_2P_1	S_2P_2	S_2P_3	S_3P_1	S_3P_2	S_3P_3
S	0.01	0.01	0.01	0.005	0.005	0.005	0.001	0.001	0.001
P	0.8 psi	1.0 psi	1.3 psi	0.8 psi	1.0 psi	1.3 psi	0.8 psi	1.0 psi	1.3 psi

4.2   Experimental Procedure

The experiment took place at the Robotics Lab of Cardiff University under the supervision of our 2 experimenters. Participants stood in a designated position before a robotic arm and started the object handover task. Participants first read the instructions and then signed the consent form. After reading the instructions, the experimenter provided information about the experimental process by reading from a script and collected basic demographic information, such as gender, through a short questionnaire.

For the experiments, we set nine sensitivity-pressure pair values, as shown in Table 1, and used eight objects with different shapes and stiffnesses (paper, fabrics, a cup, dough, strawberries, raspberries, a cable, and a prism). Aiming to investigate several aspects of our framework, we designed a questionnaire (Table 2) that consists of two questions. **Q1** has a scale of 0–10, where 0 - too sensitive, 5 - ideal, and 10 - too difficult. **Q2** has a scale from 0–10, where 0 - the object is intact, and 10 - the object is damaged. The participants perform the following experiments:

1. Each participant performs the handover tasks in a random order without knowing the sensitivity-pressure pair values.
2. After each handover, the participant answers **Q1** (Table 2) for the object in turn.
3. After each handover, the participant answers **Q2** (Table 2) for the object in turn.
4. If the robot fails to hand over the piece, the participant marks the experiment as invalid and is not required to answer questions **Q1** and **Q2**.

For each experiment, in turn, we aim to answer the following research questions:

1. Despite the random order of objects and sensitivity-pressure pairs in which the participants are asked to perform the handover tasks, is it likely that the participants will agree on which sensitivity-pressure combination results in a more pleasant handover?

2. Which sensitivity-pressure pair produces a more pleasant human-robot handover from the participant's point of view?
3. Which sensitivity-pressure pair reduces or increases the damage to the objects after handing them over?
4. What is the success rate of the proposed framework?

To validate the questionnaire, we conducted a pilot study at the beginning with three participants who carried out the experiments and answered **Q1** and **Q2**. For this analysis, the Cronbach's alpha value of each question was calculated, such that the statistical output was 0.775 and 0.852 for **Q1** and **Q2**, respectively. Since both values are greater than 0.7, the questions are considered good [22].

Table 2. Questionnaire used for the exploratory user study.

Questionnaire		Cronbach's alpha
Q1	How easy was it to hand the object over?	0.775
Q2	How damaged is the object after handing it over?	0.852

The described experiments involve the use of a screen placed on the side of the participants to provide instructions for handling various objects, as shown in Fig. 2. Once the participants verbally indicate they are ready, the researchers manually start the robot program. The positioning of the screen is strategic, as it allows the participants to receive clear visual guidance while completing the handover task (see Fig. 3). The screen will show red, indicating that placing an object is unsafe and may cause damage or harm. In this case, the participant will be instructed to refrain from placing the object and wait for further instructions. When the user indicator displays orange, it signifies that the participant can place the object between the gripper. Once the object is in place, the experimenter can close the gripper, and the participant can continue the task. Once the indicator displays a green signal, the participant can attempt to take the object.

Moreover, the instructions are essential to ensure that the participants follow the correct procedure for each object, which is critical to ensure the safety of the objects and the participants involved.

5   Results and Discussion

5.1   Results

We have organised the data in a hierarchical order to evaluate the experimental results. First, we sorted the participants' ratings for **Q1**, **Q2**, and the sensing time for all the objects. Then, we analysed the results of **Q1** by considering each object type. Lastly, we examined the findings of **Q2** by considering the different categories of objects.

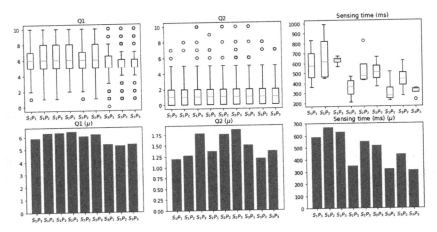

Fig. 4. This figure displays the results of each sensitivity-pressure pair for **Q1** and **Q2**, as well as the sensing time for all objects. The box plots are displayed in the upper row, while the means are shown in the bottom row.

Table 3 summarises the results of **Q1**, **Q2**, and the sensing time for all the objects (Fig. 4). For **Q1**, the results show that the participants found the handover task more comfortable for S_3. At the same time, the score deviates from 5 (5 being the ideal score as defined in the questionnaire), which indicates that the scores react proportionally to the value of S(for example, $S_1P_2 = 6.28$ and $S_3P_2 = 5.27$). At this point, the pressure value P does not seem to have a significant impact on the participants' sensation of fluency during the handover tasks. The reason behind this behaviour is that the latex layer maintains its elasticity regardless of pressure changes, which does not affect the marker's movement. For **Q2**, the participants scored higher values that correspond to higher pressure values, with the exception of S_3P_1, S_3P_1 and S_3P_1. This is because S_3 provokes the robot to open the gripper faster and produce less damage to the object. In terms of sensing times, the participants perceived a more comfortable handover when the time is below 500 ms. However, the high values for the standard deviation indicate that the time measurement requires improvement.

In Table 4, the participants' ratings for **Q1** with respect to each object are summarised. Among all the objects, raspberries and cables received the highest scores for being difficult to hand over. On the contrary, the rest of the objects obtained a rating of around 6. For all objects (Table 3), the score is closer to 5 when the sensitivity value S is lower.

Table 5 shows the participants' ratings for **Q2** with respect to each object. It can be observed that as the pressure increases for P, the participants tend to rate a higher value for **Q2**, indicating that the object is more damaged after the handover. Among all the objects used during the experiments, raspberries had the highest rates of damage, suggesting that the handover task using our approach is more challenging to execute with a fragile object like a raspberry.

Table 3. Results of each sensitivity-pressure pair for **Q1** and **Q2**, as well as sensing time for all objects and participants.

	Q1		Q2		Time (ms)	
	μ	σ	μ	σ	μ	σ
S_1P_1	5.89	1.94	1.2	1.51	586	205.1
S_1P_2	6.28	2.11	1.27	1.62	669	259.59
S_1P_3	6.32	2.22	1.78	2.55	628	45.03
S_2P_1	6.41	1.68	1.37	1.85	348	113.53
S_2P_2	6.04	2.03	1.76	2.29	550	186.88
S_2P_3	6.18	2.43	1.87	2.4	514	125.47
S_3P_1	5.37	2.01	1.5	2.21	322	130.79
S_3P_2	5.27	2.23	1.2	1.85	445	145.41
S_3P_3	5.36	2.12	1.37	1.71	312	51.03

Table 4. Results of each sensitivity-pressure pair for **Q1** obtained in the experiments.

Q1	Paper		Fabrics		Cup		Dough		Strawberry		Raspberry		Cable		Prism	
	μ	σ	μ	σ	μ	σ	μ	σ	μ	σ	μ	σ	μ	σ	μ	σ
S_1P_1	5.8	1.75	6.33	1.22	4.8	1.93	6	1.56	5.7	1.42	5.5	3.25	7.11	2.52	6	1.25
S_1P_2	6.6	2.12	6.88	2.03	5.5	2.12	6.11	0.93	5.8	2.57	6.57	1.99	7.14	2.12	6.11	2.67
S_1P_3	6.9	2.02	6.11	2.47	5.6	1.51	5.2	2.3	5.89	2.26	6.88	2.23	9	1.53	5.8	1.93
S_2P_1	6.8	1.81	5.9	1.85	6.5	1.72	5.8	0.92	5.7	1.64	7.5	2.17	6.78	1.39	6.3	1.42
S_2P_2	5.8	2.2	6.2	2.1	5.5	1.84	5.3	1.95	5.7	1.25	7.3	2.5	6.8	1.99	5.7	2.06
S_2P_3	5.8	2.66	6.78	1.86	5.3	2.41	5.2	2.04	5.56	2.13	8	1.66	7.78	2.59	5.4	2.67
S_3P_1	6.1	2.28	5.4	1.71	5.5	0.85	5.5	2.64	5.22	1.56	4	1.51	5.75	2.71	5.3	2.26
S_3P_2	4.9	1.73	5.89	2.8	4.9	2.23	4.8	2.3	4.8	2.3	5.9	2.6	6.62	2.0	4.7	1.77
S_3P_3	5.8	2.04	5.7	2.26	4.67	2.06	4.7	1.89	4.9	1.1	5.8	2.2	6.25	2.96	5.2	0.0

Table 5. Results from the experiment for every sensitivity-pressure pair for **Q2**.

Q1	Paper		Fabrics		Cup		Dough		Strawberry		Raspberry		Cable		Prism	
	μ	σ	μ	σ	μ	σ	μ	σ	μ	σ	μ	σ	μ	σ	μ	σ
S_1P_1	1.00	0.87	0.78	1.09	1.11	1.05	1.12	0.99	1.22	1.48	3.11	2.62	0.56	0.73	0.67	1.12
S_1P_2	0.60	0.84	0.50	0.71	1.40	1.43	1.44	1.13	1.44	1.51	4.00	2.51	0.57	0.79	0.60	0.70
S_1P_3	1.11	1.90	0.56	0.88	0.89	0.78	1.50	1.08	2.20	3.05	5.70	3.74	0.62	0.52	1.11	1.54
S_2P_1	1.20	1.93	0.30	0.67	1.10	1.10	1.50	1.43	1.30	1.42	3.90	2.96	1.00	1.32	0.60	0.70
S_2P_2	1.33	1.73	0.78	1.64	1.44	1.67	1.89	1.05	1.44	1.88	5.44	3.40	0.67	0.71	1.11	1.62
S_2P_3	1.56	2.01	1.33	2.18	1.67	1.87	2.22	2.05	1.50	1.77	4.67	3.46	1.33	2.55	0.67	1.00
S_3P_1	1.30	1.89	0.80	1.55	1.40	1.96	1.80	1.55	1.10	1.20	4.00	4.18	1.22	2.05	0.60	0.84
S_3P_2	0.70	1.06	0.50	0.85	1.00	1.25	1.50	1.08	0.60	0.70	3.80	3.39	1.20	1.81	0.30	0.67
S_3P_3	1.49	1.49	0.50	0.71	1.22	1.09	2.20	2.10	1.40	2.22	3.00	1.89	1.00	1.50	0.60	0.00

In terms of success rate (Table 6), the cable got the lowest success rate, followed by the Raspberry with 86% and 90%, respectively. At the same time,

Table 6. Success rates of the proposed framework for each object and the total.

Paper	Fabrics	Cup	Dough	Strawberry	Raspberry	Cable	Prism	Total
100%	96%	99%	99%	98%	90%	84%	99%	94%

the rest of the objects obtained a similar success rate of above 95% despite their shapes or sizes.

5.2 Discussion

Based on the above results, it was found that, from the participants' perspective, a lower value of S ($S_3 = 0.001$) produces a more comfortable handover. Additionally, a higher pressure value of P caused more damage to the objects after being handed over. However, there is no clear indication that the change in pressure enhanced the user's sensation of fluency while handing over the objects during the experiments. In terms of success rates, our approach encountered more difficulty with reduced-diameter objects, such as the cable, because, depending on the object's initial position while being grasped, the dot at the centre of the latex layer did not move as it did with the other objects. As a consequence, the dot-tracking module could not detect any movement of the object. Another challenging objects were the raspberries because, among all the objects, the participants noticed damage to them after performing the task, which also reflected in the success rate. Despite the shortcomings, the robot using our framework managed to hand over different objects with different sizes and stiffness with a 94% success rate.

6 Conclusion and Future Work

In this paper, we proposed an object handover framework using the vision-based tactile sensor. Overall, the experiments achieved a success rate of 94%. The exploratory user study revealed that users found the handover task more comfortable when the sensitivity value was lower. The limitations of this paper, found during the experiments, are related to reduced diameter objects (e.g., cables) and highly fragile objects (e.g., raspberries), which seem to be the most challenging objects to hand over using our approach. However, the reliability of our framework and sensor was demonstrated for handing over objects such as paper, fabrics, dough, and strawberries. For future work, we plan to improve the sensor by adding more markers to the latex layer and exploring the effects and benefits of using tactile sensing with variable pressure. Additionally, to better evaluate the performance improvement achieved by our approach, a comparison with tactile-only methods is necessary. By addressing this issue, we aim to enrich our research and establish a robust foundation for future advancements in tactile sensing systems for human-robot interaction.

References

1. Ajoudani, A., Zanchettin, A.M., Ivaldi, S., Albu-Schäffer, A., Kosuge, K., Khatib, O.: Progress and prospects of the human-robot collaboration. Auton. Robots **42**, 957–975 (2018)
2. Østergaard, E.H.: The role of cobots in industry 4.0. Universal Robots, white paper (2017)
3. Tavakoli, M., Carriere, J., Torabi, A.: Robotics, smart wearable technologies, and autonomous intelligent systems for healthcare during the COVID-19 pandemic: an analysis of the state of the art and future vision. Adv. Intell. Syst. **2**(7), 2000071 (2020)
4. Pandey, A.K., Alami, R.: Towards human-level semantics understanding of human-centered object manipulation tasks for HRI: reasoning about effect, ability, effort and perspective taking. Int. J. Soc. Robot. **6**, 593–620 (2014)
5. Nagata, K., Oosaki, Y., Kakikura, M., Tsukune, H.: Delivery by hand between human and robot based on fingertip force-torque information. In: Proceedings 1998 IEEE/RSJ International Conference on Intelligent Robots and Systems. Innovations in Theory, Practice and Applications (Cat. No. 98CH36190), vol. 2, pp. 750–757. IEEE (1998)
6. Edsinger, A., Kemp, C.C.: Human-robot interaction for cooperative manipulation: handing objects to one another. In: RO-MAN 2007-The 16th IEEE International Symposium on Robot and Human Interactive Communication, pp. 1167–1172. IEEE (2007)
7. Eguiluz, A.G., Rañó, I., Coleman, S.A., McGinnity, T.M.: Reliable object handover through tactile force sensing and effort control in the shadow robot hand. In: 2017 IEEE International Conference on Robotics and Automation (ICRA), pp. 372–377. IEEE (2017)
8. Yamaguchi, A., Atkeson, C.G.: Implementing tactile behaviors using FingerVision. In: 2017 IEEE-RAS 17th International Conference on Humanoid Robotics (Humanoids), pp. 241–248. IEEE (2017)
9. Ortenzi, V., Cosgun, A., Pardi, T., Chan, W.P., Croft, E., Kulić, D.: Object handovers: a review for robotics. IEEE Trans. Robot. **37**(6), 1855–1873 (2021)
10. Newbury, R., Cosgun, A., Crowley-Davis, T., Chan, W.P., Drummond, T., Croft, E.A.: Visualizing robot intent for object handovers with augmented reality. In: 2022 31st IEEE International Conference on Robot and Human Interactive Communication (RO-MAN), pp. 1264–1270. IEEE (2022)
11. Yang, W., Paxton, C., Mousavian, A., Chao, Y.-W., Cakmak, M., Fox, D.: Reactive human-to-robot handovers of arbitrary objects. In: 2021 IEEE International Conference on Robotics and Automation (ICRA), pp. 3118–3124. IEEE (2021)
12. Rosenberger, P., et al.: Object-independent human-to-robot handovers using real time robotic vision. IEEE Robot. Autom. Lett. **6**(1), 17–23 (2020)
13. Ardón, P., et al.: Affordance-aware handovers with human arm mobility constraints. IEEE Robot. Autom. Lett. **6**(2), 3136–3143 (2021)
14. Li, Q., Kroemer, O., Su, Z., Veiga, F.F., Kaboli, M., Ritter, H.J.: A review of tactile information: perception and action through touch. IEEE Trans. Robot. **36**(6), 1619–1634 (2020)
15. Westling, G., Johansson, R.S.: Factors influencing the force control during precision grip. Exp. Brain Res. **53**, 277–284 (1984)
16. Yamaguchi, A., Atkeson, C.G.: Tactile behaviors with the vision-based tactile sensor FingerVision. Int. J. Humanoid Rob. **16**(03), 1940002 (2019)

17. Lambeta, M., et al.: Digit: a novel design for a low-cost compact high-resolution tactile sensor with application to in-hand manipulation. IEEE Robot. Autom. Lett. **5**(3), 3838–3845 (2020)
18. Taylor, I.H., Dong, S., Rodriguez, A.: Gelslim 3.0: high-resolution measurement of shape, force and slip in a compact tactile-sensing finger. In: 2022 International Conference on Robotics and Automation (ICRA), pp. 10781–10787. IEEE (2022)
19. Wettels, N., Popovic, D., Santos, V.J., Johansson, R.S., Loeb, G.E.: Biomimetic tactile sensor for control of grip. In: 2007 IEEE 10th International Conference on Rehabilitation Robotics, pp. 923–932. IEEE (2007)
20. Reinecke, J., Dietrich, A., Schmidt, F., Chalon, M.: Experimental comparison of slip detection strategies by tactile sensing with the biotac® on the DLR hand arm system. In: 2014 IEEE international Conference on Robotics and Automation (ICRA), pp. 2742–2748. IEEE (2014)
21. Su, Z., et al.: Force estimation and slip detection/classification for grip control using a biomimetic tactile sensor. In: 2015 IEEE-RAS 15th International Conference on Humanoid Robots (Humanoids), pp. 297–303. IEEE (2015)
22. Gliem, J.A., Gliem, R.R.: Calculating, interpreting, and reporting cronbach's alpha reliability coefficient for likert-type scales. In: Midwest Research-to-Practice Conference in Adult, Continuing, and Community (2003)

Feeling Good: Validation of Bilateral Tactile Telemanipulation for a Dexterous Robot

Gabriele Giudici$^{(\boxtimes)}$, Bukeikhan Omarali, Aramis Augusto Bonzini, Kaspar Althoefer, Ildar Farkhatdinov, and Lorenzo Jamone

Queen Mary University of London, London, UK
{g.giudici,i.farkhatdinov,l.jamone}@qmul.ac.uk
https://www.robotics.qmul.ac.uk/researchteams/

Abstract. We introduce a novel bilateral tactile telemanipulation system for dexterous robots. The system is based on a leader-follower paradigm: it integrates two leader devices, a 6D manipulandum and a 3-finger exoskeleton, which allow the human operator to directly control a robot arm and dexterous robot hand simultaneously on the follower side. Tactile sensors are mounted on the four fingertips of the robot hand to collect contact data during remote object manipulation and surface exploration; the measured tactile information is translated into haptic feedback on the leader side, enhancing the performance of the human operator by increasing transparency and reducing physical and mental fatigue during teleoperation. Thanks to its rich haptic feedback, the system is particularly interesting for blind teleoperation, where visual feedback of the workspace is not available or is limited and of poor quality, as for example in the exploration of spaces with reduced illumination and in the manipulation of objects in presence of occlusions. We report the outcomes of preliminary validation experiments, which demonstrate the effectiveness of the control methodology and provide evidence supporting the feasibility of our approach.

Keywords: Teleoperation · Robotics · Tactile Sensing · Haptic Feedback · Robotics Manipulation

1 Introduction

Although the interest and effectiveness of robot teleoperation have been widely acknowledged [1,2], various technological and cost barriers have hindered research in this field, leaving many aspects unexplored. The vast bulk of research on the topic has focused on the use of artificial or human visual feedback, which has led to advancements in transparency (i.e. the ease with which one can cognitively accept a robotic arm as an extension of their own body) and dexterity in completing increasingly challenging tasks [3].

However, in recent years, significant progress has been made in the design of new tactile sensors [4], and in the development of computational techniques to extract relevant information from them during robotic manipulation and exploration [5], either in isolation of combined with visual sensing [6]. As a result, it is no longer rare to find tactile sensors used as the end effector tips of robotic arms, particularly during remote teleoperation experiences [1,7]. The prospect of combining these two technological systems along with the advancements of virtual reality [8] and wearable haptic systems [9] is driving the development and integration of devices that provide, during teleoperation, the human-operator with a sense of physical contact with remotely controlled items through haptic feedback. Although the idea is not new [10], the recent technological advancements have proven that this could be the way forward for robotic teleoperation [11,12]. Our work introduces a new tactile telerobotic setup, shown in Fig. 1, that enables fluent and effective teleoperation based on the integration of a 6D arm manipulandum with force feedback, a hand exoscheleton with force feedback, a remote robotic manipulator with a four-finger tactile hand and a virtual reality headset for visualisation of the remote environment.

Through this setup, we can record relevant aspects of the human motion and manipulation strategies, to effectively control the actions of the robotic follower, and provide feedback to the human operator for enhanced immersion in the task; additionally, valuable data about the manipulated objects can be extracted by the follower robot. Notably, the rich contact information that we gather from the follower side and we render on the operator through the leader device can either complement or completely replace visual information. The challenge of limited camera installation options or low data transmission capacities is a significant obstacle to the optimal performance and consistency of teleoperation systems. Moreover, cameras are often unable to capture images effectively under varying lighting conditions, which highlights the importance of developing effective solutions to overcome these challenges and enhance the reliability and effectiveness of teleoperation systems [13]. For this reason, a further motivation for building such a sophisticated robotic setup is to enable blind teleoperated exploration and manipulation [14], where rich haptic feedback generated solely from contact information is crucial.

We believe that this setup paves the way for a number of studies and applications, such as the digital reconstruction or classification of objects, assessing the behaviour of the human operator in performing complex activities in cooperation with a robot, and learning from the human demonstration a control policy that enables the robot to autonomously perform exploration and manipulation tasks, also in challenging environments.

The aim of this preliminary study is to evaluate the reliability of our advanced teleoperation system by conducting a sponge brick pick-and-place task. During this pilot experiment, the operator perceives, via an exoskeleton glove, feedback of contact forces that are measured through tactile sensors mounted on the fingertips of the robot and conveyed as kinesthetic haptic feedback. The Results Sect. 3.2 presents separate analyses of the teleoperation of the end effector, the finger control, and the haptic feedback experienced by the operator.

2   Telemanipulation System

The robotic telemanipulation setup depicted in Fig. 1 has been designed to offer a configuration that is as human-centric and natural as possible for everyday handling scenarios. The follower side robot (UR5 robot arm and Allegro robot hand with custom tactile fingertips) is mounted on a custom-made vertical stand, known as MARIA (the Queen Mary multi-arm robot interactive assistant), to approximately mimic the positioning of the human arm on the torso. The leader side device (Virtuose 6D arm manipulandum [15] with HGlove hand exoscheleton [16]) has been positioned to have an operating height that is compatible with the natural arm posture of a standing human adult, offering a wide range of motion to effectively telemanipulate objects placed on a tabletop in front of the follower robot. This setup is an extension of a previous setup that featured a more limited tactile feedback from the robot hand fingertips, and a simpler and cheaper leader device composed of a Leap Motion controller for hand tracking and a custom data glove for vibro-tactile feedback [17,18]; the setup was tested on telemanipulation tasks [19], demonstrating that the simple tactile feedback already reduced cognitive load, as compared to no feedback [20]. Although we did not formally compare these two setups in terms of cognitive load and task performance, we believe the current setup is even more natural and effective, based on our daily experience in the lab. The following subsections provide a detailed explanation of the devices and control strategies employed. The Robot Operating System (ROS) is utilized as the middle-ware interface for communication and control.

2.1   Human-Operator's Leader Interface

On the leader side, a combination of Virtuose 6D and HGlove [16] is used to track the position of the hand of the operator in Cartesian space and the bending of each of the fingers. In particular, Virtuose 6D is able to provide the pose of the wrist and relying on an impedance controller it is possible to generate haptic feedback on the arm of the operator. This can be used to mimic the force sensed on the follower side including the weight of the grasped object, or simply to compensate for the weight of the exoskeleton. This latter feature is crucial in reducing the muscular effort of the user during prolonged teleoperation. Additionally, it is possible to create a software-implemented constraint known as a forbidden region haptic virtual feature [21] that prevents the operator from teleoperating the follower robot in that area. Figure 1 exhibits a light blue box encompassing the non-forbidden region.

Furthermore, the movement of the fingers of the operator in the joint space can be tracked using HGlove, an exoskeleton glove. It provides a measure of the distal, proximal, and lateral movements of each of the three fingers, namely the thumb, index, and middle. Additionally, HGlove has actuators which produce kinesthetic haptic feedback for each finger on the distal and proximal joints.

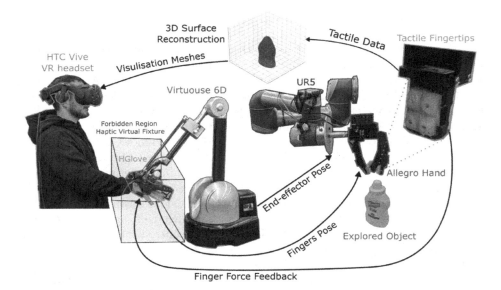

Fig. 1. Control Scheme for Bilateral Teleoperation: the end effector pose of the UR5 is controlled by the operator using Virtuose 6D while the finger movement of the Allegro Hand is controlled using HGlove. Beyond the blue box, a forbidden movement region is enforced using a haptic virtual fixture that prevents the operator from teleoperating the robot past it. Information regarding contact forces is gathered from the custom tactile sensors mounted on the fingertips of the robotic hand and used to create haptic feedback using Hglove as well as to digitally reconstruct the shape of the explored object in real-time. Finally, visualization meshes can be streamed to the operator through a display apparatus to improve the transparency of teleoperation. (Color figure online)

2.2   Robotic Manipulator Follower

For the follower side, a combination of UR5, Allegro Hand, consisting of four fingers, and customised tactile sensors [22] is proposed. To match the information received from Virtuose 6D, we found it convenient to proceed to work in Cartesian space. For this reason, we used RelaxedIK [23] as an optimiser to compute the inverse kinematics of UR5 that prevents self-collision. On the other hand, for finger control, we identified a reasonable empirical mapping to transfer information from the finger joint space of the HGlove to the finger joint space of the Allegro Hand. To ensure that this mapping remains consistent, HGlove is software-calibrated for each use to align each user's open/closed hand with the corresponding Allegro Hand configuration.

In the design of the Allegro Hand fingertips, we made the decision to customize our sensors to provide more flexibility in terms of the forces sensed as well as the shape that would be most convenient for manipulation experiments. We based our model on previous work, specifically the uSkin model [24,25], although reducing the number of sensitive taxels on each fingertip to reduce the overall size and complexity, inspired by recent work [22].

Using these tactile sensors, it is possible to estimate an averaged normal force on the four contact points from each fingertip, which can be used as force feedback to generate kinesthetic haptic feedback on the hand. Moreover, the shear forces information is crucial to obtain valuable information about the objects and about the physical interaction between the robot and the object during manipulation, that can help to recognize grasped objects [26] and to detect slip [27].

2.3   Teleoperation Architecture

The control architecture includes three components: Cartesian Tracking of the robot end-effector pose; joints control of the Allegro hand; Haptic feedback the first domain pertains to the teleoperation of the desired pose of UR5 end effector in the Cartesian space, $\hat{\mathbf{P}}_{\mathrm{UR5}}(t)$, while the second domain relates to the teleoperation of the Allegro Hand fingers using joint space control. Finally, a rule is required to render the forces measured by the sensors as haptic feedback on the fingers of the operator.

Cartesian Tracking. We define the pose of the end-effector (of either the Leader or the Follower robot arm) as a vector, $\mathbf{P} = [\mathbf{p} \ \mathbf{q}]^{\mathbf{T}}$, containing the Cartesian position $\mathbf{p} = [\mathbf{x} \ \mathbf{y} \ \mathbf{z}]$ and the quaternion orientation $\mathbf{q} = [\mathbf{q_x} \ \mathbf{q_y} \ \mathbf{q_z} \ \mathbf{q_w}]$. We define a control variable, $\Delta\mathbf{P}_{\mathrm{virt}}(t) = \mathbf{P}_{\mathrm{virt}}(t) - \mathbf{P}_{\mathrm{virt}}(t_0)$, which is the difference between the initial pose and current pose of the end-effector of the Leader robot. The control variable is mapped to a desired displacement of the end-effector of the Follower robot, $\hat{\mathbf{P}}_{\mathrm{UR5}}(t) = \mathbf{P}_{\mathrm{UR5}}(t_0) + \Delta\mathbf{P}_{\mathrm{virt}}(t)$.

Ultimately, the desired displacement of the joints of the Follower robot, $\hat{\theta}_{\mathrm{UR5}}(t) = \mathbf{RelaxedIK}(\hat{\mathbf{P}}_{\mathrm{UR5}}(t))$, is obtained through inverse kinematics computation, using the RelaxedIK solver [23], an optimizer that has demonstrated robustness for real-time teleoperation and that avoids self-collision between the robot joints.

Joints Control of the Allegro Hand. Concerning the control of the Allegro Hand joints, $\boldsymbol{\theta}^{Allegro} = \left[\theta^{\mathrm{in}} \ \theta^{\mathrm{mid}} \ \theta^{\mathrm{ring}} \ \theta^{\mathrm{th}}\right]^{\top} = [\theta_0 \ \theta_1 \dots \theta_{15}]$, an arbitrary mapping, $\hat{\boldsymbol{\theta}}_i^{finger}(t) = \boldsymbol{\theta}_i^{finger}(t_0) + \Delta\boldsymbol{\gamma}_j^{finger}\alpha_i^{finger}, i,j \in \{0,1,2,3\}$, between the joint space of the two devices was established. To this end, a variable $\Delta\boldsymbol{\gamma}(t) = \boldsymbol{\gamma}^{\mathrm{HG}}(t) - \boldsymbol{\gamma}^{\mathrm{HG}}(t_0)$, where $\boldsymbol{\gamma}^{HG} = [\gamma^{\mathrm{in}} \ \gamma^{\mathrm{in}} \ \gamma^{\mathrm{mid}} \ \gamma^{\mathrm{th}}]^T$ and $\boldsymbol{\gamma}^{in} = [\gamma_0 \ \gamma_1 \ \gamma_1 \ \gamma_2]^T$, was chosen to represent the angular deviation between the initial and current joint states of each of the fingers of HGlove. In our opinion, this choice partially addresses the vast problem of accurately mapping an exoskeleton with a robotic hand, but we opted for this strategy because we reckon that mapping in joint space is competent for power grasp tasks [28].

The main challenge of the mapping is that HGlove is composed of three joints for each finger while Allegro Hand has four. The same is also true for the number of fingers, as HGlove is composed of three fingers while Allegro Hand has four. For this reason, as illustrated in Fig. 2, we have defined a coupling as follows: the movement of the HGlove thumb controls the thumb of Allegro Hand, the movement of the index finger of HGlove simultaneously controls the index and middle finger of Allegro Hand, and finally, the movement of the middle finger of HGlove controls the movement of the ring finger of Allegro Hand.

Although having under-dimensioned finger actuators on HGlove provides an intrinsic limitation in controlling the higher-dimensional joints of the Allegro Hand, this decision has no impact on the way the operator manipulates, in fact as anticipated, the control of the fingers of the follower is defined by a unidirectional mapping between the leader and the follower. To this end, an empirical calibration of the coefficients within the aforementioned vector α, was conducted. This calibration aimed to enable the Allegro Hand to accurately mimic the finger flexion of the hand of the operator, ensuring a realistic and consistent replication. The calibration was executed to ensure that the robotic fingertips grasped objects specifically on the region equipped with sensors.

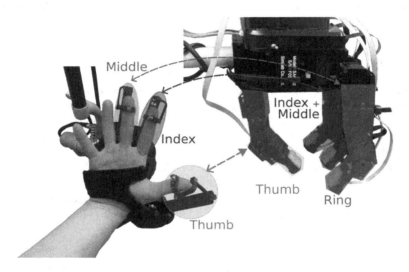

Fig. 2. Mapping of HGlove movement to Allegro Hand. The thumb of the Allegro Hand is controlled by the thumb of the Hglove (green). The index of the HGlove is coupled with the index and middle fingers of the Allegro Hand (blue). Finally, the ring finger of the Allegro Hand is paired with the middle finger of the HGlove (red). (Color figure online)

Haptic Feedback. Each of the tactile sensors mounted on the fingertips of the Allegro Hand is capable of measuring a 3D vector consisting of both shear and normal force components at four distinct points on the fingertip. While this data would prove valuable for contact analysis during manipulation, it is too voluminous to be utilized for rendering force feedback via the HGlove. To address this issue, the decision was made to use only the highest normal force value measured by each fingertip sensor, as detailed in Eq. (1). Additionally, we set a minimum threshold to distinguish disturbance caused by external magnetic fields on the sensors from a tactile force.

$$F_z^{\text{finger}} = \begin{cases} \max\{F_{z1}, F_{z2}, F_{z3}, F_{z4}\} & \textbf{if } \max\{\dots\} \geq \textbf{threshold} \\ 0 & \textbf{otherwise} \end{cases} \qquad (1)$$

Finally, we set a maximum value measured by the sensors, above which haptic force saturates at a maximum limit to ensure the safety of the operator.

3 Experimental Validation

3.1 Methods

The present study features a telemanipulation experiment which has been recorded and analyzed. The experiment consists of several distinct stages, as depicted in Fig. 3, including (b) approaching the object, (c) grasping the object, (d) moving the object on a surface of varying height, and (e) releasing the object. Through this basic experiment, the key functionalities of our setup are demonstrated, including the capability to navigate the scene, the ability to grasp, manipulate and carry objects, and the ability to render haptic feedback on the hand of the user.

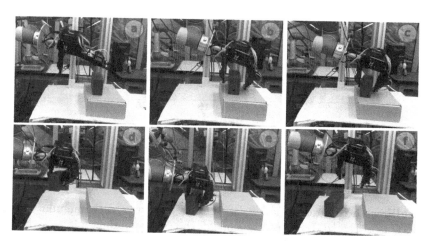

Fig. 3. Teleoperation experiment: pick and place a brick sponge. In (a & f) are shown the starting and final positions. In (b) the approach to the object is shown. In (c) the grasping of the object begins. In (d) the object is transported to a new location at a different height. In (e) the object is placed in the newly reached location.

3.2   Results

End-Effector Tracking. Figure 4 shows the trajectories in Cartesian space of the wrist of the operator connected to Virtuose 6D via HGlove and the trajectory of the end effector of the UR5 corresponding to the wrist of the UR5. The graph indicates that the robot is capable of accurately following the operator's movements. However, certain crucial aspects of the experiment require careful consideration. The z-axis trajectory reveals that the robot did not precisely mimic the operator's movement within a particular time interval. This deviation is attributable to a constraint that we imposed on the joint velocity of the robot to prevent hazardous movements; in fact, the discrepancy is observed when the movement speed of the operator increases rapidly. On the contrary, the discrepancy that can be observed on the x-axis trajectory is caused by the simultaneous data recording we perform during the experiment, which increases the computational effort and generates some packet loss in the control communication. Therefore, we have recently modified the data recording strategy to alleviate this problem, which in fact we have now solved (although not reported in this paper).

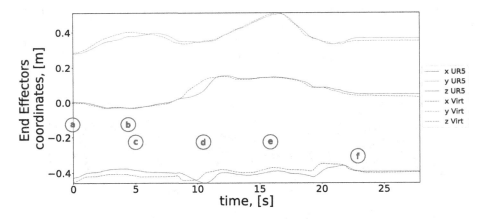

Fig. 4. Wrists trajectories in 3D Cartesian Space. The plot is labelled to emphasize the instances of pick-and-place actions depicted in Fig. 3

Controlling the Hand. The left side of Fig. 5 illustrates the angular changes of the joints of the HGLove used to control the corresponding joints of the Allegro Hand, in accordance with the coupling presented in Fig. 2. As discussed in Sect. 2.3, an empirical mapping was developed to simulate the control of the fingers of the operator, allowing for a mapping from a three-joint space of HGlove to a four-joint space on the Allegro Hand. As shown by the results, the majority of the motion corresponds to the movement of the proximal joint of both devices, which are calibrated in direct proportion to one another. Furthermore, the trajectories for all fingers, with the exception of the thumb, are comparable, as depicted in the graph. Conversely, it was determined to place a greater emphasis on the distal displacement of the thumb.

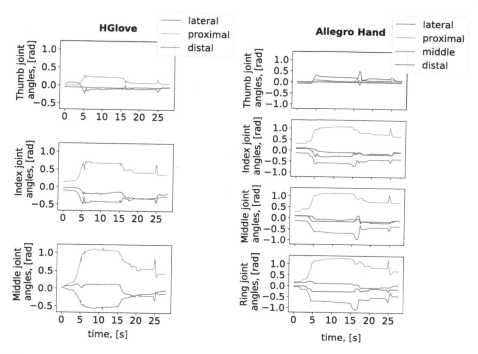

Fig. 5. Fingers Teleoperation Trajectories: The left panel shows the angular joint displacements recorded on the three fingers of the Leader exoskeleton glove, HGlove. The right panel shows the corresponding displacements observed during the pick-and-place task performed by the four fingers of the Follower robotic hand, Allegro Hand. Notably, the middle and ring fingers of the Allegro Hand were jointly controlled by only the middle finger of the Leader.

Haptic Experience. The tactile intensities measured by the tactile sensors for each fingers couple during handling are depicted in Fig. 6. While manufactured sensors are prone to disturbances due to external magnetic fields (that can lead even to negative values), the pressure exerted during manipulation generally exceeds the magnitude of such disturbances. Thus, the values obtained have been partially filtered, precluding the possibility of defining a standard unit of measurement. Nevertheless, this data proves to be highly effective in rendering exceptional haptic feedback to the operator, as evidenced by Fig. 6. Whenever a touch with a tactile intensity value higher than 30 is detected by the sensor, a feedback signal proportional to the measured touch is conveyed to the operator as kinesthetic haptic feedback. In this particular case, to render all the values greater than 200 measured by the tactile sensors a maximum force threshold of 5N was established, a value deemed safe to be rendered to the fingers of the operator [16].

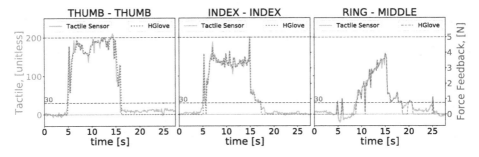

Fig. 6. The plots show haptic sensor measurements (orange) for each of the fingers used to render haptic kinesthetic feedback (blue) on the coupled fingers of the exoskeleton glove. For measurements below 30, haptic feedback is null. Conversely, it is proportional to sensor measurements up to the maximum value of 5N, which is a safe value for rendering all measurements above the threshold of 200. (Color figure online)

4   Conclusion and Future Work

In this paper, we introduce a novel tactile telemanipulation setup, in which tactile information extracted from the fingertips of a dexterous robot hand is used to generate force feedback on the human operator during remote object manipulation. The bilateral Leader-Follower control architecture is described in detail, with a focus on the haptic experience. We report the results of preliminary validation experiments that support the feasibility of our sensing, control and feedback approaches.

In previous work, we showed how remote visual sensing can be used in combination with Virtual Reality headsets to feedback to the human operator a detailed 3D reconstruction of the remote environment during telemanipulation, improving task performance and reducing cognitive load [8]. With this novel setup, we believe that similar results could be achieved without having to rely on visual sensing, but solely using tactile sensing, extending previous research on teleoperated [7] and autonomous [22, 29] robotic tactile exploration and 3D reconstruction; this would enable new application scenarios, where visual sensing is particularly challenging due to difficult lighting conditions and considerable occlusions, such as deep sea and space exploration. In addition, we believe that this setup (or, similar systems inspired by the proposed architecture) can be a powerful asset in human studies, to shed more light on the human strategies underlying physical human-robot interaction, and in robot dexterity learning from human demonstrations.

Acknowledgment. This work was partially funded by EPSRC Q-Arena grant EP/V035304/1. G. Giudici is funded by the Queen Mary University of London Ph.D. studentship.

References

1. Darvish, K., et al.: Teleoperation of humanoid robots: a survey. IEEE Trans. Robot. (2023)
2. Vitanov, I., et al.: A suite of robotic solutions for nuclear waste decommissioning. Robotics **10**(4), 112 (2021)
3. Handa, A., et al.: Dexpilot: vision-based teleoperation of dexterous robotic hand-arm system. In: IEEE ICRA, pp. 9164–9170 (2020)
4. Chi, C., Sun, X., Xue, N., Li, T., Liu, C.: Recent progress in technologies for tactile sensors. Sensors **18**(4), 948 (2018)
5. Li, Q., Kroemer, O., Su, Z., Veiga, F.F., Kaboli, M., Ritter, H.J.: A review of tactile information: perception and action through touch. IEEE Trans. Robot. **36**(6), 1619–1634 (2020)
6. Navarro-Guerrero, N., Toprak, S., Josifovski, J., Jamone, L.: Visuo-haptic object perception for robots: an overview. Auton. Robots **47**(4), 377–403 (2023)
7. Omarali, B., Palermo, F., Althoefer, K., Valle, M., Farkhatdinov, I.: Tactile classification of object materials for virtual reality based robot teleoperation. In: IEEE ICRA (2022)
8. Omarali, B., Denoun, B., Althoefer, K., Jamone, L., Valle, M., Farkhatdinov, I.: Virtual reality based telerobotics framework with depth cameras. In: IEEE International Conference on Robot and Human Interactive Communication (2020)
9. Ogrinc, M., Farkhatdinov, I., Walker, R., Burdet, E.: Sensory integration of apparent motion speed and vibration magnitude. IEEE Trans. Haptics **11**(3), 455–463 (2017)
10. Browse, R., McDonald, M.: Using tactile information in telerobotics. IEEE Trans. Syst. Man Cybern. Syst. **22**(5), 1205–1210 (1992)
11. Fishel, J.A., et al.: Tactile telerobots for dull, dirty, dangerous, and inaccessible tasks. In: IEEE ICRA (2020)
12. Liu, Y., Tsai, Y.-Y., Huang, B., Guo, J.: Virtual reality based tactile sensing enhancements for bilateral teleoperation system with in-hand manipulation. IEEE Robot. Autom. Lett. **7**(3), 6998–7005 (2022)
13. Dang, H., Weisz, J., Allen, P.K.: Blind grasping: stable robotic grasping using tactile feedback and hand kinematics. In: IEEE International Conference on Robotics and Automation 2011, pp. 5917–5922 (2011)
14. Lederman, S.J., Klatzky, R.L.: Hand movements: a window into haptic object recognition. Cogn. Psychol. **19**(3), 342–368 (1987)
15. Perret, J.: Haptic trends by haption: larger, stronger, faster. In: EuroHaptics Conference (2014)
16. Perret, J., Parent, Q., Giudicelli, B.: Hglove: a wearable force-feedback device for the hand. In: 14th Annual EuroVR Conference (2017)

17. Junput, B., Wei, X., Jamone, L.: Feel it on your fingers: dataglove with vibrotactile feedback for virtual reality and telerobotics. In: Althoefer, K., Konstantinova, J., Zhang, K. (eds.) TAROS 2019. LNCS (LNAI), vol. 11649, pp. 375–385. Springer, Cham (2019). https://doi.org/10.1007/978-3-030-23807-0_31

18. Junput, B., Farkhatdinov, I., Jamone, L.: Touch it, rub it, feel it! haptic rendering of physical textures with a low cost wearable system. In: Mohammad, A., Dong, X., Russo, M. (eds.) TAROS 2020. LNCS (LNAI), vol. 12228, pp. 274–286. Springer, Cham (2020). https://doi.org/10.1007/978-3-030-63486-5_29

19. Coppola, C., Jamone, L.: Master of puppets: multi-modal robot activity segmentation from teleoperated demonstrations. In: IEEE International Conference on Development and Learning (ICDL) (2022)

20. Coppola, C., Solak, G., Jamone, L.: An affordable system for the teleoperation of dexterous robotic hands using leap motion hand tracking and vibrotactile feedback. In: IEEE International Conference on Robot and Human Interactive Communication (2022)

21. Abbott, J.J., Okamura, A.M.: Stable forbidden-region virtual fixtures for bilateral telemanipulation. J. Dyn. Syst. Meas. Control Trans. ASME (2006)

22. Bonzini, A.A., Seminara, L., Macciò, S., Carfì, A., Jamone, L.: Leveraging symmetry detection to speed up haptic object exploration in robots. In: 2022 IEEE International Conference on Development and Learning (ICDL) (2022)

23. Rakita, D., Mutlu, B., Gleicher, M.: Relaxedik: real-time synthesis of accurate and feasible robot arm motion. In: Robotics: Science and Systems (2018)

24. Tomo, T.P., et al.: Covering a robot fingertip with uSkin: a soft electronic skin with distributed 3-axis force sensitive elements for robot hands. IEEE Robot. Autom. Lett. 3(1), 124–131 (2017)

25. Tomo, T.P., et al.: A new silicone structure for uSkin-a soft, distributed, digital 3-axis skin sensor and its integration on the humanoid robot iCub. IEEE Robot. Autom. Lett. 3(3), 2584–2591 (2018)

26. Kirby, E., Zenha, R., Jamone, L.: Comparing single touch to dynamic exploratory procedures for robotic tactile object recognition. IEEE Robot. Autom. Lett. 7(2), 4252–4258 (2022)

27. Zenha, R., Denoun, B., Coppola, C., Jamone, L.: Tactile slip detection in the wild leveraging distributed sensing of both normal and shear forces. In: 2021 IEEE/RSJ International Conference on Intelligent Robots and Systems (2021)

28. Li, R., Wang, H., Liu, Z.: Survey on mapping human hand motion to robotic hands for teleoperation. IEEE Trans. Circuits Syst. Video Technol. 32(5), 2647–2665 (2022)

29. Bonzini, A.A., Seminara, L., Jamone, L.: Improving haptic exploration of object shape by discovering symmetries. In: 2022 International Conference on Robotics and Automation (ICRA), pp. 5821–5827. IEEE (2022)

Teleoperation

Comparative Study of Hand-Tracking and Traditional Control Interfaces for Remote Palpation

Leone Costi[1(✉)], Elijah Almanzor[1], Luca Scimeca[2], and Fumiya Iida[1]

[1] Bio-Inspired Robotics Laboratory, Department of Engineering, University of Cambridge, Cambridge, UK
lc830@cam.ac.uk

[2] Department of Cancer Immunology and Virology, Harvard Medical School, Boston, USA

Abstract. Medical robotics has been widely accepted in several fields in the healthcare system. However, despite several attempts and a well-understood potential, teleoperation is still far from permeating primary care and tasks such as remote palpation, despite significant advancements in both haptic and tactile feedback. With most of the current focus on the feedback channel, the control interface has largely been overlooked. However, recent studies have proposed control interfaces so as to resemble as much as possible in-person palpation. Although hypothesized, they have not been systematically proven to be more intuitive or natural than traditional ones. In this paper, we implement a hand-guided control interface and investigate its performance, comparing it to a keyboard and a joystick-based control interface. We extract both objective and subjective measurements. We show how the hand-guided control, despite being more similar to the in-person task, achieves lower speed and worse precision, especially for point-wise target reaching. Moreover, it is perceived as less intuitive by the users, conversely to what was previously theorized in literature.

Keywords: Teleoperation · Hand tracking · Remote palpation

1 Introduction

Over the last 2 decades, the healthcare system has slowly embraced robotics and teleoperated robotics in order to perform procedures beyond human capability [16,24]. The enhanced precision and the ability to access previously unapproachable spaces have helped teleoperated leader-follower robotic technologies permeate several fields [6,31]. Moreover, even if still not commercially available, state-of-the-art literature already showcased the possible implementation

This work was supported by the SMART project, European Union's Horizon 2020 research and innovation under the Marie Sklodowska-Curie (ID 860108), and EPSRC RoboPatient project EP/T00519X/1.

F. Iida et al. (Eds.): TAROS 2023, LNAI 14136, pp. 457–469, 2023.
https://doi.org/10.1007/978-3-031-43360-3_37

of haptic feedback [2,11]. However, despite numerous attempts in developing teleoperated systems for primary care [14], teleoperated physical examination is still only explored in literature and not within clinical practice.

Physical examination is the standard routine test used by general practitioners to very the presence of potentially painful or dangerous abnormal conditions in the patient's abdomen [1,4]. The examination is composed of 4 parts: inspection, auscultation, percussion, and palpation [5,25]. Especially the latter, because of the prolonged mechanical interaction between the patient and practitioner's hand, has been accurately analyzed [19,20,26]. When designing a teleoperated platform for remote palpation, the main aim is to achieve good telepresence. To do so, most studies have focused their attention on the importance of tactile feedback [18] and on the development of the feedback channel itself [29]. Whether the tactile information is presented through visual feedback [7,17,22], vibrations [30,32], or more elaborated morphing interfaces [9,13,28], such devices are used solely as feedback channels and traditional control interfaces are used for trajectory control, resulting in a loss of telepresence. As a result, the proposed systems lack intuitiveness, which is a fundamental characteristic to achieve telepresence and effectiveness [3,27].

Nevertheless, there are studies that proposed soft control interfaces [8,12,15, 21], aimed to resemble the soft tissues touched in the remote environment. In such systems, the user is required to palpate the soft interface as if the procedure was performed in person, and the follower reproduces the hand trajectory detected by the leader. In some cases, such an interface is not only used for control but also for feedback [23]. So far, these solutions showcase 2 main drawbacks: most proposed systems have a very limited number of controllable degrees of freedom, and they can only detect the user's trajectory after the hand is placed in contact with the interface, but cannot follow the hand as it is moving through the air. All in all, the common ground of these works is the idea that a soft control interface would promote telepresence and enhance the overall performance of the device. However, there is no clear evidence that such solutions represent a more natural and intuitive control interface.

Our goal is to investigate the performance of different control interfaces during remote interaction with a soft body simulating the task of teleoperated palpation. Understanding what type of control interface results in a more natural or intuitive experience when interacting with a soft body is fundamental to avoid the user's estrangement from the task of palpation, that in turn can lead to worse overall performance and potential hazard to the patient. We aim to characterize the tested interfaces in terms of speed, accuracy, and intuitiveness both with quantitative and qualitative measures, to understand which control strategy can lead to better overall performance and higher telepresence.

This paper will showcase 3 different control interfaces: a keyboard, a joystick, and a hand-tracking algorithm. The latter, paired with a soft silicone phantom, has been developed so as to have a soft control interface able to follow the user's hand trajectory both when in contact with the soft interface itself and when moving through the air.

In the remainder of the paper, the overall system and the implementation of the different interfaces are described in Sect. 2, followed by analysis results in Sect. 3 and discussion in Sect. 4.

2   Material and Methods

The aim of this work is to investigate the performance achieved by users when remotely interacting with a soft body, during remote palpation, using 3 different control interfaces. The control interface is part of the leader of a leader-follower architecture for teleoperation and it is used to record users' input (see Fig. 1). For the purpose of this study, we implemented a unilateral teleoperated system, delivering visual feedback to the user. The follower side is composed of a highly dexterous UR5 Robotic Arm with 6 controllable Degrees of Freedom (DoF) (*Universal Robots*), a camera (*4K pro camera, Logitech*), and a 'server' workstation able to control the robotic arm via TCP/IP. On the other side, the leader is composed of a 'client' machine that achieves teleoperation by connecting to the server through a custom-made communication channel and exchanging both control and feedback data, a screen to deliver real-time visual information about the performed task, and the control interface. The communication is implemented *ad hoc* via sockets. Client and server operate asynchronously, allowing the server to run at a much higher frequency, around 125 Hz. Figure 1 showcases the schematics of the implemented unilateral teleoperated architecture.

The 3 tested control interfaces are the computed keyboard, the joystick, and a hand-tracking algorithm paired with a soft phantom. The first 2 cases represent traditional interfaces and differ only in the mapping between the pressed buttons and the motor commands, whereas the latter is a soft control interface implemented to resemble as close as possible the in-person task of palpation. All interfaces allow for an overall framerate of the system of 60 Hz. For the purpose of this study, the users are allowed to control 3 DoF: translation along x, y, and z. In all cases, the control interface retrieves the incremental motion intention of the user: at any point in time, the user can decide through the leader where to move the follower with respect to the current position as follows:

$$\vec{x}_F(t + 1) = \vec{x}_F(t) + \Delta\vec{x}_L(t) \tag{1}$$

where $\vec{x}_F$ are the x,y and z coordinates of the follower's end effector, $\Delta\vec{x}_L$ are the incremental displacement in x,y and z imposed by the leader, and t and $t + 1$ represent the current and next time step. For each axis, the incremental displacement between 2 time steps can either be 0 or a fixed $\Delta_0 = 40\ \mu m$. Forcing the follower to operate at a constant speed allows us to compare the achieved overall speed during the task when using different interfaces and isolate the effect of the interface itself rather than the speed of the follower.

When using the keyboard, individual keys are mapped to either positive or negative increments along the three axes: W and S result in positive and negative displacement along y, A, and D in positive and negative displacement along x and *Space* and *Alt* in positive and negative displacement along z, respectively

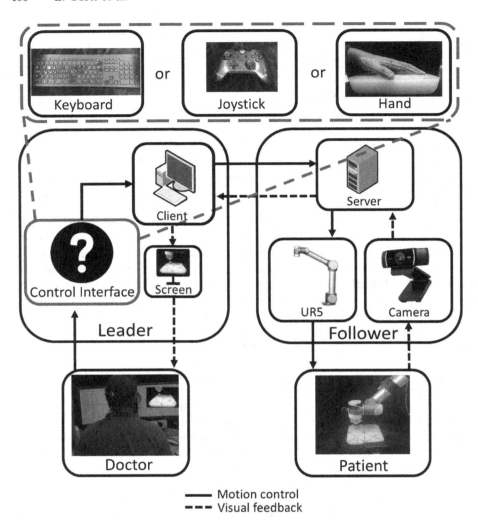

Fig. 1. Schematics of the overall unilateral teleoperated system, divided into leader and follower, showing all the components and the two communication channels, as well as the 3 investigated control interfaces.

(see Fig. 2a). Further details on this control method have been discussed in previous work [10]. On the other hand, the joystick uses the left analog to control the planar motion along the xy plane, and the 2 bumpers are used for z displacement: right bumper for positive, right bumper for negative (see Fig. 2b). The signal from the analog is digitalized in order to achieve the same constant speed achievable with the keyboard. Finally, the soft control interface implementing hand tracking and a soft phantom, from now on simply called 'hand' for simplicity, uses the relative motion of the user's hand to move the follower.

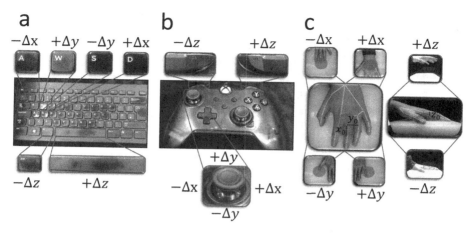

Fig. 2. The 3 tested interfaces: (a) computer keyboard, (b) joystick, and (c) hand tracking paired with a soft interface. Each interface is associated with the respective control modality. For brevity, $\Delta x = +\Delta_0$ is shortened to $+\Delta x$, and so on. The red zone in (c) represents the 'dead zone': a portion of the recorded space in which the motion is suppressed. (Color figure online)

Using the Python 3.6 library MediaPipe (version 0.8.11), the 2D position of 21 hand landmarks is identified. In order to obtain the 3D position of such landmarks, 2 cameras have been used: 1 directly above the soft phantom, to get the x and y coordinates, and one on the side, at 906o with respect to the first one, to retrieve the z coordinate (see Fig. 2c). Then, the center of the hand is computed as follows:

$$\vec{x}_c(t) = \frac{\sum_{n=1}^{N(t)} \vec{x}_n(t)}{N(t)} \tag{2}$$

where $\vec{x}_c$ and $\vec{x}_n$ are the x, y, and z coordinates of the center of the hand and the nth landmark, and N is the total number of visible landmarks at the time step t. The rest position of the user's hand $x_c(0)$ is registered at the beginning of the trial and corresponds to no movement of the follower. During the trial, the relative position of the hand's center with respect to its initial value is used to determine the incremental displacement as follows:

$$\begin{cases} \Delta x = sign(x_c(t) - x_c(0))\Delta_0 u(|(x_c(t) - x_c(0)| - x_0) \\ \Delta y = sign(y_c(t) - y_c(0))\Delta_0 u(|(y_c(t) - y_c(0)| - y_0) \\ \Delta z = sign(z_c(t) - z_c(0))\Delta_0 u(|(z_c(t) - z_c(0)| - z_0) \end{cases} \tag{3}$$

where $u(\cdot)$ is the step function, and x_0, y_0, and z_0 represent the 'dead zone': a region in which motor control is inhibited. This region is added in order to prevent follower oscillations due to indirect instabilities produced by the natural shaking of the user's hand. For this study, x_0 and y_0 are 70 pixels, and z_0 is

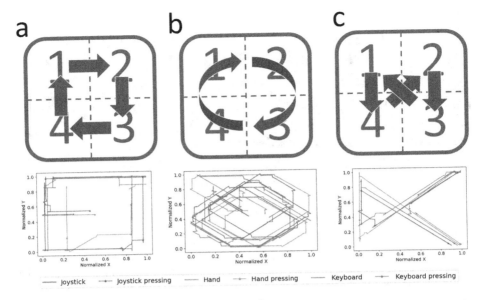

Fig. 3. Schematics of (a) task 1, (b) task 2, and (c) task 3, with executed trajectories of a single participant. Note that the order of task 3 is random and unique for every participant. Tasks 1 and 3 also report the point at which contact was made between the follower and the soft silicone phantom simulating the patient.

30 pixels. Note that the distance is given in pixels since it is recorded using a camera.

The experimental protocol is carried out on 10 users (25.2 ± 5.2 years old), of which 8 are right-handed and 2 are left-handed. 6 males and 4 females, none with previous experience in robotic navigation or remote palpation. Moreover, it is composed of 3 different tasks, each executed one time with every interface, for a total of 9 trials. Every task has a maximum duration of 2 min, followed by a 2 min rest time, for a maximum experiment time of 36 min. Every participant is given a test trial of 2 min using the hand to control the robot before the experimental trials. All tasks are executed touching a 20 cm × 20 cm flat soft phantom made of Ecoflex 00–30 (*Smooth-On*), divided into 4 quadrants to simulate the 4 quadrants in which the abdomen is divided during palpation. The first task consists of reaching and palpating the center of each quadrant in order (see Fig. 3a). The second task consists of moving the follower to draw a circle in the air 3 times (see Fig. 3b): this task is used to verify multi-DoF trajectories execution because it requires controlling more than 1 DoF simultaneously. Finally, the last task consists of reaching and palpating the center of each quadrant once more, but in a shuffled random order which is different for every participant (see Fig. 3c). The 3 tasks are always tested in the presented order, and each one is repeated 3 times, 1 with each interface. The order of the interfaces within a task is randomly assigned for each user to avoid any bias due to the learning curve of the task.

The main metrics used to analyze the results are time, distance to the target palpation target, in the case of tasks 1 and 3, and mean and standard deviation of the circumference radius for task 2. Moreover, in order to collect subjective data, a questionnaire is completed by the participants at the end of the experiments, in which they rate from 1 to 5 the perceived accuracy, speed, and intuitiveness of the 3 interfaces.

3 Results

The aim of this paper is to investigate the performance of different interfaces as control interfaces in the case of remote palpation. As already mentioned, the remote phantom used in the experimental protocol is divided into 4 quadrants, simulating the 4 abdominal quadrants explored during palpation. Every participant is asked to perform 3 different tasks (see Sect. 2) and it is evaluated on precision and speed. Figure 4a reports the required time to complete the task as a function of the user interface. Firstly, it can be noticed how the hand is significantly slower than the other 2 interfaces in task 1, but the difference is not statistically significant in tasks 2 and 3. Secondly, the joystick appears to be significantly faster than the keyboard in all tasks except task 1. To understand the cause behind such a result, Fig. 4b reports which fraction of the total time has been spent actively moving a given number of DoF as a function of task and interface. This gives an important insight into why the controller achieves faster speed, especially in task 2: the more frequent control of 2 DoF simultaneously, achieving faster the smooth circular trajectory which is desired. Such difference is probably facilitated by the presence of the analog, controlling both displacements in x and y.

As a second metric, we shift our focus to precision. In the case of tasks 1 and 3, precision can be determined by the error between the target palpation point and the actual palpated point. Figure 5a showcases the overall performance among all participants. Once again, the hand is shown to have the worst performance among all interfaces, being almost always statistically less performing except for when compared with the keyboard in task 1. Such a finding further reinforces the concept that hand-tracking showcases poor performance when trying to approach very specific points in space. Concerning task 2, the precision is characterized using 2 parameters: the mean and standard deviation of the achieved circular trajectory. The target trajectory is a circle passing by the center of each quadrant, with a radius of 7.07 cm (see Fig. 5b). The keyboard and joystick slightly undershoot the target radius, whereas the hand produces a significantly larger trajectory. Moreover, both the keyboard and joystick showcase a significantly smaller standard deviation, indicating much less deviation from the target path. Possibly, the increased variation is due to a lack of intuitiveness producing unwanted drift of the follower's end-effector.

To have a better insight into the data, Fig. 6 showcases the scatter plot of all attempts among all participants, divided based on the user interface and target point. Now, we can better understand why the hand results are less precise than

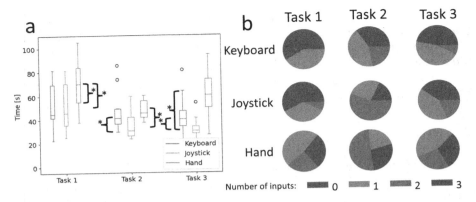

Fig. 4. (a) Total time required to complete the task as a function of the different proposed interfaces. Statistical significance under a paired t-test is highlighted using ∗. In task 1, the hand is shown to be significantly slower than both the keyboard ($p\ value = 2.6 \times 10^{-2}$) and the joystick ($p\ value = 9.8 \times 10^{-3}$). In task 2, the joystick performs significantly faster than the keyboard ($p\ value = 2.8 \times 10^{-2}$) and hand ($p\ value = 1.6 \times 10^{-2}$). Similarly, task 3 is characterized by a significantly faster performance of the joystick, compared to the keyboard ($p\ value = 2.9 \times 10^{-2}$) and the hand ($p\ value = 2.8 \times 10^{-4}$). (b) Relative time spent actively controlling a given number of DoF, as a function of the task and the interface. Blue, orange, green, and red are 0, 1, 2, and 3 simultaneously moving DoF, respectively.

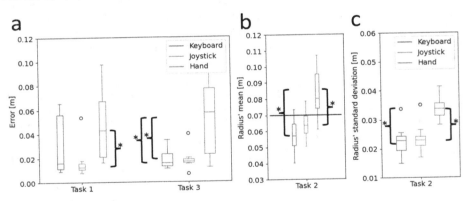

Fig. 5. (a) Error in the position of the palpated target point in tasks 1 and 3 as a function of the different proposed interfaces. (b) Mean and (c) standard deviation of the radius of the achieved circular trajectories in task 2 among all participants as a function of the control interface. The black line represents the target radius. Statistical significance under a paired t-test is highlighted using ∗. In task 1, the hand is significantly slower than the joystick ($p\ value = 8.5 \times 10^{-3}$). In task 3, the hand performs significantly worse than the keyboard ($p\ value = 3.5 \times 10^{-3}$) and the joystick ($p\ value = 5.2 \times 10^{-3}$). In task 2, compared with the keyboard and the joystick, the hand achieves a significantly greater radius ($p\ value = 1.4 \times 10^{-3}$ and 2.4×10^{-3}, respectively) and standard deviation ($p\ value = 1.0 \times 10^{-3}$ and 1.4×10^{-3}, respectively).

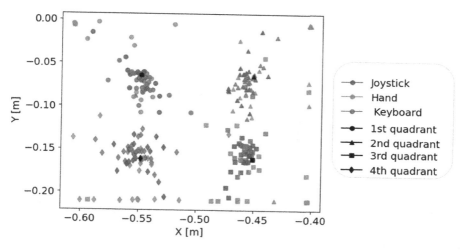

Fig. 6. 2D scatter-plot of attempted palpation. The black marker represents the target point at the center of every quadrant, and the color and shape of the markers encode the user interface and the current target.

the other 2 interfaces. There are cases in which the palpated point results to be at the edge of the phantom or in a totally different quadrant. This, paired with the high amount of time spent moving 3 DoF when not necessary (see Fig. 4b), highlights a deeper problem in controlling the interface. Unlike the keyboard and joystick, of which the errors are mostly based on user misjudgment, the hand is characterized by erroneous control, possibly due to lower intuitiveness.

To verify what is the subjective experience of the users, a questionnaire was completed after the experimental session, in which subjects were asked to rate 1–5 the following features: perceived accuracy, speed, and intuitiveness (see Fig. 7). According to the quantitative results, both perceived accuracy and intuitiveness using the hand are significantly lower than the other 2 interfaces, and the joystick is considered the fastest and most precise. All in all, the perceived performance resembles well the objective one, indicating good self-awareness of the users. Ultimately, it is clear that participants do not consider the hand intuitive nor performing, revealing the presence of the user's estrangement from the task of palpation.

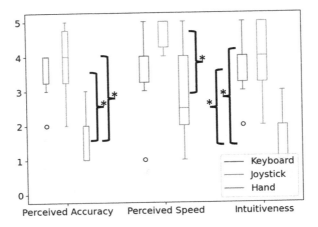

Fig. 7. Subjective feedback about perceived accuracy, perceived speed, and intuitiveness of the 3 tested interfaces. Statistical significance under a paired t-test is highlighted using ∗. Concerning accuracy, the hand is perceived to be significantly worse than both the keyboard ($p\,value = 3.7 \times 10^{-4}$) and the joystick ($p\,value = 9.1 \times 10^{-5}$). Regarding speed, the hand is perceived to be significantly worse than the joystick ($p\,value = 1.5 \times 10^{-2}$). Ultimately, the hand is considered to be significantly less intuitive than both the keyboard ($p\,value = 4.1 \times 10^{-4}$) and the joystick ($p\,value = 8.7 \times 10^{-5}$).

4   Conclusion

This work investigates the performance of different control interfaces for remote palpation. A total of 3 interfaces are tested: a keyboard, a joystick, and a hand-tracking algorithm paired with a soft palpation phantom, to simulate the in-person task. Participants perform 3 tasks consisting of moving the follower along different trajectories and palpating the remote phantom at selected points. These tasks have been evaluated both objectively and subjectively. The main finding is that, conversely to what is theorized by other work in literature, moving closer to the in-person task, allowing hand-guided control of the robot hand-effector, does not result in better performance and user feedback, and instead promotes user's estrangement, resulting in a less intuitive control strategy. However, we acknowledge that the implemented strategy is still far away from an exact replica of the in-person task, potentially resulting in an episode of 'uncanny valley'. Moreover, both the joystick and keyboard are devices very often used by the involved participant, and we endorse further studies on the learning curve of the hand-guided interface. Nevertheless, traditional interfaces have been proven more intuitive, fast, and accurate when used by people with no previous experience in medical teleoperation, and are a valid candidate for up to 3DoF teleoperation.

References

1. Alpert, J.S.: How accurate are the findings noted during a physical examination?: will physicians stop performing physical examinations? (part 2). Am. J. Med. **132**(6), 663–664 (2019). https://doi.org/10.1016/j.amjmed.2019.01.008
2. Amirabdollahian, F., et al.: Prevalence of haptic feedback in robot-mediated surgery: a systematic review of literature. J. Robot. Surg. **12**(1), 11–25 (2018). https://doi.org/10.1007/s11701-017-0763-4
3. Auvray, M., Duriez, C.: Haptics: Neuroscience, Devices, Modeling, and Applications, vol. 8618 (2014). https://doi.org/10.1007/978-3-662-44193-0_70
4. Bilal, M., Voin, V., Topale, N., Iwanaga, J., Loukas, M., Tubbs, R.S.: The clinical anatomy of the physical examination of the abdomen: a comprehensive review. Clin. Anat. **30**(3), 352–356 (2017). https://doi.org/10.1002/ca.22832
5. Cartwright, S.L., Knudson, M.P.: Evaluation of acute abdominal pain in adults. Am. Fam. Phys. **77**(7), 971–978 (2008)
6. Chen, Y., Zhang, S., Wu, Z., Yang, B., Luo, Q., Xu, K.: Review of surgical robotic systems for keyhole and endoscopic procedures: state of the art and perspectives. Front. Med. **14**(4), 382–403 (2020). https://doi.org/10.1007/s11684-020-0781-x
7. Coles, T.R., John, N.W., Gould, D., Caldwell, D.G.: Integrating haptics with augmented reality in a femoral palpation and needle insertion training simulation. IEEE Trans. Haptics **4**(3), 199–209 (2011). https://doi.org/10.1109/TOH.2011.32
8. Costi, L., Lalitharatne, T.D., Iida, F.: Soft control interface for highly dexterous unilateral remote palpation. In: 2022 9th IEEE RAS/EMBS International Conference for Biomedical Robotics and Biomechatronics (BioRob), pp. 1–8. IEEE (2022)
9. Costi, L., Maiolino, P., Iida, F.: Soft morphing interface for tactile feedback in remote palpation. In: IEEE International Conference on Soft Robotics, RoboSoft, pp. 932–937 (2022)
10. Costi, L., et al.: Comparative analysis of model-based predictive shared control for delayed operation in object reaching and recognition tasks with tactile sensing. Front. Robot. AI **8**(September), 1–15 (2021). https://doi.org/10.3389/frobt.2021.730946
11. Culbertson, H., Schorr, S.B., Okamura, A.M.: Haptics: the present and future of artificial touch sensation. Annu. Rev. Control Robot. Auton. Syst. **1**(1), 385–409 (2018). https://doi.org/10.1146/annurev-control-060117-105043
12. Dargahi, J., Xie, W.F., Ji, P.: An experimental teletaction system for sensing and teleperception of human pulse. Mechatronics **18**(4), 195–207 (2008). https://doi.org/10.1016/j.mechatronics.2007.12.001
13. Feller, R.L., Lau, C.K., Wagner, C.R., Perrin, D.P., Howe, R.D.: The effect of force feedback on remote palpation. In: Proceedings - IEEE International Conference on Robotics and Automation, vol. 2004, no. 1, pp. 782–788 (2004). https://doi.org/10.1109/robot.2004.1307244
14. Filippeschi, A., Brizzi, F., Ruffaldi, E., Jacinto, J.M., Avizzano, C.A.: Encountered-type haptic interface for virtual interaction with real objects based on implicit surface haptic rendering for remote palpation. In: IEEE International Conference on Intelligent Robots and Systems, vol. 2015-December, pp. 5904–5909 (2015). https://doi.org/10.1109/IROS.2015.7354216
15. Hernandez-ossa, K.A., Leal-junior, A.G., Frizera-neto, A., Bastos, T.: Haptic feedback for remote clinical palpation examination. In: 2nd International Workshop on Assistive Technology (IWAT2019) (2019)

16. Kakar, P.N., Das, J., Roy, P.M., Pant, V.: Robotic invasion of operation theatre and associated anaesthetic issues: a review. Indian J. Anaesth. **55**(1), 18–25 (2011). https://doi.org/10.4103/0019-5049.76577
17. Kim, J., Ahn, B., Kim, Y., Kim, J.: Inclusion detection with haptic-palpation system for medical telediagnosis. In: Proceedings of the 31st Annual International Conference of the IEEE Engineering in Medicine and Biology Society: Engineering the Future of Biomedicine, EMBC 2009, pp. 4595–4598 (2009). https://doi.org/10.1109/IEMBS.2009.5332767
18. Kim, S.Y., Kyung, K.U., Park, J., Kwon, D.S.: Real-time area-based haptic rendering and the augmented tactile display device for a palpation simulator. Adv. Robot. **21**(9), 961–981 (2007). https://doi.org/10.1163/156855307781035619
19. Konstantinova, J., Cotugno, G., Dasgupta, P., Althoefer, K., Nanayakkara, T.: Palpation force modulation strategies to identify hard regions in soft tissue organs. PLoS ONE **12**(2), 1–24 (2017). https://doi.org/10.1371/journal.pone.0171706
20. Konstantinova, J., Li, M., Mehra, G., Dasgupta, P., Althoefer, K., Nanayakkara, T.: Behavioral characteristics of manual palpation to localize hard nodules in soft tissues. IEEE Trans. Biomed. Eng. **61**(6), 1651–1659 (2014). https://doi.org/10.1109/TBME.2013.2296877
21. Lalitharatne, T.D., et al.: Face mediated human-robot interaction for remote medical examination. Sci. Rep. **12**(1), 1–14 (2022). https://doi.org/10.1038/s41598-022-16643-z
22. Li, M., et al.: Evaluation of stiffness feedback for hard nodule identification on a phantom silicone model. PLoS ONE **12**(3), 1–18 (2017). https://doi.org/10.1371/journal.pone.0172703
23. Li, M., Luo, S., Nanayakkara, T., Seneviratne, L.D., Dasgupta, P., Althoefer, K.: Multi-fingered haptic palpation using pneumatic feedback actuators. Sens. Actuat. A: Phys. **218**, 132–141 (2014). https://doi.org/10.1016/j.sna.2014.08.003, http://dx.doi.org/10.1016/j.sna.2014.08.003
24. Mehrdad, S., Liu, F., Pham, M.T., Lelevé, A., Farokh Atashzar, S.: Review of advanced medical telerobots. Appl. Sci. (Switz.) **11**(1), 1–47 (2021). https://doi.org/10.3390/app11010209
25. Mehta, M.: Assessing the abdomen. Nursing **33**(5), 54–55 (2003). https://doi.org/10.1097/00152193-200305000-00050
26. Palacio-Torralba, J., Reuben, R.L., Chen, Y.: A novel palpation-based method for tumor nodule quantification in soft tissue—computational framework and experimental validation. Med. Biol. Eng. Comput. **58**(6), 1369–1381 (2020). https://doi.org/10.1007/s11517-020-02168-y
27. Racat, M., Capelli, S.: When interfaces make it real. In: Racat, M., Capelli, S. (eds.) Haptic Sensation and Consumer Behaviour, pp. 65–93. Springer, Cham (2020). https://doi.org/10.1007/978-3-030-36922-4_3
28. Roke, C., Melhuish, C., Pipe, T., Drury, D., Chorley, C.: Lump localisation through a deformation-based tactile feedback system using a biologically inspired finger sensor. Robot. Auton. Syst. **60**(11), 1442–1448 (2012). https://doi.org/10.1016/j.robot.2012.05.002, http://dx.doi.org/10.1016/j.robot.2012.05.002
29. Salud, L.H., Pugh, C.M.: Use of sensor technology to explore the science of touch. Stud. Health Technol. Inform. **163**, 542–548 (2011). https://doi.org/10.3233/978-1-60750-706-2-542
30. Talasaz, A., Patel, R.V.: Remote palpation to localize tumors in robot-assisted minimally invasive approach. In: Proceedings - IEEE International Conference on Robotics and Automation, pp. 3719–3724 (2012). https://doi.org/10.1109/ICRA.2012.6224649

31. Troccaz, J., Dagnino, G., Yang, G.Z.: Frontiers of medical robotics: from concept to systems to clinical translation. Annu. Rev. Biomed. Eng. **21**, 193–218 (2019). https://doi.org/10.1146/annurev-bioeng-060418-052502
32. Tzemanaki, A., Al, G.A., Melhuish, C., Dogramadzi, S.: Design of a wearable fingertip haptic device for remote palpation: characterisation and interface with a virtual environment. Front. Robot. AI **5**(JUN), 1–15 (2018). https://doi.org/10.3389/frobt.2018.00062

5G-Based Low-Latency Teleoperation: Two-Way Timeout Approach

Burak Kizilkaya[✉][ID], Olaoluwa Popoola[ID], Guodong Zhao[ID],
and Muhammad Ali Imran[ID]

School of Engineering, University of Glasgow, Glasgow, UK
b.kizilaya.1@research.gla.ac.uk,
{olaoluwa.popoola,guodong.zhao,muhammad.imran}@glasgow.ac.uk

Abstract. Recent advances in communications and robotics enable myriad teleoperation applications, empowering real-time remote operation in various application areas such as healthcare, education, manufacturing, and aerial manipulation. The main problems in teleoperation systems are the time delay and packet loss caused by poor network conditions. Ultra-reliable Low-Latency Communication (URLLC), one of the key services of fifth-generation cellular communications (5G), is expected to enable real-time teleoperation by mitigating latency and reliability issues of pre-5G communications. In this study, we develop a 5G-enabled teleoperation testbed to conduct experiments on communication latency and packet loss, demonstrating the current capabilities of 5G communications for teleoperation applications. Furthermore, we propose a two-way timeout approach to reduce the communication latency. The proposed approach reduces the end-to-end (E2E) latency by limiting the waiting time for new packet reception. Extensive latency and packet loss experiments are conducted to demonstrate the superiority of the proposed approach compared to the benchmark approach without a timeout. The experimental results corroborate that the proposed approach can reduce E2E latency by up to 65% and improves overall reliability.

Keywords: Teleoperation · Robotics · 5G · URLLC · Low-Latency

1 Introduction

Advances in communications and robotics uncover myriad teleoperation applications in various areas such as medical diagnosis and surgery [6], aerial manipulation [22], learning and education [12], nuclear industry [17], and space teleoperation [19]. A typical bilateral teleoperation system enables the remote environment manipulation over communication systems while empowering the sense of touch and telepresence over haptic communications. In general, such systems utilize a controller with a haptic interface that a human operator uses to control the remote robot/teleoperator. The operator's inputs are sampled and transmitted over the communication system to be executed by the teleoperator to

F. Iida et al. (Eds.): TAROS 2023, LNAI 14136, pp. 470–481, 2023.
https://doi.org/10.1007/978-3-031-43360-3_38

accomplish a task. In bilateral teleoperation, the operator receives the feedback signal, which closes the control loop. One of the main problems in teleoperation is the time delay introduced by hardware, computation, and communication systems which degrades the teleoperation performance [13], and real-time control becomes unstable. This issue has been investigated extensively in existing literature regarding communications and control theory perspectives.

Regarding communications, current advancements in 5G provide high data rates, low communication latency, and ultra-reliable exchange of information, with teleoperation being one of the most important scenarios of ultra-reliable low-latency communications (URLLC) [2]. Communication studies optimize communication system parameters to provide better solutions in terms of communication reliability and latency, which in turn enables better teleoperation performance [7,8,18]. In [18], prediction is performed to mitigate time delays in control systems, where authors jointly optimize prediction and communication systems to minimize wireless resource consumption. Similarly, a predictive actuation framework is proposed in [7], where lost packets are predicted at the receiver to minimize the age of information (AoI) and transmit power. In [8], communication and prediction systems are optimized jointly to achieve better user-experienced delay and system reliability in haptic feedback enabled teleoperation considering communication quality of service (QoS).

From a control theory perspective, control parameters are optimized under perfect and imperfect wireless channel assumptions [3,15,20]. In [20], a control scheme switching approach is proposed based on Quality of Experience (QoE). The proposed switching approach selects the best-performing control scheme adaptively considering QoE. In [15], a passivity-based control approach is proposed for bilateral teleoperation, which achieves stable control of a legged manipulator under time delays caused by the communication system. A reinforcement learning approach is proposed in [3] and integrated with Model Mediated Teleoperation (MMT) to mitigate the effects of long time delays.

On the other hand, various other approaches are proposed to mitigate latency considering User Datagram Protocol (UDP) and Transmission Control Protocol (TCP) for real-time applications [11,14,16,21]. In [11], a UDP-based streaming method is proposed with Forward Error Correction (FEC) for real-time video streaming applications to guarantee timeliness and low packet loss rate. In [21], a novel permutation-based encapsulation method is proposed for Internet of Things (IoT) applications where UDP and TCP are considered for application layer data encapsulation. In [14], the impacts of 5G New Radio (NR) numerologies on E2E latency are discussed, where UDP and TCP-based simulations are conducted to reveal the relationship. In [16], the performance of UDP and TCP are compared in terms of throughput, data rate, packet loss, and network latency on both IEEE-802.11p and 5G networks, where the superiority of UDP is shown in terms of latency and data rate in Vehicle-to-Vehicle (V2V) and Vehicle-to-Infrastructure (V2I) scenarios.

Considering existing literature, most of the studies either consider communication or control systems separately, and some lack E2E real-life experiments.

Therefore, the feasibility of the proposed solutions remains unclear in practical E2E teleoperation systems.

Motivated by the aforementioned issue, we develop a 5G-based teleoperation testbed with haptic feedback and conduct extensive latency and reliability experiments to investigate the current capabilities of 5G communications. With the inspiration of the information freshness concept [9], we propose a two-way timeout approach in which packets are discarded if they are not received before the timeout period to reduce the waiting time for stale information. We conduct additional experiments on the 5G network to compare conventional UDP with our proposed approach. The results of the experiments show that the proposed approach achieves better latency performance with the cost of reliability compared to benchmark UDP without a timeout. The main contributions of this study can be listed as follow.

- We design and build a 5G-enabled teleoperation testbed with haptic feedback, in which a remote operator controls a robotic arm to complete a task over 5G communications. The operator can feel the remote environment with haptic feedback enabled controller, allowing for more precise operation and increasing the sense of telepresence.
- We propose a two-way timeout approach for teleoperation systems to improve latency and reliability performance.
- We implement the proposed approach on our teleoperation testbed, where we conduct latency and reliability experiments over a 5G network.
- We present latency and packet loss measurements for the proposed approach and compare them to the benchmark protocol without a timeout. Experiment results show that the proposed approach can reduce average communication latency by up to 65%.

The rest of the paper is organized as follows. In Sect. 2, we provide system descriptions and propose a two-way timeout approach for low-latency teleoperation. In Sect. 3, we present our 5G-enabled teleoperation testbed and experiment setup. In Sect. 4, we provide our experimental results, which show the superiority of our approach, and we conclude the study in Sect. 5.

2   System Description and Two-Way Timeout Approach

In this section, we provide the system description and propose the two-way timeout approach. As seen in Fig. 1, a typical teleoperation system consists of three main domains. At the operator domain, a controller equipped with a haptic interface is used by a human operator to control a robotic arm at the teleoperator domain. To accomplish a task, the haptic controller samples the operator's inputs (i.e., control commands) and transmits them via the communication domain. In the communication domain, a server is utilized to exchange packets between the operator and teleoperator domains. In the teleoperator domain, a remote robotic arm receives control commands and provides force feedback over the communication domain. Generally, UDP is used to guarantee the required

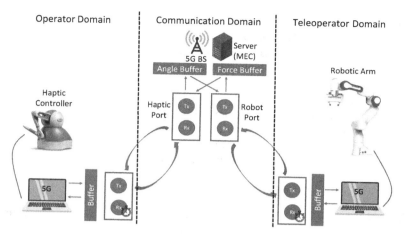

Fig. 1. 5G-enabled teleoperation system with haptic feedback

control frequency since it is more suitable than TCP for real-time applications [10].

In conventional UDP, clients request packets and wait for the response from the server. Waiting time is related to the latency and packet loss experienced in the communication domain. Since UDP is unreliable, packet losses are to be expected, which may result in communication deadlock. Deadlock can be described as the event that both the client and the server are in the receiving (Rx) state. In most cases, this is caused by packet loss in the communication domain. For example, a client transmits a packet to the server and waits for the response in the Rx state. If the transmitted packet drops, the server will also be in the Rx state, resulting in a packet exchange deadlock. In the sequel, we propose a technique to minimize communication latency and the event of a deadlock.

2.1 Two-Way Timeout Approach

As shown in Fig. 1, two clients, a haptic device and a robotic arm, communicate with the UDP server to exchange control commands and haptic feedback, respectively. In this scenario, each client sends the most recent sample to the server and waits for the most recent feedback or control command. As a result, clients can be in either the Rx or transmitting (Tx) state. We use a timeout technique at each client end (i.e., two-way timeout) to limit the waiting time in the Rx state and to mitigate the event of a deadlock. In other words, the client transmits the most recent sample and waits until the timeout threshold, τ, is reached. If no packet is received before then, it switches to the Tx state to transmit a new sample. As a result, the client is not required to wait in the Rx state for any longer than the timeout threshold τ. Please note that the timeout threshold, τ, must be adjusted according to application requirements. For example, if the required latency for an application is 10 ms, then waiting more than 10 ms is a waste of time because any packet received after the threshold will be stale. In other words, if a packet is not received before the timeout, the receiver assumes it is lost. Fresh information can thus be retrieved without wasting time waiting for stale information.

Let us denote the communication latency from the haptic device to the server as d_{hs} and the communication latency from the server to the haptic device as d_{sh}. Similarly, denote the communication latency from the robotic arm to the server and from the server to the robotic arm as d_{rs} and d_{sr}, respectively. Then, E2E communication latency (i.e., round trip latency) can be given as

$$d_{e2e} = d_{hs} + d_{sr} + d_{rs} + d_{sh}. \tag{1}$$

The proposed timeout approach limits d_{sr}, and d_{sh} by the timeout threshold τ, i.e., $d'_{sr} \leq \tau$ and $d'_{sh} \leq \tau$. In this case, the E2E communication latency becomes

$$d'_{e2e} \leq d_{hs} + d'_{sr} + d_{rs} + d'_{sh}, \tag{2}$$
$$\leq d_{hs} + d_{rs} + 2\tau. \tag{3}$$

While the timeout strategy ensures that there is no deadlock in the communication channel, it also means that packets may be discarded or dropped if they do not arrive before the timeout expires. This implies that the proposed approach has a lower level of reliability. To account for this, we denote the reliability as γ and compute the reliability using Packet Delivery Ratio (PDR), which can be expressed as

$$\gamma = R/T, \tag{4}$$

where R is the total number of packets received by the receiver and T is the total number of packets transmitted by the transmitter. To capture the overall performance, we consider a joint Cost Function (CF), defined as the cost of successfully transmitting a packet. For given E2E latency d'_{e2e}, and reliability γ, CF can be defined as

$$CF = \frac{1}{\gamma} d'_{e2e} \ (ms), \tag{5}$$

where $\frac{1}{\gamma}$ is the number of repetitions required to transmit a packet with probability 1, and d'_{e2e} is the time required to transmit a packet.

3   5G-Enabled Teleoperation Testbed with Haptic Feedback

In this study, we develop a 5G-enabled teleoperation testbed with haptic feedback[1] to enable real-time teleoperation with a sense of touch as seen in Fig. 1. At the operator domain, 3D systems haptic device is deployed as a haptic controller,

---
[1] System description: https://youtu.be/c3onK5Vh6QE.

which has the capability of 6-degree-of-freedom (DoF) positional sensing and 3-DoF force feedback. The human operator uses the haptic device to control the remote robotic arm on the teleoperator domain via the communication domain. We deployed Franka Emika Panda robotic arm as a teleoperator which is a 7-DoF serial manipulator with 1kHz control and sensor sampling capabilities. In the sequel, we explain the flow of information in each domain and describe the measurement setup.

3.1   Operator Domain

A local computer at the operator domain samples 3D positions, $\mathbf{p} = \{p_x, p_y, p_z\}$ of the haptic device's end effector at the haptic device working space. Since the coordinate systems of the robot and haptic device are different, we investigate their local coordinate systems and match their movement axes such that the Y-axis of the haptic device corresponds to the X-axis of the robotic arm (i.e., towards up), Z-axis of the haptic device corresponds to Y-axis of the robotic arm (i.e., towards to user), and X-axis of the haptic device corresponds to Z-axis of the robotic arm (i.e., towards right). Then, positions are scaled up to match the movement space of the robotic arm since one unit movement in the haptic workspace does not correspond to one unit movement in robot space, necessitating mapping. Computed position values with fixed quaternion rotations (since we only consider position control) are then fed into the inverse kinematics (IK) solver of the robotic arm, which is based on the Denavit-Hartenberg [4] parameters of the Franka Emika Panda robotic arm [1] which can be given as follows

$$\boldsymbol{\theta} = f_{ik}\left(\mathbf{p}, \mathbf{q}\right) \qquad (6)$$

where $\boldsymbol{\theta} = \{\theta_1, \theta_2, \theta_3, \theta_4, \theta_5, \theta_6, \theta_7\}$ are computed joint angles, $\mathbf{q} = \{q_w, q_x, q_y, q_z\}$ are fixed quaternion rotations, and $f_{ik}(.)$ is the inverse kinematics solver function. The same computation is performed in each sampling cycle, and the computed joint angles $\boldsymbol{\theta}$ are written into a buffer to be transmitted to the server.

3.2   Communication Domain

We deploy a UDP server in the communication domain at the 5G Base Station (BS) Mobile Edge Computing (MEC) unit. The haptic controller and the robotic arm computers are equipped with 5G dongles to access the local BS. At the UDP server, we utilize two separate ports to communicate with two clients (i.e., the haptic device computer and the robotic arm computer). In addition, we use two buffers to store the most recently received packets from the robot and haptic device. As discussed in the preceding subsection, the haptic device computer transmits the most recently computed joint angles to the server, and then the server writes them into the angle buffer as seen in Fig. 1. Most recent joint angles are transmitted to the robotic arm when a new packet request is received. New packets are requested by transmitting the most recent sample to the server. In other words, each client transmits its most recent sample, and the server receives it and updates the corresponding buffer. In exchange, the server transmits the buffer's content to the client. If the client is the haptic device, the angle buffer is updated, and the content of the force buffer is returned. If the client is the robotic arm, the force buffer is updated, and the content of the angle buffer is returned.

3.3 Teleoperator Domain

Franka Emika Panda robotic arm and a local computer reside in the teleoperator domain. Received joint angles from the server are written into a buffer for execution. The main reason for using the buffer is that the frequency of the real-time control loop is 1 kHz, which means that the control loop must be fed with new joint angles in every 1 ms. This necessitates the arrival of a new packet in every 1 ms, which is not possible in physical implementation due to communication and computation latencies. As a result, we utilize a buffer at the robot end to serve as an information source for the control loop, allowing us to run the control loop at a frequency of 1 kHz. On the other hand, we update the buffer with the latest received joint angles whenever a new packet arrives from the server. We employ a proportional integral derivative (PID) control algorithm on a local computer which computes joint angular velocity commands for received joint angles considering the difference between received joint angles and the current state of the robotic arm. Computed commands are executed using provided functions of *libfranka*, which is a C++ implementation of Franka Control Interface (FCI) [1]. This process is repeated in each control loop to enable real-time control. In addition, the robotic arm's built-in sensors are used to sample external forces applied to the robot, which are transmitted as feedback to the server, allowing us to control the robot in real-time with haptic feedback (i.e., sense of touch).

3.4 Latency Measurement Setup

One of the main challenges in latency measurements is the unsynchronized end devices. Since the E2E latency is at a milliseconds level, ensuring that the end devices are synchronised to the same clock is critical to have reliable results. One method for synchronizing end devices is to use *Network Time Protocol (NTP)* servers, in which each device synchronizes its local clock with the same NTP server, allowing time synchronization. However, even this solution has a synchronization error of tens to hundreds of milliseconds (ms) depending on the NTP server load and other communication channel characteristics [5], which is insufficient for our experiments. To overcome this difficulty, we collect exchanged packets with timestamps at the server, allowing us to perform the measurements on the same machine and eliminate the time synchronization issue. Let us denote t_c^i as the time the i-th packet received by the server from the client c. Then, the E2E latency between the server and the client c for the i-th packet becomes

$$d_{e2e,c}(i) = t_c^{(i)} - t_c^{(i-1)}, \tag{7}$$

where $d_{e2e,c}$ is the time difference between two consecutive packets, which measures the round trip time required from server to client and client to server. Then, the mean E2E latency for received N packets from client c becomes

$$d_{mean,c} = \frac{1}{N} \sum_{i=1}^{N} d_{e2e,c}(i). \tag{8}$$

On the server side, control and feedback packets are exchanged over two dedicated ports. Furthermore, two threads are running concurrently to provide real-time communication. One thread handles server and haptic device communication. Another thread runs for server and robot communication. The server buffers the received control packets from the haptic device and transmits the most recent feedback packet back. Similarly, received feedback packets are buffered, and the server returns the most recent available control packet to the robot. Since both the control and feedback buffers have a capacity of one packet, the server always has the most recently received control and feedback packets. Furthermore, the server records packet traffic from both the haptic device and the robot. Every received packet is recorded with a timestamp, providing a chronological record of packet exchanges.

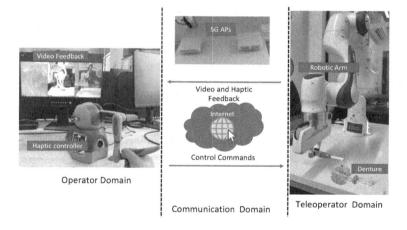

Fig. 2. Experimental setup considering remote dental inspection use case.

4   Experimental Results

In this section, we provide our experiment results considering remote dental inspection use case[2] in Fig. 2. Latency and packet loss measurements are conducted as discussed in Sect. 3-D.

---

[2] Remote dental inspection use case: https://youtu.be/afJFUwUW6Dg.

In Fig. 3a, we provide an average E2E latency comparison between the proposed approach and the benchmark UDP without a timeout. We conduct experiments for different timeout values and for the benchmark UDP, where we exchanged 10,000 packets in every experiment. As seen from the figure, the proposed approach outperforms the benchmark UDP in terms of E2E latency, where the proposed approach achieves mean E2E latency of around 5 ms while the benchmark UDP achieves mean E2E latency of around 50 ms. This is reasonable since the proposed approach reduces the waiting time in the Rx state and mitigates the long waiting time delays. On the other hand, E2E latency increases with increasing timeout period τ. This is also reasonable since the E2E latency is related to the communication latency and the timeout period.

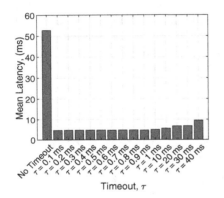
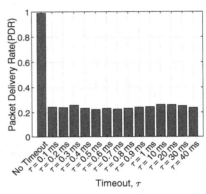

(a) Latency comparison between the proposed approach and the benchmark UDP without a timeout.

(b) Packet delivery rate comparison between the proposed approach and the benchmark UDP without a timeout.

Fig. 3. Latency and packet delivery rate comparisons.

In Fig. 3b, we provide the reliability comparison in terms of PDR. As discussed in Sect. 2, the proposed approach has a negative impact on reliability. This is because the waiting time in the Rx state is limited by the timeout period τ, which allocates very little time for packet reception. However, we must consider a joint metric CF to reveal overall performance. CF results are provided in Fig. 4a to compare the performance of the proposed approach with the benchmark UDP without a timeout. As seen from the figure, the proposed approach outperforms the benchmark UDP. In other words, the proposed approach requires less than 20 ms to successfully transmit a packet, whereas the benchmark UDP requires more than 50 ms. The results show that the proposed approach can achieve up to 65% less E2E latency under identical network conditions.

Furthermore, we provide the latency measurements in Fig. 4b for the first 300 packets to demonstrate the difference between the proposed approach and the benchmark UDP in terms of jitter, which is the deviation of the latency. The

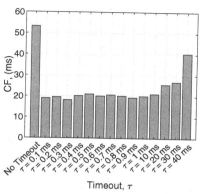

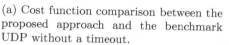

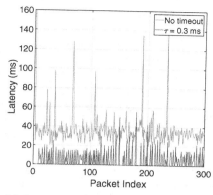

(a) Cost function comparison between the proposed approach and the benchmark UDP without a timeout.

(b) Latency values of the first 300 packets for the proposed approach with $\tau = 0.3$ ms and the benchmark UDP without a timeout.

Fig. 4. Cost function comparison and latency values for first 300 packets.

figure shows that the proposed approach reduces jitter and provides more stable and predictable network conditions.

To further evaluate the latency deviations, we provide latency distributions in Fig. 5 for the benchmark UDP (see Fig. 5a) and the proposed approach (see Fig. 5b). As seen from the figures, the proposed approach reduces the standard deviation of latency, σ, from 14.84 to 10.28 compared to the benchmark UDP which is consistent with the results in Fig. 4b and justifies them.

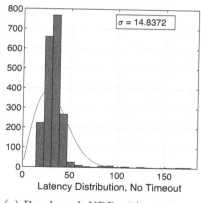

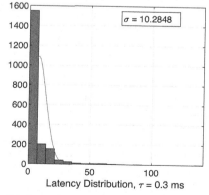

(a) Benchmark UDP without timeout

(b) Proposed approach with $\tau = 0.3$ ms

Fig. 5. Latency distributions of the proposed approach the benchmark UDP without a timeout.

5 Conclusions

In this study, we design and develop a 5G-enabled teleoperation testbed with haptic feedback, where we conduct extensive latency and reliability measurements to demonstrate the current capabilities of 5G communications. Furthermore, we propose a two-way timeout approach to maintain QoS in teleoperation systems for improved latency and reliability performance. We reduce the E2E latency by reducing waiting time in the packet reception process. The proposed approach allows for the transition between Tx and Rx states by introducing a timeout threshold for the Rx state, which improves latency and reliability performance. Experimental results are presented and compared with the benchmark UDP without a timeout. The presented results show that the proposed approach can reduce mean E2E latency by up to 65% compared to the benchmark UDP with identical communication networks.

As a future work, we will conduct more experiments to show the superiority of the proposed approach in terms of control performance, such as stability and transparency in teleoperation.

References

1. Franka control interface documentation (2017). https://frankaemika.github.io/docs/
2. Antonakoglou, K., Xu, X., Steinbach, E., Mahmoodi, T., Dohler, M.: Toward haptic communications over the 5G tactile internet. IEEE Commun. Surv. Tutor. **20**(4), 3034–3059 (2018)
3. Beik-Mohammadi, H., et al.: Model mediated teleoperation with a hand-arm exoskeleton in long time delays using reinforcement learning. In: IEEE International Conference on Robot and Human Interactive Communication (RO-MAN), pp. 713–720. IEEE (2020)
4. Denavit, J., Hartenberg, R.S.: A kinematic notation for lower-pair mechanisms based on matrices (1955)
5. Durairajan, R., Mani, S.K., Sommers, J., Barford, P.: Time's forgotten: using NTP to understand internet latency. In: ACM Workshop on Hot Topics in Networks, pp. 1–7 (2015)
6. Feizi, N., Tavakoli, M., Patel, R.V., Atashzar, S.F.: Robotics and AI for teleoperation, tele-assessment, and tele-training for surgery in the era of COVID-19: existing challenges, and future vision. Front. Robot. AI 16 (2021)
7. Girgis, A.M., Park, J., Bennis, M., Debbah, M.: Predictive control and communication co-design via two-way gaussian process regression and AOI-aware scheduling. arXiv preprint arXiv:2101.11647 (2021)
8. Hou, Z., She, C., Li, Y., Zhuo, L., Vucetic, B.: Prediction and communication co-design for ultra-reliable and low-latency communications. IEEE Trans. Wireless Commun. **19**(2), 1196–1209 (2019)
9. Kaul, S., Gruteser, M., Rai, V., Kenney, J.: Minimizing age of information in vehicular networks. In: IEEE Communications Society Conference on Sensor, Mesh and Ad Hoc Communications and Networks, pp. 350–358. IEEE (2011)

10. Kebria, P.M., Abdi, H., Dalvand, M.M., Khosravi, A., Nahavandi, S.: Control methods for internet-based teleoperation systems: A review. IEEE Trans. Hum.-Mach. Syst. **49**(1), 32–46 (2018)
11. Kim, S., Shin, S., Moon, J.: UDP-based extremely low latency streaming. In: IEEE Annual Consumer Communications & Networking Conference (CCNC), pp. 94–99. IEEE (2022)
12. Kizilkaya, B., Zhao, G., Sambo, Y.A., Li, L., Imran, M.A.: 5g-enabled education 4.0: Enabling technologies, challenges, and solutions. IEEE Access **9**, 166962–166969 (2021)
13. Liu, C.: Adaptive control of teleoperation systems with uncertainties: a survey. In: The 3rd International Conference on Robotics Systems and Automation Engineering (RSAE), pp. 5–9 (2021)
14. Patriciello, N., Lagen, S., Giupponi, L., Bojovic, B.: 5G new radio numerologies and their impact on the end-to-end latency. In: IEEE International Workshop on Computer Aided Modeling and Design of cCommunication Links and Networks (CAMAD), pp. 1–6. IEEE (2018)
15. Risiglione, M., Sleiman, J.P., Minniti, M.V., Cizmeci, B., Dresscher, D., Hutter, M.: Passivity-based control for haptic teleoperation of a legged manipulator in presence of time-delays. In: IEEE/RSJ International Conference on Intelligent Robots and Systems (IROS), pp. 5276–5281. IEEE (2021)
16. Tahir, M.N., Katz, M.: ITS performance evaluation in direct short-range communication (IEEE 802.11p) and cellular network (5G) (TCP vs UDP). In: Hamid, U.Z.A., Al-Turjman, F. (eds.) Towards Connected and Autonomous Vehicle Highways. EICC, pp. 257–279. Springer, Cham (2021). https://doi.org/10.1007/978-3-030-66042-0_10
17. Tokatli, O., et al.: Robot-assisted glovebox teleoperation for nuclear industry. Robotics **10**(3), 85 (2021)
18. Tong, X., Zhao, G., Imran, M.A., Pang, Z., Chen, Z.: Minimizing wireless resource consumption for packetized predictive control in real-time cyber physical systems. In: IEEE International Conference on Communications Workshops (ICC Workshops), pp. 1–6. IEEE (2018)
19. Wang, Z., Lam, H.K., Xiao, B., Chen, Z., Liang, B., Zhang, T.: Event-triggered prescribed-time fuzzy control for space teleoperation systems subject to multiple constraints and uncertainties. IEEE Trans. Fuzzy Syst. **29**(9), 2785–2797 (2020)
20. Xu, X., Zhang, S., Liu, Q., Steinbach, E.: QoE-driven delay-adaptive control scheme switching for time-delayed bilateral teleoperation with haptic data reduction. In: IEEE/RSJ International Conference on Intelligent Robots and Systems (IROS), pp. 8838–8844. IEEE (2021)
21. Yang, Y., Hanzo, L.: Permutation-based TCP and UDP transmissions to improve goodput and latency in the internet of things. IEEE Internet Things J. **8**(18), 14276–14286 (2021)
22. Zhang, D., Tron, R.: Stable haptic teleoperation of UAVs via small L2 gain and control barrier functions. In: IEEE/RSJ International Conference on Intelligent Robots and Systems (IROS), pp. 8352–8357. IEEE (2021)

Generative Model-Based Simulation of Driver Behavior When Using Control Input Interface for Teleoperated Driving in Unstructured Canyon Terrains

Hyeonggeun Yun[1], Younggeol Cho[2], Jinwon Lee[1], Arim Ha[1],
and Jihyeok Yun[1(✉)]

[1] Agency for Defense Development, Daejeon, Republic of Korea
jihyeok.yun@gmail.com
[2] Korea Advanced Institute of Science and Technology, Daejeon, Republic of Korea
rangewing@kaist.ac.kr

Abstract. Unmanned ground vehicles (UGVs) in unstructured environments mostly operate through teleoperation. To enable stable teleoperated driving in unstructured environments, some research has suggested driver assistance and evaluation methods that involve user studies, which can be costly and require lots of time and effort. A simulation model-based approach has been proposed to complement the user study; however, the models on teleoperated driving do not account for unstructured environments. Our proposed solution involves simulation models of teleoperated driving for drivers that utilize a deep generative model. Initially, we build a teleoperated driving simulator to imitate unstructured environments based on previous research and collect driving data from drivers. Then, we design and implement the simulation models based on a conditional variational autoencoder (CVAE). Our evaluation results demonstrate that the proposed teleoperated driving model can generate data by simulating the driver appropriately in unstructured canyon terrains.

Keywords: Teleoperated driving · Simulation model · Generative model · Driver behavior · Unstructured environment

1 Introduction

Teleoperated driving of unmanned ground vehicles (UGVs) is a prominent example of teleoperation in unstructured environments. One of the difficulties in teleoperated driving is stability, which is driving while sustaining consistent states in response to abrupt changes in the local environment [1]. In unstructured environments, ensuring stable driving is essential to reduce collision risks and increase

This work was supported by Agency for Defense Development Grant funded by the Korean Government (2023).

F. Iida et al. (Eds.): TAROS 2023, LNAI 14136, pp. 482–493, 2023.
https://doi.org/10.1007/978-3-031-43360-3_39

vehicle safety. However, teleoperation is more complex than commercial driving, as drivers lack physical feedback from the vehicle regarding speed, acceleration, and posture [2]. Furthermore, the difficulty of teleoperated driving increases in unstructured environments since roads are not standardized, and there are diverse elements, such as canyons, obstacles, and potholes. Consequently, teleoperated driving in unstructured environments requires extensive practice and is difficult for drivers.

To support teleoperated driving, previous research proposed driver assistance methods for collision avoidance and stable driving [3,4]. User studies and human-in-the-loop experiments have been used to evaluate driver assistance methods. However, conducting studies with drivers requires a huge effort and time, making repeated or iterative experiments challenging. Human-in-the-loop experiments and teleoperated driving with drivers, in particular, are high-cost. Thus, an evaluation approach based on a simulation model of users is proposed to complement the user study [5].

Previously, modeling and simulating of drivers have been studied in terms of driving behavior. Wang et al. classified and clustered driving behaviors using a machine learning-based approach for personalized compensation for speed tracking errors [6]. Li et al. proposed a human driving model that predicts the steering behavior of drivers in the teleoperation of UGVs with different speeds [7]. They used Adaptive Control of Thought-Rational (ACT-R) cognitive architecture, a two-point steering model, and a far-point control model to simulate human steering behavior. Schnelle et al. also suggested a driver steering model which can adapt a driving behavior of an individual driver [8]. Existing research has primarily centered on the development of simulation models for driving behaviors on urban roads, such as lane changing and vehicle following, using rule-based approaches. Unfortunately, these models have a limited capacity to reflect the driving behavior of multiple drivers, and their applicability to mimicking teleoperated driving of drivers in unstructured environments is also restricted.

In this paper, we solve this problem using a self-supervised generative model. Based on previous research [9], we propose a simulation model of teleoperated driving commands based on a conditional variational autoencoder (CVAE) in unstructured environments, particularly unstructured canyon terrains. First, we collected driving data from drivers using a teleoperated driving simulator, including control inputs, dynamic state information of a platform, and environmental information. The data is then used to train and validate our simulation models. Second, we design a forward simulation model and an inverse simulation model for teleoperated driving based on CVAE. CVAE is a deep conditional generative model that produces stochastic inferences based on the inputs and generates realistic output predictions [10]. We first train the forward simulation model to generate environmental information and dynamic state information, then train the inverse simulation model to generate control inputs for drivers.

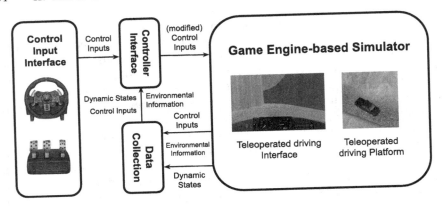

Fig. 1. Game engine-based simulator configuration with input interface

2   Teleoperated Driving Dataset Collection

Designing a teleoperated driving model requires driving data from drivers in unstructured environments. Thus, we employed an off-road teleoperated driving simulator that could reflect real-world physical effects from previous work to simulate teleoperated driving in the unstructured environment [3] (See Fig. 1). The simulator is implemented using the Unity Pro game engine and Vehicle Physics Pro automotive simulation engine. The simulator provided a truck-like wheeled platform with a Light Detection and Ranging (LiDAR) sensor that replicates Velodyne 16-channel 3-dimensional LiDAR and driving interfaces including a speedometer and a tachometer. Drivers used a Logitech G29 racing wheel as a control input interface.

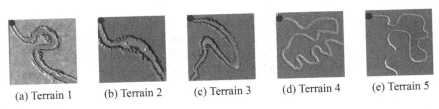

(a) Terrain 1   (b) Terrain 2   (c) Terrain 3   (d) Terrain 4   (e) Terrain 5

Fig. 2. Five terrains (maps) include both curved and linear pathways for data collection and model evaluation. Blue circle denotes the starting point of each terrain (Color figure online)

To simulate the teleoperated driving, we collected the following simulator data: control inputs, dynamic state information, and environmental information. The control inputs consisted of steering data and pedal data from the controller. The dynamic state information consisted of the current speed, orientation (yaw, roll, pitch), and current position of the platform in the simulator. The environmental information in this study refers to LiDAR Point Cloud data captured by the LiDAR sensor. The simulator stores all data every 100 milliseconds because we contemplated a generation model that utilizes environmental data.

To collect driving data, we utilized five terrains that imitated canyons and rough terrains (See Fig. 2). As we concentrated on unstructured environments and canyons, the terrains' pathways were unpaved, laneless, and surrounded by steep mountains.

We collected driving data from 5 drivers (experienced drivers) with experience using the simulator and 14 drivers (inexperienced drivers) with no experience using the simulator. The experienced drivers continuously collected driving data from three terrains (Fig. 2a, b, c). The inexperienced drivers operated the wheeled platform on the two terrains (Fig. 2d, e) to collect driving data. Since the forward simulation model needs to imitate environment and dynamic states, we employed a driving dataset of experienced drivers who could drive safely and structured for the model. The inverse simulation model needs to mimic varied drivers' behavior, hence we employed a dataset of novice drivers who could drive differently. This use of contrasting data for the two models enhances the sophistication of the deep generative model for simulating the chaotic driving behavior of drivers especially in environments where there are no obvious driving guidelines, such as lanes.

3   Teleoperated Driving Model

We implemented a teleoperated driving model based on the driving data of drivers. Our objective is to simulate the teleoperated driving of drivers so that we can readily measure and predict the teleoperated driving performance without drivers participating in teleoperated driving experiments directly. To achieve the goal, we considered a simulation model based on a deep generative model adopting a conditional variational autoencoder (CVAE). A previous study has demonstrated that a CVAE is useful at simulating physical movements based on sensor inputs and generating various outputs from given conditions [9]. We considered that a CVAE-based model could generate control inputs for multiple drivers by utilizing the relationship between current and past data.

Therefore, we designed a teleoperated driving simulation model based on a CVAE that can mimic the teleoperated driving behavior of drivers. Since we used the training and inference framework of previous research [9], we designed a forward simulation model and an inverse simulation model with a CVAE. The forward model uses the previous data from the nine-time steps and the control inputs from the current time step to generate the environmental data and dynamic state data for the current time step, and the inverse model uses the previous data from the nine-time steps and the environmental data and dynamic state data from the current time step to generate the control inputs for the current time step.

3.1   Preprocessing

We preprocessed the collected dataset in accordance with prior research in order to enhance the effectiveness of training and quality of data [3,11–13]. In preprocessing, the dataset was divided into control inputs consisting of steering input and acceleration/brake pedal input, dynamic state information consisting of orientation data and speed data, and environmental information consisting of LiDAR Point Cloud data. For each ith time step, we created a Control Vector c_i, a State Vector s_i, and an Environment Vector e_i through preprocessing.

First, by normalizing the steering input data, acceleration pedal input data, and brake pedal input data, we generate a Control Vector c_i for the control inputs [13]. The steering input data was normalized to a range of 0–1. The acceleration pedal input data was scaled to a range of 0–1, while the brake pedal input data was scaled to -1-0. They were then combined as the pedal input data, which was subsequently normalized from -1-1 to 0-1.

We create a State Vector s_i for the dynamic state information of the platform by normalizing the current speed and orientation data. The orientation data was normalized to a range of 0–1 from 0-360°, and the speed data was normalized to a range of 0–1 from 0–30 m/s, because the current speed of data did not exceed 30 m/s.

In the environmental information, an Environment Vector e_i was constructed using LiDAR Point Cloud data. The LiDAR Point Cloud data was converted to cylindrical coordinates and obstacle points were identified by detecting points with a slope greater than the threshold (which was set to 45° for this paper) along the same azimuth [11,12]. The obstacle point data was then transformed into a vector depicting the distance between the obstacle and the platform along the forward 180°. The distance values were then normalized to a range of 0–1 on the assumption that the utmost distance was 50 m.

3.2   Training and Inference Approach with Two Simulation Models

As we mentioned above, we trained two simulation models: a forward simulation model and an inverse simulation model. The forward model generates observed data derived from user interactions, while the inverse model generates user interactions derived from observed data [9,14]. Generally, the forward model is derived from principles and theories based on psychology and physics, and the inverse model is derived from a machine learning-based model based on users' behavior data. However, principles of psychology and physics do not explain the environment's change and the platform's dynamic states dependent on driving behavior. Encouragingly, empirical simulation is able to collect observed data regarding the alteration of the environment and the dynamic states in response to users' control inputs. Therefore, in our proposed model, we also used a machine learning-based model for the forward model since we thought that the observed sensor data could be derived from the control inputs and sensor data of previous time steps.

Thus, we designed two CVAE-based simulation models. The training and inference approach with two simulation models consisted of three steps.

(1) First, we create a Perception Vector by combining an Environment Vector and State. We utilize the Perception Vector and Control Vector of the previous nine-time steps and the Control Vector of the current time step as a condition vector for the CVAE, and use a Noise Vector of the same size as the Perception Vector of the current time step as input. The forward CVAE model generates the Perception vector corresponding to the current time step. To generate accurate perception vectors, we use a dataset of 102,073 time steps generated by the experienced drivers for training (Fig. 3a).

(2) Second, we use the Perception Vector generated by the forward CVAE model used in step (1) and the Perception Vector and Control Vector from the previous nine-time steps as a condition vector, and a Noise Vector of the same size as the Control Vector at the current time step as input. The Control Vector at the current time step is generated by the inverse CVAE model. To generate diverse drivers' behavior, we use a dataset of 88,955 time steps generated from inexperienced drivers for training (Fig. 3b).

(3) Third, we utilize the inverse CVAE model trained in step (2) to generate a Control Vector for the current time step from the Perception Vectors and Control Vectors of the previous nine-time steps and the Perception Vector for the current time step. The inverse CVAE model simulates the control inputs of drivers represented by the generated control vector (Fig. 3c).

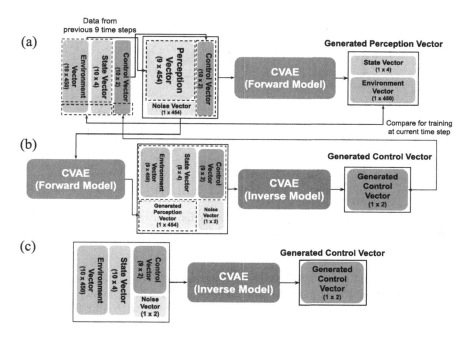

Fig. 3. Training and inference approach with a forward simulation model and an inverse simulation model

We used time-series data from ten consecutive time steps, including the current time step and the nine-time steps preceding it. The condition vector was constructed by combining the State Vector, Environment Vector, and Control Vector. We also used a random vector as a noise vector $\tilde{n}$, and the sample vector z was set to the same size as the noise vector. The dataset was divided into a training dataset for updating the model's parameters and a validation dataset for verifying the model's performance. The model was trained for 1,000 epochs using a batch size of 2,048. The initial learning rate was set to 1×10^{-3}, and it was decreased to a tenth every 300 epochs using a step decay scheduler in order to enhance training performance. Mean Squared Error (MSE) function and Kullback-Leibler (KL) divergence were used for loss functions, whereas variational autoencoder (VAE) and CVAE typically use Binary Cross Entropy (BCE) function and KL divergence for loss functions. In addition, since it is crucial to restoring the vector at the current time step based on previous information, we only compared a loss between generated vector at the current time step $c_{gen,t}$ for training. The training was conducted on a graphics processing unit (GPU) server equipped with the NVIDIA Tesla A100.

3.3   Model Architecture

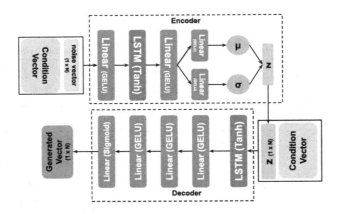

Fig. 4. CVAE-based teledriving model architecture for a forward simulation model and an inverse simulation model. N is the size of the generated vector to simulate

The architecture of the CVAE-based teleoperated driving model is illustrated in Fig. 4. Our model comprises an encoder with four Linear layers and a Long Short Term Memory (LSTM) layer, as well as a decoder with four Linear layers and an LSTM layer.

In the encoder, we first generate a Condition Vector $q = (q_{t-9}, q_{t-8}, ..., q_t)$ and a Noise Vector $\tilde{n} \in \mathbb{R}^N$ where t represents the current time step and N represents the size of the generated vector to simulate. Then, the combination of Noise Vector $\tilde{n}$ and Condition Vector q generates an input vector $x = (q_{t-9}, q_{t-8}, ..., q_t \oplus \tilde{n})$ where $\oplus$ represents concatenation. We first extract time-series features x_{enc} from x with two Linear layers and an LSTM layer.

$$x_{enc} = Linear_{enc,2}(LSTM_{enc}(Linear_{enc,1}(x))) \tag{1}$$

Then, two Linear layers generate a mean vector μ and a variance vector σ that are typically employed in variational autoencoder (VAE).

$$\mu = Linear_{enc,3}(x_{enc}) \tag{2}$$

$$\sigma = Linear_{enc,4}(x_{enc}) \tag{3}$$

The model then generates a sample vector $z = (z_{t-9}, z_{t-8}, ..., z_t)$ from the mean vector μ and variance vector σ.

$$z = \mu + \sigma^2 \odot \epsilon \tag{4}$$

where $\epsilon \sim N(0, 1^2)$ and $\odot$ is an element-wise product.

In the decoder, we only need z_t, so the z_t vector and the Condition Vector q are combined to generate the vector $x' = (q_{t-9}, q_{t-8}, ..., q_t \oplus z_t)$.

Then, sequential features $r_{dec,1}$ are extracted from x' by an LSTM layer of the decoder.

$$r_{dec,1} = LSTM_{dec}(x') \tag{5}$$

Finally, four Linear layers of the decoder then generate a Vector $g_{gen} = (g_{gen,t-9}, g_{gen,t-8}, ..., g_{gen,t}) \in \mathbb{R}^N$. We use $g_{gen,t}$ vector to simulate state and environmental information or control inputs corresponding to the current time step.

$$r_{dec,2} = Linear_{dec,3}(Linear_{dec,2}(Linear_{dec,1}(r_{dec,1}))) \tag{6}$$

$$g_{gen} = Linear_{dec,4}(r_{dec,2}) \tag{7}$$

The activation function for Linear layers, excluding the last Linear layer of the decoder, was the Gaussian error linear unit (GELU) function, while the activation function for LSTM layers was the Tanh function. The last Linear layer of the decoder utilized the sigmoid function as an activation function to generate a vector in the range 0–1.

4   Model Evaluation

4.1   Evaluation Design

To evaluate the capacity of our CVAE-based teledriving model to simulate the teleoperated driving behavior of drivers, we compared the driving performance of the simulated model to that of real drivers. We collected teleoperated driving data of the simulation model from the canyon terrain (Fig. 2e) where drivers drove. As a dataset of drivers' teleoperated driving consists of a total of 28 driving data operated by 14 drivers twice, the simulation model also drove 28 times in the same terrain. After arriving at the destination, driving data was added to the dataset for purposes of comparison.

To compare the driving performance of drivers to that of the simulation model, we employed four metrics based on previous research [3, 15–17]: the standard deviation of lateral position (SDLP), the standard deviation of speed (SDS), the average speed (AvgSpeed), and the driving completion time (DCT). For all metrics, lower scores mean superior driving performance.

4.2   Evaluation Result

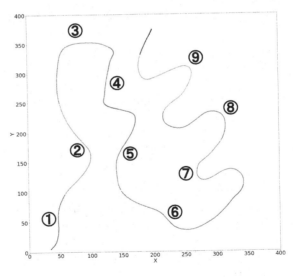

Fig. 5. Terrain sections for drivers and simulation model performance comparison

The mean and standard deviation of drivers' SDLP, SDS, AvgSpeed, and DCT are presented in Table 1, along with the simulation model. To establish a relationship between the driving performance of drivers and the simulation model, the experiment terrain was divided into nine sections (see Fig. 5). We conducted a

Table 1. Comparison results on average performance of drivers and simulation model in each section. Bolded p-values indicate $p < 0.05$

(a) Comparison results on SDLP and SDS

Section	SDLP (m)			SDS (m/s)		
	Mean (SD)		p-value	Mean (SD)		p-value
	Drivers	Model		Drivers	Model	
#1	0.72 (0.29)	0.48 (0.04)	**<0.01**	3.58 (0.75)	3.08 (0.09)	**<0.01**
#2	1.08 (0.38)	1.23 (0.20)	0.12	1.14 (0.46)	1.02 (0.18)	0.27
#3	1.19 (0.25)	1.24 (0.15)	0.41	2.57 (0.83)	2.10 (1.02)	0.09
#4	1.69 (0.63)	2.02 (0.71)	0.11	1.89 (0.68)	2.44 (1.06)	**0.04**
#5	1.11 (0.38)	1.06 (0.34)	0.60	2.22 (0.67)	2.57 (1.34)	0.25
#6	1.47 (0.27)	1.03 (0.29)	**<0.01**	1.32 (0.46)	1.21 (0.30)	0.33
#7	1.39 (0.40)	1.32 (0.24)	0.51	2.71 (1.26)	1.66 (0.92)	**<0.01**
#8	1.25 (0.34)	1.41 (0.55)	0.20	2.78 (1.57)	2.80 (1.32)	0.96
#9	1.51 (0.40)	1.44 (0.26)	0.52	2.83 (1.30)	2.69 (1.43)	0.70

(b) Comparison results on AvgSpeed and DCT

Section	AvgSpeed (m/s)			DCT (sec)		
	Mean (SD)		p-value	Mean (SD)		p-value
	Drivers	Model		Drivers	Model	
#1	8.72 (1.54)	6.14 (0.23)	**<0.01**	11.34 (2.24)	15.58 (0.61)	**<0.01**
#2	12.76 (1.89)	11.81 (0.34)	**0.04**	14.40 (2.15)	15.51 (0.43)	**0.03**
#3	11.63 (1.40)	10.30 (0.87)	**<0.01**	20.09 (2.35)	22.95 (2.24)	**<0.01**
#4	8.52 (1.74)	7.65 (2.10)	0.14	8.60 (3.88)	11.23 (3.96)	**0.03**
#5	10.22 (1.47)	10.61 (1.81)	0.43	16.15 (2.52)	15.73 (3.78)	0.66
#6	13.47 (1.76)	11.82 (1.04)	**<0.01**	18.63 (2.51)	21.33 (1.86)	**<0.01**
#7	8.85 (1.81)	9.27 (1.27)	0.31	20.29 (6.14)	18.99 (3.32)	0.32
#8	9.00 (2.63)	9.34 (1.65)	0.57	20.76 (8.44)	19.08 (3.77)	0.34
#9	8.63 (1.90)	8.91 (1.90)	0.60	25.51 (7.01)	26.12 (8.42)	0.77

Welch's T-Test to determine whether there is a statistically significant difference within each of the nine sections.

According to the findings presented in Table 1.a, there was a significant difference between the drivers and the simulation model in SDLP for the two sections ($p < 0.01$ for section #1 and $p < 0.01$ for section #6), however, no statistically significant difference was observed between the drivers and the simulation model for the other sections. In the case of SDS (see Table 1a), the significant difference was observed for the three sections ($p < 0.01$ for section #1, $p = 0.04$ for section #4, and $p < 0.01$ for section #7), however, there was no significant difference between the drivers and the simulation model for the other sections.

Meanwhile, according to the findings presented in Table 1b, there was a significant difference between the drivers and the simulation model in terms of AvgSpeed for the four sections ($p < 0.01$ for section #1, $p = 0.04$ for section #2, $p < 0.01$ for section #3, and $p < 0.01$ for section #6). However, there was no significant difference between the drivers and the simulation model for other sections. In the case of DCT (see Table 1b), the significant difference was observed for the five sections ($p < 0.01$ for section #1, $p = 0.03$ for section #2, $p < 0.01$ for section #3, $p = 0.03$ for section #4, and $p < 0.01$ for section #6), but there was no significant difference between the drivers and the simulation model for other sections.

Based on the results, we found that there were differences between the drivers and the simulation model for early section or section primarily consisting of straight roads (section #1, #2, #3, and #6) in driving performance. The observed phenomenon can be attributed to the fact that the sections consist primarily of straight roads and close proximity to the starting point, resulting in driver-specific variations in acceleration patterns. Nonetheless, no significant differences were observed between the drivers and the simulation model in the case of section primarily comprising curved roads (section #5, #7, #8, and #9). This implies that our model exhibits proficiency in accurately simulating the steering and acceleration required for driving challenging curved road conditions. In particular, the lesser difference between the drivers and the simulation model in terms of SDLP compared to AvgSpeed and DCT indicates that our model simulates steering more accurately than acceleration. Therefore, we are able to argue that our model adequately simulates drivers' teleoperated driving.

5   Conclusion

In this paper, we proposed a CVAE-based teleoperated driving model for unstructured canyon terrains. We implemented a teleoperated driving simulator for unstructured environments, enabling us to mimic teleoperated driving scenarios and collect driving data from drivers. Then, we designed a teleoperated driving model based on a CVAE-based architecture. From time-series data, the forward simulation model and the inverse simulation model generates a perception vector and a control vector at the current time step. The evaluation results demonstrated that our simulation model could reproduce drivers' teleoperated driving. This study could be expanded in the future to include a variety of off-road environments with low-friction roads, craters, and obstacles. If these studies mature, we can anticipate that our proposed simulation model, which mimics human behavior despite using a limited number of user studies, will bring about in a novel approach for dataset generation and user study.

References

1. Opiyo, S., Zhou, J., Mwangi, E., Kai, W., Sunusi, I.: A review on teleoperation of mobile ground robots: architecture and situation awareness. Int. J. Control Autom. Syst. **19**(3), 1384–1407 (2021)

2. Park, K., Youn, E., Kim, S., Kim, Y., Lee, G.: Design of acceleration feedback of UGV using a stewart platform. In: 2021 21st International Conference on Control, Automation and Systems (ICCAS), pp. 79–82. IEEE (2021)
3. Cho, Y., Yun, H., Lee, J., Ha, A., Yun, J.: GoonDAE: denoising-based driver assistance for off-road teleoperation. IEEE Robot. Autom. Lett. **8**(4), 2405–2412 (2023). https://doi.org/10.1109/LRA.2023.3250008
4. Storms, J., Chen, K., Tilbury, D.: A shared control method for obstacle avoidance with mobile robots and its interaction with communication delay. Int. J. Robot. Res. **36**(5–7), 820–839 (2017)
5. Murray-Smith, R., et al.: What simulation can do for HCI research. Interactions **29**(6), 48–53 (2022)
6. Wang, Z., et al.: Driver behavior modeling using game engine and real vehicle: a learning-based approach. IEEE Trans. Intell. Veh. **5**(4), 738–749 (2020)
7. Li, C., Tang, Y., Zheng, Y., Jayakumar, P., Ersal, T.: Modeling human steering behavior in teleoperation of unmanned ground vehicles with varying speed. Hum. Factors **64**(3), 589–600 (2022)
8. Schnelle, S., Wang, J., Su, H., Jagacinski, R.: A driver steering model with personalized desired path generation. IEEE Trans. Syst. Man Cybern.: Syst. **47**(1), 111–120 (2016)
9. Murray-Smith, R., Williamson, J.H., Ramsay, A., Tonolini, F., Rogers, S., Loriette, A.: Forward and inverse models in HCI: physical simulation and deep learning for inferring 3D finger pose. arXiv preprint arXiv:2109.03366 (2021)
10. Sohn, K., Lee, H., Yan, X.: Learning structured output representation using deep conditional generative models. In: Advances in Neural Information Processing Systems, vol. 28 (2015)
11. Choe, T.S., Park, J.B., Joo, S.H., Park, Y.W.: Obstacle detection for unmanned ground vehicle on uneven and dusty environment. In: Signal Processing, Sensor/Information Fusion, and Target Recognition XXIV, vol. 9474, pp. 433–440. SPIE (2015)
12. Li, N., Yu, X., Liu, X., Lu, C., Liang, Z., Su, B.: 3D-lidar based negative obstacle detection in unstructured environment. In: Proceedings of the 2020 4th International Conference on Vision, Image and Signal Processing, pp. 1–6 (2020)
13. Naranjo, J.E., González, C., García, R., De Pedro, T.: Cooperative throttle and brake fuzzy control for ACC + stop&go maneuvers. IEEE Trans. Veh. Technol. **56**(4), 1623–1630 (2007)
14. Moon, H.S., Oulasvirta, A., Lee, B.: Amortized inference with user simulations. In: Proceedings of the 2023 CHI Conference on Human Factors in Computing Systems, pp. 1–20 (2023)
15. Knappe, G., Keinath, A., Bengler, K., Meinecke, C.: Driving simulator as an evaluation tool-assessment of the influence of field of view and secondary tasks on lane keeping and steering performance. In: 20th International Technical Conference on the Enhanced Safety of Vehicles (ESV) National Highway Traffic Safety Administration. No. 07-0262 (2007)
16. Knapper, A., Christoph, M., Hagenzieker, M., Brookhuis, K.: Comparing a driving simulator to the real road regarding distracted driving speed. Eur. J. Transp. Infrastruct. Res. **15**(2), 205–225 (2015)
17. Neumeier, S., Wintersberger, P., Frison, A.K., Becher, A., Facchi, C., Riener, A.: Teleoperation: The holy grail to solve problems of automated driving? Sure, but latency matters. In: Proceedings of the 11th International Conference on Automotive User Interfaces and Interactive Vehicular Applications, pp. 186–197 (2019)

Implementation of a Stereo Vision System for a Mixed Reality Robot Teleoperation Simulator

Aaron Lee Smiles[✉], Kitti Dimitri Chavanakunakorn, Bukeikhan Omarali, Changjae Oh, and Ildar Farkhatdinov

Queen Mary University of London, London, UK
{a.l.smiles,c.oh,i.farkhatdinov}@qmul.ac.uk
https://www.robotics.qmul.ac.uk/

Abstract. This paper presents the preliminary work on a stereo vision system designed for a mixed reality-based simulator dedicated to robotic telemanipulation. The simulator encompasses a 3D visual display, stereo cameras, a desktop haptic interface, and a virtual model of a remote robotic manipulator. The integration of the stereo vision system enables accurate distance measurement in the remote environment and precise visual alignment between the cameras' captured scene and the graphical representation of the virtual robot model. This paper delves into the technical aspects of the developed stereo system and shares the outcomes of its preliminary evaluation.

Keywords: Teleoperation · Stereo Vision · Mixed Reality

1 Introduction

Augmented, virtual, and mixed reality have the potential to enhance the quality of human-machine interfaces in robot teleoperation. For example, virtual reality-based control interfaces combined with depth cameras can improve scene understanding [10,12], allow efficient workspace mapping for telemanipulation tasks [11], and provide easier dexterous tactile telemanipulation [5]. It was also demonstrated that using multiple visual displays and interfaces increases the cognitive load demand during teleoperating remote underwater vehicles [8]. A taxonomy of mixed reality (MR) based robot teleoperation modes for hazardous environments was proposed in [16] demonstrating MR advantages for specific use-case scenarios.

Training human operators to efficiently and safely complete remote manipulation tasks is an important aspect to which MR can contribute [1,4,7,14]. Usually such teleoperation training simulators use virtual reality (VR) to model the remote scene and the robot. However, a more enhanced training experience can be achieved if a real visual stream (live or recorded) of the remote environment can be combined with the virtual model of the robot using augmented reality

F. Iida et al. (Eds.): TAROS 2023, LNAI 14136, pp. 494–502, 2023.
https://doi.org/10.1007/978-3-031-43360-3_40

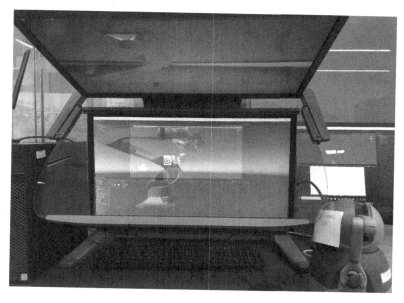

Fig. 1. 3D PluraView stereo display as part of the experimental setup with Touch haptic controller for teleoperating the virtual model of a remote robot-manipulator. The visual scene on the screen shows a combined view of the virtual robot and the stereo view from the remote environment or its emulator.

(AR), MR and stereo vision. Stereo vision allows improved scene understanding through the addition of depth perception and enables correct virtual robot geometry and motion alignment with the visual representation of the remote environment as demonstrated in surgical vision applications [9].

The aim of this work is to present a stereo vision-based robot teleoperation simulator and validate the stereo vision component of the system. The stereo vision system is based on earlier works [2,13] and is extended to include egocentric stereo vision and an MR-based robot simulator. The materials presented in the following sections are preliminary work demonstrating the integration of the stereo vision system with a virtual robot teleoperation simulator.

2 Implementation

2.1 System Overview

The stereo vision-based teleoperation interface built for this study is shown in Fig. 1. It comprises a stereo display to represent video flow from a remote robot's cameras (PluraView 3D[1]), a desktop haptic interface (Touch haptic interface[2]) and a custom-designed MR-based robotic manipulator simulation. The aim of

---

[1] www.3d-pluraview.com.
[2] www.3dsystems.com/haptics-devices/touch.

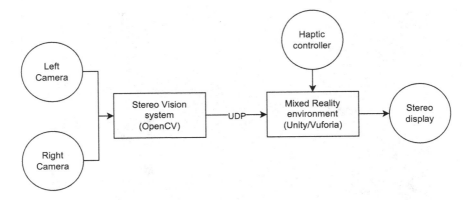

Fig. 2. High-level system diagram describing the flow of the system. The two mono camera inputs are used to create the stereo vision system in OpenCV, which sends the processed images and distance estimate data via UDP sockets into Unity. The Unity environment renders a simulated robotic end effector, which can be controlled via the haptic controller, in AR using the Vuforia plugin in the images from the webcams. These augmented camera images are then displayed on the stereo display, including the distance estimate, which can be viewed in 3D.

the proposed simulator is to provide a robot teleoperation training environment that combines a virtual remote robot model with the stereo visual flow (live or pre-recorded) from a remote physical environment. Such a simulation system provides a realistic training environment as a stereo representation of the remote physical environment is used, as well as the overall system is low-cost and safe as a virtual model of the robot is used.

A high-level flow diagram depicting the main components and inputs/outputs is shown in Fig. 2. The proposed operation workflow for the stereo vision subsystem consists of first obtaining camera images from a pair of stereo webcams. The stereo images rectified with OpenCV are sent to the Unity 3D platform used for rendering the stereo view of a remote scene is displayed using the 3D PluraView stereoscopic screen. Desktop Touch haptic controller is used to operate the simulated robotic end-effector. The 3D model of the robot is rendered in augmented reality (AR) using the Vuforia Unity plugin[3]. A Model Target is generated of a real object using the Vuforia Model Target Generator[4], so the Vuforia engine can recognise the object in the camera and trigger an AR event (a Unity GameObject) that is the same, or near-identical, distance as the real object from the virtual and real cameras. The stereo distance data of the real object from OpenCV is sent to Unity via UDP, which is then deducted from the virtual end-effector distance from the virtual object.

---

[3] https://library.vuforia.com/getting-started/vuforia-engine-package-unity.

[4] https://library.vuforia.com/objects/model-targets.

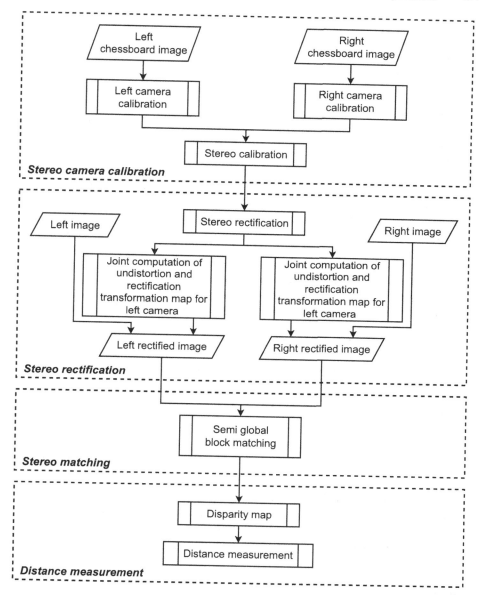

Fig. 3. Flow diagram of the proposed stereo vision distance measuring system.

2.2 Stereo Vision

The stereo vision system is used to estimate the distance to the remote scene's objects using two cameras (Logitech C505) with the optical axis aligned to be parallel. The stereo cameras were set horizontally as close as possible to the

human interpupillary distance (IPD) (average 63 mm), as this also conforms to
the zone of comfort [15]. The video flow processing used in the proposed system
is similar to earlier works [2,6,13] and represented as a flowchart in Fig. 3 and
in the following items:

- **Cameras calibration** is performed by capturing a batch of checkerboard
  images from different angles to infer the focal length and optical centres of
  the camera (intrinsics). The calibration should not be *biased* towards any
  corner or region, so we calibrate with images of the chessboard everywhere in
  the field of view.
- **Rectification and undistortion of the images** is achieved by removing
  barrel or pincushion lens distortion. This step rectifies the stereo images based
  on epipolar geometry [2], re-projecting the stereo image planes onto a common
  plane that is parallel to the line between the cameras.
- **Block/feature matching** is performed by searching for similar graphical
  features between left and right images (horizontally). Block matching is used
  to generate a disparity map between the left and right stereo images. Here we
  calculate the similarity for *each* block in the image, searching for correspondence along horizontal epipolar lines using a window, or "block", commonly
  a sum of absolute difference (SAD) window. The best match is chosen by the
  pair with the lowest SAD score.
- **Distance estimation from disparity map** produces a depth map that we
  can use to calculate the distance to the objects in a remote scene, z, based on
  the focal length, f, baseline stereo camera distance, b, and disparity, d, using
  $z = \frac{fb}{d}$ [6].

2.3 Stereo Display

The stereo display (3D PluraView) is used in the robot teleoperation simulator
to provide realistic visual feedback with a sense of depth. Parallax images are
images that are passed through your left and right eyes to create a sense of
depth. All 3D stereo media involves a pair of parallax images that pass to the
left and right eyes of a viewer separately and concurrently [3]. By combining two
images into a cross-polarised image, the 3D PluraView monitor (Fig. 1) is able
to produce stereoscopic visual feedback. The images are displayed from different
fixed angles and combined by a beam-splitter mirror in the centre, which is
viewed with passive polarised filter glasses. The stereo camera images are used
here to create 3D egocentric views of a remote scene.

The 3D model of the robotic end effector was imported into Unity and augmented to the raw camera images using the Vuforia Unity plugin. The model of
the manipulator was controlled using the haptic controller (the haptic controller's
stylus position was used as a reference position for the robot's end-effector).

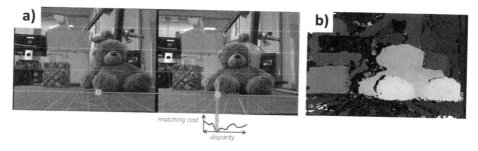

Fig. 4. a) Dense stereo block matching. The scanline (blue) is shown across the left and right images. The left image shows the target/reference block (yellow). The right image shows the scanline (blue), best matching block (yellow), and second-best matching candidates (red). The bottom image shows a plot for the Sum of Absolute Difference (SAD) between the reference block and the sliding window along the scanline in the right image. **b)** An example of stereo block matching and the disparity image obtained with OpenCV.

3 Validation of the Stereo Cameras System

An experiment was conducted to evaluate the accuracy of distance estimation to remote environments objects with the help of the implemented stereo vision system. The cameras were calibrated and the root mean squared reprojection errors were 0.0131 px for the left camera and 0.0131 px for the right, at a baseline distance of 6.3 cm. An example of stereo matching using image disparity is shown in Fig. 4b.

To validate disparity-to-depth estimation for the second study, we conducted a series of distance measurements with the system on objects of different materials as shown in Fig. 5a: a patterned cardboard box, metal bottle, clear bottle, white bottle, fabric teddy toy, and a grey 3D printed plastic part with a rough texture, almost like rough stone or concrete. A tape measure (used for ground truth) was placed in front of the cameras, and object distance measurements were taken at 18 different distances from the cameras within the range at which the system could obtain a reading, which was approximately 45–130 cm. Ten readings were taken at each distance.

The results are shown in Fig. 5. Root mean squared error (RMSE) of distance estimation for each object was: box, 14.57 cm; clear bottle, 16.34 cm; white bottle, 1.01 cm; metal bottle, 2.03 cm; teddy toy, 1.95 cm; 3D printed part 2.5 cm. The average RMSE for all objects was 9.13 cm.

Most disparity-to-depth results in the experiment showed to be normally distributed, besides some outliers due to noise in the disparity map. The clear bottle showed inconsistent readings, often returning 0 cm, or a null reading, as the disparity map had difficulty finding matches due to transparency, but performed accurately on those that it matched.

Overall, the system performed well. The aggregate RMSE was 9.13 cm, but this is skewed by the noisy pixel outliers and transparent bottle. In comparison,

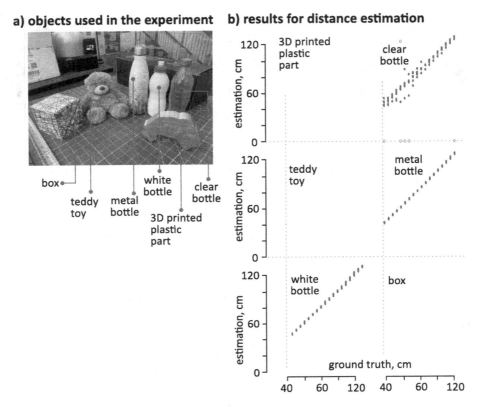

Fig. 5. a) The objects used for estimating distance using the stereo vision sub-system. From left to right: a patterned cardboard box, teddy toy, metal bottle, white bottle, clear bottle, and a 3D printed plastic part. b) Results from testing the stereo vision system to estimate the distance of various objects/materials at different distances.

the white bottle had an RMSE of 1.01 cm. In practice, when we track an object and estimate its distance, a mask is used, and the distance of the object is estimated from an average of the points in the disparity mask, which negates the error due to noise or gaps in the disparity map.

4 Conclusion

This paper presented an experimental prototype of a stereo vision-based simulator for robotic teleoperation. The study evaluated the performance of the stereo vision system that is integrated into the simulator.

Stereo vision was conducted using unsynchronised cameras since the ROV cameras are separated. The stereo camera baseline used here was 63 mm, which demonstrated sufficiently accurate distance estimations within 1.2 m range. Having a larger baseline distance between the cameras will increase the operational range. For example, the cameras on the remotely operated robot at the UK National Oceanography Centre are attached over a meter apart.

While a stereo vision system was validated, validation of the teleoperation system was out of the scope of this paper. Future work will be dedicated to validating the teleoperation system through subjective user studies. Additional mixed reality human-computer/-robot interaction features will be investigated. In future, we aim to adapt such teleoperation training systems to robot teleoperation in extreme environments [17].

Acknowledgements. Aaron Smiles was funded by the UKRI EPSRC EngD Data-Centric Engineering CDT at Queen Mary University of London (reference 2601988). The work was partially co-funded by the UKRI EPSRC Q-Arena grant EP/V035304/1. We thank Kaustubh Sadekar, Yik Lung Pang, and the National Oceanography Centre for their feedback.

References

1. Adami, P., et al.: Effectiveness of VR-based training on improving construction workers' knowledge, skills, and safety behavior in robotic teleoperation. Adv. Eng. Inform. **50**, 101431 (2021)
2. Adil, E., Mikou, M., Mouhsen, A.: A novel algorithm for distance measurement using stereo camera. CAAI Trans. Intell. Technol. **7**(2), 177–186 (2022)
3. Dodgson, N.: Autostereoscopic 3D displays. Computer **38**(8), 31–36 (2005)
4. Farkhatdinov, I., Ryu, J.H.: Development of educational system for automotive engineering based on augmented reality. In: International Conference on Engineering Education and Research (2009)
5. Giudici, G., Omarali, B., Bonzini, A.A., Althoefer, K., Farkhatdinov, I., Jamone, L.: Feeling good: Validation of bilateral tactile telemanipulation for a dexterous robot. In: Iida, F., et al. (eds.) TAROS 2023, LNAI, vol. 14136, pp. 443–454. Springer, Cham (2023). https://doi.org/10.1007/978-3-031-43360-3_36
6. Kaehler, A., Bradski, G.: Learning OpenCV 3: Computer Vision in C++ with the OpenCV Library. Reilly Media, Inc. (2016)
7. Lin, Q., Kuo, C.: On applying virtual reality to underwater robot tele-operation and pilot training. Int. J. Virtual Reality **5**(1), 71–91 (2001)
8. Livatino, S., et al.: Intuitive robot teleoperation through multi-sensor informed mixed reality visual aids. IEEE Access **9**, 25795–25808 (2021)
9. Murugesan, Y.P., Alsadoon, A., Manoranjan, P., Prasad, P.: A novel rotational matrix and translation vector algorithm: geometric accuracy for augmented reality in oral and maxillofacial surgeries. Int. J. Med. Robot. Comput. Assist. Surg. **14**(3), e1889 (2018)
10. Omarali, B., Denoun, B., Althoefer, K., Jamone, L., Valle, M., Farkhatdinov, I.: Virtual reality based telerobotics framework with depth cameras. In: 2020 29th IEEE International Conference on Robot and Human Interactive Communication (RO-MAN), pp. 1217–1222. IEEE (2020)
11. Omarali, B., Javaid, S., Valle, M., Farkhatdinov, I.: Workspace scaling in virtual reality based robot teleoperation. In: Proceedings of the Augmented Humans International Conference 2023, pp. 98–104 (2023)

12. Omarali, B., Palermo, F., Althoefer, K., Valle, M., Farkhatdinov, I.: Tactile classification of object materials for virtual reality based robot teleoperation. In: 2022 International Conference on Robotics and Automation (ICRA), pp. 9288–9294. IEEE (2022)
13. Sadekar, K.: Depth estimation using stereo camera and OpenCV (Python/C++) (2021)
14. Saliba, C., Bugeja, M.K., Fabri, S.G., Di Castro, M., Mosca, A., Ferre, M.: A training simulator for teleoperated robots deployed at CERN. In: ICINCO (2), pp. 293–300 (2018)
15. Shibata, T., Kim, J., Hoffman, D.M., Banks, M.S.: The zone of comfort: predicting visual discomfort with stereo displays. J. Vis. **11**(8), 11 (2011)
16. Szczurek, K.A., Prades, R.M., Matheson, E., Rodriguez-Nogueira, J., Castro, M.D.: Mixed reality human-robot interface with adaptive communications congestion control for the teleoperation of mobile redundant manipulators in hazardous environments. IEEE Access **10**, 87182–87216 (2022)
17. Vitanov, I., et al.: A suite of robotic solutions for nuclear waste decommissioning. Robotics **10**(4), 112 (2021)

Author Index

F. Iida et al. (Eds.): TAROS 2023, LNAI 14136, pp. 503–505, 2023.
https://doi.org/10.1007/978-3-031-43360-3

Printed in the United States
by Baker & Taylor Publisher Services